CU00704355

EXPANDING THE BOUNDARIES OF INTELLECTUAL PROPERTY

EXPANDING THE BOUNDARIES OF INTELLECTUAL PROPERTY

INNOVATION POLICY FOR THE KNOWLEDGE SOCIETY

Edited by

ROCHELLE COOPER DREYFUSS

DIANE LEENHEER ZIMMERMAN

HARRY FIRST

OXFORD
UNIVERSITY PRESS

This book has been printed digitally and produced in a standard specification in order to ensure its continuing availability

OXFORD
UNIVERSITY PRESS

Great Clarendon Street, Oxford OX2 6DP

Oxford University Press is a department of the University of Oxford.
It furthers the University's objective of excellence in research, scholarship,
and education by publishing worldwide in

Oxford New York

Auckland Bangkok Buenos Aires Cape Town Chennai
Dar es Salaam Delhi Hong Kong Istanbul Karachi Kolkata
Kuala Lumpur Madrid Melbourne Mexico City Mumbai Nairobi
São Paulo Shanghai Taipei Tokyo Toronto

Oxford is a registered trade mark of Oxford University Press
in the UK and in certain other countries

Published in the United States
by Oxford University Press Inc., New York

© Rochelle Dreyfuss, Diane Zimmerman,
Harry First, and the Contributors 2001

The moral rights of the author have been asserted

Database right Oxford University Press (maker)

Reprinted 2004

ISBN 0-19-829857-9

CONTENTS

ACKNOWLEDGEMENTS

The chapters in this volume are based on essays that were first presented at a Conference sponsored by the Engelberg Center on Innovation Law and Policy and New York University School of Law. The Conference, which was held at La Pietra, a villa in Florence, Italy, provided a unique opportunity for contributors to test their theories, consider opposing viewpoints, and modify their positions. The final product therefore owes a great deal not only to those who contributed to this volume, but also to the practitioners, academics, and judges who were present at the Conference but did not memorialize their input in writing. We also owe a debt of gratitude to Alfred B. Engelberg, whose vision and generosity created the Center, to Dean John Sexton, who made the lovely setting of La Pietra available to us and helped in too many ways to make a full accounting feasible, and to Judge Pauline Newman of the US Court of Appeals for the Federal Circuit for encouraging us to bring this project to fruition. We must also thank Leslie Freij, Alexandra Pietropinto, Nicole Fenchel, Ken Kidd, and Patricia Prior, who handled the administrative side with supreme skill, and to our researchers, Mirela Roznovschi of the NYU Law School Library, Robert Pfister and Lawrence Frank of the NYU Law School Class of 2001, and Dan Dudis and Matthew Gabin of the NYU Law School Class of 2002.

INTRODUCTION

We live, as the Chinese might say, in interesting times. We are witnessing a social change at least as fundamental as that of the eighteenth century, when an agrarian economy, dependent on land and livestock, was transformed into an industrial society. At that time, the advent of mechanization led new sets of natural and human resources to emerge as significant. Populations mobilized and urbanized; goods and production processes became more complex; international power structures realigned; cultural and moral outlooks shifted. In the end, a profound legal reordering took place. Property, tort and labor law were reformulated to deal with novel types of wealth and risk; contract and securities law were recast to meet the demands of entrepreneurship; criminal law was codified to account for new forms of social dislocation; and juridic authority was reconceptualized to reflect changes in the relationships among nations, and between each nation and its citizens.

Under traditional measures, growth from industrialization has now slowed. With the move from farm to factory played out, society has found a new source for its productivity gains: information production and management. The signs of the new order—of what might be called the Knowledge Society—are everywhere. Space satellites and imaging technologies now monitor, and will soon control, environments both remote and near; medical scanning devices and genomics are expected to play similar functions in more intimate settings. Thanks to discoveries in chemistry, pharmacology, and materials science, data can now be stored in convenient molecular, magnetic, and electronic packages, where value can be harnessed through advances in telecommunication and computer science. The monetary value of these developments can be gauged from the ever-expanding role that patented, copyrighted, and trademarked goods play in the global economy. But the significance of these achievements is far greater. With affordable health care, cheap electronic publication, accurate resource management, and universal communication, the quality of life will soar.

Coping with the dislocations that these developments produce will not, however, be easy. Participating in the Knowledge Society will be a challenge for both individuals and nations, for it will require unprecedented levels of intellectual sophistication and a highly advanced technological infrastructure. Social and business practices must change as associations become more a matter of machine interoperability than of personal interaction. Concepts of autonomy will be required to accommodate new tracking and surveilling methodologies. As knowledge is rendered fluid through its transference from material objects to other media; as workplaces, markets, and public fora are replaced by remote visualization, geographic distances and national borders will be less relevant. The transformation of the Knowledge Society—the shift from the physical to the virtual—will, just like the move from the agrarian to the industrial, alter both international and personal relations. And it, too, will provoke dramatic changes in law.

The legal problems engendered by this transformation have yet to fully surface. Nations have only begun to grapple with the problems of imposing law on an environment in which actions can be undertaken anonymously and results reified anywhere. Individual rights within this new space are beginning to evolve; the issues that have already crystallized foreshadow the many more that will arise as intangibles assume the role that real estate held in a farm economy and that tangible property played after industrialization. Debates over these issues deserve scrutiny not only by lawyers, but by society as a whole, because it is in these discussions that the norms of the Knowledge Society will take shape.

Not surprisingly, the first of the debates to emerge distinctly are those directly linked to the recognition of intellectual products as the Knowledge Society's core source of wealth. Thus, the legal system has long understood that first mover advantages were not alone enough to encourage and finance creative production. In the industrial age, antitrust law was used to stimulate competition and a series of proprietary rights—copyrights, patents, and trademarks—were developed to extend the time in which competitors were insulated from other market entrants. But the entrepreneurs of the Knowledge Society argue that these regimes are no longer apposite, that as the economy becomes dependent on an increasingly diversified portfolio of information products and as the production and distribution of these products change, the contours of law must also be reconfigured.

Thus, there is a new appreciation for the values of sharing information. Stressing the benefits of allowing competitors to collaborate on research projects, coalesce around product standards, combine technical capacities, bundle components, and pool intellectual property rights, knowledge entrepreneurs argue that the standards of antitrust enforcement must relax. Simultaneously, however, they are demanding new private rights: the expansion of existing intellectual property regimes and the adoption of new ones. In many cases, legislators and courts are reacting favorably to their claims. Antidilution and anticybersquatting measures have been enacted to supplement the protection that trademark law traditionally affords against consumer confusion. The term of copyright has been lengthened, and rights regarding digitized products strengthened. Patents are now used to protect software, business methods—even sports moves. Sui generis measures—laws specifically aimed at products as diverse as semiconductor chips, databases, industrial design, artistic performances, computer programs, and genetic maps—have either been enacted or are under active consideration. Theories of misappropriation, trade secrecy, and publicity are being promoted so that profits in advances too marginal to qualify for other forms of recognition can nonetheless be captured.

Legislatures are similarly responding to the shift from the physical to the virtual. They are crafting rules to facilitate electronic commerce and adopting codes focused on the problems of licensing intangibles. Because modern dissemination technologies can make it difficult to observe unauthorized takings, governments are improving enforcement capabilities and enhancing deterrence measures. Self-help methods—encryption, monitoring, and tracing techniques—have been approved and backed by penalties for circumvention. Infringement, once viewed as a civil wrong among individuals, is increasingly perceived as a crime against society, as counterfeiting and economic espionage, punishable by both penalties and incarceration.

In some ways, the most important changes are those occurring in the international arena. Because there are no borders in virtual space, territorially-bound legislation is increasingly seen as problematic. The Berne Convention, the Paris Convention and the Trade Related Aspects of Intellectual Property Agreement (TRIPS Agreement) of the General Agreement on Tariffs and Trade establish and enforce worldwide intellectual property norms; membership of the organizations administering these instruments, the World Intellectual Property Organization (WIPO) and the World Trade Organization (WTO), are now at an all-time high. The Patent Cooperation Treaty, the Madrid Protocol on trademarks, and regional treaties like the European Patent Convention, the European Community Patent Convention, the African Industrial Property Convention, the African Regional Industrial Property Organization, and the Eurasian Patent Convention, are taking internationalization one step farther. They lower the cost of international protection by allowing innovators to acquire rights in all signatories on the basis of a single application and examination.

But although these and like proposals have enjoyed considerable currency with lawmakers, they are not uncontested. The opposition is neither as well organized nor as well-heeled as are the industrial players. It arises, however, from many sources: from scholars and scientists; from writers and musicians; from institutions, such as libraries, schools, and research centers; and from developing nations. With the rising popularity of appropriation art and rap music, the artistic and literary possibilities unleashed by the computer and the Internet, and the availability of open source code (such as Linux) and the capacity to share files (as with Napster's software), even ordinary consumers are becoming aware of the many disadvantages of strong intellectual property regimes.

User groups see the needs of the Knowledge Society differently. Literary deconstructionists have long questioned the core concepts of authorship and originality in copyright. Historians of science have similarly come to see a challenge to patent law's notion of inventorship in the changing membership of research groups and the automation of many research processes. Economists argue that since knowledge is cumulative, enhancing the value of one generation of intellectual products necessarily increases costs to the next generation of innovators. They warn that unless lawmakers keep these offsetting effects in mind when adjusting the balance struck between creators and those who follow in their path, the production of knowledge will, in fact, be slowed. User groups ask whether, in an era when the costs of information production and distribution are decreasing, worldwide acceptance of traditional intellectual property norms is rising, and network effects reward firms who share technical standards, innovators actually need new kinds of protection to earn an adequate return on their investments. Further, users are concerned that facilitation of private arrangements can do real harm. If fragile, these arrangements impose new monitoring and litigation costs. If stable, they take information out of the public domain, fragment the knowledge base, and make entry into information industries more difficult.

There is another objection to expanding protection: international obligations fall especially hard on developing nations. Because their indigenous creative communities tend to be small, these countries do not export creative products and so cannot enjoy the benefits of strong international intellectual property protection. At the same time, however, these countries must bear the cost of such protection. The price of copyrighted, patented, and trademarked goods can increase to the point where access becomes limited, technological development is retarded, and the fruits of the Knowledge Society put out of reach.

This book examines the debate over the boundaries of intellectual property rights from a variety of perspectives. Because both innovators and users base their claims on factual assertions, it is tempting to look to empirical research to resolve the important questions that the knowledge transformation raises—to study the benefits that attach to being first to market; to determine the ratio between the return available under current rights regimes and the revenue requirements of emerging knowledge industries; to estimate how the growth in markets and the internationalization of intellectual property systems will affect revenue; and to investigate the stability and costs of private ordering regimes. Several of the chapters included here take this approach to study a variety of enterprises and organizational structures, each producing advances of different degrees of creativity. These contributions demonstrate that empiricism can be informative. However, they also show that it cannot be definitive. The impossibility of conducting controlled experiments, the complexity of the economy, the inherent unpredictability of innovation, all make it difficult to ground decisions about intellectual property rights purely in factual determinations.

The inadequacy of empiricism raises important questions of advocacy. What else should count as an appropriate argument in this debate? How far should the experience of particular industries be extrapolated to other situations? Does the persistence of attempts to create new rights say anything about the need for them? Is encouraging innovation the only goal, or are there other core social policies—for example, commitments to free expression, personal autonomy, and democracy—that should inform a debate that is, in essence, about control over cultural goods? Here, the issues are not only about the legitimacy or the adequacy of each approach, but also about the efficacy of particular arguments in specific arenas. Several of the chapters in this volume explore these issues as they arise in a series of settings, in courtrooms, in national legislatures, and in the treatymaking process.

Some of the contributions focus on questions of implementation. Lawmakers have many tools available to shape the legal environment to conform to their policy choices. Since intellectual property laws themselves strike a balance between the profit needs of knowledge producers and the access interests of information users, optimum innovation capacity could, at least in theory, be achieved solely through the way that these regimes are configured. But many believe that competition doctrine should not be ignored. The powerful analytical methods that were honed in the industrial age to understand markets for products could be extended by the Knowledge Society to scrutinize markets for innovation. With both competition law and intellectual property law in play, the creative environment would, perhaps, be even more effectively regulated. And for further fine tuning, norms embodied in basic laws, such as rights recognized in constitutions or human rights treaties, could also be consulted.

Important as these issues are, what pervades this volume is a conversation on a larger theme—on the attitude to be taken towards the opportunities presented by the knowledge transformation. Some of the contributors are what might be called 'information pessimists'. They see the dual moves of expanding intellectual property rights, on the one hand, and providing innovators with a high degree of transactional autonomy, on the other, as something of a double whammy. The parts of the public domain that are not nibbled away by formal rights regimes or common law theories, are appropriated contractually, with the help of lax competition policies and flexible licensing codes. The innovators who stand on these new rights—those who refuse to share their discoveries with those possessing complementary resources—delay commercialization, block improvements, and slow fundamental research. At the same time, those who do disseminate what they learn, do so through pools and other private arrangements that stifle competition, suppress superceding inventions, and otherwise impose negative externalities on both consumers and the next generation of innovators. To pessimists, society needs a safeguard: the protective net must be porous enough to permit advances to filter out of private hands and fall into the public domain.

'Information optimists', in contrast, see powerful synergies in the coupling of strong rights with contractual freedoms. Because ownership of intellectual property rights is a mark of success in the innovative enterprise, patents, copyrights, and trademarks help those with inventive and entrepreneurial capacities to identify one another. Laws promoting transactional flexibility permit these individuals to tailor collaborative agreements to the specific needs of their particular intellectual endeavors. Under this view, transactional autonomy is the answer to the problems that strong regimes engender, for if these regimes misallocate rights or benefits, collaborators can always redistribute them contractually, in accordance with their own perception of how rewards, credit, and control should be apportioned. By the same token, strong rights can compensate for inadequacies in contract law. With ownership of these rights firmly in hand, innovators can share information safe in the knowledge that should their dealings fall apart, exclusivity will not be lost. To optimists, strong rights are, in a sense, the coin of the Knowledge Society's realm.

Needless to say, none of the questions raised here are fully answered by this book; nor is the battle of visions resolved. However, each of the chapters presents issues that an information-based economy will face and each contributes to the jurisprudence that this new society must evolve. Parts I and II demonstrate the arguments that can be made in favor of, respectively, expanding rights and nurturing private ordering regimes. Part III takes up countervailing considerations, setting out theories in support of a strong public domain. Parts IV and V focus on implementation issues: Part IV examines legal rules that might cabin these trends; Part V sets out essays by eminent jurists who have confronted these issues in their courtrooms. Their insights into the impact that these and like arguments have on the adjudicatory process is sure to be of assistance to the advocates, policymakers, judges, and legislators who have the primary task of constructing a legal order appropriate to the Knowledge Society.

BIOGRAPHIES

Yochai Benkler
Yochai Benkler is an Associate Professor at the New York University School of Law. He is the Director of the Information Law Institute and faculty co-director of the JSD program. Professor Benkler teaches information law and policy in the digital environment, communications law and property law. His research focuses on the effects that laws regulating information production and dissemination on the distribution of control over information flows, knowledge, and cultural production in the digital environment. He has written about rules governing infrastructure, such as telecommunications and broadcast law, rules governing private control over information, such as intellectual property, privacy, and e-commerce; and constitutional law. Before coming to NYU, Benkler clerked for Associate Justice Stephen Breyer of the US Supreme Court, and had earlier been an associate in the corporate practice group of Ropes & Gray in Boston. He received his J.D. from Harvard Law School and his LL.B. from Tel-Aviv University. At both schools he was an editor of the Law Review.

William Cohen
William Cohen is Deputy Director for Policy Planning at the Federal Trade Commission and is one of the authors of the Antitrust Guidelines for Collaborations Among Competitors issued in April 2000 by the FTC and the US Department of Justice. Previously, he served as Project Director for Innovation in conjunction with the FTC's Hearings on Global and Innovation-Based Competition and the ensuing staff report entitled 'Anticipating the 21st Century: Competition Policy in the New High-Tech, Global Marketplace'. Between 1989 and 1995 Mr. Cohen was chief attorney advisor for antitrust to FTC Chairman Janet D. Steiger. Before joining the staff of the Federal Trade Commission, he was a member of the Washington, D.C. law firm Short, Klein & Karas, P.C.

Kenneth W. Dam
Kenneth W. Dam is the Max Pam Professor of American and Foreign Law at the University of Chicago Law School. He has published extensively on intellectual property, antitrust, and international economic law. In addition to his scholarly activities, he has served as IBM corporate Vice President for Law and External Affairs from 1985 to 1992, as Deputy Secretary of State from 1982 to 1985, and as Provost of the University of Chicago from 1980 to 1982. Prior to 1980 he was a law professor and, from 1971 to 1974, served in several economic positions in government. He is a board member of the Council on Foreign Relations and the Brookings Institution, co-chairman of

the Aspen Strategy Group, and chairman of the German-American Academic Council.

Susan S. DeSanti

Susan DeSanti is Director of Policy Planning at the Federal Trade Commission. She is one of the principal authors of the FTC/DOJ Competitor Collaboration Guidelines and is responsible for organizing the FTC's workshop on Business-to-Business Electronic Marketplaces. She also had responsibility for organizing the FTC's Hearings on Global and Innovation-Based Competition and for producing the 1996 FTC staff report entitled 'Anticipating the 21st Century: Competition Policy in the New High-Tech, Global Marketplace'. Currently, Policy Planning staff are working on the FTC's Joint Venture Project to clarify and update antitrust policies regarding joint ventures and other forms of competitor collaborations. Ms. DeSanti previously served as senior attorney advisor to FTC Chairman Robert Pitofsky and to former Commissioner Dennis Yao and as Assistant Director for Policy and Evaluation in the Bureau of Competition of the FTC. Prior to joining the Federal Trade Commission, Ms. DeSanti was a partner at the Washington, D.C. law firm of Hogan & Hartson, where her practice centered on antitrust litigation and counseling and other regulatory matters. She has held a variety of positions in the American Bar Association Antitrust Section and is a frequent speaker on antitrust issues, especially as they relate to innovation and intellectual property. She received her J.D. cum laude in 1981 from Boston University School of Law, where she was a member of the Law Review.

Thomas Dreier

Thomas Dreier, Dr. iur. (Munich), M.C.J. (NYU), is a Professor of Law at the University of Karlsruhe, Germany, where he is the Director of the Institute of Information Law and where he teaches civil law and information law. From 1983 to 1999 he was a member of the research staff (head of department since 1987) at the Max-Planck Institute for Foreign and International Patent, Copyright and Competition Law, Munich, Germany, where he was responsible for research and policy advising on copyright and dissemination of digital works, on computer programs, databases, cable and satellite distribution. Prof. Dreier was a consultant to the EU Commission on copyright questions regarding cable and satellite in the course of drafting Directive 93/83/EEC (1990–93); he also was a Member of the German Governmental Delegation at the Diplomatic Conference for the Conclusion of an International Treaty on the Protection of Intellectual Property in Respect of Integrated Circuits, Washington, D.C. (1989). In 1985, Prof. Dreier, who was admitted to the New York Bar in 1984, worked as an associate with the New York firm of Radon & Ishizumi. On various occasions,

Prof. Dreier has lectured on civil law and copyright law at the Universities of Munich (Germany), Toulouse (France) and St. Gallen (Switzerland) and has recently been invited as a Visiting Global Professor of Law at the New York University School of Law (2002). He is vice-chairman of the German national group of the *Association littéraire et artistique internationale* (ALAI). He studied law at the Universities of Bonn (1976–78; 79–82), Geneva (1978–79) and New York (1982–83), and art history at the University of Munich (1986–93).

Rochelle C. Dreyfuss

Rochelle Cooper Dreyfuss is a Professor of Law at New York University School of Law and Director of the Engelberg Center on Innovation Law and Policy. Her research and teaching interests include intellectual property, civil procedure, privacy, and the relationship between science and law. She holds B.A. and M.S. degrees in Chemistry and spent several years as a research chemist before entering Columbia University School of Law, where she served as Articles and Book Review Editor of the Law Review. After graduating, she was a law clerk to Chief Judge Wilfred Feinberg of the US Court of Appeals for the Second Circuit and to Chief Justice Warren E. Burger of the US Supreme Court. During her time at NYU, she has served as a member of the New York City Bar Association, the American Law Institute, and BNA's Advisory Board to USPQ. She was a consultant to the Federal Courts Study Committee and to the Presidential Commission on Catastrophic Nuclear Accidents. She is a past-Chair of the Intellectual Property Committee of the American Association of Law Schools. She has visited at the University of Chicago Law School and Santa Clara School of Law. In addition to articles in her specialty areas, she has co-authored casebooks on civil procedure and intellectual property law.

Frank H. Easterbrook

Frank H. Easterbrook is a Judge of the US Court of Appeals for the Seventh Circuit and a Senior Lecturer at the Law School of the University of Chicago. Before joining the court in 1985, he was the Lee and Brena Freeman Professor of Law at the University of Chicago, where he taught and wrote in antitrust, securities, corporate law, jurisprudence, and criminal procedure. He has published two books and more than 50 scholarly articles in these fields. His most recent book, *The Economic Structure of Corporate Law* (with Daniel R. Fischel), was published in 1991. Judge Easterbrook also engaged in economic and legal consulting work through Lexecon Inc. He served as Co-Editor of the Journal of Law and Economics from 1982 to 1991 and a member of the Judicial Conference's Standing Committee on Rules of Practice and Procedure from 1991 to 1997. Before joining the faculty of the Law School in 1979, Judge Easterbrook was Deputy Solicitor General of the

United States. He holds degrees from Swarthmore College (B.A. with high honors, 1970) and the University of Chicago (J.D. cum laude, 1973), and is a member of the American Academy of Arts and Sciences, the American Law Institute, the Mont Pelerin Society, Phi Beta Kappa, and the Order of the Coif.

Rebecca S. Eisenberg

Rebecca S. Eisenberg is a graduate of Stanford University and Boalt Hall School of Law at the University of California, Berkeley, where she was articles editor of the California Law Review. Following law school she served as law clerk for Chief Judge Robert F. Peckham on the US District Court for the Northern District of California and then practiced law as a litigator in San Francisco. She joined the University of Michigan Law School faculty in 1984. Professor Eisenberg regularly teaches courses in intellectual property and torts and has taught courses on legal regulation of science and legal issues in the Human Genome Project. She has written extensively about patent law as applied to biotechnology and the role of intellectual property at the public-private divide in research science, publishing in scientific journals as well as law reviews. She has received grants from the program on Ethical, Legal, and Social Implications for the Human Genome Project from the US Department of Energy Office of Biological and Environmental Research for her work on private appropriation and public dissemination of DNA sequence information. Professor Eisenberg has played an active role in public policy debates concerning the role of intellectual property in biomedical research. In 1996 she chaired a workshop on intellectual property rights and research tools in molecular biology at the National Academy of Sciences, and in 1997–98 she chaired a working group on research tools for the National Institutes of Health and is a past member of the Working Group on Ethical, Legal, and Social Implications of Human Genome Research. Professor Eisenberg is the Robert and Barbara Luciano Professor of Law. She spent the 1999–2000 academic year as a visiting professor at Stanford Law School.

Niva Elkin-Koren

Dr. Niva Elkin-Koren is a Senior Lecturer at the University of Haifa School of Law. She received her LL.B. from Tel-Aviv University School of Law in 1989, her LL.M. from Harvard Law School in 1991, and her S.J.D. from Stanford Law School in 1995. She teaches Contract Law, Intellectual Property, Electronic Commerce and related courses and seminars. Her research focuses on the legal institutions that facilitate private and public control over the production of information. She explores issues such as information policy, privacy, intellectual property, law and technology, and e-commerce.

Harry First

Harry First is Chief of the Antitrust Bureau of the Office of the Attorney General of the State of New York, on leave from his position as Professor of Law at New York University School of Law and the Director of the law school's Trade Regulation Program. At NYU, Professor First's teaching interests have included antitrust, international and comparative antitrust, and innovation policy. He is the co-author of law school casebooks on antitrust and on regulated industries, as well as the author of a casebook on business crime. He is also the author of numerous articles involving antitrust law, with a recent emphasis on international trade and competition issues. Professor First has twice been a Fulbright Research Fellow in Japan and has served as an Adjunct Professor of Law at the University of Tokyo. Prior to entering law teaching, Professor First was an attorney with the US Department of Justice, Antitrust Division; prior to his current position he was Counsel to Loeb & Loeb in New York City. Professor First earned his B.A. and J.D. from the University of Pennsylvania.

Jane C. Ginsburg

Jane Ginsburg, Morton L. Janklow Professor of Literary and Artistic Property Law, has been a member of the Columbia Law School faculty since 1987. She teaches Legal Methods, Copyright Law, and Trademarks Law, and is the author or co-author of casebooks in all three subjects. Recent lectures and articles on domestic and international copyright subjects have explored the legal implications of electronic creation and distribution of works of authorship. Professor Ginsburg has taught French and US copyright law and US legal methods and contracts law at the University of Paris and other French universities. A graduate of the University of Chicago (B.A. 1976, M.A. 1977), she received a J.D. in 1980 from Harvard, and a *Diplôme d'études approfondies* in 1985 and a Doctorate of Law in 1995 from the University of Paris II.

P. Bernt Hugenholtz

Bernt Hugenholtz is Professor of Law and Co-Director of the Institute for Information Law of the University of Amsterdam. In 1989 he received his doctorate cum laude from the University of Amsterdam, where he defended his thesis on copyright protection of works of information. He has written numerous books, studies, and articles on topics involving copyright and information technology, notably on the protection of computer software and databases, and on copyright problems relating to the emerging digital net-worked environment. Prof. Hugenholtz is chairman of the Intellectual Property Task Force of the Legal Advisory Board of the European Commission, and editor-in-chief of the Information Law Series, published by Kluwer Law International.

Sir Robin Jacob

Sir Robin was appointed to the Bench in October 1993. He was senior Judge of the Patents Court from January 1995 to October 1997. He is now Supervising Judge for Chancery matters in Birmingham, Bristol and Cardiff. He remains a Judge of the Patents Court and continues to take intellectual property cases on a regular basis. Before coming to the Bar in 1967 he obtained a science degree (principally in physics) from Cambridge University and a law degree from the London School of Economics. He was appointed a Queen's Counsel in 1981, having for the previous five years been the counsel who represented the Comptroller of Patents and the Government in the courts in intellectual property matters. Sir Robin's practice at the Bar was principally, though not exclusively, concerned with intellectual property in all its forms—from chasing counterfeiters to large scale (often multinational) disputes between large corporations. He regularly appeared before a wide variety of tribunals both in England and elsewhere. He appeared in the Euroepan Court of Justice, the European Commission and disputes in Hong Kong and Singapore on a number of occasions, and, in one major case, in Australia. At the Bar he had much experience of working with US attorneys and of parallel disputes in the United States, United Kingdom and other jurisdictions. He is in frequent contact with judges from many jurisdictions. Until his appointment as a Judge of the High Court, Sir Robin was appointed to hear appeals from the Trade Marks Registrar and was a Deputy Chairman of the Copyright Tribunal. For many years Sir Robin has been an author or editor of a number of legal textbooks, including *Kerly* (the leading UK work on trade marks) and the *Encyclopaedia of European and UK Patent Law*.

Bennett M. Lincoff

Bennett M. Lincoff is Senior Counsel at Darby & Darby in New York City, and a member of the firm's Internet/New Media/E-commerce practice group. He was formerly the Director of Legal Affairs for New Media at ASCAP (the American Society of Composers, Authors and Publishers), the world's largest music performance rights organization. He launched ASCAP's Internet initiative by developing and authoring the organization's Internet license agreement. That agreement, which authorizes webcasters to transmit performances of the music in ASCAP's repertory, was the first systematic and comprehensive structure for licensing online uses of any form of copyrighted content. Mr. Lincoff also co-chaired the delegation of the American Bar Association to the meetings of the World Intellectual Property Organization in Geneva, Switzerland. Those deliberations resulted in two new worldwide treaties regarding online use and protection of copyrighted works. He also served as a member of the coalition of copyright owners in the interindustry negotiations which ultimately led to passage of the Digital Millennium

Copyright Act in the United States. Mr. Lincoff is a frequent guest speaker and panelist at conferences on the issues presented by Internet uses of copyrighted works, and has written widely on that subject.

Robert P. Merges

Prof. Merges is the Wilson Sonsini Goodrich & Rosati Professor of Law at U.C. Berkeley (Boalt Hall) School of Law. Prof. Merges teaches mainly in the area of Intellectual Property and Contracts; his primary scholarly interest is in economic aspects of intellectual property rights, especially patents. He is the author or co-author of several leading student casebooks in intellectual property law. Prior to his academic career, Prof. Merges practiced law in Palo Alto, California, working primarily with technology-related startup companies. Before law school he also worked in Silicon Valley for VisiCorp (seller of the VisiCalc spreadsheet) and Intel. He received a B.S. from Carnegie-Mellon University; a J.D. from Yale Law School in 1985; and LL.M. and J.S.D. degrees from Columbia Law School.

Jon O. Newman

Judge Jon O. Newman is a judge on the US Court of Appeals for the Second Circuit (New York, Connecticut, and Vermont), where he has served for 20 years, including four years as Chief Judge. He previously served in the District of Connecticut for eight years as a federal District Judge and five years as United States Attorney. Judge Newman's career includes private law practice and staff positions in the Executive and Legislative Branches of the federal government, and in state government. He has taught law courses in the United States and consulted on court reform in numerous countries. Judge Newman has written several opinions and law review articles in the field of copyright.

Walter W. Powell

Walter W. Powell is Professor of Education and affiliated Professor of Sociology at Stanford University, and Director of the Scandinavian Consortium on Organizational Research. He joined the Stanford faculty in July 1999, after previously teaching at the University of Arizona, MIT, and Yale. He has been a fellow at the Center for Advanced Study in the Behavioral Sciences and been a visiting faculty member several times at the Institute for Advanced Studies in Vienna and the Santa Fe Institute. Prof. Powell works in the areas of organization theory and economic sociology. He is currently engaged in research on the origins and development of the commercial field of the life sciences. With his collaborator Ken Koput, he has authored a series of papers on the evolving network structure of the biotechnology industry. Powell and Koput have developed a longitudinal database that tracks the development of biotechnology worldwide from the 1980s to the present. With Jason Owen-Smith, Prof. Powell is studying the role of universities in transferring basic science into commercial development by science-based companies, and the consequences for universities of their growing involvement in commercial enterprises.

Jerome H. Reichman

Jerome H. Reichman graduated from the University of Chicago (B.A.) under the Hutchin's early admissions program in 1955, and attended the Yale Law School, where he received his J.D. degree in 1979. Since then he has taught at the University of Michigan, Ohio State University, the University of Florida, the University of Rome, Italy, and Vanderbilt University, where he was a tenured professor of law in the field of contracts and intellectual property. He became the Bunyan A. Womble Professor of Law at Duke University Law School on July 1, 2000. Prof. Reichman has written and lectured widely on all aspects of intellectual property law, including comparative and international intellectual property law. He is one of six co-authors preparing a commentary on the Agreement Concerning Trade-Related Aspects of Intellectual Property Laws (TRIPS Agreement) (edited by Paul Goldstein and Joseph Straus), to be published by Oxford University Press.

F. M. Scherer

F. M. Scherer is Aetna Professor Emeritus at the John F. Kennedy School of Government, Harvard University, and visiting professor at Princeton University. He has also taught at the University of Michigan, Northwestern University, Swarthmore College, the Central European University, and the University of Bayreuth. In 1974–76, he was chief economist at the Federal Trade Commission. His undergraduate degree was from the University of Michigan; he received his M.B.A. and Ph.D. from Harvard University; he holds an honorary doctorate from the University of Hohenheim, Germany. His research specialties are industrial economics and the economics of technological change. His current research is on the economics of musical composition between the years 1650 and 1900. He is past president of the Industrial Organization Society and the International Joseph A. Schumpeter Society, and past vice president of the American Economic Association and the Southern Economic Association. He is a member of the *Journal of Economic Literature* board of editors. He won the Lanchester Prize of the Operations Research Society of America in 1964 and the O'Melveny & Myers Centennial Research Prize in 1989.

Carl Shapiro

Carl Shapiro is the Transamerica Professor of Business Strategy at the Haas School of Business at the University of California at Berkeley. Prof. Shapiro has published extensively in the areas of industrial organization, competition policy, the economics of innovation, network economics, and competitive strategy. Prof. Shapiro served as Deputy Assistant Attorney General for Economics in the Antitrust Division of the US Department of Justice during 1995–96. He founded the Tilden Group, an economic consulting company, and is now a Senior Consultant at Charles River Associates. Prof. Shapiro has consulted extensively for a wide range of private clients as well as for the US Department of Justice and the Federal Trade Commission. He is the author, with Hal R. Varian, of Information Rules: A Strategic Guide to the Network Economy; see www.inforules.com.

Hanns Ullrich

Hanns Ullrich, Prof. Dr. iur., born 1939 (Jena/Thuringen), graduated from the University of Tubingen in 1964. He received a Dr. iur. (Freie Universität Berlin 1969), M.C.J. (New York University 1971/1975), and Dr. iur. habil (Munich 1982). Prof. Ullrich became Professor at the Universität der Bundeswehr Munich in 1985, in the chair for civil law, commercial law, and business law. He has been Head of the Institute of Comparative Business Law, Technology Law and Law of Public Procurement, and visiting professor at the College of Europe, Bruges (Belgium). He is currently at the European University Institute/Florence (Italy).

Diane P. Wood

Diane P. Wood is a Circuit Judge on the US Court of Appeals for the Seventh Circuit, Chicago, Illinois, and a Senior Lecturer in Law at the University of Chicago Law School, where she teaches in the field of international economic law. Prior to her appointment in 1995 to the Court, she served from 1993 to 1995 as deputy Assistant Attorney General in the Antitrust Division of the US Department of Justice, where she was responsible for international antitrust policy and enforcement, as well as the Division's appellate litigation. From 1981 until 1995, she was a professor at the University of Chicago Law School. In 1990, she was named to the Harold J. and Marion F. Green Professorship in International Legal Studies, becoming the first woman to hold a named chair at the school. She served as Associate Dean of the Law School from 1989 through 1992.

Diane L. Zimmerman

Diane Leenheer Zimmerman is Professor of Law at New York University School of Law where she teaches courses in copyrights, innovation policy, tort law, and First Amendment law. She writes and lectures on a variety of topics, including intellectual property, press freedoms, privacy and defamation, religious freedom, commercial speech, regulation of pornography, and women's rights. In recent years, much of her scholarship has focused on the interface between intellectual property rights and the First Amendment. Prof. Zimmerman was also the Reporter on Gender for the Second Circuit Task

Force on Gender, Racial and Ethnic Fairness, and co-authored a major study on the subject of race and gender in federal litigation that issued in December 1997. She was the Distinguished Lee Visiting Professor of Constitutional Law at the College of William and Mary in 1994, has also taught in the Law and Society program at the Aspen Institute, and for several years was special counsel to Skadden, Arps, Slate, Meagher & Flom in the area of products liability. She holds a J.D. from Columbia University, and was law clerk to the Hon. Jack B. Weinstein in the Eastern District of New York. Prior to attending law school, she was a writer and reporter for Newsweek and the New York Daily News, and also studied English and Comparative Literature at the Graduate Faculty of Columbia University.

TABLES OF CASES

European Community

European Court of Human Rights

European Court of Justice (ECJ)—alphabetical

European Court of Justice (ECJ)—numerical

Court of First Instance (CFI)—alphabetical

Court of First Instance (CFI)—numerical

TABLES OF LEGISLATION

International Treaties and Conventions

TABLES OF EC/EU LEGISLATION

Regulations

PART I

EXPANDING THE PRIVATE DOMAIN

Part I explores claims for expanding the boundaries of intellectual property law. There are two ways in which such claims sound. One is as a demand to enlarge the scope of standard forms of protection, copyright, patent and trademark law. Courts, for example, have been asked to interpret such rights broadly: to construe patent claims to cover inventions that go beyond the inventor's exact embodiment to encompass other advances made with the same insight; to hold that a copyright is infringed by paraphrasing and other nonliteral copying; to find that even noncompetitive, nonconfusing uses of trademarked material violate a trademark holder's rights. The second kind of claim is for new rights, for rights that protect innovations that are not creative enough to be covered by the standard regimes. Both sorts of claims are explored here.

F.M. Scherer, of the Kennedy School, makes an empirical argument for expanding the traditional regimes of copyright and patent law. Those who oppose strengthening protection argue that declines in the cost of developing and distributing information products mean that investments in innovative activities can be fully recouped through first mover advantages and existing protection. Professor Scherer argues, however, that recoupment is not an adequate measure of the return necessary to spur the optimum level of creativity. His examination of data in both the technological and artistic sectors demonstrates that in the creative industries, the likelihood of commercial failure is extraordinarily high and difficult to predict. Furthermore, risks cannot easily be laid off through diversification. As a result, the contours of the law must insure that successful products generate high returns, returns sufficient to compensate for these effects.

The other chapters in this Part deal with the issue of protecting sub-patentable and subcopyrightable works. J.H. Reichman uses a hypothetical research project (an attempt to produce new kinds of tulips) as a way of illustrating the problem of providing incentives to develop incremental innovations. He advocates a new form of protection which, he claims, will reward innovation without undermining the ability of developers to cumulate marginal developments and build on one another's insights. Jane Ginsburg focuses one question of database protection. Made up principally of public-domain facts, databases represent the quintessential noncopyrightable (or weakly copyrighted) work that is costly to create, yet easy to copy. She uses current proposals to demonstrate how a regime to protect such works can provide innovators with the benefits they seek while preserving a creative environment that allows others to continue to push forward the frontiers of knowledge.

1

THE INNOVATION LOTTERY

F. M. SCHERER*

During the past several years Dietmar Harhoff (University of Munich) and I have been collecting and analyzing quantitative data on the size distribution of rewards realized by individuals and organizations carrying out technological innovations. From our new evidence and insights by other scholars on the economics of individuals' gambling behavior, it is possible to propose a theory of incentives for innovation in technology and other creative endeavors. Our findings provide support for a half-century-old obiter dictum by the renowned Austrian (and later Harvard University) economist Joseph A. Schumpeter. Characterizing the admixture of chance, ability, and energy that sustains innovation and technological progress in a capitalistic economy, Schumpeter wrote:

Spectacular prizes much greater than would have been necessary to call forth the particular effort are thrown to a small minority of winners, thus propelling much more efficaciously than a more equal and more 'just' distribution would, the activity of that large majority of businessmen who receive in return very modest compensation or nothing or less than nothing, and yet do their utmost because they have the big prizes before their eyes and overrate their chances of doing equally well.[1]

Schumpeter's conjecture was based upon little more than casual empiricism. In this chapter I summarize the relevant new evidence and tread, perhaps too incautiously, into the realm of theory-building.

* Aetna Professor of Public Policy Emeritus, John F. Kennedy School of Government, Harvard University; visiting professor, Princeton University.
[1] JOSEPH A SCHUMPETER, CAPITALISM, SOCIALISM, AND DEMOCRACY 73–74 (1942).

I. Profits and their Possible Size Distributions

During the early 1960s, while seeking to understand the links between market structure and technological innovation, I happened onto some data from a small survey asking holders of US invention patents about the profitability of their inventions. Analyzing the profit data, I found their statistical distribution to be 'skew' and indeed highly skew, with most of the observations lying in the range of low profit values but 'with a very long tail into the high value side'.[2] A simple test suggested that the data might conform to what is called a Pareto distribution, to whose peculiar properties the mathematician Benoit Mandelbrot was at the time directing attention.[3]

A statistical size distribution is essentially a systematic array of numerical observations drawn through sampling, conventionally shown by plotting on the horizontal axis of a graph the range of observation values (eg, profits) and on the vertical axis the relative frequency with which those values occur in the sample. Figures 1.1(a) and 1.1(b) illustrate two such distributions created using my computer's random number generating program. The array in Figure 1.1(a) is typical of a 'normal' distribution. It resembles a symmetric bell-shaped curve, with the largest and smallest observation values occurring with much lower frequency than those in the middle of the distribution (ie, near the sample mean, or average value). Figure 1.1(b), on the other hand, reflects a particular kind of skew distribution known as a log normal distribution.[4] By far the greatest mass of observations occurs at relatively low values, but the distribution has a long thin right-hand 'tail' of large values occurring with very low frequency.

The length and thickness of the tail determine the degree of skewness characterizing a distribution. The longer the tail, the more skew the distribution is. Some general classes of skew distributions are more skew than others. The Pareto distribution I believed I had found in the 1960s for patented invention profits is more skew, ie, with a longer and fatter tail, than the typical log normal distribution illustrated in Figure 1.1(b). The differences between skew distributions can be characterized through a simple graph (Figure 1.2) popularized by Benoit Mandelbrot. The coordinates are logarithmic. On the

---

[2] F M. Scherer, *Firm Size, Market Structure, Opportunity, and the Output of Patented Inventions*, 55 AM. ECON. REV. 1098 (1965).

[3] Benoit Mandelbrot, *New Methods in Statistical Economics*, 71 J POL. ECON. 421 (1963).

[4] It is called log normal because if one takes logarithms of the observation values, the logarithmic values exhibit a symmetric normal distribution pattern. Indeed, Figure 1.1(b) was created by taking the 1,000 values used in Figure 1.1(a) (from a random number program generating normally distributed values with mean zero and a standard deviation of 1) and using them as exponents in the expression 10^n, where n is the value of a Figure 1.1(a) observation. Since the logarithm to base 10 of 10^n is n, the distribution of n is normal while 10^n is skew-distributed. The mean (average) value of the distribution in Figure 1.1(b) is 10.50; the median value is 1.11.

(a) Normal distribution

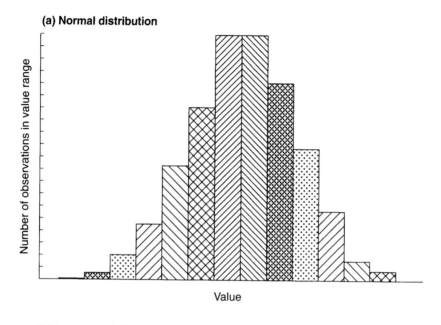

(b) Log normal distribution

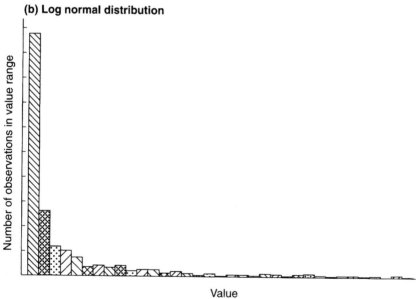

Fig. 1.1: Comparison of normal and (skew) log normal distributions

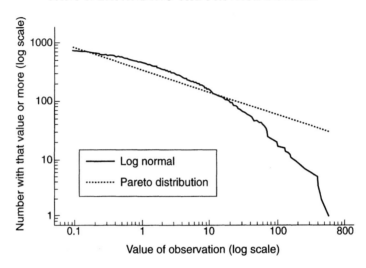

FIG. 1.2: Pareto plot of simulated log normal and Pareto distributions

horizontal axis, one identifies the values of the observations (eg, profits). The observations are ranked from most valuable to least valuable, and on the vertical axis, one plots the number of observations with values equal to or greater than any given horizontal axis value.

The solid curve in Figure 1.2 traces the log normal distribution plotted in Figure 1.1(b). The most valuable observation (number 1 on the vertical scale) has a value of 570; 18 observations have values of 100 or more; and 172 observations have values of 10 or more. The dotted straight line shows a Pareto distribution fitted to the data underlying Figure 1.1(b).[5] The simplest Pareto distributions plot as straight lines on doubly logarithmic graphs, which is why such graphs are called Pareto graphs. The dotted Pareto distribution line conforms fairly closely to the solid log normal distribution curve over the less valuable observations ranked from 100 to 1,000. However, it diverges ever more sharply from the downward-bending log normal distribution in the right-hand tail of high-value observations. Indeed, the most valuable log normal observation of 570 is only the 30th most valuable observation on the Pareto line. If the Pareto line were extrapolated linearly, one would find the value of the most valuable observation (number 1 on the vertical axis) to be 2.94 million, and the second most valuable observation (number 2 on the vertical) 520,000. True Pareto distributions have extremely large 'outliers' relative to the mass of observations.

[5] Specifically, a straight line was fitted by least squares to the observations, yielding the equation log rank = 2.585 − 0.3996 (log value of observation). The slope value 0.3996 is called the Pareto alpha or the Pareto slope coefficient.

Skew distributions exhibit ill-behaved sampling properties. Statisticians' 'law of large numbers' states that the mean (average value) of a sample of observations should converge ever more closely to some 'true' average value as one draws ever larger samples. But with skew distributions, this convergence operates at best slowly, and it may not happen at all. Pareto distributions are extreme in their non-conformity to the law of large numbers. Indeed, Pareto distributions with high but plausible degrees of skewness do not conform at all.[6] Rather, as one draws ever larger samples, there is a chance that one will come up with an extremely large observation value (such as the 2.94 million value extrapolated from the Pareto distribution of Figure 1.2) that is so large relative to all previous observations that it 'blows' the sample mean to a much higher value. For the Pareto distribution illustrated in Figure 1.2, the sample average is 1,004 if the largest observation is excluded but rises to 2,947 if it augments the other 999 observations. What this means in practical terms is that it is very hard or maybe even impossible to secure stable average profit returns by pursuing portfolio strategies eg, pooling many research and development projects into a portfolio.

II. The Profits from Technological Innovation

My discovery that the distribution of profits associated with patented inventions might exhibit sampling instabilities like those described in the previous paragraph has been gnawing at me for three decades.[7] My interest was sustained in part by others' findings, from studies of the rates at which fees are paid to keep patents in force in some national jurisdictions, that the distribution of patent values is indeed highly skew. Returning to the scene of the crime, I joined Dietmar Harhoff to conduct surveys ascertaining through direct queries the estimated value of 776 German and 222 US inventions on which German patent protection was maintained for a full 18-year term following applications filed in 1977.[8] We confirmed that even for patents considered valuable enough to warrant paying German renewal fees escalating over time to a cumulative total of DM 16,075 (roughly $6,825 at 1977 exchange rates), most of the inventions are of only modest value, while a few yield blockbuster rewards. Among the 776 German patents—already self-selected from the seven times larger cohort of contemporary patents not

---

[6] This is true when the so-called Pareto slope coefficient has an absolute value less than 10. The slope coefficient for the Pareto distribution in Figure 1.2 is shown in n. 5 above to be 0.3996. Thus, asymptotically (as ever larger samples are drawn, and the straight dotted line in Figure 1.2 shifts in parallel upward), the sample mean diverges toward infinity.

[7] Acquaintances of long standing might observe that quite a lot of me has been gnawed away in the interim

[8] Dietmar Harhoff et al., *Exploring the Tail of Patent Value Distributions* (working paper), Center for European Economic Research, Mannheim, Germany (1998).

renewed to full term—the most valuable 78 (ie, the top ten percent) accounted for an estimated 88 percent of all 776 patents' economic value to their holders. For the smaller but even more select group of US inventions, which were patented both in Germany and the United States, the top 22 accounted for 81 to 85 percent of the 222 patents' value. The best of the best conferred economic prizes measured in the billions of dollars or Deutschmarks.

Figure 1.3 plots the German patent value distribution on doubly logarithmic (ie, Pareto) coordinates. If the size distribution were Paretian, it would plot as a straight line on the chosen coordinates. In fact, downward concavity reveals that there is less skewness than for the Pareto case. A statistical analysis provides the strongest support for a log normal distribution like the solid-line distribution in Figure 1.2.[9]

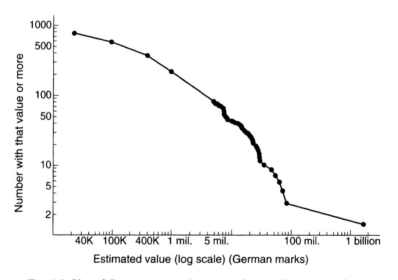

FIG. 1.3: Plot of German renewed patent values on Pareto coordinates

In a parallel survey of the license royalties obtained by six research-oriented US universities on their patent portfolios during four years of the early 1990s, I found that a single bundle, comprising the three Cohen-Boyer gene splicing patents, yielded 24 to 33 percent of the total royalties obtained from 350 to 486 individual bundles of licensed technology. The top six bundles, ie,

[9] For the log normal data underlying Figure 1.2, the 100 largest observations (ie, the top 10 percent) accounted for 76.9 percent of total sample values. By this concentration measure, the Figure 1.2 data are somewhat less skew than the German patent data.

making up one to two percent of the sample members by number, generated from 66 to 76 percent of total sample patent royalties.[10]

Confirmation of the rewards skewness phenomenon comes from information on the discounted present value of quasi-rents (ie, the discounted surplus of sales revenues over estimated production and marketing outlays) realized by companies from new pharmaceutical chemical entities marketed during the 1970s and early 1980s in the United States following Food and Drug Administration approval.[11] The most profitable 10 percent of those product introductions contributed 48 to 55 percent of total sample quasi-rents. Among eight sets of data on which reward size distribution data were obtained, the two drug quasi-rent samples exhibited the least skewness. Their distributions were much less skew than Pareto distributions and somewhat less than the log normal distribution, but more than plausible alternative skew distributions such as the negative binomial or the Weibull.[12]

Further insights emerge from evidence on the outcomes of investments in that most dynamic of US industrial sectors, new high-technology ventures. Surveys of 1,053 investments by venture capital funds in individual venture capital targets reveal a highly skew distribution of outcomes. Some 59 to 62 percent of the ultimately realized returns came from the most successful 10 percent of investments by number.[13] A Federal Reserve Board staff study of 225 venture capital partnerships formed between 1980 and 1986 revealed a weighted-average internal rate of return on investment as of 1993 averaging 7.95 percent, with a weighted-average median of 5.58 percent.[14] Finding the mean in excess of the median or mid-sample value, which occurred for every individual year of fund formation as well as in the aggregate, is another indication of distribution skewness. So also is the high variability over time of median rates of return, ranging from 1.6 percent (for partnerships organized in 1981) to 13.2 percent (for 1980-vintage funds). When the distribution of outcomes is skew, as we have seen, atrophied operation of the law of large numbers makes it hard to diversify away random sampling variability by forming portfolios of numerous investments.

To sharpen insights on the performance of new high-technology ventures, an exhaustive sample was drawn of venture fund-backed companies that floated initial public common stock offerings (IPOs) in the 1983–86 period and that operated in specified high-technology fields.[15] Typically, new

---

[10] F. M. Scherer, *The Size Distribution of Profits from Innovation*, 49/50 ANNALES D'ECONOMIE ET DE STATISTIQUE 495 (1998).

[11] See Henry Grabowski & John Vernon, *A New Look at the Returns and Risks to Pharmaceutical R&D*, 36 MGMT SCI. 804 (1990); *Returns on New Drug Introductions in the 1980s*, 13 J. HEALTH ECON. 383 (1994).

[12] See Scherer, n. 10 above.   [13] Ibid.

[14] GEORGE W. FENN ET AL., THE ECONOMICS OF THE PRIVATE EQUITY MARKET (1995). The weighted-average standard deviation was 9.60 percent.

[15] A more complete analysis is presented in F M. Scherer et al., *Uncertainty and the Size Distribution of Rewards from Technological Innovation*, 10 J. EVOLUTIONARY ECON. 175 (2000).

companies supported by venture capital partnerships attempt IPOs only after they have made appreciable progress toward achieving technical and market success, and so they tend to be more mature investments than those discussed in the previous paragraph. A hypothetical first-day investment of $1,000 was made in the common stock of the 110 sample companies whose stock continued to be traded on a public market after the IPO date.[16] Dividends were reinvested and stock splits were tallied. By the end of 1995, 52 of the 110 companies remained as independent entities. The value of their stocks as of 31 December 1995, along with proceeds (reinvested temporarily in the NASDAQ index) from the liquidation of drop-out company stocks, was as follows:

52 surviving companies	$417,002
23 acquired companies	96,400
35 delisted companies	21,178
Total terminal value	$534,580

Had the same $110,000 been invested in the NASDAQ index in January 1983, investors would have had $501,908. Thus, investors in our sample of high-technology companies increased the value of their initial investment by a substantial multiple, earning on average a 12.2 percent return on their investment, but fared only slightly (and not statistically significantly) better than investors in a complete portfolio of NASDAQ company stocks.

For our present purposes, the key point is this: as the years progressed from the time of the initial investments analyzed here, the distribution of outcomes became more and more skew. By the end of 1995, the best-performing 11 companies (10 percent by number of the initial sample) contributed 62 percent of the investors' total portfolio value. Figure 1.4 shows how the value of individual company investments changed over time. It is limited to 10 companies, including the five most successful full-term survivors and five others selected randomly. The share values for the random choices cluster so tightly below $2,000 that they are largely indistinguishable. Had one invested $1,000 in Adobe Systems, Concord Computing, and Amgen, on the other hand, one would have had shares valued at $77,565, $74,130, and $55,980 respectively by the end of 1995. The cross-sectional distribution of full-term survivors as of December 1995, plotted in Figure 1.5 on doubly logarithmic coordinates like those used in Figures 1.2 and 1.3, exhibits a concave log normal scatter of values not unlike the one observed for German patents, except that there is no single extremely large outlying value. Skew-distributed samples commonly exhibit such erratic behavior in their right-hand tail.

---

[16] Twenty-one IPO companies left no discernible trace of stock trading in stock exchange records To standardize the investments for timing differences, $1,000 was 'parked' in the NASDAQ index as of 1 January 1983, with the proceeds being invested on the date of any sample company's IPO.

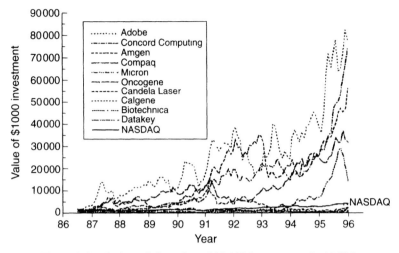

FIG. 1.4: Evolution of the value of $1,000 investments in 10 IPOs

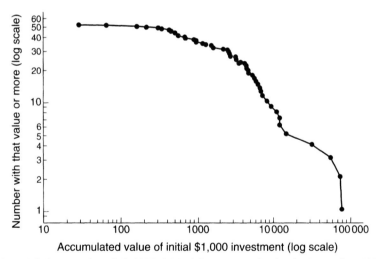

FIG. 1.5: Pareto plot of 52 1983–86 IPO investments' value in December 1995

Thus, we conclude that there are striking regularities in the distribution of rewards to technological innovation. A minority of 'spectacular winners' appropriate the lion's share of total rewards, as Schumpeter predicted. The size distribution of rewards is highly skew, with a long right-hand tail. The distributions do not appear to be Paretian, contrary to my 1965 hypothesis; the log normal distribution characteristically provides a better fit. The rewards from individual patents exhibit more skewness, ie, the top 10 percent capture a higher total share of payoffs, than the rewards from innovations such as new drugs, which may be covered by numerous product and process patents, or investments in high-technology startup companies, which sometimes market multiple innovations and hence average out some of the variability associated with individual innovations.

III. Innovation in Popular and Not-So-Popular Culture

Not all innovation is technological. Innovation also occurs in cultural domains, eg, in the composition or performing of music, the production of motion pictures, and the writing of books. We supplement our insights here by analyzing fragmentary data from the first two of these branches.

From *Billboard* magazine, data were obtained on the US sales of the 70 best-selling popular music albums and single recordings in 1997.[17] The best-selling album, with sales of 5.3 million estimated by sampling, was by the Spice Girls; the best-selling single, with sales of 8.1 million units, was Elton John's 'Candle in the Wind', commemorating the death of Britain's Princess Diana. It is known (also from *Billboard*) that approximately 613 million music albums and 134 million singles records were sold in 1997. The best-selling album accounted for 0.86 percent of total album sales; the best-selling 70 albums (all with sales of 1 million or more) for 21.0 percent. The best-selling single recording gained 6.1 percent of singles sales; the 70 best-sellers (with sales of 500,000 or more) 55.0 percent of singles sales. It is not known how many albums and singles were offered in total during 1997. A crude extrapolation from the (nearly log normal) distribution of data on the top 70 albums suggests that 1,000 albums accounted for 60 percent of total album sales, with average sales for individual albums in the bottom decile of this best-selling group averaging approximately 123,000. A similar extrapolation reveals (with somewhat larger uncertainty) that 800 records sufficed to account for 98 percent of total singles sales, with the least successful hundred of those 800 averaging sales of roughly 10,000 each. Even though individual winners did not capture the lion's share of sales, the top 10 winners surpassed the sales of records ranked 800th in the distribution by approximately 25 times on average for albums and 250 times for singles. Clearly, it is much more lucrative to be a top winner.

Figure 1.6 plots on doubly logarithmic coordinates the size distribution of sales for the top 70 records of 1997. For both albums and singles, some concavity is evident, although the extreme 'Candle in the Wind' outlier reverses the curvature for singles, just as an extreme value does in the distribution of German patents (Figure 1.3).

---

[17] *Best-Selling Records of 1997*, BILLBOARD MAGAZINE, January 31, 1998, at 76.

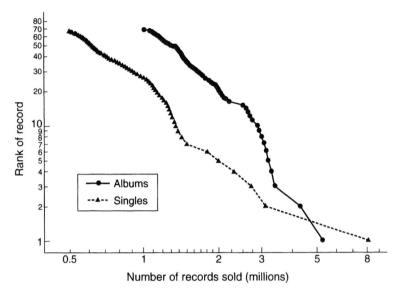

FIG. 1.6: Pareto plot of leading popular record sales in 1997

These statistics are for individual records. Another article in *Billboard* arrays the cumulative total record sales outside the United States over 50 years through December 1997 for the 48 most successful recording groups affiliated with one of the leading popular record companies, Atlantic Records.[18] The highest-selling group, Led Zeppelin, achieved career sales of 29.6 million records, more than twice those of the second-ranked group and 34 times those of the 48th-ranked artist. Led Zeppelin's sales comprised 17.6 percent of the sales of all 48 leading groups. This and other evidence reveals more skewness in career record sales than for the distributions across individual records, but less than what was observed for any group of technological innovations.

The success of classical music composers, tallied not in lifetime financial rewards but in the attention posterity has paid them, also appears to follow a skew distribution. From the Schwann *Reference Guide to Classical Music* for Fall 1996, the number of records currently available was estimated for 686 composers born between 1650 and 1840.[19] The measure used was linear centimeters of record listings, with five lines of type per centimeter on average and the typical record entry running from one to three lines. A list of the eight leaders yields no major surprises:

---

[18] *Atlantic's International Best-Sellers*, BILLBOARD MAGAZINE, January 17, 1998, at A–28.
[19] A posthumous record count is analogous to the publication citation counts used to assess the influence of scholars. See DEREK J. DE SOLLA PRICE, LITTLE SCIENCE, BIG SCIENCE (1963).

W. A. Mozart   1,656 cm
L. Beethoven   1,262 cm
J. S. Bach   1,190 cm
J. Brahms   644 cm
P.I. Tchaikovsky   568 cm
F. Schubert   553 cm
F. Chopin   497 cm
F. J. Haydn   461 cm

Mozart alone commands 11.3 percent of the recordings; the top eight composers 46.8 percent, and the 69 composers comprising the top 10 percent by number 87.8 percent.[20] These values, reflecting a high degree of skewness, are broadly consistent with those observed for the profits or royalties from technological innovations.[21] Figure 1.7 plots the distribution function on doubly logarithmic coordinates. For the vast majority of composers, it is close to a

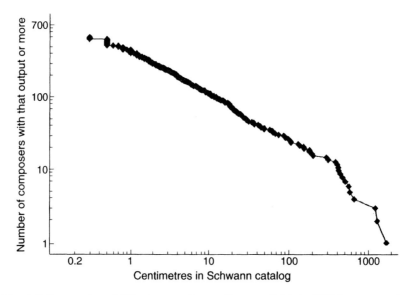

FIG. 1.7: Pareto plot of 686 composers' recordings available in 1996 (composers born between 1650 and 1840)

---

[20] Mozart's leadership is even stronger when composers are arrayed in order of records per year of working life, with the working life defined (somewhat inaccurately for the case of Mozart) to begin at age 16. The top eight composers by this criterion accounted for 57.1 percent of the total distribution.

[21] In ongoing research, I am attempting to assemble data on the the size distribution of composers' earnings during their lifetimes. On Mozart, for which the documentation is particularly rich, see W. J. Baumol & Hilda Baumol, *On the Economics of Musical Composition in Mozart's Vienna*, 18 J. CULTURAL ECON. 171 (1994).

straight line, consistent with a Pareto distribution, departing from the Pareto form and bending downward only for 13 leaders.

Arthur DeVany and W. D. Walls compiled statistics on the distribution of revenues for motion pictures (most of them readily forgotten) appearing among the Top 50 list in *Variety* magazine between May 1985 and January 1986.[22] Over the entire nine-month period surveyed, the top 10 percent of market-leading films by number generated approximately 60 percent of total sample revenues. Again, a skew distribution is revealed. The distribution was strongly concave relative to doubly logarithmic coordinates and hence inconsistent with a Pareto law, but more skew than a log normal distribution.

IV. An Ideal Reward System?

From the compilation of evidence reviewed here, it would appear that Schumpeter was correct at least statistically: the big prizes from innovation are thrown to a small minority of winners, while the majority of innovative efforts confer only modest rewards. For new drug chemical entities and investments in high-technology startups, on which the evidence is most complete, the median project yields less than the capitalized cost of capital funds invested, but losses on the majority of projects are more than offset by gains from the most successful projects. We ask now whether Schumpeter might also have been correct in his conjecture that a skew distribution of rewards motivates innovative activity 'more efficaciously' than a more 'just' system of rewards, which presumably would bestow returns more or less closely proportional to the investments seeking them.

Skew reward distributions are particularly risky because it is difficult to make random deviations cancel each other out and converge on some stable average value by forming diversified portfolios containing numerous investments.[23] Most of received investment theory assumes that investors are risk-averse. If innovation requires investment and investors are risk-averse, how can a highly skew distribution of rewards be conducive to innovation?

The assumption that investors are risk-averse is difficult to square with the widespread and long-standing popularity of sweepstakes lotteries in the

---

[22] Authur DeVany & W D. Walls, *Bose-Einstein Dynamics and Adaptive Contracting in the Motion Picture Industry*, 106 ECON. J. 1493 (1996).

[23] How difficult it is was shown by computer simulations in which hypothetical random samples were drawn repeatedly from the skew distribution of new drug quasi-rents estimated by Grabowski and Vernon. Even when new product introductions were pooled to the full US industry-wide level (ie, with a single entity introducing 18 new products annually, each yielding profits over a 21-year span), annual profit swings as large as plus-or-minus 25 percent of long-run industry averages remain. See F. M. Scherer & Dietmar Harhoff, *Technology Policy for a World of Skew-Distributed Outcomes*, 29 RES. POLICY 559 (2000).

United States and other nations.[24] The larger in absolute value the prize, captured at infinitesimal odds, the more enthusiastic individuals' participation appears to be. With an actuarial value of payoffs well below the sum of players' bets—eg, for state sweepstakes lotteries, roughly half the stakes on average—such lotteries, like most other forms of gambling, are not 'fair' gambles.[25] Yet people flock to play.

Investing in high-technology startup companies is similar to (but less extreme than) lotteries in the skewness of rewards and the relatively low probability (well below 0.1) of a really big payoff. But they are strikingly different in the sense that venture investment tends, given reasonable diligence, to yield discounted returns exceeding actuarially the value of the stakes invested. Thus, at least historically, they have been 'fair' gambles. Perhaps that is difference enough to distinguish between buying sweepstakes tickets and investing in the innovation lottery. (Whether high-technology stock returns will continue to exceed investments in the future as more and more naive investors plunge into the high-technology game remains to be seen.) But let us probe further to see whether more can be discerned.

That people embrace high-stakes gambles but engage more or less simultaneously in the risk-averse behavior associated with paying an administrative premium for insurance has long fascinated economists. In a seminal paper, Milton Friedman and L. J. Savage showed that a consumer may rationally choose both to buy insurance against risks that would reduce her wealth and accept unfair gambles on the off chance of a sizeable wealth increase. Their argument is illustrated in Figure 1.8, which assumes that 'utility' (whose measurement problems need not detain us) is derived from consumption and that consumption is facilitated by wealth. Friedman and Savage postulated that the utility function, ie, the mathematical relationship between an individual's utility and her wealth, has the peculiar ogive shape shown by the heavy solid line U(W) in Figure 1.8. Suppose the consumer's initial wealth position is W_o, yielding (read horizontally over to the vertical axis) utility realization U_o. Now suppose the consumer can invest in a 'fair' lottery ticket whose cost, if with relatively high probability she fails to draw the winning combination, leaves her with lower wealth W_L. But if she wins the lottery (with low probability), she is propelled to much higher wealth W_W (yielding correspondingly higher utility U_W). The straight line segment ACB shows a locus of expected utility values given by the probability of winning P_W times the utility U_W from winning plus $(1 - P_W)$ times the utility U_L from being at the loser's

[24] See, eg, CHARLES T. CLOTFELTER & PHILIP J. COOK, SELLING HOPE: STATE LOTTERIES IN AMERICA (1989); Matthew Breuer et al., *State Lotteries: The Determinants of Ticket Sales*, 8 WAGNER REV. 15 (1997); Gregory Bresinger, *The Lottery Racket*, 16 FREE MARKET 1 (1998). The irrationality of lotteries appears to be one of the few things on which economists of all ideological persuasions agree.

[25] A fair gamble is one in which the actuarial value of the prize, ie, the value of the prize times the probability of winning it, equals the value of the bets.

wealth level W_L. If the odds are such that the probability-weighted expected wealth outcome is $\overline{W}$, the expected utility (read horizontally from point C on the expected value line ACB to the vertical axis) of that outcome is exactly the same as the utility U_0 from not entering the lottery and remaining with certainty at wealth level W_0, then our consumer will be indifferent between playing and not playing. But if the 'cost' of a lottery ticket (eg, in the form of less than 'fair' odds) is less than $W_0 - \overline{W}$, so that the probability-weighted expected value of the consumer's post-lottery wealth is greater than $\overline{W}$, the consumer will realize higher expected utility participating in the lottery than not participating. This happens because substantial increases in wealth yield disproportionately large increases in utility (ie, marginal utility is increasing with increases in wealth), outweighing the actuarial value of the modest decrease in utility associated with buying a ticket and losing. By similar reasoning, it can be shown that from an initial wealth position W_0, the consumer faced with some small probability of losing much of her wealth (eg, because her house burns down) but able to insure against that contingency by paying a premium for insurance will, within some range of insurance costs, choose to buy the insurance. The reason is that, in the concave-downward (low-wealth) segment of the consumer's utility function, wealth losses entail disproportionately large sacrifices of utility, the avoidance of which is worth paying more than the actuarial value of insurance.

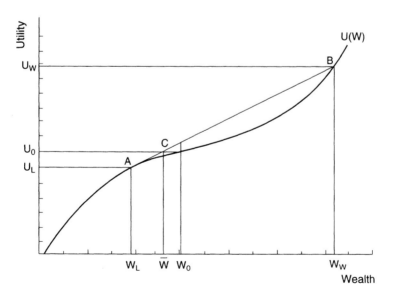

FIG. 1.8: Utility function consistent with buying insurance and betting in lotteries

Friedman and Savage speculate that real-world individuals' utility functions often have upward-bending curvature at wealth levels much higher than those currently attained, implying increasing marginal utility of wealth, because a big wealth increase moves the consumer to a new, much higher material and social status. Such a large change in effect fulfills their optimistic, or perhaps wildly optimistic, dreams. Certainly, something like that explains the propensity of lower-income citizens to spend disproportionate amounts of their income playing the lottery, in effect gambling on an escape from poverty.[26] It is also consistent with anecdotal evidence about the motives of high-technology firm entrepreneurs, who see a successful startup as the principal means of becoming truly wealthy. In this respect, sweepstakes players and technological entrepreneurs may be more similar than their conventional demographic characteristics imply.

Lotteries, of course, are not the only form of gambling to offer the possibility of large payoffs at low odds. Horse racing provides a rich environment for analyzing risky choices. There is evidence that the actuarial returns from bets on 'long shots' tend to be lower than on better-rated horses, suggesting (given the way parimutuel odds are set) that some bettors have a positive preference for long shots. Noting that the same individuals place bets on multiple races and often bet on more than one horse per race—portfolio strategies that pool and hence reduce risks, conventionally defined—Golec and Tamarkin question previous studies' inference that such bettors are risk lovers. They argue that one must distinguish between two commonly confounded aspects of risk: the variance (technically, the second moment of a statistical distribution), which measures the average variability of sample observations around their mean, and the skewness (the third moment), which, as we have seen, measures asymmetries associated with very long tails on one side of the distribution.[27] Golec and Tamarkin test the hypothesis that it is skewness (the third moment), not variance (the second moment, and the more conventional measure of risk) that the long-shot bettors embrace.[28] In a statistical analysis of 2,309 races, they find persuasive evidence that bettors are simultaneously variance-averse and skewness-loving.

This discovery, which is consistent with the utility function shape exhibited in Figure 1.8, might equally well explain the behavior of high-technology

---

[26] See CLOTFELTER & COOK, n. 24 above, at 95–104. It is for this reason that their book is titled 'Selling Hope'.

[27] Statisticians distinguish four main moments, or mathematical characterizations, of sample distributions. The first moment, or mean, characterizes the sample's central tendency; it is the sum of observation values divided by the number of observations. The second moment, or variance, characterizes the degree to which observations deviate from the mean; the third moment, the skewness of the distribution of observations, was clarified earlier; and the fourth moment, the 'peakedness' or height of the distribution compared to the length of its tails.

[28] Joseph Golec & Maurry Tamarkin, Bettors Love Skewness, Not Risk, at the Horse Track, 106 J. POL. ECON. 205 (1998).

entrepreneurs, inventors, and (to the extent that financial motives play a role) creators of popular culture. In high technology, those who commit their fortunes and most of their waking hours to pioneering a new venture forego the option of placing multiple bets enjoyed by horse race bettors. But high-technology 'angels', like horse players, simultaneously bet on long shots and pursue variance-reducing multi-investment portfolio strategies. At this stage, the proposition that those who invest in high technology derive positive utility from the skewness of rewards is offered as hypothesis, not as a demonstrated phenomenon. The most one can say is that it is intuitively plausible. Testing it rigorously is likely to be more difficult than with horse racing, since all of the skewness evidence presented in this chapter was derived ex post, and it is unclear whether the ex ante skewness potential of specific high-technology investments or classes of bets can be measured empirically.

V. Intellectual Property Implications

In the evidence that the rewards from innovation are skew-distributed and that at least some risk-takers are skewness lovers there are implications for intellectual property policies. However, several caveats need to be recognized.

For one, especially in the arts but to some extent also in the realm of technology, creative activity is often driven by non-pecuniary motives. To be sure, an artist, author, or inventor must keep body and soul together, but as long as that condition is met and the incremental costs of creation are not large, the uncertain prospect of spectacular payoffs may be more of a 'nice to have' fringe benefit than a necessary incentive. On this, preferences undoubtedly differ. Franz Schubert first composed a work for money at the age of 19. Ten to 12 years later he was still offering publishers his work for 'a moderate remuneration'.[29] Beethoven, on the other hand, was notoriously avaricious, playing publishers off against one another to gain desired publication fees for specific compositions and segmenting his markets geographically, with different publications for England, France, and the various German-speaking territories. Franz Joseph Haydn toiled most of his career on a handsome salary that provided no special incentive compensation for his prodigious creative output, but went for the big prizes when his patron Prince Nicolaus Esterhazy died and he was invited to London by impresario Johann Peter Salomon. Aaron Copland is said to have testified in a deposition on copyright royalties that he would pay people to listen to his music. As an author who has often purchased copies of my work at appreciable out-of-pocket cost and distributed them free to colleagues, I empathize. My daughter helps support

---

[29] FRANZ SCHUBERT'S LETTERS AND OTHER WRITINGS 30, 122–23, 135 (Otto Erich Deutsch ed., 1974).

her six children with the modest fees she receives playing bluegrass fiddle professionally, but dreams of the affluence a hit record would bring.

Although individual high-technology entrepreneurs may, like racetrack bettors and sweepstakes lottery players, be skewness-lovers, it seems less likely that decision-making in well-established corporate organizations conforms to the hypothesis. For the employed inventor, a particularly successful contribution can bring a sizeable bonus and promotion to a higher income bracket, but nothing remotely approximating the rewards populating the right-hand tail of the profit distributions Dietmar Harhoff and I have been surveying. For the research and development manager who drives an invention to commercial success, the fraction of benefits appropriated personally is similarly modest.[30] When corporate hierarchies must decide whether or not to invest substantial sums on the commercial development of an invention, risk aversion, not skewness affinity, is almost surely the behavioral norm. Such motivational differences may have much to do with the propensity observed during the first half of the twentieth century for a disproportionate share of the boldest technological innovations to originate outside the laboratories of large corporations,[31] and, more recently, for high-technology startups to be among the most prolific contributors to US technological dynamism.

To the extent that investments in technological and artistic creation are motivated by the longshot hope of a very large reward, intellectual property policies should sustain and reinforce that incentive system, not undermine it. This implies a role for strong patents and copyrights. But from that basic precept two more nuanced implications can be drawn.

First and most obvious, patents and copyrights ought not to be revoked or weakened simply because an innovator has made 'too much' money from his creation, for the prospect of a large reward is a crucial feature of the skewness-based incentive system. This does not mean that *any* weakening of intellectual property rights is necessarily counter-productive, for an expectation that patents or copyrights can be enforced fully has more relevance for some actors—notably, those who conform to the skewness-loving paradigm—than for others. There is compelling evidence that patent rights are not very important as a prerequisite for research and development investments in many (but not all) well-established industries.[32] The early market occupancy, reputational, and learning curve advantages of being a first mover are in

[30] For an early statement of this managerial risk aversion hypothesis, see WILLIAM J. FELLNER, COMPETITION AMONG THE FEW 172–73 (1949).

[31] See, eg, JOHN JEWKES ET AL., THE SOURCES OF INVENTION (1959); F. M. Scherer, *Schumpeter and Plausible Capitalism*, 30 J. ECON. LITERATURE 1416 (1992).

[32] See Richard C Levin et al., *Appropriating the Returns from Industrial Research and Development*, Brookings Papers on Economic Activity (No. 3) 783–832 (1987); Wesley J. Cohen et al., *Appropriability Conditions and Why Firms Patent and Why They Do Not in the American Manufacturing Sector* (working paper), Carnegie-Mellon University (June 1997).

many instances much more important. Because of these non-patent advantages, the enforcement of compulsory patent licensing in more than 100 US antitrust settlements does not appear to have had much, if any, adverse impact on the target companies' investments in research and development.[33] Fine-tuning is needed in remedying antitrust abuses and avoiding impediments to further innovation caused when one inventor has a powerful position blocking the advances of others who could otherwise make significant improvement inventions. In particular, policymakers should be particularly cautious in avoiding the early erosion of rights for that class of innovators or creators for whom the uncertain hope of large rewards was a plausibly significant motivational factor.

A second implication follows. Although exceptions exist, there is reason to believe that the enforcement of intellectual property rights is biased in favor of large, well-established organizations, whose behavior conforms least well to the skewness paradigm, and against the independent innovators who conform most closely. David does occasionally slay Goliath in the courtroom, but more often than not, a well-heeled corporation can afford to persevere in costly litigation until the financially weaker party submits—if not in absolute defeat, then in a settlement that yields less than the spectacular reward that might otherwise have been achieved by an independent innovator.[34] If the skewness hypothesis is anywhere near correct, there ought to be policy adjustments to remedy the imbalance.

There may also be implications for international economic policy. Just as the larger payoffs available with statewide (and perhaps also nationwide) lotteries encourage more intensive participation than smaller city-based lotteries,[35] the larger rewards attainable by selling innovative products in a global marketplace probably strengthen incentives for both skewness-loving and risk-averse actors. There is much to be said therefore for continuing efforts to harmonize national intellectual property systems and, as under the single-filing-locus system endorsed by many European Union nations, to reduce the costs of securing protection outside one's home nation.

---

[33] See F M. SCHERER, THE ECONOMIC EFFECTS OF COMPULSORY PATENT LICENSING Ch. IV (1977).

[34] The nerd's prayer: 'Oh Lord, help me to capture the market with my killer app; but if Thou willst otherwise, let me at least sell out to Microsoft'.

[35] See Philip J Cook & Charles T. Clotfelter, *The Peculiar Scale Economies of Lotto*, 83 AM. ECON. REV. 634 (1993); *The Massachusetts State Lottery*, John F. Kennedy School of Government case study C16–91–1025.0 (1992).

OF GREEN TULIPS AND LEGAL KUDZU: REPACKAGING RIGHTS IN SUBPATENTABLE INNOVATION

JEROME H. REICHMAN*

How to enable entrepreneurs to appropriate the fruits of their investments in cumulative and sequential innovation without impeding follow-on innovation and without creating barriers to entry has become one of the great unsolved puzzles that the law and economics of intellectual property rights needs to address as the new millennium gets underway.[1] This chapter draws briefly from my earlier works to identify some of the key historical difficulties encountered in protecting small grain-sized innovations that do not rise to the

* Bunyan A. Womble Professor of Law, Duke Law School. I wish to thank Rochelle Cooper Dreyfuss for her encouragement and inspired editing; the participants at the NYU-Engelberg Center's Innovation Law and Policy Conference, Villa La Pietra, Florence, Italy (June 1998), at the Duke Faculty Workshop (April 1999), and at the Vanderbilt Law Review's Symposium on the Law and Economics of Intellectual Property Rights (April 2000); the Kapor Family Foundation, which supported much of the underlying research; and my colleagues—Pamela Samuelson, Mitchell D. Kapor and Randall Davis—whose collective insights inform every page.

[1] See eg, WILLIAM KINGSTON, DIRECT PROTECTION OF INNOVATION (W. Kingston ed. 1987); James Bessen & Eric Maskin, *Sequential Innovation, Patents and Imitation,* (MIT Working Paper No. 00–01, Jan. 2000, http://papers.ssrn.com/paper.taf? Abstract id = 206189); Mark Janis, *Second Tier Patent Protection,* 40 HARV. INT'L. L. J. 151 (1999); Pamela Samuelson, Randall Davis, Mitchell D. Kapor, & J. H Reichman, *A Manifesto Concerning the Legal Protection of Computer Programs,* 94 COLUM. L. REV. 2308 (1994) (hereinafter *Manifesto*); Richard R. Nelson, *Intellectual Property Protection for Cumulative Systems of Technology,* 94 COLUM. L. REV. 2674 (1994); Rochelle C. Dreyfuss, *Information Products: A Challenge to Intellectual Property Theory,* 20 N.Y.U. J. INT'L L. & POL. 897 (1988).

level of novel and nonobvious inventions or original and creative works of authorship.[2] It then examines these difficulties through the lens of a hypothetical 'green tulip' problem, which encapsulates certain recurring investment dilemmas that afflict entrepreneurs operating under the hybrid intellectual property regimes available under both domestic and international intellectual property systems. Without focusing on the technical operations of any of these hybrid regimes in detail, the green tulip exercise will demonstrate why, from a structural perspective, they tend systematically to thwart the most socially desirable outcomes, especially with regard to follow-on innovations. The chapter goes on to show how innovators and second comers working on common technical trajectories could better resolve these same problems by a more rational allocation of their collective costs of research and development.

From a broader perspective, I seek to refocus the attention of legal and economic analysis on the potential benefits of liability rules over property rules in the subpatentable environment and to emphasize the role of the public domain in a technological universe in which the funding of small scale applications of know-how to industry is increasingly critical to entrepreneurial success.[3] I will suggest that a crucial test of any socially desirable regulatory model for small scale innovation is the extent to which measures that deter free-riding appropriation also retain a capacity to enrich—rather than diminish—the public domain.[4] Besides demonstrating the high but often hidden opportunity costs that inherently result when a proliferation of hybrid regimes of exclusive property rights govern small scale innovation, this chapter concretely illustrates the ways in which an alternative regime built on compensatory liability principles could stimulate investment without chilling follow-on innovation and without creating legal barriers to entry. It ends by

---

[2] See eg, J. H. Reichman, *Charting the Collapse of the Patent-Copyright Dichotomy: Premises for a Restructured International Intellectual Property System*, 13 CARDOZO ARTS & ENTERTAIN. L.J. 475 (1995); J.H. Reichman *Legal Hybrids Between the Patent and Copyright Paradigms*, 94 COLUM. L. REV. 2432 (1994) (hereinafter *Legal Hybrids*).

[3] For the classic discussion of liability and property rules, see Guido Calabresi & A. Douglas Melamed, *Property Rules, Liability Rules, and Inalienability: One View of the Cathedral*, 85 HARV. L. REV. 1089, 1092 (1972); more recent work includes Louis Kaplow & Steven Shavell, *An Economic Analysis of Property Rules Versus Liability Rules*, 109 HARV. L. REV. 713 (1996); Ian Ayres & Eric Talley, *Solomonic Bargaining: Dividing a Legal Entitlement to Facilitate Coasean Trade*, 104 YALE L. J. 1027 (1995). For the view that property rules are always socially more desirable for large grain-sized intellectual creations, see Robert P. Merges, *Contracting into Liability Rules: Intellectual Property Rights and Collective Rights Organizations*, 84 CALIF. L. REV. 1293 (1996). This chapter takes the opposite approach for small grain-sized innovation.

[4] See, eg, David Lange, *Recognizing the Public Domain*, 44 LAW & CONTEMP. PROBS. 147 (1981). For renewed attention to the role of the public domain in intellectual property law generally, see, eg, JAMES BOYLE, SHAMANS, SOFTWARE, AND SPLEENS 155–57 (1996); Yochai Benkler, *Free as the Air to Common Use. First Amendment Constraints on Enclosure of the Public Domain*, 74 N.Y.U. L. REV. 354 (1999); Julie Cohen, *Lochner in Cyberspace: The New Economic Orthodoxy of 'Rights Management'*, 97 MICH. L. REV. 462 (1998); Jessica Litman, *The Public Domain*, 39 EMORY L.J. 965 (1990).

noting ways in which the compensatory liability rules proposed to address the puzzle of small grain-sized innovation generally would also go a long way toward answering hard questions about how to protect applications of traditional biological and cultural knowledge to industry, which are of increasing importance to developing and least-developed countries.

I. Historical Models: The Creation of Legal Kudzu[5]

So long as innovators can keep their knowhow under actual or legal secrecy, and the resulting innovations are relatively difficult to copy, they expect a period of natural lead time in which they may try to recoup their investments and turn a profit. Since the earliest days of the industrial revolution, however, it was clear that investors in some small scale applications of intangible knowhow to products sold in the open market would suffer from a chronic shortage of natural lead time.[6] As far back as the seventeenth century, for example, producers of textile and fabric designs had voiced complaints about a lack of legal protection against unauthorized imitations.[7] During the nineteenth century, when the dominant patent and copyright paradigms crystallized, these complaints gave way to more robust demands by manufacturers of goods produced in series for new laws to protect both novel appearance designs of useful articles (i.e. nonfunctional, three-dimensional product configurations) and novel functional shapes that improved the utility of hand tools and everyday household articles.[8] Because entrepreneurs who developed innovative industrial designs falling within either category could not keep their noncopyrightable and subpatentable knowhow secret once it had been embodied in products distributed in the open market, slavish imitators could reduce their natural lead time to zero without incurring any significant research and development costs of their own.

By the late twentieth century, it was clear that the vulnerability of industrial designs to slavish imitation had merely foreshadowed a wave of small scale technical innovations whose similar predicament would destabilize the

---

[5] Kudzu is a Japanese vine. Brought to the United States to prevent soil erosion, it has spread uncontrollably over the southern states.

[6] Although the worldwide intellectual property system has always experienced difficulties in stimulating investment in some types of small scale innovation, traditional legal scholarship perceived these shortcomings as a pesky but relatively minor problem that exerted little adverse influence on its core operations, the patent and copyright regimes. See, eg, 2 STEPHEN P. LADAS, PATENTS, TRADEMARKS, and RELATED RIGHTS: NATIONAL AND INTERNATIONAL PROTECTION 828–31 (1975).

[7] See, eg, BRAD SHERMAN & LIONEL BENTLY, THE MAKING OF MODERN INTELLECTUAL PROPERTY LAW—THE BRITISH EXPERIENCE, 1760–1911 (1999), citing the earliest statute to deal explicitly with the legal protection of designs, the Calico Printers' Act of 1787, 27 GEO. III c. 38 (1787).

[8] See, eg, LADAS, n. 6 above, at 828–30, 837–40 (industrial design laws), 949–51 (utility model laws); SHERMAN & BENTLY, n. 7 above, at 64–67, 77–94; JANIS, n. 1 above (utility models).

patent-copyright dichotomy on which the worldwide intellectual property system was, by then, firmly grounded.[9] Computer programs, integrated circuit designs, biogenetically engineered organisms, new plant varieties and, most recently, electronically generated databases all create conditions favoring market failure, similar to those that had afflicted investors in both ornamental and functional designs at a much earlier period.[10] In place of the breakthrough or 'pioneer' inventions of the past, which still dominate our thinking about patents (and about related contractual rights as well), it is the routine engineers' cumulative and sequential working out of shared or common technical trajectories[11] that increasingly drives the post-modern economy, in Silicon Valleys and their equivalents throughout the world.

As in the past, what the routine engineer produces is essentially technical knowhow: that is to say, a store of information about methods or processes of production that confers some commercial advantages on those who possess it. What primarily differentiates the production of today's cutting-edge technical knowhow from most of the knowhow generated during the industrial revolution, however, is the chronic inability of those who invest in its commercial exploitation to keep it secret from would-be competitors. In this state of affairs, second comers can rapidly reproduce any incremental innovation borne on or near the face of a product without incurring appreciable costs in reverse-engineering the innovator's technical knowhow by proper means and without conferring any appreciable lead time advantages on those who first performed the underlying research and development. The vulnerability of small grain-sized innovation to free-riding duplicators under these conditions breeds fears of market failure that border on panic. The dilemma is that, while unbridled competition would be likely to induce suboptimal investment, lessening competition by accommodating these innovations under traditional patent and copyright paradigms tends to stretch these regimes to their breaking points.

---

[9] See Paris Convention for the Protection of Industrial Property, Mar. 20, 1883, *as last revised,* July 14, 1967, 21 U.S.T. 1583, 828 U.N.T.S. 305; *revised,* July 24, 1971, 828 U.N.T.S. 221; Berne Convention for the Protection of Literary and Artistic Works, Sept. 9, 1886, *as last revised,* July 24, 1971 *(amended* 1979), 828 U.N.T.S. 221; Agreement on Trade-Related Aspects of Intellectual Property Rights, Apr. 15, 1994, Marrakesh Agreement Establishing the World Trade Organization, Annex 1C, 33 I L.M. 1197 (1994) (hereinafter TRIPS Agreement).

[10] See, eg, *Manifesto,* n. 1 above, at 2332–65 (computer programs); Rebecca S. Eisenberg, *Proprietary Rights and the Norms of Science in Biotechnology Research,* 97 YALE L. J. 177 (1987) (biotechnology); Henrique Freire de Oliveira Souza, *Genetically Modified Plants: A Need for International Regulation,* 6 ANN. SURV. INT'L. L. 129 (2000) (plants); J. H. Reichman & Paul Uhlir, *Database Protection at the Crossroads. Recent Developments and Their Impact on Science and Technology,* 14 BERKELEY TECH. L. J. 793 (1999) (data). See generally, Wendy J. Gordon, *Asymmetric Market Failure and Prisoner's Dilemma in Intellectual Property,* 17 U. DAYTON L. REV. 853 (1992).

[11] See, eg, Robert P. Merges & Richard Nelson, *On the Complex Economics of Patent Scope,* 90 COLUM. L. REV. 839 (1990); Merges, n. 3 above; Giovanni Dosi, *Technological Paradigms and Technological Trajectories: A Suggested Interpretation of the Determinants and Directions of Technical Change,* 11 RES. POLICY 147, 147–62 (1982).

The typical legislative response to this threat of market failure is to enact sui generis regimes of exclusive property rights, built on modified patent and copyright principles, which afford target classes of investors fixed periods of artificial lead time. In other words, when faced with the risk of suboptimal investment in small scale applications of knowhow to industry, legislators and administrators turn instinctively to a property rule—they assume that some efficient admixture of modified patent and copyright principles will resolve every problem. In this climate, the European Union has recently taken steps to strengthen and harmonize the design protection laws of its member countries and to mandate utility model laws that will confer patent-like protection on small scale (ie less than nonobvious) innovation generally.[12] Other miniature legal monopolies, derived from the same historical matrix that the early design and utility model laws first established, are routinely enacted, in Europe and elsewhere, to protect ever smaller fragments of innovative contributions. Recent examples include sui generis laws protecting integrated circuit designs, plant breeders' varieties, boat hull designs, and computer-generated databases.[13]

My first articles examined these historical models, namely design protection laws and utility model laws. I tried to understand why the design laws had uniformly failed to live up to the expectations placed in them, why no consensus solution to the quest for a model design protection law had emerged to light after so much time and effort, and why sometimes local industry could prosper despite the lack of such protection.[14] Those studies revealed an inherent tension between relatively weak and relatively strong forms of design protection that triggered recurring cyclical movements between states of perceived underprotection and states of perceived overprotection.

In more recent articles, I tried to explore the root causes of this cyclical pattern and of the other infirmities that my study of hybrid regimes brought to

---

[12] See Directive 98/71/EC of the European Parliament and of the Council of 13 October 1998 on the Legal Protection of Designs, 1998 O.J. L289/28 (hereinafter EC Directive on Designs); Graeme B. Dinwoodie, *Federalized Functionalism: The Future of Design Protection in the European Union*, 24 AIPLA Q.J. 611 (1996); Janis, n. 1 above, at 158–78; J.H. Reichman, *Electronic Information Tools—The Outer Edge of World Intellectual Property Law*, 24 INT'L REV. INDUS. PROP. & COPYRIGHT L. (IIC) 446 (1993).

[13] See, eg, the Semiconductor Chip Protection Act of 1984, 17 U.S.C. §§ 901–914 (integrated circuit design); the International Convention for the Protection of New Varieties of Plants, Dec. 2, 1961, 33 U.S.T. 2703, 89 T.I.A.S. 10199, *as amended* 1991, <http://www.upov.int/eng/con vntns/1991/content.htm> (hereinafter UPOV) (plant varieties); 17 U.S.C. 1301–1332 (vessel hulls); Directive 96/9/EC of the European Parliament and of the Council of 11 March 1996 on the Legal Protection of Databases, 1996 O.J. L77/20 (databases).

[14] In addition to my articles cited earlier, see J.H. Reichman, *Design Protection and the New Technologies: The United States, Experience in a Transnational Perspective*, 19 U. BALT. L. REV. 5 (1989) (hereinafter *Design and New Technologies*); J.H. Reichman, *Design Protection After the Copyright Acts of 1976: A Comparative View of the Emerging Interim Models*, 31 J. COPYRIGHT SOC'Y 267 (1984), J.H. Reichman, *Design Protection in Domestic and Foreign Copyright Law: From the Berne Revision of 1948 to the Copyright Act of 1976*, 1983 DUKE L.J. 1143.

light, particularly the economic and doctrinal contradictions associated with the ever-growing practice of rewarding less than nonobvious innovation with powerful exclusive property rights.[15] Combining historical and comparative analysis with some basic insights of the law and economics literature, I concluded that what undermined the hybrid intellectual property regimes was not just their ad hoc, technology-specific birthmarks or the inability of legislatures to craft appropriate admixtures of modified patent and copyright principles. It was, rather, that from the oldest to the newest, most of these regimes suffered from a common structural defect: namely, that legal theory had blindly, and by a series of historical accidents, committed itself to solving the puzzle of small scale innovation by means of a property rule, whereas the problems entrepreneurs actually faced resulted from the failure of a liability rule for which some functional equivalent was badly needed and long overdue.

Since publishing those articles, I have gained new insights into the puzzle of small scale innovation from the critical attention given to my previous work;[16] from ongoing efforts to adapt my proposed regime to the needs of developing countries in order to stimulate local innovation;[17] and, above all, from practical experience in seeking to defend the interests of science and education against overly broad legislative proposals to protect databases.[18] The single most important insight gleaned from all these sources—and the one that most compels me to write this chapter—is that the hybrid regimes of exclusive property rights uniformly saddle the process of follow-on innovation with unacceptably high social costs.

To be sure, there is continuing debate about the ability of even the mature patent and copyright paradigms satisfactorily to balance public and private interests in promoting follow-on innovation. While this is not the place to discuss that topic,[19] I stress at the outset that a different calculus of social costs

[15] See, eg, *Legal Hybrids*, n. 2 above; *Manifesto*, n. 1 above; *Electronic Information Tools*, n. 12 above.

[16] See, eg, *Symposium: Toward a Third Intellectual Property Paradigm*, 94 COLUM. L. REV. 2559 (1994).

[17] See, eg, J. H. Reichman, *From Free Riders to Fair Followers: Global Competition Under the TRIPS Agreement*, 29 NYU J. INT'L L. & POL. 11 (1996/1997).

[18] See Reichman & Uhlir, n. 10 above; J. H. Reichman & Pamela Samuelson, *Intellectual Property Rights in Data?*, 50 VAND. L. REV. 51 (1997).

[19] A worldwide concern to stimulate risky investments in patentable inventions and original works of authorship has nonetheless elicited an internationally binding set of baseline entitlements that initially favor inventors and authors, while subjecting them to countervailing ambiguities in doctrines controlling the scope of protection. These offsetting doctrines vary in strength from one jurisdiction to another and often within single jurisdictions at different times, and there is no consensus about how to draw the lines in specific cases or with respect to certain subject matter categories of protection. Even so, the social costs of assigning inventors and authors exclusive rights to 'equivalent inventions' and 'derivative works' are attenuated in practice by judicially limiting the range of equivalents in crowded fields or when competitors have added significant value of their own, and perhaps above all, by encouraging resort to private contractual agreements to overcome the ambiguities otherwise built into legal rules governing the scope of protection.

and benefits applies when small grain-sized innovation is at stake. Without the big social pay-offs expected from major innovations, patentable inventions and copyrightable works of authorship, one must question the use of powerful exclusive rights to elicit technical contributions within the reach of routine engineers, which entrepreneurs would usually need to make any way simply to maintain a competitive advantage.[20] There is likewise a more compelling need to seek alternative solutions to the problem of appropriability so as to encourage investment without necessarily entitling the first or the second comer to all the returns from follow-on innovation. Indeed, it is precisely the legislative inability to solve the problem of follow-on innovation in the subpatentable environment that largely accounts for the recurring cycles of perceived under- and overprotection in the first place.

In what follows, I will try to demonstrate why a liability rule correctly addresses this critical problem of follow-on innovation at the subpatentable level. Using a single, hypothetical problem—the green tulip problem— against which we can test the prototypical models underlying all the sui generis regimes of intellectual property rights, I propose concretely to demonstrate why a property rule fails to solve the problem of follow-on applications of subpatentable knowhow to industry and why a properly crafted liability rule would solve that same problem with fewer social costs and without impoverishing the public domain.

II. The Green Tulip Problem: Unpacking Rights in Subpatentable Innovation

We turn now to the green tulip problem. Before proceeding, however, I need to clarify that the ensuing discussion about the investment dilemmas that hypothetical plant breeders might face when evaluating the uncertain market prospects for a new variety—the green tulip—is not put forward with a view to illustrating the vagaries of existing plant variety protection laws as such. On the contrary, for the purpose of this exercise I have deliberately assimilated all the hybrid regimes built around modified patent and copyright principles, both past and present, to two simple historical models or prototypes, a strategy that ignores the many nuanced features that actually distinguish such regimes in practice.

One basic model provides relatively weak protection against copying to small grain-sized innovations under a low eligibility requirement of originality.

---

[20] See Matthew Nimetz, *Design Protection*, 15 COPYRIGHT L. SYMP. (ASCAP) 79 (1967) (who nicely made this point in the context of legal and economic analysis of design protection laws). See generally Edmund W. Kitch, *The Nature and Function of the Patent System*, 20 J. L. & ECON. 265 (1977); A. Samuel Oddi, *Un-unified Economic Theories of Patents—The Not-Quite-Holy Grail,* 71 NOTRE DAME L. REV. 267 (1996).

Known historically as a 'copyright approach', I prefer to call this type of regime 'a copyright-like approach' to distinguish it from full copyright protection (such as France gives to industrial designs) and because it would not typically protect against unauthorized follow-on creations in the way that the mature copyright paradigm prohibits unauthorized derivative works.[21] The second basic model or 'patent-like approach' would typically condition eligibility on some form of novelty higher than an originality standard, though lower than the nonobviousness standard of the mature patent paradigm; and it would confer a so-called absolute right that, at least in principle, would prohibit the making of unauthorized, follow-on innovations even in the absence of slavish imitation.[22]

In the real world of hybrid intellectual property rights, matters quickly become more complicated. For example, courts hostile to specific legal monopolies or generally concerned about weakening competition may, by interpretation, elevate the threshold of eligibility or, by declining to see equivalent creations in practice, narrow the scope of protection against follow-on creations. Conversely, courts hostile to free-riding or imbued with natural property right views may, by a process of interpretation, lower a nominally stiff eligibility requirement or impede follow-on imitations in the name of 'copying' even when the statute provides no formal basis for that result. Moreover, in crafting any given hybrid exclusive right, legislatures may deliberately blur the admixture of ingredients so that one cannot confidently classify it as either a 'copyright-like' or a 'patent-like' regime.[23]

Nonetheless, for the purpose of the green tulip exercise, we shall keep matters simple by assuming perfect judicial compliance with our perfectly crafted prototypical models. We shall also relax the threshold of eligibility to the point where it usually ceases to impinge on the analysis, that is, by assuming that all the small scale innovations in question would normally meet any requirements of originality or novelty that might apply.[24]

---

[21] Real-world examples might include the UK's 1842 Ornamental Design Act, see SHERMAN & BENTLY, n. 7 above, at 64–67; the German Law Concerning Copyright in Designs and Models of 1876, see UMA SUTHERSANEN, DESIGN LAW IN EUROPE 173 (2000); the French Design Law of 1806, ibid. at 135–36; and the UK's utility model law of 1843 (soon repealed), SHERMAN & BENTLY at 64, 67.

[22] Examples might include: the UK's Registered Designs Act 1949, as last amended by the Copyright, Designs and Patents Act 1988, see SUTHERSANEN, n. 21 above, at 276–303; the Benelux and Nordic Design Laws, ibid at 128–34, 506–14, 323–28; and the EC Directive on Designs, n. 12 above.

[23] For examples, see *Design and New Technologies*, n. 14 above.

[24] If either of these prototypes appeared likely to produce socially positive responses to our hypothetical investment dilemmas, we could profitably descend into an examination of the more nuanced structural details. In reality, however, neither of these historical prototypes yields socially justifiable results, and so we need not further encourage the quest for some unattainably perfect admixture of patent and copyright principles by closely scrutinizing specific hybrid regimes in these pages.

Two further caveats must also be borne in mind. First, even if the only option available to legislators were a choice between a bad copyright-like regime and a bad patent-like regime, the calculus of social costs and benefits would differ significantly in the two cases, and different countries might logically exercise their limited options differently, depending on their own cultural needs and level of technical sophistication. Secondly, we will close our eyes to the ways in which the existence and character of any given sui generis regime affects the willingness of courts and legislatures to expand or contract the domestic patent and copyright laws to accommodate borderline cases.

However important all these matters are in the real world operations of specific hybrid regimes, we ignore them here and concentrate instead on the two prototypical approaches. By applying these abstract regulatory models to a hypothetical but characteristic problem of follow-on innovation, we can expect to obtain a generic picture of the social costs and benefits more or less attributable to all approaches. By thus isolating a common set of problems and solutions and identifying a common set of errors or flawed results, the green tulip exercise reveals a basis for reforms that might put an end to the current tendency to multiply ad hoc, technology-specific mixtures of modified patent and copyright principles.

A. Stating the problem

The hypothetical problem concerns three firms of established plant breeders who regularly grow and sell flowers and who, from time to time, introduce novel varieties bred from their own stocks. One of the firms, Breeder A, develops a green tulip for the first time ever. However, this firm gains little commercial success from its innovative variety because the consuming public does not appreciate green tulips enough to buy them.

Shortly thereafter, Breeder B develops a red, white, and green tulip by combining Breeder's A green tulip variety with stocks of his own. This new variety of tulip scores a commercial success in the relevant market segment, largely because Italian-Americans love it. Subsequently, other breeders (collectively designated 'Breeder C') cash in on B's success by using A's and B's varieties to produce an array of tulips in new color combinations built around a green foundation.

FIG. 2.1: The green tulip problem

Tulip Breeder A	Tulip Breeder B	Other Breeders (C)
Breeds a green tulip for the first time ever, but there is no consumer market	Breeds a red, white, and green tulip using A's technology; he gains commercial success	Other breeders cash in on this success and extend the technology to new color combinations

The purpose of this hypothetical green tulip problem is to clarify the ways in which existing intellectual property regimes that deal with small grain-sized innovation articulate the relations between innovators and second comers. The core questions bear on the extent to which different regimes enable the first comer, Breeder A, to appropriate more or less of the fruits of his initial investment by participating in the gains from other breeders' follow-on applications of the technical knowhow that was initially generated.

To address these questions, I must rely on certain basic assumptions that underlie the rest of the exercise. First and foremost, we assume that the traditional intellectual property regimes are not available. The green tulip variety represents a small grain-sized innovation, based on cumulative and sequential knowhow, that falls below the prevalent standard of nonobviousness applicable under relevant domestic patent laws, ie it is subpatentable by definition. Trade secrecy is not operative because the technical knowhow at issue, once embodied in the product, is available to the world. Any breeder examining the tulip can understand how to produce it from available exemplars, and neither copyright nor unfair competition laws impede breeders from engaging in such learning activity. We further assume, however, that even though the green tulip makes only a small advance over technical solutions already known to other plant breeders in the relevant markets, it is enough to satisfy the threshold eligibility requirements of our prototypical hybrid intellectual property regimes. Finally, we assume that all the firms appearing in our exercises operate within a single territorial unit, and only territorial laws apply.

B. Standard legal solutions

If one reviews all the hybrid intellectual property regimes that deviate from the mature patent and copyright paradigms for likely solutions to the problem of Breeder A's vulnerability to other breeders' appropriating the fruits of his investment, one can identify three basic factual patterns that recur with sufficient regularity as to merit particular attention. Two of these patterns flow from the basic regulatory models identified above, namely, a relatively weak copyright-like form of protection and a relatively stronger, more patent-like approach. A third factual pattern arises when no baseline entitlements govern a specific type of innovation and the fate of relevant investments depends entirely on free market conditions. This last situation is the raw or primordial state of affairs that we shall look at first.

1. The raw state of affairs
In the raw state of affairs, there is no exclusive property right in subpatentable technical innovation of any kind, and free competition prevails. Under these conditions, Breeder A has no legal right to protect the fruits of his investment; Breeders B and C may free-ride on the former's investment to their hearts'

content. In the worst case scenario (which interests us here for purposes of sharper comparisons), the free-riding second comers take the market altogether. Unless A's other commercial activities prove more successful, A may go out of business or avoid further investment in risky research and development, despite the objective commercial success of a follow-on innovation built around his own earlier innovation.[25]

In such a case, both the relevant technical community and the public at large will have lost Breeder A's potential for developing further innovative contributions. This negative result follows in part because Breeder A failed to share in the fruits of at least one major commercial success and also because he received no direct or indirect contributions to his sunk costs of research and development from either B or C.

2. Hybrid copyright-like solutions apply

If we assume that Breeder A's legislature had responded to complaints about the raw state of affairs by enacting a sui generis regime loosely derived from the copyright model, then Breeder A could presumably invoke a weak intellectual property right against the 'copying' of his innovative product. This model, however, typically denies protected innovators any claim to rights in follow-on innovation, such as B's red, white, and green tulip, especially when the second comer has invested funds, time, and effort of his own to obtain it.

From an economic perspective, this approach is similar to the unfair competition laws of some countries.[26] In principle, courts operating under such regimes remain free to hold that a second comer's follow-on product appropriated too much of the first comer's creative or technical contribution, and such decisions can help to establish a jurisprudence of market-destructive conduct over time. In practice, however, no two judges see alike in these matters, and courts may balk at engrafting a pseudo-derivative work right onto a copyright-like regime that lacks this legislative specification and that operates with a low threshold of eligibility. Moreover, experience with industrial design laws demonstrates that if the legislature does specify a derivative work right (even by inference), courts may elevate the eligibility requirements by interpretation so as to narrow the anticompetitive effects of such regulatory action after the fact.[27]

To the extent that our prototypical regime removes or glosses over uncertainties in the ways that such laws have actually been applied in the past, the creator of the green tulip in our hypothetical problem, Breeder A, would wind

---

[25] For example, the producers of the 'VisiCalc' spreadsheet went out of business after the follow-on product, 'Lotus 1–2–3', went on the market.

[26] See ANSELM KAMPERMAN SANDERS, UNFAIR COMPETITION LAW—THE PROTECTION OF INTELLECTUAL AND INDUSTRIAL CREATIVITY 24–66 (1997).

[27] An example is the treatment of German design laws, see SUTHERSANEN, n. 21 above, 556–57. See also ibid at 197 (noting that courts rejected softer 'subjective novelty' standard that academics preferred in favour of 'objective relative novelty').

up with a very weak claim for relief. As long as neither Breeder B nor Breeder C slavishly imitated Breeder A's variety, but instead acts as a value-adding (or, in some dubious usage, 'transformative') user, B or C would not likely infringe under this prototypical regime, which does not protect against the making of derivative varieties.

In the worst-case scenario, the absence of any right to control follow-on innovation or value-adding uses of his technical contribution thus means that Breeder A's position is, in the end, not appreciably better than it was under the raw state of affairs. Nevertheless, B's (and C's) success comes with something of a free ride on A's initial investment. Breeder A may again be forced to exit from the market because he failed to share in the commercial success of succeeding applications of his green tulip technology, or he may lack sufficient capital to invest in further risky ventures that depend on research and development.

3. Hybrid patent-like solutions apply

If we assume that Breeder A's legislature had, instead, responded to the vulnerability of small scale innovators by adopting a regime loosely identified with the patent model, then that regime would, at least in theory, protect qualifying innovators against value-adding users who appropriate all or a substantial part of the first comer's technical knowhow. Here, in other words, Breeder A could invoke a stronger right that would allow him to interdict the production of unauthorized follow-on (or derivative) varieties, notwithstanding the small grain-size of his own initial innovation.

Real world examples of such a regime might include many present-day design protection laws, all utility model laws that cover small (ie less than nonobvious) inventions generally, or even the latest model law of plant breeders' rights that was negotiated at the international level in 1991.[28] In actual practice, however, courts applying these laws tend, at the infringement stage, to narrow the range of protected equivalents when the alleged infringer adds substantial value of his own to the underlying innovation. Because utility model laws (and some design laws) are not subject to any qualifying examination of the prior art, and because in that case, even the eligibility requirements are tested retroactively at the infringement stage, any serious judicial resistance to the recognition of an appreciable range of equivalents tends to reduce their impact to that of a codified form of unfair competition.[29]

But to the extent that our prototypical patent-like response solves these real-world infirmities, Breeder A will be in a good position. He will be able to control unauthorized follow-on varieties, such as the red, white, and green tulip, so long as they are deemed impermissibly derivative of, or equivalent to,

---

[28] See, eg, Janis, n. 1 above, at 151–54; UPOV, 1991 amendment, n. 13 above.
[29] See *Designs and New Technologies*, n. 14 above, at 133–36.

his underlying technical contribution. In this situation, Breeders B and C will need a license from Breeder A in order to develop follow-on products that apply A's earlier technology.

Now, however, it is the constraint on B and C that becomes problematic. It puts Breeders B and C at the mercy of Breeder of A's willingness to deal, and it requires them to negotiate with A over price at a time when B and C have the greatest uncertainty about the risks they face in extending A's innovation to untried commercial applications. Neither Breeder B nor C may yet know whether, and at what cost, they can successfully apply Breeder A's technical knowhow to follow-on products. Above all, they may be unable to estimate the potential for commercial success of the proposed follow-on product without committing to the license ex ante, which discloses their market potential to A (who may then simply copy it),[30] or risking an infringement action ex post by proceeding without authorization.[31]

To reduce the costs of such a system, the legislature could relax the first comer's grip on follow-on applications by denying the innovator a right to prevent independent creation.[32] In such a case, structural adjustments to the law may attempt to distinguish between unauthorized follow-on productions that result from 'copying' the protected innovation and those that result from permissible forms of 'independent creation'. But even if this softer, more pro-competitive variant of the patent-like model were applied, it would not significantly improve the plight of Breeders B and C. Either they must acquire Breeder A's permission (which could be denied), or they must independently repeat the costs of critical development efforts that Breeder A had already sustained and then proceed to incur the further investment costs associated with applying that technology to follow-on products. But Breeder A's own product—the green tulip—did not score a commercial success and Breeder B's costs and risks in developing the red, white, and green tulip could seem disproportionately high absent some way to test the market for that project. Furthermore, Breeder A could launch a harassing infringement action questioning Breeder B's good faith, and the latter might have difficulty proving independent creation. Even under these circumstances, Breeders B and C are

---

[30] The problem of bargaining over secret information is often called 'Arrow's disclosure paradox', after Kenneth J. Arrow, *Economic Welfare and the Allocation of Resources for Invention*, in THE RATE AND DIRECTION OF INVENTIVE ACTIVITY 609 (National Bureau of Economic Research ed. 1962), discussed in Robert P. Merges, *Of Property Rules, Coase, and Intellectual Property*, 94 COLUM. L. REV. 2655, 2657–58 (1994).

[31] On ex ante versus ex post bargaining over the right to follow-on products in the context of patentable inventions, see Suzanne Scotchmer, *Standing on the Shoulders of Giants: Cumulative Research and Patent Law*, 5 J. EC. PERSPECTIVES 29 (1991); Suzanne Scotchmer, *Protecting Early Innovators: Should Second-Generation Products Be Patentable*, 27 RAND J. EC. 322 (1996). I take no position in this chapter on proposals to reform patent laws.

[32] German design law once again furnishes an example, see SUTHERSANEN, n. 21 above, at 201.

thus unlikely to develop follow-on products absent a license from Breeder A, in which case they face the same constraints on licensing that were set out above.

In the worst-case scenario, Breeders B and C may logically decide to avoid using the green tulip technology altogether, rather than run the risks of dealing with Breeder A up front. All that Breeders B and C bring to the table is an untried business idea that Breeder A might be perfectly capable of implementing without any present or future technical inputs from them. Faced with the decision to risk dealing with A or investing their resources in developing novel varieties of their own that would themselves qualify for protection under the same regime, they will more logically make the latter decision.

Here the small grain-size of the innovation makes spending the time and money to negotiate a contractual transaction less attractive than would be the case with respect to a large grain-sized invention covered by the domestic patent laws, where cross-licensing to obtain a technically difficult solution makes sense. With regard to subpatentable innovation, however, follow-on applications usually lie within the reach of routine engineers, especially if there is a market opening, and some basis (even if only a hunch) for predicting a chance of commercial success. Once a green tulip exists that bears Breeder A's technical knowhow literally on its face, a red, white, and green tulip becomes a statistical probability, and there is mainly a first mover advantage to be obtained. Because the market for routine innovation tends to be fast-moving and dynamic, in other words—precisely because it encounters fewer technical obstacles—Breeders B's and C's ideas for follow-on applications are most valuable as potential business strategies (not as technical outcomes), but they also remain filled with uncertainty as to whether consumers will in fact respond favorably to their initiatives.

The end result is that Breeders B and C will tend to avoid follow-on applications of the green tulip technology, especially if they require ex ante disclosures to A, lest A free-ride on their initiatives. Unless A and B nonetheless agree to prospect and develop a red, white, and green tulip together (collectively or under a licensing arrangement), despite the risk of premature divulgation of B's business idea and/or of his own technical knowhow, the public may not obtain such a tulip, the cycle of cumulative innovation may be broken, and, carrying matters to an extreme, both A and B may fail for lack of other commercial successes.

Moreover—and this point is easily overlooked—all other participants in the relevant breeder community are then deprived of the potential technical benefits that might have flowed from an influx of new investments. In other words, if Breeders B and C decline to invest in follow-on applications because of Breeder A's powerful hybrid intellectual property right, the rest of the relevant technical community may also suffer directly or indirectly from the loss of a potential stream of new investments that was thus prematurely aborted.[33]

C. Critiquing the standard solutions

The historical section of this chapter described the cyclical nature of approaches to small grain-sized innovation, and the green tulip exercise helps to pinpoint the precise nature of the flaws that produce this phenomenon. One problem that the exercise reveals is that while copyright-like regimes inherently tend to offer too little incentive to first comers, any patent-like solution tends to provide too much. In the exercise, the patent-like solution gave Breeder A a relatively strong legal monopoly for undertaking an investment in routine innovation motivated by his own business judgment (in this case, erroneous) about market opportunities. Since he likely would have made that investment anyway, the public obtained no significant creative contribution in return for rewarding Breeder A with monopoly rights. While the public arguably stood to benefit from the green tulip innovation (despite the tepid initial consumer response), solving the free-rider problem by misbundling exclusive property rights imposed burdensome transaction costs on the relevant technical community, frustrated entrepreneurial initiative, and saddled the public with the social costs of misdirected, top-down incentives that deny equally capable second comers access to inputs from the public domain.

More generally, any system that protects subpatentable applications of technical knowhow to industry by means of a property right (even if it is a hybrid) will tend to reward individual creators and innovators as if they had delivered big grain-sized innovation. In reality, the individual's quantitative creative contribution over and above investment will typically be small (despite its potentially great commercial value) precisely because the relevant technical community had cumulatively shared and sequentially developed the basic knowhow of which the individual contribution partakes. None of the hybrid solutions takes account of the community's role in the process of developing subpatentable innovation through minuscule additions to the common stock of technical knowhow that accrue from combined efforts to work through prevailing technical trajectories. Indeed, because they remain perversely structured around hybrid admixtures of patent and copyright principles that recognize only the contributions of individual creators, these solutions may actually undermine the community's own interests by artificially restricting access to the public-domain inputs on which it collectively depends.

---

[33] For more insights into this problem in the context of patentable and copyrightable works, see Mark A. Lemley, *The Economics of Improvement in Intellectual Property Law*, 75 Tex. L. Rev. 989 (1997); Merges & Nelson, n. 11 above.

This kind of system also creates barriers to entry. Second comers must negotiate permissions and pay monopoly prices, even when contemplating risky follow-on innovations of their own, and even when such follow-on innovation actually vindicates or validates the first comer's own investment. The need to bargain around an exclusive property right perversely complicates routine business transactions and adds new risks of disclosure and infringement litigation, to the innate risks of predicting market success.

Phrased differently, the platform of hybrid intellectual property rights as currently structured lacks any systematic capacity to promote the needs, especially the investment needs, of the relevant technical community as a whole. Motivated by self-interest, the members of this community would presumably continue to invest in future applications of their shared technical knowhow, with a concomitant expansion and deepening of that same knowhow, but for the free-rider problem, the attendant risk of market failure, and the divisive influence of the hybrid exclusive rights elicited to cure it. By rewarding individuals with strong exclusive property rights for routine applications of the community's technical knowhow to industry, the system tends to make that shared knowhow artificially scarce.

On the positive side of the ledger, of course, hybrid exclusive property rights also attenuate the social costs of market failure by encouraging investment in routine innovation that might not otherwise take place in the raw state of affairs. This explains the tenacity of utility model laws, which—despite their obvious economic contradictions—continue to be adopted throughout the world. But once it is clear how much these systems cost, the burden of demonstrating lower social costs overall should logically fall on those advocating the imposition of top-down measures. They must show that diminishing access to the public domain will do less harm than leaving innovators to take their chances in a 'malcompetitive' business environment, that solving market failure by proliferating legal kudzu is truly worth the candle, and that different, less individualistic approaches, would not yield greater benefits at lower social costs.

As tiny bundles of small scale innovation covered by strong intellectual property rights and strong contractual rights thus multiply, they divide up the community's shared knowhow into ever smaller parcels that are withdrawn from the public domain. This produces a tangled web of property and quasi-property rights that in itself constitutes a barrier to entry and a disincentive to further small scale innovation. The transaction costs of reconstituting contractually the chain of sequential knowhow previously available from the public domain become correspondingly high and increasingly prohibitive.[34] In the long term, these hybrid intellectual property regimes, and the suffocating

---

[34] See Michael A. Heller, *The Boundaries of Private Property*, 108 YALE L.J. 1163 (1999); Michael A. Heller & Rebecca S. Eisenberg, *Can Patents Deter Innovation? The Anticommons in Biomedical Research*, 280 Sci. 698 (May 1, 1998).

weed-like thicket of exclusive rights they breed, threaten to throttle more innovation than they could ever possibly stimulate.

III. Solving the Green Tulip Problem

To arrest the pendular swings between states of chronic under- and overprotection that investors in small scale innovation increasingly face under
present-day conditions, a new type of intellectual property regime is needed.
Such a system would break with the tradition of multiplying hybrid exclusive
property rights. While it would empower entrepreneurs to prevent free-riders
from rapidly appropriating the fruits of their investment, it would also avoid
measures that impoverish the public domain or that foster legal barriers to
entry. Such a system could also serve as a buffer or transitional zone between
the mature patent and copyright paradigms on the one hand, and unbridled
competition on the other.

A general purpose innovation law meeting these criteria could be built on
liability principles, suitably modified. This system would create a limited
period in which investors were entitled to defray their research and development costs through compensatory contributions from second comers who
borrowed subpatentable knowhow for industrial applications of their own.
This system would not, however, endow small scale innovators with an exclusive right to control second uses. In what follows, I state the tenets of this
proposal and show how, by combining the right set of legal incentives to
invest with the benefits of free competition, a liability regime could resolve the
dilemmas facing the green tulip protagonists and all similarly situated
investors.

A. Mechanics of a compensatory liability regime

To achieve the desired goals, the proposed compensatory liability scheme
requires a basic set of default rules that obligate second comers to pay equitable compensation for borrowed improvements over a relatively short
period of time. With reference to the green tulip hypothetical, for example, we
saw that Breeder A's main complaint in the raw state of affairs was that
Breeders B and C could swiftly turn the subpatentable knowhow resulting
from A's investment into commercially successful follow-on products without contributing to the underlying costs of research and development that
had yielded a green tulip in the first instance.

Breeder A could not properly lodge any patent or copyright claims because
the green tulip did not qualify either as a nonobvious invention or as an original work of authorship. Yet, because his innovative knowhow was embodied in the green tulip variety itself, which any other breeder could purchase

and reproduce, Breeders B and C could move immediately into adjacent market segments without incurring significant research expenses of their own. Moreover, even if the green tulip had scored a commercial success on its own merits, Breeders B and C might have captured that initial market segment as well, because they had lower costs and Breeder A would have obtained no natural lead time from actual secrecy or from the operations of trade secrecy law.

1. A functional substitute for natural lead time

My proposal responds to this dilemma by providing a functional substitute for the chronic lack of natural lead time that afflicts today's investors in small scale innovation. It entitles Breeder A to a specified period of artificial lead time during which the use of his innovative green tulip knowhow requires compensation but not authorization. If, during the specified period of time, Breeder B borrows Breeder A's innovative knowhow, he must compensate Breeder A according to the formulas discussed below,[35] which are aimed at roughly measuring the value added to B's products by the features or components borrowed from A. In this way, Breeder B would contribute directly to Breeder A's costs.

Let me emphasize that while Breeder A would thus obtain some legal entitlement, his entitlement operates as a true liability rule and not as an exclusive property right. The whole idea is to recreate some functional equivalent of the natural lead time that once made competition with respect to most forms of subpatentable innovation feasible. Thus, Breeder A does not have the right to hold out: Breeder B need not seek Breeder A's permission to make use of his green tulip variety, and Breeder A cannot deter second comers from borrowing his small scale innovation so long as they remain willing to pay and the term of protection has not expired.

Follow-on innovation is further encouraged because the operative period of legal liability is short. If Breeder B remains patient and waits until that period expires, he may treat the green tulip variety as a free input from the public domain. Moreover, an impatient Breeder B who possesses sufficient technical knowhow of his own can independently generate a green tulip variety and need not compensate Breeder A at all. In that case, there would be no free-riding. On the contrary, Breeder B's application of that technique to the red, white, and green variety will then further contribute to the relevant technical community's aggregate investment in research and development, which will presumably furnish the basis for other improvements in the field.

Other breeders (Breeder C) are treated like Breeder B. They remain free to extend Breeder B's improved red, white, and green variety to other follow-on products without seeking authorization. However, any rapid borrowing of

---

[35] See below at pp. 43–5.

the claimed technical knowhow pertinent to either the green tulip or the red, white, and green variant during the terms in which Breeder A's and Breeder B's rights are protected will require other breeders (C) to compensate both Breeders A and B according to the applicable formulas. If some of the breeders who fall in category C wait until Breeder A's rights have expired, they need to compensate only Breeder B, and then only for the added value to their products of his specific contribution. If all of the breeders in category C waited long enough, or if they all demonstrably generated follow-on varieties by dint of their own investments in the relevant research and development without borrowing protected knowhow, none of them would become liable to Breeders A or B.

The element of free-riding is attenuated in all these cases by the obligation to contribute to the underlying costs of research and development either directly (via compensation) or indirectly by regenerating the knowhow in question with likely improvements. If neither Breeders B nor C borrow the small grain-sized innovation within the applicable period of liability and accordingly pay nothing at all to Breeder A, the latter will nonetheless have benefitted from a period of artificial lead time in which to emulate B's red, white, and green variety and C's other successful follow-on products. Whether Breeder A generates these competing products by virtue of his own independent efforts, without compensating B or C, or opts instead quickly to borrow back their improvements with a payment of compensatory liability depends entirely on A's business judgment and technical capacity. However, his decisions cannot be skewed by B's or C's refusal to authorize competing small scale innovations for lengthy periods of time under top-down exclusive property rights.

This system does, however, retain some residual element of free-riding: at the expiry of a relatively short period of protection, each breeder's small scale innovation will lapse into the public domain where all competitors remain free to use it without incurring compensatory liability. But this is precisely what free competition entails. In a healthy competitive environment, any second comer can access any subpatentable innovation for purposes of reverse-engineering the underlying process of manufacture by proper means, because the time and money required to accomplish the task of reverse-engineering overcomes the inherent risk of market failure. It is only in an environment in which incremental innovation bears the entrepreneur's knowhow on (or near) its face—where the costs of reverse engineering are negligible—that a problem arises. The proposed compensatory liability regime would solve it by imposing functionally equivalent costs: it channels funds that might otherwise have been spent on the task of reverse-engineering to defray directly the first mover's real costs of research and development.

If Breeders B and C choose to wait out the period of protection and thus make no compensatory liability payments, they stand in the shoes of 'healthy' competitors, whose only barriers to entry are natural lead time and the state of the art available to all other routine engineers. Their autonomous investments in small scale innovations that improve existing products (and strengthen their own competitive prospects) will then redound to the benefit of the entire technical community. This follows because, even though on this scenario they owe nothing to Breeder A, all other breeders who share the common stock of technical knowhow (including Breeder A) are themselves free to borrow back any new incremental additions to subpatentable knowhow that patient Breeders B and C may contribute in return for equitable contributions to their respective development costs.

2. Implementing a liability rule

I have elsewhere outlined a legal framework for implementing a general purpose innovation law along these lines, which Professor Pamela Samuelson and I have referred to as a 'modified liability regime', and which I now prefer to call a 'compensatory liability regime'.[36] Our previous work suggested that such a regime would benefit from certain constitutive elements that are discussed and amplified below.

a. Main features   Some of these elements are fairly straightforward. First, there must be a subject matter denomination of the protectable bundles of commercially valuable information, which we call an 'industrial compilation'. Secondly, the regime will need a loose standard of novelty more or less equivalent to that which courts apply in trade secrecy cases. A third element is the period of artificial lead time available to entrepreneurs claiming protection for any given 'industrial compilation'. A fourth element is a national registration system for making these claims known. Mediatory dispute and arbitral settlement arrangements should also be built into the system.   ·

In principle, a compensatory liability regime would thus be crafted in general terms, so as to accommodate small scale innovation from all sectors of industry. One advantage of this approach, however, is that, over time, codified variants might be tailored to meet the needs of particular industries; eg, a database protection law could benefit from certain structural nuances not needed for the bulk of subpatentable innovation without gutting the liability regime as a whole.[37] In this and other respects, the compensatory liability regime constitutes a 'third intellectual property paradigm', whose basic principles can be systematically developed without undermining the operations of the patent and copyright laws within their traditional spheres of influence.[38]

Other constituent elements of a compensatory liability regime would include criteria for infringement; a menu of users' liabilities; a list of defenses, including misuse; and rules governing the relations between this regime and other laws, particularly unfair competition law. Also desirable is the encouragement

---

[36] See *Legal Hybrids*, n. 2 above; *Manifesto*, n. 1 above.
[37] See Reichman & Samuelson, n. 18 above.   [38] See *Symposium*, n. 16 above.

of sectoral agents (or quasi-collection societies) on an industry by industry basis, which would facilitate collective action on licensing, dispute resolution, and ancillary rule-making procedures of interest to particular sectors. Some of these issues are amplified below.

b. Infringement An implementing statute should set out the applicable standard of infringement, and I have elsewhere endorsed a 'substantial identity' criterion for this purpose.[39] However, the underlying purpose of the liability rule should affect the way courts apply that standard. Since the goal here is to defray the research expenses of earlier innovators, courts must ensure that virtually any use of a qualitatively or quantitatively significant component within the specified term of protection would infringe, in the sense of triggering a duty to pay.[40]

Some difficulties in proving use might arise, especially in countries where opportunities for discovery are sparse, although the small scale of the innovation at issue and the brevity of the liability period should help to alleviate such problems. At bottom, once a complainant satisfies a 'substantial identity' test, the onus should shift to the defendant. The latter can then rebut the possibility of use thus raised by producing evidence of independent development. Codifying the relative burdens of proof in such cases is a good idea, for which there are analogies in existing law.[41]

c. Compensatory remedies In theory, a liability rule could objectively require every user to contribute a proportionate share of the costs of development from which he benefitted or to pay the value that the borrowed fruits of this development added to his own products. This rule seems consistent with the goal of defraying a first comer's costs, and it would also integrate some unjust enrichment principles into the framework.[42] Such a rule could, however, be difficult to implement.[43] Thus, a better alternative would be to require the parties to negotiate, subject to a requirement of arbitration, should negotiations fail. This system could be made more manageable and efficient by reducing the duty to compensate to a set of royalties levied on a fixed percentage of the offender's gross revenues that varied within a specified range of options.

---

[39] See *Manifesto*, n. 1 above.

[40] Cf the EC's Directive on Databases art. 8(1), n. 13 above, which adopts a 'quantitative or qualitative' component test, but within the ambit of an ultra high-protectionist exclusive property right.

[41] See, eg, TRIPS Agreement, n. 9 above, art. 34.

[42] See, eg, Wendy J. Gordon, *On Owning Information: Intellectual Property and the Restitutionary Impulse,* 78 VA. L. REV. 149 (1992). This is the calculus used in the sole existing liability regime that operates somewhat along the lines of the compensatory liability regime discussed here, see Italian Copyright Law, Law No. 633 of April 22, 1941, *as amended through* July 29, 1989, art. 99, *codified as* Codice Civile sec. 2578, *reprinted in* Codice del Copyright—Il Diritto D'Autore Fra Arte e Industria 7 (Gustavo Ghidini ed. 1995).

[43] Procedural complications are easy to conjure up if plaintiffs must identify many users and join them all in a single lawsuit, or if the defendants held liable in one case sought contributions from others.

For example, a three-pronged sliding scale of royalty options could simple-mindedly distinguish between small, medium, and large contributions to added value that entailed corresponding duties to pay.[44] A slightly more refined system might recognize a fourth category applicable to an 'extra large' quantum of technical knowhow added (without authorization) to the follow-on product in question. Whether these percentage options should fall into a very modest range (say, 3–6–9 percent) or into a range with more bite (say 5–10–15 percent or higher) is an issue best deferred to more empirical investigation.

A number of factors combine to make this approach (or, in default, an arbitrator's decision to the same effect) more socially desirable than a nominally more serious assessment of the real value added in single cases. First, by insisting that Breeder B share in the costs of Breeder A's research and development, we are intentionally structuring a de facto legal partnership arrangement embracing all the members of the relevant technical community. One goal is to ensure that this partnership arrangement outperforms the zig-zag, hit-or-miss decisions that result when courts use unfair competition laws to fill gaps in domestic intellectual property systems. As work on patent pools demonstrates, a sliding scale of percentage royalties expresses this venture partnership principle (and the sharing of scientific and technical information that it implies).[45]

A second reason for preferring a relatively uncomplicated scale of percentage royalties is that, even if we were serious about quantifying real value added to follow-on innovation, the single source of greatest value added to any small scale innovation is always the public domain. In the green tulip exercise, for example, the bulk of the value resides in the common store of plant breeders' knowhow (or in this case, of specific tulip breeding knowhow) that Breeders A, B, and C share in common with all the other breeders at work on the existing technical trajectory. Any of these breeders can freely make use of any of the cumulative and sequential innovations that enrich the public domain without owing any dues to anybody.

If, on top of this giant, Breeder A's green tulip technique adds a new and commercially valuable fragment to that common store of knowledge, it is fitting that Breeders B and C contribute a tangential percentage of the revenues resulting from exploitation of that fragment in recognition of Breeder A's real development costs. But given the preponderant weight of the public-domain layer in all small scale applications of knowhow to industry, we do not want

---

[44] Of course, second comers like Breeder B might quarrel with Breeder A about whether the latter was entitled to a relatively 'large', 'medium', or 'small' percentage of Breeder B's revenues from sales of his red, white, and green tulip, given that the valuation of Breeder A's prior technical inputs (into a commercially unsuccessful green tulip) must also take account of the cost of Breeder B's own technical inputs (into a successful red, white, and green tulip) as well as the value of his superior marketing skills. In this scheme, failure to agree on this issue would be taken up by the arbitrator.

[45] See, eg, Merges, n. 11 above, 45; see also Merges, Chapter 6 below.

the compensatory mechanism to undervalue the technical community's own contribution to every follow-on innovation. From this angle, a sliding scale of relatively modest percentage royalties expresses the concept of floating, de facto partnerships, while respecting the shared ownership of the commons that unites all those engaged in technical and scientific pursuits.

The small scale of allowable percentages would also discourage resort to arbitration or to appeal of the results of arbitration to the courts. Moreover, because most of the relevant players in the different sectors of industry are likely to alternate as both borrowers and lenders of subpatentable innovation over time, their mutual self interest pushes toward accommodations with which both lenders and borrowers can live.

Finally, a preference for a set of modest percentage royalties over other more aggressive valuation methods harmonizes with the principle that the period during which any borrower remains liable for equitable contributions to the costs of research and development should be short in an absolute sense. This follows because the primary purpose of the proposed default rules is to overcome the chronic shortage of natural lead time under present-day conditions, and not to create legal monopolies or other incentives to invest where none are needed. One should also emphasize that the transaction costs of implementing the proposed set of default rules need not prove onerous or burdensome precisely because only a finite number of industry players are ever involved at any given time, and the system focuses mainly on payments and adjustments between players on given market segments.

d. Defenses   In practice, once a compensatory liability regime is legislatively set in motion, parties opting into the system would normally prefer to strike their own bargains while treating the baseline statutory entitlements as a point of reference for this and other purposes, including litigation. The ex-ante disclosure problem that hinders deal-making between Breeders A and B under present-day conditions, for example, would give way to an environment in which both parties (and all other industry players) knew that Breeders B and C could legally apply Breeder A's green tulip knowhow to follow-on products only by paying compensatory dues.

In many ways, this propensity to deal is a major benefit of the proposal. Experience suggests that industry-approved standard-form contracts, perhaps administered by a single authorized agent, may develop, and these would further tend to reduce overall transaction costs. If public, such deals will also furnish data about the industry's own valuations of follow-on innovations, and arbitrators could use these data in contested cases. Actual experience could eventually lead legislatures to modify the initial statutory entitlements to reflect more accurately these bargained-for results.

At the same time, facilitating transactions among competitors also raises the danger of anticompetitive agreements, such as agreements that unduly benefit Breeders A, B, and C at the expense of those who would buy their tulips or who would enter the market as their competitors. It seems advisable, therefore, to include in the statute a list of anticompetitive acts that would furnish defenses to infringement actions, along with codified standards of misuse that would further clarify the limits of privately negotiated contracts arising under the compensatory liability regime.[46] An accompanying series of safe harbors should likewise provide entrepreneurs with guidance on types of agreements that are considered to promote innovation and competition.[47]

e. Relationship to unfair competition laws Although the proposed compensatory liability regime should obviate the need for other sui generis intellectual property rights to protect subpatentable innovation, some doctrines of unfair competition should retain their vitality. The first is trade secrecy law: there is nothing in a compensatory liability regime that is inconsistent with allowing entrepreneurs who are capable of keeping all or part of their subpatentable innovations secret from taking their chances under trade secrecy law. The innovator's lead-time calculus would then vary with the second comers' abilities to reverse engineer the process underlying the relevant products by honest means. If such an entrepreneur declined to use trade secret protection and opted into the compensatory liability system, he would be wagering that the potential returns accruing from its period of artificial lead time would exceed expected earnings under a variable (and disappearing) period of natural lead time. Of course, few investors will actually enjoy the luxury of such a choice, given that the impetus for this proposal was the chronic shortage of natural lead time that afflicts investments in most of today's commercially valuable applications of knowhow to industry.

General norms of unfair competition law are a different matter. As I have shown, the notion that unfair competition law can alleviate the investment dilemmas attributed to the phenomenon of incremental innovation bearing knowhow on its face is both historically anachronistic and empirically untenable. Historically, unfair competition law constitutes an amorphous 'urground' or basic set of principles that identify and try to rectify recurring instances of market failure. These very principles led to the codification of patent and copyright laws, but they also led to the epicycles of hybrid regimes. Empirically, unfair competition norms enabled courts to adopt temporary measures to alleviate the tensions that arise from gaps in the domestic systems of innovation. Over time, however, when legislatures fail to intervene (or when they choose to intervene inopportunely), courts applying these amorphous principles tend to become part of the problem rather than agents of any

---

[46] A similar approach is found in proposed US database legislation, see H. R. 1858, 106th Cong. 1st Sess. (1999) § 106, and HOUSE REP. No. 106–350 (Part I) (1999).

[47] See J.H. Reichman & Jonathan A. Franklin, *Privately Legislated Intellectual Property Rights: Reconciling Freedom of Contract with Public Good Uses of Information*, 147 U. PA. L. REV. 875 (1999).

real solution. Inevitably, judicial decisions are ad hoc and prompted by the judges' own views about the morality of copying and the importance of free competition.

The compensatory liability regime explored in this chapter aims to improve upon these historical failures while avoiding recourse to hybrid exclusive property rights that seldom do better than unfair competition law and that cumulatively undermine the competitive ethos. There is, nonetheless, at least one point where the principles of unfair competition and compensatory liability properly converge. Here I refer to the situation in which the second comer rapidly appropriates the innovator's small grain-sized technical contribution in order to compete head to head in the same market segment, without producing any value-adding product. In terms of the green tulip exercise, this is the situation in which Breeder A's green tulip scored a commercial success and, by appropriating the relevant technical knowhow without incurring the costs of research and development, Breeder B undersells Breeder A and captures the initial green tulip market as well as adjacent market segments for follow-on varieties.

This is the one situation in which it makes sense for a compensatory liability regime to undertake a more aggressive calculus of the real value added to Breeder B's product by his rapid duplication of Breeder A's technical contribution. Even here, however, there are other ways of addressing the underlying threat of market failure from a compensatory liability angle that may better respect the common public-domain denominator of both products and that may better preserve the benefits of competition.

A relatively simple solution, for example, is to codify measures that block Breeder B's ability to undertake this act of wholesale or slavish imitation in the same market segment for a fixed period of artificial lead time, after which head-to-head competition may be allowed without any further duty to make compensatory contributions to research. On this approach, Breeder B could not *duplicate* the green tulip variety for, say, a period of three years, even though his *value-adding* operations would remain permissible but subject to compensatory liability payments.

The advantages of this solution are its low transaction costs and its neutral impact on follow-on innovation. However, it tends to slow the pace of direct competition and further to skew the benefits of such competition by imposing a relatively long blocking period that lacks any firm empirical foundation. Another, more refined way to address the problem is to reduce the prohibition against wholesale duplication for purposes of head-to-head competition to such a short blocking period that it could withstand any critical economic evaluation, while requiring the second comer to pay compensatory contributions to the costs of research and development for the remainder of a specified period of artificial lead time. For example, the statute could block Breeder B's wholesale duplication of the green tulip for, say, one year, and then allow him to enter that market segment on condition that he make compensatory payments for an additional period, say, two years.

Here, moreover, the calculus of those contributions could arguably have still more bite, to reflect the fact that there is no value-adding operation that redounds to the benefit of the technical community as a whole. This can be achieved either by imposing a higher percentage royalty than would ever apply in a case of follow-on innovation, or by extending the period of compensatory liability beyond that applicable to follow-on innovation, or by some combination of the two. For example, after a one-year blocking period, Breeder B's wholesale duplication of Breeder A's green tulip might bear a higher percentage royalty than that applicable to follow-on innovation, and the duty to pay it might last for a longer term than that governing the case of follow-on applications (say, four years rather than three). In any event, the mere threat of such regulatory sanctions should encourage greater reliance on negotiated transactions to resolve conflicts over acts of slavish imitation, like those envisioned earlier for follow-on innovations.

B. Implications of a compensatory liability regime

The compensatory liability regime outlined above would solve the green tulip problem and make it unnecessary to enact more hybrid exclusive property rights to address market failure in the technology-specific fashion of the past. However, one could conceivably achieve similar results outside of the intellectual property system, for example, by rooting the proposed default rules in contract law or in trade regulation law. What matters is not the specific legal regime chosen to implement the proposal, but rather the end result: namely, a set of off-the-rack liability rules allocating contributions to the costs of research and development for unauthorized uses of subpatentable innovations within a specified period of time.

In this context, a paramount consideration is that any new approach to the puzzle of small scale innovation should focus on the relevant technical community as a whole and not on the individual innovator, whose inducement to invest hinges on market-determined variables rather than on the need to overcome exceptionally high technical barriers. If the risk of market failure that collectively discourages investment in small scale innovation were otherwise attenuated, it should suffice to free individual entrepreneurs operating within the relevant technical communities to follow their own business instincts— that is, to make pro-competitive business decisions about the direction of such investments—without the spur of ad hoc legal monopolies. Conversely, the growth of any given technical community's store of shared knowhow in the absence of balkanizing exclusive property rights depends on a continuing and adequate flow of investment across the given field of endeavor, which serves to nourish the innovative activities of single players as their needs arise.

This investment model differs from that applicable to large grain-sized innovation (especially patentable inventions), in which context a major technical advance by any single player tends to elevate the level of competition as a whole and to redirect the flow of investment to new objectives that lie beyond the scope of the prior art. In what follows, I will attempt to clarify the deeper implications of my approach to small scale innovation in light of the findings derived from the green tulip exercise.

1. Amplifying investment without impoverishing the public domain
Within the relevant community of small grain-sized innovators at work on a common technical trajectory, all the players can add to the cumulative stock of knowhow at different times by dint of their individual business decisions, and each is likely to operate as either a lender or a borrower of incremental innovation at different times or intervals. So long as the stock of shared knowhow continues to grow, today's innovator who borrows another's subpatentable technical innovation tomorrow in order to meet and trump the evolving state of competition periodically injects both investment and knowledge into an ongoing community-wide enterprise. The proper goal of a reformed system is mainly to inhibit second comers operating within the confines of given technical trajectories from free-riding by obliging them to contribute, directly or indirectly, to the first comers' costs of research and development. These costs have facilitated the second comers' specific follow-on innovation and have also produced a small, incremental addition to the cumulative stock of shared technical knowhow, which potentially benefits all firms operating in the same market segment.

However, one should not assimilate the second comers' duty to pay compensation under this approach with the compensatory duties that arise when compulsory licenses derogate from the patentee's (or the copyright owner's) legal monopoly under existing intellectual property systems.[48] In principle, compulsory licenses cut back on proprietary control in order to promote certain overriding public interest goals, and the rationale for imposing them remains inherently controversial. In contrast, the 'automatic license' that, under my proposal, entitles an investor to compensatory liability for follow-on applications by second comers during a specified period of time fully expresses the entitlement in question and does not constitute an artificial limitation upon an exclusive property right. As I conceive it, the power to *control* follow-on applications of subpatentable innovation (as distinct from an entitlement to equitable compensation for certain uses) is simply not a constituent feature of a regime that is based on modified liability principles. I stress nonetheless that the first comer's entitlement to compensation, although weaker than the corresponding exclusive property rights that the

---

[48] See, eg, TRIPS Agreement, n. 9 above, art. 31.

patent and copyright paradigms afford, remains an *entitlement*: correctly perceived, it is an entitlement that takes the form of an automatic license without the power to exclude.[49]

One should not assume that, despite the comparative weakness of the proposed liability regime, a rightholder would necessarily collect a lesser stream of revenue from follow-on applications of protected small scale innovation than would accrue if some hybrid exclusive property right covered the same innovation. The very power to exclude unlicensed follow-on applications often pits the first comer's interest in preserving a legal or factual monopoly against the second comer's business instincts regarding potentially profitable applications. As the green tulip problem illustrates, an aggressive second comer's applications—if freely allowed subject to a compensatory liability rule—might yield far more in overall income than the first comer would have obtained if he or she had denied the license or granted it exclusively to a more congenial licensee. This possibility of unexpected returns arises especially when several second comers become interested in multiple follow-on applications that could produce a cumulative benefit well in excess of what the first comer's own business plan might otherwise have yielded. In the green tulip exercise, for example, the endeavors of Breeders B and C created, in effect, a lottery payout to A, in the form of royalties on novel tulips having multiple color combinations.

Breeder A benefits in another way, for nothing impedes a first comer from borrowing back the second comers' successful follow-on applications, like those that Breeders B and C developed for their own innovative purposes. In that event, of course, Breeder A must himself contribute to the development costs of Breeders B and C by paying compensation to them, but they have no capacity to deny him this right. But by borrowing back the features that Breeders B and C added to their own small-scale innovations, Breeder A positions himself to compete with them on related or potential market segments, without suffering or imposing free-rider costs.

I do not mean to imply that Breeder A, as a single enterprise, is always better off under a liability rule than he would have been under a property right. The point is rather that the relevant technical community (and society as a whole) are cumulatively better off under such a regime, while Breeder A is not always or necessarily worse off. At the same time, Breeder B—pushed by his own business instincts and pulled by the compensatory liability regime that protects his follow-on innovation—retains sufficient incentives to play the game. In other words, once Breeder B opts to make equitable contributions to Breeder A's costs, he puts himself in a position to collect similar contributions not only from Breeder C, but even from Breeder A, who will often want to exploit the second comer's follow-on innovation quickly, so as to keep up with the state of the art or move it forward.

---

[49] I am indebted to Professor James Blumstein of Vanderbilt Law School for this insight.

The automatic license that characterizes the proposed compensatory liability regime thus eliminates the economically unjustifiable tendency of hybrid regimes of exclusive property rights to allocate ownership of follow-on applications to either the first comer (at the expense of others) or to second comers (at the expense of the initial innovator). Instead, first comers will have to calculate their business strategies knowing that second comers must pay compensation for follow-on applications of the small scale innovation in which they plan to invest (within a specified period of time) and knowing also that they themselves are entitled to borrow back any such follow-on applications in return for compensatory liability. At the same time, the second comer's legal ability freely to borrow the first comer's subpatentable innovation within specified periods of time is limited in practice by the need to calculate the impact on profitability of his contributions to the first comer's costs. Within the specified time limits of the applicable regime, this automatic license should empower all the relevant players at work on the shared technical trajectory to move back and forth between the status of lenders and that of borrowers as their business instincts dictate, unimpeded by artificial legal barriers encumbering access to subpatentable innovation.

2. Other applications

This proposed compensatory liability regime was articulated with the historical problems of the developed industrial world in mind, but it will prove beneficial in other contexts as well. Thus, the development of the Internet, digitization, and electronic commerce pose new challenges to small scale innovation. These advances reduce the cost of copying, shrink lead time, and increase the risk that small scale innovators will take matters into their own hands and create totally unregulated states of artificial lead time through encryption and adhesion contracts. If enforceable, these electronically imposed standard form contracts could degenerate into a basis for asserting private rights that override all the public-interest safeguards that have ensured access to the public domain under traditional intellectual property laws. They could balkanize the information commons and reintroduce conditions that impede the flow of information.[50]

However, the enactment of a general purpose innovation law on modified liability principles would lessen these risks because it would offer those who innovate in this environment a way to alleviate market failure without impoverishing the public domain. Indeed, these developments may themselves contribute to the operation of the liability regime: online communication will expedite claim registration, help innovators find the knowhow they need, facilitate negotiations, and promote the use of standardized terms.

---

[50] See Reichman & Franklin, n. 47 above. See generally *Symposium, Intellectual Property and Contract Law for the Information Age*, Part I, 87 CAL. L. REV. 1 (1999); Part II, 13 BERKELEY TECH. L. J. 809 (1998).

Monitoring use and collecting royalties will likewise prove easier to organize and less costly to implement online.

The compensatory liability regime proposed in this chapter would also help to cure some of the major problems afflicting the domestic patent laws in certain developed countries. Thus, the mere existence of such a liability regime would alleviate pressures on the patent systems of countries where the level of nonobviousness has been pushed downwards in order to provide some refuge for commercially valuable, small scale innovations of importance to local industries. A liability regime for small scale applications of knowhow to industry would allow the intellectual property authorities and the courts to restrict the dominant patent-copyright dichotomy to truly nonobvious inventions and original works of authorship.

Furthermore, the proposed compensatory liability regime would help to solve some pressing needs of the developing countries. In particular, such a regime would provide these countries with new means of stimulating local innovation that would avoid the pitfalls and contradictions of existing design protection laws and utility model laws. More important, this regime could easily be modified to enable developing countries to protect the folklore and traditional knowhow of indigenous people.[51] As with small scale innovation, the goal is to reward both first comers (in this case, the relevant indigenous community) and second comers (those who build on the community's cultural and technical heritage), without impeding access to the pubic domain or the flow of new products. With small amounts of tinkering, a compensatory liability regime could be used to encourage use of traditional knowledge without denying the relevant indigenous communities the right to a fair share of the proceeds.

IV. Conclusion

The objective of the green tulip exercise was to expose the structural flaws underlying prior legal solutions to the problem of small scale innovation. The analysis showed that property-based rules cannot work. They return to the first comer too little or too much, they impede follow-on developments, ignore the significant contributions of the public domain, balkanize the knowledge base, and increase transaction costs.

A modified liability rule would resolve these difficulties. Within a designated period of artificial lead time, firms are permitted to borrow one

---

[51] See, eg, Thomas Cottier, *The Protection of Genetic Resources and Traditional Knowledge: Towards More Specific Rights and Obligations in World Trade Law*, 1 J. INT. EC. L. 555 (1998); Rosemary J. Coombe, *Intellectual Property, Human Rights, & Sovereignty: New Dilemmas in International Law Posed by the Recognition of Indigenous Knowledge and the Conservation of Biodiversity*, 6 INDIANA J. GLOBAL LEGAL STUDIES 59 (1998).

another's subpatentable innovations, but only when they contribute to the costs of development. When this occurs, the short-term commercial success of any player in the relevant technical community should either have produced new investment in new innovation or a flow of contributions back to other members of the technical community in exchange for investment in follow-on applications of their own subpatentable innovation during the very recent past. The success of multiple players in the relevant technical universe should correspondingly augment the flow of investment and technical information to that universe as a whole, as players participate in the industry-wide virtual partnership that a liability rule supports.

As a result, development decisions would be properly rooted in business judgments about the state of competition, the likelihood of commercial success, and the comparative economies that would result from expending costs in reverse engineering as compared with the payment of equitable compensation. They would not be skewed by top-down legal monopolies that slow the pace of competition and make the public pay for technical advances that would have been achieved anyway in the absence of market-destructive appropriations.

US INITIATIVES TO PROTECT WORKS OF LOW AUTHORSHIP

JANE C. GINSBURG*

Since the US Supreme Court swept away 'sweat copyright' in its 1991 *Feist* decision,[1] producers and consumers of works of low authorship, primarily compilations of information and, particularly, digital databases, have debated whether US law still affords these works effective protection.[2] For the first 200 years of US copyright law, Congress, courts, and compilers seem to have concurred that copyright supplied a needed incentive to gather and publish useful information, and courts condemned competitors who copied even scantily (if at all) original compilations.[3] Today, 'thin' copyright protection remains available, but it covers only those original contributions (if any) that the compiler brings to the public domain information. Moreover, *Feist* makes clear that padding the compilation with original added value will not

* (Part I of this article is based in part on Jane C. Ginsburg, *Copyright, Common Law, and Sui Generis Protection of Databases in the United States and Abroad*, 66 U. Cin. L. Rev. 151 (1997). Thanks to Bruce Joseph in general, and especially for many of the ideas in Part III B; to Christelle Bousquet Wu, Columbia Law School J.D. 2000, for research assistance with Part III A; and to Allison Engel, Columbia Law School J.D. 2000, for general research assistance.

[1] *Feist Publications, Inc. v. Rural Tel. Ser. Co., Inc*, 499 U.S. 340 (1991).

[2] See U.S. Copyright Office, Report on Legal Protection for Databases (August 1997) at <http://www.loc.gov/copyright/reports>

[3] See, eg, Jane C. Ginsburg, *Creation and Commercial Value· Copyright Protection of Works of Information*, 90 Colum. L. Rev. 1865, 1873–93 (1990) (surveying history of US copyright protection of works of information).

flesh out the skeletal figure beneath: the information, stripped of selection, arrangement, or other copyrightable frills, remains free for the taking.[4] The vulnerability of information compilations today to copying therefore raises the question whether sufficient incentives persist to undertake the labor and investment of compiling and disseminating databases. Digital media make the question all the more pressing, since the medium's amenability to instantaneous replication sharply diminishes the 'lead time advantage' that producers of valuable, but unprotected, information goods have historically enjoyed over competitors.[5]

On the other hand, provisions added to the Copyright Act in 1998 to protect against the circumvention of technological access and anticopying controls on copyrighted works may serve to prevent unlicensed copying, even of portions of minimally original digital databases. Because the new provisions may make it possible to bootstrap unprotected information to coverage by combining it with protected expression, they may fill some of the gap *Feist* left in protection. By the same token, however, they may also fill the gap to overflowing: it is not yet clear that (or how) the fair use balance built into copyright law will apply to technological controls. Thus, while we should seek to preserve incentives to compile information, these provisions may overcompensate for copyright's post-*Feist* failings.[6]

A better way to address the problem would be to enact legislation specifically tailored to afford limited reproduction rights in unoriginal databases. In fact, some form of database bill has been proposed in every session of Congress since 1996.[7] None, to date, however, has come close to passage.

---

[4] See, eg, *BellSouth Adver. & Publ'g Corp. v. Donnelly Info. Publ'g, Inc.*, 999 F.2d 1436 (11th Cir. 1993) (en banc), *cert. denied*, 510 U.S. 1101 (1995) (listings of business-rate telephone service subscribers not copyrightable); *Key Publications, Inc. v. Chinatown Today Publ'g Enters. Inc.*, 945 F.2d 509 (2d Cir. 1991) (original directory of New York-area Chinese businesses not infringed when second comer copied listings but did not substantially appropriate either the selection of businesses included, or their arrangement); *Cantor v. NYP Holdings, Inc.* 51 F. Supp. 2d 309 (S.D.N.Y. 1999) (newspaper article on celebrity graduates of New York City schools did not infringe copyright of book on same subject by what it borrowed because defendant did not take plaintiff's principle of selection and arrangement); *Skinder-Strauss Assocs. v. Mass. Continuing Legal Educ., Inc.*, 914 F. Supp. 665, 674–75 (D. Mass. 1995) (original legal directory contains much uncopyrightable information, such as standard calendar, list of important holidays, national map; copying these does not constitute copyright infringement).

[5] See, eg, RESTATEMENT (THIRD) OF UNFAIR COMPETITION § 38 cmt. C ('The originator of valuable information or other intangible assets normally has an opportunity to exploit the advantage of a lead time in the market. This can provide the originator with an opportunity to recover the costs of development and in many cases is sufficient to encourage continued investment'); Stephen Breyer, *The Uneasy Case for Copyright: A Study of Copyright in Books, Photocopies, and Computer Programs*, 84 HARV. L. REV. 281 (1970).

[6] I have elsewhere considered how state misappropriation and contract rules might cover compilations of information, as well as the extent to which federal law does, or should, preempt those protections. See Jane Ginsburg, *Copyright, Common Law, and Sui Generis Protection of Databases in the United States and Abroad*, 66 U. CIN. L. REV. 151 (1997).

[7] See, eg, the 'Collections of Information Antipiracy Act', H.R. 354, 106th Cong. (1999) (Judiciary Committee Bill); 'Consumer and Investor Access to Information Act of 1999', H.R.

This chapter will examine current US copyright doctrine on protection of works of 'low authorship', before turning to the potential impact on database protection of the 1998 anticircumvention measures. In the last section of this chapter, I will draw on the 1996 European Union Database Directive,[8] and on several Member States' implementing laws, as well as on some features of bills proposed in the US to outline a model statute that would create a special misappropriation claim. The proposed statute would protect against the copying of substantial portions of a collection of information assembled by substantial investment of monetary or other resources.

I. Protection Under the Copyright Act: Copyrightable Subject Matter and Scope Since *Feist*

To appreciate why copyright after *Feist* no longer secures the commercial value of information compilations, it may be helpful to analyze some of that decision's implications. *Feist* stresses that copyright protects only the selection or the arrangement of information contained within a compilation. The 'facts themselves' remain free, as do the other elements that section 102(b) of the Copyright Act excludes from the subject matter of copyright. These include ideas, processes, and methods of operation.[9] Moreover, trite, banal, or 'garden variety' selections or arrangements of information lack the required minimal originality.[10] Thus, an alphabetical or exhaustive listing of all telephone subscribers or local businesses will not 'make the grade'.[11] It follows, by contrast, that a novel or imaginative selection—for example, a directory of all the hard-to-find frescos in Florence, or a listing of the restaurants with the worst service in New York City—should qualify (although the component facts themselves do not).

Or should it? Perhaps the universe-defining criterion that governs the selection is just an unprotectable 'idea'. The Second Circuit confronted this quandary in a case concerning a compilation of used car resale values.[12] Judge Leval recognized that the recharacterization of the selection or arrangement of a compilation from original contribution to public domain idea would mean that:

[v]irtually nothing will remain of the protection accorded by the statute to compilations, notwithstanding the express command of the copyright statute [that

---

1858, 106th Cong. (1999) (Commerce Committee bill); 'Collections of Information Antipiracy Act', H.R. 2652, 105th Cong. (1998); 'Database Investment and Intellectual Property Antipiracy Act of 1996', H.R. 3531, 104th Cong. (1996).

   [8] Council Directive 96/9/EC, 1996 O.J. L77/20 (hereinafter Directive).
   [9] 17 U.S.C. § 102(b) (2000).   [10] *Feist Publications*, n. 1 above, 499 U.S. at 358–59.
   [11] Ibid at 362–64.
   [12] CCC *Info. Servs., Inc. v. Maclean Hunter Mkt. Reports, Inc.*, 44 F.3d 61 (2d Cir. 1994).

compilations are included within the subject matter of copyright] . . . Given the nature of compilations, it is almost inevitable that the original contributions of the compilers will consist of *ideas*. Originality in *selection* for example, will involve the compiler's idea of the utility to the consumer of a limited selection from the particular universe of available data.[13]

Despite discerning the paradox, the court did not fully resolve it. Rather, the Second Circuit eluded the 'idea' trap by distinguishing between 'ideas that undertake to advance the understanding of phenomena or the solution of problems', and those that are 'infused with the author's taste and opinion'.[14] The latter kind of 'idea' is not an 'idea' in the forbidden section 102(b) sense. Instead, it is a 'soft' idea, whose privatization by copyright is tolerable because it 'do[es] not materially assist the understanding of future thinkers.'[15] The court came close to acknowledging that an 'idea' in copyright law is not an epistemological but a legal conclusion, informed by public policy notions of what is necessary to stimulate creation of works in the first place, while still leaving room for subsequent innovation.[16]

How does the distinction between 'hard' and 'soft' ideas or facts work? The information in the second kind of compilation I posited—New York City restaurants with the worst service—would seem to fall in the 'weaker, suggestion-opinion category'[17] that should be protected against copying of substantial subjective aspects of the compilation. By contrast, the first compilation, of hard-to-find frescos in Florence, might be characterized as problem solving. That is, the point of the directory is to identify where these obscure frescos may be found. The directory thus furnishes a solution to the problem of locating the hard-to-find. If this characterization is correct, then that compilation may be freely copied (assuming it contains no original arrangement). The 'idea' of its selection may have been clever and unusual, but it is too objective to receive the protection extended to 'soft' selections.

Does this make sense? Why should copyright cover only mushily subjective selections, throwing useful, and even novel, but objective, universe-defining criteria to the wolves? The distinction relates to copyright's obsession with facts. In copyright law, the facts shall be made free because no one should own the 'building blocks' essential to all authors.[18] Subjective presentations are merely 'approximative statements of opinion'.[19] That makes them not only author-intensive, but less necessary to subsequent creators.

---

[13] Ibid at 70 (emphasis in original; citations omitted).   [14] Ibid at 71.   [15] Ibid.

[16] Cf *American Dental Ass'n v. Delta Dental Plans Ass'n* , 126 F.3d 977 (7th Cir. 1997) (a 'taxonomy', a system of classification, of dental procedures held not an 'idea' or 'system' under § 102(b): 'There can be multiple, and equally original, biographies of the same person's life, and multiple original taxonomies of a field of knowledge. Creativity marks the expression even after the fundamental scheme has been devised').

[17] See *CCC Info. Servs.*, n. 12 above, 44 F.3d at 73.   [18] Ibid at 71.   [19] Ibid.

This formulation invites challenge.[20] I will note, but not press, the observation that there is much subjectivity even in apparently 'objective' presentations of fact;[21] but whatever its post-modern appeal, that observation is unlikely to change the legal conclusion that even a false fact purveyed as a true fact will be treated as a fact nonetheless.[22] The second objection deserves more attention: subjective information is easily objectified. For example, my belief that the restaurants listed in my compilation offer the worst service in New York City is subjective. But it is also an objective fact that I believe that these restaurants offer miserable service. In one recent controversy, a defendant who copied plaintiff's used car valuations argued that it used them in this objective way. Indeed, defendant tried to push objectification even further, by borrowing not only plaintiff's set of valuations, but also another rating service's valuations, and then adding the average of the two.

The Second Circuit rejected the objectification sleight of hand, recognizing that it posed the same risk of 'vitiat[ing] the inducements offered by the copyright law to the makers of original compilations'[23] as did characterizing the selection as an unprotectable 'idea'. The objectification technique may give greater pause, however, when the objectifier is not the copying defendant, but a state or local authority. For example, the car valuation defendant further contended that, whatever the initial subjectivity of plaintiff's ratings, they had become public domain facts because state car insurance statutes or regulations refer to those valuations in setting rates. When governments adopt the compiler's 'suggestions' in ways that affect the conduct of (or costs to) the governed, perhaps due process considerations should overcome claims of private ownership.[24]

[20] For further examination of 'soft' ideas and their implications for copyright protection of informational works, see, eg, Dennis S. Karjala, *Copyright in Electronic Maps*, 35 JURIMETRICS J. 395, 408–11 (1995).

[21] See, eg, Michel Foucault, *Nietzsche, Genealogy, History*, in FOUCALT, LANGUAGE, COUNTER-MEMORY, PRACTICE: SELECTED ESSAYS AND INTERVIEWS 138–64 (Donald F. Bouchard ed.; Donald F. Bouchard & Sherry Simon trans., 1977); SANDY PETREY, REALISM AND REVOLUTION: BALZAC, STENDHAL, ZOLA AND THE PERFORMANCES OF HISTORY (1988); Jane C. Ginsburg, *Sabotaging and Reconstructing History. A Comment of the Scope of Copyright Protection in Works of History After Hoehling v. Universal City Studios*, 29 J. COPYRIGHT SOC'Y USA 647 (1982).

[22] See, eg, *Oxford Book Co. v. College Entrance Book Co.*, 98 F.2d 688 (2d Cir. 1938); *Nester's Map & Guide Corp v. Hagstrom Map Co.*, 796 F. Supp. 729, 733 (E.D.N.Y. 1992); *Houts v Universal City Studios, Inc.*, 603 F. Supp. 26 (C.D. Cal. 1984); *Mosley v. Follett*, 209 U.S.P.Q. 1109 (S.D.N.Y. 1980); *Huie v. Nat'l Broad. Co.*, 184 F. Supp. 198 (S.D.N.Y. 1960).

[23] *CCC Info. Servs.*, n. 12 above, 44 F.3d at 73. See also *Castle Rock Entertainment v. Carol Publ'g Group, Inc.*, 955 F. Supp. 260 (S.D.N.Y. 1997), aff'd,150 F.3d 132 (2d Cir. 1998) (rejecting defense that trivia quiz book about 'Seinfeld' TV series merely reproduced 'facts' about the shows; events and characters held not 'facts', but creations of the show's writers).

[24] See, eg, *Building Officials & Code Adm'rs Int'l, Inc. v. Code Tech , Inc ,* 628 F.2d 730 (1st Cir. 1980) (querying whether policy that precludes copyright for state statutes should also apply to regulations, even when these are based on a privately developed, and copyrighted, model building code). Cf *Del Madera Props. v Rhodes & Gardner, Inc.*, 637 F. Supp. 262 (N.D. Cal. 1985) (distinguishing government-approved document—a privately generated subdivision map—from self-executing norms, such as building codes), aff'd, 820 F.2d 273 (9th Cir. 1987).

Of course, there are competing due process considerations. As Judge Leval stressed, to hold that a state's incorporation by reference or adoption of subjective valuations 'results in loss of copyright . . . would raise very substantial problems under the Takings Clause of the Constitution'.[25] Had the valuations been commissioned by the state or local government, the public document claim would seem stronger. But an incorporation by reference rule such as that urged by the car valuation defendant would mean that the government put the private compiler to its own expense, then 'rewarded' it by adopting its proposals—thereby confiscating the compiler's copyright.[26]

Assuming that a 'soft' fact compilation is copyrightable, what is the scope of its protection? The compilation would be original not only with respect to its governing principle of selection, but also with respect to much of its information. For example, every restaurant listing in my compendium of 'the worst . . .' is 'infused with opinion' or it would not be in my compilation. Does this mean that I may prevent not only wholesale copying from my compilation, but also more discrete appropriations? This was not an issue in the car valuation case, since the defendant there copied the work in its entirety. But the court's analysis suggests that infusions of opinion can make a thin copyright fat again.[27]

As a practical matter, probably not. For example, if a third party is recycling my restaurant listings into a bland, opinionless collection of New York City eateries, then she has not taken the quality that made my listings protectible: their subjectivity. She has engaged in the *Feist*-approved activity of stripping the original contribution from the compilation in order to reshuffle the information. She may have saved herself some time and effort by consulting my listings, but *Feist* reminds us that taking advantage of another's time-saving labors is 'neither unfair nor unfortunate' as a matter of copyright law.[28] If 'soft' facts yield a 'fatter' copyright, then it would only be with respect to partial copying that includes the subjectivity of the original listings.

The kind of compilation that involves subjectivity in each item included and that is most likely to be subject to copying would be one whose listings correspond to evaluations. For example, the AMA Guide to Impairment lists values corresponding to varieties of physical injuries.[29] If a third party copies all the Guide's valuations, then even 'thin' copyright principles will justify a

---

[25] *CCC Info. Servs.*, n. 12 above, 44 F.3d at 74; *Accord Practice Management Info. Corp. v. American Med. Ass'n*, 121 F.3d 516, 520 (9th Cir. 1997) (AMA 'guide to impairment' codes used to evaluate the cost of injuries for Medicaid reimbursement).

[26] Cf H.R. REP. No. 94–1476, at 60 (1976) (House Report accompanying 17 U.S.C. § 105) ('works of the United States government' are not protected by US copyright, but 'the committee here observes . . . publication or use by the government of a private work would not affect its copyright protection in any way').

[27] See also Karjala, n. 20 above, raising similar questions.

[28] *Feist Publications*, n. 1 above, 499 U.S. at 350.

[29] See *Practice Management*, n. 25 above, 121 F.3d at 516.

finding of infringement. If, however, the third party copies only some of the values corresponding to gastro-intestinal damage, then arguably, an infringement could be found only on the basis that each individual evaluation enjoyed protection.[30] The question is whether this kind of copying is likely to occur to a meaningful extent.[31] I do not have an answer to that question, but I suspect that it could become more likely in a digital environment. If so, then copyright may still afford meaningful protection to subjective compilations, although it will be of little help to collections of information gathered or organized according to familiar objective criteria. On the other hand, as the next part suggests, new legal protection for technological controls may change the digital environment from one susceptible to widespread copying to one that resists unauthorized reproductions.

II. Protection Against Circumvention of Access and Anticopying Controls

In October 1998, Congress passed the Digital Millennium Copyright Act (DMCA),[32] adding, among other things, a new Chapter 12 to title 17 of the U.S. Code. New § 1201 of the Copyright Act defines three violations: (a)(1) to circumvent technological protection measures that control 'access' to copyrighted works (effective October 28, 2000); (a)(2) to manufacture, disseminate or offer devices or services that circumvent access controls; and (b) to manufacture, disseminate, or offer devices or services that circumvent a technological measure that 'effectively protects a right of the copyright owner'.[33] While these provisions address protection of copyrighted works, the question arises whether a database producer who password-protects, encrypts or otherwise technologically protects the contents of a minimally original compilation could rely on § 1201 to insulate those contents from copying, even if the material sought to be reproduced is not copyrightable. Answering that question requires close analysis of the new provisions.

---

[30] Cf *Key Publications, Inc. v Chinatown Today Publ'g Enters., Inc.*, 945 F.2d 509, 516–117 (2d Cir. 1991) (directory of Chinese businesses held sufficiently original as a whole, but not infringed, because defendant substantially copied neither the selection, nor the arrangement of businesses).

[31] Another question is whether the evaluations, whatever their subjectivity, should be protected when, because of the publisher's market power, the evaluations become the standard for the industry, cf *Practice Management*, n. 25 above, 121 F.3d at 516 (impairment codes copyrightable, but AMA held to have misused its copyright); but cf *CCC Info. Servs.*, n. 12 above, 44 F.3d. 61 (evaluations that become a standard because of government adoption remain protectable).

[32] Pub. L. No. 105–304, 112 Stat 2860 (1998) (adding §§ 512 and 1201–1203 to the Copyright Act of 1976).

[33] 17 U.S.C. § 1201 (2000).

A. Section 1201(a): Protection of technological measures controlling access to copyrighted works

Subsection 1201(a) sets out a right to prevent circumvention of technology used to control access to a copyrighted work. The right is articulated separately and treated differently from the circumvention of technology used to protect a 'right of the copyright owner' under Title 17 (for instance, to authorize or prohibit reproduction, creation of derivative works, distribution, public performance/display; subsection (b) covers these rights, see below).[34] The DMCA thus distinguishes between access to the work, and acts done in relation to the work once it is accessed. 'Access' under the DMCA, however, does not mean mere acquisition of a copy of a work. Indeed, the text indicates that 'access' is distinct from a 'right of the copyright owner under this title'.[35] The difference becomes apparent if one compares the consequences of protecting a measure controlling 'access to *a work*' with a measure controlling 'access to *a copy of* a work'. The latter corresponds to 'access' in the traditional copyright sense of the right to distribute copies of the work; the former is the new right introduced in the DMCA.

The following example illustrates the difference between 'access to a work' and 'access to a copy of a work'. Suppose I purchase a CD-ROM containing a copyrighted database, such as a 'Worst Restaurants' compilation. Suppose also that to view the listings, I must register with the producer, using the modem in my particular computer. The producer in turn communicates a password to me. A technological measure included in the CD-ROM recognizes my password and my computer. Thenceforth, each time I wish to look up a restaurant, I must enter my password, and consult the listings on the same computer.

In this scenario, by purchasing the CD-ROM, I have acquired lawful access to a *copy* of the work. Section 101 of the Copyright Act defines 'copies' as 'material objects' in which 'a work' is fixed. The CD-ROM I purchased is a material object. But I do not access 'the work' until I have entered the password from the correct computer. Thus, when the law bars circumvention of controls on access to the 'work', 'access' becomes a repeated operation, whose controls will be substantially insulated from circumvention under the text of section 1201(a). I would therefore not be permitted to circumvent the access controls, even to perform acts that are lawful under the Copyright Act, such as privately viewing the listings on another computer, or lending my CD-

---

[34] 17 U.S.C. § 1201(a)(1) prohibits direct acts of circumvention, but did not go into effect until October 28, 2000. 17 U.S.C. §1201(b) prohibits the manufacture or distribution or offering of devices or services primarily designed to circumvent access controls. 17 U.S.C. §1201(b) took effect upon enactment, October 28, 1998.

[35] Compare 17 U.S.C. § 1201(a) with § 1201(b). See also 17 U.S.C. § 1201(f), (g) (permitting circumvention for purposes of reverse engineering and encryption research if, inter alia, the user 'lawfully obtained the right to use a copy').

ROM to a friend or colleague—acts permitted to the owner of the copy under the 'first sale doctrine' codified in section 109(a) of the Copyright Act, and under section 117, which allows the owner of a copy of a computer program to use it in any computer.

This analysis indicates that, in granting copyright owners a right to prevent circumvention of technological controls on 'access', Congress may in effect have extended copyright to cover 'use' of works of authorship, including minimally original databases. In theory, copyright does not reach 'use'; it prohibits unauthorized reproduction, adaptation, distribution, and public performance or display (communication to the public) when these acts exceed the bounds of fair use. Not all 'uses' correspond to these acts. But because 'access' is a prerequisite to 'use', by controlling the former, the copyright owner may well end up preventing or conditioning the latter.

Note, moreover, that § 1201(a) governs 'a work protected under this title'; it does not specify how *much* of the work must be 'protected under this title', nor does it distinguish 'thin copyright' works from more creative endeavors. As a result, to benefit from § 1201(a), it appears that, so long as a database producer does not merely encrypt raw public domain documents or unoriginal listings of information, but instead packages the information with copyrightable trappings, such as a new introduction, or minimally original reformatting,[36] the database would be a copyrighted work, however scant the copyrightable overlay. This suggests that the copyrightable figleaf a database producer affixes to an otherwise unprotectable work could, as a practical matter, obscure the public domain nakedness of the compiled information.

Section 1201 does include a variety of exceptions to the prohibition on access-circumvention, but these are extremely specific, and none directly apply to databases.[37] Worse, the extraordinarily narrow drafting of the exceptions defeats attempts to discern from them an overall legislative policy regarding the kinds of access control circumventions that should offset copyright owners' enhanced ability to control the use of their works. Indeed, if anything, the proliferation of special case exceptions prompts the negative inference that any access circumvention not expressly exempted is prohibited.

Arguably, § 1201(c) accords courts residual authority to expand exceptions to access control. That provision specifies that nothing in § 1201 affects 'defenses to copyright infringement, including fair use, under this title'.[38] But a violation of § 1201(a) is not copyright infringement, it is a new violation for which the DMCA provides distinct remedies.[39] Nonetheless, circumvention

---

[36] See, eg, *Maljack Prods., Inc v. UAV Corp.*, 964 F. Supp. 1416 (C.D. Cal. 1997), *aff'd on other grounds sub nom*; *Batjack Prods. v. GoodTimes Home Video Corp.*, 160 F.3d 1223 (9th Cir. 1998) (panning and scanning).

[37] See 17 U.S.C. § 1201(d)–(j) (2000).   [38] 17 U.S.C. § 1201(c) (2000).

[39] See 17 U.S.C. § 1203 (2000). Remedies for copyright infringement are set forth at §§ 502–510.

claims remain copyright-dependent, since § 1201 covers only measures that protect access to copyrighted works. Perhaps, a court could be persuaded that the challenged act of circumvention (or use of an access-circumvention device) would not under the circumstances lead to copyright infringement, because—as in the case of a 'copyrightable figleaf' covering a collection of public domain information—whatever access to a copyrighted work the act or device permits is incidental and necessary to access unprotected data. 'Accessing' the copyrighted work will generally involve making a digital copy in temporary memory, but, under these circumstances, the copying would probably be considered fair use.[40] Perhaps, under appropriate circumstances, the act of accessing should be deemed fair use as well.

Lest this analysis forebode the end of research, it is important to point out the potential availability of another safety valve, one not requiring the judicial activism of interpolating a fair use exception into the access circumvention provisions. Section 1201(a)(1)(B) may temper the risk of overprotection of unoriginal databases. That provision states that the prohibition on circumvention of access controls shall not apply to persons who are users of a copyrighted work which is in a particular class of works, if such persons are, or are likely to be in the succeeding three-year period, adversely affected by virtue of such prohibition in their ability to make non-infringing uses of that particular class of works under this title. Section 1201(a)(1)(C)(D) directs the Librarian of Congress to publish, at three-year intervals, classes of works whose non-infringing use would be adversely affected; as to those classes, the access-circumvention prohibition would not apply during the ensuing three years. 'Figleaf' databases may be a good candidate for inclusion in the 'particular class'.[41]

That said, however, one must recognize that not all databases that § 1201(a) might otherwise overprotect are plainly of the 'figleaf' variety. It will not always be easy to distinguish the pretextual copyrightable figleaf from a substantial authorship contribution. For example, what if the copyrightable work is one that blends subjective elements with public domain elements? Recall the 'Worst Restaurants' compilation: the database as a whole is protectable because of its subjective selection. Subsets of listings may also be protectable, at least to the extent that the copier incorporates the collection's subjective aspects. It is harder to claim in this instance that the producer's resort to access controls abusively insulates information from free access,

---

[40] Cf *Sega Enters. v. Accolade, Inc.*, 977 F.2d 1510 (9th Cir. 1992) (intermediate copying of video game console's operating system held fair use when copying afforded only means to access unprotected 'ideas' of system in order to create a compatible applications program).

[41] The Copyright Office has issued a Rulemaking in connection with its determination of classes of works exempted from 17 U.S.C. § 1201(a)'s protection of access controls. See *Exemption to Prohibition on Circumvention of Copyright Protection Systems for Access Control Technologies*, 65 FR 64555,<http//www.loc.gov/copyright/1201/anticirc.html> (October 21, 2000). The report evokes the problem of minimally original databases, but concludes that no adverse impact has yet been shown. See 65 FR at 64566 & n.8.

thereby warranting the collection's inclusion in a 'class of works' whose circumvention the Librarian's rulemaking should exempt.[42]

The § 1201(a)(1)(C) and (D) rulemaking may fall short in another way. As the statute is written, the exemption of classes of works appears to apply only to direct acts of circumvention of access controls: distribution of circumvention devices remains prohibited, even if the devices' *use* in connection with access to listed classes of works would be lawful. Since many users may well require such a device in order to engage in permitted access circumvention, the rulemaking may also need to consider the means by which the relevant public will be able to obtain the benefits of the Librarian's listing of classes of works.

Access controls may not, however, pose the most serious threat to research and other noninfringing uses of databases. Access is a predicate to copying or further communication of a database's contents, but once access has been lawfully (albeit repeatedly) obtained, impediments to extracting (copying) information from within the database will come not from the access barrier that the user has already crossed, but from technological inhibitions on copying. These technological measures are governed by a different provision of the DMCA, to which we shall now turn.

B. Circumvention of technological protections of (traditional) rights under copyright

The DMCA also addresses technological protection of the post-access rights of reproduction, adaptation, distribution, public performance or display. Here, the law targets the producers and suppliers of circumvention devices and services rather than the actions of the end-user. This distinction, however, may not be significant in practice since many end-users may not be able to circumvent the protections themselves. As with section 1201(a), section 1201(b) does not ban all devices that are capable of being used for circumvention. Manufacture and distribution of post-access circumvention devices and services are prohibited only if they are 'primarily designed' or have 'only limited commercially significant purpose or use other than' to circumvent 'protection afforded by a technological measure that effectively protects a right of a copyright owner under this title in a work or a portion thereof' or if they are 'marked' as circumvention devices.[43]

---

[42] The Copyright Office might, however, require as part of copyright management information under § 1202(c)(8) that copyright owners distinguish copyrightable from public domain components; decrypting only the public domain components would not violate 17 U.S.C. § 1201(a). This marking requirement would be feasible only where the public domain elements are not the objects of copyrightable added value, such as editorial alterations or enhancements. Cf 17 U.S.C. § 403 (2000) (form of copyright notice for compilations including works of the US Government). See discussion below.

[43] See 17 U.S.C. § 1201(b)(1)(A)–(C) (2000).

The prohibition's specification that it addresses measures that effectively protect '*a right of a copyright owner under this title*'[44] appears to make this subsection less stringent than the subsection concerning access controls. The exclusive rights under copyright set forth in section 106 of the Copyright Act are expressly made 'subject to sections 107 through 121', sections that set forth a variety of exceptions to and limitations on copyright, including fair use.[45] If the circumvention device is designed for or can be put to commercially significant noninfringing use, then it is not a violation of § 1201(b) to sell the device or to offer the circumvention service.

With respect to circumvention services, these may be tailored to defeat only those technological measures that would otherwise prevent the copying of public domain information. Circumvention devices, however, (including devices employed by those who render otherwise legitimate circumvention services) probably cannot be made to distinguish between circumventions for fair use purposes or for purposes of extracting unprotected information on the one hand, and circumventions aimed simply at obtaining unauthorized copies on the other. But were the device exculpated simply because it is capable of being put to a noninfringing use,[46] then, as a practical matter, the noninfringing use tail would wag the copyright infringement dog.

Section 1201(b) thus seems to lead to an impasse: it is permissible to circumvent anticopying controls in order to make noninfringing use, but the software or device needed to engage in the circumvention cannot be disseminated because it can all too easily be put to infringing use. There may be two ways out. First, the software or device might be marketed only to those users, such as libraries and universities, who will employ them for noninfringing purposes. This approach, however, may put too much faith in the good conduct of those users.

Secondly, at least for those works that contain elements drawn from the public domain, such as copyright-expired text or images, it may be possible to mark the work in a way that would permit a circumvention device to recognize and override the protection only of the public domain portions. Copyright owners may not be eager to facilitate noninfringing use, but the DMCA offers a means to encourage, albeit not compel, this kind of marking. Other provisions of the DMCA prohibit the removal of or tampering with 'copyright management information' that the copyright owner elects to

---

[44] Ibid (emphasis supplied).

[45] See generally *Quality King Distribs., Inc. v. L'Anza Research Int'l, Inc.*, 523 U.S. 135 (1998) (holding exclusive rights in § 106 are inherently limited by 17 U.S.C. §§ 107–121).

[46] Cf *Sony Corp. of Am. v. Universal City Studios, Inc.*, 464 U.S. 417, 442 (1984) (the producer or distributor of a device used to copy protected works incurs no liability for contributory infringement if the device is 'widely used for legitimate, unobjectionable purposes. Indeed, it need merely be capable of substantial non infringing use'). It seems clear from 17 U.S.C. § 1201 that Congress intended to impose a standard stricter than the 'merely capable' test.

include with distributed copies of the work.[47] Section 1202(c) defines copyright management information, and provides a residual category of 'Such other information as the Register of Copyrights may prescribe by regulation'.[48] The Copyright Office might include within the definition of copyright management information a requirement that copyright owners distinguish copyrightable from public domain components. The 1976 Copyright Act has already implemented a similar concept: the provisions concerning copyright notice specifically provide that the evidentiary benefits of copyright notice will not apply to works 'consisting predominantly of one or more works of the United States Government' (under § 105, these works enjoy no copyright protection) unless the copyright notice 'includes a statement identifying, either affirmatively or negatively, those portions . . . embodying any work or works protected under this title'.[49] If the Copyright Office required the marking of works consisting not only of works of the US Government, but also of other public domain works or identifiable components, then circumvention software or devices that target only the public domain elements would not violate § 1201(b).

Admittedly, this marking requirement would be considerably more difficult to apply when the database includes works, such as a translation or new edition, that adds copyrightable value to the public domain elements, or otherwise interweaves unprotected facts with copyrighted expression. Nonetheless, it helps, at least in part, to avoid a law-buttressed technological lockup of unprotected information contained in copyrighted databases. Ultimately, however, indirect approaches like the one just discussed, cannot provide a full response to the potential problem of overprotection of databases. Moreover, bootstrapping database protection to technological protection measures does not afford a comprehensive intellectual property regime, even from the point of view of information providers, especially those who disseminate print, as well as digital compilations. It would be preferable to attack the issue directly, by devising a statute carefully tailored to ensure meaningful incentives to gather, organize, and disseminate information, without unduly encumbering research and derivative uses of the collected information.

III. A US Statute for Database Producers and Users

The United States is not the only country to confront the incompatibility of copyright with protection of unoriginal databases and to perceive a corresponding need to devise appropriate protection for databases. The European Union responded in 1996 by enacting a Directive that, on the one hand,

---

[47] See 17 U.S.C. § 1202 (2000).   [48] 17 U.S.C. § 1202(c)(8).   [49] 17 U.S.C. § 403.

harmonized copyright protection of databases to a *Feist*-like standard, and enacted sui generis protection on the other.[50] Member States were to have implemented the Directive's provisions by the end of 1998.[51] In the United States many database statutes have been proposed in the years since *Feist*, but none have passed, nor is it clear that passage is imminent.[52] In the absence of US legislation, I outline and in some respects criticize the European approach, but will draw on it, and on several of its national implementing laws, to propose several points that I believe a US database statute should address.

A. The EU Database Directive

The EU Database Directive comes in two parts.[53] The first addresses copyright protection of databases; the second establishes a sui generis regime to

---

[50] Directive, n. 8 above.

[51] Austria, Bundesgesetzblatt [BGBl] 1998/25 modifying the Urheberrechtsgesetz BGBl 1936/111 on the Copyright to Works of Literature and Arts as well as on Related Proprietary Rights; Belgium, Law of August 31, 1998 concerning the protection of databases; France, Code de la propriété intellectuelle, art. L 341-1–343-4; Denmark, Act No. 407 dated 26 June 1998 (amending the copyright statute); Finland, Law of 3 April 1998, came into force 15 April 1998 (FFS 1998, page 963); Germany, Information and Communication Services Act, art. 7, 1997 BGBl. I, 1870, 1877 *et seq.*; Italy, Law No. 22/4/1941, n. 633, Title II-bis; Netherlands, Act of 8 July 1999 implementing Directive 96/9/EC of European Parliament and Council of 11 March 1996 concerning the legal protection of databases (Staatsblad 1999–303); Spain, Law incorporating Directive 96/9/CE on the Legal Protection of Databases; Sweden, Law amending the Law (1960: 729) on copyright in respect of literary and artistic works, (SFS 1997: 790); United Kingdom, Copyright and Rights in Databases Regulations (SI 1997/3032). Directive 96/9/EC.

For commentary on these laws, see, eg, Alain Strowel, *La loi du 31 aout 1998 concernant la protection des bases de données*, JOURNAL DES TRIBUNAUX, No. 5924, pp. 297–304 (1999) (Belgian law); Philippe Gaudrat, *Loi de transposition de la directive 96/9 du 11 mars 1996 sur les bases de données: dispositions relatives au droit d'auteur, Chronique de législation et de jurisprudence françaises, Droit des nouvelles technologies*, 51 REVUE TRIMESTRIELLE DU DROIT COMMERCIAL (RTDCom) 598 (1998); Philippe Gaudrat, *Loi 98–536 du 1er juillet 1998 portant transposition de la directive 96/9/CE du Parlement Européen sur les bases de données: le champ de la protection par droit sui generis, Chronique de législation et de jurisprudence françaises, Droit des nouvelles technologies*, 52 RTDCom 86 (1999); Philippe Gaudrat, *Loi 98–536 du 1er juillet 1998 portant transposition de la directive 96/9/CE du Parlement Européen sur les bases de données: les caractères du droit sui generis, Chronique de législation et de jurisprudence françaises, Droit des nouvelles technologies*, 52 RTDCom 398; J. Lorimy, *Loi du 1er juillet 1998 portant transposition en droit interne de la directive 'base de données' du 11 mars 1996*, DROIT INFORMATIQUE ET DES TÉLÉCOMS 1999/2, p. 100 (France); Michael Lehmann, *The European Database Directive and its Implementation into German Law*, 29 INT'L REV. INDUS. PROP. & COPYRIGHT L. [IIC] 776 (1998); L. Gimeno, *Protection of Compilations in Spain and the UK*, 29 IIC 907 (1998); Simon Chalton, *The Effect of the E.C. Database Directive on the United Kingdom Copyright Law in Relation to Databases: A Comparison of Features*, 6 E.I.P.R. 278 (1997); S. Chalton, *The Copyright and Rights in Databases Regulations 1997: Some Outstanding Issues on Implementation of the Database Directive*, 5 E.I.P.R. 178 (1998); S. Lai, *Database Protection in the United Kingdom: The New Deal and Its Effects on Software Protection*, 1 E.I.P.R. 32 (1998).

[52] See n. 7 above.

[53] This chapter does not purport to offer an exhaustive or systematic critique of the Directive. For in depth and critical examinations of this text, see, eg, Mark Schneider, *The European Union*

protect the 'substantial investment' in the compiling, verification or presentation of information against 'extraction' or 'reutilization' of a 'substantial part' of the database contents.[54] The Recitals and several of the implementing laws specify that the 'substantial investment' may be of financial, material, or human resources.[55] The incorporation of data into another database that is made available to the public constitutes 'reutilization'.[56] Extraction occurs when all or a substantial part of the contents are transferred, for example to paper or a disk.[57] Indeed, extraction also occurs if the user simply downloads a 'substantial part' of the contents to RAM to view on screen, since 'extraction . . . shall mean the permanent or *temporary* transfer'.[58] This does not mean that ordinary consultation of a database necessarily triggers a violation of the extraction right. Ordinary consultation does not involve downloading substantial parts of the contents, since usually only a relatively few items are consulted at a time.

The EU text also contains limited user rights to extract or reuse insubstantial parts of a database's contents for any purpose.[59] The Directive further specifies that contracts purporting to override these rights are invalid.[60] The Directive does not include a general fair use-type exception, but it permits Member States to make further exceptions for private copying of non-electronic databases, and for 'extraction [from any database] for the purpose of illustration for teaching or scientific research, as long as the source is indicated and to the extent justified by the non-commercial purpose to be achieved'.[61] This exception does not, however, entitle the extractor to 'reutilize' the copied material.[62] This means, for example, that a professor may download and display substantial excerpts from a database in the course of classroom instruction, but may not incorporate them into a new and different database that will be disseminated to the public, even if the source is indicated

Database Directive, 13 BERKELEY TECH. L.J. 551 (1998); J.H. Reichman & Pamela Samuelson, *Intellectual Property Rights in Data?*, 50 VAND. L. REV. 51, 76–95 (1997); G.M. Hunsucker, *The European Database Directive: Regional Stepping Stone to an International Model?*, 7 FORDHAM INTELL. PROP. MEDIA & ENT. L.J. 697 (1997); Lionel M. Lavenue, *Database Rights and Technical Data Rights: The Expansion of Intellectual Property for the Protection of Databases*, 38 SANTA CLARA L. REV. 1 (1997); W.R. Cornish, *1996 European Community Directive on Database Protection*, 21 COLUM.–VLA J. L. & ARTS 1 (1996).

[54] Directive, n. 8 above, at art. 7.2.

[55] See Recital 40; Belgium, Law of August 31, 1998 concerning the protection of databases, art. 3.1; France, Code de la propriété intellectuelle, art. L 341–1; Spain, Law incorporating Directive 96/9/CE on the Legal Protection of Databases, art. 133.1.

[56] See Directive, n. 8 above, at art. 7.1.   [57] Ibid at art. 7.2(a).

[58] Ibid (emphasis supplied); Recital 44.

[59] Directive, n. 9 above, at arts. 8, 15, 7.5. However, these texts also prohibit 'repeated and systematic' extraction or reutilization of insubstantial parts of a database's contents that conflicts with a normal exploitation of the database. Ibid at art. 7.5.

[60] Ibid at art. 15.   [61] Ibid at art. 9(b).

[62] This point is stressed by Prof. Reichman and Paul Uhlir. J.H. Reichman & Paul Uhlir, *Database Protection at the Crossroads: Recent Developments and Their Impact on Science and Technology*, 14 BERKELEY TECH. L.J. 793, 803 (1999).

and the dissemination is for nonprofit educational purposes. This could be problematic for nonprofit researchers, particularly scientists, who excerpt from databases, incorporating the copied material into new and different information compilations.

The term of protection in the EU is 15 years from creation, but 'any substantial change . . . which would result in the database being considered to be a substantial new investment' entitles the changed database to another 15 years.[63] The sui generis protection is independent of (but can be cumulated with) copyright protection.[64] It is also limited to databases produced by EU nationals or corporate domiciliaries,[65] or to those made in countries offering 'comparable protection'.[66]

How would the Directive apply to my 'Worst Restaurants' database (assuming it qualified for protection in the EU)? Because the sui generis right is independent of copyright, the availability of copyright protection for the subjective features of my database does not affect its entitlement to sui generis protection. Whether my database is so protected depends on whether I have made a 'substantial investment' in gathering, verifying, or presenting the information. For a database of this kind, it would seem that my investment qualifies in many ways. The gathering of the information required human resources (going to the restaurants and determining which had the worst service), financial resources (paying for meals and poor service), and technical resources as well.

Indeed, at first blush, it would seem that almost *any* database containing large amounts of data should easily meet the 'substantial investment' criterion. But some kinds of 'obtaining' of the information may not qualify as 'substantial investment'. For example, telephone companies do not go out and collect subscriber information; subscribers furnish it to the service. Similarly, databases comprising government-generated information, such as census data, may entail a 'substantial investment' by the government employees who gather and systematize the data, but not by the private sector database producer who simply incorporates it.[67] The database producer may still qualify for protection, but only on the basis of the value added through verification or presentation of the contents.

If only this value added justifies protection, shouldn't the scope of protection be limited to the extraction or reutilization of the value added? While such a restriction considerably curtails the reach of the new property right, it is consistent with the rationale for sui generis protection. The justification,

---

[63] Directive, n. 8 above, at art. 10.   [64] Ibid at art. 1.4.
[65] Ibid at art. 11.   [66] Ibid, Recital 56.
[67] The Directive does not address whether or not databases produced by governmental entities are excluded from coverage. The Berne Convention leaves it to Member States to determine whether protection may be granted to government texts, see Art. 2.4; cf 17 U.S.C. § 105 (2000) (no copyright in works of US Government).

after all, for the special legislation is the need to supply an incentive to undertake the investment of compiling information products.[68] If the investment in acquiring the information is not in fact substantial, why should the information (apart from the value added) be protected? Before it can claim protection for the information, the database producer should be required to demonstrate the substantiality of its investment in obtaining the data.[69] Because more and more information is becoming readily accessible at the click of a mouse, it should become increasingly important to ascertain whether the compiled information truly required a substantial investment to collect.[70]

Moreover, the database producer should also be required to show that the 'extracted' or 'reutilized' portion captures the substantial investment. But neither the Directive, nor most of the Member State implementing laws, appear to distinguish between copying from a protected database, and copying material whose inclusion in that database required a substantial investment. The Spanish law appears to come closest to the latter standard; it entitles the database producer to prohibit 'the extraction and/or reutilization of the whole or of a substantial part of its contents, evaluated qualitatively or quantitatively, so long as the obtaining, the verification or the presentation of that content represents a substantial investment from a qualitative or quantitative point of view'.[71]

Similarly, while the Directive and implementing laws authorize successive 15-year terms of protection for new substantial investments in databases, they do not specify how the user may distinguish between newer and older investments.[72] Suppose I updated my 'Worst Restaurants' compilation at annual intervals, so that after 15 years the contents of my database have substantially changed. (One may imagine that if the restaurants are as poor as I contend, at least some of them may have gone out of business.) Suppose further that each annual update, taken separately, might not suffice to constitute a new substantial investment; may I nonetheless cumulate the 15 years to claim a new substantial investment in toto? Even if I may so receive the benefit of a

---

[68] See, eg, Directive, Recitals 7–10.

[69] Cf Cornish, n. 53 above, at 10 (regarding documentation of substantial incremental changes to a database).

[70] I am grateful to Joram Lietaert Peerbolte, Columbia Law School LLM 1997, J.D. 1999, for the arguments in this and the preceding paragraph. See *The European Database Directive* (February 1997) (unpublished paper) (on file with author). Mr Peerbolte would also reject claims of 'substantial investment' from database producers who invested in acquiring or generating the information for a purpose other than creating a database, then subsequently recycled the information into a database. For example, a television station may invest in planning the programming of each day's broadcasts: its primary purpose for the investment is to organize and fill the broadcast day; a secondary purpose is to publish a guide to the daily programs. I believe this contention is appealing, but it may be difficult in practice to distinguish primary from secondary purposes for information-gathering.

[71] Spanish Law, art. 133 (translation mine).

[72] See Recitals 54, 55 (burden of proof on database proprietor to show substantial new investment; verification may qualify).

new 15-year term, the new investments are not supposed to create additional protection for the old. Old listings, therefore, are free for substantial taking. But how are my users to know which material was generated by my new substantial investment? Here again, neither the Database Directive nor its implementing law offers guidance as to how to distinguish the freely copyable material generated by the old investment from the still-protected material produced with the new investment. If anything, the Directive's recognition that 'substantial verification of the contents of the database' may constitute a substantial new investment[73] suggests that, even when the content remains largely the same after 15 years, the effort expended to ensure that the same content was still accurate entitles the database to a new 15-year period of protection. As a result, protection may end up being perpetual.[74]

Thus, the Database Directive, like the DMCA, presents a significant risk of overprotection. While the Directive's provisions establishing inalienable user rights offer an important check on the market power of database producers, the scope of these rights, as well as of other exceptions, may not suffice to offset the risks of information privatization that the Directive poses. This brief analysis of some of the problems the Directive raises, however, helps sharpen our inquiry into what a US database statute should look like.

B. Proposal for a modest US database law

1. Objectives

Let us start by envisaging the goal of a US statute protecting databases. The legislation should endeavor to supply the incentive, arguably stripped away by *Feist*, to expend the 'sweat' needed to create useful collections of information. In essence, the old 'sweat copyright' was a form of unfair competition protection against free-riders whose copying enabled them to compete against the original compiler without incurring the compiler's information-gathering costs. The clearest case for sweat copyright arose over copiers who resold essentially the same compilation, although some of the sweat copyright decisions extended protection against a variety of derivative compilations as well.[75] The rationale for these extensions had more to do with the perceived unfairness of 'reaping where one had not sown'[76] than with competition *per se*, since the derivative compilation exploited markets different from those filled by the initial compilation.

---

[73] Recital 55.   [74] See Lehmann, n. 51 above, at 790.
[75] See generally, Ginsburg, n. 3 above, at 1893–1907 (reviewing cases).
[76] The phrase comes from *Int'l News Serv. v. Associated Press*, 248 U.S. 215 (1918), a case that concerned both free-riding and direct competition (in news information), but was subsequently extended by state courts to a broader range of allegedly unfair acts of copying for commercial purposes. See Douglas G. Baird, *Common Law Intellectual Property and the Legacy of International News Service v. Associated Press*, 50 U. Chi. L. Rev. 411 (1983).

But the less creative the work at issue, the less justified is a broad scope of derivative works protection, since derivative work rights concern not only extension into potential markets, but the refashioning of the work of *authorship* into new versions and formats.[77] Where there is no authorship, the only considerations in determining whether to afford protection against noncompetitive (or indirectly competitive) free-riding are economic: how broad a scope of protection is needed to induce the production of useful collections of information? Will a broad scope of protection discourage the reworking of the information into new and different collections of information?

These twin questions counsel a limited scope of derivative works protection. In keeping with a purely unfair competition approach, it would not be appropriate to grant the information-gatherer rights with respect to all markets for which the information *could* be licensed. Rather, rights should be confined to distribution of the collected information in markets the compiler is currently exploiting, or in those markets that the compiler has current and demonstrable plans to exploit.[78]

There are additional reasons to constrain any unfair competition-based protection for databases. A broad scope of protection may not only forestall the production of desirable derivative databases; it may also unduly hamper *use* of the data by scientists, educators and researchers. Such a special database statute would risk running afoul of the policies and limitations set forth in the Constitution's patent-copyright clause.[79] The clause empowers Congress to 'promote the progress of science and useful arts' by securing the limited monopolies of patent and copyright. But legislation that frustrates that progress would seem at least in tension with constitutional objectives.[80] More significantly, a copyright-like, or super-copyright-like, scope of protection for databases would conflict with the constitutional restriction on Congress's power to enact intellectual property laws that the Supreme Court enunciated in *Feist*. By repeatedly proclaiming that originality is a constitutional requirement,[81] the Court has arguably stripped Congress of power

---

[77] See generally Ginsburg, n. 3 above, at 1885–93 (discussing rationales for derivative works protection); Ralph S. Brown, *The Widening Gyre: Are Derivative Works Getting Out of Hand?*, 3 CARDOZO ARTS. & ENT. L.J. 1865 (1984); Paul Goldstein, *Derivative Rights and Derivative Works in Copyright*, 30 J. COPYRIGHT SOC'Y USA 209 (1983). For a more economics-oriented justification for derivative work rights, see, eg, William M. Landes & Richard A. Posner, *An Economic Analysis of Copyright Law*, 18 J. LEGAL STUD. 325, 353–57 (1989).

[78] This standard is taken from *National Basketball Ass'n. v. Morotola, Inc.*, 105 F.3d 841 (2d Cir. 1997).

[79] U.S. CONST. art. I, §8, cl. 8. Impediments to the creation of derivative databases may also raise First Amendment concerns.

[80] Cf *Rosemont Enters., Inc. v. Random House, Inc.*, 366 F.2d 303, 306–07 (2d Cir. 1966) (justifying copyright fair use doctrine as, inter alia, a constitutionally-inspired corrective, lest enforcement of copyright in particular circumstances frustrate the goal of promoting the progress of knowledge).

[81] See Goldstein, n. 77 above (*Feist* pronounces a constitutional originality requirement 'no fewer than thirteen times').

under either the patent-copyright clause, or under the commerce clause, to enact a copyright-like statute for non-original databases.[82]

2. Outline of a federal database statute

a. Protected subject matter   First, the statute should define a database in a manner that avoids overlap with works of authorship (other than compilations). A database statute is intended to protect unoriginal collections of information; it would be undesirable were the statute to end up providing a kind of super-copyright by protecting against copying regardless of the nature of the work. A database is a collection of discrete items of information (including documents), but not every 'collection' is a database. Otherwise, a novel could be recharacterized as a collection of words, a musical composition a collection of notes, or a computer program a collection of instructions.

On the other hand, overlap with copyrightable subject matter is appropriate to the extent that the database is also a copyrightable compilation. Since the statute would protect the investment in information-gathering, it would be undesirable to deny database protection to those collections of information that required not just money, but imagination, to compile. A database statute should restore incentives to produce exhaustive compilations that may lack originality; it should not provide a perverse incentive to forego originality on the theory that unoriginal compilations will now enjoy broader protection than copyright affords.[83]

The 'substantial investment' that qualifies for protection should be of money or labor expended in gathering the information. It may be problematic to extend protection as well to substantial investments in organizing and/or maintaining the information. First, if the organization meets copyright standards of originality, the database will already enjoy copyright protection. If the organization does not, then the organizational principle is likely to be so banal or rote that it could be accomplished by a computer program (that may itself be protected by copyright). Paying for the computer program to organize the information seems outside the investment that the statute should seek to foster. With respect to maintenance, there may be sufficient incentives outside the statute to expend resources to maintain the accuracy of an already-created database. That is, the statute may be necessary to spur creation of the database in the first place, but once the database exists, the producer's interest in retaining a market for it will provide incentives for its

---

[82] I developed this argument more fully in Jane C. Ginsburg, *No 'Sweat'? Copyright and Other Protections of Works of Information After Feist v. Rural Telephone*, 92 COLUM. L. REV. 338, 369–84 (1992). For more recent treatment of this question, see, e.g., William Patry, *The Enumerated Powers Doctrine and Intellectual Property: An Imminent Constitutional Collision*, 67 GEO. WASH. L. REV. 359 (1999).

[83] If the database qualifies both for copyright and for special statutory protection, and if the copyright and database statutes offer different remedies, query whether the producer should be able to cumulate remedies, or must elect.

upkeep. On the other hand, where a producer takes an obsolescent, preexisting public domain database and invests in its substantial updating, that expenditure of resources may be a kind we wish to encourage.

Regardless of the investment made, some databases should not be protected at all, or should enjoy more limited protection. Databases produced by government entities should remain in the public domain.[84] Databases produced with government grants might, at the grantor's option, be placed in the public domain, subjected to mandatory licensing, or left to the general statutory regime. The problem of privately produced databases that are the sole source for the collected information will be discussed in connection with the scope of protection.

b. Scope of protection: prohibited acts As discussed earlier, the statute should not prohibit copying per se, but copying that captures the substantial investment made by the database producer and that redisseminates the copied material to the public in substantially the same form as it was taken from the copied database. The wrongful act, after all, is not simply copying, but usurpation, through nontransformative copying, of the database producer's market for the work. That usurpation occurs when the copyist, who did not incur the first producer's information-gathering costs, sells substantial parts of the database at a price below the first producer's. By contrast, 'use' of the database, including by copying, should not itself violate the statute so long as the copying does not turn into promiscuous 'sharing' of substantial parts of the substantial investment made in the database.

c. Scope of protection: permitted acts A broad scope of derivative works protection would not be appropriate. We should seek to encourage the creation of new and different databases, even if they gather much of their information from prior sources. If, however, the statute defines the cognizable harm as the copying and redissemination of substantial parts of a database in which there was substantial investment, substituting the copy for its source, then perhaps no additional exception for 'transformative' copying is needed.

Indeed, if the threshold for protection is high enough, no special exemptions for 'permitted acts' should be required. Nonetheless, we may wish to single out some kinds of exploitations for indulgence. The European Directive lists among 'permitted acts' extraction (but not reutilization) for non-commercial teaching and scientific research.[85] A similar exception would be appropriate for a US law, although the bar on redissemination should distinguish between, for example, making the database available without authorization to all students enrolled in a course (prohibited), and including

---

[84] State universities, however, should not, for purposes of the database statute, be considered government entities; otherwise, as producers of databases, they would be at a disadvantage compared with private universities.

[85] Directive, n. 8 above, at art. 9(b).

substantial parts of a database to support the conclusions of a study that interprets information from the database, and that is made available to the public (permitted).

d. Mandatory licensing   When a database is or becomes the only source for the collected information, it may be appropriate to require the producer to license the contents at fair and reasonable rates. The European Commission had, in an earlier version of the Directive, included such a provision, but, in the final version, simply left the question to general norms of European competition law.[86] 'Sole source' databases include those whose compilers have generated the information, and those whose compilers have acquired the information from sources, which subsequently become unavailable.

e. Duration   What is a duration sufficient to recoup the substantial investment made in producing the database and generate a reasonable profit thereafter? The commercial life of some databases, such as stock quotations, may be very short, while the life expectancy of others, such as directories of college alumni/ae, may be considerably longer. Since it is rather difficult to assign a term of years, perhaps the European Union's 15-year period is as good as any. At least, a US 15-year standard would be 'comparable' with the EU's. The duration difficulty lies perhaps more in the term's extendability than in its initial determination. If protection lasts 15 years, but can be indefinitely renewed through subsequent investments made in maintaining the database, then the term is, potentially, forever. At most, only the new additions to the database should lay claim to an additional 15 years; the old information, even if verified, should no longer enjoy protection.

f. Formalities   This brings us to the problem of formalities. It is very well and good to say that 'old information', or information from government sources, or information otherwise unstamped by the producer's substantial investment, should remain free for copying and redissemination. But, how is a user to know what is what? I earlier suggested that the database producer be required to mark public domain components of a database so that users could extract them without violating legal protection of technological anticopying measures.[87] Similar requirements might apply to dating the components of the database, and to identifying components drawn from government sources, as well as other unprotected materials.[88]

In addition to notice, a deposit requirement may also be appropriate. The requirement not only would make it possible for users to acquire information

---

[86] Compare Directive, n. 8 above, at art. 13, Recital 47, with Amended Proposal for a Council Directive on the Legal Protection of Databases, COM (93)464 final.

[87] See text accompanying nn. 47–49 above.

[88] H.R. 354 requires a notice identifying the source of government information included in a protected database, see § 1408(b). In addition, without imposing an explicit requirement of notice regarding the dating of a database's components, the bill places the burden on the producer to show that copied material is no more than 15 years old, see §. 1409(d).

from expired databases (which might otherwise have vanished), but also would have archival benefits.

g. Relationship to other laws   Finally, it is necessary to consider how much, if any, preemption of other laws is appropriate. US database bills have generally preserved 'the law of contract'. But this may be problematic in the context of mass-market licenses that contract into more stringent protection than that posited here. The Database Directive voids any agreement in which the user forgoes the right to extract and reutilize *in*substantial parts of a database (so long as these extractions do not cumulatively become substantial).[89] A similar curtailment of contractual prerogative may be appropriate for a US statute as well, at least when the contract was not the result of arm's-length bargaining. Indeed, a US statute might extend the realm of inalienable user rights to the components the statute excludes from coverage: expired databases, government information, and information whose collection did not require a substantial investment. This does not mean that database producers must give this information away for free, any more than the public domain principle in copyright law means that conventional publishers must give away copies of public domain works. It does mean, however, that producers may not prevent the subsequent copying and redissemination of collected information for whose initial distribution they have been paid.

IV. Conclusion

In the United States, after *Feist*, some statutory protection of nonoriginal databases may be desirable; not only to foster these collections' production, but to temper producer resort to other means of protection, both contractual and technological. The European Union's 1996 Database Directive affords a partial model for the United States, but it also leaves open too many questions regarding the subject matter and scope of protection. The proposal outlined here attempts to follow some of the Directive's provisions, together with more stringent specification of 'substantial investment' and cognizable harm. Finally, the proposed formalities should make the user rights set forth in the Directive and further detailed here possible to implement in fact by clearly identifying the database components for which no protection is available.

---

[89] Directive, n. 8 above, at arts. 7.5, 8.1, 15.

PART II

THE GROWTH OF PRIVATE ORDERING REGIMES

It is easy to assume that public law is the sole vehicle for establishing the scope of the rights possessed by those with 'intellectual products.' After all, we know that copyright and patent law represent a legislative effort to balance a broad set of conflicting policies (perhaps not always in the best way, as many of the authors in this book would argue). Antitrust law, as well, brings its own set of public policies to the balance, placing limits on the scope of intellectual property rights so as to reflect the legislative concern with preserving a competitive process. Whatever the ultimate balance struck by legislatures (and the courts) in these areas, however, we take that balance to be the result of serious public decisionmaking.

The chapters in Part II remind us that the scope and effect of intellectual property rights is significantly affected by the conduct of private decisionmaking. Public policy might encourage widespread dissemination of copyrighted works, but privately controlled technology can readily thwart that policy. Public policy might seek to control the licensing practices of intellectual property rightsholders to encourage competition, but private 'rights controlling' associations may bring their own policies to bear when ordering the relations among rightsholders.

Carl Shapiro's chapter, the first in this Part, explores the rich world of standard-setting organizations, an area of private ordering that has become increasingly significant for network industries. In addition to describing some of the most important of these standard-setting organizations, Shapiro also reviews the economic costs and benefits of such efforts, fitting the policy concerns that they raise into the legal framework of antitrust and intellectual property law. Kenneth Dam's chapter explores the issues raised by technological self-help, including efforts at encryption and technologies that allow only limited use of copyrighted works. Robert Merges describes the workings of a number of important patent pools, arguing that these 'private collective organizations' effectively create a system of 'private liability rules' which improve on the potentially overly-fragmented system of rights created by the patent laws. In the final chapter in this Part, Bennett Lincoff focuses on perhaps the oldest of private collective rights organizations, music performance rights societies. He describes the importance and value of this private effort and suggests the changes these organizations must make to cope with the emergence of Internet distribution of music.

4

SETTING COMPATIBILITY STANDARDS: COOPERATION OR COLLUSION?

CARL SHAPIRO*

We live in a world built on product standards. You can make sense of these words because we share a common language. I can fax you this chapter because our fax machines obey a common protocol. I can (probably) share computer files with you because our computers employ various standardized hardware and software formats. And I can e-mail you the file containing this chapter because of an intricate web of standardized Internet protocols. A great deal of the information economy is driven by standards.

The need for product standards is not new. In biblical times the lack of a standardized language wreaked havoc at the Tower of Babel. The US Constitution called for Congress to establish a system of standard weights and measures. During the US Civil War, the Navy managed to standardize the diameters for bolts, nuts, and screw threads, but only at Navy yards. More recently, during the great Baltimore fire of 1904, fire fighters called in from neighboring cities were unable to fight the blaze effectively because their

* Transamerica Professor of Business Strategy, Haas School of Business, and Professor of Economics, University of California at Berkeley. Portions of this chapter rely heavily on my joint paper with my colleague Michael L. Katz, *Antitrust in Software Markets*, in COMPETITION, CONVERGENCE AND THE MICROSOFT MONOPOLY (Kluwer 1999), which can be obtained at http://haas.berkeley.edu/~shapiro/software.pdf. This chapter also draws on Chapter 8 of my book with HAL R. VARIAN, INFORMATION RULES: A STRATEGIC GUIDE TO THE NETWORK ECONOMY, see www.inforules.com.

hoses would not fit the Baltimore hydrants. The following year, national standards for fire hoses were adopted.[1]

Standards are an inevitable outgrowth of *systems*, whereby *complementary products work in concert to meet users' needs*. Systems are all around us. Communications systems are a prominent example. For the language 'system' to work requires that individuals seeking to communicate learn the same language; my training in English is complementary with your training in English, but not with your training in Italian. Likewise, my fax machine or modem is complementary with your fax machine or modem if they utilize the same transmission and compression protocols. Happily enough, the International Telecommunications Union (ITU) has established universal standards for faxes and modems, including intergenerational compatibility. Prior to these standards, rival incompatible fax protocols failed to gain popularity. The telephone network and the Internet require a myriad of standards to function properly.

The need for standards creates an imperative for various firms to work together to develop, establish, endorse, and promote those standards. Sometimes these alliances are strictly among companies selling complementary components that work together to form a system, as when Intel and Microsoft team up to make sure that their chips and operating system function smoothly in concert. More often, however, companies that compete directly with one another agree on compatibility or interface standards to build sufficient support for a new technology, as when Sony and Philips jointly established and licensed the CD standard, and when modem manufacturers around the world agree on a new modem standard at the ITU. Such cooperation naturally raises the spectre of antitrust sanctions: where does legitimate cooperation end and collusion begin? That is the topic of this chapter.[2]

---

[1] See Achsah Nesmith, *A Long, Arduous March Towards Standardization*, SMITHSONIAN, 176 (March 1985), for an entertaining description of standard setting through the ages.

[2] For other discussions of the issues discussed herein, see David Balto, *Networks and Exclusivity: Antitrust Analysis to Promote Network Competition*, 7 GEORGE MASON LAW REVIEW 523–76 (1999); Nicholas Economides & Lawrence J. White, *Networks and Compatibility: Implications for Antitrust*, in 38 EUROPEAN ECON. REV. 651 (1994); Joseph Farrell & Michael Katz, *The Effects of Antitrust and Intellectual Property Law on Compatibility and Innovation*, ANTITRUST BULL. (1998); Joseph Farrell & Garth Saloner, *Standardization, Compatibility, and Innovation*, 16 RAND J. ECON. 70 (1985); Joseph, Farrell and Garth Saloner, *Installed Base and Compatibility: Innovation, Product Preannouncement, and Predation*, 76 AM. ECON. REV. 940 (1986); Federal Trade Commission, *Competition Policy in the New High-Tech Global Marketplace*, STAFF REPORT (1996); Richard Gilbert & Carl Shapiro, *Antitrust Issues in the Licensing of Intellectual Property: The Nine No-No's Meet the Nineties*, BROOKINGS PAPERS ON ECONOMICS: MICROECONOMICS (1998); Michael Katz & Carl Shapiro, *Network Externalities, Competition and Compatibility*, 75 AMER. ECON. REV. 424 (1985); Michael Katz & Carl Shapiro, *Technology Adoption in the Presence of Network Externalities*, 94 JOURNAL OF POLITICAL ECONOMY 822 (1986); Michael Katz & Carl Shapiro, *Product Compatibility Choice in a Market with Technological Progress*, 38 OXFORD ECON. PAPERS 146 (1986); Michael Katz & Carl Shapiro, *Product Introduction with Network Externalities*, 40 (1) J. INDUS. ECON. 55 (1992); Michael Katz

I. Standard Setting in Practice

A. Some examples of standards

Standards are not new, but they are growing in importance. Why? Because standards are especially important in the sector of the economy that is growing most rapidly, the sector encompassing information, communications, and entertainment, or ICE. Information systems require standards for the storage, retrieval, and manipulation of information, be it a corporate database, a spreadsheet, an inventory management system, or a library of images. Whether the message is voice, data, or a video signal, communications cannot take place without standards linking the parties sending and receiving the messages. And entertainment systems are built on standards, such as the CD standard for music or the new standard for digital television.

Before launching into the economics and the law surrounding standards, it is useful to simply list some examples of standards, both de facto and de jure standards. Most of the standards listed are successful ones, but not all. Others are still struggling for supremacy. Most of these examples illustrate the need for cooperation to establish successfully new standards. The examples also are suggestive regarding the impact of standards on competition.

In the area of consumer electronics: the old 33⅓ rpm standard for LP records; the Sony/Philips standard for CD players and disks; the VHS standard for video cassette players; the Sony mini-disk and digital audio tape (DAT) standards; the Philips digital compact cassette technology; the emerging standard for digital video disks (DVD); the NTSC and PAL standards for television transmission and reception; and the new HDTV standard for digital television.

In the computer hardware realm: the earlier 5¼ inch floppy disk drive standard; the newer 3½ inch floppy disk drive standard; yet newer high-capacity drives such as the Zip drive by Iomega; the VGA video display standard; various buses that transport data from one component to another; and the Intel x86 microprocessor architecture.

& Carl Shapiro, *Systems Competition and Network Effects,* 8 (2) J Econ. Perspectives 93 (1994); Joel I. Klein, *Cross-Licensing and Antitrust Law* www.usdoj.gov/atr/speeches (1997); Joel I. Klein, *The Importance of Antitrust Enforcement in the New Economy,* www.usdoj.gov/atr/speeches (1998); Mark Lemley & David McGowan, *Legal Implications of Network Economic Effects,* 86 Calif. L. Rev. 479 (1998); Samuel R. Miller, *Antitrust and Competitor Collaboration in the Computer Industry,* Fed. Trade Comm'n, Hearings on the Changing Nature of Competition in a Global and Innovation-Driven Age (Oct. 26, 1995); Jeffrey Rohlfs, *A Theory of Interdependent Demand for a Communications Service,* 5 (1) Bell J. Econ. 16 (1974); Carl Shapiro, *Antitrust in Network Industries,* www.usdoj.gov/atr/speeches (1996); U.S. Dept. of Justice & Fed. Trade Comm'n, *Antitrust Guidelines for the Licensing of Intellectual Property,* April 1995, http://www.usdoj.gov/atr/public/guidelines/ipguide.htm; U.S. Dept. Justice & Fed. Trade Comm'n, *Antitrust Guidelines for Collaborations Among Competitors,* April 2000, http://www.ftc.gov/os/2000/04/ftcdojguidelines.pdf.

In the computer software realm: the Microsoft Windows operating system; the MPEG standard for compressing video data; Adobe PostScript, a page description language; Adobe Acrobat, a standard for making documents 'portable'; and the *lack* of a single version of UNIX.

In the financial world: the standards required for consumers to be able to make purchases or obtain money at a large network of locations: the standards for ATM cards and networks; the standards for the acceptance and processing of credit cards; and the standards embodied in smart cards.

In the communications realm: a multitude of standards that permit the operation of an integrated worldwide telephone system; the fax and modem standards noted above; a welter of Internet protocols; the Ethernet standard for local data networks; the GSM standard for wireless telephone systems; and many, many more.

B. Formal standard-setting bodies

Most standard setting takes place through formal standard-setting processes established by various standards bodies. Never before have such cooperative, political processes been so important to market competition. There are hundreds of official standard-setting bodies throughout the world. Some, like the Underwriter's Laboratory, which sets safety standards, are household words. Others, like the International Telecommunications Union (ITU) seem far removed from everyday experience but exert significant, behind-the-scenes influence. Some are independent professional organizations, like the Institute of Electric and Electronic Engineers (IEEE); others are government bodies, like the National Institute of Standards and Technology (NIST).

And these are only the *official* standard-setting bodies. On top of these, we have any number of unofficial groups haggling over product specifications, as well as various Special Interest Groups (SIGs) that offer forums for the exchange of information about product specifications. For example, there are 36 SIGs operating under the auspices of the Association for Computing Machinery (ACM) alone, including SIGART (artificial intelligence), SIG-COMM (data communications), SIGGRAPH (computer graphics), and SIGIR (information retrieval).

Participants often complain about the formal standard-setting process: it is slow, it is too political, it doesn't pick the 'best' technology, and so on. But history proves that the consensus process of formal standard-setting is time and again critical to launching new technologies. The telecommunications industry, for example, has relied on the ITU to set international standards, starting with the telegraph in the 1860s, through radio in the 1920s, to a panoply of standards today, from the assignment of telephone numbers, to protection against interference, to data protocols for multimedia conferencing. Whether you consider formal standard-setting a necessary evil or a godsend, it is here to stay.

Formal standard setting is designed to be open to all participants and to foster consensus. This sounds good, but often results in a very slow process. The HDTV story is one example: it took roughly 10 years to set a technical standard for digital television in the United States, and HDTV is yet to be adopted in the United States on a commercial scale.

A fundamental principle underlying the consensus approach to standards is that they should be 'open', with no one or few firms controlling the standard. Thus, a quid pro quo for the inclusion of a participant's technology in a formal standard is a commitment by that participant to license any of its patents *essential* to implementing the standard on 'fair, reasonable, and nondiscriminatory' (FRND) terms. Note that this duty does *not* extend to *nonessential* patents, which can lead to an amusing dance in which companies claim that their patents merely cover valuable enhancements to the standard and are not actually essential to complying with the standard.

The openness promise of a formal standards body is a powerful tool for establishing credibility. However, be aware that most standards bodies have no enforcement authority. Aggrieved parties must resort to the courts, including the court of public opinion, if they feel the process has been abused. In the United States at least, the result has been a variety of private lawsuits involving patent misuse and/or antitrust claims.

The granddaddy of organizations setting standards for information infrastructure is the International Telecommunications Union (ITU).[3] The ITU grew out of the International Telegraph Convention of 1865, signed by 20 European countries to coordinate use of the telegraph. It became an agency within the United Nations in 1947. The key part of the ITU for telecommunications standards is the International Telephone and Telegraph Consultative Committee (CCITT).

The ITU is notoriously slow, in part because there are so many member countries, and in part because companies in each country must first work to reach a national consensus which is then communicated to the ITU. For example, for some ITU Recommendations, the Telecommunications Industry Association (TIA) communicates the interests of American companies to the State Department, which then formally represents the United States at the ITU. The ITU's strong tradition and insistence on an open consensual process also slows things down. Some observers have suggested that the ITU will have to speed up or cede power to regional standards organizations keen on swifter adoption of new technologies.

The fact remains, however, that the ITU plays a crucial role in setting standards that truly require a worldwide consensus, such as standards for fax

---

[3] See http://www.itu.ch.

machines, modems, the public switched telephone system, and the use of spectrum. The ITU also has clear rules requiring companies to license any patents essential to a standard. Oddly, however, the ITU steadfastly refuses to broker agreements among companies with rival or complementary patent portfolios. Those deals have to be cut in a sidebar, not formally under ITU auspices.

Within the United States, the American National Standards Institute (ANSI)[4] is the umbrella organization most widely responsible for promoting formal standard setting. ANSI's aim is to promote and facilitate voluntary consensus standards. ANSI does not itself promulgate standards, but rather helps establish consensus among qualified groups. ANSI's guiding principles are consensus, due process, and openness. Some 175 distinct entities are currently accredited by ANSI and some 11,500 American National Standards have been approved under ANSI oversight. ANSI has established an Information Infrastructure Standards Panel to facilitate development of standards critical to the Global Information Infrastructure. ANSI also has helped establish, with some government financing through the National Institute of Standards and Technology (NIST), the NSSN, a Web-based information resource on standards, including a database pointing to over 100,000 standards currently in use.[5]

ANSI is the US representative of the two major non-treaty international standards organizations, the International Organization for Standardization (ISO)[6] and the International Electrotechnical Commission (IEC).[7] The ISO is a worldwide federation of national standards bodies, one from each of about 100 countries, dating back to 1947. The ISO seeks voluntary, industry-wide, global consensus—no small feat! ISO standards cover everything from film speeds to standardized freight containers, to safety, to symbols for automobile dashboard controls. The ISO covers all areas except electrical and electronic engineering, which is the responsibility of IEC. The ISO and the IEC handle the field of information technology together through a joint technical committee, JTC1.

Finally, it is important to bear in mind that a great deal of standard setting takes place through less formal cooperative arrangements among firms. Indeed, a day hardly goes by without some announcement of an alliance, joint venture, or other agreement that high-tech firms have entered into to adopt and promote certain would-be standards. A company like RealNetworks, which develops multimedia software, is continually lining up support for its RealPlayer audio player and associated formats.[8] In these less formal cases of standard setting, which may involve standards wars, firms that have not been invited to participate in the establishment of standards (or who are denied

---

4 See http://www.ansi.org.   5 See http://www.nssn.org.
6 See http://www.iso.ch.   7 See http://www.iec.ch.
8 See www.realnetworks.com.

compatibility with the standard) may complain at their exclusion, and all manner of licensing and cross-licensing arrangements can be found.

II. The Impact of Cooperative Standard Setting

As illustrated by the examples listed above, antitrust concerns have clearly not prevented many cooperative standard-setting efforts from proceeding forward. Indeed, even the fiercest enemies often team up in the software industry to promote new standards. For example, in 1997 Microsoft and Netscape, two companies hardly known as cozy partners, agreed to include compatible versions of Virtual Reality Modeling Language (developed by Silicon Graphics) in their browsers. This agreement was expected to make it easier for consumers to view 3-D images on the Web. Earlier, Microsoft agreed to support the Open Profiling Standard, which permits users of personal computers to control what personal information is disclosed to a particular website, and which had previously been advanced by Netscape, along with Firefly Network, Inc. and Verisign Inc.

But neither is cooperative standard setting immune from antitrust scrutiny. In the consumer electronics area, for example, the Justice Department investigated Sony, Philips, and others regarding the establishment of the CD standard in the 1980s. Cooperative efforts to set optical disc standards have also been challenged in private antitrust cases, on the theory that agreements to adhere to a standard are an unreasonable restraint of trade:

[d]efendants have agreed, combined, and conspired to eliminate competition . . . by agreeing not to compete in the design of formats for compact discs and compact disc players, and by instead agreeing to establish, and establishing, a common format and design . . .[9]

Does cooperation lead to efficient standardization, increased competition, and additional consumer benefits? Or is cooperative standard setting a means for firms collectively to stifle competition, to the detriment of consumers and firms not included in the standard-setting group? Answering these questions and evaluating the limits that should be placed on cooperative standard-setting efforts requires an analysis of the competitive effects of such cooperation in comparison with some reasonable but-for world. Inevitably, an antitrust analysis of cooperative standard setting involves an assessment of how the market would likely evolve *without* the cooperation. One possibility is that multiple, incompatible products would prevail in the market, if not for the cooperation. Another possibility is that the market would eventually tip to a single product, even without cooperation. Even in this latter case, an

---

[9] 'Second Amended Complaint', *Disctronics Texas, Inc., et al. v. Pioneer Electronic Corp. et al.*, Eastern District of Texas, Case No. 4:95 CV 229, filed August 2, 1996, at 12.

initial industry-wide standard can have significant efficiency and welfare consequences, for three reasons: (1) cooperation may lock in a different product design than would emerge from competition; (2) cooperation may eliminate a standards war waged prior to tipping; and (3) cooperation is likely to enable multiple firms to supply the industry-standard product, whereas a standards war may lead to a single, proprietary product.

A. The costs and benefits of compatibility and standards

I begin by laying out the costs and benefits of achieving compatibility. I then turn to the legal treatment of cooperation to set compatibility standards.

1. Greater realization of network effects

When all users are on a single network, the size of the network is maximized and so is the realization of network benefits. For communication networks, users benefit from the fact that any given user can communicate with any other. For hardware-software networks, users benefit from the fact that firms supplying components have access to a large market for their software. This is likely to lead to increased entry and variety, and greater price and innovation competition in the supply of individual components.

2. Buyers are protected from stranding

When products are compatible, a consumer does not fear being stranded when he or she chooses to make a purchase from a particular supplier. When a consumer buys a television set in the United States, for example, he or she knows that it is compatible with the signals sent out by local broadcasters—the Federal Communications Commission (FCC) sets standards that all television receivers must meet. In contrast, neither the FCC nor anyone else set AM stereo standards for years. The result was consumer confusion and a reluctance to buy. Incompatibility between the Sony mini-disc and the Philips digital compact cassette led to a similar result.

3. Constraints on variety and innovation

The need to adhere to a standard imposes limits on firms' product design choices. Unlike the first two effects of standardization, this effect is a cost. Limits on design choices can lead to static losses from the reduction in variety. And they can lead to dynamic losses as firms are foreclosed from certain paths of R&D that could result in innovative new products that could not comply with the standards. Note that these limits impose costs both at the time a new product is created, and later when it is possible to introduce a new generation offering greatly enhanced performance. In the latter case, firms must confront the issue of whether to preserve intergenerational compatibility.

4. *Impact on competition*

In the presence of network effects, compatibility can fundamentally affect the nature of competition. The importance of compatibility stems from the fact that compatible products constitute a single network. Increased adoption of one vendor's product does not create a competitive advantage for that vendor relative to its rivals because the rivals' products also benefit from the larger network size. In contrast, when products are incompatible, different brands constitute different networks. Consequently, the increased adoption of one brand creates a larger network for that product but not for competing products. Thus, increased adoption of a particular product creates an ongoing competitive advantage for that product by raising the value of that brand relative to brands that are not part of that network.

This fact has several consequences. To illustrate, suppose that everyone expects the market to tip eventually. If these expectations are correct, then eventually there will be a single network, whether or not firms agree to common standard. In this setting, there are two ways to achieve industry-wide compatibility. One is for firms to agree up front to a common standard. The other is for firms to battle for dominance. Under incompatibility, firms will *compete for the market.* Firms may make big investments and incur initial losses as the attempt to become the dominant network. In contrast, under compatibility, firms will *compete within the market.* Network effects do not provide a means for a firm to pull ahead of its rivals and perhaps even become a monopolist. Instead, firms will compete along other dimensions, such as price, product features, and post-sales service.

This suggests an overall pattern. Cooperative standard setting mutes the intense front-end competition characteristic of a standards war, while permitting greater competition later in the life of a product, since multiple firms can provide products that comply with the standard. In other words, cooperative standard setting tends to decrease competition along some dimensions, and in the near term, while increasing competition on other dimensions and in the future. On net, compatibility can either increase or decrease competition, depending on market conditions. To see how standardization affects competition, we must compare the evolution of a market with and without the compatibility of competing products.

One must be careful in applying this analysis of competitive effects. Generally, it does not give a clear answer, but rather suggests a tradeoff: ex ante versus ex post competition, you can have one but not both. There is, however, an important set of situations in which compatibility gives rise to increased competition at all points in time. These situations arise when the entire product category would fail to take off in the absence of standardization. This can happen if consumers withhold making initial purchases (or if producers of complementary components refrain from making investments) because they are too worried about being locked in to the wrong choice.

5. *Weighing the benefits and costs*

This discussion should make it clear that there are no easy or general answers regarding the impact of cooperative standard setting on competition, efficiency, and consumer welfare. Still, I believe that this economic framework helps frame the key questions and gives insight into the proper scope for collective standard setting. As a general matter, antitrust analysis of interfirm cooperation should assess the harm to third parties who are not part of the agreement. The leading candidates are consumers, those offering complements, and suppliers of the product who do not control and/or participate in the standard-setting process.

The clearest case favoring standard setting arises when collective action is essential to get the bandwagon moving at all. This could happen if two or more firms have crucial intellectual property that must be contributed to develop a successful product; see the section below on cross-licensing and patent pools. This also could happen if consumers simply would not adopt any product without the unified support of a number of suppliers. In these situations, collective standard setting benefits consumers as well as the vendors.

Collective standard setting also is likely to be desirable, even if multiple suppliers could offer competing products, so long as network effects are strong and the standard does not unnecessarily restrict product variety. Because of the network effects, total efficiency is greatest when there is a single network; the best one can hope for is to achieve this result while enabling several firms to offer compatible programs. If variety can still flourish within the standard, the outcome can be very efficient and preserve considerable competition even while exploiting network effects.

Cooperation becomes more problematic if the participants agree to standards that compel each to pay royalties to the others. This may simply be a form of induced collusion. One sign of this may be agreements where one piece of intellectual property from each member of the coalition is included in the standard. Of course, this pattern may also reflect the fact that the parties are getting together to resolve blocking intellectual property rights, in which case cooperation is necessary to move forward at all. To distinguish the cartel situation from the patent unblocking situation, the key question is whether a successful product could be launched by one or a subset of the parties without infringing the intellectual property rights of the others.

Another pattern worthy of antitrust attention arises when a subset of firms in an industry adopt a standard that encompasses their intellectual property rights and makes it necessary for anyone producing to that standard to make payments to those firms. This can be a means for that set of firms jointly to monopolize the market. Such concerns can be alleviated if the firms agree to license their intellectual property openly on fair and reasonable terms, as required by numerous standard-setting organizations including the American National Standards Institute and the International Standards Organization.

B. Legal treatment of cooperative standard setting

The question of whether firms should be allowed, or even encouraged, to set standards cooperatively is part of the broader issue of collaboration among competitors, a storied area within antitrust law. Most of the case law deals with *quality and performance standards* rather than *compatibility standards*.[10] Existing cases have also tended to focus on the standard-setting *process* itself, rather than the outcomes of cooperative standard setting.

Antitrust liability has been found for participants in a standard-setting process who abuse that process to exclude competitors from the market. One leading case is *Allied Tube & Conduit Corp. v. Indian Head, Inc,*[11] in which the Supreme Court affirmed a jury verdict against a group of manufacturers of steel conduit for electrical cable. These manufacturers conspired to block an amendment of the National Electric Code that would have permitted the use of plastic conduit. They achieved this by 'packing' the annual meeting of the National Fire Protection Association, whose model code is widely adopted by state and local governments.[12] The other leading case is *American Society of Mechanical Engineers v. Hydrolevel Corp,*[13] in which the Supreme Court affirmed an antitrust judgment against a trade association. In this case, the chairman of an association subcommittee offered an 'unofficial' ruling that plaintiff's product was unsafe, and this ruling was used by plaintiff's rival (who enjoyed representation on the subcommittee) to discourage customers from buying plaintiff's product.

Antitrust risks associated with excluding a rival from the market appear to be less of a problem for an 'open' standard, but could arise if the companies promoting the standard block others from adhering to the standard or seek royalties from outsiders.

As the Supreme Court has noted, '[a]greement on a product standard is, after all, implicitly an agreement not to manufacture, distribute, or purchase certain types of products'.[14] To date, this type of reasoning has not been used to impose per se liability on standard-setting activities. Indeed, I know of no successful antitrust challenges to cooperation to set compatibility standards. The closest case of which I am aware is *Addamax Corporation v. Open*

---

[10] See James Anton & Dennis Yao, *Standard-Setting Consortia, Antitrust, and High-Technology Industries*, 64 ANTITRUST L. J. 247 (1995), for a more complete discussion of the legal treatment of performance standards.

[11] 486 U.S. 492 (1988).

[12] As described in Samuel R. Miller, HIJACKING THE STANDARD-SETTING PROCESS—THE ANTITRUST RISKS 5 (Folger & Levin Firm, San Francisco, CA, May 1996): 'The defendants recruited 230 people to join the standard-setting association and attend the meeting at a cost of more than $100,000. The steel group voters were instructed where to sit and how and when to vote by group leaders who used walkie-talkies and hand signals to facilitate communication' (*citing Allied Tube & Conduit Corp*, 486 U.S. at 496–97).

[13] 456 U.S. 556 (1982).

[14] *Allied Tube & Conduct Corp.*, n. 11 above, 486 U.S. at 500.

Software Foundation, Inc.[15] In *Addamax*, the District Court refused to grant summary judgment on behalf of the Open Software Foundation, an industry consortium formed to develop a platform-independent version of the UNIX operating system. OSF conducted a bidding to select a supplier of security software. After failing to be selected, Addamax brought antitrust claims against OSF, Hewlett Packard, and Digital Equipment Corporation, asserting that OSF had chosen the winner not based on the merits but to favor specific companies and technologies. The *Addamax* case looks problematic (although, admittedly, the court was only permitting a rule-of-reason claim to go forward), inasmuch as the primary purpose of OSF was to permit its members to team up to offer stronger competition against the leading UNIX vendors, Sun Microsystems and AT&T, and there was no evidence suggesting that OSF's failure to pick Addamax was based on its members' desire to control the market in which Addamax itself operated.

I believe that the antitrust risks faced by companies that are trying to set compatibility standards are minor as long as the scope of the agreement is limited to standard setting. While the law has typically looked for integration and risk sharing among collaborators in order to classify cooperation as a joint venture and escape per se condemnation, these are not very helpful or useful screens for standard-setting activities. The essence of cooperative standard setting is not the sharing of risks associated with specific investments, or the integration of operations, but rather the contribution of complementary intellectual property rights and the expression of unified support to ignite positive feedback for a new technology.

C. Policy implications

What does this analysis tell us that antitrust enforcers should look for when deciding whether to allow cooperative standard setting?

- *Do the firms in the proposed standards coalition have market power?* Answering this question is made difficult by the fact that the product may not yet have been brought to market. The analysis must thus focus on capabilities. In this sense, the inquiry is akin to conducting a market power analysis for a merger case based on potential entry effects. If the firms collectively lack market power and there are firms that jointly or individually could put forth competing standards, then the cooperation is unlikely to harm competition.
- *Does the coalition have open or closed membership?* Open membership defuses the danger that the firms involved will exclude others from the

---

[15] 888 F. Supp. 274 (D.Ma. 1995). The court subsequently held that even assuming an antitrust violation, Addamax would not have been entitled to damages, see 964 F.Supp.549 (D.Ma. 1997), *aff'd,* 152 F. 3d 48 (1st Cir. 1998).

market, but increases the likelihood that the members collectively do or will possess market power. 'Small' open groups thus are the least worrisome. 'Large' open groups can also be highly pro-competitive, especially if the members are not restricted in their ability to compete independently of each other and even outside of the standard.

- *Do members of the coalition possess blocking patents or other intellectual property rights?* If two or more companies each have patents that are essential to production of goods, then some form of cooperation is far more likely to be desirable. Cooperation is not essential; the firms might be able to license each other and third parties separately. However, separate licensing is prone to higher royalty rates than collective licensing because an owner of intellectual property rights acting individually fails to take into account the harm it does to holders of complementary intellectual property rights when it raises its license fees. (See the Technical Appendix below.)
- *Are royalties required to adhere to the standard?* Such royalties will tend to raise the price of any product complying with the standard. Royalties that reward owners of blocking patents or copyrights are easily defensible, but royalties can have cartel-like effects.
- *Is coordination critical to the launch of the product?* Cooperation is desirable in those situations where the product would fail to take off in the absence of standardization. Of course, the difficulty in applying this standard is to determine whether standardization really is needed. Indications that either buyers or the suppliers of complementary components strongly favored standards can provide very valuable evidence.
- *What ancillary restraints are placed on members of the standards coalition?* Is a member firm allowed to produce products that do not adhere to the standard? If there are no limitations, then cooperation is less likely to harm competition. It is important to recognize, however, that there may be good reasons to limit members' ability to produce non-standard products.

III. Standard Setting and Intellectual Property Rights

I now look more closely at two intellectual property issues that frequently arise in the context of standard setting: the use of cross-licenses and/or patent pools; and the duties of participants to license their patents on 'reasonable' terms.

A. Cross-licenses and patent pools

All too often in high-tech markets, several firms control property rights that must be combined to bring products to market. In other words, blocking patents are not unusual. This is especially true in a standard-setting context:

if multiple firms own patents that are essential to comply with the product standard, they each can block all others from making compatible products. For precisely this reason, standard-setting bodies require participants to license any essential patents on reasonable terms.

The case in which multiple firms control patents essential to a standard is amenable to formal economic analysis. In essence, any manufacturer seeking to produce a compliant product must obtain a license from each rights holder to avoid facing an infringement action. This is a classic case in which the manufacturer requires each of several inputs in fixed proportion. The Technical Appendix below sketches out the most basic theory of the pricing of such complementary inputs. As shown there, prices are higher if these patents are controlled and licensed separately than if they are under consolidated control. (The Appendix only covers the case of two essential patents, but the theory extends naturally and easily to multiple essential patents. The greater the number of such patents, the more important it is to coordinate their pricing to avoid stifling product demand.)

The basic theory of complements shown in the Technical Appendix gives strong support for competition authorities to welcome either cross-licenses or patent pools to clear such blocking positions. If the two patent holders are the only companies capable of manufacturing compliant products, a royalty-free cross-license is ideal from the point of view of (ex post) competition, but *any* cross-license is superior to a world in which the patent holders fail to cooperate, since neither could proceed in that world without infringing on the other's patents. Alternatively, if the patent holders see benefits from enabling many others to make compliant products, a patent pool, under which all the blocking patents are licensed in a coordinated fashion, can be an ideal outcome. The simple theory in the Technical Appendix suggests that coordinating such licensing can lead to *lower* royalty rates than would independent pricing of the patents. Of course, the best outcome of all may be for other manufacturers and perhaps large users to insist on low or nominal royalties as a quid pro quo for supporting the standard in the first place.

An excellent illustration of how the enforcement agencies can successfully handle intellectual property in the standard-setting context comes from the Justice Department's June 1997 approval of the proposal by Columbia University and nine companies to create a clearinghouse to offer a package license of patents needed to meet the MPEG-2 video compression standard developed by the Motion Picture Expert Group. The portfolio will only contain patents found to be truly essential to the MPEG-2 standard. The MPEG-2 standard is used in many forms of digital transmissions, including digital television, direct broadcast satellite, digital cable systems, personal computer video, DVD, and interactive media. It was important to the Justice Department that the pool was restricted to blocking patents, which are complements, not substitutes, as determined by an independent expert. The scope of the cooperation endorsed by the Justice Department was to unblock patent positions, and to reduce transactions costs through the use of a clearinghouse. Similar reasoning was applied by the Justice Department in two business review letters involving Digital Versatile Disk (DVD) standards.[16]

Another interesting case involving a patent pool is the March 1998 Federal Trade Commission complaint against Summit Technology, Inc. and VISX, Inc. two firms that market lasers to perform a new, and increasingly popular, vision correcting eye surgery, photorefractive keratectomy. According to the FTC: 'Instead of competing with each other, the firms placed their competing patents in a patent pool and share the proceeds each and every time a Summit or VISX laser is used'. A key issue for analysis is whether the companies indeed held *competing* patents or alternatively *blocking* patents, and just what the standard will be for defining 'blocking' patents.[17]

B. Hidden intellectual property rights

Firms are sometimes accused of hiding intellectual property rights until after the proprietary technology has been embedded in a formal standard. I view this issue primarily as one of contract law. Standard-setting groups should— and often do—have provisions in their charters compelling members either to reveal all relevant patents (thus giving others fair notice and the opportunity to design around those patents) or to commit to licensing any patents embedded in the standard on 'reasonable' terms.

In some cases, however, the precise requirements imposed by a standard-setting group may be unclear. In these circumstances, if the standard affects non-participants, including consumers, there is a public interest in clarifying the duties imposed on participants in a fashion that promotes rather than stifles competition.

1. Dell Computer and the VESA VL-bus standard

One leading US example of this type of antitrust action is FTC's consent agreement with Dell Computer Corporation, announced in November 1995. Although the case involved computer hardware, it is important for a wide

---

[16] First, in December 1998 (see http://www.usdoj.gov/atr/public/press_releases/1998/2120. htm), the Department approved a proposal by Philips, Sony, and Pioneer jointly to license patents necessary to make discs and players that comply with the DVD-Video and DVD-ROM standards. Secondly, in June 1999 (see http://www.usdoj.gov/atr/public/press_releases/ 1999/2484.htm), the Department approved a joint licensing scheme relating to the DVD-Video and DVD-ROM standards; this second arrangement includes patents held by Toshiba (the licensing entity), Hitachi, Matsushita, Mitsubishi, Time Warner, and Victor Company of Japan.

[17] The companies subsequently dissolved their pooling venture, agreed not to fix prices for their lasers and patents, and agreed to cross-license their patents on a royalty-free basis. See *In Re Summit Technology*, 1999 FTC Lexis 23 (Feb. 23, 1999).

range of standard-setting activities. The assertion was that Dell threatened to exercise undisclosed patent rights against computer companies adopting the VL-bus standard, a mechanism to transfer data instructions between the computer's CPU and its peripherals such as the hard disk drive or the display screen. The VL-bus was used in 486 chips, but it has now been supplanted by the PCI bus. According to the FTC:

> During the standard-setting process, VESA [Video Electronics Standard Association] asked its members to certify whether they had any patents, trademarks, or copyrights that conflicted with the proposed VL-bus standard; Dell certified that it had no such intellectual property rights. After VESA adopted the standard—based in part, on Dell's certification—Dell sought to enforce its patent against firms planning to follow the standard.[18]

There were two controversial issues surrounding this consent decree: (a) the FTC did not assert that Dell acquired market power, and indeed the VL-bus never was successful; and (b) the FTC did not assert that Dell *intentionally* misled VESA. My analysis suggests that anticompetitive harm is unlikely to arise in the absence of significant market power and that the competitive effects are not dependent on Dell's intentions.

2. *Motorola and the ITU V.34 modem standard*

Another good example of how competition can be affected when standard-setting organizations impose ambiguous duties on participants is the case of Motorola and the V.34 modem standard adopted by the International Telecommunications Union. Motorola agreed to license its patents essential to the modem standard to all comers on 'fair, reasonable, and non-discriminatory terms'.[19] Once the standard was in place, Motorola then made offers that some industry participants did not regard as meeting this obligation. Litigation ensued between Rockwell and Motorola, in part over the question of whether 'reasonable' terms should mean: (a) the terms that Motorola could have obtained ex ante, in competition with other technology that could have been placed in the standard; or (b) the terms that Motorola could extract ex post, given that the standard is set and Motorola's patents are essential to that standard.

These issues are best dealt with by the standard-setting bodies, or standard-setting participants, either by making more explicit the duties imposed on participants, or by encouraging ex ante competition among different holders of intellectual property rights to get their property into the standard. Unfortunately, antitrust concerns have led at least some of these bodies to

---

[18] See http://www.ftc.gov/opa/9606/dell2.htm. Another important case involving the disclosure of patent applications in the standard-setting process is *Wang Lab. v. Mitsubishi Elec. Amer.*, No. CV92–4698 JGD (C.D. Cal. 1993).

[19] I served as an expert in this matter retained by Rockwell; the views stated here do not necessarily reflect those of any party to the case.

steer clear of such ex ante competition, on the grounds that their job is merely to set technical standards, not to get involved in 'prices', including the terms on which intellectual property will be made available to other participants. The ironic result has been to embolden some companies to seek substantial royalties after participating in formal standard-setting activities.

IV. Conclusion

Standard setting is here to stay, with a vengeance. As more and more products work in conjunction to form systems, interface standards play a bigger and bigger role in the economy. And, as computer and communications systems encompass a larger portion of economic activity, compatibility standards become an ever-more important aspect of competitive strategy. Intellectual property law and antitrust law must adapt to keep pace with these changes.

Clearly, there is an enormous amount of cooperative standard setting, little of which is impeded by antitrust concerns. At the same time, some very thorny issues arise when firms control intellectual property essential to a standard: what is the duty to disclose the existence of such rights, how do we interpret duties to license such property on 'fair, reasonable and non-discriminatory' terms, and how are competition authorities to treat cross-license and patent pools that arise in the context of new product standards? Generally, patent holders should be given wide latitude to fashion arrangements to cooperate to clear blocking patents.

Technical Appendix: Pricing of Components and Systems

1. The model

Consider a situation in which two components, A and B, are used in fixed proportions to constitute a system. Let the unit cost of components A and B be c_A and c_B respectively. Call the unit cost of a system $c_S \equiv c_A + c_B$. By making c_A and c_B invariant with respect to the institutional setting (see below), we are assuming that there are no economies or diseconomies of scope if the system is assembled within one firm vs. two. The focus here is thus entirely on pricing incentives for a given cost structure. The results here are well-known in the fields of microeconomics and industrial organization, but their implications for antitrust may not be fully appreciated. The treatment here is intended to illustrate some standard theoretical results, not to break new ground.

There are many examples of (actual or nearly) fixed-proportion components in the information sector, including (a) a computer and a monitor, (b) a computer and an operating system, or (c) a microprocessor and a chipset within the computer. We explore here the pricing of the components, and the system, in three different institutional settings.

The first setting is that of an *integrated firm* that manufacturers and assembles the entire system. Call the unit cost of the system $c_S \equiv c_A + c_B$. Call the price of the system to consumers, to be set by the seller, p_S.

The second setting is a *vertical chain* in which firm A manufacturers and sells component A to firm B, which then combines the A component with the B component and sells the resulting system to consumers. Firm B sets the system price p_S. In this case, call p_A the price for component A that firm A charges to firm B.

The third setting involves the *complements*: each of the two firms, A and B, sells its component to the consumer, which then combines the components into a system. In this case, call the prices charged by the two firms p_A and p_B; the system price faced by the consumer is $p_A + p_B$.

Consumers ultimately care about the total price of the system, p_S, which governs the demand for systems. Call this demand relationship $x_S = D(p_S)$, where x_S is unit sales of systems, and the demand function, $D(\cdot)$ is downward sloping, exhibits declining marginal revenue, and satisfies the usual regularity conditions for oligopoly theory. We will illustrate our results using the constant-elasticity demand curve, $D(p_S) = P_S^{-\epsilon}$. Note for use below that in this special case

$$-\frac{D(p_s)}{D'(p_s)} = pS/\epsilon.$$

Note also that in general $-D(p_S)/D'(p_S)$ is equal to the difference between price and marginal revenue at the price p_S, or, equivalently, at output level $D(p_S)$.

2. Integrated firm

With a single, integrated, firm, we have a standard monopoly pricing problem. The firm's problem is to pick p_S to maximize

$$D(p_S)(p_S - c_S)$$

The standard solution can be written as

$$p_s - c_s = -\frac{D(p_s)}{D'(p_s)}$$

With constant-elasticity demand, this gives the standard markup rule

$$p_s = \frac{c_s}{1 - 1/\epsilon}$$

3. Vertical chain

If firm A sets a single, uniform price p_A selling to firm B, which in turn sets a single uniform price selling to consumers, we have the standard 'chain of monopolies' problem. A standard result is that prices are higher under this structure than with an integrated monopolist.

The resulting price is obtained in two steps. First, consider how firm B prices the system for a given price p_A set by firm A. Effectively, firm B now has a unit cost of each system of $p_A + c_B$. Naturally, this leads to a higher system price to consumers than would unit costs of $c_A + c_B$, as in the integrated case just above. Firm B thus prices according to the rule

$$p_S - (p_A + c_B) = -\frac{D(p_S)}{D'(p_S)}$$

With constant-elasticity demand, substituting for $-D/D'$ gives

$$p_S\left(1 - \frac{1}{\epsilon}\right) = p_A + c_B$$

The next step is to determine A's optimal pricing, given B's demand as reflected in the equation just above. This is analogous to the Stackelberg problem in standard oligopoly theory. Firm A sets p_A to maximize $D(p_S)(p_A - c_A)$, where p_S is determined by the relationship just above. In the case of constant elasticity of demand, using the linear relationship between p_S and p_A noted above, a series of calculations leads to the following expression for the resulting systems price:

$$p_S = \frac{c_S}{(1 - 1/\epsilon)^2}$$

4. Complements

If firms A and B each set prices independently for their components, the problem is analogous to Cournot oligopoly, as opposed to the Stackelberg solution just derived. Firm A sets p_A to maximize

$$D(p_A + p_B)(p_A - c_A)$$

taking p_B as given. Since $dp_S/dp_A = 1$ in this situation, the resulting first-order condition is simply

$$D(p_S) + D'(p_S)(p_A - c_A) = 0$$

Firm B does likewise, giving the analogous condition for p_B of

$$D(p_S) + D'(p_S)(p_B - c_B) = 0$$

Adding up these two first-order conditions gives

$$2D(p_S) + D'(p_S)(p_S - c_S) = 0$$

which can be rewritten as

$$p_S = c_S - 2\frac{D(p_s)}{D'(p_s)}$$

Note that this equation is identical to the equation for the integrated firm, except for the factor of two on the right-hand side. In the special case of constant-elasticity demand, we have

$$p_s = \frac{c_s}{1 - 2/\epsilon}$$

Notice that this special case becomes internally inconsistent if the elasticity of demand is less than two. (Each firm will want to set arbitrarily high prices.)

5. Pricing comparisons

We know that in general the system price set by the integrated firm is lower than the price under the vertical chain or complements. The intuition behind this result is as follows. Lower prices for one component generate a positive external effect of the owner of the other component. These externalities are internalized through integration, leading to lower prices. However, this intuition alone does not tell us whether the prices are highest under complements or the vertical chain.

In the case of constant elasticity of demand, the resulting systems prices are

$$p_s^I = \frac{c_s}{1 - 1/\epsilon}$$

for the integrated firm,

$$p_s^v = \frac{c_s}{\left(1 - 1/\epsilon\right)^2}$$

for the vertical chain, and

$$p_s^c = \frac{c_s}{1 - 2/\epsilon^2}$$

for the independent pricing of complements. Direct comparison of these prices reveals that the system price is lowest for the integrated firm, somewhat higher for the vertical chain, and highest of all under the complements arrangement.

In the case of constant elasticity of demand, prices are lower under the vertical chain than under complements because the upstream firm, which we have denoted by firm A, recognizes that firm B will *raise* its own component price in response to A's higher price. Put differently, the system price will go up by more than one unit, for every unit increase in p_A. Another way to say this is that firm B's reaction curve (optimal p_B as a function of p_A) is upward sloping. (This follows from the fact that a monopolist facing constant elasticity of demand, firm B, more than passes through any increases in unit costs, p_A.) Recognizing this reaction, firm A sets a lower price under the vertical chain than under complements pricing. It follows that the systems price is lower, because firm B is setting its optimal component price given p_A under either the vertical chain or complements structure.

More generally, the comparison of system prices between the vertical chain and complements depends upon whether the reaction curve of firm B is upward or downward sloping. Put differently, prices are higher under complements if and only if cost increases are more than passed through to final consumers. Formally, this occurs if and only if $dp_S/dp_A > 1$ in the vertical chain setting. (We always have $dp_S/dp_A = 1$ in the complements setting.) Since in general the vertical chain systems price is given by

$$p_s + \frac{D(p_s)}{D'(p_s)} = p_A + c_B$$

the comparison hinges on the derivative of the left-hand side of this equation with respect to p_S. A few steps of calculus tell us that prices are higher in the complements case if and only if the ratio $D(p_S)/D'(p_S)$ is declining in p_S, which is equivalent to

$$D'(p_S)D'(p_S) < D(p_S)D''(p_S)$$

(For simplicity, I am assuming that these various conditions hold or fail uniformly at all points on the demand curve.) This condition is always met for constant elasticity of demand.

Note, however, that the condition just provided always *fails* for linear (or concave) demand. Under those conditions, prices are higher in the *vertical chain* setting.

We can illustrate these points by solving the linear case explicitly. Suppose that demand for systems is given by $D(p_S) = K - p_S$. For simplicity, and without (further) loss of generality, let c_A and c_B equal zero. The integrated firm maximizes $(K - p_S)p_S$, which involves a systems price of $K/2$. Under complements, firm A maximizes $(K - p_A - p_B)p_A$, which gives a reaction curve of $p_A = (K - p_B)/2$. Solving for the equilibrium prices gives $p_A = p_B = K/3$, for a systems price under complements of $2K/3$.

Finally, under the vertical chain arrangement, firm B's response to p_A is $p_B = (K - p_A)/2$, so firm A, the first mover, maximizes $(K - p_A - (K - p_A)/2)p_A$. The solution to this is given by $p_A = K/2$, causing B to set a component price of $K/4$, with a resulting systems price of $3K/4$. In this case, the systems price responds *less* than one-for-one to increases in p_A, so firm A is led to set a higher price under the vertical chain than under complements. In the linear case, firm A charges $K/2$ for its component, rather than $K/3$, an increase of $K/6$. However, firm B lowers its component price in response from $K/3$ to $K/4$, a decrease of only $K/12$ (the slope of B's reaction function is only $1/2$). As a result, the final systems price rises from $2K/3$ under complements to $3K/4$ under the vertical chain, an increase of $K/12$.

5

SELF-HELP IN THE DIGITAL JUNGLE

KENNETH W. DAM*

A word about my title: 'Digital Jungle' is designed to evoke a content provider's perspective on the dangers to be run in putting valuable content on the Internet. 'Self-help' refers to an expanding set of technologies and systems designed to protect content from unauthorized copying and to facilitate electronic commerce involving content. I use 'content' broadly to include text, data, images, audio, video, and all of the other media that patrons of the Web are familiar with.

There may be a jungle out there, but if so it is an exceedingly fertile one. From every perspective the Internet is growing at an astonishing rate and in steadily more diverse directions. I see no reason to repeat all of the projections on the opportunities for creation of online communities, the flourishing of political speech in totalitarian states, and the potential growth of online publishing and electronic commerce. The projections and estimates grow steadily, on the basis of faster than anticipated adoption.

* Max Pam Professor of American and Foreign Law, University of Chicago Law School. I should like to thank for their comments and suggestions the participants in the conference that New York University Law School's Engelberg Center on Innovation Law and Policy held in La Pietra, Italy, in June 1998 and in addition, Eliot Dam, Jack Goldsmith, William Landes, Douglas Lichtman, Henry H. Perritt, Jr., Richard Posner, and Cass Sunstein. And for generous support of the research for this chapter I thank The Sarah Scaife Foundation Fund and The Lynde and Harry Bradley Foundation Fund.

One issue is whether self-help systems will play an important positive role, especially in the development of commercial applications and more generally in the growth of electronic commerce. The question that interests many intellectual property specialists is whether self-help systems may go too far—by interfering, for example, with 'user rights'.[1] In my view, self-help systems will not only reduce the incidence of copyright violations and be one of the crucial success factors in electronic commerce but, more specifically, these systems are likely to evolve to meet most of the concrete objections of those who criticize such systems from an intellectual property doctrinal point of view.

Self-help systems will never meet, however, the goals of those who believe that they should be 'free'. Nor should we expect them to meet those goals. On the contrary, it would be an error in economic policy to adopt rules that would de facto incapacitate self-help systems. In any case, it is not my purpose to debate with those who, in the name of user rights or of freedom of the Net, would effectively emasculate copyright. I take copyright law as given and as desirable and indeed necessary intellectual property law. Since self-help systems can greatly limit unauthorized copying of copyrighted materials, there is not necessarily any need to rewrite copyright law to fit the online environment. But I do not limit the value of self-help systems to protection of copyrighted content. Self-help systems also protect uncopyrightable and uncopyrighted (including public domain) materials. And because they do so by facilitating contracting between content providers and users, they should not be viewed as conflicting with the intellectual property law of copyright.[2]

The views one brings to the table in this area depend a great deal on where one enters the thicket of legal, ethical, and policy issues involved. My own perspective is that electronic commerce can, if promoted through appropriate

---

[1] Many intellectual property commentators have analyzed the issue as one of copyright law. Those who dislike self-help systems often have the conception that fair use should necessarily be interpreted as broadly as possible. Exaggerating only a little, one can say that in their eyes the key principle, especially in the online world, should be free use, and that copyright should be considered an exception. This theme is especially strong in the writings of those who emphasize 'user rights'. For critical comments on the user rights approach, see Jane C. Ginsburg, *Authors and Users in Copyright*, 45 J. COPYRIGHT SOC'Y 1 (1997).

[2] See *ProCD, Inc. v. Zeidenberg*, 86 F.3d 1447 (7th Cir. 1996). Compare *Aronson v. Quick Point Pencil Co.*, 440 U.S. 257 (1979). The view stated in the text concerning the relationship between contract and copyright is obviously controversial. I state it as a conclusion as to the desirable policy outcome and do not, in this comment, attempt to deal with all of the technical legal issues raised by a number of writers on this subject. I do note, nevertheless, that the case law finding preemption of contracts by intellectual property law is quite limited. References to the shrink-wrap cases are irrelevant because the issue in those cases is whether there is a contract in the first place. Finally, the notion that 'click-on' instantaneous contracts are contracts of adhesion and therefore somehow invalid finds little support in the case law. See Tom W. Bell, *Fair Use vs. Fared Use: The Impact of Automated Rights Management in Copyright's Fair Use Doctrine*, 76 N.C. L. REV. 557, 607–8 (1998). Even if they were contracts of adhesion, that would mean only that courts could scrutinize the contracts more closely for ambiguities or for unconscionable terms and conditions. See, eg, *Fireman's Fund Insurance Co. v. M.V. DSR Atlantic*, 131 F.3d 1336 (9th Cir. 1998).

legislation and left relatively free from impediments to free and open contracting, be as important to the next century as the industrial revolution was to the late eighteenth and early nineteenth centuries. I base this unprovable conjecture on the twin propositions that our society is predominantly and increasingly a service society, and that the service portion of the society is increasingly based on information. Electronic commerce may be useful for groceries and the host of other things that can now be ordered on the Net for delivery through the mails and delivery services, but the big payoff lies in information, which can not only be ordered but delivered electronically.

Mine is not, I suspect, the perspective of most intellectual property scholars. Most of those who write on self-help are particularly interested in copyright law. I shall not attempt to deal here with all of the copyright and even constitutional points that have been raised to question the propriety and legality of using self-help systems.[3] Those are important issues but, as I shall argue, they place too much weight on one side of public policy scales.[4]

The current state of legislation is that the Congress, in the Digital Millennium Copyright Act of 1998, recognized the need to protect both self-help systems against circumvention and fair user rights in the context of such protection. In an all too typical compromise, the Congress, unable to balance these two somewhat conflicting objectives, delegated the task to the Librarian of Congress, who is to determine in a rulemaking proceeding the extent of a fair user exception to the Act's general prohibition against circumvention of any 'technological measure that effectively controls access to a work protected' under the Act.[5] Because the Act protects only copyrighted works and the Congress specifically dropped any protection of databases, the legislation

---

[3] One line of concern about self-help systems is that they involve possible invasion of a user's privacy. See Julie E. Cohen, *Some Reflections on Copyright Management Systems and Law Designed to Protect Them*, 11 BERKELEY TECH. L.J. 161, 183–87 (1997). Privacy for online users is a general concern that needs to be dealt with, and it is in no way limited to self-help systems. The Digital Millennium Copyright Act, discussed below, deals in part with this concern by allowing circumvention of a self-help system to the extent that it 'contains the capability of collecting or disseminating personally identifying information reflected in the online activities of a natural person' without allowing that person an ability to opt out of the collection or dissemination of that information: 12 U.S.C. § 1201.

[4] A different issue is how much self-help systems will actually contribute to the growth of electronic commerce in information. Clearly there are a variety of business models for providing information on the Web, not all of which require the same protection of content. Dyson, in an illuminating discussion, concludes that selling copies through self-help systems is unlikely to be the dominant business model because 'there's all that competing stuff for free': ESTHER DYSON, RELEASE 2.0: A DESIGN FOR LIVING IN THE DIGITAL AGE, at 154 (1997). Many business models involve free use of content to sell something in the offline world. This does not mean, however, that self-help systems will not play a crucial role in one important part of what seems destined to become an enormous online market. On the question of business models, the fact that copy-protection systems for software fell out of favor due to buyer resistance should, of course, make one cautious about predicting unqualified market success for self-help systems. See Henry H. Perritt, Jr., *Property and Innovation in the Global Information Infrastructure*, 1996 U. CHI. LEGAL F. 261, 303–4.

[5] 17 U.S.C. § 1201(a)(1)(A).

says nothing about self-help systems in the uncopyrightable database context. After considering the nature of self-help systems and the values at stake in their use, I shall review briefly this legislation.

I. Self-Help Systems

The two most important factual points about self-help systems are, first, they are here now, and secondly, they are, of course, still quite primitive compared to what experience suggests they are likely to become. I shall describe briefly what now exists and what one can expect, especially with the right incentives, only a few years from now. Both because of the demand for self-help systems and the rapid growth of sophistication in software programming, one may expect them to be much more sophisticated in the next few years (especially if government and the courts do not get in the way). The special importance of the rapid evolution in self-help technology is that it holds out the possibility of helping to achieve the objectives of both the proponents and opponents of self-help systems.

These systems are often called copyright management systems, but the underlying information need not be copyrighted. It may be protectable, say as a trade secret, where the use of such a system will help the trade secret owner to demonstrate that all reasonable steps have been taken to keep the information secret (or, better still, to avoid the leakage of the information in the first place and hence the necessity for litigation). Or the underlying information may not be protectable at all. It may be just a compilation or purely factual, or indeed it could be information for which a third party owns the copyright—for example, it may be pirated content.[6] I shall use the phrase 'self-help systems' rather than 'copyright management systems' for two reasons. They can and will be used for noncopyrighted content. And the word copyright is likely to make us dwell too much on copyright doctrine rather than on the underlying goals and values we would like to promote in an information society.

I also avoid the term 'rights management systems' because I see little reason to get into a case-by-case analysis as to whether the content is copyrightable or otherwise independently protectable by legal action. After all, telephone books have a convenience value, even if not copyrightable. We surely would not argue that because telephone books in tangible form

---

[6] In the last case, self-help systems may be used to facilitate piracy. Thus, a music pirate might send copyrighted music to a wide circle, whether for personal or commercial reasons, within a cryptolope in order to avoid being detected by the copyright owner. See the discussion of cryptolopes below.

normally cannot be copyrighted, it should be lawful simply to steal them. To permit outright theft would make consumers worse off, not better off, because although theft may be just an economic transfer, the 'sweat of the brow' investment in time and money required to generate them warrants encouragement. This is not a legal argument nor necessarily a plea for intellectual property protection for telephone books, but simply an observation that allowing people to protect by their own means what they create is usually socially optimal where the law does not provide a cheaper, more effective remedy.[7] That is the central argument, for example, for allowing freedom to use encryption to protect private communications, even though some who do so may be drug dealers or terrorists. So, too, society not only allows those with houses, apartments, and cars to lock them but increasingly favors such self-help through various legal and contractual (for example, insurance) measures.

II. What Can Self-Help Systems Do?

In the simplest application, self-help systems enable a content provider to transmit content to a potential reader (or viewer, listener, etc.) by posting it on a website, e-mailing it, etc., while preventing anyone from accessing it without, say, paying the content provider (for example, by giving a credit card number or, in newer electronic commerce applications, by using digital cash). Note that I use the concept of a 'content provider' in the broadest possible sense to include all forms of information and without distinction as to whether or not the information is legally protected against access by unintended recipients through intellectual property rights.

A. Encryption

Normally, the basic technology is encryption. The encrypted content is placed within a digital envelope (called a cryptolope by IBM and a DigiBox by

---

[7] Most scholars of intellectual property law have supported the Supreme Court decision in *Feist Publications, Inc. v. Rural Telephone Service Co., Inc.*, 499 U.S. 340 (1991), in rejecting the 'sweat of the brow' doctrine as the basis for copyright protection. I do not believe it necessary to enter into that question to analyze contract protection for self-help systems. But it is worth noting that scholarly approbation of the *Feist* doctrine is by no means unanimous. For skeptical thoughts on *Feist*, see, for example, Rochelle Dreyfuss, *A Wiseguy's Approach to Information Products: Muscling Copyright and Patent into a Unitary Theory of Intellectual Property*, 1992 SUP. CT. REV. 195, 209–20 (1993). For a general argument in the patent law context for state law protection of unpatentable innovation on grounds somewhat analogous to 'sweat of the brow', see Douglas Gary Lichtman, *The Economics of Innovation: Protecting Unpatentable Goods*, 81 MINN. L. REV. 693 (1997).

InterTrust)[8] so that the content provider can indicate in unencrypted text on the envelope what a potential reader has to do to decrypt the content.[9]

B. Digital watermarks

Another class of self-help systems involves placing a digital watermark on an image so that any copies can be identified not just as originating with the content provider but as being copied from an image transmitted to a specified party. The idea is to discourage sending the copy on to a third party who might make copies unauthorized by the content provider. This technique, which can be thought of as an application of the cryptographic technique of hiding messages within other messages by slightly altering the intensity or color of pixels ('steganography'), can also work for music but not normally for alphanumeric text (although fonts might be minutely altered for this purpose). Digital watermark technology may be combined by a content provider with a search program that roams the net looking for the provider's watermark, thereby ferreting out unauthorized use of the content in webpages.[10] One can well imagine the development of ASCAP/BMI types of rights companies that would roam the Net to find copies via watermarks and obtain payments for the authors. Since the equivalent of watermarks can be used to insert inaudible information within audio,[11] it may be that ASCAP and BMI themselves will come to fulfill the same function on the Net that they perform with regard to radio and TV.

One of the common misunderstandings about self-help systems is the assumption that they exclusively benefit content providers to the detriment of

---

[8] For detailed descriptions of the self-help technologies discussed in this chapter, one can contact the providers of those technologies. For a brief discussion of each technology, the best single source is a compendium of such providers in Information Technology Association of America, *Intellectual Property Protection in Cyberspace: Towards a New Consensus*, WEST'S LEGAL NEWS, December 12, 1996, *available in* 1996 WL 710185. This compendium includes the URL and mail address of each provider. Other useful sources include Eric Schlachter, *The Intellectual Property Renaissance in Cyberspace. Why Copyright Law Could Be Unimportant on the Internet*, 12 BERKELEY TECH. L.J. 15, 38–48 (1997); Bell, n. 2 above, at 567. See also I. Trotter Hardy, *Project Looking Forward: Sketching the Future of Copyright in a Networked World* (May 1998) <http://www.loc.gov/copyright/docs/thardy.pdf>.

[9] Obviously, the development of a nationwide public key infrastructure, something this and prior administrations have done little or nothing to foster, would enable much more varied ways of using encryption to protect content. For example, once the intended recipient had paid or otherwise met the requirements of the content provider (say by membership in a designated group or by establishing credit arrangements), the content provider could send the content encrypted with the intended recipient's public key and only the intended recipient could decrypt it. See CRYPTOGRAPHY'S ROLE IN SECURING THE INFORMATION SOCIETY 375–76 (Kenneth W. Dam & Herbert S. Lin eds., Nat'l Acad. Press 1996).

[10] The Stanford Copy Analysis System (SCAM) developed by the Stanford Computer Science Department performs this kind of search of web and FTP sites and Usenet newsgroups. See n. 8 above.

[11] MusiCode by ARIS performs this function. See n. 8 above.

users. But watermarks are not just for content providers; they can enhance a user's capabilities. For example, a graphic artist using a program like Adobe Photoshop can use a watermark reader to determine the source of a water-marked photo, enabling the user to communicate directly with the original photo owner, facilitating agreement on enhancements to the photo for a particular kind of use.[12]

The foregoing applications involve hiding watermarks for future detection. However, in some applications, where the watermark does not detract from the usefulness of the image (say for blueprints or other utilitarian images), watermarks may be made readable by the human eye in order to facilitate not just rights clearances but normal research conventions. One can imagine such applications facilitating academic research, where the visible watermark attached to a historical document gives citation material that does not disappear when the document is cropped or poorly copied. Still another class of watermarks may be used to protect moral rights. A 'fragile' watermark technique can be used by a content provider, say an artist, to determine whether an image has been tampered with.[13]

C. Invisible messages

Self-help systems can attach messages to content (say to a webpage) that are not visible to the eye, but that nonetheless make it impossible to copy the content or that allow only a single copy, or that send a message back to the content provider indicating how many copies are being made.[14] Much of the debate about circumvention and 'stripping off' involves this class of self-help systems.

A subset of this class involves locking mechanisms. Content can be locked so that it has to be unlocked by each recipient. Thus, if the content provider transmits content to an original recipient who unlocks it (say by payment) and then retransmits it (forwards it) to a friend, the friend will receive a locked copy and cannot unlock it without paying. Thus, each recipient, whether or not a recipient intended by the content provider, must pay.[15] Similarly, it would be possible to require payment for each hard copy made.

These locking and similar invisible message technologies can easily evolve to enable the objectives of those who worry that self-help systems will spell an

---

[12] The Digimarc digital watermark reader is such a program. See n. 8 above.

[13] See the discussion of IBM watermark technologies in Fred Minzer et al., *Safeguarding Digital Library Contents and Users*, D-LIB MAG. (December 1997) <http://www.dlib.org/dlib/december97/ibm/12lotspiech.html>.

[14] The Xerox Digital Property Rights Language (DPRL) is an example. See n. 8 above. For a conceptual discussion of the use of digital rights languages, see Mark Stefik, *Shifting the Possible: How Trusted Systems and Digital Property Rights Challenge Us to Rethink Digital Publishing* 12 BERKELEY TECH. L.J. 137, 140 ff. (1997).

[15] For example, the SoftLock system, see n. 8 above.

end to doctrines promoting access, such as fair use and first sale. For example, technology can allow a recipient to 'loan' an authorized copy to a particular third person for a particular period of time or indeed to 'sell' it to a third person.[16] During the period of the loan or after the sale the copy is no longer accessible by the recipient and is accessible only by the particular third person. Thus, self-help systems can support, from a practical standpoint, a digital version of the objective of the first-sale doctrine. As we will see later, this is just one of a number of ways in which self-help systems can facilitate implementation of many of the ideas underlying pro-competitive and fair use ideas embedded in copyright and other intellectual property law.

Similarly, self-help systems can facilitate the kinds of negotiations that copyright law itself contemplates. For example, content can be accompanied by recipient-readable copyright information that will enable those who are anxious to establish their right to make derivative works to contact the original content provider.[17]

The foregoing are just a few variations on the concept of a self-help system. So long as the integrity of the self-help technology is maintained, almost any conceivable combination or variation of the ideas just discussed is possible. Many bells and whistles can be added, and some of them will help resolve policy conflicts over the propriety of self-help systems.[18] But before discussing the ways in which self-help systems can deal with these policy conflicts, it is important to understand the vulnerabilities of such systems.

III. The Robustness of Self-Help Systems

Any electronic online system is vulnerable to attack. That is close to an axiom in the field of computer security.[19] So too, therefore, are self-help systems vulnerable. In the typical case, electronic online systems are attacked by non-parties (for example, a third party intercepting a message). But in the case of

---

[16] See Stefik, n. 14 above, at 147–48.

[17] For example, the NetRights attribute system, see n. 8 above.

[18] In one sense self-help systems, no matter how complex, are not new but simply more sophisticated versions of techniques for conditioned access. Conditioned access systems have been around for some time, first on specialized proprietary systems such as Lexis and Westlaw, then on general closed services such as America Online, and finally on the Internet. In the Internet environment, access is sometimes conditioned on payment (say by providing a credit card number) but often just in return for registration, where the registrant is required to provide personal information, which when packaged together with information from other registrants constitutes valuable information that the content provider is able to sell to third parties. Obviously the ability to sell this information provides an incentive for the creation and making available of the content. Moreover, this content subject to conditioned access is often, perhaps usually, uncopyrightable. Thus, self-help systems constitute simply a further evolution of what has existed for some time without much controversy (except for concerns about privacy).

[19] PETER G. NEUMANN, COMPUTER-RELATED RISKS (1995).

self-help systems, an additional important vulnerability lies in the prospect that an intended recipient of content may have an interest in defeating the conditions of access (for example, copying without paying).

Inevitably other technologies will arise to defeat self-help systems. For example, computer programs can be written to detect and, either automatically or at the discretion of a content recipient, strip off invisible messages and controls. Similarly, one can anticipate the rise of software technologies to detect digital watermarks and to wash them out. Some technologies developed for other purposes can degrade watermarks. For example, compression techniques are normally 'lossy', that is, they involve eliminating some information and thus may destroy some information in a watermark, information that is not restored when an image document is subsequently expanded (decompressed).

The fact that technologies used to defeat self-help systems may and probably will have other uses suggests that care should be taken in any legislation designed to protect self-help systems from attack. The Digital Millennium Copyright Act wisely limits its prohibition with respect to circumventing technology to that which is 'primarily designed or produced for the purpose of circumventing protection' and which 'has only limited commercially significant purpose or use other than' circumvention.[20]

Can anything general be said about the vulnerabilities of self-help systems? One key point is that although self-help systems work and are likely to be defeated only occasionally, with minor consequences for their utility, some self-help systems depend heavily on their robustness for their usefulness. For example, some integrity uses (say in photojournalism) require time stamps to determine when the digital original was taken; where the photograph is sufficiently controversial that its integrity is open to question, the time stamp needs to be robust against hostile attack. Similarly, someone who posts content (say artwork) on the Web may use time stamps to be able to prove subsequently when it was posted, say in a contest over who was first; here again, the time stamp must be robust.[21]

The warfare analogy of a race between offense and defense comes readily to mind. For those who sympathize with content providers, one can view the copier as the attacker, with the content provider responding to copying by using 'defensive' self-help systems. Then offensive techniques will arise to overcome the defenses to copying (or to alteration) not authorized by the content provider, and so on ad infinitum.

---

[20] 17 U.S.C. § 1201(b)(1). Aside from any arguments about user rights, this provision reflects a broader technology policy that it is unwise to declare any technology unlawful, especially in the electronics realm, in view of the rapid progress in the field that constantly builds on recent technologies developed for quite different initial uses. A fortiori one should not criminalize use of a technology that has benign uses simply because it also has harmful uses.

[21] The WebArmor system is designed to meet this need. See n. 8 above.

IV. Fair Use and Self-Help: Legislation and Standards

The Digital Millennium Copyright Act enacted in October 1998 takes the first step in addressing the relationship between fair use and self-help systems. It applies only to copyright and therefore leaves open the question of noncopy-rightable content, such as databases lacking sufficient creativity to be copyrightable.

Recognizing the vulnerability of self-help systems, the Act prohibits circumvention of any 'technological measure that effectively controls access' to a copyrighted work as well as the manufacture, importation, or offer to the public of any technology primarily produced for the purpose of such circumvention.[22] But since such measures against circumvention may affect the exercise of fair use rights, the statute establishes a system for determining whether users of particular classes of works are 'adversely affected by virtue of such prohibition in their ability to make noninfringing uses of that particular class of works'.[23] Users of such classes of works are not subject to the circumvention prohibition. The mechanism to be used to determine what those classes of works are is a rulemaking proceeding carried out by the Librarian of Congress. In that rulemaking proceeding, the Librarian is to consider the impact of the circumvention prohibition on 'criticism, comment, news reporting, teaching, scholarship, or research'. Those six categories are, of course, the kinds of potential fair use mentioned in the preamble to the Copyright Act's fair use provision.[24] The fair use provision does not, however, grant fair use rights automatically to users in those six categories but rather sets forth four factors to be weighed in determining whether fair use status is to be accorded. The Digital Millennium Copyright Act also sets forth factors for the Librarian to apply, but they are different and include 'such other factors as the Librarian considers appropriate'.[25] In short, the impact of the Act on self-help systems remains somewhat up in the air. And since the rulemaking proceeding is to be repeated each three years, that impact will perhaps remain up in the air for some time.[26]

The American Law Institute Tentative Draft (April 15, 1998) of the UCC Article 2B on licenses (now transformed into the Uniform Computer Information Transaction Act, or UCITA) permits self-help systems in the

---

[22] 17 U.S.C. § 1201(a)(1)(A).   [23] 17 U.S.C. § 1201(a)(1)(B).
[24] See 17 U.S.C. § 107.   [25] 17 U.S.C. § 1201(a)(1)(C).
[26] The Digital Millennium Copyright Act also contains a narrowly drafted exemption from the circumvention prohibition to nonprofit libraries, archives, and educational institutions to gain access to a commercial work solely for the purpose of determining whether to acquire a copy in an otherwise lawful way. See 17 U.S.C. § 1201(d)(1).

commercial law context.[27] A review of its various provisions and of the reporters' notes suggests some principles that could be useful in more general regulation of self-help systems. One is that the content provider might be required to make the content recipient, including someone who independently finds the content provider web site, aware of the limitations on the ability to copy, transfer, or alter the file containing the content. But it would be possible to go further to encourage or even require a content provider to take technical steps to facilitate some kind of negotiation between licensor and licensee in certain defined 'fair use' types of situations. Indeed, one can imagine a scenario in which a recipient upon clicking, for example, a reviewer button would thereby obtain unrestricted access but be representing that access is for the purpose of writing a review and that copies will not be used for non-review distribution. Since the putative reviewer could later be legally held to this representation, content providers who seek reviews for their own success would likely find this kind of 'fair use' button access attractive.[28]

This fair use access principle can be generalized. The market failure explanation for fair use, which is that fair use normally involves a market failure situation precluding negotiation between the parties,[29] leads to the conclusion that by making negotiations automatic, transactions costs can be reduced greatly through electronic means.[30] Of course, where we are talking about derivative works, the content provider will want special payment, but at least self-help systems can, as suggested earlier, facilitate contact between the content provider and the person seeking to create derivative works. In academia and many technical fields, transformative uses will be favored by content

[27] See <http://www.nccusl.org/uniformact_factsheets/uniformacts-fs-ucita.htm>. Section 2B–310 of the April 15, 1998, draft states that a party 'entitled to enforce a limitation on use of information which does not depend on the existence of a breach of contract' may utilize a 'restraint' (defined as a 'program, code, device, or similar electronic or physical limitation that restricts use of information') under certain defined circumstances. Subsection (b)(2) makes clear that restraints may be used to prevent uses not granted by license whether they involve 'uses . . . inconsistent . . . with rights under informational property rights law' or, more controversially, 'uses . . . inconsistent with the agreement'; in other words, § 2B–310 places contract on a par with copyright with regard to self-help. In this respect art. 2B is consistent with the approach of *Aronson v. Quick Point Pencil Co.*, 440 U.S. 257 (1979), and *ProCD, Inc. v. Zeidenberg*, 86 F.3d 1447 (7th Cir. 1996), recognizing that contract applies between the parties, whereas copyright offers protection against third-party uses of intellectual property. Since art. 2B involves commercial law, it does not deal squarely with a major potential use of self-help systems, especially those employing encryption, which is to prevent copying where there is no contract and no intellectual property right. Another relevant provision is § 2B–716 (electronic self-help), limiting the right of an information licensor to use electronic means to exercise rights under § 2B–715 in the case of a breach by an information licensee.

[28] See William M. Landes & Richard A. Posner, *An Economic Analysis of Copyright Law*, 18 J. LEGAL STUD. 325, 358–59 (1989), indicating why publishers as a class benefit from even unfavorable reviews. The same principle is likely to apply to electronic content providers.

[29] See Wendy J. Gordon, *Fair Use as Market Failure: A Structural and Economic Analysis of the Betamax Case and Its Predecessors*, 82 COLUM. L. REV. 1600 (1982); Landes & Posner, n. 28 above, at 357–61.

[30] I. Trotter Hardy, *Property (and Copyright) in Cyberspace*, 1996 U. CHI. LEGAL F. 217.

providers so long as the accessing recipient agrees to give appropriate recognition (say by citing the source) to the content provider; a 'citation button' can be used to make the appropriate contractual commitment to give such recognition where use is made.[31]

Some readers may leap to the conclusion that such fair use buttons should be required. I believe such regulation would be unwise, and for three reasons. First, some such arrangements will arise spontaneously because it is in the interest of the content provider in many cases to make them. Secondly, such a requirement may undercut some desirable effects of some self-help technologies, such as the use of invisible digital watermarks in tracing the origin of knock-off copies sold to the public. Thirdly, the technological add-ons may raise the costs of self-help systems in some instances to an extent that would make them less useful in achieving their desirable goals. On the other hand, in the Librarian of Congress rulemaking proceeding envisaged by the Digital Millennium Copyright Act, one possible outcome would be to find that no person can be 'adversely affected' by the Act's circumvention provision 'in their ability to make noninfringing uses' to the extent that self-help systems provide fair use buttons.

In any case, some content providers may find that fair use buttons or related devices are in their own interest and therefore may want to encourage other content providers to use similar devices. If so, the development of industry standards is likely to be a preferable and more flexible approach, allowing different kinds of content providers to approach the fair use issue in quite different ways, thereby avoiding the deficiencies of a one-kind-fits-all legislative or rulemaking approach.[32]

---

[31] Of course, in some fair use situations, such as parody, agreement would often not be possible even at zero transactions costs, and therefore self-help systems are unlikely to provide for, say, a 'parody button'. See *Campbell v. Acuff-Rose Music, Inc.*, 510 U.S. 569, 592 (1994). In other words, even with the much lower transactions costs that electronic means provide, few content providers are likely to want, at least ab initio, to consider licensing a parody.

[32] See Frank H. Easterbrook, *Cyberspace and the Law of the Horse*, 1996 U. CHI. LEGAL F. 207, 214. Among the reasons that content providers might utilize the standards process are that industry-developed standards may (1) be more user friendly, enhancing user understanding and acceptance; (2) reduce the costs of implementation as off-the-shelf software incorporates the standards; and (3) avoid free-riding by content providers who find competitive advantage in being less open to fair use. It should be noted that it is private-sector standardization rather than legislation and regulation of the often proposed information superhighway variety that has led to nearly all of the progress in private networking and the Internet. See generally Joel R. Reidenberg, *Lex Informatica: The Formulation of Information Policy Rules through Technology*, 76 TEX. L. REV. 553 (1998); Lawrence Lessig, *Reading the Constitution in Cyberspace*, 45 EMORY L. J. 869, 896 (1996) (on the crucial importance of 'rules, or laws, inscribed in the software itself— the code, we might say').

V. Moral Rights and Deterrence

Criticisms of self-help systems often contrast providers' private quest for greater revenues with the public interest values embodied in the concept of fair use. Usually completely overlooked is that self-help systems can also serve purposes akin to moral rights, first by assuring *attribution* to the author, artist, or composer, and secondly by ensuring the *integrity* of documents, images, and music. The value of the attribution function is fairly straightforward, and means of achieving it through self-help systems have already been discussed above.

Integrity is a much less appreciated function. Self-help systems can harness the feature of digital copies that they will normally all be identical with one another. Self-help systems can help ensure that identity for the protection of the reputation of an author, artist, or composer. But many other integrity concerns that crop up repeatedly in a complex modern society can potentially be met by self-help systems. For example, they can also help protect against liability where distortion of the digitized information might lead to liability concerns, for example, a digitized human X-ray. Problems involving alteration of evidence in litigation or of digitized scientific data in scientific misconduct disputes can be avoided by linking source and time stamps to documents through invisible messages that can only be removed by a determined attacker. So too distortion of photographs and archives in political-historical contexts can be avoided by such techniques and by source and time information included in digital watermarks.

Still another little-appreciated function of some kinds of self-help systems is deterrence. Self-help systems are normally thought of as protecting the content provider. But where, for example, artistic works are involved, some self-help systems can protect artists who do not even use self-help systems. Take the invisible digital watermark. Pirates who become aware that such watermarks are being used to trace piracy would naturally choose to copy those artistic works that do not contain a watermark and avoid those works that do contain a watermark. But since watermarks are invisible to them, piracy of all artistic works posted on the Web will be deterred (at least in part), not just those works that actually contain the watermark.

As revealed in this invisible watermark example, self-help systems belong to a class of measures recently the subject of considerable economic research involving what may be called 'unobservable victim precaution'.[33] Such precautions produce positive externalities because they are unobservable. For example, in a study of LoJack, a hidden radio-transmitter device used for

---

[33] Ian Ayres & Steven D. Levitt, *Measuring Positive Externalities from Unobservable Victim Precaution: An Empirical Analysis of LoJack*, 113 Q. J. ECON. 43 (1998).

retrieving stolen vehicles, Ayres and Levitt found that the use of LoJack in a community results in a sharp decrease in auto theft at the same time that the rate of other kinds of crime in the community remains unchanged. Moreover, the authors calculated that those auto owners who use LoJack capture only one-tenth of the benefits of their use, yet the marginal social benefit of an additional unit of LoJack is 15 times greater than the marginal social cost in high-crime areas. Needless to say, Ayres and Levitt conclude that LoJack is underused.[34] Viewing invisible watermarks as an inexpensive application of the principle of unobserved victim precaution, one could easily conclude that the use of hidden watermarks, far from being viewed as a threat to the purposes of the copyright system, should be positively encouraged because it will deter a broad class of piracy involving images and audio.[35]

VI. Concerns About Self-Help Systems

At the outset of any discussion of objections to electronic online measures, it is useful to consider analogies from earlier periods. For example, self-help systems are sometimes analogized to commercial self-help remedies such as repossession. But other nonelectronic self-help technologies and techniques are perhaps more relevant to the general case of using electronic self-help systems to protect content. All kinds of technologies make it difficult for users to copy, even where they are entitled to do so.

The lock on my office door may make it difficult for even the most well meaning scholar or journalist to copy part of a manuscript or document, indeed even where copying would surely constitute fair use under the copyright statute. Similarly, simple business methods can make access in fact difficult. Indeed, even 'widely copied' content will be difficult to copy if the copier cannot, because of technology, access the material. Any company may have hundreds, even thousands of copies of highly sought after information available in the hands of its employees and customers (let us say in a beta test period). Imagine, for example, how many unauthorized users might like to copy the early source code on the next Windows version (which is likely to be already available to scores of application programming firms). Most, if not all, of that source code would be unprotectable under *Computer Associates International, Inc. v. Altai, Inc.*[36] and other software copyright decisions. Yet

---

[34] Ibid. See Ayres & Levitt for citations to other economic work bearing on positive externalities from unobserved victim precaution.

[35] The Ayres-Levitt study involves unobservable precautions and implies that they will have a salutary effect even if they do not work perfectly. Even more obviously observable self-help precautions will deter misappropriation even if they can be defeated by clever hackers. See Lessig, n. 32 above, at 897: 'But from the fact that "hackers could break any security system", it no more follows that security systems are irrelevant than it follows from the fact that "a locksmith can pick any lock", that locks are irrelevant'.

[36] 61 F.3d 6 (2d Cir. 1995).

firms like Microsoft use a network of beta test confidentiality agreements to make the source code available to some firms but to prevent access by others. In considering the concerns that have been raised about self-help systems, a question worth considering is why electronic self-help systems should be treated differently from other more primitive, but often highly effective, technologies and business methods.[37]

VII. The Role of Contract in Online Information Systems

In one important sense, an analysis of self-help issues as copyright issues presents much too narrow a framework. Perhaps the academic writing revolves around copyright and fair use because copyright doctrine is widely taught and understood. But with self-help systems, content is going to be charged for whether or not the content provider has any intellectual property rights in the content. It is the convenience of access that people will pay for. (Of course, they would rather not pay for it if they could avoid it, but that is another question.) For example, much of the content will be purely factual. There will be no pretense of copyright. In the worlds of business, personal investment, and, increasingly, personal entertainment, information—especially convenient just-in-time information—is of great value. People want it and want it now and will pay for it. In short, in an information-based services-oriented society, convenience is a driving factor behind contract. The exclusivity of the information, and especially the property rights in it, are not the economic basis driving the explosion of online contracting for information. In short, self-help systems can become an important facilitating device in an information-based service society.

---

[37] One possibility would be to distinguish between published and unpublished material, limiting the power of a copyright holder to use self-help systems with regard to published materials on the ground that once published, materials should be generally available on the same terms to all. The examples in the text concerning locked offices and beta testing involve unpublished materials where there is arguably a stronger case for allowing self-help protection. However, the Copyright Act specifically states that the 'fact that a work is unpublished shall not itself bar a finding of fair use if such finding is made upon consideration of all the above factors': 17 U.S.C. § 107. Publication still plays some role, however, in fair use doctrine where the unpublished nature of materials has been found to be a factor in denying a fair use defense in an infringement action. See *Harper & Row v. Nation Enterprises*, 471 U.S. 539 (1985); and, for an analysis, William M. Landes, *Copyright Protection of Letters, Diaries, and Other Unpublished Works: An Economic Approach*, 21 J. LEGAL STUD. 79 (1992). But this distinction, even if recognized, would not preclude the use of self-help systems for content provided only subject to the self-help system (that is, otherwise unpublished). Nor does it address the use of self-help systems outside the realm of copyrighted material. In any event, nothing in the law of fair use requires a copyright holder to continue publishing or to refrain from charging once a copy has been given away free or at a lower price. Indeed, if a work has already been published, there are presumably copies of the copyrighted work 'out there' available to the fair user so that there is no absolute need for the fair user to access new copies being made available only under self-help systems. Nothing in copyright law requires a copyright owner to make special arrangements to facilitate copying by a fair user.

Information is, for this purpose, much like tangible things that people want and will pay for. One has to ask what possible justification could be advanced for interfering with the market system by in effect legitimizing third-party actions that make transacting more difficult or more costly. Surely noncopyrightable information is as much an economic good as unprotectable functional tangible products whose design can be freely copied (provided one can get close enough to them to actually copy without violating unrelated laws, such as those against trespassing). By increasing transactions costs, a prime result will likely be that less content will be provided. Higher costs mean less supply, for reasons obvious even to those offended by economics. This conclusion is not affected by placing the label 'public domain' on the content. To say that something is in the public domain is to say that it is not protected by copyright, not that one who has it has to make it easy to copy and cannot take measures to make it more difficult to copy. The Louvre has the Mona Lisa, a prototypical public domain painting, but surely the Louvre is not required to allow students and artists (or even art reviewers and parodists) to set up easels for copying it or to allow them to take photographs or even to admit them without charge to the museum so that they can copy covertly.

What most people have in mind who would like to limit self-help systems is, I suspect, that thought and ideas should be disseminated as broadly as possible. Although that objective surely underlies the institution of copyright, it is not clear that it means that the copyright owner should be under a greater obligation to facilitate copying or even to avoid steps to make copying harder just because some user may be a fair user. Such a principle would, if applied without qualification, have unforeseeable ramifications. Would such a principle mean that an author or publisher should be required to print a minimum number of copies so that those who wished to photocopy would more easily be able to find one to copy? Would it mean that a motion picture company would be required to make movies available in videotape form and could not simply limit their availability to conventional movie theaters? Would someone who republishes a book in the public domain have, a fortiori, an even stronger obligation to make the republished book easily available for copying?

All of this kind of analysis is great fun and games. But it is a reasonable conjecture that self-help systems will facilitate, not stem, the spread of ideas. This conclusion is based in part on the belief that most people do not like the idea of transgressing others' rights, though many will do so if they perceive that it is difficult to obtain permission or to make payment.

Self-help systems will make small payments easy and efficient. When digital cash becomes common for storing in a computer or on a smart card insertible in a computer, users can effectively pay the small amount that will be charged for the right to make a copy. Indeed, digital cash can become the small change of the information economy; it can be available for micropayments and, especially important in the realm of ideas, can preserve the anonymity of the payer (just as I can buy a newspaper or a political tract with pocket change without revealing my identity).

VIII. Self-Help and Social Norms

On another plane, self-help systems will also facilitate the change in public mores that will be required to make paying for information seem to be the thing to do rather than an encroachment on freedom. (In the realm of tangible information goods, most people would rather pay for a daily paper than steal a copy from a newsstand even if they were sure that they would not be caught; yet many of those same people will simply take a copy if there is nobody around to receive payment).[38] The notion that online information should be free is one that, I predict, well prove to be heavily influenced by the ease of payment, an important element of transactions costs. Technology can promote ethics and the public good by reducing transactions costs.[39]

My argument in this respect is inspired by recent work on social norms.[40] Much of the social norm discussion emphasizes the role of government in promoting desirable social norms and widespread adherence to them. What I argue here is that in the self-help systems context private contracting can be the vehicle for promoting the development of such social norms and adherence to them. The technology of self-help systems lowers transactions costs (especially when coupled with digital cash through increasing the convenience of payment) and thereby reduces undesirable social behavior such as free-riding appropriation of content created by others. As transactions costs go down (including convenience going up), it is easier for people to do what they intuitively feel is the 'right thing' (that is, paying or obtaining permission for copying content others have created). As more people do this 'right thing',

---

[38] I recognize that physically taking a copy of a newspaper may in some cases deprive another reader access to that newspaper copy, unlike the online case where my downloading or copying information does not affect other users. (The difference is not so great in practice as in the classroom since theft from a newsstand usually simply reduces the return to the publisher or distributor by the amount of money the thief fails to pay.) The point, however, is that the decision to take with or without paying is one that is heavily influenced by the ease of paying.

[39] To use a well-known analogy, many people now find it natural to segregate their trash even though it takes time and effort when previously they found it an outrageous infringement on their personal freedom to be asked to do so. The change is not merely the result of public preaching about the environment. It also has to do with the various techniques—different colored trash containers and the like—that municipalities have used to make the separation easier, faster, and more convenient. In the trash case, transactions costs of high-minded acts have been reduced by municipal assistance measures.

[40] See, e.g., CASS SUNSTEIN, FREE MARKETS AND SOCIAL JUSTICE 32–69 (1997). On social norms, see generally Eric A. Posner, *Efficient Norms*, NEW PALGRAVE DICTIONARY OF ECONOMICS AND THE LAW 19 (Peter Newman ed. 1998).

others are more likely to be motivated to do it as well, thereby further strengthening the influence of what until now has been in the online context a quite shaky social norm. This argument is independent of the additional point that self-help systems, by making piracy difficult, encourage content creators to provide more content in the widely available low-cost environment.[41]

Even on the intellectual property home turf of copyright, a key point is that self-help systems can also be developed that will facilitate some of the core ideas behind copyright by inducing people to abide voluntarily with the policy behind those ideas. The first-sale rule, for example, is not one that limits just the rights owner; it also has implications for users. Users could be induced to live by the spirit of the first-sale doctrine through self-help systems that, as previously discussed, make it difficult to transfer a downloaded file without submitting to the erasure of their own file. Most of us do not photocopy a book before lending it to a friend, not just because it is 'wrong' to do so, but also because it is inconvenient.

Similarly, it is probable that some kinds of content providers, at least in the realm of ideas, will want to facilitate transformative uses so long as acknowledgment of their own work is made. Self-help systems may contribute to the academic ethic by, as suggested above, allowing users to copy a file by clicking on a button that constitutes acknowledgment of their duty to cite the copied work if it is included in their own future work. To fail to make the citation will weigh on most academics' minds, and failure to cite under such circumstances may indeed affect the copier's academic reputation.

For content providers, workable technological arrangements to accommodate fair users would be a win-win solution. They would receive protection against piracy while, by recognizing the public policy goals of fair use principles, accommodating what is likely to be political opposition to self-help systems.

One can of course invent situations where it is difficult to imagine the technology that could accommodate the fair user, but anyone who sells technology short by saying 'it can't be done' has very little experience with technology. And even if there is a one-off situation that can be invented in the classroom, it does not follow that fair users as a class will not be far

---

[41] Computer and software technology, by lowering transactions costs (including enhancing convenience), can be expected to contribute to more optimal social behavior in other realms as well. For example, James T. Hamilton, in CHANNELING VIOLENCE 302–3 (1998), makes a persuasive case that the combination of privately developed systems of TV ratings using the privately developed PICS standard together with privately developed V-chip technology could reduce exposure of some children to violent TV programming: 'The rating system reduces the transaction cost to parents of determining program content, so that they do not have to bear extensive costs of investigating the content of unfamiliar programs or movies [while the] V-chip technology dramatically lowers the costs of acting upon the ratings information'. On the private development of the PICS standard, see Reidenberg, n. 32 above, at 558–60.

ahead because the added security for content and the ease of payment by users will greatly increase the content available.[42]

Some critics will of course object categorically to any system that is used, especially on the Net, to charge for access. The fact that information can be a public good often obscures the appropriate analysis. Too often noneconomists draw the conclusion that, since one person's use of information does not raise the costs of another person's use, such uses should be free. But the problem is of course that information is costly to produce and often costly to distribute. Hence, we have the patent and copyright systems. Contract, backed up by self-help systems, can solve the public goods problem by generating the resources necessary to fund the production and distribution of information. With competition in the content provider industries, there is no more reason to expect monopoly returns than there is in tangible goods industries. On the contrary, competition and the desire to be first to market with new kinds of content can be expected to drive per-use prices down sharply, just as they often do for software, which also has public goods characteristics. Indeed, in this sense, contract with self-help may be superior in some circumstances to copyright and patent protection.

With regard to fair users as a class, I have serious doubts that there will in practice prove to be a serious 'fair use' problem, even if I am wrong in predicting (see earlier discussion) that self-help systems will evolve to accommodate many classes of fair users, such as reviewers. All that will be precluded by most self-help systems is the ability to use a computer software cut-and-paste function. It will still be possible to use the fair use techniques of yesteryear of simply writing down what is on the screen, or, if one copy is permitted, to 'cut and paste' (using old-fashioned nonvirtual scissors and paste) from that copy. This example suggests that technology will in general put fair users ahead of where most of them were little more than a decade ago and in the typical case put them far ahead because of the greater volume of content available. The problem that self-help systems solve is to permit society to benefit from the lower transactions costs of online delivery and of the much lower search costs of putting information buyers and sellers together while at the same time lowering costs of misappropriation and free-riding on the creation and distribution of convenient information.

---

[42] An important question is what, other than the inconvenience (high transactions costs) of obtaining permission and making payment, accounts for the widespread belief within American society that uncompensated copying of materials on the Net by end users is unobjectionable and should even be sacrosanct. Professor Ginsburg has addressed this question in passing in discussing the relative rights of authors and users. See Ginsburg, n. 1 above, at 17–18. I do not have a good answer to this puzzle, but no doubt it has something to do with several generations brought up on videotaping, audiocassette copying, and photocopying. Perhaps anthropologists and sociologists can tell us whether such attitudes are irreversible. But I insist that we will never know for certain unless obtaining permission and making payment become a great deal more convenient.

IX. Conclusion

In sum, if we refrain from the kinds of regulation and legal rules that discourage self-help systems, fair users as a class are likely to benefit because the amount and quality of content available over the Net will expand at a far greater rate for the reasons previously given. The challenge is thus how to harness self-help systems technology to further the broad societal aims implicit in the fair use concept without adopting measures that will make it more difficult or costly to implement such systems.

6

INSTITUTIONS FOR INTELLECTUAL PROPERTY TRANSACTIONS: THE CASE OF PATENT POOLS

ROBERT P. MERGES*

In this Chapter I hope to accomplish three things: briefly summarize trends in the economic theory of intellectual property rights (IPRs); describe some ideas of my own on the emergence of IPR exchange institutions, and describe how an emphasis on institutions fits into existing theory; and ground these issues in a discussion of collective IPR licensing, in particular, patent pools. I begin with a discussion of how transactions have crept into intellectual property theory, and then turn to an examination of actual institutions that have evolved out of the need for various industries to conduct a large volume of IPR transactions.

* Wilson Sonsini Goodrich & Rosati Professor of Law and Technology, University of California at Berkeley (Boalt Hall) School of Law

I. The Theoretical Literature

Economists have been arguing the merits of IPRs since at least the eighteenth century, though serious theorizing began only in the nineteenth.[1] From the beginning, the literature was concerned primarily with the ultimate question of whether IPRs could be justified. As a simplifying assumption, and no doubt in part as a reflection of real-world conditions, individual property rights were assumed to be roughly coextensive with economic markets. A patent, for example, was conceived as a property right over a single, coherent product occupying a distinct economic market. Eli Whitney's patent on the cotton gin is a canonical example. Likewise a copyright was discussed as a property right over a particular book or map. In this way, debate over the consequences of IPRs could be conducted in the language of economics: IPRs were legally-granted 'monopolies', whose distortionary effects on competitive markets could be defended or attacked in familiar cost-benefit terms. This view of IPRs can be described as a simple 'tradeoff model': it sought to determine whether the costs of monopoly outweighed the benefits of legal inducements to create new works.

A. IPRs and transaction costs

In this early theory, the transactional role of IPRs is limited to facilitating product markets. The promise of a patent leads to the creation of the cotton gin, for example, and thence to a market for it.[2] Likewise with copyright: in the prototypical example, legal protection enables an author to sell his or her book to readers.[3] This 'one property right per marketable work' image of things simplified discussion, to be sure. Under it, the only relevant question is one of net effects: is the increased effort that the prospect of an exclusive right calls forth worth what Jefferson called 'the embarrassment' of a state-backed monopoly?[4] Commentators assumed that the reward took the form of exclusivity in a discrete end-product market.

---

[1] See generally Machlup, *An Economic Review of the Patent System, Study No. 15 of the Subcomm. on Patents, Trademarks, and Copyrights of the Senate Comm. on the Judiciary*, 85th Cong., 2d Sess. (1958) (economic overview of patent system as whole); Paul A. David, Intellectual Property and the Panda's Thumb: Patents, Copyrights and Trade Secrets in Economic Theory and History, *in* GLOBAL DIMENSIONS OF INTELLECTUAL PROPERTY RIGHTS IN SCIENCE AND TECHNOLOGY 19 (Mitchel B. Wallerstein et al. eds., 1993).

[2] See Machlup, n. 1 above; WILLIAM NORDHAUS, INVENTION, GROWTH AND WELFARE (1969).

[3] See Stephen Breyer, *The Uneasy Case for Copyright: A Study of Copyright in Books, Photocopies, and Computer Programs*, 84 HARV. L. REV. 281 (1970), for a summary of the older literature.

[4] The phrase is from a letter from Thomas Jefferson. See XIII WRITINGS OF THOMAS JEFFERSON 335 (Andrew J. Lipscomb ed., 1903).

This image lay undisturbed in the minds of economists until the important paper by Kenneth Arrow in 1962. In this paper, Arrow shifted the focus from product markets to markets for *information*, in keeping with his research agenda at the time.[5] Patents became, in Arrow's hands, a mechanism for encouraging information disclosure. Without such protection, the buyer of information, who presumably needs access to it to determine its worth, would never pay anything; or else, she would have to be content to buy it without seeing it—an arrangement not conducive to a robust market.

Arrow thus recognized that IPRs occupy a related, but separate, set of markets from the assets that embody them. Indeed, IPRs play a crucial role in creating the *possibility* of exchange in these markets. Implicit in Arrow's theory is that one firm may need to purchase informational inputs from another firm—and that patents facilitate this process. Arrow set the stage for a new type of theory, one that recognized the need to assemble information and property rights from disparate sources in the process of bringing a product to market. In this new theory, IPRs do not simply *reside* in marketable products; they are the subject of markets in their own right. They serve a *transactional* function, encouraging and perhaps even enabling, the integration of pieces of information produced by disparate, independent firms. By focusing on markets for information, Arrow eliminated the assumption that property rights were coextensive with economic markets for final (tangible) products.

It took some time for this insight to sink in. One indication that things had begun to change was a series of papers on patent scope. Merges and Nelson, Scotchmer, and others became interested in how property rights were allocated among sequential innovators in various industries.[6] This literature had as its chief concern the role of property rights in dividing the spoils—and setting the stage for private bargaining—between early (pioneer) inventors and follow-on improvers. Typically, papers in this genre explore how the details of IPR rules and doctrines affect the bargaining environment facing the sequential innovators. Property rights are important because they necessitate and structure transactions. The pioneer-improver paradigm reinvigorated thinking about how economic agents integrate disparate IPRs, so that viable products can reach the market.

The recently developed 'anticommons' theory, which is associated with Michael Heller and (as applied to IPR problems) with Heller and Rebecca Eisenberg, advances this theme by more explicitly analyzing interactions

[5] See Kenneth J. Arrow, *Economic Welfare and the Allocation of Resources to Invention*, in THE RATE AND DIRECTION OF INVENTIVE ACTIVITIES (Richard R. Nelson ed., 1962), *reprinted in* ESSAYS IN THE THEORY OF RISK-BEARING (1974).

[6] See Robert P. Merges & Richard R. Nelson, *On the Complex Economics of Patent Scope*, 90 COLUM. L. REV. 839, 888–93 (1990) (hereinafter Merges & Nelson, *Patent Scope*); Suzanne Scotchmer, *Standing on the Shoulders of Giants: Cumulative Research and the Patent Law*, 5 J. ECON. PERSP. 29 (1991).

between property rights and transactions.[7] The basic idea is that granting too many property rights of too small a scale can preclude effective exploitation of economic resources. Heller defines an 'anticommons' as an economic resource that is covered by a large number of individual exclusionary rights. Businesspeople must bundle numerous rights to make good use of the resource.[8] If various impediments to bargaining are present, this may prove difficult; as a result, the resource may be underutilized.[9] Heller applies this notion to a number of situations, with special attention to retail stores in postcommunist Russia. In a separate article, Heller and Eisenberg deploy anticommons theory in a critique of patents on short fragments of human genes:

The problem we identify is distinct from the routine underuse inherent in any well-functioning patent system. By conferring monopolies on discoveries, patents necessarily increase prices and restrict use—a cost society pays to motivate invention and disclosure. The tragedy of the anticommons refers to the more complex obstacles that arise when a user needs access to multiple patented inputs to create a single useful product. Each upstream patent allows its owner to set up another tollbooth on the road to product development, adding to the cost and slowing the pace of downstream biomedical innovation.[10]

The authors present two 'current examples in biomedical research': the creation of 'too many concurrent fragments of [IPRs] in potential future products', and rules permitting 'too many upstream patent owners to stack licenses on top of the future discoveries of downstream users'.[11]

More recently, Heller has turned to solutions.[12] He argues that various property doctrines forestall anticommons by preventing excessive fragmentation of rights. As examples, Heller identifies doctrines as diverse as minimum lot size zoning in real estate law, and the utility requirement in patent law. Describing the latter example, and elaborating on his article with Eisenberg, Heller explains:

---

[7] See Michael A. Heller, *The Boundaries of Private Property*, 108 YALE L.J. 1163 (1999) (hereinafter Heller, *The Boundaries of Private Property*); Michael A. Heller & Rebecca S. Eisenberg, *Can Patents Deter Innovation? The Anticommons in Biomedical Research*, 280 SCI. 698 (1998) (hereinafter Heller & Eisenberg).

[8] See Michael A. Heller, *The Tragedy of the Anticommons: Property in the Transition from Marx to Markets*, 111 HARV. L. REV. 621 (1998) (hereinafter Heller, *The Tragedy of the Anticommons*).

[9] 'If people hold multiple rights to exclude each other from a resource, they must incur the transaction costs of finding out with whom to negotiate. Despite the presence of transaction costs, people will be able in many cases to negotiate with each other to overcome an anticommons and put the property to more efficient use . . . On the other hand, even if the number of parties and transaction costs are low, the resource still may not be efficiently used because of bargaining failures generated by holdouts, as sometimes seems to happen with Moscow storefronts': ibid at 674 (footnotes omitted). Heller's references to 'transaction costs' here and elsewhere reveal a tight connection with the economic theorizing of Oliver Williamson. See, e.g., OLIVER WILLIAMSON, THE MECHANISMS OF GOVERNANCE (1998); THE ECONOMIC INSTITUTIONS OF CAPITALISM (1985).

[10] Heller & Eisenberg, n. 7 above, at 699.   [11] Ibid.

[12] Heller, *The Boundaries of Private Property*, n. 7 above.

To give an intellectual property example, patent law only weakly prevents excessive fragmentation in biomedical research. Old-fashioned boundary doctrines, such as the 'utility' requirement in patent law, have not kept pace with technological change. Rebecca Eisenberg and I have argued that creating property rights in isolated gene fragments seems unlikely to track socially useful bundles of property rights—a form of excessive 'physical' fragmentation.[13]

The emphasis on obstacles to bundling, and solutions rooted in close attention to 'boundary problems', highlights the transactional orientation of anticommons theory. This is a break with past IPR theory, as we have seen. But it also represents a break with received wisdom in the general economic theory of property rights. Indeed, the explicit emphasis on transactions is an attempt not only to move IPR theory more into alignment with observed features of the commercial world, but also to do the same for the more general economic theory of property rights. In the process, almost without noticing it (and certainly without commenting on it), the newer transactional theory of IPRs holds the potential partially to bridge the gap between the general literature on property rights and the more specialized work on IPRs.

Property rights theory in economics has not traditionally been especially concerned with bargaining among multiple rightholders. Ronald Coase, Harold Demsetz, and other earlier theorists worried primarily about the initial grant of rights to *individual owners*. For them, property rights are the solution of choice when one person's actions affect the wellbeing of others. Thus Coase argued the benefits of establishing clear entitlements where land holdings adjoined spark-emitting railroads, and where farms were set amidst roaming livestock.[14] Demsetz studied rights over fur-bearing animals in colonial North America. He applauded the switch from common use to private ownership when the economic value of furs increased. In other early papers, Demsetz argued that economic actors refine property rights to keep pace with developments in enforcement and monitoring costs.[15] While Coase and Demsetz showed some concern for the costs of moving rights around, this was not their primary focus. They emphasized the scope and content of property rights: the state's definition of the rights of property holders.

The newer transactional theories depart from this tradition. They worry a great deal about what owners do with their property rights *after* the state grants them. Heller has for the most part emphasized 'tragedies', or transactional *failures*;[16] so too Heller and Eisenberg with respect to patents.[17] Multiple, discrete rights give many owners the right to exclude, which creates

[13] Ibid at 1174–75.
[14] See Ronald Coase, *The Problem of Social Cost*, 3 J. L. & ECON. 1 (1960).
[15] See Harold Demsetz, *Toward a Theory of Property Rights*, 57 AM. ECON. REV. 347 (1967).
[16] See Heller, *The Boundaries of Private Property*, n. 7 above; Heller, *The Tragedy of the Anticommons*, n. 8 above.
[17] See Heller & Eisenberg, n. 7 above.

the conditions for failure in their example because of the high costs of bundling together the necessary rights. Heller identifies bargaining failures, holdup problems in particular, as a key reason for anticommons tragedies. As he points out, in many settings rights are held by parties who will not undergo repeat interactions. A one-shot bargaining game results, where some party must assemble disparate rights to move forward with a valuable economic project. This is a setting ripe for holdups and bargaining breakdown, as the economic literature has long recognized.[18] This is true even in cases where only a few parties must bargain to strike a deal,[19] and notwithstanding that private contracting sometimes achieves bundling.

These successful bargained-for solutions were the subject of my article on 'Bargaining into Liability Rules'.[20] I found that multiple private rightholders bargained with each other in forming collective rights organizations in a number of industries. In many cases the resulting arrangements started as simple bilateral contracts between parties that had (or expected to have) repeated interactions with each other. Some such contracts matured into full-blown, freestanding administrative entities responsible for widescale licensing of large bundles of members' intellectual property rights. This 'repeat-play' feature is somewhat similar to the 'close knit' societies examined so skillfully by property theorist Robert Ellickson, although in the cases Ellickson studied formal entitlements play a relatively minor role in structuring most negotiations.[21]

Economist Gary Libecap has explored dysfunctional bargaining in the setting of oil field 'unitization'.[22] Libecap's studies center on oil fields governed by separate claims, held by independent owners. Potential efficiencies await owners who agree to treat the entire oilfield as a single 'unit'. For example, such an agreement can prevent wasteful 'pumping races' which are expensive and result in lower oil yields. But Libecap's research shows that despite the presence of gains from cooperation, owners of oil field claims often fail to reach agreement.

Anticommons theory tells a series of similar cautionary tales about the doleful effects of too many overlapping property rights. Other recent theory

---

[18] See Guido Calabresi & A. Douglas Melamed, *Property Rules, Liability Rules, and Inalienability: One View of the Cathedral*, 85 HARV. L. REV. 1089, 1092 (1972); GARY LIBECAP, CONTRACTING FOR PROPERTY RIGHTS (1989); Robert P. Merges, *Of Property Rules, Coase, and Intellectual Property*, 94 COLUM. L. REV. 2655 (1994) (hereinafter Merges, *Of Property Rules and Coase*).

[19] See Heller, *The Tragedy of the Anticommons*, n. 8 above, at 674.

[20] Robert P. Merges, *Contracting into Liability Rules: Intellectual Property Rights and Collective Rights Organizations*, 84 CAL. L. REV. 1293 (1996) (hereinafter Merges, *Contracting into Liability Rules*).

[21] See ROBERT ELLICKSON, ORDER WITHOUT LAW: HOW NEIGHBORS SETTLE DISPUTES (1991) (hereinafter ELLICKSON, ORDER WITHOUT LAW); Robert Ellickson, *Property in Land*, 102 YALE L.J. 1315, 1329 (1993) (hereinafter Ellickson, *Property in Land*).

[22] See LIBECAP, n. 18 above.

is more optimistic: it examines voluntary exchange among disparate rightholders, recounting examples of what might be called transactional *success* stories.[23] In one respect the optimists and anticommons 'pessimists' agree: the key issue is the cost of integrating disparate rights. But the optimists describe situations where rightholders establish formal and informal mechanisms—loosely, 'institutions'—to bring these costs down. One example is the emergence of collective copyright licensing organizations, such as ASCAP.[24] This organization, and others like it, serves two functions. It gathers together a large number of musical composition copyrights, which permits it to issue a 'blanket license' for all songs in its repertoire. This reduces transaction costs for large-volume users of music, such as radio and television stations. In addition, ASCAP distributes a share of the blanket licensing fees as payments to individual copyright holders. It does so using a complicated formula based on the estimated number of uses of each composition, determined through a combination of internal rate-setting procedures and sophisticated sampling techniques. ASCAP is governed by weighted voting rules, under which each member has a vote in proportion to the number of copyrights it has contributed and the value of each, as determined by past royalty distributions.[25]

Patent pools are a second example of an IPR-based collective rights organization. A patent pool is an arrangement among multiple patent holders to aggregate their patents. A typical pool makes all pooled patents available to each member of the pool. Pools also usually offer standard licensing terms to licensees who are not members of the pool. In addition, the typical patent pool allocates a portion of the licensing fees to each member according to a pre-set formula or procedure.

In both copyright collectives and patent pools, rightholders combine far-flung property rights into useable bundles, overcoming the tragedy of the anticommons while preserving the incentives that come with these rights. In basic terms, the optimists assume nothing more than that conventional economic principles apply. With 'gains from trade' to be had, the parties figure out a deal that makes everyone better off. (Even pessimists concede this will often be true.)[26] The only twist is a nod in the direction of transaction cost

---

[23] See, eg, Merges, *Contracting into Liability Rules*, n. 20 above; Peter Grindley & David J. Teece, *Managing Intellectual Capital: Licensing and Cross-Licensing in Semiconductors and Electronics*, 39 CAL. MGMT. REV. 2 (1997).

[24] 'ASCAP' stands for the American Society of Composers, Authors, and Publishers. It is a collective rights organization that acts as a nonexclusive licensing agency for the owners of musical composition copyrights. It, along with Broadcast Music Incorporated (BMI), issues most of the public performance licenses that permit copyrighted songs to be played on radio and television, in bars and restaurants, and in most other public places.

[25] See Merges, *Contracting into Liability Rules*, n. 20 above, at 1338–40.

[26] 'Despite the presence of transaction costs, people will be able in many cases to negotiate with each other to overcome an anticommons and put the property to more efficient use . . . On the other hand, even if the number of parties and transaction costs are low, the resource still may

economics: for optimists, an institution creates a mechanism that lowers the average cost of transactions enough to make ongoing exchange worthwhile. In terms of traditional entitlements theory, this amounts to no more than a large helping of Coase, with a serving of Ellickson on the side.

The preceding, and in particular the optimist-pessimist terminology, implies that rival theorists differ only in the attitudes they bring to their studies. This is not really so, the theories do interpret things differently, but more importantly, at least to date, they *interpret different things*. Anticommons theory as applied to IPRs has concentrated on patents for short gene sequences. These are held by numerous entities that are both far-flung and (for the most part) small. Their value, furthermore, is as yet highly uncertain. In many cases researchers do not yet know if a particular gene corresponds to (or 'codes for') anything useful, let alone a highly valuable protein product. But anticommons theorists believe that *when* a gene is found to be valuable, it may be devilishly difficult for scattered, self-interested rightholders to agree on an effective multilateral licensing scheme. In the worst case, patients may be deprived of therapies that might help.[27]

The optimists have not for the most part studied the gene fragment 'business', which in any case is still forming. They have instead concentrated on two types of industries: (1) established, technology-intensive industries, where the lineup of players is fairly stable, technological complementarities are common, and patent pools are a familiar sight on the industrial landscape; and (2) industries where IPR-producers are widely scattered but buyers need to buy in bulk, which creates demand for large *packages* of IPRs—music collectives (such as ASCAP) being the classic example. In the first case, firms organize patent pools to regularize frequent interactions. In the second, IPR holders create collectives such as ASCAP to bundle individual rights into more marketable packages.

Only recently has property rights scholarship honed in on the importance of transactions. And with so few data points, it is too early to decide on a general rule of pessimism or optimism. (We do know that each seems right in at least some cases so far.) We must begin to collect a list of factors that typically accompany anticommons tragedies, on the one hand, and institution-forming successes on the other. (This chapter's Conclusion takes a tentative step in this direction.)

---

not be efficiently used because of bargaining failures generated by holdouts, as sometimes seems to happen with Moscow storefronts.': Heller, *The Tragedy of the Anticommons*, n. 8 above, at 674.

[27] See Eisenberg, Chapter 9 below.

B. IPRs and property-liability rule theory

For a transaction cost optimist, collective organizations such as ASCAP and patent pools are fascinating and instructive. They reveal what brings individual rightholders together to resolve transactional bottlenecks. Soon after coming together, one of the first things they do is to settle two issues of valuation: the rates licensees will pay for access to the entire pool; and rules for dividing the spoils among the pool's members. In the case of licensing rates, the price(s) are the same for all takers, or at least for all licensees of similar size.[28] Through their collectively-determined prices, these institutions operate in much the same way as a compulsory license.[29] Essentially all comers are welcome to use the right(s), so long as they pay the preestablished price.

Of course, there is one major difference between private collectives and conventional, statutory compulsory licenses: in these organizations, the members, and not Congress or a court, set the price. This almost always involves extensive negotiations; sometimes, ongoing adjustments are carried out via a permanent administrative structure. The point is, however, that the collective organizations present a simple, coherent menu of prices and other terms to licensees—and that they do so after extensive internal consultation.

Group action like this is interesting not only for its internal dynamics, however. It also sheds light on a discussion central to entitlement theory, which is known as the Calabresi-Melamed Framework. The essence of this Framework is this: Calabresi and Melamed assign all legal entitlements to one of two rules, 'property rules' and 'liability rules'. The former are best described as 'absolute permission rules': one cannot take these entitlements without prior permission of the owner. The rightholder, acting individually, thus sets the price. Most real estate fits this description.

By contrast, liability rules are best described as 'take now, pay later'. They allow for non-owners to take the entitlement without permission of the owner, so long as they adequately compensate the owner later. In the Calabresi-Melamed Framework, ex post adequate compensation is deemed 'collective valuation'. And in their examples, it is always a court that performs the valuation. The government's power of eminent domain—where a state agency takes property, and a court determines the fair price for it—is the classic example of a liability rule. As another example, parties to a contract are usually said to possess this sort of right; they can breach the contract if they like, so long as they pay damages after the fact (ex post) sufficient, in the eyes of a court, to compensate the other party for the breach.

The organizations studied in this chapter present what might seem a paradox in light of the literature on entitlements: they produce what look like lia-

---

[28] See discussion below at III A and B, for a description of differential royalty rates for different classes of licensees.

[29] This is a license, granted by law, from a rightholder to a user.

bility rules to users, but they are based on IPRs—quintessential property rule entitlements.[30]

It is not a paradox, however; and it is certainly not coincidence. The gist of my argument is that the high costs of repeat contracting—both among members, and between members and users—drive the rightholders to pool their property rights in a collective organization. The relatively uniform terms offered by this organization then lower the costs of exchange with users. At the same time, the organization's internal rules for dividing up royalties save on member-to-member transaction costs. Rightholders establish these organizations in response to high transaction costs. In other words, property rule entitlements engender a liability rule-like regime based on private, though collective, determinations of economic value.

The organizations I study here therefore contribute the following important insight: they show that valuation of an entitlement can occur not just at the levels of the individual, on the one hand, or the government, on the other, but also on the level of a private collective organization. These institutions are intermediate forums for the valuation of entitlements. Because these organizations offer a fixed menu of terms to all comers, and because the menu is determined by the members and not the government, I call them 'private liability rule' organizations. Similarly, I call the process of creating them 'contracting into liability rules', because the contracting parties start with property rule entitlements, and wind up subject to a collectively-determined liability rule.

C. The effects of lower enforcement costs

The decision to found or join collective IPR institutions turns on exchange and enforcement costs. If the institution lowers the cost of exchange and enforcement, it makes sense to join. If not, it is better for each rightholder to stick to private enforcement.

Although economic theorizing about the choice of enforcement methods is still in its infancy, one model of this choice deserves mention here. Thrainn Eggertson, summarizing a field study and associated model by B.C. Field,[31] makes the insightful observation that institutions can substitute for private property rights.[32] Where a collective institution lowers the cost of excluding trespassers (or infringers), it can be used to augment private enforcement of

---

[30] For an explanation of why intellectual property rights are almost always property rule entitlements, see Merges, *Of Property Rules and Coase*, n. 18 above.

[31] Barry C. Field, *The Evolution of Property Rights*, 42 KYKLOS 319 (1989). The version of the Field paper cited by Eggertson is an earlier, unpublished draft.

[32] THRAINN EGGERTSON, ECONOMIC BEHAVIOR AND INSTITUTIONS 257 (1990). But see Ellickson, *Property in Land*, n. 21 above, at 1329 ('In sum, a shift from group to individual ownership of land substitutes the relatively cheap systems of self-control and boundary monitoring for the relatively costly system of pervasive intragroup monitoring'). Ellickson thus *assumes* that group monitoring is always more expensive. See also ibid at 1398 (ease of monitoring boundary crossings compared to difficulty of monitoring activities of group member on collective land).

property rights. Field's model relates to decisions regarding the optimal parcel size for real property holdings by members of a community. He is concerned with showing that, where community members must police against damage from trespassers, efficiency is not necessarily served by small parcel sizes. (This is so even though, for well-understood reasons, small parcel size is associated with significant advantages.) It makes sense, under certain circumstances, for individuals to in a sense cede some property rights to the community, in the form of sharing in larger parcels rather than owning smaller ones outright. In some cases this creates efficiencies in enforcement against trespassers. Hence overall efficiency—taking into account one transaction cost, the cost of enforcement—is improved.

Models such as this help explain some features of IPR institutions. Firms in an industry are faced with the decision whether to rely on individual rights to exclude infringers or pool rights in a collective organization. They trade off enforcement costs associated with individual rights against the costs of founding and participating in the institution. Although joining such an institution involves ceding some individual control, it may lower costs overall. If so, firms will decide to join.

II. Emergence of Exchange Institutions in the Presence of Property Rights: Patent Pools

As an illustration of unadorned private liability rules, few institutions compare to the patent pool. Multiple patent holders assign or license their individual rights to a central entity, which in turn exploits the collective rights by licensing, manufacturing, or both. In addition, and most importantly, the pool regularizes the *valuation* of individual patents, making, as the Supreme Court put it, 'a division of royalties according to the value attributed by the parties to their respective patent claims'.[33]

Patent pools, like collective rights organizations in copyright, thus serve to regularize technology transactions. Indeed, at least one court has noted the similarity between ASCAP and patent pools.[34] Like ASCAP, their basic economic rationale is that they significantly reduce the transaction costs of exchanging rights when compared to a series of one-shot licensing deals. When they are not being used as a cover for a cartel,[35] they add significantly

[33] *Standard Oil Co. (Ind.) v. United States*, 283 U.S. 163, 167–68 (1931) (emphasis added).

[34] See *Columbia Broad. Sys., Inc. v. ASCAP*, 562 F.2d 130, 133 n.17 (2d Cir. 1977) ('There is, moreover, some analogy to the patent pooling cases . . . [O]n the surface, the pool of copyrights may be analogized to a pool of competing patents').

[35] On pools and cartels, see George Priest, *Cartels and Patent License Arrangements*, 20 J.L. & ECON. 309 (1977); CARL KAYSEN & DONALD TURNER, ANTITRUST POLICY: AN ECONOMIC AND LEGAL ANALYSIS 164 (1959) (role of patent pools in Gypsum, Masonite, and Hartford-Empire glass cartels).

to the efficient operation of the patent system,[36] as many industries have discovered over time.[37]

In many cases, pools are creatures of necessity. For example, where different firms hold patents on the basic building blocks of the industry's products, they will have to cross-license to produce at all.[38] This was the case, for example, with the aircraft industry in the early days of the twentieth century, and with sewing machines.[39] And it applies with equal force to the standards-driven industries of today, for example, in the manufacture of various types of digital media products (see below). Even where no single patent or set of patents is essential, however, firms in an industry often find that they engage in such frequent negotiations that a regularized institution with formal rules, or even general guidelines, is helpful in reducing transaction costs. An example of a pool such as this is the one formed by the early shoe machinery industry.[40] The economic literature on institutions explains this quite well; repeat-play makes it easier to reach agreement on any particular issue, because disparities tend to balance out over many transactions.

Patent pools function according to liability rules. Typically firms are required to license into the pool all patents covering technology of use in the industry.[41] In exchange, pool members are permitted to use any other member's technology. Sometimes the cross-licensing is royalty-free, as with the

---

[36] I am not the first to make this point. See Alfred Kahn, *Fundamental Deficiencies of the American Patent Law*, 30 AM. ECON. REV. 975 (1940) ('All things considered, it must be concluded that the pool is a distinct improvement over the patent law as originally contemplated in effecting technological advance under modern conditions').

[37] See *Pooling of Patents: Hearings on H.R 4523 Before the House Comm. on Patents*, 74th Cong. 1140, 1144–45 (1935) (hereinafter Patent Pooling Hearings) (report by Charles A. Welsh, Jr., economist): 'In all of the following major industries which the committee has included within the scope of its activities some form of patent consolidation are [sic] in use in an attempt to circumvent the existence of patent deadlocks and overlapping inventions: Automobile, agricultural machinery, aviation, building equipment and supplies, chemicals, communications, electrical-equipment industries, food industries, glass, machinery and machine equipment, mining, munitions, oil, office equipment and machinery, paper, radio, railroad equipment, rubber, steel, scientific instruments, utilities'.

[38] See, eg, *United States v. Birdsboro Steel Foundry & Mach. Co., Inc.*, 139 F. Supp. 244, 108 U.S.P.Q. 428 (W.D. Pa. 1956) (defendants were justified in entering into agreement to cross-license patents for cooling beds used in steel mills, where, in absence of such agreement, cooling beds embodying the best features of both defendants' patents could not lawfully be made, and neither the defendants nor the public could obtain any benefit without agreement); *International Mfg Co , Inc. v. Landon, Inc.*, 336 F.2d 723, 142 U.S.P.Q. 421 (9th Cir. 1964) ('No commercially feasible [swimming pool cleaning and filtering] device could be manufactured under one of the patents without infringing the other. For this reason, Cavenah and Pace were found to be blocking, or interlocking, patents').

[39] See IS NEW TECHNOLOGY ENOUGH?: MAKING AND REMAKING U.S. BASIC INDUSTRIES 31 (Donald A. Hicks ed., 1988).

[40] See Ross Thomson, *Invention, Markets, and the Scope of the Firm: The Nineteenth Century U.S. Shoe Machinery Industry*, 18 BUS. & ECON. HIST. 140, 143 (1989) ('Patent control further strengthened [the] competitive positions [of the three largest firms] via pooling for the three major dry-thread firms (in conjunction with Elias Howe)').

[41] See Merges & Nelson, *Patent Scope*, n. 6 above, at 888–93.

great bulk of automobile patents in the auto industry pool. In other cases, members must pay licensing fees. Often these fees are calibrated to reflect the significance of the technology being licensed; for administrative convenience, the technology in the pool is usually divided into several broad classes.[42] The first licensing pool, among members of the sewing machine industry beginning in 1856, operated under these sorts of rules, as have many others including the aircraft and automobile pools.[43]

All patent pools share one fundamental characteristic: they provide a regularized transactional mechanism in place of the statutory property rule baseline which requires an individual bargain for each transaction. In most other respects, however, they vary all over the lot. They range from huge industry-wide institutions with dozens of members, and encompassing hundreds of patents, to relatively simple arrangements that look like nothing more than multilateral relational contracts. Although at the latter extreme they border on terrain outside the scope of this chapter—being not so much liability *rules* as elaborate installment contracts—the larger pools are plainly the sort of large-scale private institutions at the heart of our enterprise. So we begin with them.

A. Mega-pools

The most well-documented industry-wide pools arose in the automobile and aircraft industries around the turn of the twentieth century. In these cases representatives of the various members participate in the valuation of the patented technology. Each licensee of pooled technology is charged a royalty that is agreed upon by the pool committee.[44] This basic structure appears in pools covering not only autos and aircraft, but also sewing machines,

---

[42] See, eg, George Bittlingmayer, *Property Rights, Progress, and the Aircraft Patent Agreement*, 31 J.L. & Econ. 227 (1988) (describing accounting system for aircraft pool); William Greenleaf, Monopoly on Wheels 242–247 (1961) (describing automobile patent pool administration).

[43] See Floyd L. Vaughan, The United States Patent System 62–67 (1956); Merges & Nelson, *Patent Scope*, n. 6 above, at 888–91; Bittlingmayer, n. 42 above, at 227–8.

[44] Even these committees take on variable forms. See, eg, *Suni-Citrus Prods. Co. v. Vincent*, 170 F.2d 850, 854 (5th Cir. 1948) (suit regarding pool constituted as trust involving patents owned by private inventor and State of Florida): 'The trust agreement, between Vincent, the State and the Trustee, purported to pool certain patents by assigning them to the trustee, and to create a trust committee under whose directions the trustee would act. The powers of the committee included: the right to fix royalties; the right to include, in licenses, price fixing limitations upon the licensed products covered by the Neal patent when the prices had been fixed by members of the committee appointed by the State or other state representatives acting by virtue of legal authority in the State of Florida; and the right to include, in the licenses, price restrictions on products manufactured and sold in the State of Florida if and when these prices are fixed by virtue of legal authority in the State of Florida. The trust agreement also fixed the percentage of royalties to be paid to the person entitled'.

bathtubs, door parts, seeded raisins, coaster brakes, and a variety of other technologies.[45]

The rationale for pools with these more sophisticated administrative structures is well described in this passage from the 1935 Congressional Patent Pooling Hearings:

These various institutions have differed materially in the type of organization created by the agreements. Perhaps the loosest of all is the automobile manufacturers agreement, and obvious [sic] the most severe restrictions are imposed where the patents pass into the hands of a single owner, yet all these agreements have in common the principle that *within the industry, the individual monopoly created by patents is abolished in the form it is provided by statute and a different system is substituted more in harmony with the needs of that industry* . . .

[I]n the airplane cross-licensing agreement, after completely abolishing the monopoly of the individual inventor and opening every patent to every member of the association, it provides that a board of arbitrators may decide in any case what reward should be paid to individual patent owners and this is based not upon *the official determination of patentability by the Patent Office, but upon the unofficial determination of the importance of the invention by a board of arbitrators.*[46]

Actually, not all patent licensing requests were 'arbitrated' under the aircraft pool. In its earliest incarnation, the pool's chief functions were to eliminate ruinous litigation and divide royalties on patents existing at the time of the pool's formation according to a set formula.[47] Apart from the 'foundational'

---

[45] See VAUGHAN, n. 43 above, at 40–50.

[46] Patent Pooling Hearings, n. 37 above. On the general theme of the superiority of 'private ordering' in patent pools, see Willis B. Rice, *History of Patent Law*, in Patent Pool Hearings, n. 37 above, at 537. Despite the hostile tone of the pooling hearings, industry representatives sung the praises of administrative pooling arrangements. Consider the Testimony of Sidney R. Kent, President of Fox Film Corporation of New York:

'[Representative] McFarlane: That brings us to this question. Do you think that a private corporation, having primarily a monetary interest, is a better group to have charge of and supervision of pooling of patents, rather than a governmental agency that might arbitrate and try to be fair to the industry as a whole?
Mr. Kent You will not be offended with me if I answer that very frankly, will you Congressman—
Mr McFarlane: Go ahead.
Mr. Kent: When I say to you that governmental operation of anything, from the standpoint of industry or manufacture, can not possibly be as efficient as private manufacture . .
Mr. Kent: [M]y personal opinion   . is that if all the industry in this country were run as efficiently as the Bell Telephone and American Telephone and Telegraph . . . then we would have a pretty efficient set-up, both Government-wise and every other wise   . That is my personal opinion.'

Ibid at 501, 529–30.

[47] See JACOB A. VANDER MEULEN, THE POLITICS OF AIRCRAFT 28 (1991) (original pooling agreement called for $100 per airplane to major patentees, Glenn Curtiss and the Wright Brothers, up to a maximum of $1 million). The original agreement was amended to reflect the growing prosperity of the industry soon thereafter. See *Manufacturers Aircraft Ass'n, Inc. v. United States*, 77 Ct. Cl. 481, 487 (1933): 'The [pooling] agreement required the plaintiff to pay the remaining 87½ per centum of the royalties received from all sources in declared proportions of 67½ per centum to the Wright-Martin Aircraft Corporation and 20 per centum to the Curtiss-Burgess Airplane & Motor Corp., Inc. The agreement also contained a provision to the effect that within the period prior to November 1933, whenever and if said 87½ per centum payments to Wright and Curtiss

patents of Glenn Curtiss and the Wright Brothers, which earned millions of dollars in royalties for their holders under the pooling agreement,[48] most licensing was conducted on a royalty-free basis, with mutual forbearance from infringement suits as the real payment for the exchange.[49]

Patents added to the pool after its formation were divided into two classes. Normal patents were licensed into the pool for all to use, with no special royalty payout going to the inventor or firm.[50] Exceptional patents did earn ongoing royalties, in an amount determined by a formal arbitration procedure; under the original contract creating the pool, known as the Manufacturers Aircraft Association (MAA), members agreed:

To submit claims for compensation in respect to airplane patents or patent rights hereafter acquired to a board of arbitrators consisting of one member appointed by the board of directors of the Association (Inc.), another by the subscriber making the claim, and a third by the other two, who shall determine the total amount of compensation, if any, to be paid for the same, and the rate of royalty to be paid toward such compensation by any subscriber desiring to take a license under such patent. (Art. V, pp. 4–5).

To waive all claims as against each other for infringements prior to July 1, 1917 (Art. XIV, p. 13); to make various reports and to keep various accounts, etc.[51]

Since compensation requests were in practice limited to exceptional patents,[52] arbitrated valuations were by definition rare.[53] This two-tiered approach to valuation is of course quite rough; but the repeat-play nature of exchange under the terms of the pool tended to smooth out any discrepancies in the parties' valuation in an individual transaction.[54] The general sense

had equalled a maximum of $2,000,000 for each, the rate of royalty to be paid to plaintiff was automatically to change to a sum not exceeding $25 an airplane'.

[48] See VANDER MEULEN, n. 47 above, at 57.

[49] See Manufacturers Aircraft Association–Antitrust Laws, 31 Op. Att'y Gen. 166, 169 (1917) (hereinafter Attorney General, MAA Opinion) (prepared at the request of the Secretary of War, who had asked for a ruling on the legality of the MAA under the antitrust laws).

[50] See, eg, Patent Pooling Hearings, n. 37 above, at 775 (statement of Frank H. Russell, President of the Manufacturers Aircraft Association): 'Any member company, to become a member, after he has bought a share of stock has to agree to exchange all patents which he may have either for nothing, or, if he feels that the patent has cost him a lot of money or is of great advantage to the art, or is bringing something to the development in the process which did not previously exist, he has the right to ask for a special royalty, and that reference is then sent to a board of arbitration which is made up of a member representing him or himself, a member of the association, and a third member who is selected by the other two'.

[51] Attorney General, MAA Opinion, n. 49 above, at 169.

[52] See Patent Pooling Hearings, n. 37 above, at 775 (statement of Frank H. Russell).

[53] For example, a requested arbitration involving Boeing's patented design for low-wing, twin-engine transport planes, said to have been used by Douglas and Lockheed, was noteworthy enough to warrant special mention in a history of the aircraft industry of the 1930s. See VANDER MEULEN, n. 47 above, at 101.

[54] Cf ibid at 27–28 ('the agreement . . . was . . . an opening of the patents' use to most anyone, but under organized conditions that would facilitate the industry's development'); Attorney General, MAA Opinion, n. 49 above, at 170 (the MAA, 'instead of restraining trade facilitates competition among the subscribers of that association').

seemed to be that although one member might make out well on one technology—eg, by getting free access to a very valuable invention—the member on
the short end of the deal would make up the difference in future transactions.
Some measure of the transaction cost savings engendered by the pool may be
reflected in the fact that the major patent holders, Wright and Curtiss, low-
ered the royalty they were receiving before formation of the pool.[55]

From the point of view of internal dynamics and administration, the MAA
looked surprisingly like ASCAP; voting was weighted by the economic value
of the patents contributed by the founding members. According to the
Attorney General's report clearing the MAA of antitrust problems:

If all the manufacturers had been given equal voice in the Association (Inc.) the
smaller manufacturers together would have been enabled to control the Association
(Inc.), to wit, the agent of the parties in whose responsibility and vigilance the Wright-
Martin and Curtiss corporations are so vitally interested. This conflict of interest
accounts for the adoption of the voting trust agreement under which the Wright-
Martin and Curtiss corporations named one trustee, the smaller manufacturers
another trustee, and a party not favorable to either interest, namely, a member of the
Advisory Committee, was selected for the third trustee.[56]

A corresponding governance structure, weighted to reflect the respective
patent holdings of the founding members, was built into the auto industry
patent pool when it was formed in the early twentieth century.[57] But the similarities do not stop there: the two institutions also shared a massive scale (the
auto pool had 79 members and 350 patents when formed, and over 200 members and 1,000 patents in 1932);[58] a two-tiered patent classification scheme;[59]
an arbitration procedure for exceptional patents;[60] and an institutionalized
end to ubiquitous litigation.[61]

As with the MAA, most members seemed content to rely on the blanket,
royalty-free cross-licensing that was also available under the pool.[62] What
arbitration there was took place in a committee of knowledgeable industry

[55] See Attorney General, MAA Opinion, n. 49 above, at 167 ('The royalties to be paid under
the cross-license agreement in respect to the patents of both the Wright-Martin and Curtiss corporations are materially lower than those previously demanded by the Wright-Martin
Corporation alone').

[56] Ibid at 172.

[57] See GREENLEAF, n. 42 above, at 246 (because of perception that original structure favored
small manufacturers, 'certain alterations in the agreement made concessions to the major manufacturers').

[58] See ibid at 245–46.

[59] In addition to the two tiers, many related groups of patents were excluded. See ibid at 245
('Not included were the following categories of patents: design and special styling; special classes
of motor vehicles, such as trucks, tractors, fire-engines, ambulances, and motor-buses').

[60] See ibid ('Not included were . . . basic and revolutionary patents').

[61] See ibid ('The plan . . . in large measure fulfilled the hope that the industry would be free of
the heavy burdens of patent litigation').

[62] See ibid ('[E]ach signatory enjoyed reciprocal privileges of free licensing . . . The plan operated with unqualified success').

participants.[63] The arrangement was lauded far and wide as a success, even by no less an opponent of the patent system as Walton Hamilton.[64]

In fact, Hamilton spoke of the success of the automobile pool as proof of the creaky substructure of the patent system. 'A heterodox chapter', he concluded, 'challenges the whole theology of the patent system'.[65] It was as if the need to reconstitute the property rights by contract—the need to create an administrative apparatus to deal with the rights—proved the irrelevance or inadequacy of those rights.

But the thrust of this section of the chapter is to read the institution of patent pools as a sign of success, not failure. Without the property rights, backed by the threat of production-choking injunctions, the advantages conveyed by the pool would never have been realized. And note: those advantages extended far beyond a cessation of patent hostilities. They included the institutionalized exchange of all manner of *unpatented*. technical information,[66] and the creation of a framework for the crucial task of standardizing sizes and configurations for car parts.[67] All this followed from the industry's establishment of the contractual liability rule, or institution. A recognition of these advantages lies behind the language of a Congressional report on patent pools from 1935:

Each of these [patent pooling] agreements therefore represents the perhaps unformulated, but nonetheless definite and considered judgment of the leaders in that industry that it cannot exist under the patent law in the form in which that law was designed, and that progress demands a substitution for the law as created by statute and *the substitution of a new system of law by contract*.[68]

It is hard to improve on this formulation: patent pools as a form of contractual governance that '*substitutes*' for life under property rule entitlements, ie, for 'patent law in the form in which that law was designed'.

---

[63] Telephone interview with George Frost, Patent Lawyer, General Motors (retired), former General Motors representative to the American Automobile Manufacturers Association (AAMA) (November 2, 1994).

[64] See Walton Hamilton, *Patents and Free Enterprise, reprinted in Temporary National Economic Committee,* 76th Cong., Investigation of Concentration of Economic Power 122 (Senate Comm. Print 1941): 'It is hard to think of a form of cooperation between competitors which has brought as much benefit to the public as the cross-licensing agreement in respect to the automobile. The members of the trade are freed from the trouble and expense of struggling with patent problems. Their whole energies can go into improving their product, perfecting the process of manufacture, devising methods of marketing'. For more on Hamilton's general views of patents and monopoly, see ibid (pointing to corporate abuses of patents and stressing system's contribution to monopoly).

[65] Ibid.

[66] See GREENLEAF, n. 42 above, at 246 (noting that original pool design benefitted small companies especially, and 'quickened the spread of technological knowledge to the far corners of the industry').

[67] See ibid at 250 (calling standardization the 'most enduring and massive contribution of the Selden controversy'). The Selden controversy concerned George Selden's claim to be the exclusive inventor of the gasoline automobile. See generally ibid.

[68] Rice, n. 46 above, at 1128 (emphasis added).

B. Small, contract-based pools

Once we begin looking at patent pools as contractual substitutes for statutory entitlements, we can expand our field of vision beyond the auto and aircraft 'mega-pools'. At that point a host of smaller, more modest pools, targeted at specific industry sectors or technologies, come into view. Besides the great diversity in organizational forms, what is striking about these prosaic pools is that each one, regardless of the particular industry or the scale of the institution, embraces the twofold principle of their larger cousins: (1) consolidate property rights in a central entity (ie, the contract); and (2) establish a valuation mechanism—often a simple formula—to divide up the royalty stream. Most small scale pools are often nothing more than multilateral contracts incorporating these two basic elements.[69]

Before examining small scale pools in depth, we must return to a distinction first raised in the Introduction to this chapter above. Smaller, technology-specific pools might seem to lack the kind of complex administrative structure present in the larger pools we have discussed. One might even question how a simple contract can create a true liability *rule,* since this term seems to imply a legal regime that applies uniformly to anyone who might take or use a legal entitlement.

Typically, we would associate a liability rule with a more formalized administrative structure formed as an association of many rightholders. This separate entity typically offers a bundle of its members' property rights to all comers, just as in the simple licensing agreement just described. In addition, members grant the entity the power to add new property rights to the bundle licensed to customers, and in some cases to remove others found no longer necessary to making the relevant product; to restructure royalty payments accordingly; and in some cases to settle disputes among members about which property rights to include, and the value of respective members' rights (and hence royalty payments). The formal administrative entity created to deal with these problems is at the heart of a 'private liability rule' system. Members cede to this entity some of the decisional rights they obtain when the state grants them property rights. They in turn are bound to at least some degree by the organization's administrative decisions. Each property owner grants to the central entity the power to allow other members of the organization to use those property rights. The entity grants to sublicensees and customers—to all comers, typically—similarly open-ended rights. And each member gives the central entity power to modify the terms on which the

---

[69] Indeed, a small line of cases deals with the enforceability of executory pooling agreements. See *S. & B. Rubber & Chem. Corp v. Stein,* 7 N.Y.S.2d 553 (Sup. Ct. 1938) (ordering specific performance of pooling agreement); *Dial Toaster Corp. v. Waters-Genter Co.,* 233 N.W. 870 (Minn. 1930) (pooling contract calling for pool entity to license pooled patents 'on the best royalty basis obtainable' held too uncertain to permit specific performance decree).

members deal with each other, as well as the power to determine (or adjust) royalty rates charged to sublicensees and customers. Such an entity brings about a true liability *rule* as that term is used in the foundational entitlement literature: acting as a group, rather than an individual, it sets a pre-determined price for an entitlement.[70]

With this in mind, we might sensibly distinguish between small scale, bilateral contracts and large scale institutions. The problem with this approach is that the two are not all that different to start with in some respects, and what differences there are often blur over time. This occurs because large patent pools—those that spawn freestanding administrative entities—often begin life as humble contracts. This happens by a sort of natural growth process: recall ASCAP with its nine founding members, and the auto pool, formed around a single, pioneering patent. Because the large oaks of formal institutions often grow from the small acorns of bilateral contract, we must often look for the roots of true liability rule institutions in simple contracts.

To take one example, noteworthy simply because of its simplicity, consider a pooling agreement drawn from the davenport bed industry of the 1930s:[71]

On November 3, 1916, a written agreement was entered into between the owners of . . . various patents [pertaining to folding davenport beds and similar devices], which provided for the granting of an exclusive license to the Seng Company . . . to manufacture and sell under all of said pooled patents, the specified royalties to be divided in stated proportions among the parties to said agreement. Of the total amount of said royalties, 33 per cent was allotted to the Pullman Couch Company . . . The license contract of November 3, 1916, was signed by the Davoplane Bed Company and also by the Pullman Couch Company, as well as by [two inventors], individually. The Pullman Couch Company 'submitted' 13 patents to be controlled by the pool agreement, including two of the Bostrom patents, and the Davoplane Bed Company 'submitted' 7 patents, including one of the Bostrom patents. [An individual inventor] likewise 'submitted' one patent.[72]

This simple contract integrated at least three transactions that would otherwise have been negotiated separately. More importantly, it translated the contribution of each of the three patent holders into a precise percentage of the royalty stream.[73] The pool's exclusive licensee, the Seng Company, paid a

---

[70] See Calabresi & Melamed, n. 18 above, at 1106–7 (describing a liability rule entitlement such as property subject to the state's eminent domain authority as an entitlement subject to a 'collective determination' of value, as opposed to a strictly private 'market' valuation).

[71] *Kramer v. Comm'r*, 27 B.T.A. 1043, 1045 (1933). The description is drawn from a tax case apparently concerned with the income from the divided royalties. The case does not explain how several different entities came to own numerous patents issued to one inventor, the industrious Bostrom.

[72] Ibid.

[73] Royalty-free exchanges are also common, as in the case of the auto pool (described below). One case describes a patent pool that set up a royalty-free exchange of patents between two firms that concentrated on different technologies, but which occasionally made inventions relating to the other firm's 'core' technology. The pool allowed mutual access to patents in the 'core'

fixed percentage to one entity (the pool) in assembling the 'patent inputs' required to manufacture a state of the art davenport bed.[74] Pool members then split the royalty according to the formula in the pooling agreement.[75] Thus did the patentees substitute a collective contractual framework for individually-bargained transactions.[76]

This is by no means an unusual arrangement; a host of cases reveals similar contract-based pools in industries ranging from movie projectors (Edison's famous 'Motion Picture Patents Corporation')[77] and hydraulic

technology of each firm. See *Cutter Lab., Inc. v. Lyophile-Cryochem Corp.*, 179 F.2d 80, 91–92 (9th Cir. 1949) (upholding legality of pool that was the raison d'etre of the defendant Lyophile-Cryochem Corporation): 'Sharp & Dohme, Inc., a corporation engaged in the manufacture and sale of drugs, owned a series of patents on processes, products, containers and machinery within the field of freeze-dried drugs, including the Reichel patent in suit. The F. J. Stokes Machine Co., which manufactures machinery and apparatus used in the manufacture of drugs, owned a similar series of patents, including the Flosdorf patent in suit. These two companies formed the appellee Lyophile-Cryochem Corporation, to which they agreed to transfer the exclusive power to issue licenses under all patents within the freeze-dried drug field which each party then owned or might in the future acquire, and they agreed to endeavor to acquire such patents from any of their employees who might be connected with new inventions within the field. They also agreed to cause the new corporation "to grant licenses to others on such terms as, consistently with the maintenance of the strength of its patent rights and the good reputation of the products made pursuant to the patents, shall encourage maximum sales of the products and minimize sales resistance, and such licenses shall not be unreasonably withheld" '.

The court later explained: 'Stokes, interested in the manufacture of freeze-drying apparatus, conducts research for improvements in that apparatus. In the course of that research, it incidentally discovers improvements in freeze-drying processes and freeze-dried medical products. It is entitled to a patent monopoly on those improvements, but it cannot directly exploit those patents without going outside its normal field, which is machinery. Sharp & Dohme, on the other hand, is in a position to exploit the improvements. Moreover it is faced with the same problem, for it is in no position to exploit directly the improvements in machinery which it discovers in the course of its research. It is consistent with the spirit, as well as the letter, of the patent laws that each of these two companies should arrange to use the other in order to reap the rewards to which it is entitled as patentee and yet which it is in no position to reap by itself': ibid at 93.

[74] Although the davenport bed pool was set up to cater only to the Seng Company as an exclusive licensee, many pools license multiple manufacturers. See, eg, *Emile Indus , Inc. v. Patentex, Inc.*, 478 F.2d 562, 565 (2d Cir. 1973) (patent pool in women's hosiery production equipment) (alterations in original): 'Burlington and Chadbourn created Patentex in 1955 "to acquire title [from them] to patents and methods of manufacturing women's stretch stockings and processing yarns used in their manufacture . . . [Patentex] license[d] other hosiery manufacturers under their patents and in turn receive[d] royalties for their use." Thus, in return for royalty payments, Burlington and Chadbourn allowed their competitors to employ knitting technology which they had patented'.

[75] For an example of a nascent pool that was seemingly organized before the parties truly reached agreement in these issues, see *Dial Toaster Corp v Waters-Genter Co.*, 233 N.W. 870, 871 (1930) (specific performance decree sought on contract to pool toaster patents; 'Plaintiff asserts that anything from 25 to 35 cents a toaster would be a reasonable royalty. Defendant put the figure much higher').

[76] Cf *Baker-Cammack Hosiery Mills, Inc. v. Davis Co.*, 181 F.2d 550, 85 U.S.P.Q. 94 (4th Cir. 1950). The pool in this case involved a corporation formed in 1946 to pool the 15 patents beneficially owned by three firms in the men's hosiery industry, thereby enabling prospective licensees to deal with only one licensing source.

[77] See Ralph Cassady, Jr., *Monopoly in Motion Picture Production and Distribution: 1908–1915*, 32 S. CAL. L. REV. 325 (1959). Cassady describes in depth the complicated division

pumps,[78] to swimming pool cleaners[79] and synthetic polypropylene fiber production.[80] In the davenport bed pool, and all the pools described in these

of royalty income among the participants, spelled out in the 1908 agreement between Armat, Biograph, Edison and Vitagraph, under which the four firms assigned 'all of the patents of any importance in the early-day motion picture industry': ibid. at 331. The agreement also specified the royalties that were to be paid into the pool by licensees of the pool's patents, ie, movie exhibitors. On the role of the MPPC in the structure of the early film industry, see Catherine E. Kerr, *Incorporating the Star. The Intersection of Business and Aesthetic Strategies in Early American Film*, 64 Bus. Hist. Rev. 383, 390–91 (1990). For a good fictional account of the battle between the 'patent' (ie, MPPC pool) and 'non-patent' forces in the early movie industry, see the movie 'Nickelodeon' (Columbia 1976).

[78] *Kobe, Inc. v. Dempsey Pump Co.*, 198 F.2d 416, 420 (10th Cir. 1952) (70 patents in pool; 'The royalties exacted were a percentage of the proceeds of the sale of all pumps manufactured by licensees of [the pool entity]').

[79] *International Mfg. Co., Inc. v. Landon, Inc.*, 336 F.2d 723, 729 (9th Cir. 1964) (emphasis added): 'The trial court found that, although the two patents were issued at different times, they together covered only a single article. No commercially feasible device could be manufactured under one of the patents without infringing the other. For this reason, Cavenah and Pace were found to be blocking, or interlocking, patents.

Landon's first efforts to license manufacturers under the Cavenah patent alone were frustrated by the manufacturers' unwillingness to accept Cavenah without also being licensed under Pace. In order to end this impasse, Robert M. Pace, then owner of the Pace patent, and Landon entered an agreement whereby (1) the Pace patent was assigned to Landon, (2) Landon granted Robert Pace a royalty-free, non-exclusive license under both patents, (3) Landon promised to license the patents collectively only, and (4) *Landon and Robert Pace agreed to share royalties according to a set formula.*

No attempt was made to limit the number of licenses issued pursuant to this agreement. All licenses were offered under uniform terms and conditions to all who wished licenses'.

[80] *Studiengesellschaft Kohle m.b.H. v. Dart Indus., Inc.*, 666 F. Supp. 674, 678 (D. Del. 1987): 'Ziegler Pool Licenses . . . , granted jointly by Ziegler and Montecatini, gave licensees rights under both Ziegler and Montecatini patents at the standard sliding scale royalty rate of 5.5%. Montecatini, later known as Montedison, owned patents closely related to Ziegler's. Ziegler was to receive 30% of the royalties received under the Pool Licenses'.

See also *United States v. Gen. Instrument Corp.*, 87 F. Supp. 157, 181 (D.N.J. 1949) (radio vacuum tubes): '[T]he grant on said three Letters Patents shall proceed from the Radio, Condenser Company instead of the Condenser Development Corporation, it being understood that the royalties payable thereon and on the remaining patents of said licenses be payable to the second contracting party, the said royalties being in turn payable by the Condenser Development Corporation one half to the Radio Condenser Company and the other half to the General Instrument Corporation'.

Sometimes, the contractual division of royalties is left unspecified, or at least open to negotiation—creating a pool by 'relational' contract. See *United States v. Birdsboro Steel Foundry & Mach. Co , Inc* , 139 F. Supp. 244, 254 (W.D. Pa. 1956). In *Birdsboro* the court upheld the legality of a pool between defendant Birdsboro and another firm Mesta, where Birdsboro had the right to manufacture steel mill cooling beds for both semi-finished products and merchant mills, Mesta had the exclusive right to sell into the merchant mill market, and Birdsboro was to manufacture cooling beds for Mesta to sell in the merchant mill market, subject to the following 'fair pricing' clause in the pooling agreement: 'The prices at which Birdsboro shall sell cooling beds to Mesta shall be fair and reasonable, and comparable in general to prices paid by Mesta to Birdsboro for cooling beds already bought, with due allowance made for general increases or decreases in the cost of labor and materials, taxes, etc. In any event, the prices charged by Birdsboro shall be such as to enable Mesta to sell in competition with equipment offered by others, and to allow Mesta a reasonable profit for such resale in competition; *Provided*, however, that Birdsboro shall not be required to manufacture cooling beds at competitive prices which shall result in a loss to itself. Should Birdsboro be unwilling to accept the order from Mesta for

sources, the simple administrative—ie, contractual—structure ought not to divert attention from the significant conservation of transaction costs.

Despite differences in complexity and scale, these simple patent pools share several important features with the 'mega-pools' for autos and aircraft studied earlier: expert valuation (in the form of negotiated royalty splits); a centralized transactional mechanism; and one-stop licensing for the non-member licensees. Surely the negotiated valuation of intellectual property rights that is the essence of these contractual pools differs substantially from a true 'collective valuation' mechanism as suggested by the term 'liability rule'. Hence small-scale pools cannot realistically be deemed private 'liability rules'. Yet even though they do not represent a fundamental reconfiguration or transformation of entitlements, they are worth studying because of the features they share with true, full-blooded private liability rule systems.

As we have seen, the chief characteristic of small scale, contractual patent pools is that they regularize a set of transactions and thereby reduce transaction costs. To be sure, regularizing transactions does not eliminate entirely all sources of high transaction costs in exchanging patents. The historical record shows pool members negotiating at length, usually over the valuation of particularly important patents. The extensive cross-licensing agreement between DuPont and Imperial Chemical Industries (ICI) of Great Britain, which resembled a pool in complexity due to the magnitude of each firms' chemical research efforts, provides several examples.[81] Although the agreement lasted for more than 10 years, there were disputes over an implicit contractual arrangement whereby certain 'exceptional' inventions were placed outside the licensing framework created by the agreement.[82] For these inventions— which included nylon and neoprene for DuPont, and polyethylene for ICI— the originating firm kept exclusive rights. According to an authoritative history of DuPont, this caused serious friction during the term of the agreement.[83] And there is evidence from a case involving another pool that, as one

a cooling bed on that account, then Mesta shall have the right, notwithstanding anything herein stated in the contrary, to build such cooling bed itself or to have it built by others. Mesta shall use its best efforts to obtain such prices as to enable Birdsboro to make fair profits on the cooling beds herein contemplated. Mesta shall in no case quote prices for cooling beds without first having obtained prices from Birdsboro, unless such quotation is made based upon standard prices then in force between Mesta and Birdsboro': ibid at 254. Here the price adjustment under the fair pricing clause effectively caps the implicit royalty Birdsboro can charge on the technology it contributed to the pool, which is a rough form of apportionment.

[81] See DAVID HOUNSHELL & JOHN SMITH, SCIENCE AND CORPORATE STRATEGY: DUPONT R & D, 1902–1980, 193–205 (1988).

[82] See ibid at 199; WILLIAM READER, IMPERIAL CHEMICAL INDUSTRIES: A HISTORY 53 (1975) ('[T]here was a clause allowing either party to remove a "major invention" from the agreement altogether, so that they could make special terms').

[83] Even so, the arrangement proved basically workable, breaking down only when the US Government dissolved the arrangement as an antitrust violation. See *United States v. Imperial Chem. Indus., Ltd.*, 105 F. Supp. 215 (S.D.N.Y. 1952).

might predict, pool members act strategically in an effort to maximize their share of the pool's revenues.[84]

Even apart from the continuing transaction costs attendant on operation of a pool, the costs of initially negotiating a pooling agreement will often be steep. These are a product of (1) differing assessments of the technological merits of the contributions of the members of the pool, (2) private information held by each member concerning the precise characteristics of the technology and the details of the patent position (all relevant prior art, etc.), and (3) strategic bargaining possibilities created by the negotiations over the potentially large 'pooling surplus' that may result from the creation of the pool.[85] The fact that pools have arisen so often in the past despite these costs says a great deal about the cost *savings* firms expect from these institutions. The lengthy negotiations between firms trying to create a single DVD pool, and ultimately the dual pools that formed, serve as a modern reminder.

It is also worth noting that some pools have been formed only with the help of a 'visible hand' to overcome the collective action problem inherent in group bargaining. In several cases where technology useful to the military was not being developed because of a logjam of conflicting property rights, the lurking threat of the eminent domain power contributed to the formation of patent pools.[86] In at least one case, a long-term industry patent pool was

---

[84] See *Hazeltine Research, Inc. v. Zenith Radio Corp.*, 239 F. Supp. 51, 72 (N.D. Ill. 1965) (emphasis added): 'The dominant radio and electronics companies in Great Britain set up the British Patent Pool into which flow thousands of patents owned or controlled by the members and those affiliated with them in the plan. Among these companies are Electric & Musical Industries Ltd., General Electric Company, Ltd., Marconi's Wireless Telegraph Co. Ltd., Philips Electrical Ltd., Pye Ltd., Murphy Radio Ltd., Rank Cintel Ltd., Standard Telephone & Cables Ltd., Gramophone Co. Ltd., E.K. Cole Ltd., and Cossor Ltd. The Hazeltine inventions and patents have been funneled into the Pool pursuant to an agreement with General Electric Co. Ltd. and the share of the Pool's income allocated to these patents is split between General Electric Co. Ltd. and Hazeltine. Pursuant to this arrangement British inventions controlled by General Electric Co. Ltd. are licensed to Hazeltine for exclusive licensing use in its American territory and are included in its United States package licensing activities. *The Hazeltine-General Electric Co. Ltd. exclusive agreements were specifically devised to get the Hazeltine patents into the British Patent Pool in a manner which would provide for G.E.C. maximum bargaining power vis-a-vis the other Pool members on the division of the Pool income'*.

[85] See Scotchmer, n. 6 above; Stefan Fölster, *Firms' Choice of R&D Intensity in the Presence of Aggregate Increasing Returns to Scale*, 13 J. ECON BEHAV. & ORG. 387 (1990). On the possibility of bargaining breakdown in IPR transactions, see Robert Merges, *Intellectual Property Rights and Bargaining Breakdown: The Case of Blocking Patents*, 62 TENN. L. REV. 75 (1994) (hereinafter Merges, *Bargaining Breakdown*).

[86] Bittlingmayer, n. 42 above, at 230–32; Dykman, *Patent Licensing within the Manufacturer's Aircraft Association (MAA)*, 46 J. PAT. OFF. SOC'Y 646 (1964) (describing formation of industry licensing pool, at behest of government, because, '[n]o one would license the other under anything like a reasonable basis'). See generally Merges & Nelson, *Patent Scope*, n. 6 above. See also *Gen. Tire & Rubber Co. v. Firestone Tire & Rubber Co.*, 489 F.2d 1105, 1140 (6th Cir. 1973) (describing a dispute arising from a World War II patent pool formed at the request of the US Government and administered by the Reconstruction Finance Corporation (RFC) in the area of synthetic rubber research). The pool in this case was formed immediately after Pearl Harbor, according to the court, by the signing of contracts between the RFC and the big four of the

formed in the wake of the government's forced licensing; this pool itself embodied an interesting governance structure built on an industry-wide practice of technology exchange through IPR licensing.[87] The emergence of these pools suggests an interesting avenue for future government policy: encouraging firms to contract around their patents as an alternative to more forceful government intervention, eg, a compulsory licensing scheme.

C. Recent pools in consumer electronics: MPEG–2 and DVD

Recently, a number of companies have joined together to form patent pools encompassing various aspects of digital media used in consumer electronics products. The MPEG–2 pool, covering patents on data compression technology, came first in 1995; followed by a pair of related pools concerning Digital Versatile Discs (DVDs). The Antitrust Division of the Department of Justice has finalized and approved all three pools in business review letters. The MPEG–2 pool and the DVD patent pools illustrate an important recent variant on the themes discussed in this section and will be described in detail. These pools join together some features of both the mega-pools and the simpler, contract-based pools. They thus represent an interesting new breed of patent pool: they are less comprehensive than the 'mega-pools', since they are concerned only with one technology, rather than *all* patents in an industry. Yet they are more substantial than pools based on simple cross-licenses, because they include various adjustment mechanisms, most importantly for adding new patents and recalibrating royalty shares. Most importantly, they carry forward crucial features of pools from the past, and thus continue to demonstrate the viability of private institutional solutions to the transaction costs imposed by widespread patent blockages in established industries.

rubber industry (Goodyear, U.S. Rubber, Goodrich and Firestone), both to manage and operate the synthetic rubber plants and to pool patents and conduct research for the government, the results of which would be shared royalty-free with the government and its 'nominees' (ie the other rubber companies participating in the research agreements). The organizing contract for the pool read in part as follows: '7. Contractor hereby grants to RFC and its nominees (1) a royalty-free license to utilize without limitation any information or invention (whether or not patented) resulting from the research authorized by this contract, including the right to reproduce, disclose to others, and publish all such information or inventions, and including the right to make, use and sell thereunder, and (2) a royalty-free license to use any information or invention to which RFC or its nominees are entitled under the provisions of paragraph 5 above, including the right to reproduce, disclose to others, and publish all such information or inventions, but limited to the utilization of the same in the production, use or sale of general purpose synthetic rubber suitable for use in the manufacture of transportation items such as tires or camel-back, and (3) a royalty-free license with respect to any information or invention made available under the provisions of paragraph 6 above, limited to the utilization of the same in the manufacture, use or sale of rubberlike polymers, copolymers, mixed polymers and interpolymers of the compositions defined in paragraph 3 above': ibid at 1143.

[87] See Bittlingmayer, n. 42 above, at 232 (in 1917, following United States entry into World War I, 'Congress passed legislation that would have condemned the patents', thus spurring the parties to negotiate an agreement).

1. MPEG–2

The MPEG–2 pool began as an agreement among nine patent holders[88] to combine 27 patents that are needed to meet an international standard known as MPEG–2 video compression technology. The Moving Picture Experts Group of the International Standards Organisation (ISO) and the International Electrotechnical Commission established the MPEG-II standard in 1995.[89] The pool was an outgrowth of the creation of this standard. Under the pooling agreement, the patent holders all license their MPEG–2 patents to a central administrative entity known as MPEG LA, based in Denver. MPEG LA is essentially a licensing agent; it administers the pool on behalf of the members. MPEG LA licenses the group's patent portfolio to third parties who will manufacture products to meet the MPEG–2 standard. Like many pools, the MPEG group has grown: it now includes 14 patent holders and 56 essential patents.[90]

The MPEG–2 pool reflects many of the essential features of the mega-pools of yesteryear. These include 'one-stop shopping' for patent/technology inputs into manufacturing processes;[91] an institutional structure reflecting weighted

---

[88] Current essential patent holders who are members of MPEG–2 (either by themselves or through related entities) are Columbia University, Fujitsu, General Instrument, Matsushita, Mitsubishi, Lucent, Philips, Scientific-Atlanta and Sony.

[89] On the economic importance of standard-setting committees, see Joseph Farrell & Garth Saloner, *Coordination Through Committees and Markets*, 19 RAND J. ECON. 235 (1988).

[90] See MPEG LA <http://www.mpegla.com>.

[91] By the beginning of 1998, Columbia University, ComStream, DX Antenna, Divicom, Dooin Electronics, Fujitsu, Gunzameory Computer, Kenwood, Matsushita/Panasonic, Mitsubishi, NDS, NTT, NextLevel, Nippon Steel, Philips, Pioneer, Samsung, Sampo, Sanyo, Scientific-Atlanta, Sharp, Sony (several divisions), Tadiran, Toshiba and JVC/Victor were all licensees.

Manufacturer royalty rates are as follows:

Consumer products (TV set top boxes, computers and the like) which incorporate an MPEG–2 encoder or decoder pay a royalty rate of $4.00 per product (Arts 2.2, 2.3, 3.1.1, 3.1.2). Consumer products which incorporate both an encoder and decoder such as a camcorder are licensed for a total royalty of $6.00 (Art. 3.1.4).

Packaged media such as DVD or other optical discs or magnetic tapes: for consumer use ($.04 per disc or medium per 'MPEG–2 Video Event', eg, feature length film) or commercial use ($.40 per disc or medium per 'MPEG–2 Video Event').

'Distribution Encoding Products'—generally those used in real time broadcasts and cable transmissions—are $4.00 per device per channel which is incorporated in the device. (Arts 2.5, 3.1.3). Royalty rates for 'Transport or Program Stream Products' such as multiplexers are $4.00 times the greater number of inputs or outputs.

Thus, for example, the royalty due from a film studio on a DVD disc sold to consumers incorporating a single 'MPEG–2 Video Event' would be $.04, or 0.16% of the retail price, assuming a price of $25.00. If the disc incorporates a patent of each essential patent holder where the disc is manufactured or sold, the gross pro rata royalty for each essential patent holder would be $.0044, not considering any applicable taxes and licensing costs. The royalty due from a camcorder manufacturer which incorporates both an encoder and decoder would be $6, or 0.15% of the retail price, assuming a price of $400. If the camcorder incorporates a patent of each essential patent holder where the unit is manufactured or sold, the gross pro rata royalty for each essential patent holder would be $.67, not including any applicable taxes and licensing costs.

representation among patentees; expert administrative valuation procedures for (a) determining royalty splits among members and (b) 'blanket' licensing charges to licensees; a negotiation framework for determining whether new technologies merit addition to the pool; and a pre-agreed procedure for settling disputes.

In every sense, MPEG LA is an institution, as opposed to a simple one-time transfer of rights. It has a governance structure and a set of internal rules (codified in a formal 'charter').[92] Most importantly from the point of view of the framework described here and in my 1996 *California Law Review* article, there is a permanent administrative procedure for evaluating new technologies. The pool is charged with determining whether new patented technologies are appropriate for inclusion in the pool.[93] (To give some sense of the complexity involved, the MPEG lawyers began by studying over 8,000 patent abstracts, owned by over 100 companies and inventors; narrowed the field to 800 patents, and eventually identified the 27 Essential Patents, most of which also have foreign counterparts.)[94] New patents are being added all the time as they are being granted by patent offices around the world.[95] There is also a mechanism for recalibrating the internal royalty split among members in light of the new technology when a new patent is included in the pool.[96] This is an

[92] The 'Amended and Restated Limited Liability Company Agreement of MPEG LA', cited extensively in Letter from Joel I. Klein, Acting Assistant Attorney General, Department of Justice, Antitrust Division, to Gerrard R. Beeney, Esq. (June 26, 1997) <http://www.usdoj.gov/atr/pubdocs.html> (hereinafter MPEG–2 Review Letter).

[93] The licensors' request for a Business Review from DOJ says: '[E]xtreme care has been taken to insure that the proposed licensing program includes only blocking or essential patents and a structure has been devised both to remove from the program any patents hereafter shown to be non-essential and to include at a later date any other patents that are deemed essential'.

Cf Sabra Chartrand, *The Federal Government Will Allow a Group of Companies to Unify Administration of 27 Patents*, N.Y. TIMES, June 30, 1997, at D8 ('Mr. [Baryn] Futa [president of MPEG LA, the corporate entity that administers the MPEG–2 pool] said that 27 patents "is only an introductory number" and that more would be added').

[94] See Barry Fox, *Replicators Risk Drowning in a Growing Pool of Patents*, ONE TO ONE, Mar. 18, 1998, at 63.

[95] According to the trade press, for instance: 'Lucent Technologies (Bell Labs) and Toshiba are expected to join [the pool] soon and add more patents' ibid.

[96] From the MPEG–2 'Request Letter' preceding the DOJ Review Letter: 'The Agreement establishes an Administrative Committee (Article 3) consisting of a representative of each licensor. The Administrative Committee has responsibility for selecting the Licensing Administrator, and reviewing certain activities of the Licensing Administrator. The Licensing Administrator, however, and not the Administrative Committee or individual licensors, has exclusive responsibility to identify and solicit potential portfolio licensees, audit sublicensees, determine back royalties which potential licensees may owe, bring actions to enforce a Portfolio License and other licensing administration matters (Article 3.5.4). The Agreement Among Licensors also provides the formula for apportioning royalty income among licensors (Article 5.1) as well as a basis for dividing any joint expenses or liability which may arise (Article 5.2, 5.3). The licensors agree to reimburse certain of the expenses which were incurred by CableLabs in connection with the patent search and other efforts to organize the proposed licensing program (Article 5.3.2). The Agreement also provides the procedures for removing existing or adding new essential patents to the Portfolio License—whether such new patents are held by the original licensors or other

example of an internal 'liability rule', ie, a set of rules and norms for determining the value of a new, patented technology. The administrative structure of the pool substitutes technical expertise by the members (and the pool's staff) for that of the courts. This effectively converts members' property rights from 'property rule' entitlements to administratively-determined liability rule entitlements.

Like the older mega-pools, the MPEG–2 pool separates patents into different classes, to ease administration. The backbone of the organization is what the charter calls 'Essential Patents:' the basic complementary technologies that in effect comprise the MPEG–2 standard. The charter also recognizes another type of patented technology, which it calls 'Related Patents'. These are technologies that implement, build on, or employ the MPEG–2 standard in electronic components, software, and the like.[97] Related Patents are classic improvement patents: technologies embodying them would infringe the MPEG–2 standard if unlicenced, but they add value in some way, for example, by applying MPEG–2 in a new electronic device or application (such as, apparently, the Internet).

As a mechanism for integrating Related Patents into the pool, the MPEG–2 pool has some novel features. The charter allows individual MPEG–2 members to 'opt out' of the pool with respect to a single licensee. The purpose of this provision, called 'Partial Termination', is to provide bargaining leverage to an MPEG–2 member that is negotiating for a license to a complementary patent held by an MPEG–2 licensee. Any MPEG–2 member thus can partially terminate when the licensee has (a) brought a lawsuit or other proceeding against the MPEG–2 Licensor for infringement of a licensee patent and (b) refused to grant the MPEG–2 Licensor a license under that patent on 'fair and reasonable terms and conditions'.[98]

entities—and provides that any new licensor will reimburse the original licensors $25,000 for certain start-up expenses which the original licensors incurred (Articles 2, 6)'.

There is a cap on the upward revision of royalty rates over the short term, however: 'The Portfolio License expires in 2000, but each licensee is given the option to renew the license for an additional period of five years (Art. 6.1). Licensees are assured that royalties will increase, if at all, by no more than 25% for the five year renewal period': MPEG–2 Review Letter, n. 92 above.

[97] The MPEG–2 Charter, at § 1.23, defines The Portfolio license, like several of the relevant documents, defines 'MPEG–2-Related Patent' as 'any Patent which is not an MPEG–2 Essential Patent but which has one or more claims directed to an apparatus or a method that may be used in the implementation of a product or a service designed in whole or in part to exploit the MPEG–2 Standard under the laws of the country which issued or published the Patent'.

[98] MPEG–2 Portfolio License, § 6.3. The rationale for this provision is stated in MPEG–2's Review Letter request to the DOJ: 'This provision is critical to prevent Portfolio licensees from taking unreasonable and unfair advantage of the fact that each Portfolio licensor already has agreed to license its patents on open, non-discriminatory terms at what would likely be a fraction of the royalties that would be payable if patents were licensed individually outside the Portfolio License. Without this provision, a Portfolio licensee could—while enjoying the considerable benefits of the Portfolio License—attempt to extract unreasonable terms for licensing its patent as a result of already being licensed under the Portfolio. Article 6.3 merely "evens the playing field", puts the parties back into the bargaining position each would have been in but for the Portfolio

The role of the partial termination right in encouraging patent right integration is explained in the Department of Justice Review Letter that cleared the pool of antitrust concerns (discussed in more detail below):

[T]he partial termination right may have procompetitive effects to the extent that it functions as a nonexclusive grantback requirement on licensees' Related Patents. It could allow Licensors and licensees to share the risk and rewards of supporting and improving the MPEG–2 standard by enabling Licensors to capture some of the value they have added to licensees' Related Patents by creating and licensing the Portfolio. In effect, the partial termination right may enable Licensors to realize greater returns on the Portfolio license from the licensees that enjoy greater benefits from the license, while maintaining the Portfolio royalty at a level low enough to attract licensees that may value it less. This in turn could lead to more efficient exploitation of the Portfolio technology.[99]

The Department of Justice concluded that the partial-termination clause appeared unlikely to be anticompetitive because of the 'potentially significant procompetitive effects and the limited potential harm it poses to Portfolio licensees' incentives to innovate'.[100]

2. DVD

A DVD is a high volume digital storage medium said to be the successor to Compact Disc (CD) technology. DVD discs can hold more than seven times as much data as CDs. The market for DVD hardware and software is projected to be worth more than $28 billion by 2001.[101] As with MPEG–2, a multi-firm standards group declared a standard for DVD technology. Also as with MPEG–2, multiple firms hold important patents on the elements of this standard. In late 1995, it was reported that four 'core' DVD[102] developers of a 10-member DVD consortium would enter into a patent pooling agreement to administer the licensing of DVD patents.[103] The core members, Philips, Sony, Matsushita and Toshiba, reportedly extended an open invitation to secondary patent holders claiming rights to DVD-related patents.[104]

License, and creates no competition issues. The individual licensor's patents are only withdrawn from the Portfolio License when and if the licensee refuses to grant a license to the Portfolio licensor on fair and reasonable terms. Moreover, the ISO undertaking signed by each essential patent holder-licensor insures that the licensee will be able to obtain a license under the essential patent at issue, just not necessarily on the terms offered in the Portfolio License. Any potential licensee which objects to this provision remains free to negotiate individual licenses from essential patent holders'.

[99] MPEG–2 Review Letter, n. 92 above.   [100] Ibid.

[101] See *The Future of DVD Has Yet to be Decided* (June 29, 1999), <http://www.dvdinsider. com/news/database/view.asp?ID=679>.

[102] DVD stands for 'digital video discs', high-capacity compact discs capable of storing feature-length films as well as music and other forms of entertainment.

[103] See *Four Companies to Oversee DVD Patent Pool*, CONSUMER ELECTRONICS, Dec. 18, 1995, at 14.

[104] See ibid; see also *Sony, Philips Break Ranks, Prepare DVD Licensing Fees*, OPTICAL MEMORY NEWS, Aug. 13, 1996.

In August, 1996, after a period of failed negotiations among the core consortium members, Sony and Philips announced that they would form their own DVD pool, with Philips to be the licensor.[105] Philips stated that '[t]here were so many differences of opinion that we could not wait for these to be settled'.[106] Pioneer Electronics subsequently joined this three-firm pool. Six months later, Hitachi, Matsushita, Mitsubishi, Time Warner, Toshiba and JVC formed their own patent pool. Industry analysts warned that without a single, unitary pool, the price of DVD technology would increase since a piecemeal licensing system would push the cost of the technology higher.[107] One industry analyst reported that '[t]he hope within the industry had been that [through a patent pool] everyone would take a little less for the common good'.[108]

The Department of Justice recently cleared both DVD patent pools. The Sony, Philips and Pioneer pool received its clearance in December 1998. Even though the formation of these separate patent pools precluded the opportunity for a one-stop-shop for DVD licensing, the Antitrust Division recognized that the patent pools would at least reduce DVD-related transaction costs. Now companies that want to manufacture DVD discs or equipment have only to deal with these two pools, instead of the ten separate firms that formed them. The Division reached similar conclusions after reviewing the arrangements of the two pools: '[I]t appears that the proposed arrangement is likely to combine complementary patent rights, thereby lowering the costs of manufacturers that need access to them in order to produce discs, players and decoders in conformity with the DVD-Video and DVD-ROM formats'.[109]

The story of the DVD patent pool is revealing. First, it provides a clear example of the relationship between standard setting and patent pools. As with MPEG-2, the DVD pools grew out of industry standard setting organizations. In some instances companies participating in standard setting are required to agree in advance to license any patents essential to the standard on 'a fair and nondiscriminatory basis on reasonable' terms.[110] Even where there is no formal requirement along these lines, past practice exerts a powerful influence: having seen standards coalesce into pools, consumer electronics companies may simply expect this as the natural progression. It might not be stretching things to say that this industry is characterized by a norm of standard-setting, and then pooling. In any event, as a practical matter they often go hand in hand.

---

[105] See Andrew MacLellan, *Philips, Sony Pooling DVD Patents*, ELECTRONIC NEWS, Aug. 5, 1996, at 4.
[106] Ibid.   [107] See *Sony, Philips Break Ranks*, n. 104 above.   [108] Ibid.
[109] Letter from Joel I. Klein, Assistant Attorney General, Department of Justice, Antitrust Division, to Carey R. Ramos (June 10, 1999) <http://www.usdoj.gov/atr/pubdocs.html> (hereinafter Toshiba Review Letter).
[110] Mark A. Lemley & David McGowan, *Could Java Change Everything? The Competitive Propriety of a Proprietary Standard*, 43 ANTITRUST BULL. 715 (1998).

So in the normal course of events, firms begin to move toward standard setting and pool formation when they recognize patent blockages in a promising
new technology. The next step is to address the issues identified by anticommons theory: strategic behavior and cognitive bias. Pool organizers employ a
number of tactics to minimize the threat of strategic behavior. One is to hire
an independent patent expert to evaluate the patents of the various aspiring
pool members. For example, the owners of the patents in the MPEG–2 Patent
Portfolio employed an independent patent expert to identify the essential
patents to be included in the portfolio.[111] The DVD patent owners also
retained patent experts to perform similar reviews in the separate patent
pools.[112] Indeed, the DVD pools call for *standing* experts to perform periodic
evaluations of prospective new patents for the pool.[113]

Presumably one reason for hiring an independent patent expert is to prevent strategic posturing. Independent review puts limits on bargaining. A
company will find it difficult to argue that its technology is the key to the standard, and thus deserves the lion's share of pool revenue, if the independent
expert finds otherwise. Independent experts also presumably cut down on the
impact of the parties' 'cognitive biases'. A second opinion, particularly from
a disinterested agent of the (presumably) neutral patent pool organization, is
likely to be a powerful corrective to an intransigent pool member adamant
about the importance of its contributions to the pool. It is no coincidence, for
example, that the independent expert hired by one of the two DVD pools is
required to be an expert in DVD technology.

Another technique for limiting strategic behavior is aimed at licensees.
Pool members understand that the licensee-manufacturers have a strong
incentive to acquire patents that cover one or more features of the standard.
A licensee of the pool that happened to have a patent application covering
some aspect of the technology pending when the standard was announced
might acquire such a patent, for instance. Such a patent, which would by definition be necessary for lawful use of the standard, are called 'Essential
Patents'. A calculating licensee could use such a patent to extract concessions
from the pool members, given that those members would have to license any
new patents on 'essential' features of the technology falling within the standard. The Review Letter for the Sony DVD pool describes the pool organizers' response to just this threat:

The grantback provision is likely simply to bring other 'essential' patents into the
Portfolio, thereby limiting holdouts' ability to exact a supracompetitive toll from
Portfolio licensees and further lowering licensees' costs in assembling the patent rights

---

[111] See MPEG–2 Review Letter, n. 92 above.
[112] See Letter from Joel I. Klein, Assistant Attorney General, Department of Justice,
Antitrust Division, to Gerrard R. Beeney (December 16, 1998) <http://www.usdoj.gov/atr/pub-
docs.html> (hereinafter Sony Review Letter); Toshiba Review Letter, n. 109 above.
[113] Sony Review Letter, n. 112 above; Toshiba Review Letter, n. 109 above.

essential to their compliance with the Standard Specifications. While easing, though not altogether eliminating, the holdout problem[114] the grantback should not create any disincentive among licensees to innovate.[115]

The MPEG–2 pool agreement contained a similar grantback provision. The grantback obliges licensees to make available to all pool participants an essential patent at a 'fair and reasonable royalty'.[116] A licensee firm thus cannot hold back its own essential patents and simultaneously benefit from the cost savings afforded by the portfolio license. Thus the parties see the grantback clause as a way to limit future opportunism. In terms of the theory described earlier, licensees must agree in advance to be bound by the grantback if they are to receive a license. Potential holdouts are prevented ex ante, by prior agreement of the parties.

The DVD pools also preempt similar bargaining issues among pool members. The Sony Review Letter speaks of a confidential royalty allocation formula among the pool members, and the Toshiba pool has a more elaborate set of 'Ground Rules for Royalty Allocation'.[117] The DVD pools thus have many characteristics of the older mega-pools. Put succinctly, they are operational institutions whose core missions are to regularize the valuation of key manufacturing patents.

However, in the DVD case two pools formed. As with the oil field unitization studies by Gary Libecap discussed earlier in this chapter, even though the parties all understood there would be significant gains from reaching agreement, they were unable to split amicably the 'cooperative surplus'. Each entity among the group has its own agenda or strategy. Toshiba, for example, stated initially it did not want to commit unless all 10 members of the consortium agreed.[118] Other firms obviously had different agendas; thus the impasse that resulted in dual patent pools. The time and expense involved in negotiating such a patent pool are evident. Although industry participants realized that an efficient licensing mechanism might be necessary because many separate entities held essential patents, various differences caused the pooling effort to bog down.

To summarize, the DVD pools represent the continuation of the tradition of industry-wide institution formation as a response to patent bottlenecks.

---

[114] Any non-manufacturing owner of an 'essential' patent, in contrast, can still be a holdout, having no need for either Portfolio License.

[115] Sony Review Letter, n. 112 above.   [116] MPEG–2 Review Letter, n. 92 above.

[117] See Sony Review Letter, n. 112 above; Toshiba Review Letter, n. 109 above.

[118] Cf Video Notes, Video Wk., Nov. 3, 1997 (Toshiba has now joined with five other companies—Hitachi, JVC, Matsushita, Mitsubishi, and Time Warner—to form its own pool). The prospect of dueling pools each possessing essential complementary patents poses interesting possibilities. It may enhance the bargaining position of its members vis-à-vis the other pool, and thus be a prelude to a single pool. It may also slow the introduction of new technology, as licensees must negotiate with two entities. In effect, this situation mirrors the case of blocking patents. The same bargaining dynamic holds, with the added complication that each of the bargaining entity is a coalition of multiple firms. See Merges, *Bargaining Breakdown*, n. 85 above.

The standing expert review, grantback provisions, and 'Ground Rules for Royalty Distribution' are all earmarks of an ongoing, functioning institution designed to overcome the inherent problems of valuing complementary patents.

The DVD pools show the continuing importance of a 'visible hand' in helping to overcome collective action problems. In this case, it was the hand of the Department of Justice that motivated Sony and Philips to strike out on their own to form a pool. Sony and Philips had previously felt the close scrutiny of the Department of Justice: in 1995, after investigating the highly profitable pooling of Sony and Philips CD technology, the Department of Justice reached a settlement with both parties.[119] The result of the settlement was that Philips-Sony could no longer force licensees to take a blanket license of the entire CD patent pool portfolio; rather, companies were allowed to obtain licenses under individual patents or groups of selected patents.[120] Philips officials stated that formation of the Sony-Philips DVD pool was 'necessary to avoid being "accused of illegal behavior", noting that U.S. law says [that] holders must make patents available on [a] nondiscriminatory basis.'[121] In reference to the Department of Justice's questioning of Philips, Philips responded '[w]e don't want to have a collision with the Department of Justice'.[122]

3. Other new pools

Perhaps inspired by the successful founding of these pools, a spate of other technologies (including digital video broadcasting,[123] synthetic fibres,[124] flat panel speakers,[125] and next-generation dynamic RAM memory chips)[126] have been gathered into patent pools in recent years. The ubiquity of patent pools on the industrial landscape demonstrates that this is an institutional mechanism capable of simplifying transactions in a wide variety of industries. As more and more IPRs are issued, potential transaction costs will grow as well, making pools even more important.

---

[119] See *Justice Dept. Examining DVD Patent Situation*, AUDIO WK., Jan. 8, 1996.

[120] See ibid.

[121] MacLellan, n. 105 above. 'The law says we have to make our patents available in a non-discriminatory and timely manner. If this drags on too long, and we release the patents too soon before we introduce our product, that is illegal. Time was running out': ibid.

[122] *Philips and Sony Offering DVD Patent Licenses*, CONSUMER ELECTRONICS, Aug. 5, 1996, at 10. In addition, an industry insider speculated that Sony and Philips had an additional purpose—that of compelling the other eight consortium members to get into the patent pool. See Scott Berinato, *Licensing Disputes Said to Delay Sony DVD*, PC WK., Sept. 9, 1996, at 33.

[123] See Fox, n. 94 above.

[124] See Paul Durman, *Courtaulds Ends Patent Dispute*, THE TIMES (London), Jan. 8, 1998 (describing patent pool for synthetic fibre 'Tencel').

[125] See *Speaker Patent Fight Averted*, CONSUMER ELECTRONICS, Dec. 8, 1997, at 1.

[126] See Andrew Maclellan, *Consortium Incorporates to Push SLDRAM Technology*, TECHWEB NEWS, Jan. 28, 1998 (pool with 24 patent holder-members).

D. Quasi-pools: A positive role for patents as 'bargaining chips'

Despite occasional roadblocks, patent pools often do take shape; and when they do, as we have seen, they serve to collect a host of beneficial transactions under one roof. But talk of these transactional advantages leads naturally to a further question: can *informal* exchange norms also serve to regularize exchange in an industry? To put it another way, if pools can sometimes 'substitute' for property entitlements, and if simple contracts can sometimes take the place of pools, can informal exchange norms emerge that serve some of the same functions as actual contracts?

In the semiconductor, consumer electronics, and chemical industries patents have long been used as bargaining chips.[127] They facilitate technology trades, or at least settle or fend off infringement suits in a convenient way.[128] In other words, these industries have evolved a norm under which patents are used primarily as 'currency' in cross-licensing.[129] In an operational sense, then, a loose 'liability rule' exchange system prevails;[130] the legal right to exclude is rarely enforced fully, and firms therefore do not always seek permission of the rightholder first. Often they appear to go on about their business, sometimes infringing other firms' patents in the process, with the intention of 'settling up' later. Since industry members share a sense of the worth of individual patents, it is easy for firms to 'trade off' infringement liabilities when they 'settle up'. Remaining 'balances' are then paid off in money damages. Indeed, firms share such an understanding of how the process works that they sometimes institutionalize the arrangement in advance by means of extensive cross-licensing agreements.

There are thus two key indicators that the operative norm at work in these industries deviates from the structure of the initial property rule: permission is not always sought first; and each firm agrees roughly on the value of individual patents. Perhaps this norm emerged because of economic forces in the industry such as rapid development and mutually interdependent research efforts. Under certain circumstances it would be rational systematically to forgo full enforcement of property rights, in exchange for reciprocal forbearance from competitors. In any event, these industries have developed

[127] See JOHN TILTON, INTERNATIONAL DIFFUSION OF TECHNOLOGY: THE CASE OF SEMI-CONDUCTORS 16 (1971); HOUNSHELL & SMITH, n. 81 above.

[128] See INTELLECTUAL PROPERTY RIGHTS IN SCIENCE, TECHNOLOGY AND ECONOMIC PERFORMANCE (Frank Rushing & Connie Brown eds., 1990) ('[I]n each of these industries [that ranked patents low on the scale of appropriation mechanisms in a survey] at least half of the patentable inventions were patented. The reason seems to be that the prospective benefits of patent protection, including (besides royalties) whatever delay is caused prospective imitators and the use of patents as bargaining chips, are judged to exceed costs').

[129] See, eg, *Intel Corp. v. ULSI Sys. Tech., Inc.*, 782 F. Supp. 1467 (D. Or. 1991) (dispute over cross-license involving patented 80387 microprocessor math coprocessor), *rev'd*, 995 F.2d 1566 (Fed. Cir. 1993).

[130] See Merges & Nelson, *Patent Scope*, n. 6 above, at 888–93.

exchange regimes based on property rule entitlements (patents) that have many earmarks of a well-functioning liability rule. Again, as we saw with both large scale pools and their smaller, contract-based cousins, predictable expert valuation rules substitute for individuated arms-length bargains.

It is of course not incidental that informal norms, and the patent pools whose operation they emulate, appear to work when they are run by a close-knit group of experts with shared understandings of the technology, industry, and entitlements structure. These industries approximate the 'close-knit' groups Ellickson elucidates so well.[131]

My positive account of industry cross-licensing norms contrasts with traditional descriptions. Some commentators, for instance, have argued that when patents serve only as bargaining chips they serve no useful purpose, except possibly to restrict entry into an industry.[132] Others, while not condemning the practice outright, have appeared puzzled by this use of patents; it seems anomalous in light of accepted theories of patent protection, which emphasize the need for incentives to offset the public goods aspects of technology and the products that embody it.[133]

III. Antitrust Review of Patent Pools

As the Antitrust Guidelines demonstrate, recent antitrust enforcement policy has begun to reflect the growing awareness that patent pooling can confer net social gains. The burden of this chapter is to describe how those gains come about, out of a background of strong property rights and high transaction costs. I have also tried to show that patent pools are in no sense unique—that, to the contrary, they are illustrative of a whole family of transactional institutions based around intellectual property rights. In so arguing, I have thus tried to connect this family to the larger study of economic institutions, of which it is undoubtedly a part.

The MPEG and DVD pools raised a number of important antitrust issues. Since anticompetitive activity represents the 'dark side' pool formation, this section briefly addresses those issues.

Some MPEG–2 members were initially hesitant to form the pool because they feared that the royalty scheme would raise antitrust problems.[134] This

---

[131] Ellickson, *Property in Land*, n. 21 above; Ellickson, ORDER WITHOUT LAW, n. 21 above.

[132] See, eg, Cecil Quillen, *Proposal for the Simplification and Reform of the U.S. Patent System*, 21 AM. INTELL. PROP. L. ASS'N Q.J. 189 (1993).

[133] See David, n. 1 above.

[134] In this regard, General Instrument, a member of the group, voiced its distaste for the royalty scheme. Time Warner, a non-member, stated that '[m]aking such demands through a consortium of hardware manufacturers, some of whom have been included despite their ownership of unessential patents, smacks of price fixing, collusion and an attempt to monopolize': *Greed on the I-Way*, INFO. L. ALERT, Mar. 24, 1995, at 1.

concern highlights the continuing importance of antitrust issues on the formation of pools. Despite their apparent transactional advantages, patent pools—at least formal ones—were relatively rare from the 1940s until recently. It might be thought that this poses a challenge to the thesis that stronger IPRs encourage the formation of transactional mechanisms.

To the contrary, the explanation for the decline in patent pools can be found in government antitrust policy. Ever since myriad forms of interfirm cooperation were condemned in the 'trust-busting era',[135] firms have been reluctant to initiate industry-wide arrangements of every ilk, including pools.[136] Antitrust enforcement is a threat to a patent pool from three directions. First, government enforcement activity has often led to significant liability and operating restrictions under consent decrees.[137] Secondly, the threat of an antitrust suit by a licensee or would-be pool participant could put powerful downward pressure on the pool's royalty prospects. Thirdly, and perhaps most importantly, the threat of an antitrust suit by a *member* of the pool could be used to influence royalty or use negotiations. The threat of destabilizing intervention into the private ordering system could quite plausibly compromise the integrity of a pool's valuation procedures, thus undermining a major advantage of the pool arrangement. Given this multidirectional threat, even the latent (and, increasingly, historically distant) threat of government antitrust action appears to have been enough to make pool formation prohibitively risky.[138]

To be fair, however, it is at least plausible that the declining popularity of patent pools owes its origins in part to the fact that most pools were in fact cartels, which are now more vigorously pursued by antitrust authorities.[139] Nevertheless, the relative scarcity of pools on the present landscape—

---

[135] These are reviewed in Donald Turner, *Legal Restrictions on Exploitation of the Patent Monopoly: An Economic Analysis*, 76 YALE L.J. 267 (1966).

[136] See Thomas Jorde & David Teece, *Innovation, Cooperation and Antitrust: Striking the Right Balance*, 4 HIGH TECH. L.J. 1 (1989).

[137] See, eg, Bittlingmayer, n. 42 above (describing break-up of aircraft pool under the weight of a consent decree).

[138] Note in this respect that explicit antitrust 'safe harbors' for industry-wide research consortia have contributed to the success of this form of R&D organization. See Jorde & Teece, n. 136 above.

[139] I mean to suggest that antitrust enforcement activities directed at patent pools have not always, or even usually, been misguided. In some cases, pools were so clearly masking cartels that they had to be broken up. See, eg, *United States v. Nat'l Lead Co.*, 63 F. Supp. 513, 522–523 (S.D.N.Y. 1945), *aff'd*, 323 U.S. 319 (1947), where the Antitrust Division produced a gun that was not only smoking, but also screaming and flashing: 'Cornish, president of [National Lead], finds himself obliged to contribute to the correspondence [on the formation of the pool] . . . The subject under discussion is apparently the proposed arrangement with the Blumenfeld companies: "May I call the proposed combination, for simplicity, a cartel?" And he defines it. "The whole purpose of the cartel is to obtain a monopoly of patents so that no one can manufacture it excepting the members of the cartel, and so can raise the prices by reason of such monopoly to a point that would give us much more profit on our present tonnage, but also prevent a growth in tonnage that would interfere with their greater profits in lithophone"'.

especially given the increasing presence and strength of patents in many industries—suggests a classic case of excessive deterrence. Surely the optimal patent pooling policy is not completely laissez faire; but just as surely, it is not to discourage all pools. Although this is not the place to set out a complete test to determine the appropriate antitrust standard to apply, the tools do seem at hand to construct such a test. George Priest's 1977 article, stressing the degree of technological integration as the key indicia of a pro-competitive pool, is certainly a good starting point.[140] To this might be added the thought that the determinations necessitated by the Priest approach are not at all unmanageable; they amount to no more than a large scale application of standard tests for patent infringement.[141] Where industry members are seen pervasively to infringe each other's patents, and where valuation and exchange mechanisms appear to serve no ulterior purpose beyond setting compensation for these infringements, a real working pool is in effect.

At a minimum, pools which reduce the volume of licensing and lead to greater technological integration ought to be considered presumptively legal, whereas pools that do not add to interfirm technology adoption ought to be suspect. Surprisingly, though one might suppose that such a test would be difficult to administer, a quick review of the reported cases suggests otherwise. Perhaps fortuitously, the pools described in the case law seem to fall fairly readily on one side of the line or the other.[142]

Although revising the antitrust test applied to patent pools would be a good start, we should go further. To bring about the full benefits of contractual liability rules in the patent sphere, it may actually make sense for the government to contribute to the formation of pools and other exchange mechanisms. European policymakers recently did just this with respect to

---

[140] Priest, n. 35 above.

[141] On these tests, see ROBERT P. MERGES, PATENT LAW AND POLICY Ch. 8 (1992).

[142] A different set of issues is presented where the pool is created out of a research program funded by the government. Fairness and access issues are more compelling under those circumstances. See Testimony of Jerry Rogers, CEO of Cyrix, Inc. (a small semiconductor company excluded from Sematech, the large (partly) government-financed R&D consortium for the industry), reprinted in Semiconductor Industry: CEO Testifies on Challenges Facing U.S Firms, EDGE, Aug. 5, 1991: 'Innovation sometimes depends on access to "patent pools"—licensing of multiple items of intellectual property that are interrelated but whose patents are held by various parties. Established companies with substantial patent portfolios can often swap their patent rights to gain access to these patent pools.

Smaller companies, although they possess innovative intellectual property, have not had the time to obtain patent rights. Therefore, they have fewer patents with which they can barter, thus either: 1) they can pay a 10–20 percent royalty to each patent holder in the pool; or 2) they can trade products, turning over the rights to all their innovative intellectual property and products before they are granted manufacturing in return.

"If entrepreneurial companies like Cyrix can be assured of a level playing field that gives us the same access to tax-supported research that large companies enjoy", said Rogers, "and if we can be assured of protection—not victimization—by the nation's patent laws, I am sure that we can make an even more substantial contribution to the nation's competitive strength in the years ahead" '.

CD-ROM patents.[143] One can imagine a similar effort in the United States, for example a small group of technology exchange officers, perhaps working out of the Patent Office, whose function is to help bring together firms wishing to explore the possibility of pooling. Such an effort would also give the government a chance to prevent the most egregious misuses of pooling arrangements. At the very least, government policy should be neutral when an industry proposes the formation of a patent pool. The key to antitrust enforcement should be the bona fide efforts of people in the industry—including engineers and researchers—to value the technology administratively. Although court valuation is ineffective, as I have argued, court *oversight* of the institution charged with valuation ought to be tractable. Perhaps where it is not, where bona fide technology valuation cannot be separated from cartelization, market division, and the like, pools should be restricted or abolished.

A series of papers by antitrust scholars Thomas Jorde and David Teece in recent years lend credence to these conclusions. Jorde and Teece argue in favor of liberal antitrust treatment of all manner of interfirm cooperation, including but by no means limited to joint ventures and 'information sharing'. While they generate their predictions from a Schumpeterian-innovation framework, and couch them more in terms of antitrust policy, in broad terms we share the conclusion that policy ought to generally favor interfirm cooperation.[144]

[143] See Europe Advances Digital *Gear*, WALL ST. J., Dec. 21, 1992, at A6: 'The European Community Commission tentatively approved cross-licensing and other agreements between electronics companies to encourage development of digital compact cassettes and players. Firms and researchers may make, use or sell the products patented to other partners in the group. The EC said its move could restrict competition through pooling of patents, know-how and common specifications, but would advance technology and serve consumers'.

See also Nick Louth, *Sony and Philips to Let Market Referee Audio Fight*, REUTERS FIN. REP., Oct. 9, 1991: 'Philips said earlier it will pool patents with Sony over the latter's minidisc, while Sony for the first time endorsed the Dutch group's digital compact cassette (DCC). "Ultimately it is left to the consumer to decide," said analyst Angela Dean of brokers Morgan Stanley in London. The pooling of patents gives each firm access to the other's patents in the minidisc area. Analysts believe it would make no sense for Philips to hinder minidisc development by costly patent disputes when it expects to win in the market anyway. By contrast, and to illustrate that the inhospitality tradition in the U.S. may not be dead, n. that the Antitrust Division of the U.S. Department of Justice has announced an investigation of patent licensing practices in the CD-ROM field'.

See also Dennis Kneale, *Sony-Philips Pact on CD-Licensing Fees is Target of U.S. Antitrust Investigation*, WALL ST. J., July 12, 1994, at A3: 'Justice Department officials in recent weeks have sent out subpoenas to more than a dozen companies requesting documents outlining their dealings with Sony and Philips. The two companies signed a pact in the late 1970s to cross-license each other's basic patents on CD technology, according to industry executives. The agreement designated Philips to handle enforcement, collect fees from vendors and split the proceeds with Sony . . . The two companies' aggressive licensing program has enabled them to collect millions of dollars a year in patent fees while ensuring that new developments are compatible with the CD players they make and sell'.

[144] See David Teece, *Information Sharing, Innovation, and Antitrust* (Haas School of Business, U.C. Berkeley, working paper, 1993); Jorde & Teece, n. 136 above (extolling virtues of cooperative R&D and marketing efforts).

A. The Department of Justice's new outlook

Recent developments on the antitrust enforcement front show that Jorde and Teece are being heard. The potentially beneficial effects of patent pools are duly noted in the Department of Justice and Federal Trade Commission 'Antitrust Guidelines for the Licensing of Intellectual Property', issued in 1995.[145]

Although the Guidelines state (not surprisingly) that the Department of Justice intends to maintain its vigil over the anticompetitive effects of patent pools (ie, collective price or output restraints, price fixing, and market division), they also speak to the significant pro-competitive benefits which patent pools may provide. In fact, the section on pools and cross-licensing begins:

Cross-licensing and pooling arrangements . . . may provide procompetitive benefits by integrating complementary technologies, reducing transaction costs, clearing blocking positions, and avoiding costly infringement litigation. By promoting the dissemination of technology, cross-licensing and pooling arrangements are often procompetitive.

Additionally, in apparent response to its position that '[a]nother possible anticompetitive effect of pooling arrangements may occur if the arrangement deters or discourages participants from engaging in research and development, thus retarding innovation', the Guidelines state that 'such an arrangement can have procompetitive benefits, for example, by exploiting economies of scale and integrating complementary capabilities of the pool members, (including the clearing of blocking positions), and is likely to cause competitive problems only when the arrangement includes a large fraction of the potential research and development in an innovation market'.

The Guidelines' section on patent pools ends by providing the following 'safe-harbor'-like example:

Situation: [T]wo of the leading manufacturers of a consumer electronic product hold patents that cover alternative circuit designs for the product. The manufacturers assign several of their patents to a separate corporation wholly owned by the two firms. That corporation licenses the right to use the circuit designs to other consumer product manufacturers and establishes the license royalties. [T]he manufacturers assign to the separate corporation only patents that are blocking. None of the patents assigned to the corporation can be used without infringing a patent owned by the other firm.

Discussion: [T]he joint assignment of patent rights to the wholly owned corporation in this example does not adversely affect competition in the licensed technology among entities that would have been actual or likely potential competitors in the absence of the licensing arrangement. Moreover, the licensing arrangement is likely to

---

[145] US Department of Justice and Federal Trade Commission, *Antitrust Guidelines for the Licensing of Intellectual Property—1995,* 4 Trade Reg. Rep. (CCH) ¶13,132 (Apr. 11, 1995).

have procompetitive benefits in the use of the technology. Because the manufacturers' patents are blocking, the manufacturers are not in a horizontal relationship with respect to those patents. None of the patents can be used without the right to a patent owned by the other firm, so the patents are not substitutable. [T]he firms are horizontal competitors in the relevant goods market. In the absence of collateral restraints that would likely raise price or reduce output in the relevant goods market or in any other relevant antitrust market and that are not reasonably related to an efficiency-enhancing integration of economic activity, the evaluating Agency would be unlikely to challenge this arrangement.

B. The MPEG–2 and DVD review letters

The Justice Department's approach is evidenced in its treatment of the MPEG–2 pool. The Antitrust Division of the Department of Justice issued a Business Review Letter approving this pool. The Division concluded:

Like many joint licensing arrangements, the agreements . . . for the licensing of MPEG–2 Essential Patents are likely to provide significant cost savings to Licensors and licensees alike, substantially reducing the time and expense that would otherwise be required to disseminate the rights to each MPEG–2 Essential Patent to each would-be licensee. Moreover, the proposed agreements that will govern the licensing arrangement have features designed to enhance the usual procompetitive effects and mitigate potential anticompetitive dangers.[146]

The Antitrust Division first analyzed the patent pool in general. It highlighted the limitation of the Portfolio to 'technically essential patents' as determined by an independent expert as a feature that 'reduces the risk that the patent pool will be used to eliminate rivalry between potentially competing technologies'. The independent expert also plays a continuing role as an arbiter of essentiality when a new patent is submitted for inclusion in the portfolio. Patents adjudicated to be invalid or unenforceable will be deleted from the pool.

The division next analyzed whether the arrangement facilitated collusion and concluded that it did not. MPEG LA is prohibited from transmitting confidential information among the licensors and licensees. The division concluded that it appeared 'highly unlikely that the royalty rate could be used during that period as a device to coordinate the prices of downstream products' since the contemplated royalty rates would likely make up a tiny fraction of the prices of MPEG–2 products.

The Antitrust Division also found pro-competitive the features concerning the use by and rights of the licensees:

The conditioning of licensee royalty liability on actual use of the Portfolio patents, the clearly stated freedom of licensees to develop and use alternative technologies, and the

---

[146] MPEG–2 Review Letter, n. 92 above.

imposition of obligations on licensees' own patent rights that do not vitiate licensees' incentives to innovate, all serve to protect competition in the development and use of both improvements on, and alternatives to, MPEG–2 technology.

A law review article by DOJ staffers provides additional insight into how the Division viewed the MPEG–2 pool.[147] The article stresses the characterization of the horizontal, rather than vertical, structure of the pool. 'The pooling arrangement promises to bring together complementary inputs (the 27 MPEG–2 patents), reduce double-marginalization problems and transaction costs (by creating a mechanism for one-stop shopping for most of the patents required to meet the MPEG–2 standard), and promote the dissemination of new technology'.[148] This characterization is based on the premise that the patents in the portfolio are essential to the implementation of the MPEG–2 standard and are complementary.

The DOJ staffers also emphasize the safeguards that render the MPEG–2 pool 'unlikely to harm competition under a vertical theory—excluding or disadvantaging rivals or facilitating collusion'.[149] The article points out several provisions of the arrangement that reduce the likelihood that the pool will anticompetitively disadvantage rivals:

First, the agreement commits the licensors to extend the portfolio license on nondiscriminatory terms to any party requesting a license. Second, no person was prevented from submitting a patent for possible inclusion in the pool, and no person identified as having an essential patent was excluded from participation in the pool. Third, although MPEG LA only licenses the portfolio as a package, all of the pooled patents may be licensed from the pool members individually. This provides a 'safety valve' against the pool being used to create a 'two-level entry' problem.

Like the MPEG–2 pool, the Antitrust Division concluded that two recently-formed pools for DVD technology were not likely to be anticompetitive. Indeed, it would have been quite a surprise had the Department of Justice concluded otherwise, given the many similarities between the MPEG–2 and DVD pools. The pools for both include only essential patents—those required to implement a widely-accepted technological standard. Also in both, an independent patent expert determines 'essentiality' on the basis of objective evaluation procedure. Both pools call for royalties that are small relative to the total costs of manufacture. In addition, licensing is nondiscriminatory, and individual licensees are free to strike deals with each patent holder. Finally, because of the structure and scope of the pool, innovation does not appear to be hampered.

---

[147] Willard K. Tom & Joshua A. Newberg, *Antitrust and Intellectual Property: From Separate Spheres to Unified Field*, 66 ANTITRUST L.J. 167 (1997).
[148] Ibid, at 219–21.   [149] Ibid.

C. Complementarity and transaction costs

The recently-approved pools will serve as a guide to action in other industries. But of course future pools will likely differ from MPEG–2 and DVD in at least some respects. Which features will be deemed 'essential', and how far may future pools vary yet still receive favorable treatment?

An exhaustive account of possible variations would be pointless. But one important variable is worth discussing. The two recent pools grew out of industry standard setting. While this is a common practice, not all technological blockages result from standards. Indeed, not all potential patent pools are the result of *strict* blockages. Should these pools be encouraged, too?

This comes down to a question of whether the transactional benefits of pooling outweigh the potential social costs. These costs, which would follow from the anticompetitive potential that follows from pooling, would likely take the form of restricted entry in the relevant industry, and ultimately higher consumer prices. Antitrust treatment of this issue would follow the Antitrust Guidelines cited earlier.

What economists call 'strict complementarity' provides an appealing reason to approve a patent pool.[150] In such a situation, none of the bargaining parties can realize *any* return on their assets in the absence of agreement. In such a case, the gains from cooperation are very large: in theory, *all* benefits of a given technology depend on agreement among the parties. But many times the patent landscape in an industry falls far short of strict complementarity. To take one example, assume there are two components that are essential for the proper functioning of a given product. Each of two firms holds a key patent on each of the components. Imagine it is possible for end-users physically to integrate the two components, but that it is much better if a manufacturer integrates the components into one marketable product. (Either it is cheaper to do so, or the resulting product works much better, or both.) In such a scenario, the patents are not strictly complementary. Both patentees can realize some economic gain by selling the components directly to end-users. But both can also realize much higher returns if they cross-license the patents and manufacture integrated products for sale to end-users.

What if the two firms in this scenario want to form a patent pool? I would argue that traditional 'rule of reason' analysis ought to be applied during antitrust review. The gains from permitting integration ought to be weighed against the potential costs. And the same is true for the related case, where more than two manufacturers want to joint the pool. Specifically, as I have

---

[150] See, eg, Joel Klein, *Cross-Licenses, Patent and Copyright Pools and the U.S. Antitrust Laws*, 73 COPYRIGHT WORLD 44 (1997). Cf Dennis W. Carlton & J. Mark Klamer, *The Need for Coordination Among Firms, with Special Reference to Network Industries*, 50 U. CHI. L. REV. 446 (1983); Gene M. Grossman & Carl Shapiro, *Research Joint Ventures: An Antitrust Analysis*, 2 J.L. ECON. & ORG. 315 (1986).

argued throughout this chapter, antitrust authorities should recognize the potential for considerable savings in transaction costs that follow from industry-established transactional mechanisms. Thus some features of the recent MPEG–2 and DVD pools might be deemed essential. In particular, 'open membership' and nonexclusive licensing (ie, licensees' right to take individual licenses from pool members outside the setting of the pool) are important mechanisms for preventing anticompetitive harm from pooling. But I would argue that strict complementarity, based on industry standards, should not be deemed essential to future pools.

IV. Conclusion

Patent pools continue to pose intriguing challenges to theorists of property rights. They challenge us to ask: should property rights be granted with some view toward post-grant transactions? And why are oil field unitization, Moscow retail property, and perhaps gene fragment patents, different from established, technologically sophisticated industries? The three former cases exemplify an inability for multiple complementary rightholders to bargain to an effective solution, while the latter often develop an effective mechanism (the patent pool) to do just that. Why is that?

This is a young branch of theory, and we have as yet few data points. But a brief summary of transactional characteristics may be attempted. The idea is not to settle the debate, if such it is, but merely to take stock of what we know so far. In that spirit, consider Figure 6.1, which compares anticommons (Moscow store fronts, gene fragment patents), oil field unitization, and successful IP transaction institutions.

The way forward from here is obvious. We need both more data, and more nuanced theory to account for it. And we also need a better understanding of when and how government policy can be brought to bear on these issues. For example, we are just beginning to see how patterns of post-grant transactions affect the economic impact of various property right entitlements. This will have obvious implications for our thinking about the proper contours of property right grants. At the same time, it is likely that in certain cases it will be very difficult or impossible to see far enough down the road to predict the post-grant landscape. In such cases, we must be sensitive to the need for rules and doctrines that permit the 'visible hand' of government to prod or even force parties into transactions. This may be the only way effectively to reconcile a proliferating array of property rights with society's need to assemble rights into useful bundles.

Fɪɢ. 6.1: Summary of transactional characteristics

Case Study	Number of contracting parties	Repeat players or one-shot exchange	Property right valuation features
Anticommons (Moscow property, gene fragment patents)	Many	One-shot	High uncertainty
Oil field unitization	Few to many	One-shot	High uncertainty; parties' actions may influence value of holdings
IPR exchange institutions (patent pools, ASCAP)	Pools: usually few ASCAP: many	Repeat players	Pools: acceptance of technology specialists' valuations ASCAP: rights valuable only in large bundles

A PLAN FOR THE FUTURE OF MUSIC PERFORMANCE RIGHTS ORGANIZATIONS IN THE DIGITAL AGE

BENNETT M. LINCOFF*

I. Introduction: The Web is Alive with the Sound of Music—Maybe

Collective management of music performance rights has been the standard practice since 1851 when SACEM,[1] the French rights society, was established. Today, a worldwide network of affiliated performance rights organizations (PROs) is in operation. Each functions within its own territory as a clearinghouse, making markets between those who own copyrighted music and those whose public performance of it requires the owner's authorization. Music users pay fees to local PROs for licenses to perform any of the millions of works in the aggregate repertory of all the affiliated organizations and, in

---

* The author formerly served as the Director of Legal Affairs for New Media at ASCAP (the American Society of Composers, Authors and Publishers). The views expressed in this chapter, however, do not necessarily reflect those of ASCAP, its Board of Directors, counsel, management, employees or members.

[1] SACEM is the *Societe des Auteurs, Compositeurs et Editeurs de Musique*. See generally <http://www.sacem.fr>.

turn, PROs distribute these fees, after deducting their costs, as royalties to writers and music publishers.

Collective management has been a boon for music owners and users alike. Through it, music users can minimize their costs by obtaining authorization to perform a vast repertory of copyrighted works in a single transaction at reasonable fees. Alternatively, they would incur the additional expense of contacting and negotiating with individual copyright owners to secure the rights they need. In addition, through so-called 'blanket licensing', music users are freed from the burden of scrutinizing every performance they make. Such scrutiny would otherwise be required to avoid even unintentionally infringing conduct.

In the absence of collective licensing, the majority of music copyright owners may find it difficult, if not impossible, to locate, negotiate with, and license the numerous and far-flung users of their works. However, through well-managed collective licensing structures, copyright owners, large and small, can enjoy a reliable means of receiving a fair royalty for performances of their creative works.

With collective licensing through the affiliated PROs, the whole is greater than the sum of its parts: the value of the right of access to this aggregated repertory is greater than the cumulative value of the right of access to each of the works comprising the repertory.[2]

Prior to the Internet, public performances, as such, did not involve the reproduction or distribution of music or any rights in sound recordings in which the performed works may have been embodied.[3] Streaming media[4] and the ability of end-users to download and retain perfect digital copies permit, for the first time, the simultaneous exploitation of both performance and distribution rights. Online transmissions also may involve the distribution and digital performance rights in sound recordings; and the loading of music and sound recordings onto a server's hard drive also count as reproductions.

The Internet will maximize the opportunities to exploit every category and combination of rights in music. However, new technology also may blur the distinctions between different rights. It may not be possible to know whether end-users only listen to online performances or also download them.

---

[2] See *BMI v. CBS*, 441 US 1, 21–22 (1979).

[3] Live performances at clubs, hotels and concert venues, performances of recorded music in restaurants, bars and retail establishments, and broadcast performances all undoubtedly promoted music sales However, these performances did not involve 'copying' the music; rather the music was copied or distributed in sheet music or in the form of sound recordings. No independent protection was afforded to performance rights in sound recordings in the USA until 1995; and the right then enacted is limited to digital audio transmissions. See Digital Performance Right in Sound Recordings Act of 1995, Pub. L. No. 104–39, 109 Stat. 336 (1995), amended by Digital Millennium Copyright Act, Pub. L. 105–304, 112 Stat. 2860 (1998).

[4] Streaming media technology enables end-users to hear music simultaneously with its transmission, allowing computers to function like radios—or, if there is a video component to the transmission, like televisions.

Moreover, efforts to prevent widespread unauthorized downloading may prove futile. Technological protections beget countermeasures, and news of a successful hack will be available instantly to anyone who cares. In any event, whatever technological fix the music industry devises for newly-made recordings, it cannot protect existing works already in the public's hands. Because of the Internet, the market for authorized sales of individual sound recordings can be ruined in a nanosecond. Accordingly, it will be difficult to sustain a revenue model based on music sales with thin margins and driven by hits.

On the other hand, the Internet and its attendant technologies create a market in which performance rights licensing for music may gain substantially as a revenue source. The market for performance rights constantly refreshes itself. People seem never to tire of listening to the music they like most. The success of radio and music television is proof of this. Moreover, whether or not a particular webcaster is licensed has no effect on the market for performance rights over all. Unlike the distribution right, the performance right cannot be subverted by a single unauthorized webcaster or Internet end-user. Through the Internet, performances could be made available from countless sources, all the time, everywhere, to anyone with online access.

Webcasters clamor for a 'one-stop shop' for their music licensing needs. They seek a single source from which to obtain all Internet rights in musical works and sound recordings. Because the separate rights involved have different owners, it is unlikely that a universal 'one-stop shop' will be in operation anytime soon. Indeed, antitrust laws may prohibit the 'one-stop shop' altogether. Also problematic are divisions within the music industry—particularly between record labels and music publishers—concerning ownership, valuation and collective administration of the different rights involved.

Record labels are doing what they can to preserve their some US $40 billion in annual worldwide revenue from the sale of recordings.[5] Many have launched their own websites to offer secure digital downloads. In addition, working through the Recording Industry Association of America (the RIAA),[6] the record labels have become gatekeepers of online performances of recorded music. The webcasting provisions of the Digital Millennium Copyright Act (DMCA) grant a statutory license to 'eligible' webcasters who operate, essentially, as the online equivalent of traditional radio broadcasters.[7] All others are

---

[5] For 1998, the International Federation of the Phonographic Industry (IFPI) reported worldwide sales of US $38.67 billion. See <http://www.ifpi.org/music_stats/index.html>.

[6] See generally <http://www.riaa.com>.

[7] 17 US.C. § 114(d)(2)(C)(i)–(ix), (j)(2), (j)(4), (j)(6), (j)(7), (j)(13); H.R. REP. No. 105–796, at 80–88 (1998). To be 'eligible' for the statutory license, a webcast must be 'nonsubscription' and 'noninteractive' and must meet additional programming restrictions and user interface requirements. Webcasts are 'nonsubscription' if no fee is required from users to recieve them. Webcasts are 'interactive' and, therefore, not 'eligible' for the statutory license, if they allow users, on request, to recieve transmissions of particular recordings (except for requests that particular recordings be webcast for particular reception by the public at large where the webcast does not

relegated to free market negotiations with record labels who may refuse to grant digital performance rights in the sound recordings they own.[8] None of this, however, will meaningfully reduce the threat of unauthorized downloading.[9] But it will result in fewer licensed webcasts with fewer performances of fewer works. And this will slow the growth of license fees that music copyright owners and record labels will earn from online performances of recorded music.

Of course, not all online performances will be of music embodied in copyrighted sound recordings. The Internet is particularly well-suited to offer live performances as well. Moreover, not all sound recordings are copyrighted. Those created prior to 15 February 1972 are not protected under federal copyright law[10] and, therefore, are not subject to the record labels' rights under the DMCA. In addition, performances of theme, background, bridge, cue and other incidental music used in television programming and movies do not involve sound recordings as a general matter. For all of these, rights must be obtained from the copyright owners of the underlying musical works being performed or from their licensing representative, such as the PRO to which they belong.

For their part, many music publishers already have established an online presence. Their trade association, the National Music Publishers Association, is offering mechanical rights licenses where downloading clearly is

substantially consist of recordings performed within one hour of a request or at specifically designated times).

The DMCA's programming restrictions prohibit webcastors from: (1) webcasting, in any three hour period, more than three songs (or more than two in a row) from the same recording, or more than four songs (or more than three in a row) by the same artist; (2) publishing advance program schedules or making prior announcements of the titles of recordings or the artists to be webcast (other than immediately prior to their transmission); (3) webcasting archived programs (those which are always accessed at their beginnings) which are less than five hours, or webcasting programs which are greater than five hours if archived for more than two weeks; (4) webcasting continuous, or looped programs, which are less than three hours; (5) webcasting more than three times in two weeks any program shorter than one hour that is announced in advance and which contains recordings in a predetermined order; (6) webcasting an advertisement for a particular product or service every time it transmits a particular recording or artist, unless they are affiliated; or (7) webcasting any bootleg recording.

The DMCA's user interface requirements mandate that webcasters: (1) cooperate with record labels to prevent end-user scanning of webcasts for particular recorings; (2) employ available technology to disable end-users from downloading (and not to suggest that end-users download) webcasts; (3) accommodate and not interfere with copyright management information encoded in recordings they webcast; and (4) identify in on-screen text the title of the song and album and the artist at the time it is webcast.

⁸ Not all sound recording copyright owners necessarily want to limit online performances of their works. A growing number of artists and independent record labels are themselves webcasters and are making their recordings more widely available for performances in this new medium.

⁹ Every website and every end-user in the world is potentially a source for the unauthorized distribution of copyrighted sound recordings.

¹⁰ Sound Recording Act of 1971, Pub L. No. 92–140, 85 Stat. 391 (1971), amended by Pub. L. No. 93–573, 88 Stat. 1873 (1975).

involved.[11] In addition, music publishers, as copyright owners, can aggregate the reproduction, performance and distribution rights in their musical works into a newly-created hybrid, an online transmission right, which they can offer webcasters directly. In this way, each music publisher can establish its own 'one-stop shop', making available a worldwide grant encompassing the necessary array of rights in its musical works. It remains to be seen whether, and to what extent, music publishers will offer webcasters this new form of online transmission right or will license reproduction, performance and distribution rights directly but separately. Were either of these practices to become widespread, it could disintermediate PROs altogether from the online music marketplace.

The worldwide reach of Internet performances coupled with the ability of webcasters to originate their transmissions from the territory with the lowest Internet license fees may lead to competition among national PROs of an entirely new kind. This new competition could erode the cooperative foundation upon which the PROs' network of affiliation has, until now, been based.

Currently, the PROs are not fully able to administer Internet performance rights in the music they represent. They do not yet have a definitive basis for determining which among them is authorized to license webcast performances involving more than a single territory, nor a means to resolve conflicting claims to royalties arising from performances contained in transborder communications.

If PROs hope to retain their function and position in the music-licensing environment of the future, they must reexamine their concept of territoriality as it applies to licensing webcasters and distributing Internet royalties to their songwriter and music publisher members.

Two changes are indicated. First, each PRO should be authorized to act on behalf of all the affiliated organizations to grant webcasters worldwide performance rights for transmissions originating in the territory of the PRO issuing the license. Secondly, the PROs will need to adopt royalty distribution rules that conceive of each webcast as two performances—one in the territory from which the webcast originates, and one in the territory where it is received. If these turn out to be two different countries, then, as I will show, a way must be found to divide the publishers' share of the royalties so that copyright owners of the work in the two territories involved will be treated fairly. These changes are inextricably linked; so, too, are the consequences of failing to take adequate and timely action.

---

[11] See generally <http://www.nmpa.org>.

II. How Performance Rights Organizations Currently Obtain Rights, License Users, and Distribute Royalties

Writers and music publishers grant their local PRO the right to administer performances of their works worldwide. Initially, therefore, each PRO obtains worldwide rights to works created and owned by its own members, but no rights in works owned by members of other organizations.[12] Given this, the inherent value of licenses that any PRO can offer, acting separately, is limited by the relative number of sought-after works in its domestic repertory. Also, it is neither efficient nor cost effective for PROs to license music users or monitor performances occurring outside their home territories. To do so would require creation and maintenance of rights management infrastructures in foreign territories. It also might involve regulation under foreign legal regimes.

Therefore, the PROs have created a network for collective management of their members' rights in all territories in which participating organizations operate.[13] Each PRO grants those with which it is affiliated authorization to license and monitor performances of works owned by its members when occurring in the other's territory. For example, GEMA (the German PRO)[14] grants SOCAN (the Canadian organization)[15] authorization to administer performances of German music in Canada and, in turn, SOCAN grants GEMA the same right with respect to Canadian music in Germany. In this way, music users can obtain authorization from a local organization, on a territory-by-territory basis, to perform any and all works from what is, essentially, a worldwide repertory of music.

Of course, music users are not required to do business with PROs. They can obtain the rights they need directly from the copyright owners of the works they wish to perform. The extent to which copyright owners may license

---

[12] Occasionally, copyright owners affiliate simultaneously with PROs in two or more territories When this happens, one organization receives worldwide rights except for performances occurring in the territories of the other PROs to which the copyright owner belongs; and the other PROs receive domestic performance rights only.

[13] CISAC, the Confederation Internationale des Societe D'Auteurs et Compositores, is the governing body of the world's affiliated copyright collecting societies, with 180 member organizations in 95 countries. See generally <http://www.cisac.org>.

[14] GEMA is the Gesellschaft fur musikalische Auffuhrungs-und mechanische Vervielfaltigungsrechte. See generally <http://www.gema.de>.

[15] SOCAN is the Society of Composers and Music Publishers of Canada. See generally <http://www.socan.ca>.

[16] In the United States, writers and music publishers grant their PROs non-exclusive rights Elsewhere, they grant exclusive rights, but are permitted to withhold rights with respect to any category or categories of music user. In the United States, it is only the music publisher, as copyright owner of the works involved, who has authority to license music users directly. Elsewhere, both the writer and music publisher have that authority.

music users on their own depends on the PRO to which they belong.[16] ASCAP[17] and BMI,[18] the two principal US PROs,[19] only permit their members to license performances of their works directly on a user-by-user basis. The European organizations allow it on an industry-by-industry basis. This difference may gain added significance as technology allows copyright owners to connect even with the most physically remote webcasters performing their works. Absent some change, individual European music copyright owners will be able to establish comprehensive Internet licensing strategies, whereas ASCAP and BMI members will not.

PROs distribute royalties based on surveys of licensed performances. Most monitoring is limited to samples, although a few surveys rest on a census of licensed performances. Some rely on play lists or similar data prepared by licensees; others on movie cue sheets and published program guides; and still others on remotely made recordings of television and radio broadcasts and cable and satellite transmissions. Each PRO establishes its own practices for monitoring performances and its own rules governing the calculation and distribution of royalties.

Generally, however, royalties are divided equally between the writer and music publisher. If the work is of domestic origin, the PRO that licensed its performance pays the writer's and publisher's shares to its own members. If the work is of foreign origin, it pays the writer's share to whichever PRO the writer belongs (for subsequent distribution to him), but, normally, it will pay the publisher's share to a member of its own who has been designated to act as the subpublisher of the work within the territory where the performance occurred.[20] If no domestic subpublisher for a work of foreign origin has been designated, then both the writer's and publisher's shares are paid to the appropriate affiliated foreign PRO.

This structure works well for performances which begin and end in a single territory. It authorizes the PRO in that territory to act on behalf of all the affiliated organizations to license the music user in question. It also establishes that the party who owns local rights in the work for the territory where its performance occurs is entitled to receive the publisher's share of royalties.

But PROs do not have a consistent basis for administering rights in works contained in performances which involve more than a single territory.

---

[17] ASCAP is the American Society of Composers, Authors and Publishers. See generally <http://www.ascap.com>.

[18] BMI, is also known as Broadcast Music, Inc. See generally <http://www.bmi.com>.

[19] ASCAP and BMI dominate the market for music performance rights in the United States There are, however, several smaller organizations including, for example, SESAC, which also function as PROs and which, between them, may have a 2 or 3 percent market share.

[20] To facilitate administration of rights in their works worldwide, music publishers enter into agreements with publishers in other countries, called subpublishers, to represent the publisher's interests in the subpublisher's territory. In exchange for a fee typically measured as a percentage of revenues collected, the subpublisher will register the publisher's works with the local PRO and collect performance and other royalties on its behalf.

Decisions regarding rights administration for transborder broadcasts and satellite transmissions turn on the nature of the transmission technology involved and on the inclination of the affiliated PROs to cooperate with each other.

Broadcasts are diffuse and freely available to anyone operating a radio or television set close enough to the broadcast tower. As a practical matter, one cannot know with certainty in which territory audience members are located or whether a particular broadcast performance was received in a territory other than the one from which it originated. Accordingly, it is difficult to quantify the interests of the PROs in territories where transborder broadcasts can be received. However, the reach of transborder broadcasts is limited to the spillover occurring between contiguous territories. Therefore, the PROs treat these broadcasts as if they begin and end entirely within the territory from which they originate. That is, the PRO in that territory has authority to license the broadcaster in question and to distribute royalties as it would for other performances occurring locally.

Satellite transmissions are different. They are available only to subscribers whose identity and location are known in advance of the transmission. They are directed narrowly and specifically to territories falling within the satellite footprint chosen by the program service. This may or may not include the territory from which they originate. Programming and advertising can be targeted on a territory-by-territory basis. Therefore, it is possible to quantify the interests of the PROs in each territory involved in transborder satellite transmissions of particular programs. Accordingly, the PROs have agreed that, prior to granting other than domestic performance rights, the organization in the territory from which the satellite transmissions originate must consult each organization in the territories in which transmissions may be received about the terms and conditions of licensing and the basis on which royalties will be distributed for the performances involved.

III. The Licensing Needs of Webcasters and the Consequences of Failing to Meet Them

Nearly every webcast performance of a musical work brings with it the possibility of worldwide liability. Not only may these performances be infringing if unauthorized in the territory from which they originate, they also may be infringing if not authorized for territories in which they are received. Thus, the PROs' traditional practice of limiting the licenses they grant to a single territory, or proceeding on an ad hoc basis, is not suitable for the Internet. It imposes an untenable choice on webcasters, large and small, whose transmissions are available for reception worldwide. Each must either enter into separate agreements with every PRO in the world and pay multiple license fees calculated on inconsistent bases, or enter into a single agreement with its local PRO for domestic performance rights only, and risk an unknown quantum of infringement liability under foreign legal regimes.

To the extent that webcasters are aware of this problem, they view it with considerable alarm. Their only alternative is to obtain rights on a song-by-song or catalog-by-catalog basis directly from music copyright owners.

Failure to grant webcasters worldwide rights will result in decreased copyright compliance because transborder Internet performances will proceed without authorization for territories in which they are received. License fee collections also may decline. If webcasters are granted domestic performance rights only, they may want to exclude from the base against which their license fee is calculated any revenue attributable to access by end-users located outside the territory for which the webcaster's performances are authorized. The same negative effect on fee collections might result if license fees were calculated on a pay-per-play rather than a percentage of revenue basis. Finally, as will be discussed more fully below, failure to grant webcasters worldwide rights will make it harder for PROs to monitor online performances of the works they license.

A. How the affiliated Performance Rights Organizations, acting together, can grant webcasters the worldwide performance rights they need

There are two ways in which the PROs, acting together, can grant webcasters worldwide performance rights. Either each PRO can obtain authority to grant rights for webcasts originating in its territory, or authority to grant rights could be given to the PRO in the territory where the webcaster's principal place of business is located. In either case, the grants made would include all works in the aggregate repertories of all affiliated PROs. Each organization could conduct its licensing activities separately, offering agreements with terms and conditions appropriate to local market circumstances. Neither harmonization of disparate national law nor agreement on licensing structures or rates and tariffs would be necessary.

The first solution—allowing each affiliated PRO to grant worldwide performance rights for webcast transmissions originating in its territory—is simplest. Thus, for example, JASRAC (the Japanese PRO),[21] acting on behalf of all affiliated organizations, would have authority to grant worldwide rights to any webcaster whose transmissions originate in Japan.

This approach would meet the needs of most webcasters. For some, however, such a license may not be feasible. These include webcasters whose transmissions originate from a territory where no PRO operates, or where the

---

[21] JASRAC is the Japanese Society for Rights of Authors, Composers and Publishers. See generally <http://www.jasrac.or.jp>.

PRO is not affiliated with those granting worldwide rights, or where the PRO grants worldwide rights but, for some reason, has not licensed the webcaster in question. In such circumstances, all PROs should be free to license any performances that occur by virtue of the receipt of these webcasts in their respective territories and to initiate infringement litigation against webcasters who fail or refuse to obtain such licenses.

This approach would benefit webcasters who want to comply with copyright laws. They could obtain worldwide rights to nearly all copyrighted music in a single transaction with the PRO in the territory where their website is located. It also would provide a structure for enforcing rights against those unable or unwilling to obtain a worldwide grant.

Nevertheless, it is unlikely that most PROs will support this solution because it may encourage webcasters to use foreign host servers, resulting in transmissions originating from the territory with the lowest Internet license fees. If such migration occurs, the PRO in the webcaster's home territory loses license fee revenues it otherwise would have earned and, in turn, its members receive fewer royalties. In theory, each PRO could avoid this loss by refusing to affiliate with any other organization which, in its view, charges unacceptably low Internet license fees. In practice, however, this may prove unworkable.

Website migration is significant only because the United States is the territory to which webcasters might be expected to flee. ASCAP and BMI operate in a highly regulated marketplace pursuant to anti trust consent decrees.[22] The fees they charge are subject to review and adjustment by a federal court.[23] As a consequence, performance rights license fees in the United States often are lower than elsewhere.

Moreover, actions taken on their own initiative may lead ASCAP and BMI to depress Internet license fees further than the courts that review their rates might require. For example, ASCAP charges webcasters who operate their own music servers a license fee based on a percentage of revenue each derives from its site.[24] On the other hand, webcasters who rely on music content aggregators, such as broadcast.com, to host and serve their music transmissions pay no license fee to ASCAP at all.[25] Rather, the music aggregator pays

---

[22] See *United States v. ASCAP*, 1950–1951 Trade Cases (CCH) Par. 62,595 (S.D.N.Y. 1950) (the Amended Final Judgment); *United States v. BMI*, 64-Civ. 3787 (S.D.N.Y., December 29, 1966), as amended November 18, 1994.

[23] See *United States v. ASCAP*, 1950–1951.

[24] ASCAP Experimental License Agreement for Internet Sites on the World Wide Web, Release 3.0 Though denominated 'Experimental', this agreement is that which ASCAP offers to webcasters.

[25] Broadcast.com, originally known as AudioNet, was, in 1995, the premiere Internet music content aggregator. Its founder, Mark Cuban, recognized the opportunity presented by the early reluctance of radio group owners to underwrite development of their stations' websites. Cuban offered station managers free hosting of their music content on his service, thus enabling radio stations to retransmit their broadcasts live on the Internet using streaming media technology provided by AudioNet. A link on the stations' website allowed end-users to access its webcasts through a page on AudioNet's website dedicated to that radio station's content. AudioNet made its money by selling advertising on the station's page on AudioNet.com.

ASCAP a license fee based on a percentage of the aggregator's own revenue, and pays an additional flat dollar amount for each of its webcaster clients.[26] None of the revenue earned by the aggregator's webcaster clients is included in the base against which the aggregator's ASCAP license fee is calculated.[27]

This circumstance is an unhappy one for non-US PROs. Not only do they lose license fees when their domestic webcasters migrate to the United States; but, for webcasters who rely on music content aggregators,[28] ASCAP, at least, may collect only a token license fee payment wholly unrelated to the revenue earned by the webcaster from its online performances of music. The loss occasioned by this licensing practice is likely to increase as convergence of media continues.

There is unlikely to be anything the non-US PROs can do to remedy this situation. The ASCAP and BMI repertories are vast. Together, they probably comprise the majority of the most frequently performed works worldwide. The domestic repertories of the non-US PROs contain far fewer sought-after works. Accordingly, licenses offered by PROs affiliated with ASCAP and BMI depend, in large part, on inclusion of the US repertory for their value.

Several of the non-US PROs, led by the largest of the continental European organizations, advocate an alternate solution—one which offers webcasters the worldwide rights they need but does not encourage website migration. They want each affiliated PRO to be authorized to license those webcasters whose principal place of business ('economical residence' in European parlance) is within its territory. Thus, the website of an entity with its principal place of business in Paris would obtain rights through an agreement with

---

[26] For 2001, these payments ranged from US$10 to US$1,000 for each webcaster served by an ASCAP-licensed content aggregator. See ASCAP Experimental License Agreement for Internet Aggregators, subpara. 7(b).

[27] ASCAP first issued its License Agreement for Internet Aggregators in mid-1998. During my tenure, however, it sought to license aggregators and their webcaster clients separately, though with the same form of agreement, charging each a fee based on the revenue it derived from performances jointly undertaken. See, ASCAP Experimental License Agreement for Internet Sites on the World Wide Web, Release 2.0, subparas 3(b), 4 and 6(a).

The License Agreement for Internet Aggregators illustrates a different approach. It allows the aggregator's relationship with ASCAP to inure to the benefit of the aggregator's webcaster clients. It is curious that ASCAP voluntarily adopted this form of agreement which so closely tracks the structure that the ASCAP rate court imposed on it for licensing the cable industry. Cablecasting involves two licensable performances: one by the program service when it transmits its signal to the headends of the cable systems which carry it, and the other by the system operators who transmit those signals to viewers' homes. ASCAP is required to offer the program services licenses which, as they say, 'run through to the viewer'. The separate performances made by the system operators do not require separate licenses from ASCAP. Accordingly, for these cable performances, ASCAP receives license fee payments from the program services, but receives nothing from the system operators. See *United States v. ASCAP*, 782 F.Supp. 778 (S.D.N.Y. 1991), *aff'd per curiam*, 956 F.2d 21 (2d Cir. 1992), *and cert. denied*, 504 US 914 (1992). Yet the bulk of cable industry revenues is earned by the system operators, not the program services.

[28] For a description of what a 'content aggregator' does, see n 25 and accompanying text above.

SACEM, and pay SACEM's prevailing license fees, regardless of where the webcaster's transmissions originate or are received.

This proposal, too, has several shortcomings. First, it will increase the cost of licensing and cause delay because extensive research may be needed to determine the principal place of business of each webcaster before a license may be offered.[29] Secondly, it will result in PROs authorizing performances with which they have no nexus because the performances begin and end in territories other than that of the PRO issuing the license.[30] Thirdly, it will be perceived as unfair by webcasters who decide to locate on a foreign host server for reasons unrelated to consideration of performance rights licensing fees, only to find themselves paying different rates from others using the same server.[31]

Finally, the proposal provides no guidance in a number of important situations. For example, what should happen when websites are operated in partnership by corporations with their principal places of business in different territories?[32] How should foreign subsidiaries be treated?[33] It does not

[29] Unlike radio and television broadcasters and cable and satellite operators, webcasters currently are not regulated as such by governmental agencies. There is no registry or index of legal entities operating websites. There is no obligation to disclose the legal identity of a webcaster when obtaining a domain name. Domain names themselves are often fanciful and do not necessarily identify their legal owners. Moreover, an entity's principal place of business is not necessarily in the territory in which it is incorporated, nor in which its registered office is located. The research required—to be done on a worldwide basis—to determine the principal place of business of the hundreds of thousands of webcasters already in operation will quickly overwhelm the resources of the PROs.

[30] Under this proposal, webcasts originating from a server located, for example, in London, England, and operated by a webcaster with its principal place of business in Rome, Italy, would be licensed by the Italian PRO, SIAE (the Societa Italiana degli Autori ed Editori) (see generally <http://www.siae.it>), even if every transmission from the site were received in South Africa (or, for that matter, in any territory other than Italy).

[31] Under this proposal, two webcasters whose transmissions originate from the same server located, for example, in Lisbon, Portugal, offering similar content and deriving equivalent revenue may pay dramatically different license fees merely because one has its principle place of business in Norway and so would be licensed by TONO, the Norsk selskap for forvaltning av fremforingsrettigheter til musikkverk, the Norwegian PRO (see generally <www.tono.no>), while the other has its principle place of business in Ireland and so would be licensed by IMRO, the Irish Music Rights Organization (see generally <www.imro.ie>).

[32] Under this proposal, it would be unclear whether, for example, the Danish PRO, KODA (Selskabet til Forvaltning af Internationale Komponistrettigheder I Danmark) (see generally <http://www.koda.dk>), or IMRO would be authorized to license a webcaster whose transmissions originate from a server in Amsterdam, the Netherlands, which was operated by a partnership comprised of one company with its principal place of business in Copenhagen, Denmark, and another with its principal place of business in Dublin, Ireland.

[33] If the PRO with authority to license a particular webcaster is determined by reference to the principal place of business of the parent corporation, then, for example, Spain's SGAE (the Sociedad General de Autores y Editores) (see generally <http://wwwsgae.es>), would have authority to license the webcasts of a French subsidiary of a Spanish corporation even though the principal place of business of the website operator (the French subsidiary), and the server from which that website's transmissions originate, are both in Lyon, France. If the determination is to be made by reference to the territory in which the subsidiary has its principal place of business, then the proposal provides no help with respect to websites operated by foreign

address treatment of webcasters who are nationals of territories where copyright protection is inadequate, or where no PRO is in operation. The proposal could expose affiliated PROs to regulation by every foreign country if they were deemed doing business there as a collecting society. Finally, the proposal might not survive anti-trust scrutiny in the United States. The ASCAP and BMI consent degrees compel these organizations to license music users who submit written requests for licenses.[34] Therefore, neither ASCAP nor BMI may refuse a license to a webcaster whose transmissions originate in the United States merely because they have agreed with foreign rights organizations to do so.

B. Interdependence, factionalism, and the possibility of a free-for-all

For many decades, the affiliated PRO's have been, as they are now, highly interdependent. They rely on each other for their mutual success. The non-US organizations depend on the depth, breadth, and worldwide popularity of US music for a large part of the value of the licenses they offer. And ASCAP and BMI depend on the efforts of the non-US PROs to license foreign performances of US music.[35] There is every reason to expect, therefore, that these organizations will find some way to respond as a group to the challenges and opportunities presented by the Internet. But they have not yet done so.

In the meantime, an alternative has arisen. In January 2000, BMI and the British, Dutch, French and German PROs (PRS,[36] BUMA,[37] SACEM and GEMA, respectively) announced the imminent signing of an 18-month interim agreement by which each would be authorized to offer webcasters worldwide performance rights to the works in their combined repertories.[38] This will enable webcasters to obtain worldwide rights to a significant portion of the most widely-performed music of Anglo-American and European origin.[39]

---

subsidiaries located in copyright havens (whether established there specifically for the purpose of avoiding payment of license fees, or for some unrelated business purpose).

[34] See, eg, ASCAP's Amended Final Judgment, §§ VI and IX(A).

[35] ASCAP, for example, reported that US$130 million of the US$424.4 million it distributed in royalties for 1998 was attributable to payments received from affiliated non-US PROs for performances in their territories of works from ASCAP's domestic repertory. See *ASCAP In The News: 1998 ASCAP Revenues Exceed Half Billion Dollar Mark* (last modified February 8, 1999) <http://www.ascap.com/press/meeting-020899.html>. BMI does not publicly disclose its revenues or the amounts it distributes to its members. However, BMI does claim to be closing the gap between its earnings and ASCAP's, and to be approaching over all parity with the older, larger organization.

[36] PRS is also known as the Performing Rights Society. See generally <http://www.prs.co.uk>.

[37] BUMA (Buma/Stemra/Cedar) is the Netherlands Copyright Organization. See generally <http://www.buma.nl>.

[38] Emmanuel Legrange, *Rights Groups Team Up*, BILLBOARD MAGAZINE, Feb. 5, 2000, at 10.

[39] Not included would be that portion of the US repertory administered by ASCAP, nor any music from anywhere other than England, France, Germany or the Netherlands.

Such a grant, while not ideal, will be sufficient for those willing either to forego performances of works not included in the combined repertories of the five participating PROs, or to obtain authorization to perform excluded works directly from the copyright owners.

According to BMI's press release announcing the joint agreement, 'licenses will be granted by each society based on the territory indicated by a website's URL (e.g. ".fr" [for France] to be licensed by SACEM, ".com" or ".net" [for the United States] to be licensed by BMI; etc)'.[40] At first blush, it appears that this agreement bestows authority to license webcasters on the PRO in the territory from which the site's webcasts originate. However, BMI's press release also alludes to 'sufficient safeguards to prevent efforts by web music providers to limit or evade copyright liability'.[41] Given the European organizations' perspective, it is unlikely that these 'safeguards', whatever they may be, will operate in any way other than, for example, to preserve SACEM's opportunity to license Radio France even if Radio France's website were hosted on a server in Cleveland, Ohio (thus becoming <www.radiofrance.com> and, otherwise, licensable by BMI) rather than one in Paris (where it would be <www.radiofrance.fr> and licensable by SACEM).

Nevertheless, BMI may be able to participate in this new alliance without violating its antitrust consent decree because it may not need to refuse requests for a license from European webcasters whose transmissions originate in the United States. The matter simply may not come up.

Although BMI and its European partners have 'combined' their repertories for purposes of worldwide Internet licensing, ASCAP is the US PRO with authority to administer rights to most European music.[42] As a result, BMI's webcaster license can include rights to only a small portion of the works in the repertories of the British, Dutch, French and German PROs. On the other hand, a license from any of these four European organizations would include rights to all works in their combined repertories, plus that portion of the US repertory administered by BMI. Thus, even if not compelled to do so, European webcasters operating in the United States may chose licenses from the PRO in their home territory, rather than the BMI license, because they would get authorization to perform more European works of importance to their end users back home. Of course, the result might be different if ASCAP also were participating in this new alliance.

BMI's initiative gives it a competitive advantage over ASCAP. Because ASCAP offers domestic performance rights only, webcasters may seek to

---

[40] *MIDEM Hums "Music and the Internet" Theme* (last modified February 10, 2000) <http://www.bmi.com/musicworld/news/archive/200002/20000210109.asp>.

[41] Ibid.

[42] Under preexisting agreements between ASCAP and the British, Dutch, French and German PROs, ASCAP is designated as the default US PRO to administer rights in their music. In order for BMI to represent these works, the European writer must affirmatively instruct his or her PRO to deviate from the standard practice.

exclude from the base against which their ASCAP license fee is calculated any revenue attributable to foreign access to their sites. ASCAP's revenues also would decline if US webcasters, interested primarily in US music and eager for worldwide rights, rely on music available through a BMI license and music they are able to license directly from copyright owners. In addition, BMI no doubt will claim leadership among US PROs in licensing online performances of the music it represents. This may well draw more writers to BMI, enlarging its membership rolls, expanding the number of works in its repertory, and increasing the value of the BMI license for all music users.

In response, ASCAP could proceed independently, offering webcasters worldwide rights to the many works in its own vast domestic repertory. Or it could ally itself with one or more European PROs excluded from BMI's alliance, thus establishing a competing joint operation for Internet licensing.

BMI's alliance with PRS, BUMA, SACEM and GEMA may be a breakthrough. It also may prove to be the first step leading to a disestablishment of the larger network of affiliated PROs. Were that to occur, it would result in substantial dislocation in the marketplace for music performance rights. For example, the non-US PROs would lose authority to administer rights in US music; and because they have no substitute for the US repertory to offer music users, they would suffer a decline in license fee collections over all. This, in turn, would inure to the detriment of European writers and music publishers who would receive correspondingly smaller royalty payments.

ASCAP and BMI, and the writers and music publishers they represent, may fare better. In addition to offering webcast licenses, they could establish an alternate means of licensing foreign performances of their members' music. For example, ASCAP could ally itself with a single European PRO which could serve as ASCAP's continental European licensing agent for all purposes. Operating from the European partner's home offices, this new combination could function efficiently by selectively licensing only broadcasters and cable and satellite operators, foregoing the many businesses and other music users PROs traditionally approach. This subset of music users is the easiest to identify and locate and also pays the highest license fees.[43] In this way, ASCAP could maintain the bulk of its license fee revenues derived from performances of its members' music in the lucrative European market. BMI could do the same.

C. Royalty distribution fundamentals for the digital age

Everyone would be better served, however, if the PROs maintained their network of affiliation and adapted it to the new circumstances of the digital age.

---

[43] The overhead associated with efforts to license bars, restaurants, hotels, retail stores and other business establishments is quite high, and the license fees these music users pay are relatively modest by comparison with the fees paid by those in the broadcasting, cable and satellite industries.

Webcasters could then readily obtain the worldwide rights they need. Writers and music publishers in every territory could enjoy a reliable means of receiving royalties for online performances of their works and consumers could be assured of full, immediate and uninterrupted access to online performances of the music they most want to hear.

But, for this to happen, the PROs first must settle on criteria for determining which among them shall have authority to license which webcasters. They also must modify their royalty distribution rules to accommodate the conflicting claims of music copyright owners in cases of webcasts involving more than a single territory. Publishers in the territory where a webcast performance originates and those with rights in the territory where it is received both may claim entitlement to royalties arising from the same transmission. Giving all the royalties to one group of music publishers—and none to the other—will not gain support from PROs whose members will lose money they believe to be theirs by right.

These circumstances require adoption of royalty distribution rules that treat each webcast as two performances. One performance occurs in the territory where the server from which the webcast originates is located, and the other in the territory of the end-user receiving the transmission. The traditional practice of paying the publisher's share of royalties to the party who owns local rights for the territory where the performance occurs can be applied in the webcasting context in the following way. The PRO that issues the license would pay half of the publisher's share to the rights owner in the territory where the webcast originates. The remaining 50 percent would be paid to the rights owner for the territory where the webcast is received. If both occur in the same territory, then the publisher for that territory would be entitled to both halves. If two territories are involved, then the rights owner for the second territory would receive the second half of the payment. The writer's share of royalties would be paid as they are now. Whether performance of a work occurs in one territory or another, the identity of the writer or writers entitled to that share remains the same.

D. The willing cooperation of webcasters is indispensable to monitoring online performances

Collective management of music performance rights in the digital age begins and ends with the ability to monitor online transmissions. Knowing which works have been performed and by whom underlies licensing, enforcement, contract administration and royalty distribution. Initially, it is necessary to determine which webcasters are performing music in order to know who may need a license. If a license is refused, identification of works performed without authorization is necessary for an infringement action. Once licensed, performance data may be needed to calculate the fees due from each webcaster.

And, knowing specifically which works were performed by each licensed web-caster is necessary in order to know which writers and music publishers are entitled to receive royalty payments.

Internet performances are digital and occur in a networked environment. Because of this, writers and music publishers, dissatisfied with the PROs' sample surveys which credit only a fraction of performances in traditional media, may demand that Internet monitoring encompass a full census of licensed performances. Only if the PROs conduct such a census can they forego surrogate measures for calculating royalties and allow payments to correspond precisely with licensed webcast performances.

It may be possible, eventually, to monitor Internet performances remotely, reliably, and accurately. However, at this time, existing techniques do not permit a systematic and comprehensive survey of Internet performances. There is no Internet equivalent of movie cue sheets or television program guides. One can determine which works are available to be performed on particular websites at particular times by accessing these sites directly. But doing so tells a PRO nothing about which works actually have been performed or how often. Nor can PROs rely on remote recording of webcasts. Unlike broadcast, cable and satellite channels, over which only a single work can be performed at a time, every work on a website can be performed simultaneously in separate transmissions to different end-users.

An Internet survey will take time to develop and deploy. Cost, accuracy, ease of use, and degree to which it approaches a census of licensed performances all are important considerations. The implementing technology must work on all systems and across platforms. It also must be ubiquitous and, therefore, cannot be proprietary or dependent on the use of a particular music server or player.

As a starting point, the PROs have created a universal numbering system by which a unique identifying code can be assigned to each musical work. An International Standard Work Code (ISWC) number will be issued for each newly-created work when it is first registered with a PRO.[44] Numbers also will be assigned to preexisting works already in the PROs' repertories.[45] The PROs have aggregated their ISWC codes into a single database stored on a server in New York City.[46] By cross-referencing these codes with other information in the PROs' databases, it is possible to determine a work's title, and to identify its writer, publisher, and any performing artist who may have recorded it. The reverse also is true. By knowing a work's title, and either its writer, publisher or performing artist, it is possible to derive its ISWC code.

An Internet survey also will require development of a means for marking music files with their identifying codes, and a technology for tracking online

---

[44] See generally <http://www.cisac.org/cisac/index2e.htm>.   [45] Ibid.   [46] Ibid.

performances of marked works. It is here that the PROs need the willing cooperation of webcasters.

Watermarking, the process of encoding individual music files with their corresponding ISWC numbers, requires access either to the digital audio files or to the recordings from which they were made. However, the PROs' only connection to musical works is that they administer performance rights in them; they do not exercise dominion and control over the physical objects in which music is embodied. In any event, nearly all existing recorded popular music already has been widely distributed in digital form through the sale of CDs without the data needed for online performance monitoring encoded on them. Webcasters are able to 'rip' these CDs, turning them into digital audio files, and transmit them on the Internet in unmarked form. Even were the music industry to mark newly-made recordings, the technology would not help in monitoring the use of previously distributed unmarked works.

Despite this, or perhaps because of it, the solution to marking digital music files lies with webcasters. They select the works to be made available for performances on their sites and operate the servers from which online transmissions originate. Webcasters are in the best position to mark music for online use; they could affix copyright management information, including ISWC codes, to music files before loading them onto their servers.

To facilitate the quick and accurate matching of digital files with the ISWC codes for the musical works they contain, the PROs must provide webcasters with ongoing, open access to their databases. The PROs may be reluctant to do this, however. They are concerned that, by making their databases transparent, it will be easier for webcasters to identify, locate and contact music copyright owners to license works directly. It is more likely, however, that copyright owners themselves will initiate direct licensing if the PROs fail to take available steps which would enable them to mark music in an efficient manner.[47]

In their effort to track online performances, the PROs have relied on robots, spiders, sniffers, and other webcrawlers. These programs locate websites which offer designated types of sound files, such as '.wav', '.ram', or '.mp3' files, and may assist licensing and enforcement efforts. But they are currently of limited use. As already noted, because existing music is not watermarked, it cannot be tracked effectively by searchbots. Searchbots are also unable to distinguish between files containing musical works and those containing other sounds, such as speech. They are unable to determine how many musical works are contained in a given sound file. They are unable to identify specific musical works merely by reference to the name of the file in which the works are contained. Moreover, they operate too slowly to capture

---

[47] If the information in the PROs' databases has such value, some Internet entrepreneur eventually will obtain financing, hire a roomful of music enthusiasts, and create a parallel database to be made available for a fee or free to all on an advertiser-supported website

the vast and growing number of ephemeral performances occurring online every moment. And, as technological tools, searchbots can be defeated by technological countermeasures.

As with watermarking, the solution to tracking online performances also lies with webcasters. Webcasters maintain server log files which document activity on their sites. Performance data can be stored there for subsequent retrieval and analysis. If webcasters were to provide PROs with ongoing, open access to the relevant portions of their log files, the PROs could gather all the highly granular information necessary to support their Internet survey and royalty distribution systems. The logs could disclose which works were performed, when and how often. And, by noting each end-user's Internet Protocol address, the logs also could identify the territory in which each webcast performance was received.[48] Of course, because gathering data about end-users without their knowledge and consent raises serious privacy concerns, the PROs and the webcasters acting on their behalf should scrupulously avoid linking particular Internet Protocol addresses with individual end-users by name or by other personal identifying information.

As a group, webcasters constitute a new community of music users. Individually, their experience with PROs varies widely. Some have, or have had, licenses for performances in other media or at other venues. Many have no prior experience with PROs, and know little about their structure or methods of operation. Under these circumstances, PROs have the opportunity to foster mutually supportive relationships where none existed previously.

IV. Conclusion

The Internet directly links every constituency important to the PROs' success in the digital age. In this network of networks, no issue stands alone, nothing can be treated in isolation, and stop-gap measures may not work. By implementing the changes suggested in this chapter, the PROs would bring a measure of predictability, rationality and fairness to that segment of the online music marketplace over which they have greatest influence. And, in doing so, they may preserve a role for themselves as that marketplace develops.

---

[48] The PROs may want to work together with webcasters to develop specialized software for managing data in server log files. This could simplify the task for webcasters and benefit the PROs through standardization. In addition, it would increase transparency in the relationships among the affiliated PROs and between each organization and its writer and music publisher members. If every PRO were able to access the relevant portions of licensed webcasters' server log files, then each PRO could verify the thoroughness and accuracy of performance statements received from affiliated organizations in other territories. In the same way, songwriters and music publishers could verify performance statements they receive from their own PROs.

PART III

THE CLAIMS OF THE PUBLIC DOMAIN

Contributors to Parts I and II have shown the advantages that can accrue to innovators through stronger intellectual property laws alone or through a combination of strong legal regimes and intensive reliance on patterns of private ordering. In Part III, however, we take account of the costs that new legal rights and increased utilization of private contract and self-help technologies impose, both on the public (that is, the user population or target audience for innovations) and on future innovators who need access to earlier learning as the foundation for their own new works.

Niva Elkin-Koren addresses the potential effect on consumers and on intellectual property policy of allowing the enforcement of so-called shrinkwrap and clickwrap contracts under which digital works are licensed to the public. These standard form contracts are imposed unilaterally by copyright owners on each purchaser of their product, without the opportunity to negotiate terms, or even, in many instances, for the consumer to know in advance of installing the work in her computer, what the terms actually are. Much of Professor Elkin-Koren's discussion is triggered by a recently promulgated model law in the United States, known as the Uniform Computer Information Transaction Act or 'UCITA'.[1] Professor Elkin-Koren expresses concern that the UCITA approach, if widely adopted in the United States and elsewhere, will facilitate enforcement of terms that will displace, for works in digital form, many of the standard rights that consumers of intellectual property have traditionally been expected to enjoy as part of the statutory 'bargain' between owners and users of copyrighted works.

Rebecca Eisenberg and Walter Powell both point to problematic aspects of expanded reliance on patents, and in particular on patenting of basic research tools, for the kinds of information flows that have historically been critical to successful biomedical research. Professor Eisenberg draws on her experience as chair of the National Institutes of Health Working Group on Research Tools to examine the negative effect of the transaction costs incurred in negotiating licenses to use proprietary tools for industrial, academic, government, and nonprofit research. The difficulty, as a practical matter, in negotiating over rights to use these tools for research projects with uncertain future payoffs threatens to act as a brake on investigatory activities of a kind that have, in the past, provided high social returns. Professor Powell, who has studied the ways in which the biotechnology industry has utilized formal and informal networks of information exchange between players in private industry and researchers in academic and nonprofit settings, similarly expresses concern over the price that may be exacted in the form of decreased future innovation as researchers and academic institutions

---

[1] The model act was adopted by the National Conference of Commissioners on Uniform State Laws in 1999 as a proposed amendment to the Uniform Commercial Code. For information on the model act, and the status of its adoption by various states, see <http://www.nccusl.org/uniformacts_factsheets/uniformacts-fs-ucita.htm>.

become more proprietary about their discoveries in basic science and seek to patent them.

Finally, Yochai Benkler examines the impact of higher levels of proprietary rights on freedom of speech and on the production of new informational works. He argues that the impact of increased rights regimes is to discourage new entrants into the field and to center the production of such works more and more in the hands of large mass media firms. Because these firms already have great financial resources, and in addition, control a vast repertory of copyrighted works, they can outbid smaller producers for needed inputs, and also can recycle their inventory of owned works into a variety of derivative products at a lower cost than would be incurred by competitors. In the long run, he argues, this route will lead to fewer works being produced, and to an increased tendency of those works to use and reuse preexisting stocks of owned expression.

A PUBLIC-REGARDING APPROACH TO CONTRACTING OVER COPYRIGHTS

NIVA ELKIN-KOREN*

Not long ago, book publishers and record companies, movie producers and software publishing-houses, perceived cyberspace as the biggest threat ever to their hegemony over the market for content. Many pages of law review articles and committee reports were devoted to the challenges created by digital technology to the interests protected by copyright law. Cheap and easy copying, we were warned, would bring about the death of copyright and signal the end of the content industries.

Then, technology came to the aid of copyright owners. Copyright management systems increasingly allow producers physically to control and manage

* Senior Lecturer at the University of Haifa School of Law.

information distributed digitally, and also allow them to set the terms, by means of contracts, that govern the use of information. Legislators, too, have been recruited to strengthen the statutory rights of content owners in the new information market.

Today, the emerging copyright landscape is governed primarily by privately generated norms, the enforceability of which are backed up by legislation. The recently enacted Digital Millennium Copyright Act (DMCA)[1] in the United States provides legal support for copyright management systems by prohibiting the development and use of technologies designed to circumvent them.[2] The Uniform Computer Information Transaction Act ('UCITA') in the United States, a model law proposed by the Commissioners on Uniform State Laws, provides legislative support for industry-promulgated contractual restrictions on the use of information.

Together, these developments provide a privileged status to private ordering and displace the traditional norms of copyright: the rule-making process regarding the use of information is privatized, and the legal power to define the boundaries of public access to information is delegated to private parties. The immediate outcome of this process is to turn large chunks of what was once in the public domain into private goods. What seems to be missing from recent developments is a public-regarding interest in securing not only the rights of current copyright owners, but also those of the public in having the greatest feasible level of unrestricted access to information.

The proliferation of self-help technologies for safeguarding and regulating the use of copyrighted materials, coupled with increasing reliance on private control rather than public law, threatens to undermine the principles of information policy which have served us well up to now. Private ordering alone cannot ensure an important goal of information policy—the continued existence of the public domain.[3]

While the threats to the public domain are raised both by contracts and self-help technologies, contracts are often conceived as a lesser problem. Since contracts must be enforced by courts, courts, it is thought, will have the opportunity to test the validity of the restrictions on access against existing

---

[1] Digital Millennium Copyright Act, Pub. L. No. 105–304, 112 Stat. 2860 (1998).

[2] This anticircumvention legislation was implemented in the WIPO Copyright Treaty, a treaty concluded at Geneva, Switzerland, on December 20, 1996 by a Diplomatic Conference of the World Intellectual Property organization ('WIPO'). See WIPO Doc. CNR/DC/94 (Dec. 23, 1996). The legislative history of the statute suggests that advocates of the DMCA hoped that other WIPO signatories would follow the same approach in implementing the Treaty.

[3] Elsewhere I have argued that contracts cannot protect the public interest in the public domain. See Niva Elkın-Koren, *Copyrights in Cyberspace—Rights Without Law,* 73 Chi.-Kent L. Rev. 1155, 1187–89 (1998). Other commentators have taken a similar position. See Mark A. Lemley, *Intellectual Property and Shrinkwrap Licenses,* 68 S. Cal. L. Rev. 1239, 1291 (1995); J. H. Reichman and Jonathan Franklin, *Privately Legislated Intellectual Property Rights: Reconciling Freedom of Contract with Public Good Uses of Information,* 147 U. Pa. L. Rev. 875 (1999).

legal norms. Consequently, it has been suggested that courts can mitigate any hazardous effect of contracts under established legal doctrines, applied on a case-by-case basis.[4]

This chapter will examine the adequacy of existing legal doctrines to deal with contracts that govern access to information. It concludes that these doctrines are unlikely to address the threats to the fundamental objectives of information policy posed by private ordering. In particular, it argues that contract doctrine is ill-equipped to deal with the problem of the enforceability of restrictive terms. It suggests, therefore, that regulators must assume an active role in limiting the enforceability of restrictive terms to safeguard public access to information. After explaining why existing contract law will not sufficiently guarantee a commons in information (the public domain), I move on to discuss the shortcomings of other current and proposed US and European laws as limits on the overexpansion of owner's rights through the use of standard form contracts. I conclude by outlining some principles for a regulatory approach to restrictive terms.

I. On Restrictive Terms and Information Policy

A. What are restrictive terms?

By 'restrictive terms', I mean those terms defined by standard form contracts governing the use of information products that limit or prohibit uses of a work that would be otherwise permitted by copyright law. Copyright law not only defines a set of exclusive rights granted to owners, but also defines the privileges of users. Such privileges limit the rights of owners by warranting some degree of free access to, and certain uncondensed uses of, copyrighted materials. For instance, copyright law prohibits the unlicensed reproduction of a work of authorship. Therefore, when a copyright owner licenses someone to make a single copy of her computer program, she is merely exercising her exclusive right under copyright law. On the other hand, copyright law may privilege the purchaser of a copy to adapt the program to the extent necessary to run it on a particular machine. If the license prohibits such adaptation, it applies what I am calling a restrictive term to the use of that computer program.[5]

---

[4] See Lorin Brennan, *The Public Policy of Information Licensing*, 36 Hour. L. Rev. 61 (1999); Mark A. Lemley, *Symposium: Beyond Preemption: The Law and Policy of Intellectual Property Licensing*, 87 Cal. L. Rev. 111 (1999). This approach was also adopted by the drafters of UCITA as further discussed below.

[5] For instance, such provisions, if enforceable, might prevent consumers from adapting their copy of a program for the year 2000, although they are privileged to do so under section 117 of the US Copyright Act of 1976. See 17 U.S.C § 117 (providing that the owner of a copy of a computer program is entitled to adapt the program to the extent necessary to run it on a particular machine).

Similarly, reading is currently privileged under copyright law, and the owner of a copy is free to read it without needing specific permission from the copyright owner.[6] If, however, a contract provides that a new license is necessary for each and every reading of the work, that, too, would qualify as a restrictive term.

Restrictive terms are typically defined by standard form contracts drafted unilaterally by the information provider and offered to users on a take-it-or-leave-it basis. Often such contracts become binding upon the mere use of the product,[7] a neutral action that scarcely indicates any meaningful assent.[8] This type of contract exhibits none of the characteristics that have led commentators to argue that contracts are superior to government regulations. The hypothesis that a contract regime will generate the optimal set of rules for information use assumes that contracts are voluntarily entered, reflect the bilateral assent of the parties, and occur in a competitive market. None of these conditions are met where standard form contracts are used to impose restrictive terms on access to information.

Restrictive terms in standard form contracts are universal; they are not the outcome of negotiation, and are not tailored to address the interests of particular parties. Therefore, no variety exists in the type of terms and conditions that apply to any given work. In most cases, such terms will uniformly govern all access to a particular product. In fact, some restrictions may be valuable to the information provider only because they are applicable to everyone who gains access to the informational product.[9]

There is no perfect competition over the 'terms and conditions' in the same way we may expect competition over the price of goods in a competitive market.[10] Indeed the terms and conditions attached to the sale or licensing of an

---

[6] See Jessica Litman, *The Exclusive Right to Read*, 13 CARDOZO ARTS & ENT. L.J. 29 (1994).

[7] See *ProCD, Inc. v. Zeidenberg*, 86 F.3d 1447, 1452 (7th Cir. 1996). This approach was further incorporated into UCITA, as discussed below.

[8] There are other reasons to enforce standard form contracts, such as reduced transaction costs. It does not follow, however, that terms in standard form contracts reflect the will of the parties, or the aggregated will of consumers.

[9] Corporations are using standard form contracts not only to reduce transaction costs involved in mass-market negotiations but also to serve the organizational structure of the corporation. Uniformity is essential in order to exercise control over the consequences of the transaction, particularly when the firm is using intermediaries for distributing its products and does not bargain directly with its customers. Standardization also preserves the internal hierarchical structure of firms. When contracts are standard, they leave no discretion to subordinates. See T.D. Rakoff, *Contracts of Adhesion: An Essay in Reconstruction*, 96 HARV. L. REV. 1173, 1121–25 (1983) (arguing that firms are using standard form contracts to stabilize their external market relationships and to serve the needs of their complex organizational structure). These considerations are somewhat different in the context of online commerce that facilitates direct marketing and may transform the traditional corporate structure.

[10] Online distribution may, however, enhance competition over terms and conditions by facilitating information exchange, and reduce transaction costs associated with consumer's collective action. Online distribution may lower the cost of searching and comparing various versions of contracts by enabling automatic search and the use of various electronic agents. See Niva

information product may be reflected in the contract price, but they lack the comprehensibility of prices. Therefore, consumers cannot respond to this information in the way they normally do to price variations in other products.

Furthermore, because the fiction of assent is attributed to the formation of standard form contracts, competition over terms is unlikely to develop. Also, if, as claimed, a contract can be valid even when potential users are not informed of the license terms until they have completed the transaction, information providers have no incentive to reveal the license restrictions in advance, and users are even less likely to develop a demand for particular usage rights. As a result, norms generated by such standard form contracts become pervasive. Their general applicability renders them a form of 'private legislation', governing all would-be users of the information product.[11]

B. Why can't contracts govern information policy?

The enforceability of restrictive terms means that decisions regarding information policy are left to the market. What are the consequences of replacing the regulatory regime of copyright law with that of the market?

Information providers, as profit maximizers, can be expected to use their control over their information products to restrict any free or potentially competitive use. That would result in privatizing information that is currently unprotected under copyright law.

Contract advocates argue that market forces of supply and demand will guarantee the optimal level of information use. Use restrictions will reflect actual user preferences. Some users will prefer to pay less in return for limited rights; others may be willing to pay more for greater rights. If users are unwilling to pay for more expensive licenses, there is no benefit in having the law require that they be granted these greater rights.[12]

The problem with this argument is that markets for information are unlikely to reflect the actual value of information, and may, therefore, undercut the fundamental objectives of information policy. Copyright law is based on several assumptions about the production of information and the desirable restrictions on information use. It recognizes that, to stimulate the production of information, potential creators need appropriate incentives. Such incentives are provided in the form of limited exclusive rights over copyrighted works. Copyright policy recognizes, however, that a vital public

Elkin-Koren and Eli M. Salzberger, *Law and Economics in Cyberspace*, 19 INT'L REV. L. & ECON. 1, 17–18 (1999).

[11] Friedrich Kessler first coined the term 'private legislation' in 1943: Friedrich Kessler, *Contracts of Adhesion*, 43 COL. L. REV. 629 (1943).

[12] For this view, see, eg, Frank H. Easterbrook, *Cyberspace and the Law of the Horse*, 1996 U. CHI. LEGAL F. 207; Trotter Hardy, *Property (and Copyright) in Cyberspace*, 1996 U. CHI. LEGAL F. 217; Tom W. Bell, *Fair Use v. Fared Use. The Impact of Automated Rights Management on Copyright's Fair Use Doctrine*, 76 N.C. L. REV. 557, 564 (1998).

domain is a powerful engine that stimulates production of further information.[13]

The public domain is a common. Information is considered in the public domain when it is subject to no private rights of exclusion and all are privileged to use it.[14] The public domain thus consists of information products that are unprotected by copyright law (such as facts), or any usage of works that falls outside the scope of copyright exclusive rights (such as reading) or is privileged under copyright exemptions (such as fair use).[15]

Because information is developed incrementally and often by reference to existing works, progress requires exposure to contemporary information products. By securing widespread access to information independent of economic means, the public domain increases the likelihood of further innovation and development. Furthermore, innovation and development require some level of sharing and exchange that are less likely to occur when all information is subject to exclusive property rights.[16] The public domain thus facilitates alternative and supplementary forms of authorship alongside the proprietary competitive model.

Aside from serving as an engine for innovation, the public domain further facilitates the coexistence of a copyright regime with the principles of freedom of speech[17] and democratic values. Indeed, a very strong and comprehensive

---

[13] An increasing body of research focuses on the centrality of the public domain to information policy. See Yochai Benkler, *Free as the Air to Common Use: First Amendment Constraints on Enclosure of the Public Domain*, 74 N.Y.U. L. Rev. 354 (1999); Jessica Litman, *The Public Domain*, 39 Emory L.J. 965, 968 (1990) ('The public domain should be understood not as the realm of material that is undeserving of protection, but as a device that permits the rest of the system to work by leaving the raw material of authorship available for authors to use'); Lawrence Lessing, *Intellectual Property and Code*, 11 St. John's J. Legal Comment. 635, 638 (1996).

[14] This way of describing the public domain is based on the legal definition of a common property regime in which 'multiple owners are each endowed with the privilege to use a given resource, and no one has the right to exclude another'. See Michael A. Heller, *The Tragedy of the Anticommons: Property in the Transition From Marx to Markets*, 111 Harv. L. Rev. 621, 623–24 (1998). Such a definition draws on Hohfeld's terminology: property rights are defined in terms of 'rights of exclusion' and the 'common' is defined in terms of privileges. See generally Wesley Newcomb Hohfeld, Fundamental Legal Conception as Applied in Judicial Reasoning and Other Legal Essays (Walter Wheeler Cook ed., 1923). See also Benkler, n. 13 above, at 360 ('[I]nformation is in the public domain if all users are equally privileged to use it'); Litman, n. 13 above, at 968 ('The public domain consists of those aspects of copyrighted works which copyright does not protect'). The definition of the 'public domain' may have some implications for the information policy derived from copyright law.

[15] Note that under the US 1976 Copyright Act, 'fair use' is defined as a limitation on the exclusive rights: 17 U.S.C. § 107.

[16] Debora J. Halbert, Intellectual Property in the Information Age: The Politics of Expanding Ownership Rights (1999) (arguing that once property rights are granted, sharing is less likely, and litigation over the boundaries of the property rights is the most likely outcome).

[17] For an analysis of the inconsistency between copyright and free speech principles, see Diane L. Zimmerman, *Information as Speech, Information as Goods: Some Thoughts on Marketplaces and the Bill of Rights*, 33 Wm. & Mary L. Rev. 665 (1992). For a more traditional view of this conflict, see Melville Nimmer, *Does Copyright Abridge the First Amendment Guarantees of Free Speech and Press*, 17 UCLA L. Rev. 1180 (1970) (discussing the idea/expression dichotomy as a

property rights regime in information may severely impede democratic goals by centralizing control over the production of information and setting limits on free flow of information.[18] By preserving a pool of information that is freely[19] accessible to the public, the public domain mitigates some of the negative effects involved in the concentration of ownership over information. In this sense, a copyright paradigm that preserves a vital public domain may itself stimulate freedom of speech.

The public domain thus produces a social good—added value for society as a whole. The increment of social good, however, is often an insignificant factor in each individual transaction for information goods, and therefore would rarely influence the parties' choice of contractual terms. Market exchanges reflect the immediate interests of the parties involved and cannot reflect the public utility and the benefits to society as a whole.[20] Nevertheless, widespread restrictions on access to information do create negative externalities for society, but because it is not a party to discrete market transactions, public utility is unlikely to be accounted for in market processes. Consequently, reliance on contracts alone cannot guarantee that the public domain will continue to exist. This suggests that some public regulation of contract terms is necessary.

II. Limitations on Freedom of Contract: Can They Secure Public Access to Information?

Modern contract law does set some limits on freedom to contract.[21] Are these limits in US and European laws enough to secure and preserve the historical balance between owner's rights and the public good? Can they sufficiently secure the public domain?

---

guarantee against conflicts between copyright law and freedom of speech); Jessica Litman, *Symposium: Copyright Owners' Rights and Users' Privileges on the Internet: Reforming Information Law in Copyright's Image*, 22 DAYTON L. REV. 587 (1997) (arguing that the idea-expression dichotomy balances First Amendment considerations and interests protected by copyright law). Freedom of speech considerations may further limit the rights granted to copyright owners under copyright law. See Paul Goldstein, *Copyright and the First Amendment*, 70 COL. L. REV. 983 (1970) (proposing a First Amendment exception to copyright).

[18] See Benkler, n. 13 above. Elsewhere I discuss the potential effect of copyright law on social dialogue and democratic ideals, see Niva Elkin-Koren, *Cyberlaw and Social Change. A Democratic Approach to Copyright Law in Cyberspace*, 14 CARDOZO ARTS & ENT. L. J. 215 (1996).

[19] I mean free in the sense of no restrictions. It does not necessarily follow that such use would be 'free of charge'. Use of information in the public domain may still involve costs. See Bell, n. 12 above, at 580–81.

[20] HUGH COLLINS, THE LAW OF CONTRACT 230–33 (1997).

[21] For a historical overview from a comparative standpoint of the development of modern contract law and the limitations on freedom of contract, see K.M. Sharma, *From 'Sanctity' to 'Fairness': An Uneasy Transition in the Law of Contracts?*, 18 N.Y.L. SCH. J. INT'L & COMP. L. 95 (1999).

The validity of restrictive terms may be tested under contract law or as a copyright question under intellectual property law. Below I discuss some of the limits set on freedom of contract, and examine their applicability to restrictive terms in contracts for information goods.

A. Challenging the validity of restrictive terms under contract law

The governing principle of contract law is 'freedom of contract'. This means that parties should be free to fix the terms of their contract and to shape their transactions as they choose. It further assumes that parties are free to choose when, whether and with whom they wish to enter a contract.

Standard form contracts fall far from this ideal. They are offered on a take-it-or-leave-it basis, often on the assumption that the offeree will not even read the terms. Such contracts have nevertheless been enforced for efficiency reasons. They dramatically reduce transaction costs by eliminating the need for suppliers to negotiate and draft individualized documents, as well as by reducing the time it would take for consumers to familiarize themselves with a new set of terms in each transaction.

Modern contract law has, however, increasingly restricted freedom of contract, recognizing that under certain circumstances, such as in mass-market transactions, strict application of this principal may seriously compromise consumers' interests. Courts and legislators have further elaborated various legal doctrines to limit freedom of contract for considerations of fairness and public policy.

The following discussion reviews some of the exceptions to freedom of contract under US and European law. It highlights some of the fundamental tensions between conventional contract doctrines and the demands of new information markets. I conclude that the limitations designed to address traditional issues in contract law are inadequate to salvage the objectives of public information policy.

US contract law enforces standard form contracts subject to limited exceptions. These exceptions create procedural safeguards, such as providing that enforceability depends on an opportunity to read. The rationale of such exceptions is that, if a party has an opportunity to read the contract terms, she can make a rational choice about whether to expend the resources to find out what it says, or, by default, be held to agree to the terms.

The limits on enforceability, however, are pretty messy. The exceptions are not strictly distinguishable from one another, and their rationales and standards overlap. They address the concerns regarding standard form contracts by voiding terms in three types of circumstances: if they are unconscionable, if there is no true assent to a particular term, or if the term contravenes public policy.[22]

---

[22] See John D. Calamari & Joseph M. Perillo, The Law of Contracts 382–83 (4th ed. West 1998) for the rationale of providing limited enforceability to terms in contracts of adhesion

The doctrine of unconscionability, codified in section 2–302 of the Uniform Commercial Code (UCC),[23] allows the court to refuse to enforce a single provision or an entire contract.[24] Unconscionability may exist whenever terms are grossly one-sided and the disadvantaged party shows that it is unreasonable to presume that she voluntarily agreed to such terms. For example, she may have been ignorant of the meaning of the contract terms or of the risk involved, or may have had no realistic alternative to that particular risk allocation.[25] An agreement may also be held non-binding if the party had no opportunity to review the terms before committing to the contract.

In the case of contracts of adhesion,[26] the courts may refuse to enforce a contract that is prepared in advanced by one party and offered on a take-it-or-leave-it basis to the other party who has no reasonable alternative but to accept it. In determining whether the contract is one of adhesion, the two most important factors are its standardized form and gross disparity in bargaining power.[27] This doctrine seeks to ensure that both parties entered the contract voluntarily, and that the contract indeed reflects their will. It also is driven by a second rationale. Although courts ordinarily assume that the parties have read and understood their contracts, in contracts of adhesion, where, realistically, courts recognize the absence of true and meaningful assent, there is no safeguard against unconscionable terms or terms that contravene public policy. Consequently courts may strike them down.[28] Normally, the party seeking to void a contract term on this ground must show that the contract is an adhesion contract and that the term either violates reasonable expectations[29] or is unconscionable.

(arguing that modern contract law has limited the duty to read in adhesion or other standard form contracts based on three grounds: the absence of true assent to a particular term; that a term is contrary to public policy; and that a term is unconscionable).

[23] UCC § 2–302. Indeed, the Official Comment explicitly states that unconscionability shall not apply in cases involving mere inequalities in bargaining power, but disparities of power have been an important element in the adjudication related to unconscionability. See CALAMARI & PERILLO, n. 22 above, at 374.

[24] The proposed section 111 of UCITA incorporates this doctrine: 'If a court as a matter of law finds the contract or any term thereof to have been unconscionable at the time it was made, the court may refuse to enforce the contract, or it may enforce the remainder of the contract without the unconscionable term, or it may so limit the application of any unconscionable term as to avoid any unconscionable result': UCITA § 111(a).

[25] See CALAMARI & PERILLO, n. 22 above, at § 9.40.

[26] See Rackoff, n. 9 above.

[27] STEVEN EMANUEL & STEVEN KNOWLES, CONTRACTS 370 (1993–94 ed.). Disparities of bargaining power may result in contracts that do not reflect the parties' will. Instead such contracts may merely reflect an exercise of power by one party over the other. If that is the case, there is no justification for enforcing the contract in favor of the party that enjoys the power advantage. Enforcing the license in such circumstances would be neither efficient nor just.

[28] CALAMARI & PERILLO, n. 22 above, at 385.

[29] The standard for 'reasonable expectations' is normally based upon whether the plaintiff understood the contract or the disputed provision. For a review of the origins of the reasonable expectations doctrine in American contract law, see DAVID W. SLAWSON, BINDING PROMISES, THE LATE 20TH CENTURY REFORMATION OF CONTRACT LAW 49–54 (1996).

A third doctrine allows courts not to enforce surprising terms in an otherwise enforceable contract.[30] A term will be deemed surprising if the drafting party had reason to believe that the user, had she known about it, would not have manifested assent.[31] This doctrine is not limited to consumer transactions. It may also apply, in principle, to business transactions, although, in practice, courts are reluctant to use it very often to uphold challenges in such situations.[32]

For several reasons these doctrines are likely to offer only limited help in policing restrictive terms. First, the interactive and malleable nature of online distribution facilitates prior notice of the contract terms. Procedural safeguards such as an opportunity to read, are not useful to secure the rights of users participating in electronic commerce. Until recently, lack of an 'opportunity to review the terms' was a ground for refusing to enforce shrink-wrap licenses accompanying computer programs.[33] The license was inserted in the software package and could often be reviewed by the potential user only after the purchase was concluded. The Seventh Circuit is a notable exception. In the case of *ProCD Inc. v. Zeidenberg* the court found a license enforceable despite the fact that the licensee had the opportunity to read it only after paying for the product. Online contracting, however, makes it feasible to provide users with an opportunity to read the terms and conditions before entering a contract. It also provides various ways for explicitly manifesting users' con-

---

[30] Note, however, that under the Restatement (Second) of Contracts, enforceability of standard form contracts is the rule. Whenever a party manifests assent to a standard form contract, the terms will become binding even in the absence of any negotiation. Only unfairly surprising terms will be unenforceable: RESTATEMENT (SECOND) OF CONTRACTS, § 211(1) ('Except as stated in subsection (3), where a party to an agreement signs or otherwise manifests assent to a writing and has reason to believe that like writings are regularly used to embody terms of agreements of the same type, he adopts the writing').

[31] Under § 211 of the Restatement (Second) of Contracts, 'surprising terms' would not constitute part of the agreement: RESTATEMENT (SECOND) OF CONTRACTS, § 211(3) ('Where the other party has reason to believe that the party manifesting such assent would not do so if he knew that the writing contained a particular term, the term is not part of the agreement').

[32] Similarly, the International Institute for the Unification of Private Law Principles validate standard form terms subject to exclusion of surprising terms: UNIDROIT Principles of International Commercial Law, art. 2.19 (1994). There are two differences between the US approach and the UNIDROIT approach. The first difference has to do with the focus of UNIDROIT on standard terms rather than on standard contracts—this places a heavier burden on licensors, and subjects more contracts to regulation, even negotiated contracts that include standard terms. A second difference is the focus of UNIDROIT on the expectations of the licensee compared with a US approach focus on the perspective of the licensor. R. Nimmer criticizes the UNDIROIT approach, arguing that '[u]nlike the Restatement, this places the emphasis on the expectations of the assenting party and creates, one suspects, an impossible burden on a licensor who must structure its forms to fit diverse transactions and diverse contexts, especially in the mass market': RAYMOND NIMMER, INFORMATION LAW § 11.12[4][a] (1999).

[33] See, eg, the district court opinion in the *ProCD* case discussed above, which was overruled by the Court of Appeals ('I conclude that because defendants did not have the opportunity to bargain or object to the proposed user agreement or even review it before purchase and they did not assent to the terms explicitly after they learned of them, they are not bound by the user agreement'): *ProCD, Inc. v. Zeidenberg*, 908 F. Supp. 640, 655 (W.D. Wis. 1996).

sent to the terms as a precondition for gaining access to the product.[34] It is therefore unlikely that courts would accept challenges to standard form contracts in online settings based on this ground.[35]

Online contracting further challenges the concept of a 'duty to read'. A procedural rule that concerns itself with whether consumers have had an opportunity to read a contract before being bound by it seeks to address a problem of lack of information. The underlying assumption is that if a particular term is important to the potential user, she will try to get a license that will address her needs. Cyberspace in general, and online distribution in particular, swamps users with masses of information that users are required to study.[36]

Users in online transactions may have the physical opportunity to read the terms governing access to information, but they may lack the attention span necessary to absorb such information and to make proper choices. It is simply impractical for people to read and understand the large volume of contracts they must enter on a daily basis. They are unable to make meaningful choices for each and every information product consumed. Information on the costs and benefits of each term of use is likely to be prohibitively expensive while, in the majority of cases, the expected benefit to users from modifying a particular term is likely to be low.

Another reason for the inadequacy of the US contract doctrine to deal with restrictive terms relates the nature of information transactions. The technical opportunity to read a standard form contract does not necessarily mean the user has a *reasonable opportunity* to understand it. Reading and comprehending license terms is critical in information transactions since the 'product' in such transactions is the license itself and the deliverable is often a bundle of abstract rights to use an intangible product.[37] The information

---

[34] A license may be posted on the gateway to a website and may provide that, by clicking the Accept button, the user agrees to the terms and conditions, such as registration, obtaining a password, or paying prior to access. A website may also simply provide that the use is subject to the terms and conditions made available on the site, and that the use of the services or product constitutes acceptance.

[35] Online contract formation, except when executed by electronic agents, does not involve any unique difficulties. In fact, online contracts are likely to be enforceable under existing laws, especially under objective doctrine. Online contracting provides the parties with better opportunities to read the contract terms than the average consumer would have when she purchases a computer program subject to a shrinkwrap license in a store, or signs forms to open a bank account while other customers line up behind her. Online transactions allow a user to read a document over and over again, to increase the size of the font, to print it out, to think it over.

[36] Electronic commerce involves the processing of masses of information regarding transactions. A purchaser in a department store may touch the product, measure its size, appreciate its color, pick up the product, pay for it in cash, and take it home in a bag. A purchaser in an online transaction must rely on information provided by the vendor. The product is described; she then submits information regarding the product of her choice, places an order, pays by providing her credit card or subscriber account number, and the information (the product) is downloaded into her computer.

[37] See Wendy J. Gordon, *An Inquiry into the Merits of Copyright: The Challenges of Consistency, Consent, and Encouragement*, 41 STAN. L. REV. 1343, 1378–84 (1989) (discussing the ramifications of the lack of physical boundaries in copyrightable subject matter).

product lacks physical boundaries and the proper authorizations necessary to make specific uses of the product may not be self-evident. When a user does not sufficiently understand the license, she doesn't really know what she has purchased.

The legal description of permitted uses and restrictions may be unintelligible to potential users of software, video games, or online newspapers. Most people would have more difficulty comprehending the exact scope of their rights to use a computer program than to assess the utility or limitations inherent in the purchase of a chair, a silver ring, or other tangible products. To understand the limits set by a contract on the use of a video one might have to understand the technical meaning of a 'public performance' or a 'derivative work'. Did the video provider reserve his right to control any derivative work created by the user? If so, does presenting the licensed work on a divided screen create a derivative work? Does adapting a computer program to the year 2000 constitute a derivative work? What is an unprotected idea and what is a copyrighted expression? What are unprotected data and what constitutes prior knowhow?

In sum, restrictive terms may not be understood at first sight, and may require legal advice that can often turn out to be more expensive than the product itself. Furthermore, people use informational works in many contexts and for various purposes. It may be difficult to predict ex ante all the usages one would wish to make. It is even more difficult to attach a value to all the prospective uses. Accordingly, consumers lack sufficient incentives to gain deeper understanding of such terms and to quantify their value.

Thus, contract rules that ask whether the user has had an opportunity to read the contract seem beside the point if users do not understand it, and probably could not without legal advice. Enforcing such contracts is hardly justifiable under contract theory because under such circumstances we can no longer be confident that the exchange indeed renders both parties better off. Unless the courts adopt more substantive requirements under the 'opportunity to read' rubric, this exception may not effectively limit the enforceability of restrictive terms in online transactions.

Finally, current US contract law may be inadequate to deal with restrictive terms for reasons related to business practices and to the structure of the information market. As the use of restrictive terms in information transactions becomes a common industry practice, it cannot be said to violate the 'reasonable expectations' of users. A restrictive term widely used by an industry is unlikely to be found by a court to be 'bizarre or oppressive'[38] or to constitute 'unfair surprise'. Clearly, parties acquiring software or visiting a website expect a form license as part of the deal.[39] Also, it may be difficult to

---

[38] RESTATEMENT (SECOND) OF CONTRACTS, § 211, cmt. f (1997).
[39] See UCC § 2–302 Official Cmt.

prove that a restrictive term is so one-sided as to be unjust towards the user. An examination of the unfairness of a term focuses on the circumstances of a particular bargain.[40] If a user pays less for a more restricted right of use, the transaction may be considered fair in contract terms, even if it is socially detrimental because it prevents a use, such as criticism, that has public value. The concern with restrictive terms goes beyond the fairness of a particular bargain because, cumulatively, they may compromise the interest of society as a whole.[41]

In summary, US contract law enforces terms in standard form contracts unless they fail to meet certain procedural requirements. These exceptions, designed to guarantee sufficiently informed and voluntary consent, are inappropriate for addressing the risks involved in the general enforceability of restrictive terms.

European contract law, by contrast, reflects a general skepticism towards mass-market transactions and takes a stricter approach to standard form contracts.[42] Under European law, therefore, restrictive terms are more likely to be subject to regulation, although this regulation aims at addressing traditional consumer concerns rather than concerns about information policy. European contract law is defined by the national laws of the European Union Member States, though in specific fields, such as commercial transactions that affect competition and consumer contracts, it has been affected by relevant European Community legislation.

Consumer contracts in Europe are regulated under the EC Directive on Unfair Terms in Consumer Contracts (the 'Unfair Terms Directive'). Unfair terms in a consumer contract do not bind the consumer.[43] A term is considered unfair if it has not been individually negotiated[44] and contrary to the requirements of good faith if it causes a significant imbalance in the parties'

---

[40] See COLLINS, n. 20 above, at 230–31

[41] Another consideration in standard contract doctrine is lack of alternatives. To void a restrictive term on this ground would require the user to show she had no alternative to entering this contract. This may depend on the particular circumstances. As a general matter, if terms become pervasive and are used by all providers of the same product, and if that product has no close substitute, then a user can show that she had no reasonable alternative. It would be easier to establish the lack of alternatives when the producer exercises a monopoly power.

[42] See generally MICHAEL H. WHINCUP, CONTRACT LAW AND PRACTICE, THE ENGLISH SYSTEM AND CONTINENTAL COMPARISON 163–85 (1996).

[43] See Council Directive 93/13/EEC, art. 6(1), 1993 O.J. L95. Under the Directive, a contract may continue to bind the parties if it can exist without the unfair terms.

[44] See ibid, at art. 3(2). A term shall always be regarded as not individually negotiated where it has been drafted in advance and the consumer has not been able to influence the substance of the term. Also: 'notwithstanding that a specific term or certain aspects of it in a contract has been individually negotiated, these . . . shall apply to the rest of a contract if an overall assessment of the contract indicates that it is a pre-formulated standard contract'. The Directive excludes four categories of contract: contracts relating to employment, succession rights, rights under family law, and organization of companies or partnership.

rights and obligations to the detriment of the consumer.[45] The Directive contains a non-exclusive list of unfair terms.[46]

The Directive, however, may have only limited applicability to restrictive terms because it explicitly excludes from coverage terms that define the main subject matter of the contract.[47] Because the permissions and restrictions actually define the nature of what will be delivered in information transactions, restrictive terms may be exempt from the Directive on the ground that they 'define the product'.

Another shortcoming of the Directive for governing restrictive terms is that it applies only to consumer transactions, narrowly defined as those involving an individual (rather than a corporation) who acquires products for her own personal consumption and not for business or professional use.[48] The rationale behind this regulatory approach is that government should decrease the effect of disparities in bargaining power between sellers/suppliers and consumers. Unfortunately, such disparities are not limited to individual consumers facing a wealthy corporate producer. They also exist whenever one party is in a position to control the contract terms that will govern access to her product or service.

The disparities in bargaining power often result from systematic information asymmetries. The producer who specializes in the particular business typically understands the product better than the prospective user. The provider of an operating system for a medical apparatus is in the best position to know all its functions and advantages, as well as the limitations and risks involved in using it in various environments. The user, even if it is a large hospital, is unlikely to acquire comparable knowledge.[49] The producer is also better placed to accumulate experience as to the legal validity of the terms and conditions, by becoming involved in litigation or following the laws and the case law related to its products.[50] Consequently, the producer is likely to develop a better understanding of the license terms and their significance to any individual product and circumstances. The restrictive terms in the license may reflect an attempt to capitalize on this advantage.

More limitations, though applicable only to computer programs, are set out by the EC Directive on the Legal Protection of Computer Programs. This Directive explicitly invalidates contract provisions that prohibit a lawful user of a computer program from making a back-up copy of the program to the

---

[45] See ibid, arts. 2(a), 3(1).   [46] See ibid, art. 3(3); Annex.

[47] See ibid, art. 1(2). Other terms not covered by the Directive are the price and those terms required by statute or regulation.

[48] See ibid, art. 2(b).

[49] For a discussion of disparities of power between users and producers, see SLAWSON, n. 29 above, at 26–29 (describing the producer-consumer relationship as vertical).

[50] See ibid (using a broad definition of consumers and arguing that producers can spread the cost of informing themselves about the laws affecting their products; consumers lack this cost-spreading opportunity and, therefore, are less likely to invest in acquiring such information).

extent necessary for its use.[51] It also invalidates restrictions on the rights of a lawful user to decompile the program for a noncommercial purpose.[52] Similar limitations on contractual restrictions are set out in Article 15 of the EC Directive on the Legal Protection of Databases.[53] This provision invalidates any attempt to contract around Articles 6(1)[54] and 8[55] of the Directive which allow lawful users to extract and reutilize insubstantial parts of the database for any purpose.

In addition to these Directives, several European states regulate standard form contracts in both business and consumer transactions. These laws treat unfair terms as voidable in business transactions and as void in consumer transactions.[56] The German Standard Contract Terms Act of 1976,[57] for instance, imposes a general duty of fairness and requires provisions in standard form contracts to be both reasonable and clear. In addition, the Act includes both a 'black list' of terms, which are prohibited and void, and another list of terms that are permissible only under certain circumstances.[58]

The law of the United Kingdom may also offer limited redress for restrictive terms under its Unfair Contract Terms Act 1977 (the 'Unfair Terms Act').[59] Section 3 of the Unfair Terms Act applies to any transaction in which one party deals on the other's written standard terms of business. The drafter is not entitled to render a contractual performance substantially different from what was reasonably expected of him. Unexpected terms would be valid only if reasonable in light of the total circumstances.[60] A user might rely on

[51] Council Directive 91/250/EEC, art. 5(2), 1991 O.J. L122.

[52] Ibid, at art. 9(1) (any contractual provision contrary to Article 6 or to the exceptions provided for in Article 5(2) and (3) shall be null and void).

[53] Council Directive 96/9/EC, art. 15, 1996 O.J. L77 ('Any contractual provision contrary to Articles 6 (1) and 8 shall be null and void').

[54] Ibid, art. 6(1) ('The performance by the lawful user of a database or of a copy thereof of any of the acts listed in Article 5 which is necessary for the purposes of access to the contents of the databases and normal use of the contents by the lawful user shall not require the authorization of the author of the database').

[55] Ibid, art. 8 ('The maker of a database which is made available to the public in whatever manner may not prevent a lawful user of the database from extracting and/or re-utilizing insubstantial parts of its contents, evaluated qualitatively and/or quantitatively, for any purposes whatsoever').

[56] MICKLITZ & BOHLE, FIVE-AND-A-HALF YEAR GERMAN STANDARD TERMS ACT: AN INTERIM SURVEY FROM THE POINT OF VIEW OF CONSUMER PROTECTION, IN UNFAIR CONTRACT TERMS IN CONSUMER CONTRACTS 111 (T. Bourgorgnie ed. 1983).

[57] Gesetz zur Regelung des Rechts der Allgemeinen Geschäftsbedingungen, v. 9.12.1976 (BGBl. I).

[58] Similarly, Dutch Civil Code arts. 6.231–4 to –7 regulates the use of suppliers' standard written terms. General terms are annulled if unreasonably onerous. Article 6.236–7 sets out a black-list of types of terms considered unreasonably onerous for consumers. For an overview of limitations on government supervision over unfair terms in civil law, see WHINCUP, n. 42 above, at 184–90.

[59] The Unfair Contract Terms Act 1977 in the UK was supplemented by the Unfair Terms in Consumer Contracts Regulations 1994 (SI 1994/3159), implementing the European Union Directive discussed above, see text accompanying nn. 51–55 above.

[60] See Unfair Contract Terms Act 1977, s. 3(2)(b) (i), (ii) (Eng.).

this provision to argue that the information producer failed to perform as reasonably expected by imposing overly restrictive limits on the use of the information provided. Two difficulties arise: one is that the property conveyed or licensed is defined by the terms that set out the restrictions;[61] the other is that it could be hard to prove that restrictive terms were not reasonably expected if their use were to become an industry standard.

Thus, contract law in Europe as well as in the United States seems ill-equipped to address the problem of restrictive terms. It is concerned with protecting the expectations of the parties or aiding a party who is structurally disadvantaged in the bargaining process. It is not geared to protect the public interest by preserving an adequate level of unrestricted access to information—the goal that is the central tenet of information policy.

The fundamental tenet of contract law is that private ordering is a fair and efficient process for effectuating the establishment of norms. Classic contract doctrine recognizes no universal or social values beyond 'freedom of contract' and the procedural safeguards are designed to secure it. By its very nature, then, contract doctrine does not provide a standard for distinguishing 'good' terms from 'bad' ones. The 'good' is defined by reference to the parties' preferences. Consequently, one must look outside contract law for justifications permitting intervention in the allocation of risks fixed by the parties.

Public policy doctrine may provide a limited substantive ground for invalidating restrictive terms in a contract. In the USA, a contract term may be voided if it is contrary to the public interest as reflected in federal or state statutes. One source of public policy may be intellectual property statutes or decisions.[62] There are also indications that a public policy test may be applicable to information licenses under European laws. For instance, the Dutch Supreme Court refused to enforce a provision that purported to prohibit a legal acquirer of a publication from reusing the printed materials in subsequent reading portfolios, on the ground that this term violated the exhaustion doctrine in Dutch copyright law.[63] The German Act Against Restraints on Competition[64] may also provide a basis for invalidating contract provisions.

---

[61] This was acknowledged by the drafters of UCITA, although they did not draw the same operative conclusions from the observation. In a sale of goods, the buyer owns the subject matter (eg, the toaster); ownership creates exclusive rights in the item purchased. In contrast, when the subject matter is computer information, a person who acquires a copy may own the diskette, but does not own the information or rights associated with it. Instead, the person's rights to use the information depend on contract terms and intellectual property rights. Terms of the agreement determine what the purchaser obtains beyond the diskette: UCITA, Prefatory Note, p. 4.

[62] See Lemley, n. 4 above, at 151–67. Restraints may also be based on competition regulation. For further discussion, see text accompanying nn. 89 to 98 below.

[63] See *De N V Drukkerij de Spaarnestad v. Leesinrichting Favoriet*, HR, 25 January 1952, No. 95, described in *Contracts and Copyright Exemptions*, Institute for Information Law, Amsterdam, *Contracts and Copyright Exemptions* (visited June 21, 2000) <http://www.impri matur.alcs.co.uk/legal.htm>.

[64] *Gesetz gegen Weltbewerbsbeschränkungen, v. 20 2 1990* (BGB1. I S.235).

Section 20 of the Act covers agreements for the acquisition or use of patents, patent applications, and registered designs, and applies by analogy to agreements for the acquisition and use of secret knowhow under section 21. Restrictions imposed by a licensor are invalid if they are broader than those provided for by law.[65]

Relying on a public policy limitation, however, poses several problems. First, it requires courts to develop information policy on a case-by-case basis, a time-consuming and inefficient process. Secondly, the process requires users to show that a particular restrictive term is contrary to public policy and thus imposes a prohibitively heavy burden on them. Furthermore, because there is no well-defined criterion for judging what is contrary to public policy, uncertainty about the validity of terms is inevitable. Resolving that uncertainty imposes high transaction costs and creates a chilling effect that induces compliance with restrictive terms even when they are contrary to public policy.[66] Finally, the court's discretion under contract doctrine is limited by contract law principles that give priority to private ordering and freedom of contract rather than the goals of information policy.[67] Unless an explicit definition is provided for what is contrary to information policy, the public policy exception may prove ineffective for mitigating the negative effects of restrictive terms.

B. The shortcomings of contract doctrine: lessons from UCITA

Some of the same shortcomings seen in traditional contract doctrine are also reflected in a recently introduced US model code for information transactions. UCITA (formerly UCC2B)[68] assumes that information transactions require special treatment because they differ substantially from transactions in tangible goods.[69] The drafters analyzed these differences.[70] The product in information transactions is a package of rights to use the information, rather than an object. Information in digital form, the drafters assumed, is more susceptible than are tangible goods to alteration and to the creation of perfect

---

[65] See MARGET VAN WESTERHALT, GERMANY, INTERNATIONAL INFORMATION TECHNOLOGY LAW, CENTER FOR INTERNATIONAL LEGAL STUDIES, (S. Cotter ed., 1997).

[66] For the significance of certainty in the context of intellectual property, see Craig Allen Nard, *Certainty, Fence Building, and the Useful Arts*, 74 IND. L.J. 759 (1999).

[67] Also, copyright cases in the USA are litigated in federal rather than in state courts.

[68] The National Conference of Commissioners on Uniform State Laws and the American Law Institute announced on April 7, 1999, that legal rules for computer information transactions would not appear as Article 2B of the Uniform Commercial Code, but as a separate model act called the Uniform Computer Information Transactions Act ('UCITA').

[69] UCITA, Prefatory Note, pp. 4–5.

[70] Some differences, of course, were overlooked by the drafters, for instance, that information may be shared at no cost and that its use and distribution involves some important externalities. The attempt to define a deliverable product, rather than considering alternative business models for distributing information, served to justify the legislative model ultimately advanced in UCITA.

copies.[71] In fact, to use a digitally delivered information product, one must first copy it. These factors led the drafters to believe that the interests of information providers require further protection. The drafters overlooked, however, a central characteristic of information, that is, the important externalities involved in any allocation and use of it. But, despite the acknowledged differences, the drafters ended up treating information just like a tangible good and applied the same approach that governs all other fields of commerce.[72] Consequently, the overall effect of UCITA is to equate information and tangibles and to facilitate the propertization of information.

UCITA's purpose is to facilitate electronic commerce in information by establishing coherent and predictable legal rules that will lower transaction costs.[73] Believing that the main obstacle to electronic commerce is lack of clarity in the legal rules, UCITA offers a set of default rules that apply to computer information transactions[74] in the absence of an agreement to the contrary between the parties.

(1). What does it do?

The Reporter's Note acknowledges that by making standard form contracts for information products enforceable, UCITA may de facto facilitate the enforceability of producers' rights not merely against parties to the contract but also against the world-at-large.[75] It also acknowledges a fundamental public interest in preserving the public domain. Nonetheless, UCITA's interpretation of the public interest is extremely narrow.[76]

---

[71] See UCITA, Prefatory Note, at 4.   [72] Ibid at 3.

[73] The drafters perceive the greatest danger in the dramatic growth of information technology and electronic commerce to be the 'lack of uniformity and lack of clarity of the legal rules governing online transactions'. This, the drafters believe, may 'engender uncertainty, unpredictability, and high transaction costs': ibid at 8. The drafters recognize the relevance of the First Amendment to the commercialization of information: 'What law does here affects not only the commercialization of information, but also the social values its distribution has always had in society. Informational content does not become something entirely different if the provider or author distributes it commercially'. But, they argue, that 'commercialization is not inconsistent with the role of information in political, social and other venues'. These values require, it is argued, that contract law support the distribution of information: ibid.

[74] The definition of a 'computer information transaction' under UCITA covers any agreement for creating, modifying, transferring or licensing computer information, such as software, data and databases, or informational rights in computer information. See UCITA, § 102.

[75] UCITA, Reporter's Notes, at 66.

[76] Ibid. Acknowledging the public interest in preserving a public domain, and the significance of the public domain to the objectives of information-policy is unusual in copyright legislative discourse. Such a perspective was completely absent from other official documents addressing copyright law in the information age. See, eg, U.S. DEP'T OF COMMERCE INFO. INFRASTRUCTURE TASK FORCE, INTELLECTUAL PROPERTY AND THE NATIONAL INFORMATION INFRASTRUCTURE: THE REPORT OF THE WORKING GROUP ON INTELLECTUAL PROPERTY RIGHTS (1995) ['White Paper']. For a review of the legislative history of the public policy limitations, see Pamela Samuelson and Kurt Opsahl, *Licensing Information in the Global Information Market: Freedom of Contract Meets Public Policy*, 8 EUR. INTELL. PROP. REP. 386, 390–91 (1999). This perspective is certainly not the only

As a general matter, UCITA takes the position that the use of restrictive terms is entirely appropriate in information transactions, and it facilitates the enforceability of such terms. It makes licenses binding, even in the absence of affirmative negotiation or opportunity to read the terms and conditions before committing to the contract. Subject only to limited public policy restraints, standard form license restrictions would routinely be enforceable under the new model code.

The limited exceptions to enforceability of terms is set out in section 105. This provision purports to preserve the current balance between contract law and other bodies of law, such as intellectual property, consumer protection, competition, and trade regulation laws. These exceptions are not ones defined by UCITA but ones that may apply because of the actions of other bodies of law.

Subsection 105(a), for instance, says that '[a] provision of this [Act] which is preempted by federal law is unenforceable to the extent of the preemption'. As discussed below, the circumstances under which restrictive terms in standard form contracts are preempted are unclear and have been the subject of conflicting court decisions. UCITA does not clarify this legal uncertainty and makes no determination as to whether preemption doctrine applies to contracts. In fact, the Reporter's Notes take the narrow view that preemption doctrine should come into play only when federal rules explicitly regulate specific contract terms.[77]

Subsection 105(b) allows a court to void or limit enforcement of a contract if any of its provisions violate a fundamental public policy that is superior to the policy favoring enforcement.[78] This section was put in at the November 1998 meeting of the Article 2B Drafting Committee in response to what was referred to as the Public Policy Motion.[79] It was intended to allay concerns

plausible interpretation of copyright law. An alternative view of intellectual property advocates maximizing propertization. See Easterbrook, n. 12 above; Bell, n. 12 above. For a discussion critical of this approach see Mark A. Lemley, *The Economics of Improvement in Intellectual Property Law*, 75 TEX. L. REV. 989, 994–95 (1997).

[77] Subsection (a) refers to preemptive federal rules, but other doctrines grounded in First Amendment, copyright misuse and other federal law may limit enforcement of some contract terms in some cases. In general, however, except for federal rules that directly regulate specific contract terms, no general preemption of contracting arises under copyright or patent law: UCITA, Reporter's Notes, p. 67.

[78] 'If a term of a contract violates a fundamental public policy, the court may refuse to enforce the contract . . . to the extent that the interest in enforcement is clearly outweighed by a public policy against enforcement of the term'. UCITA, art. 105(b). This language resembles Restatement (Second) of Contracts, § 178, comment b: 'In doubtful cases . . . a decision as to enforceability is reached only after a careful balancing, in light of the circumstances, of the interest in the enforcement of the particular promise against the policy against the enforcement of such terms . . . Enforcement will be denied only if the factors that argue against enforcement clearly outweigh the law's traditional interest in protecting the expectations of the parties, its abhorrence of any unjust enrichment, and any public interest in enforcement of the particular term'.

[79] See Brennan, n. 4 above, at 63. For an overview of the legislative history of this section, see Pamela Samuelson and Kurt Opsahl, n. 76 above, at 391.

regarding the potential negative effects of UCITA on policies promoting innovation, competition, and freedom of expression.

But what terms should be considered against public policy? The Reporter's Notes explicitly acknowledge that information transactions may implicate innovation and competition policies, and the right of fair comment,[80] but refer the courts to federal laws, including copyright and patent statutes, for guidance on the appropriate limits on contract terms. The courts are instructed to avoid overriding a contract term in the absence of a legislative declaration of a particular policy. They are also told to refrain from overriding terms on the basis of purely 'local' policies. Consequently, a claim against restrictive terms is limited to those public policies explicitly defined by state and federal legislation.[81]

Finally, the Reporter's Notes direct the courts to balance against these particular public policy considerations the fundamental public policy of the UCC, which is to enforce private ordering.[82] Thus, the Notes suggest that 'private parties ordinarily have sound commercial reasons for contracting for limitations on use and that enforcing private ordering arrangements in itself reflects a fundamental public policy enacted throughout the Uniform Commercial Code and common law'.[83] Enforcing standard contracts, and strengthening the reliability of contractual obligations, are thus treated by UCITA as weighty public policy goals in and of themselves.

(2). Proclaimed neutrality and actual preference

UCITA claims neutrality with respect to policies governing the use and distribution of information. It takes the position that information policy questions should be left to international treaties and to Congress.[84] At the same time, UCITA reflects an explicit commitment to the market and to 'freedom

---

[80] UCITA, Reporter's Notes, p. 68 ('Innovation policy recognizes the need for a balance between conferring property interests in information in order to create incentives for creation and the importance of a rich public domain upon which most innovation ultimately depends. Competition policy prevents unreasonable restraints on publicly available information in order to protect competition. Rights of free expression may include the right of persons to comment, whether positively or negatively, on the character or quality of information in the marketplace').

[81] Ibid.

[82] Ibid at 70. In determining whether to deny enforcement of a provision that violates public policy, courts are directed to consider: the potential effect of enforcement or invalidation on the interests of each party and on other fundamental public interests; the interest in protecting expectations arising from the contract; the purpose of the challenged term; the strength and consistency of judicial decisions applying similar policies in similar contexts; the nature of any express legislative or regulatory policies; and the values of certainty of enforcement and uniformity in interpreting contractual provisions. See ibid at 68.

[83] Ibid at 70.

[84] The Reporter's Notes conclude that 'it is clear that limitations on the information rights of owners that may be imposed in a copyright regime where rights are conferred that bind third parties, may be inappropriate in a contractual setting where courts should be reluctant to set aside terms of a contract': ibid at 67.

of contract', notwithstanding that it applies to situations where 'freedom' is quite limited—standard form contracts, mass-market transactions, and contracts made by electronic agents.

No doubt, 'freedom of contract' serves an important public goal. If contracts express autonomous choices made by individuals, then the enforcement of contracts facilitates personal autonomy. If contracts allow private ordering to replace government regulation, then the enforcement of contracts facilitates personal liberty. If contracts guarantee that customers will only pay for what they want, then enforcement of contracts facilitates efficiency.

Standard form contracts, however, have little to do with 'freedom'. The goal of freedom of contract most clearly advanced by the draft is freedom from regulation. It pays very little respect to the autonomous choice of the parties who have actually entered the contract. Yet, it is only when parties exercise their free and voluntary choice in a contract that the enforcement of contracts may be said to be efficient and just. When contracts fail to manifest such free and voluntary choice, it is no longer justifiable for the state to give such weight to enforcing them.

(3). What are the ramifications?

UCITA gives priority to freedom of contract and to market processes for defining the marketplace in which information is disseminated and acquired. The narrow limits on enforcement of contracts recognized by UCITA for protecting consumers[85] and licensees[86] are weak. Indeed, when enforceability of restrictive terms is the rule, and the exceptions are insufficient to secure the public interest, the effect of UCITA is to facilitate producers' efforts to expand their rights.

The model act, as currently drafted, suffers two major shortcomings: one is procedural and the other is substantive. UCITA creates a presumption that all terms in a contact for the transfer of an information product are valid. The burden of proof that a term is invalid for reasons of public policy is imposed on the user.[87] This allocation of the burden of proof provides the information providers who draft the license with a considerable advantage.

---

[85] 'Consumer' means an individual who is a licensee of information or informational rights that the individual at the time of contracting intended to be used primarily for personal, family, or household purposes. The term does not include an individual who is a licensee primarily for profit-taking, professional, or commercial purposes, including agriculture, business management, and investment management other than management of the individual's personal or family investments: UCITA § 102(16).

[86] Ibid § 102(43) ('"Licensee" means a transferee in a license or other agreement under this Act').

[87] 'A term or contract that results from an agreement between commercial parties should be presumed to be valid and a heavy burden of proof should be imposed on the party seeking to escape the terms of the agreement under subsection (b)': UCITA, Reporter's Notes, at 69.

Uncertainty increases the cost involved in any legal dispute. Individual users and small businesses are highly sensitive to the costs of such uncertainty. Therefore, in case of doubt, such users are likely to conform to questionable terms rather than to challenge them.

In particular, occasional users who are subject to many different restrictions under various licenses, each involving a relatively low value, are unlikely to dispute the terms. For one thing, users normally will lack the financial resources necessary to undertake litigation. Some arguments in favor of invalidating terms in contracts like these—for example, that the contract poses a threat to competition—are particularly difficult to prove; it would be prohibitively expensive for an individual consumer to attempt to establish that a particular producer exercises monopoly power. In fact, the antitrust laws usually leave this kind of anticompetitive behavior for the government to prove and prosecute.

Users may also lack sufficient incentives to challenge a restrictive term when it does not affect their immediate interests, or when its effect is relatively small. This does not mean, of course, that the term at issue is insignificant in terms of its negative externalities for society as a whole.

Finally, the presumption of validity, and the limited grounds for invalidating terms, ex post, in particular cases does not provide producers with any incentive to draft contracts that are fair and that comply with other public goals. Because enforcement is a matter of state law and invalidation will turn on the particular circumstances established by the user, invalidating a provision in one standard form contract does not necessarily mean that this same term in other contracts will also be invalidated. Expected damages are also relatively small. Moreover, the mere appearance of a term in a printed license will increase the chances that risk-averse users will conform to them. The fact that all terms are presumed to be enforceable by UCITA strengthens this bias.

A more substantive shortcoming is the approach taken by the model law to information policy. The drafters of UCITA acknowledged three fundamentals of information policy: innovation, competition, and freedom of speech. The Reporter's Notes explicitly recognize that establishing a rich public domain and preventing unreasonable restraints on information are central means for achieving these goals.[88] Yet, UCITA fails to provide adequate means for securing these goals.

To support a vital public domain and reasonable access to information, occasional users of information need to feel confident that they can safely

---

[88] Innovation policy recognizes the need for a balance between conferring property interests in information in order to create incentives for creation and the importance of a rich public domain upon which most innovation ultimately depends. Competition policy prevents unreasonable restraints on publicly available information in order to protect competition. Rights of free expression may include the right of persons to comment, whether positively or negatively, on the character or quality of information in the marketplace: ibid, at 68.

access and use information in ways that are not explicitly restricted by law. The ex post approach adopted by UCITA promotes not user confidence but self-restraint. In other words, it has a chilling effect.

UCITA does succeed, of course, in reducing uncertainty for producers about the extent to which they can secure their interests by the use of restrictive terms. It does so by making all terms presumptively enforceable. While the coherent and predictable legal regime sought by the drafters is undoubtedly desirable, it should not necessarily require that the public-regarding aspects of information policy be diminished. Ideally, UCITA should reduce uncertainties for information users, too. It should make free flow of information the rule, and permissible restrictions on use should be clearly defined. This would require the adoption of an ex ante approach for invalidating restrictive terms. The law should make clear in advance the sorts of provisions that are invalid, rather than leaving the determination ex post to the courts.

III. Restrictive Terms as a Copyright Question

Copyright law itself may limit attempts to contract around legislative norms. When standard form contracts impose greater barriers to the use of online materials than copyright law does, the doctrines of copyright misuse and preemption may come into play.

A. The abuse of intellectual property rights

Copyright misuse is a theory adopted from patent law and applied by US courts only in recent years. It derives from the equitable doctrine of unclean hands, and does not require the defendant who asserts it in a copyright infringement action to show that she has been injured by the misuse. Courts will find copyright misuse when the copyright is used in a manner that violates the public policy underlying the law.[89] Misuse claims have been asserted where the copyright owner engages in allegedly anti-competitive practices,[90] as well as where the owner attempts to expand the protection of her intellectual property beyond that granted by copyright. Misuse may also be claimed when contractual restrictions violate antitrust law.[91]

---

[89] See *Lasercomb Am., Inc. v Reynolds*, 911 F.2d 970, 978 (4th Cir. 1990).

[90] See *Practice Mgmt Information Corp. v AMA*, 121 F.3d 516, 521 (9th Cir. 1997), *amended by* 133 F.3d 1140 (9th Cir.1998) (finding copyright misuse where the license was made contingent upon an undertaking by the licensee not to use a competing work).

[91] There are conflicting authorities on whether copyright misuse requires an actual antitrust violation. See *Reliability Research Inc. v. Computer Associates Int'l, Inc.*, 793 F. Supp. 68, 69 (E.D.N.Y 1992). In some cases, courts have required a showing of an antitrust violation. See, *e.g.*, *Service & Training, Inc. v. Data General Corp*, 963 F.2d 680 (4th Cir. 1992); *BellSouth Advertising & Publ. Corp. v. Donnelley Information Publ. Inc.*, 933 F.2d 952, 960–61 (11th Cir.

Thus, use of restrictive terms may be a copyright misuse. In *Lasercomb*,[92] for instance, the US Court of Appeals for the Fourth Circuit upheld a copyright misuse defense because a restrictive clause in a license prohibited the development or sale of any software competitive with the licensor's for a period of 99 years. The court found that the restriction went beyond protecting the expression, and sought instead to restrict the use of the idea embodied in the copyrighted software. Thus, the court concluded that Lasercomb had attempted to use its copyright 'in a manner adverse to the public policy embodied in copyright law'.[93]

Copyright misuse, however, is hardly ever raised as a defense in civil law countries.[94] Abusive licensing practices in intellectual property are addressed under antitrust laws or unfair competition rules. One of the central cases involving an abusive licensing practice is *Radio Telefis Eireann v. E. C. Comm'n (Magill TV Guide Ltd. intervening)*.[95] Here, the European Court of Justice held that a refusal to license a third party to publish weekly listings of television and radio programs was an abuse of a dominant position and contrary to Article 86 of the EC Treaty.[96]

1991); *Reed-Union Corp. v. Turtle Wax, Inc.*, 77 F.3d 909 (7th Cir. 1996). Other courts, however, do not require this. See *Lasercomb*, n. 89 above, 911 F.2d 970; *Practice Management Info. Corp.*, n. 90 above, 121 F.3d 516. This question is also controversial among scholars. See Lemley, n. 4 above, at 151–53 (arguing that copyright misuse is not based on antitrust principles); Maureen A. O'Rourke, *Drawing the Boundary Between Copyright and Contract: Copyright Preemption of Software License Terms*, 45 DUKE L.J. 479, 550 (1995) (arguing that copyright misuse may prevent full-blown antitrust litigation).

[92] The Court in *Lasercomb* wrote: 'Lasercomb undoubtedly has the right to protect against copying of the Interact code. Its standard licensing agreement, however, goes much further and essentially attempts to suppress any attempt by the licensee to independently implement the idea which Interact expresses'. See *Lasercomb*, n. 89 above, 911 F.2d at 978.

[93] This reasoning is not entirely accurate. Copyright misuse doctrine applies to things protected by copyright. When we are dealing with contracts or licenses, the problem may fall outside the scope of copyright law. It is not a misuse of the copyright that is at stake, but instead, contractual practices that, regardless of whether copyright protection is granted or denied, may undermine the goals of copyright policy. A similar difficulty is suffered by preemption doctrine.

[94] For a discussion of 'abusive' exercises of intellectual property rights under the European competition rules, and the 'misuse' of intellectual property rights under the rules on the free movement of goods, see INGE GOVAERE, THE USE AND ABUSE OF INTELLECTUAL PROPERTY RIGHTS IN E.C. LAW 85–89 (1996); *Contracts and Copyright Exemptions*, n. 63 above, at 22–24.

[95] Case 69/89 *Radio Telefis Eireann v. E. C. Comm'n. (Magill TV Guide Ltd. intervening)*, *reproduced in* 24 IIC 83 (1993), *confirmed by* Cases 241/91 P and 242/91 P, RTE and *ITP v. Commission of the European Communities* (holding that the mere refusal to grant a license, even if it is the act of an undertaking holding a dominant position, cannot in itself constitute an abuse of a dominant position; however, exceptional circumstances such as refusal may involve abusive conduct).

[96] 25 March 1957, Rome, Treaty Establishing the European Economic Community (as amended by Subsequent Treaties), Art. 86 ('Any abuse by one or more undertakings of a dominant position within the common market or in a substantial part of it shall be prohibited as incompatible with the common market in so far as it may affect trade between Member States. Such abuse may, in particular, consist in: (a) directly or indirectly imposing unfair purchase or selling prices or unfair trading conditions; (b) limiting production, markets or technical development to the prejudice of consumers; (c) applying dissimilar conditions to equivalent transactions

Misuse doctrine helps to incorporate the objectives of information policy into contract discourse and litigation. But copyright misuse only applies if the work is covered by copyright, and may, therefore, not be applicable to contracts involving works that are unprotected.[97] Also, the number of cases that have actually refused to enforce a contract or a contract term as a copyright misuse is still relatively small, and how the doctrine will develop remains unclear. Finally, copyright misuse doctrine is a defense that has thus far only been recognized in copyright infringement actions. A successful claim depends on a showing of abuse of the right under particular market circumstances. Therefore, the findings of courts in such cases only apply to the parties involved and may have no effect on other licensees. Consequently, both copyright misuse and antitrust claims may be of limited significance in policing standard form contracts.[98]

B. Harmonization and uniformity in copyright policy

Lastly, contract provisions that conflict with copyright law may be preempted. In the United States, copyright preemption guarantees a homogeneous federal copyright law system by preventing overlapping or conflicting state protection. Similar considerations underlie the EC Directives on computer programs and on databases discussed above.[99]

Arguably, to achieve homogeneity, preemption doctrine should prevent state legislators from providing extra protection for works of authorship that Congress purposely left in the public domain.[100] What works were purposely left in the public domain, and should therefore be unprotected is, however, a highly controversial issue.

Preemption takes two forms. One rests on the Supremacy Clause of the US Constitution and ensures that legitimate exercises of federal power will supplant conflicting state legislation. The other is codified in section 301 of the Copyright Act of 1976 and expressly preempts any state law claim that

---

with other trading parties, thereby placing them at a competitive disadvantage; (d) making the conclusion of contracts subject to acceptance by the other parties of supplementary obligations which, by their nature or according to commercial usage, have no connection with the subject of such contracts').

[97] Lemley, n. 4 above, at 157.

[98] Ibid, 192 (acknowledging that most courts have rejected copyright misuse claims).

[99] Harmonization measures were taken in the case of new technologies, such as computer programs, whereas most traditional copyright subject matters were thought of as enjoying a sufficient level of harmonization under international treaties, particularly the Berne Convention. The term of copyright protection was harmonized by adopting the model used in German law. Germany, until harmonization, provided the longest term of copyright protection granted by a Member State—70 years after the death of the author. See Council Directive 93/98/EEC, 1993 O.J. L290. See *also* GOVAERE, n. 94 above, at 55–56.

[100] See *ProCD v Zeidenberg*, 86 F.3d 1447, 1453 (7th Cir. 1996), citing from the Supreme Court in *Bonito Boats, Inc. v. Thunder Craft Boats, Inc.*, 489 U.S. 141 (1989) (applying the same principle under patent laws).

conflicts with federal copyright law. Because contracts are creatures of state law, they could be overridden if it were established that the enforcement of the contract would conflict with copyright policy.[101]

Preemption doctrine, however, may not be sufficient to address concerns about an overexpansion of owner's rights via contracts. Using the doctrine to limit restrictive terms raises several difficulties. While some courts have taken the position that preemption doctrine may bar the enforceability of some contract terms,[102] others have held that a simple two-party contract, by its very nature, cannot interfere with copyright policy. The argument is that contract law creates rights against parties to the contract only, whereas copyright law creates exclusive rights against the world.[103] Elsewhere I have argued that this distinction is no longer valid or useful because information producers using technological protective devices are able to govern all access to their materials by the same standard form contract.[104]

A second obstacle to the use of preemption doctrine is that it does not provide a clear answer about what constitutes an interference with copyright policy. State-created rights in the subject matter covered by copyright are preempted only if they are 'equivalent to any of the exclusive rights within the general scope of copyright'.[105] In other words, states cannot add on their own copyright-like rules to works covered by the federal scheme. However, what remains unclear is which unprotected works are covered by copyright law in that Congress purposely decided to inject them into the public domain, and which works are entirely outside copyright and may be subject to state regulation. This confusion is another reason preemption doctrine could be of limited significance in policing standard form contracts.

IV. Outlining the Principles of a Regulatory Approach to Contracting Copyrights in Mass-Market Transactions

As the preceding discussion suggests, private contracts alone cannot sustain the public domain. The concern with the public domain is unrelated to the particular circumstances of specific contract but rather to the general public good. Therefore it is not adequately addressed by contract law. The problem is further complicated by the fact contract law differs, not just between countries but also within the United States and the European Union.

---

[101] 17 U.S.C. § 301.

[102] See, eg, the district court in *ProCD v. Zeidenberg*, 908 F. Supp. 640, 658 (W.D. Wis.), rev'd 86 F.3d 1447 (7th Cir. 1996) (holding that when 'a contract erects a barrier on access to information' that should be accessible under copyright law, it alters the 'delicate balance' created by the law; such a license, the court held, would 'step into territory already covered by copyright law').

[103] See *ProCD*, 86 F.3d 1447.

[104] See Niva Elkin-Koren, *Copyright Policy and the Limits of Freedom of Contract*, 12 BERKELEY TECH. L.J. 93 (1997).

[105] 17 U.S.C. § 301.

Furthermore, existing legal doctrines are inadequate to minimize the negative externalities caused by restrictive terms in contracts, and even if we expand the grounds, the law of contracts will still be insufficient to handle the job.[106] Challenges to particular terms, even if successful, invalidate only the particular contract before the court. Although repeated findings of invalidity may eventually influence the drafters of future contracts, that is a slow and uncertain way to protect the public interest against such restrictions.

How may the long-term objectives of information policy be secured? Restrictive terms in information transactions resemble private regulation and, therefore, require regulators to take an active role to minimize their damaging impact on the public domain. What form should regulatory intervention take in a contract regime? The law should create a presumption that restrictive terms are invalid unless the licensor can show adequate justification for their enforcement in particular cases. Such a presumption would serve as a safeguard for the public interest in preserving some level of free access to works. At the same time, it would leave room for information providers to show that, in particular market circumstances, the use of restrictive terms should be permissible. This approach relies on several assumptions that are discussed in more detail below.

A. The legal rule should focus on the behavior of information providers

In a contract regime, information producers control the drafting process. Users rarely draft any terms, and, indeed, hardly read the form contracts. They know they are unlikely to understand the terms, and even if they did, that they would have a negligible chance of changing them.[107] But there is no need for users to review the terms. To do so would be inefficient. What is necessary is to make sure that users are not held to obligations whose enforcement is not socially beneficial.

Information producers who draft the contracts are better situated to secure their interests and to predict and prepare in advance for the risk that some terms will be invalidated. When a court invalidates a contract ex post, it actually changes the bargain between the parties. But if the legal rule were presumptively to invalidate restrictive terms, a rationale drafter would take this into account when drawing up the contract. A presumption of invalidity places the burden of proof on the person who can best assess the benefits and risks embodied in any of the contract terms and is best able to understand the impact of any given term on the ability to exploit their informational works. Since producers execute a large number of similar contracts over time, they have an incentive to collect information about the implications and legal validity of the terms they draft.

[106] This is essentially the suggestion proposed by Reichman and Franklin, see n. 3 above.
[107] See SLAWSON, n. 29 above, at 30.

Yet, simply presuming restrictive terms to be void would not entirely eliminate the chilling effect created by such terms. Provisions whose legal validity
is uncertain are nevertheless included in contracts because contract terms do
not simply define the rights of users. They also communicate the expectations
of the drafter by means of a text that sounds authoritative; that is, they serve
to declare and deter. In most cases, users will do what the contract says and
not question it. Consequently, producers would retain an incentive to use
such terms, hoping that users will comply with them.

The experience of countries that limit the enforceability of unfair terms in
standard form contract[108] shows that information providers are unlikely to
give up restrictive terms altogether. This may further be inferred from the
history of shrink-wrap licenses in the past 20 years. Shrink-wrap licenses continued to be routinely used by software providers even though their enforceability was denied in the United States by many courts. Nevertheless, a clear
legal rule would assist users in recognizing invalid terms, and, over time, such
restrictions should gradually disappear

B. The law should permit the use of standard form contracts for information products in the interest of efficiency

The law should not entirely prevent contracts involving use of copyrights.
Giving information producers the power to tailor a bargain that accommodates their particular interests is socially beneficial. Negotiated contracts that
manifest a meaningful assent allow particular consumers and providers to
adjust the rights of access to their specific needs. Contracts facilitate greater
flexibility than may be achieved under a generally applicable copyright rule.
Negotiated transactions, which reflect informed consent and free choice, are
unlikely to inflict the kind of damage created by generally applicable terms in
standard form contracts. To the extent that a genuinely individualized agreement compromises the public interest, traditional legal doctrines are capable
of addressing it.

Restrictions should, therefore, only apply to non-negotiated terms. This
does not mean that the law should discourage the use of standard form contracts as a general matter. Rather it should exploit their advantages. These

---

[108] In Israel, for instance, a number of statutes limit the enforceability of terms in standard
form contracts. See, eg, Sale (Housing) Law, 5733–1973, § 7A ('There will be no contracting out
of the provisions of this law but for the benefit of the consumer'). Experience shows, however,
that construction companies routinely incorporate such prohibited terms into their contracts.
The rationale seems obvious. Merely incorporating such terms does not violate the law. The
chances that a dispute over the validity of such terms will be litigated is low, and, in any event,
such a case would probably be settled. Even if terms are held to be void, the finding will apply
only to the parties to the dispute, and will not affect the validity of terms in other standard form
contracts. At the same time, including such provisions would allow construction companies to
manage their risk in most transactions.

contracts significantly reduce transaction costs. Furthermore, allowing providers to use contracts to subdivide the market and to tailor prices and licenses to different market segments may be a socially beneficial way to promote access to information.[109] But if this practice becomes the rule, and no alternative access to information is available, it may also enhance social segregation and the development of new classes of information 'haves' and 'have-nots'.

C. The legal rule should shift the burden of proof

Holding restrictive terms presumptively invalid would be a better legal strategy than invalidating such terms altogether. We currently lack sufficient information on the provisions providers are likely to include in their contracts. It is also unclear what effects specific provisions that seem to expand copyrights will have on the public domain. What legal policy should we adopt in the face of uncertainty? Some believe that, absent information about the kind of rights that would evolve under a contract regime, the law should refrain from intervening at all, and allow providers to exit freely from copyright law into contract law.[110] However, the preceding analysis suggests that restrictive terms are unlikely to be socially beneficial. Hence, the appropriate compromise would be to allow providers to show that, in particular market circumstances, such terms are justifiable. Once we acknowledge that restrictive terms can impose negative externalities on society as a whole, we need to adopt a legal strategy to secure the public interest. Waiting for individual users to challenge the enforceability of terms in court is inefficient. In many cases individual users may lack adequate incentives to dispute the validity of a term. Perhaps it does not particularly affect their immediate interests, or has such a slight effect on their ability to use the product that the benefits of challenging it would be outweighed by the cost of litigation. It does not follow, however, that such restrictions are insignificant. Once such a term becomes prevalent, it may negatively affect society as a whole.

The cost of litigation may further be a barrier to legal challenges by users. That is particularly true under the American Rule, which imposes the cost of litigation on both parties (the plaintiff and the defendant) regardless of the litigation outcome. Restrictive terms set limits on actions by users, and consequently challenges are likely to occur when a suit is brought by the producer for breaking the contract. Users, as defenders, are likely to avoid litigation

---

[109] Several commentators believe that contracts enhance access to information. By providing opportunities for arbitrage that does not exist under a copyright regime, contracts allow providers to differentiate among consumers. Thus customized contracts, it is argued, will allow providers to reduce the price of access by charging a lower price for each use. See Bell, n. 12 above; William Fisher III, *Property and Contract on the Internet*, 73 CHI.-KENT L. REV. 1203, 1234–40 (1998).

[110] Bell, n. 12 above, at 562.

even if they believe they can show in court that a particular restriction is void. That is because they would wish to avoid incurring nonrecoverable litigation costs. The negative presumption may therefore be more efficient.

D. The legal rule should address the needs of global electronic commerce

Electronic commerce and the global marketplace for information require some common legal understandings for doing business internationally. It is necessary to establish legal certainty, not only within national laws, but also in the international arena. UCITA adopts a contract-based solution. It provides a set of default rules that the parties can modify by contract. If UCITA is adopted by the states, the United States is likely to move for its global implementation.

UCITA's reliance on contract law does not provide an adequate framework for dealing with restrictive terms on a global basis. First, contract law is diverse. Considerable differences exist in Europe among EU Member States in the law of contracts and the same is true among US states. Certainly, there are differences between US and European contract doctrine. The contract model would not, therefore, provide a relatively clear, uniform, and predictable set of rules to facilitate planning by players in a global market.

The contract model does allow contracting parties freely to choose the law they want to govern their agreement.[111] This leads, however, to forum-shopping, allowing licensors to choose the jurisdiction whose law is most favorable to them. National governments are also likely to be more vulnerable to pressure from the international business community to create a contract regime friendlier to corporate interests. Finally, the contract model does not provide an adequate jurisprudential framework for developing information policy. The contract model requires courts to deal with information policy as part of contract law. Information policy requires some expertise, however, and familiarity with the complexity and peculiarity of information transactions. Information policy must be informed by a broader view of the public interest. Contract litigation, in contrast, is likely to focus on such matters as freedom of contract and the parties' expectations. Copyright laws reflect information policy, and may therefore provide a better setting for balancing conflicting interests and disputes regarding use and access to information.

Of course, there is also considerable diversity in copyright law. Copyright law in the United States is fairly uniform, but in Europe it varies across the Member States. There are also fundamental differences between European and US copyright laws. The *droit d'auteur* regime perceives copyright as a natural right of authors and as a reward for their intellectual efforts. It is

---

[111] There are further differences between the US and European approaches to choice of law in contracts. See Friedrich K. Juenger, *Contract Choice of Law in the Americas*, 45 Am. J. Comp. L. 195 (1997).

designed to protect the author's interests in her work as an 'extension' of her personality. The US approach to copyright law is utilitarian, justifying property rights as a vehicle to promote the advancement of the arts and sciences by providing authors with incentives to create. Nevertheless, copyright policy has reached some level of harmonization through international treaties.

A presumption against restrictive terms is consistent with current European thinking, as reflected in the Computer Program Directive. The presumption is also congruent with long-standing European traditions that limit freedom of contract and are suspicious of claims that standard forms and market processes safeguard the public welfare. European law reflects more awareness and consideration of disparities of power between individuals and corporations, litigation costs, and the fallacy of market equality. The fact that copyrights under *droit d'auteur* are broader and stronger and are based on a natural rights tradition should not be an obstacle to limiting the legal power of producers to enforce restrictive terms.[112]

The place to imbed the presumption against restrictive terms is in the copyright law itself. Indeed, the law should explicitly set out which users' rights may not be overridden by standard form contracts. Access is one of the core tenets of copyright law, and protecting it should be the focus of legislative efforts. Copyright law should be redesigned to address the concerns of information policy in a privately ordered market for information. Information policy for the new information economy must focus on progress. The major challenge for copyright law in past centuries was to provide adequate incentives for the creation of new content; the challenge for copyright policy in the new information economy is to secure reasonable access by the public.

---

[112] In fact, some countries, such as Germany, impose public obligations on the owner of any property including intellectual property.

BARGAINING OVER THE TRANSFER OF PROPRIETARY RESEARCH TOOLS: IS THIS MARKET FAILING OR EMERGING?

REBECCA S. EISENBERG*

As intellectual property claims proliferate in rapidly advancing fields of technology, new research paths often cross the boundaries of many prior patents. Without an exemption from infringement liability,[1] subsequent innovators need licenses from multiple predecessors to pursue such research projects. Whether this state of affairs promotes innovation or retards it is an empirical question of considerable complexity.

Suzanne Scotchmer's work on cumulative innovation highlights an important policy consideration: patent boundaries are a significant determinant of the relative returns to investment at different stages in the course of cumulative innovation.[2] Broad patents on early innovations permit their owners to

* Robert & Barbara Luciano Professor of Law, University of Michigan Law School. I am grateful to John Barton, Rochelle Cooper Dreyfuss, Ronald Mann, and workshop participants at New York University Law School, Engelberg Center on Innovation Law and Policy, Conference at Villa La Pietra, Florence, Italy (June 1998); the Biotechnology Industry Organization annual meeting, New York (June 1998); the American Type Culture Collection Patent Seminar, Virginia Center for Innovative Technology (September 1998); the Mayo Clinic (October 1998); and the University of California at Berkeley (May 1999) for helpful comments on earlier drafts of this chapter.

[1] The US patent statute does not generally exempt research activities from infringement liability, although it includes a narrow exemption for the use of a patented invention 'solely for uses reasonably related to the development and submission of information under a Federal Law which regulates the manufacture, use, or sale of drugs or veterinary biological products': 35 U.S.C. § 271(e)(1).

[2] See Suzanne Scotchmer, *Standing on the Shoulders of Giants: Cumulative Research and the Patent Law*, 5 J. ECON. PERSP. 29 (1991); Jerry R. Green & Suzanne Scotchmer, *On the Division of Profit in Sequential Innovation*, 26 RAND J. ECON. 20 (1995).

capture, through license transactions, the value that their innovations contribute to second generation technologies, ensuring that the incentives of early innovators reflect this value. Although the cost of getting licenses from prior innovators diminishes the profitability of second generation innovations,[3] Scotchmer argues that subsequent innovators can still recover an adequate return if they negotiate the terms of licenses before they incur research and development (R&D) costs.

This analysis highlights the importance of transactions between prior and subsequent innovators to permit valuable research to go forward across the boundaries of prior patent claims. In a recent article focusing on biomedical research,[4] Michael Heller and I argue that too many patent rights on 'upstream' discoveries can stifle 'downstream' research and product development by increasing transaction costs and magnifying the risk of bargaining failures. Just as too few property rights leave communally held resources prone to overuse in a 'tragedy of the commons', too many property rights can leave resources prone to underuse in what Heller calls a 'tragedy of the anticommons'.[5] The greater the number of people who need to be brought to agreement in order to permit a research project to proceed, the greater the risk that bargaining will break down or that transaction costs will consume the gains from exchange.

Other commentators have noted that such bargaining failures are not inevitable. In a world of costless transactions, people could avoid commons or anticommons tragedies by trading their rights. Robert Merges has documented the development of numerous institutions that reduce the transaction costs of negotiating through a thicket of intellectual property rights in different industries, including the ASCAP copyright collective and the recent MPEG patent pool.[6] If owners and users manage to negotiate mutually agreeable license terms, then a proliferation of patents can promote equitable distribution of the value of cumulative and interdependent innovations without unduly inhibiting future research.

Is bargaining failure in the market for intellectual property licenses a hypothetical problem that sophisticated institutions and well-functioning markets

---

[3] Scotchmer worries more about preserving the incentives of early innovators on the assumption that the stand-alone value of their innovations will be small relative to that of the later innovations that they facilitate. On the other hand, it may be that patent incentives are more important in the later stages of cumulative innovation than in the early stages (eg, if early innovations are relatively cheap or are subsidized by the government), whereas subsequent innovations are relatively expensive or more dependent on private sector investment—and if so, it may make more sense to limit the rights of early innovators so that subsequent innovators can capture a larger share of the value of cumulative efforts.

[4] See Michael A. Heller & Rebecca S. Eisenberg, *Can Patents Deter Innovation? The Anticommons in Biomedical Research*, 280 Sci. 698 (1998).

[5] See Michael A. Heller, *The Tragedy of the Anticommons: Property in the Transition from Marx to Markets*, 111 Harv. L. Rev. 621 (1998).

[6] See Robert P. Merges, *Contracting Into Liability Rules: Intellectual Property Rights and Collective Rights Organizations*, 84 Cal. L. Rev. 1293 (1996). See also Merges, Chapter 6 above.

are likely to avoid, or is it something to worry about? In biomedical research, there is evidence that the problem is real. In 1997–98, I served as chair of the National Institutes of Health (NIH) Working Group on Research Tools (the Working Group), a group charged with investigating difficulties encountered by researchers in obtaining access to proprietary research tools—materials, information and methods—for use in biomedical research.[7] The Working Group gathered information from scientists, university technology transfer professionals, and private firms in the pharmaceutical and biotechnology industries.[8] Within these communities, there seems to be a widely-shared perception that negotiations over the transfer of proprietary research tools present a considerable and growing obstacle to progress in biomedical research and product development. Scientists report having to wait months or even years to carry out experiments while their institutions attempt to renegotiate the terms of 'Material Transfer Agreements' (MTAs), database access agreements, and patent license agreements. University technology transfer professionals report that agreements presented for the transfer of research tools impose increasingly onerous terms. They say that the burden of reviewing and renegotiating each of a rapidly growing number of agreements for what used to be routine exchanges among scientists is overwhelming their limited resources. Private firms—both large, established pharmaceutical firms and small, young biotechnology companies—also report growing frustration with the administrative burden of renegotiating the terms of agreements for the transfer of research tools and with attendant delays in research. Some even

---

[7] See *Report of the National Institutes of Health (NIH) Working Group on Research Tools, Presented to the Advisory Committee to the Director* (June 4, 1998) <http://www.nih.gov./news/researchtools/ index.htm>.

[8] Many of the individuals who spoke with members of the Working Group were concerned about maintaining confidentiality. As a result, both the discussion in this chapter and the Report of the Working Group avoid the use of specific examples and citations to conversations with specific individuals. The discussion in text is drawn from communications with representatives of many academic institutions and private firms. I also include quotations from some of these conversations as recorded in my own notes, although without attribution to specific individuals or institutions. The private firms that provided information to the Working Group include: Affymetrix; Amgen; Arena Pharmaceuticals; Ares-Serono; Bristol-Myers Squibb; CEPH; Cephalon; DuPont; Ergoscience; Genentech; Genetics Institute; Guilford Pharmaceuticals; Hoechst Marion Roussel; Hoffmann-La Roche; Human Genome Sciences; Ligand Pharmaceuticals; Megabios; Merck; Millennium; Parke-Davis; Pfizer; Pharmacopeia; Schering-Plough; SmithKline Beecham; Vical. The academic institutions that provided information to the Working Group include: Allegheny Health, Education and Research Foundation; The Bowman Gray School of Medicine, Wake Forest University; University of California; California Institute of Technology; University of Chicago; University of Cincinnati; Columbia University; University of Connecticut; Harvard University; University of Illinois at Urbana-Champaign; Indiana University; University of Iowa; Johns Hopkins University; University of Louisville; Massachusetts General Hospital; Massachusetts Institute of Technology; Miami University; University of Michigan; University of Pennsylvania; Princeton University; University of Rochester; Rutgers University; University of South Carolina; Stanford University; State University of New York; Tulane University Medical Center; University of Washington; Washington University; University of Wisconsin-Madison; Yale University.

confided that in internal discussions they have questioned whether it is worth their while to continue to exchange research tools with university scientists. Although there are many points on which they disagree, most people from each of these quarters seem to agree that the problem is growing rather than diminishing.

Why, in this setting, is it proving so difficult to arrive at mutually agreeable bargains between prior and subsequent innovators? If transaction costs are consuming the gains from exchange, why haven't the communities that confront this problem figured out mechanisms for reducing these costs?[9] Answers to these questions about transactions for the transfer of biomedical research tools may shed some light on broader questions about how far we can rely on bargains among sequential innovators to allocate new technologies to socially valuable uses. If prior and subsequent innovators find it difficult to negotiate the terms of transactions for the transfer of intellectual property, then perhaps initial allocations of intellectual property rights matter, not only because they determine the distribution of returns across various stages of cumulative innovation, but because they either promote or retard the efficient dissemination of prior discoveries to subsequent innovators.

I. Background

Current problems in the exchange of biomedical research tools arise in the context of dramatic institutional and cultural changes in biomedical research that have not yet come to rest. One important policy shift has come from passage of the 1980 Bayh-Dole Act[10] and subsequent Congressional directives that encourage universities and other recipients of federal research funds to patent the results of federally-sponsored research.[11] The result has been a dramatic increase in patent filings from institutions that, in an earlier era, were more likely to make their discoveries freely available.[12] Two dimensions of this change are particularly relevant to current problems surrounding the exchange of research tools. First, it has expanded and diversified the types of *institutions* claiming proprietary rights in their discoveries, as academic and nonprofit institutions have established technology transfer offices to patent

---

[9] The Association of University Technology Managers has attempted to streamline transactions for the transfer of biomedical research tools by creating a Uniform Biological Materials Transfer Agreement (UBMTA). See 60 Fed. Reg. 12771 (1995). Many universities have approved the use of the UBMTA in principle, but few seem actually to use it. More recently, in response to the Report of the Working Group, NIH has created guidelines on research tools that include a proposed form agreement. See 64 Fed. Reg. 72090 (1999).

[10] 35 U.S.C. §§ 200–211.

[11] See Rebecca S. Eisenberg, *Public Research and Private Development: Patents and Technology Transfer in Government-Sponsored Research*, 82 VA. L. REV. 1663 (1996).

[12] See Rebecca Henderson et al., *Universities as a Source of Commercial Technology: A Detailed Analysis of University Patenting 1965–1988*, 80 REV. ECON. & STAT. 119 (1998).

faculty inventions and to market them to commercial firms. Secondly is a corresponding expansion and diversification in the types of *discoveries* that are the subject of proprietary claims to include the early-stage discoveries, considerably removed from product development, that typically emerge from government-sponsored biomedical research. The domain of proprietary exchange has thus become more diverse in terms of both the participants and the objects of exchange.

A related, contemporaneous change has been the emergence of commercial biotechnology firms in market niches that lie somewhere between fundamental academic research and end product development. These biotechnology firms differ from established pharmaceutical firms in important ways. Many of these firms have academic scientists as founders, retain strong scientific and financial ties to academic institutions, and rely on government grants for research funding. Lacking end products for sale to non-research consumers, some of these firms survive in the private sector by selling research tools and the research capabilities of their scientific personnel to other institutions, especially to major pharmaceutical firms. The evolving profit strategies of biotechnology firms often depend heavily on intellectual property rights in discoveries that are primarily inputs into further research. These firms are motivated to exchange research tools with other institutions, but they also need to preserve the competitive and financial value of their research tools.

The shifting balance of public and private funding for biomedical research is another factor with an important bearing on exchanges of research tools.[13] In the past decade, despite steady increases in federal funding for health-related research,[14] private funding overtook public funding as the principal source of support for biomedical research in the United States.[15] Although public funding remains the principal source of support for university-based biomedical research, public-private boundaries are blurring as relationships between academic institutions and private firms proliferate in the life sciences.[16] Collaborative research that pools research capabilities and funds from different institutions in the public and private sectors is increasingly

---

[13] See National Science Board, *Science & Engineering Indicators—1998* (1998) (hereinafter 1998 Indicators) <http://www.nsf.gov/sbe/srs/seind98/start.htm>.

[14] See ibid ch. 4, at 3.

[15] See *National Institutes of Health: Source of Funds, Medical and Health Related R&D: Fiscal Years 1986–1995* (visited September 1, 1999) <http://www4.od.nih.gov/ofm/PRIMER97/page6. stm>. According to these data, from 1986–1995, government funding for medical and health-related R&D doubled, from $7,924 million to $15,846 million, while industry funding for medical and health-related R&D more than tripled, from $6,192 million to $18,645 million. These data indicate that industry funding first exceeded government funding in 1992.

[16] See David Blumenthal et al., *Relationships Between Academic Institutions and Industry in the Life Sciences—An Industry Survey*, 334 N. Eng. J. Med. 368 (1996) (finding that 90 percent of companies conducting life science research in the United States had relationships involving the life sciences with academic institutions).

common, not only in the life sciences[17] but across all fields of research.[18] Mature pharmaceutical firms, biotechnology start-ups, and academic institutions find themselves sometimes collaborating and sometimes competing to achieve overlapping research goals. As a result, it is often difficult to tell when an academic researcher is a commercial competitor.

In this environment, many institutions that develop new materials, methods, and information for use in research regard these tools as valuable intellectual property. By restricting access to new research tools, some institutions seek to capture their value through sales and licenses to researchers in other institutions, and some seek to preserve a competitive advantage in subsequent stages of research by withholding these resources from their rivals entirely. At the same time, many scientists and institutions at least purport to embrace traditional scientific norms calling for widespread sharing of research tools to promote scientific progress, especially when they seek access to tools that have been created by others.

Some of these scientists and institutions resolve the dissonance between the norms they would apply to the tools created by others and the norms they abide by in disseminating their own tools through the use of carefully crafted definitions of the term 'research tool'. The term 'research tool' would seem to connote a user perspective, indicating something that is not yet an end product and has its primary value as an input into further research. Yet a user's research tool may be a provider's end product. Some products that are currently used in research might also have markets, actual or potential, among nonresearch consumers. A pharmaceutical compound might be used in academic research, and a DNA sequence that is associated with disease might be marketed as a diagnostic product at the same time that it is used in further research to understand its role in a disease pathway. Some biotechnology firms make a business out of developing and supplying proprietary materials, information and methods that are useful primarily, if not only, in further research; to these firms research tools *are* end products.

Some major pharmaceutical firms that earn profits by selling proprietary drugs to nonresearch consumers have been outspoken supporters of improving access to research tools throughout the research community.[19] But what these firms mean by 'research tools' is the biological materials that they use in

---

[17] See Walter W. Powell et al., *Interorganizational Collaboration and the Locus of Innovation: Networks of Learning in Biotechnology*, 41 ADMIN. SCI. Q. 116 (1996). See also Powell, Chapter 10 below.

[18] See 1998 Indicators, n. 13 above, at 4–28 to 4–32.

[19] A research director of a major pharmaceutical firm said that 'we consider this a matter of enlightened self-interest—no one can own them all, so we really should figure out ways to make them accessible'. He conceded that his firm will not supply materials to a competitor, noting that it is important to 'distinguish enlightened self-interest from stupidity', but said that if a competitor were willing to make the materials itself and simply needed a license to avoid patent infringement, the firm would provide an 'unblocking license' for a nominal fee.

the course of drug discovery, not the end products that they sell (or hope to sell) to consumers.[20] The same firms are quite restrictive about disseminating their own proprietary therapeutic products to researchers. A scientific liaison for a biotechnology firm that makes transgenic animals, noting that there are different levels of security for different types of materials, states that 'any type of proprietary material is not a research tool' and 'our transgenics are proprietary'. A representative of a biotechnology firm that sells therapeutic proteins has two different form agreements—a simple form with few restrictions that it uses for 'things that aren't proprietary products in development', and a more restrictive form that it uses for materials that the firm has identified as potential products.

Institutions tend to be high-minded about the importance of unfettered access to the research tools that they want to acquire from others, but no institution is willing to share freely the materials and discoveries from which they derive significant competitive advantage. Thus many of the people that spoke with the Working Group were eager to establish that the term 'research tool' means something other than their own institution's crown jewels. Those firms whose crown jewels could only be characterized as 'research tools' insisted that they were different in kind from ordinary research tools and therefore called for different terms of exchange.[21] When one institution's research tool is another firm's end product, it is difficult to agree upon a universe of materials that should be exchanged on standardized terms.

Some proprietary research tools have been widely distributed under license agreements that permit subsequent research to go forward while preserving a return for the patent owner. Two outstanding examples of fundamental importance to biomedical research are the recently-expired Cohen-Boyer patents on recombinant DNA technologies, jointly owned by Stanford University and the University of California,[22] and the patents on the polymerase chain reaction (PCR) owned by Hoffmann-La Roche.[23] Both are

[20] A representative of a major pharmaceutical firm defined 'research tool' as 'something that gets you on the path of doing drug discovery, not a chemical entity or product, but an assay, or a target, or genetic information encoding a target, cell line, or other materials used in the research process'. A senior executive from another major pharmaceutical firm acknowledged that such a broad definition of 'research tool' would extend to materials that 'may be a quite meaningful competitive differentiation, particularly to a small company that makes a living through the identification of [drug] targets'. He added that even for large companies, 'if you have a series of molecular species that have given you the ability to resolve a disease pathway ahead of your competitors, that has competitive value, and you don't want others to use the tools after you've invested time and money to get there'.

[21] A lawyer for a biotechnology firm that earns most of its revenue from selling tools used in the analysis of gene expression stated that 'while on the surface it might look like what we have is a simple research tool, the value [of the product] is orders of magnitude more than what any other research tool might have'.

[22] See Intellectual Property Rights and the Dissemination of Research Tools in Molecular Biology: Summary of a Workshop Held at the National Academy of Sciences, February 15–16, 1996, 40–42 (1997).

[23] See ibid, 43–46.

fundamental enabling technologies that have had considerable value in research on a wide range of problems, and both have been licensed on terms that have permitted widespread dissemination and use.

One might expect these early success stories to lead the way toward the licensing of other research tools on increasingly routine and uncontroversial terms. Yet recent experience reveals precisely the opposite trend. Exchanges between universities and private firms are particularly likely to be problematic, but bargaining difficulties extend to purely academic and purely commercial exchanges as well. Although there is significant variation in the terms of agreements for the transfer of research tools, most of the conflict between providers and users of research tools focuses on the same handful of provisions over and over again.[24]

Some, but not all, of these conflicts have been relatively easy to resolve through negotiations. For example, tool providers will often modify restrictive prepublication review provisions in response to objections from the user.[25] What is surprising about these routinely renegotiated provisions is that tool providers continue to propose the more aggressive terms initially, rather than modifying the language of their draft agreements to avoid the costs of repeated renegotiations.[26]

More intractable disagreements arise over so-called 'reach-through' and 'grantback' provisions governing rights to potential future inventions made by the user of the research tool. For example, providers of research tools may seek royalties on future product sales, options to acquire exclusive or nonexclusive licenses under future patents, or even outright ownership of future inventions as a condition for making the tools available. Through such provisions, owners of research tools may seek to leverage their proprietary rights in early innovations into a share of the profits from future innovations that may be more lucrative. Or, by asking for automatic license rights to discoveries made while using their tools, they may seek to protect themselves from intellectual property claims that users might assert against them in the future. But these precommitments to extend future licenses create a problem for users of multiple research tools faced with similar reach-through demands from multiple owners. A user cannot promise an exclusive license to future discoveries more than once in the course of a research project before creating

---

[24] See Rebecca S. Eisenberg, *Streamlining the Transfer of Research Tools*, 74 ACADEMIC MEDICINE 683 (1999).

[25] For example, the provider's initial draft might require the user to submit manuscripts for pre-publication review 180 days prior to submission for publication, a period that is reduced to 60 days in the course of negotiations.

[26] One inhouse lawyer for a biotechnology firm suggested that a possible explanation for repeated use of forms that consistently need to be renegotiated may be that these forms are drafted by retained counsel that profit from the time spent in renegotiating the terms of the agreement. Another possibility is that sometimes the forms are signed in the form presented, encouraging owners to try for the same terms again.

conflicting obligations. Even past promises of nonexclusive licenses would conflict with future promises of exclusive licenses to the same discoveries. Concerned about incurring overlapping and inconsistent obligations to providers of different research tools, and reluctant to enter into agreements that disable them from licensing potential future discoveries as they see fit before they even know what the discoveries are, users balk at signing the proffered terms of access, and negotiations stall.

Although the terms of access to some high value research tools have provoked controversy,[27] the more serious bottleneck to research is the growing burden of negotiating numerous agreements for routine use of methods, materials and data in experiments. Taken individually, none of these agreements is likely to yield commercially valuable results. Nonetheless, in the aggregate, they create significant administrative delays that slow the pace of research.

II. Analysis

The investigation of the Working Group on Research Tools provides a rare opportunity to examine, from multiple perspectives, difficulties encountered in negotiating for the transfer of intellectual property. What accounts for apparently growing difficulties in establishing a market for the exchange of biomedical research tools? Four themes emerge from interviews with participants in this market, each of which I elaborate below. First, transaction costs are a greater obstacle to low-value exchanges than to high-value exchanges. Transaction costs are thus more likely to impede the transfer of research tools for use in experiments that are unlikely to yield commercially valuable results than they are to impede major research collaborations, even among the same people and institutions. Secondly, heterogeneities among institutions within the biomedical research community seem to be complicating the search for mutually agreeable terms of exchange. Universities, pharmaceutical firms, and biotechnology firms each find it relatively easy to deal with their own kind, but each finds institutions of the other kinds to be unreasonable and unrealistic in their demands and expectations. Thirdly, even within a single institution, the interests of scientists who make and use research tools and the interests of the lawyers and business people who negotiate the terms of these exchanges on behalf of the institutions that employ the scientists are not necessarily the same, and these different 'agents' do not always present a united front in negotiations. These internal conflicts complicate the bargaining process and frustrate the emergence of agreement about fair terms of

---

[27] See, eg, Eliot Marshall, *The Mouse That Prompted a Roar*, 277 Sci. 24 (1997); Jon Cohen, *Exclusive License Rankles Genome Researchers*, 276 Sci. 1489 (1997).

exchange within the biomedical research community. Fourthly, evaluation of research tools, and estimation of the contribution that they might make to potential future discoveries, is highly speculative and subjective and does not lend itself to dispassionate negotiations from agreed-upon benchmarks.

A. Transaction costs

A striking feature of the market for biomedical research tools is the sophistication of the institutions involved and the frequency with which the same parties conclude other, higher value deals.[28] How can it be that institutions with the resources and skills to establish major collaborative research agreements nonetheless stumble over mundane exchanges of research materials and techniques?

A simple explanation is that transaction costs are worth incurring for high value transactions, but not for low value transactions. Collaborative research agreements generally involve more substantial commitments of resources, and hopes for future value, on all sides of the deal than MTAs.[29] Not surprisingly, institutions involved in biomedical research give priority in the allocation of their negotiating resources to higher value transactions, while lower value transactions get deferred. As a result, the transaction cost bottleneck presents more of a problem for low value exchanges than for major collaborations.

This generalization was repeatedly confirmed by people who negotiate agreements on behalf of institutions in the private sector. Representatives of biotechnology firms and pharmaceutical firms indicated that, although routine exchanges are increasingly likely to be delayed to the point that the transaction loses its value, the exchanges of research tools that matter most to the firms' scientists generally go forward.[30] Representatives of universities, on the

---

[28] Walter Powell describes elaborate networks for pooling the resources of pharmaceutical firms, biotechnology firms, and universities to perform collaborative biomedical research. See, eg, Walter W. Powell & Jason Owen-Smith, *Commercialism in Universities: Life Sciences Research and its Linkage with Industry*, 17 J. POL'Y ANALYSIS & MGMT. 253 (1998); Powell et al., n. 17 above.

[29] As noted earlier in text, MTA is a standard abbreviation for a 'material transfer agreement' that sets forth the terms of access to a (typically unpatented) biological material. Several representatives of private companies said that they would only use an MTA if the company has little or no interest in the research of the scientist to whom it is sending a research tool. If the company anticipates that the scientist's research will yield valuable results, it would propose a more substantial relationship, perhaps involving research sponsorship or collaboration. Exchanges for which an MTA is used are thus typically of low value to the provider of the material.

[30] For example, a Vice President and General Counsel of a biotechnology company stated that 'there isn't anything that people can't get access to if they really need it', although sometimes it is cheaper and easier to design around a proprietary research tool. A representative of a different biotechnology company reported that her firm only cares about approximately 100 MTAs out of 2,000 that she processes annually, and those agreements always get done. The research director of a major pharmaceutical firm claims that his firm has never had to shut down a research project for failure to gain access to a proprietary research tool, although they sometimes

other hand, appear to be frustrated not only by the large volume of low value agreements demanding their attention, but also by the terms of access to certain high value research tools that have led to bargaining impasses.[31]

Even from the perspective of large, private firms, the value of foregone exchanges due to failed bargains over the transfer of research tools is often more than trivial. For example, a former scientist who now represents a major pharmaceutical firm in research tool negotiations indicated that, even when her firm would be willing to pay $20,000 for a license to a research tool, negotiations over contract language can take months or years, during which time the scientists often give up and turn their attention to something else.[32] The same representative indicated that when her firm receives an unsolicited request to provide a research tool, the firm is unwilling to invest any resources at all in renegotiating the terms of exchange; would-be users can take the firm's form agreement or leave it.[33] Paradoxically, such cost-driven intransigence in renegotiating the terms of agreements may slow the emergence of a consensus on what counts as fair terms of exchange. A representative of another pharmaceutical firm explained that 'the deal breaker [in negotiations over the transfer of research tools] typically isn't cost, but terms and conditions'.

The terms and conditions that are so difficult to agree upon generally involve the allocation of speculative future value and risks. If most transfers of research tools will not produce discoveries of any value, the ratio of value to transaction costs could be improved, and aggregate transaction costs reduced, by deferring the most difficult negotiations until after it becomes apparent that there is significant value at stake. Some firms try to do this—or at least suspect that other firms try to do this—by using patented research tools without a license, assuming that they can settle the matter later in the

---

have spent considerable resources inventing around patents, and sometimes have performed experiments offshore when a US license has not been available on reasonable terms.

[31] See, eg, Marshall, n. 27 above; Cohen, n. 27 above.

[32] 'We wouldn't mind paying $20,000 for a license if we thought it were something we could build a research program on . . . The biggest barrier in that price range is disagreements over legal language and the turnaround time to get that accomplished. Most university offices have long backlogs of these projects on their desks, and they have to prioritize. Rarely does it seem like our small research tool contracts make it to the top of their piles. It takes a long time for them to get back to us . . . We also have limited staff that can work on these agreements . . . If each round takes a couple of months, even though it might take only an hour or so, it ends up taking several months. I'm working on something that's taken over a year for a $20,000 research tool. We're stuck on the issue of indemnification . . . Eventually, the scientists shrug their shoulders and pick something else to work on rather than trying to work out an agreement with the university . . . It's the time delay, rather than the cost, that discourages us from going forward most of the time.'

[33] 'We have a policy that people find pretty hard. If we get an unsolicited MTA, we basically ask them to accept our MTA word for word. But if our scientist says that this is a valuable proposal and the data would be important for us, then we'll try to work it out. It's a two-tiered system. We are constrained in terms of the legal staff that we have available. Otherwise, we couldn't get any work done.'

unlikely event that they discover something significant.[34] Other firms try to achieve a similar result through the use of agreements that do not resolve difficult issues, such as the division of future intellectual property, up front. Instead, they preserve the parties' bargaining positions and obligate each side to return to the table for further negotiations in the event that a valuable discovery emerges. Although this is not always possible, a lawyer for a biotechnology company reported some success with such a strategy in negotiations over transfers of his company's libraries of combinatorial chemistry compounds to other firms planning to screen the compounds against their own proprietary biological targets. Frustrated with up-front negotiations that could take a year or longer, he began proposing simple agreements under which his firm would make its compounds available to firms that would promise to return to negotiate over any 'hits' between compounds and targets prior to filing any patent applications. He proposed such contracts to 15 firms over the course of a year and concluded seven deals on those terms. The subsequent license negotiations over rights to the 'hits' take time, 'but at least you're arguing over something that has value'.

Not all transfers of research tools can follow a strategy of deferring negotiation over the tough issues until it is known whether the results justify the transaction costs. The reason this strategy is viable for the screening transactions is that each side is in a position to withhold value after the screening is complete, and thus each side retains bargaining leverage for use in subsequent negotiations. The owner of the combinatorial chemistry libraries has intellectual property rights in the compounds that can still be enforced after the screening is complete, and the owner of the targets can disclose the existence of a hit while withholding information about which compound has hit which target. Each side thus has good reason to return to the bargaining table after a successful screening. Often, however, the owner of a research tool retains no leverage after the fact if use of the tool facilitates a valuable discovery. Tool owners are thus forced to negotiate before the research takes place if they wish to stake a claim to future value, even though at that point the value is entirely speculative.

When progress in research depends on the relatively unfettered flow of low value exchanges of information and materials among scientists, a proliferation of intellectual property claims to the objects of these exchanges may impose transaction costs that consume the gains from exchange. If owners and users are unable to reduce these transaction costs, exchanges that could have considerable value in the aggregate might not occur.

---

[34] One representative of a major pharmaceutical firm, while insisting that his own firm has a strict policy of not infringing patents, said that 'other companies just go ahead and work on the project without a license. The likelihood of success is so low, you end up buying 100,000 licenses for everything that succeeds. You spend a lot of money churning. People on the outside don't know if companies are using things on the inside. Maybe they think they can litigate it after, or get licenses retrospectively'.

B. Institutional heterogeneity

Biomedical research occurs in universities, nonprofit institutions, government agencies, small biotechnology firms and major pharmaceutical firms. Research in each of these settings both draws on and contributes to research in the other settings, yet these institutions have different missions and objectives and face different constraints. Elinor Ostrom and others have observed that heterogeneous groups have greater difficulties than homogeneous groups in reaching agreement on how to manage natural resources so as to avoid a tragedy of the commons.[35] The investigation of the Working Group on Research Tools suggests a parallel phenomenon in efforts of the heterogeneous biomedical research community to manage intellectual property rights so as to avoid a tragedy of the anticommons.[36]

Across the spectrum of institutions involved in biomedical research, people report that although they sometimes have difficulty reaching agreements within their own sector, the really serious problems arise in dealing with the other sectors. More specifically, with a few exceptions, the primary focus of complaints is difficulty negotiating the terms of access to *incoming* research tools from institutions in other sectors rather than difficulty negotiating the terms of access to *outgoing* research tools. Whether the research tool originates in a university, a biotechnology firm, or a pharmaceutical firm, it is generally the would-be user who is frustrated by the provider's terms of exchange.

Representatives of universities say that they are generally successful in negotiating with other universities, but that they find private firms unreasonable and unrealistic in their expectations of what academic institutions can promise in exchange for access to research tools. In the private sector, one hears exactly the opposite generalization—that private firms know how to do deals, but that universities are unreasonable and unrealistic in their demands. Even within the private sector, representatives of pharmaceutical firms find it relatively easy to deal with other pharmaceutical firms, but find many biotechnology firms to be unreasonable and unrealistic in their demands.

Although all sides recognize that differences in institutional resources and missions might justify asymmetrical terms of exchange, each side seems to think that the asymmetries should work in its favor. For example, universities often expect private firms to make research tools freely available to university scientists, although the same universities routinely charge private firms for access to research tools created in academic laboratories.[37] Universities feel

---

[35] See ELINOR OSTROM, GOVERNING THE COMMONS: THE EVOLUTION OF INSTITUTIONS FOR COLLECTIVE ACTION (1990).

[36] See Heller & Eisenberg, n. 4 above.

[37] In the words of the general counsel for a biotechnology firm, 'When [they seek access to a research tool from a company], universities wear the mortarboard, they want the company to pay

justified in making this distinction because their own research is for academic purposes, whereas the research done in private firms is for profit.[38] In the ethos of many university technology transfer professionals, the financial interests of their institutions converge with the public interest in scientific progress.[39] But private firms resent this claim to the moral high ground and see it as hypocritical. Some representatives of private firms challenge the claim that university research is not for profit, noting that many university scientists collaborate with private firms, and that proprietary research tools supplied to university scientists sometimes find their way into the hands of commercial competitors.[40] Others take exception to the claim that it is more fair for universities to restrict access to their research tools by commercial scientists than it is for commercial firms to restrict access to their research tools by academic scientists. Instead, they argue that university research is publicly-subsidized and should therefore benefit the taxpaying public, including private firms, while companies that pay for research with shareholder dollars have a corresponding obligation to return value to their shareholders and therefore cannot give intellectual property away.[41]

The Working Group also heard numerous complaints from representatives of all sectors of the biomedical research community that their counterparts in the other sectors are unrealistic in their demands and fail to appreciate the difficulties that they face in complying with contract terms. For example, recurring complaints among university technology transfer professionals focus on prepublication review provisions and limitations on who can work with the

all the money and take all the risk. But when they [seek to license a research tool out to a company], they scream about how they don't have any money, they're constantly ripped off by private firms . . . Universities want it both ways. They want to be commercial institutes when it comes to licensing their technology, but to be academic environments when it comes to accessing technology that others have developed. Sit down with a university and they will insist that they have discovered the holy grail and it's worth all the tea in China. But if they need something, they are academic institutions who are being impeded. They throw the same things in the way of small companies'.

[38] This attitude was particularly apparent in discussions among university technology transfer professionals at a meeting of the Association of University Technology Managers attended by members of the Working Group.

[39] A representative of a nonprofit institution told me that when, in the course of negotiations over terms of access to a research tool, a private firm tells her that they have a duty to their shareholders, she responds that she has a duty to the public.

[40] The research director of a major pharmaceutical firm claimed that academic scientists whose names would be recognizable to the firm as collaborators of its competitors sometimes use graduate students and post-doctoral fellows to get access to materials without revealing their identities. The general counsel of a biotechnology firm similarly reported that 'many companies will tell you they've been burned by professors who've made deals with multiple companies'.

[41] The words of a representative of a major pharmaceutical firm are typical of many comments from the private sector: 'It's hard to expect companies to forbear from seeking the same terms that universities are seeking. The universities don't have any moral imperative working in their favor—they aren't even accountable to shareholders'.

materials and what they can do with them.[42] They cite these provisions as evidence of a lack of appreciation for the open culture of academic research and the absence of control mechanisms within universities for ensuring compliance.[43]

University representatives also complain about prohibitions on the use of materials in research that is subject to a licensing obligation to another entity, and grantback provisions that give the provider automatic licenses under future patents. Such provisions, in their view, create conflicting obligations when multiple firms provide different research tools for use in the same project. They worry that contractual obligations to extend even nonexclusive licenses to past providers of research tools will compromise universities' stewardship over future discoveries. They point out that when these discoveries result from government-sponsored research, the Bayh-Dole Act imposes technology transfer obligations on the university.[44] In this view, the ownership rights that universities retain over discoveries made with public funds come with a corresponding trust that obligates universities to license those discoveries so as to promote transfer of technology to the private sector. Often, the best way to promote commercial development of an invention is to grant an exclusive license to a firm that promises to pursue development with diligence. But universities are unable to grant such exclusive licenses if they have previously promised nonexclusive licenses to past providers of research tools under the terms of MTAs. Precommitted licenses to future discoveries also conflict with opportunities to obtain corporate research funding for university-based research, as corporate research sponsors typically demand preferential license rights to such discoveries. Universities see the exchange of future license rights for access to a research tool as tantamount to 'free research for the company' that provides the tool. This characterization

[42] A representative of a university that many companies singled out for praise as a negotiating partner observed that Amost of these problems appear to be caused by the material provider's inexperience in dealing with a non-profit institution and its special duties and concerns'.

[43] One university technology transfer professional explained that 'scientists have a tendency to get material for one purpose and use it for something else. Nobody knows about it. It's up to the investigator to comply with reporting requirements [to the provider of a research tool]. We don't have the resources to do it . . . Research projects metamorphose all the time'. In fact, many companies are acutely aware of the risk that scientists will obtain material for one purpose and, without letting the company know what they are doing, use it for another in violation of their agreements. They seek to control this risk through the terms of their MTAs.

[44] As explained by a representative of a major research university, 'Because companies will not typically allow use of their materials in research being funded by another commercial entity, the material provider who successfully negotiates sole rights gets exclusive control of inventions whose discovery was funded by the federal government—simply by providing a sample of material . . . The provider who successfully negotiates an automatic, royalty-free, non-exclusive license has seriously damaged the ability of the research institution to promote the commercial development and marketing of any invention by offering exclusivity as an incentive to investment'.

enrages firms that see themselves as seeking a modest quid pro quo for providing free materials to university scientists.[45]

Companies complain that universities do not understand business and suffer from a 'cultural schizophrenia' about whether they are businesses or academic institutions. In the words of a lawyer for a company that was the focus of many complaints from university technology transfer professionals: '[university] tech transfer offices are not close enough to people who do deals. People out here do deals, and do them fast. University tech transfer offices take eight months to get to the point of doing a deal, and then the relevant people quit and you have to start over with someone else . . . They're overly conservative. They would rather pass up ten good deals than make one mistake'.[46] A number of private firms complained that university technology transfer offices are inadequately staffed, use inexperienced people who lack adequate authority to conclude agreements, and place considerable pressure on their staffs to bring in money for the university, giving them little incentive to spend time on smaller agreements for the transfer of research tools.[47]

---

[45] The 'free research' characterization infuriates corporate providers of research tools to universities because it suggests that the value of the research tool is zero. From another perspective, however, it may not be entirely off the mark. When asked why they provide research tools to university researchers, many representatives of private firms cited the benefit of getting interesting and reliable research results from leading experts in the field. For example, a lawyer for a small biotechnology firm explained that 'small companies can't do everything. Often what you're looking for is an expert in academia who isn't in a competing company, has lots of expertise in the area, and may be the best person in the country to work on it, giving us confidence in the results'. A senior patent counsel for a larger biotechnology firm said 'it's useful to learn as much as possible about our proteins. We'd probably miss things if we did everything internally, because we don't have expertise in all tissue types and organs. In fact, we've learned a lot from academics. We've had a number of developments come back to us, and we've licensed in a new use of a material'. In other words, companies make research tools available to university researchers because that is a cheap way of getting research done that might yield useful results for the firm. Similar motivations account for the interest of firms in receiving incoming research tools that have been developed by university scientists, notwithstanding the difficulties that they describe in negotiating with university technology transfer offices. A representative of a small biotechnology company explains: 'It's just time that we're saving by getting [a tool] from a university. If I were Merck or Pfizer, they may have their own cloning group. They know up-front that it's not worth wasting time dealing with universities. They're so resource-rich, but we're not. We have to go to the academic community'. These comments from the private sector suggest that an important motivation for exchanging materials with academic investigators, whether the firm is providing or receiving the materials, is to obtain research results while conserving the firm's own resources for other research projects.

[46] The same lawyer also expressed contempt for the competence of universities in licensing out their own technology to companies: 'We don't have any faith in the ability of universities to license technology effectively. They don't have the infrastructure, they don't understand, they don't have a clear mission. The scientific collaborators want it both ways—they want to pocket their money but remain in the ivory tower. Quite frankly I have no faith in them to license it and get value out of it, to appreciate what's valuable in it . . . We want to be in a position to control what's done'.

[47] The research director for a major pharmaceutical firm explained: 'Problems we have that are impediments to getting things done quickly are tech transfer offices not having enough people available, combined with the agenda to bring in money for university, means that it's hard to get their attention to these smaller agreements. You need to get the attention of enlightened people on both sides in order to do these low-cost agreements in a more rapid, expedient way. You need enough people with the tools of legal language at their fingertips'.

Another recurring complaint was that universities try to impose unrealistic diligence obligations on firms to achieve rapid commercial development and are unduly suspicious that firms will suppress licensed technology.[48]

Perhaps the most consistent complaint about universities from the private sector is that they overvalue their own discoveries[49] and underestimate the considerable risk and expense involved in commercial research and product development.[50] Pharmaceutical firms voice a similar complaint about biotechnology companies,[51] and biotechnology companies say the same about people who provide them with research tools.[52]

Heterogeneities within the biomedical research community appear to impede the exchange of research tools in a number of ways. Each segment of the community feels misunderstood by the others, and each feels that the differences in institutional cultures and missions should weigh in its favor. Institutions from each of the different segments of the community thus have an easier time negotiating mutually agreeable terms of exchange with their own kind than with representatives of the other segments.

C. Conflicting agendas of different agents

Quite apart from heterogeneities across the spectrum of institutions involved in biomedical research, each institution itself is a heterogeneous community employing different kinds of people whose agendas may come into conflict in negotiating the terms of transfer for research tools. This was particularly apparent for universities, perhaps because the Working Group separately sought out the views of scientists and technology transfer professionals within universities. The perceptions and concerns of these two groups differ

[48] A vice president and general counsel for a biotechnology company complained that universities 'want to revoke the license if they don't see an NDA [New Drug Application] filed [with the Food and Drug Administration] within three years. They have no idea how long it takes to go from an IND [Investigational New Drug application] to an NDA. Academic institutions are always afraid someone is going to tie up their technology. Why would I want to do that?'

[49] One lawyer for a biotechnology company politely observed that 'the academic community sometimes has less information than the company does about what kind of royalties are typical'. A less diplomatic representative of a major pharmaceutical firm said that 'university tech transfer offices have gone fantastical'.

[50] A licensing professional in a major pharmaceutical firm, citing the tendency of universities to overvalue molecular drug targets that might be used to screen potential products, explained: 'Universities don't understand the drug discovery process. They think screens are like sieves, with drugs coming out the bottom. They don't understand how much attrition there is in the path of product development'.

[51] One representative of a pharmaceutical firm said that many biotechnology companies that seek substantial reach-through royalties on future products are 'dreaming', and that 'greedy biotechs will freeze themselves out'.

[52] For example, a senior executive of a genomics company reported that clinicians who collect DNA samples from families for use in cloning disease genes often seek royalties on future products, without appreciating how much more work remains to be done to clone the genes involved in the disease pathways and identify potential drug targets.

strikingly, setting the stage for intra-institutional conflict and raising obstacles to the emergence of market norms.

Academic scientists are under considerable pressure to generate and publish research results. Their top priority when they seek access to research tools is acquiring the materials they need as quickly as possible. Scientists have limited patience for reading the terms of the agreements accompanying these tools and express considerable irritation with their institutional representatives for taking too long to get the paperwork in order. Rather than seeing these technology transfer professionals as facilitators and guardians of their best interests who enable them to gain access to research tools on reasonable terms, they see them, in the words of one scientist, as 'paper pushers who sit on these documents and try to find errors'.[53]

University technology transfer professionals, on the other hand, are primarily charged with licensing university-owned inventions out to the private sector and bringing in money to the university (whether in the form of grants or license revenues).[54] Their top priorities in reviewing agreements are to protect the university and its scientists from incurring obligations that will limit their freedom to conduct research, to preserve future opportunities to obtain research funding, and to preserve their freedom to license future discoveries on lucrative terms. From their perspective, the terms of incoming MTAs are treacherous land-mines waiting to explode beneath unsuspecting signatories. They see scientists within their institutions as naive, short-sighted, and careless in their readiness to assume legal obligations that they will later regret.[55]

---

[53] This is more of a problem for some kinds of contract provisions than for others. Technology transfer professionals in universities report that it is relatively easy to explain to scientists why they should resist draconian prepublication review provisions, but that the scientists see little point to renegotiating provisions governing more remote contingencies such as the allocation of intellectual property rights in future discoveries or the allocation of tort liability in the event of injuries. Particular difficulties arise with definitions of terms used in agreements that do not track the ordinary meaning of these terms to scientists. For example, an agreement might define 'the material' that is subject to restrictions in a way that includes modified derivatives, or it might define prohibited use for 'commercial purposes' to include use in research that is subject to a licensing obligation to another firm (including a firm that might have supplied another research tool). On a quick reading, these provisions appear innocuous to scientists, leading them to suspect that it is their own university technology transfer office, rather than the provider of the material, that is being unreasonable.

[54] In some universities, agreements governing incoming research tools are processed by an office that is primarily concerned with negotiating and administering grants for sponsored research, while in other universities they are processed by a technology transfer office that is primarily concerned with negotiating and administering license agreements for university-owned technologies. Either way, incoming research tool agreements represent an additional responsibility that adds to the workload of the professional staff without adding in any visible way to the revenues that they bring in to the university.

[55] Speaking about the university's reluctance to agree to assume tort liability under an MTA, one university technology transfer professional remarked that 'the faculty doesn't understand this issue at all, and it's hard to explain it to them. We have no real horror stories to back up our concern. But universities have endowments [that could be depleted by tort judgments], and some of these materials are actually dangerous'.

At the same time, however, technology transfer professionals must rely on the scientists to alert them to potential problems and to monitor and comply with any obligations imposed by the agreements.[56]

This divergence of perspectives within universities is not lost on those who negotiate the terms of research tool agreements on behalf of private companies. Company representatives see (and encourage university scientists to see) university technology transfer professionals as the true obstacles to the expeditious transfer of research tools, stalling research in the hope of preserving speculative future intellectual property. In the words of a scientific liaison to a biotechnology company, 'the function of the technology transfer office should be to serve the faculty, not to make money, yet they refer to faculty as children'.

But the interests of the faculty are not necessarily the same as the interests of the university. Although faculty members are employees of universities and are typically bound by contract to assign intellectual property rights in their discoveries to their employers, the agency relationship between faculty members and universities is attenuated by traditions of academic freedom that protect faculty from institutional control of their academic work. Faculty members enjoy considerable freedom to select and pursue their own research agendas—typically with external funding—and to publish their results without prior institutional approval. Whereas researchers in the private sector are often bound by confidentiality agreements or non-competition covenants that prohibit their use of information gained from working for a particular employer when they move to a new job, faculty members who move from one academic institution to another typically take their research (and grants) with them. Moves from one academic institution to another rarely lead to litigation over intellectual property rights between universities and former faculty members, although as a purely legal matter universities are generally entitled to claim ownership of the patentable inventions developed by their employees using university facilities.[57] Within the academy, faculty members who resist institutional constraints on their research feel that they are upholding a sacrosanct tradition rather than violating a fiduciary duty.

This strong tradition of faculty autonomy from institutional control of the conduct of research makes universities wary of incurring institutional obligations that rely on faculty members for compliance.[58] Yet providers of

---

[56] A technology transfer professional for a major research university noted: 'It's not really possible for a bureaucrat to recognize the problems looking at a text. You have to rely on the scientists, whose skill and integrity in these matters vary'.

[57] Litigation is more likely when a departing faculty member brings research to a private firm. See eg, *University Patents v. Kligman*, 762 F.Supp. 1212 (E.D. Pa. 1991).

[58] Some common provisions in research tool agreements, such as prepublication review provisions, prohibitions against transfer to another laboratory or institution, and obligations to disclose data to the provider, impose obligations that call for compliance on the part of the faculty scientist. Others, including payment obligations, reach-through royalties, automatic licenses,

research tools to academic scientists typically seek to bind the universities, and not just the faculty members, to the terms of their agreements. Academic scientists thus need the concurrence of university technology transfer professionals to receive incoming research tools. But if the scientists later violate the terms of the agreements, whether through inadvertence or indifference, the institution will be exposed to liability.

Faculty autonomy also limits the power of university technology transfer professionals over the terms of exchange for outgoing research tools. Although in theory the university owns these tools, as a practical matter faculty members have the power to bypass the technology transfer office when they send out their materials for use in other institutions and universities are unlikely to sue them for doing so.

Private companies typically have considerably more control than universities over the activities of their employed scientists. Nonetheless, some comments from lawyers and business people in these firms suggested there might be similar divergences of interest among the various agents involved in the transfer of research tools in the private sector. The benefits of exchanging research tools with academic counterparts—collegiality, access to data, opportunities for prestigious collaborations and publications, and scientific credibility—are often more palpable to commercial scientists than they are to the lawyers and business people whose approval is necessary to conclude the exchange. Many company representatives reported that their scientists exchange materials with academic counterparts informally without getting the approval of the firm or its lawyers.[59] This practice exceeds the authority that firms typically give scientists to send out materials under the company's form agreement, but not to vary the terms of the agreement without approval.

The practical (if not legal) ability of scientists to bypass the business and legal agents that represent their employers when they exchange research tools appears to be creating a two-tiered market. In the 'free exchange' tier, scientists deal with one another directly and impose minimal obligations and paperwork, while in the 'proprietary' tier, lawyers and technology transfer professionals haggle over terms of exchange with resulting delays in research. The existence of a free exchange tier relieves some of the pressure on the exchange system overall by avoiding the transaction costs of proprietary

---

options to acquire licenses, and indemnity provisions, call for compliance on the part of the university. Either way, the institution is likely to face liability for noncompliance. Even if the university has a formal right to seek indemnity from the faculty member, this right is unlikely to be exercised and may be of little value.

[59] The director of scientific affairs at a biotechnology company reported: 'The scientists here will often send research reagents without my knowledge . . . We have an R&D driven staff that generally think it's a waste of resources to use agreements for all the research reagents . . . It's a method of gaining good will, developing a rapport with labs that we may later have more substantial relationships with. The legal department frowns upon it. Scientists are under specific instructions not to send out anything proprietary without an MTA'.

exchange in some cases. But these two tiers are not entirely separate. Because the terms of exchange in the proprietary tier typically restrict subsequent free exchange of materials, some of the free exchange transactions may eventually give rise to liability for breach of contract. As a result, lawyers and technology transfer professionals become ever more wary of free exchange and more assiduous about restricting its domain, while scientists become ever more frustrated with proprietary exchange and more motivated to bypass its constraints.

D. Difficulties in valuation

Virtually everyone who provided information to the Working Group cited difficulties in measuring the value of access to a research tool as an obstacle to negotiating terms of exchange. Pharmaceutical firms, biotechnology firms, and universities framed the problem somewhat differently, but research tool users within each sector share the perception that tool-providers in the other sectors are asking for too much and overvaluing the contribution of particular tools relative to other inputs that contribute to future valuable discoveries.

Representatives of pharmaceutical firms argue that a fair measure of the value of both incoming and outgoing research tools is the cost of creating the tools.[60] They are often willing to pay such a sum for incoming tools up-front, but they are loath to promise to pay royalties on future product sales for access to research tools, believing that in most cases such payment terms would grossly overvalue the contribution of a research tool relative to other investments in the course of drug development.[61] They complain that universities and biotechnology firms have unrealistic expectations of making money from research tools, given that these institutions do not share in the full costs and risks of the complex process of drug discovery.[62]

[60] One representative of a major pharmaceutical firm said that his firm has a philosophy of 'making research tools available at reasonable cost' defined as 'what it would cost in time and money to reproduce [the tool]'. He contrasted this perspective with the 'gold rush mentality' of some universities that have 'inappropriate expectations' that they are 'going to be able to make money for the university' and biotechnology firms that are 'striving to jack up stock prices' with 'business plans that are strictly financial, not drug discovery'.

[61] A research director for a major pharmaceutical firm explained: 'Reach-through royalties are making everyone crazy . . . If someone makes a discovery of substantial value that was the core critical issue that gave us a competitive advantage, that has value, and if we succeed, the person who gave us that should succeed. But [only] for really critical discoveries . . . The way to judge a critical contribution is for the company to say I can't do this without it'. A high-ranking executive in another major pharmaceutical firm sees the overvaluation problem as compounded by the issuance of multiple, overlapping patents on research tools: 'You have a series of different academic labs working with a receptor and you may get lots of different claims coming from different labs. Royalty-mounting can frustrate the economic incentive to develop'.

[62] In the words of a high-ranking representative of a major pharmaceutical firm: 'Individuals in tech transfer offices in universities have had the fire lit under them to go forth and capture this presumed pot of gold. It leads them to take an unrealistic posture in asking for reach-through rights'.

Consistent with the position that they take for incoming research tools, when pharmaceutical firms set the terms of access to outgoing research tools and materials for other institutions, they do not seek promises of future royalties or even large up-front payments. They are typically more concerned about protecting themselves against future obligations than about collecting cash payments or garnering a share of future profits.[63] Their principal worries are (1) that use of the tool will compete with the firm's own work and enhance the position of a competitor who either collaborates with the user or takes a license to the user's discoveries;[64] (2) that the research will yield publications that undermine the firm's patent position[65] or generate patents that constrain the firm's freedom to develop its own products fully;[66] and (3) if the research tool is a pharmaceutical product in development, that the user's data will suggest possible harmful side-effects that create regulatory problems and add to the costs of clinical trials.[67] They therefore ask that the tool not be distributed beyond the laboratory and/or scientist to whom the firm is providing it, that the scientist explain what will be done with the material and report research results, and in some cases that the firm receive an automatic license to use any improvements for internal research purposes and/or an option to obtain an exclusive license to future discoveries. To pharmaceutical firms, these provisions are defensive measures that protect them from losing competitive ground when they make their materials available free of charge to academic scientists.

Universities that are confronted with such provisions for access to incoming research tools take a different view. From their perspective, agreements

---

[63] A representative of a major pharmaceutical firm explained that 'we don't charge academic labs anything, but we do charge companies nominal payments. We ask [universities] for a nonexclusive license for internal research to improvements that they make, disclosure of improvements, and maybe prepublication review'.

[64] A research director for a major pharmaceutical firm said that when the firm makes research tools available to academic researchers, there is a 'major risk . . . of transfer to another company . . . Scientists with the most strident voices in the debate [about access to research tools] are often those that have conflicts of interest'.

[65] In the words of a research director for a major pharmaceutical firm: 'What matters most is being informed that something has been found using this tool, so we don't just find out about it in a paper. We want the opportunity to file for patents or seek a license'.

[66] This concern is particularly significant in the case of research that might uncover new uses for pharmaceutical compounds. A representative of a major pharmaceutical firm explained: 'with a compound, we'd probably be very sensitive if we saw an experiment description that might lead to a new use. We might use a research collaboration and licensing agreement rather than a simple material transfer agreement. If someone is going out to find a new indication, and we think that we've given the essential material, it makes no sense to exclude us'.

[67] A lawyer for a major pharmaceutical firm said that 'the last thing you want to do is become obligated to do further toxicology studies'. Another pharmaceutical representative downplayed this concern, saying that although 'inadvertent activity that gives rise to concern about the compound can be very difficult to deal with, you don't want to suppress legitimate information about adverse effects'. He rated this concern as 'minor on the scale of things', although conceding that this problem is minimized because firms rarely release products in development for use as research tools.

that condition access to a research tool on license rights to future discoveries overvalue the research tool relative to potential future discoveries. If they agree to give automatic, nonexclusive licenses to providers of research tools, they will not be able to grant more lucrative exclusive licenses to their future discoveries to anyone else, regardless of the value of the discoveries. As for granting options to enter into an exclusive license, this is the compensation that universities give for full research sponsorship, not for the mere contribution of a research tool. They see promises to grant license rights to future discoveries in exchange for research tools as forced bargain sales that undervalue their future intellectual property.[68]

On the other hand, many private firms reported to the Working Group that universities frequently seek reach-through royalties on future products as payment for the outgoing research tools that they provide to the private sector. Although reach-through royalties on future product sales are not the same as grantbacks of license rights to future discoveries, both mechanisms compromise the value of future discoveries made by the user of a research tool. Universities may be more successful in imposing reach-through royalties on biotechnology firms than on pharmaceutical firms.[69]

Biotechnology firms and pharmaceutical firms tend to agree with each other that universities have unrealistic expectations as providers of research tools. They have different concerns, however, when it comes to setting the terms of access to their own outgoing research tools. In contrast to the defensive focus of pharmaceutical firms in licensing their outgoing research tools, biotechnology firms often see their own proprietary research tools as central to their evolving business strategies and as a critical source of value for the firm. Both pharmaceutical firms and universities complain that biotechnology firms overvalue their research tools and have unrealistic expectations about what they can demand for them. Pharmaceutical firms explain the tendency to overvalue research tools on the part of both biotechnology firms and universities as stemming from ignorance of the costs and risks involved in the drug discovery process. One representative of a pharmaceutical firm explained that biotechnology firms typically focus on a small number of

---

[68] A representative of a biotechnology firm suggested that concern on the part of universities about undermining the marketability of their future discoveries reflects an inflated sense of the commercial value of their own discoveries: 'Universities think they have something commercially viable when they don't. If it were viable we'd be in line for an exclusive license. So I don't think our nonexclusive licenses are really preventing them from selling anything they could otherwise sell'.

[69] In the words of a representative of a major pharmaceutical firm: 'biotechs like reach-throughs, and pharmas hate them'. This may be because biotechnology firms themselves seek reach-through royalties as compensation for providing research tools. One high-ranking officer of a biotechnology firm speculated that another reason may be that biotechnology firms expect to be able to offload reach-through royalty obligations onto a pharmaceutical firm that ultimately develops the product, although the biotechnology firm might thereby reduce its own royalties on the product.

research strategies and overvalue their chances for success. Pharmaceutical firms, on the other hand, understand that 'in this business, you've got to get a lot of shots on goal, because most of them never make it'.

Conflict over the value of research tools seems to be particularly aggravated for exchanges between biotechnology firms and universities, perhaps because both sides of the exchange are typically cash-poor. When biotechnology firms provide outgoing research tools to universities, they often seek not merely to protect themselves from competitive harm, but to profit from future discoveries made through use of their tools. In the words of a lawyer for a biotechnology firm: 'most small companies resolve it this way: If we're going to give a research tool to a company, we'll charge money. If we give it to a university, we need to get some other kind of value out of them' in the form of license rights to future discoveries. A lawyer for another biotechnology firm elaborates that since universities can't afford to pay full price for access to research tools, 'we ask them to pay with the currency they have, which is intellectual property'.[70]

In contrast to some pharmaceutical firms that express a commitment to make research tools available in order to advance science, many representatives of biotechnology firms expressed a need to justify their dissemination of research tools to shareholders and boards of directors in terms of potential profits for the company. One representative of a biotechnology firm explained that 'the promise of a possible exclusive license is how we justify throwing money away by giving out free material'.[71]

Some biotechnology firms seek grantbacks of licenses to any discoveries made through use of their research tools, without restrictions to particular fields of use contemplated by the firm. A senior patent counsel for a biotechnology firm explained that such broad rights are necessary because of the difficulty of drafting agreements that precisely allocate rights in unpredictable research results: 'Whatever they come up with is likely to either be useful with or compete with our molecule. It's hard to draft an option that only catches the things we will want an exclusive license to, so we draft it broadly'. A lawyer for another firm offered a somewhat different, and perhaps more candid, explanation: 'My biggest fear is that an academic institution is going to discover something valuable with my technology, whether I planned on it or it's totally unplanned. I want to have some opportunity to get access to the technology, to use or exploit it, or to work with the institution to jointly control disposition. It's human nature to want that, even though I'm no worse off. It's more emotional than rational'.

[70] This firm asks universities for an option to take an exclusive license to future discoveries at a predetermined royalty rate, a provision that is very unpopular with universities. He explains that 'no one knows how to value this stuff, and everyone's afraid of getting burned. They're worried that they're going to license out a blockbuster cheap'.

[71] A lawyer for another biotechnology firm put the point even more bluntly: 'A business is in business to make money for somebody. You can't have people giving things out for free'.

One senses in the remarks from representatives of all sectors that emotions are playing a large role in negotiations over the transfer of research tools. Perhaps the inherent difficulty of assessing values for research tools relative to the values of potential future discoveries makes it difficult to identify dispassionate points of reference that everyone can agree upon. Research involves investigation of the unknown; its outcome is inherently uncertain. Information that would help estimate the likely value of research using a tool is divided between the owner of the tool (who has typically worked with the tool and may already be pursuing what it considers the most promising uses) and the would-be user (who may have complementary expertise that brings into view a research plan that might or might not have occurred to the owner). If owners and users perceive each other as rivals, they may be reluctant to share information regarding their valuations and skeptical of each other's purported assessments.[72] For research that is remote from end product development, it may be some time before the commercial value of resulting discoveries becomes apparent; and even when research yields an outcome of manifest value, it may be difficult to agree on a formula for assessing how that value should be apportioned between prior and subsequent innovators.

The profitable endpoint of biomedical research is the development of a successful pharmaceutical product. A strong patent position on such a product can be quite lucrative, although such products are outliers in a distribution that includes many costly failures.[73] But many of the institutions involved in the complex enterprise of biomedical research have no expectation of ever bringing a pharmaceutical product to market themselves. Universities and many biotechnology firms specialize in earlier stage discoveries that provide a platform for the discovery of new pharmaceutical products. The challenge for these institutions is to leverage their proprietary rights in premarket discoveries into a place at the feeding trough of a new pharmaceutical product.

Given the vicissitudes of drug discovery, tools used in research that may or may not yield lucrative products typically have a low expected value to the user. The farther upstream from product development the research lies, the less likely the user is to be willing or able to pay a large up-front fee for use of

[72] Recognizing that informational asymmetries exist, owners and users of research tools may draw inferences from each other's bargaining behavior that lead them away from agreement rather than towards it. For example, an owner of a research tool may figure that if a prospective user wants to use it badly enough to invest resources in negotiating the terms of exchange, it must be valuable, and the owner will therefore hold out for favorable terms. The user's resistance to particular terms in the agreement may signal to the owner that those provisions are particularly valuable to retain, eg, if the user is reluctant to promise the owner a license to future discoveries, the user must believe it is on the verge of making an important discovery.

[73] As F.M. Scherer and his co-authors have documented, the value of innovations exhibits a highly skew distribution. See Scherer, Chapter 1 above; F.M. Scherer et al., *Uncertainty and the Size Distribution of Rewards from Technological Innovation* (March 1998) (unpublished manuscript); Dietmar Harhoff et al., *Exploring the Tail of Patented Invention Value Distributions* (1998) (unpublished manuscript)

the tool. Academic researchers may lack the resources to pay more than a trivial sum, and private firms may consider the remote prospect of future commercial gain insufficient to justify a large payment. Contingent payment mechanisms such as reach-through royalties or grantbacks of license rights in future discoveries rest on even less informed speculations about how large a share of the value of potential future discoveries is properly attributed to the use of a research tool. To the extent that these mechanisms diminish the value of future discoveries to their owners, they also undermine incentives to pursue commercial development. Owners of research tools may believe that their materials will be of considerable value in the discovery of commercial products, and manifestations of interest from researchers at other institutions are likely to confirm that belief. The result may be protracted negotiations over value that lead the parties away from, rather than towards, agreement.

III. Conclusion

The exchange of research tools within the biomedical research community often involves vexing and protracted negotiations over terms and value. Although owners and users of research tools usually manage to work out their differences when the transactions matter greatly to both sides, difficult negotiations often cause delays in research and sometimes lead to the abandonment of research plans. Transaction costs have remained persistently high in this setting as the heterogeneous institutions involved in the exchange of research tools have been unable to agree upon standardized contract language, or even to agree upon a universe of materials, information and techniques that are properly termed 'research tools'. The result has been burdensome and frustrating case by case negotiations over exchanges that in an earlier era might have occurred between scientists without formal legal agreements.

Is this a picture of market failure, or is it simply a market? Surely most markets are characterized by positive transaction costs that render some low value transactions prohibitively expensive. Why should we care if the low value end of this particular market gets bogged down in negotiations, or even fails?

One reason why we might care about this particular market is that, although the value of any particular transfer of a research tool may appear small ex ante, some such transfers, if they go forward, may prove to have been highly valuable ex post. (Indeed, it is this remote possibility, and the impossibility of distinguishing high value from low value exchanges ex ante, that motivates the parties to bargain hard over the terms of each exchange.) However skew the distribution, the aggregate social value of widespread dissemination of biomedical research tools is likely to be quite large. When biomedical research is repeatedly stalled pending negotiations over the terms of MTAs, the social cost of foregone or delayed innovations, measured in lives and health, could prove to be substantial.

This close-up picture of what goes on in the market for biomedical research tools serves as a reminder that transaction costs for transfers of intellectual property are indeed positive and not negligible. Bargaining over intellectual property rights in the context of cumulative innovation is problematic. Nonetheless, the limited context investigated by the Working Group cautions against broad generalizations about what might be happening outside that context. Do similar problems arise in other settings, including other fields of technology? The foregoing discussion suggests some features of a market for intellectual property that may impede agreement upon terms of exchange, including high transaction costs relative to likely gains from exchange, participation of heterogeneous institutions with different missions, complex and conflicting agendas of different agents within these institutions, and difficulties in evaluating present and future intellectual property rights when profits are speculative and remote.

In some settings institutions have emerged to bring down transaction costs associated with a proliferation of intellectual property rights, but in some settings they have not. It is important to weigh these costs, and the foregone value of the exchanges that they prevent, in assessing the wisdom of creating new intellectual property rights, rather than simply assuming that bargains between owners and users will bring about efficient reallocation of rights.

10

NETWORKS OF LEARNING IN BIOTECHNOLOGY: OPPORTUNITIES AND CONSTRAINTS ASSOCIATED WITH RELATIONAL CONTRACTING IN A KNOWLEDGE-INTENSIVE FIELD

WALTER W. POWELL*

The most developed economies today are undergoing a transformation from raw material processing and manufacturing to the creation, development, and application of new knowledge. As a consequence, many scholars tell us, production based on a logic of diminishing returns is being replaced by a logic of increasing returns.[1] The development of an increasing returns-based economy is buoyed by several factors. In knowledge-intensive fields, steep upfront costs in research and development (R&D) are typical, but once a new medicine or software product is successfully developed, the costs of producing additional copies are minimal. Moreover, the linkage between basic science and downstream commercial application is greatly tightened, and in fields such as biotechnology, the distinction between basic and applied science

* Professor of Education and Sociology, Stanford University.

[1] See, eg, Brian Arthur, *Positive Feedbacks in the Economy*, 262 Sci. Am. 92 (1990); Paul Krugman, *Increasing Returns and Economic Geography*, 99 J. Pol. Econ. 483 (1991); Paul Romer, *Increasing Returns and Long-run Growth*, 94 J. Pol. Econ. 1002 (1986); David Teece, *Capturing Value from Knowledge Assets: The New Economy, Markets for Know-How and Intangible Assets*, 40 Cal. Mgmt. Rev. 55 (1998).

has been rendered moot.[2] Thus, firms today are engaged in learning races, and the bulk of the rewards go to the swiftest. In such a contest, there is scant payoff, as David Teece puts it 'to penny pinching and high payoff to rapidly sensing and then seizing opportunities'.[3]

In the fields of organization theory and strategic management, scholars have been developing a knowledge-based theory of the firm.[4] In one strand of this work, scholars have focused on dynamic capabilities inherent in firms that are highly entrepreneurial, with minimal hierarchy, high-powered incentives, a clear vision, and project-based work design.[5] Others have stressed the importance of 'absorptive capacity', or the ability to make sense internally of news generated externally.[6] In fields where knowledge is developing rapidly and the sources of knowledge are widely dispersed, I have argued that the locus of innovation is found in interorganizational networks.[7] Consequently, in circumstances where the sources of scientific and technological leadership are widely distributed, it is necessary to extend the knowledge-based view of the firm to the network level and examine the capabilities of firms to manage multiple interfirm relations. In the rapidly advancing field of biotechnology, the ability to manage and orchestrate relational contracting is highly consequential.

Given the wide array of recent scientific discoveries in molecular biology and genetics and related fields, biotechnology has become an extremely diverse industry in terms of its underlying science and technology. Product-focused companies work on recombinant protein therapeutics and small molecule therapeutics, as well as gene, antisense, and cell therapeutics. Technology-focused companies offer such novel enabling methodologies as genomics, combinational chemistry, high-throughput screening, and bioinformatics. Given this diversity, not even the largest pharmaceutical companies can build a sufficiently strong research base to cover all the therapeutic areas and technical advances. Moreover, the full range of skills (eg basic

---

[2] See Walter Powell & Jason Owen-Smith, *Commercialism in Universities: Life Sciences Research and the Interface with Industry*, 17 J Pol'y Analysis & Mgmt. 253 (1998) (providing illustration of the collapse of the basic-applied divide in the life sciences).

[3] Teece, n. 1 above, at 58.

[4] See Wesley Cohen & Daniel Levinthal, *Absorptive Capacity: A New Perspective on Learning and Innovation*, 35 Admin Sci. Q. 128 (1990); Bruce Kogut & Udo Zander, *Knowledge of the Firm, Combinative Capabilities, and the Replication of Technology*, 3 Org. Sci. 383 (1992); Walter Powell, et. al., *Interorganizational Collaboration and the Locus of Innovation: Networks of Learning in Biotechnology*, 41 Admin. Sci. Q. 116 (1996); David Teece, et. al., *Dynamic Capabilities and Strategic Management*, 18 Strategic Mgmt. J. 509 (1997).

[5] See, eg, David Teece & Gary Pisano, *The Dynamic Capabilities of Firms· An Introduction*, 3 Indus. & Corp. Change 537 (1994); Teece, et al., n. 4 above.

[6] See Cohen & Levinthal, n. 4 above.

[7] See Walter Powell, *Inter-organizational Collaboration in the Biotechnology Industry*, 151 J Institutional & Theoretical Econ. 197 (1996); Powell, n. 4 above; Walter Powell, et. al., *Network Position and Firm Performance: Organizational Returns to Collaboration in the Biotechnology Industry*, 16 Res. Soc. Org. 129 (1999).

research, applied research, clinical testing procedures, manufacturing, marketing, and distribution, familiarity with intellectual property law, and experience with obtaining worldwide regulatory approval) needed to move a new medicine from the lab bench to the doctor's office is not easily assembled under one roof. So the various participants in this field—universities, government institutes, new science-based firms, research hospitals, and established pharmaceutical and chemical corporations—have turned to all manner of joint ventures, research partnerships, strategic alliances, minority equity investments, and licensing arrangements to speed the process of drug development and to compensate for their lack of internal capabilities. In the first section of this chapter, I review the industry's origins and its key participants, discussing the reasons for the emergence of this lattice-like structure of formal contractual collaborations and the even more spider-webbed structure of informal cooperation.

This universe of relational contracting unfolds in an intensely competitive context where costs are considerable (roughly $175–$300 million to develop a new biotech medicine),[8] and much of the knowledge being exchanged is tacit and not easily replicated. The participants must maneuver to form new combinations in order to access new knowledge and acquire complementary technologies and relevant skills. Competing in this fashion requires both the ability to learn from *and* across multiple relationships, and the capacity to resolve disputes in a timely manner. In the next section, I discuss the infrastructure supporting these alliances, pointing to the emergence of a dense transactional community, including university technology transfer offices, venture capital firms, and law firms that specialize in intellectual property and relationship management, that renders relational contracting feasible.

But just how durable are these networks of learning? Many observers from outside the industry suggest that these arrangements are merely reflections of the early stage in an industry's life cycle, and will eventually be replaced by more traditional organizational arrangements, typified by hierarchy and vertical integration. Those more close to the industry stress the continuing importance of basic science and knowledge-based assets that sustain collaborative practices, but note that there are significant obstacles to institutionalizing interfirm governance as a stable system, with well-defined rules of the game. In the final section below, I discuss several potential problems. In particular, concern that public science is becoming more proprietary, and that a patenting race is replacing a learning race, are looming large. I conclude with a brief discussion of whether awareness of a common fate is sufficiently broad and deep to sustain a field that is based, in large part, on relational contracting.

---

[8] Comparable costs for a new pharmaceutical drug run from $300 to $500 million. See Daniel Vasella, *Novartis' Role in 21st Century Drug Development*, 15 NATURE BIOTECHNOLOGY 485 (1997).

I. Industry Origins and Key Participants

The scientific discoveries that created the field of biotechnology had their genesis in university and government laboratories. In turn, the promising discoveries were developed into new medicines by young science-based, dedicated biotech firms, (or DBFs in industry parlance), which had a host of needs: access to scientific knowledge, huge amounts of cash to fund costly research, and the skills to move from scientific research to marketable products. Numerous barriers had to be overcome, but more importantly, new kinds of organizational arrangements had to be created, and the operations of a wide range of established institutions had to be altered. The critical participants in the evolution of the industry have been drawn from research universities, government institutes, the field of venture capital, private nonprofit medical institutes and hospitals, established pharmaceutical corporations, and the DBFs that were funded by the score in the late 1970s, and throughout the 1980s and 1990s. I briefly consider each of these actors, detailing their specific skills, resources, and interests. Out of the interactions of participants in these arenas, patterns of coalition and competition formed, and a mutual awareness of membership in a common technological community grew.

A. Research Universities

Groundbreaking research at a handful of leading universities played a critical role in biotech's emergence, but the development of biotech also triggered and coincided with dramatic changes in university practices. Discovery efforts required an interdisciplinary mixing of academic specialties in a manner, and to an extent, heretofore unprecedented in biomedical research. Universities, with an established departmental division of labor, were not initially well-equipped to respond, but DBFs, frequently started by academic researchers, were not as wedded to disciplinary conventions. To be sure, the past few years have seen many research universities make significant reorganizations in their biological science divisions, partly in response to biotechnology's development.[9] But biotechnology has further collapsed the distinction between academic and industrial research, with the consequence that fundamental research in the life sciences, such as the discovery of a fat gene, has immediate commercial relevance.

The cross-traffic between universities and biotech companies has become extensive and reciprocal, leading to the emergence of an entrepreneurial culture in the academy and a strong focus on basic science in biotech companies. A new identity has emerged—the scientist-entrepreneur. What would once

---

[9] See Wade Roush *Biology Departments Restructure*, 275 Sci. 1556, 1558 (1997) (describing developments at Berkeley and other universities).

have been regarded as inappropriate for a top university scientist is now increasingly viewed as not just legitimate, but desirable. Several factors sustain this process. One, the quality of the basic science done at commercial biotech firms is high, at least as measured by citations in the scientific literature.[10] Two, the competition for traditional sources of funds to support biomedical research is intense, and a commercial sector that values research productivity is an acceptable new venue. Three, the diffusion of new knowledge does not occur solely through technological spillovers; most of the academic-industry contact is informal and occurs on a scientist-to-scientist basis. Lynne Zucker and colleagues have shown that many 'star' scientists played a direct role in the transfer of ideas from the lab bench to the medical marketplace.[11] Finally, universities, spurred by changes in government policy such as the Bayh-Dole Act of 1980[12] allowing retention of patent rights to discoveries made with federal funds, have become much more involved in the commercialization of research.[13] The new mission of universities is, in the words of former NSF division director Daryl Chubin, to be both 'creators and retailers of intellectual property'.[14] University commercial involvement in biotech illustrates this new mandate.

B. Government Institutes

The US National Institutes of Health (NIH), the principal agency for federal involvement in the biomedical sciences, has played an enormously influential role in both funding and conducting research on new medical technologies. NIH supported the research that developed recombinant DNA technology. This technology, which uses cultured organisms as factories to produce large quantities of biologically-important proteins that would not otherwise be available, was the basis for such first generation biotech medicines as Activase, made by Genentech; Epogen, made by Amgen; and Humulin, distributed by Eli Lilly.

Approximately 60 percent of NIH's research funds are awarded to universities, but considerable efforts are devoted by the NIH to transferring scientific knowledge into the private economy. Moreover, the award of a peer-reviewed NIH grant to a DBF is highly valued for its prestige as well as

[10] See Powell, et al., n. 4 above, at 141, table 7.

[11] Lynne Zucker, et al., *Intellectual Capital and the Birth of U S. Biotechnology Enterprises*, National Bureau of Economic Research Working Paper #4653 (1994).

[12] 35 US.C. §§ 200–211.

[13] See, eg, Yong Lee, *Technology Transfer and Public Policy in an Age of Global Economic Competition*, 22 POL'Y STUD. J. 260 (1994); Linda Cohen & Roger Noll, *Privatizing Public Research*, SCI. AM. 72 (1994); Henry Etzkowitz & Andrew Webster, *Science as Intellectual Property*, in HANDBOOK OF SCIENCE AND TECHNOLOGY STUDIES, 480 (Shelia Jasanoff et al. eds., 1995).

[14] Daryl Chubin, *How Large an R&D Enterprise?*, in THE FRAGILE CONTRACT: UNIVERSITY SCIENCE AND THE FEDERAL GOVERNMENT 118, 126 (DH. Guston & K. Keniston eds., 1994).

for financial support. In recent years, however, the NIH has come under scrutiny by Congress concerning the benefits of NIH research investments. Analysts note that new medical technologies have been a major contributor to the rapid rise in health care costs over the past half-century.[15] NIH's growing support of industry-based research is viewed by critics as a welcome vehicle for 'crossing the bridge' from expensive basic science to publicly-available medical application.

C. Venture capitalists

Young research-intensive firms rarely generate significant cash flow from operating activities, particularly in fields like biotech where product development is lengthy and complex. Thus, early-stage companies must turn to outside investors. But venture capitalists provide much more than money to early-stage companies.[16] They offer information and advice, much as a management consulting firm might provide a more mature firm. They intensively monitor performance, as well as lend enhanced credibility to the firm in the eyes of third parties. Venture capitalists provide all this help to a firm in its early stages in expectation of handling an initial public offering (IPO) of the firm's stock, the timing and pricing of which determine the venture capitalist's rewards. In sum, as Professors Ronald Gilson and Bernard Black put it, by providing *both* information and capital, the venture capitalist puts 'his money where its mouth is'.[17] As a general rule, venture capitalists are repeat players, funding successive generations of high-tech companies, and are located geographically proximate to the firms they support.

D. Nonprofit organizations

Prestigious hospitals, such as Sloan-Kettering, and nonprofit research institutes, such as Cold Spring Harbor or Salk, have been actively involved in biotech, both in basic research and in clinical development. In some respects, their research roles overlap with universities and government institutes. Nonprofit institutes have been the location for basic science discoveries, which are licensed to DBFs for development and eventual marketing distribution. Leading medical centers offer not only research collaborations, but also provide a venue for joint-sponsorship of costly clinical trials, which can

[15] See Burton Weisbrod, *The Health Care Quadrilemma: An Essay on Technological Change, Quality of Care, and Cost Containment*, 29 J ECON. LITERATURE 523 (1991) (pointing out that health care is one of the few areas where technological innovation has led to higher costs).

[16] See PAUL GOMPERS & JOSH LERNER, THE VENTURE CAPITAL CYCLE (1999) (offering an excellent overview of venture capital financing); Ronald Gilson & Bernard Black, *Venture Capital and the Structure of Capital Markets: Banks versus Stock Markets*, 47 J FIN. ECON. 243 (1998) (stressing the multi-faceted role played by venture capitalists in start-up firms).

[17] Gilson & Black, n. 16 above, at 254.

defray the expenses of product development for the DBF and afford the medical center early access to promising new treatments. Affiliations with highly-regarded hospitals and institutes also transfer reputational benefits to a DBF.

E. Pharmaceutical companies

The global pharmaceutical industry has long been both research-intensive and highly profitable. Biotechnology represents a powerful alternative to traditional pharmaceutical methods of drug discovery, which as practiced for most of this century involved the laborious screening of thousands of organic compounds found naturally in soil, plants, and molds. Building on advances in molecular biology and genetic engineering, contemporary biotech firms pursue a more 'targeted' and 'orderly' approach. Focusing on the etiology of the disease at the cellular and genetic levels speeds development and saves costs.[18] Leading pharmaceutical firms also face challenges due to their over-reliance on a few blockbuster drugs, excess manufacturing capacity, and the need to consolidate their sales forces in the face of rapid growth of managed care, which obviates the need to call on doctors individually.[19] These pressures have fueled considerable merger activity in the pharmaceutical industry as the largest firms have merged with other large firms.

With respect to biotech, pharmaceuticals have also attempted to either 'outsource' their R&D to smaller DBFs or to 'cherrypick' successful young companies through acquisition. Neither effort has met with great success. Outsourcing strategies run the risk of losing core competence, without which it is not possible to evaluate the worth of a partner's efforts; on the other hand, acquisitions offer no guarantee that those acquired will choose to remain.[20] Professors David Teece and Gary Pisano put it well: 'an organization cannot improve that which it does not understand'.[21] Moreover, pharmaceutical firms have vast experience with managing clinical trials,

---

[18] See, eg, Ashish Arora & Alfonso Gambardella, *Complementarity and External Linkages: The Strategies of Large Firms in Biotechnology*, 38 J. INDUS. ECON. 361 (1990); ALFONSO GAMBARDELLA, SCIENCE AND INNOVATION: THE U.S. PHARMACEUTICAL INDUSTRY DURING THE 1980s (1995); Jerry Weisbach & Walter Moos, *Diagnosing the Decline of Major Pharmaceutical Research Laboratories: A Prescription for Drug Companies*, 34 DRUG DEV. RES. 243 (1995).

[19] See Powell, n. 7 above; Thomas Zumbroich, et al., *Re-Thinking Research, Leveraging Licensing*, 12 In Vivo 18 (1994) (discussing how changes in the structure of health care systems are reshaping the pharmaceutical industry).

[20] In my field research, I have seen DBFs refer to pharmaceutical companies who lacked a good understanding of the underlying science they were funding as 'clueless sugardaddies'. These unflattering remarks were characterized by one large firm's senior vice president for research as regrettable, but accurate. Nor has outright, uninvited takeover proven viable. In the most notable case from the 1980s, Eli Lilly's acquisition of Hybritech, not a single Hybritech employee remained two years after the deal. See ROBERT TEITELMAN, GENE DREAMS: WALL STREET, ACADEMIA, AND THE RISE OF BIOTECHNOLOGY (1989). A more common option today is a partial equity investment by a large firm in a DBF.

[21] Teece & Pisano, n. 5 above, at 550.

manufacturing, and marketing and distribution; without full information of the underlying research, those capabilities cannot be adequately exploited. Consequently, recognition of mutual need has occurred: DBFs require large firm financial support, regulatory savvy, and product development skills, while large firms need to collaborate in order to access the research prowess of DBFs and their closeness to basic science.

F. Established biotechnology firms

Although barely two decades old, biotechnology firms have brought more than 50 new medicines to market, have more than 350 medicines and therapies in various stages of clinical testing, and garnered in excess of $16 billion in sales in 1998.[22] We have shown that at the core of the industry are a small cadre of firms with considerable early success at both basic research and product development. For a number of reasons, these firms are very well-connected to other industry participants. One, the more intellectual assets a firm has, the more it has to trade with potential collaborators. Two, as these firms matured, they have spun-off dozens of early-stage R&D projects into separate entities, as both means to attract new investors and to avoid the volatile effects of costly early-stage research on the companies' only-recently stabilized financial prospects. Finally, high visibility is a magnet to others in the field. Thus, at the center of the industry are a group of bellwether firms that are highly active in collaborating with newer second- and third-generation DBFs, as well as with universities and mature pharmaceutical companies. Moreover, in recent years, several pharmaceuticals have turned to established biotech firms to be their 'talent scouts'. To wit, Roche partially acquired Genentech and Ciba-Geigy (now Novartis) took a stake in Chiron. In turn, these DBFs have used the infusion of cash to expand dramatically their connections into new areas of research.

Thus, the biotech field emerged from recognition of common opportunities and multiple resource dependencies. Interorganizational collaboration has proved particularly useful when the relevant knowledge and resources were both specialized and scattered. A biotech company is able to assemble a wide array of inputs-capital, managerial expertise, manufacturing capability, marketing knowhow, and legitimacy—by drawing on a diverse set of partners. Yet, a DBF may not need these assets, and the sponsors that bring them, at the same time, or in any particular sequence or combination. As a firm converts resources into promising lines of research, its needs evolve, and some initial partners may depart while relationships are forged with new allies. Initially productive research ideas must be developed, then tested in clinical

---

[22] See Pharmaceutical Manufacturers Association Annual Report for 1998; SCOT MORRISON & GLEN GIOVANNETTI, BRIDGING THE GAP: 13TH ANNUAL BIOTECH INDUSTRY REPORT (Ernst & Young, 1999).

settings and pushed through the regulatory process, but the time involved in each step is unpredictable. As a firm brings products to market, the bundle of activities and potential partners shifts with the new circumstances: new medicines must be safely manufactured and medical markets accessed through broad sales and distribution channels. Moreover, DBFs typically are engaged in multiple projects, each at different stages. As a result, most firms are simultaneously involved with numerous collaborators on an array of different projects and activities.

Biotechnology, then, is a knowledge-intensive field where the various participants rely on collaborative relationships to access, survey, and exploit emerging technological opportunities. As the structure of the field became shaped more and more by interorganizational relations, the nature of competition was altered. The participants had to adjust to the novel view that is was no longer necessary to have exclusive, proprietary ownership of an asset in order to extract value from it. Moreover, since a competitor on one project may become a partner on another, the playing field resembles less a horse race and more a rugby match, in which the players frequently change their uniforms. In addition, collaboration may itself become a dimension of competition. As firms turn to partners for a variety of resources, they develop a network profile, or portfolio: a pattern of ties to specific partners for certain activities. Thus, for example, an emerging biotech company may have a research grant from a branch of the National Institutes of Health, a research collaboration with a leading university, licensing agreements with other universities or nonprofit research institutes, clinical studies underway with a research hospital, and sales or distribution arrangements with a large pharmaceutical corporation. Others may have only one such relationship, or may hook up with the same partners for different activities, or with disparate partners for similar activities, or have complex relationships involving multiple activities with each partner. A firm's portfolio of collaborations is both a resource and a signal to markets, as well as to other potential partners, of the quality of the firm's activities and products.

Although collaboration may sound 'soft' and cooperative, these relationships are also very much about control, with formal agreements often specifying the scope of a relationship, intellectual property rights, the right to enforce patent rights, possible constraints over the publication of research findings, marketing strategy, and even the make-up of a firm's board of directors.[23] Control issues are resolved in a manner that reflects the needs of the various participants, the overall availability of capital, the financial health of the parties, and the research prowess of the biotech firms involved. These relationships, then, hinge on the ability to facilitate the exchange of knowledge

---

[23] See Josh Lerner & Robert Merges, *The Control of Strategic Alliances: An Empirical Analysis of Biotechnology Collaborations*, 46 J INDUS. ECON 125 (1998).

and/or resources among partners while simultaneously increasing the barriers to knowledge imitation and 'leakage' outside the network.

II. The Infrastructure of Collaboration

In many respects, modern biotechnology is not an industry or discipline per se, but a set of technologies relevant to diverse disciplines and industries. Moreover, not only is the field multi-disciplinary, it is multi-institutional as well. In addition to research universities and both start-up and established firms, government agencies, nonprofit research institutes, and leading hospitals have played key roles in conducting and funding research, while venture capitalists and law firms have played essential parts as talent scouts, advisors, consultants, and financiers. Biotechnology emerged at a time, in the 1970s and 1980s, when a dense transactional community for relational contracting was being developed.[24] This institutional infrastructure of venture capital firms, law firms, technology transfer offices, and technology talent scouts greatly facilitates a reliance on collaboration. These various intermediaries constitute the transactional infrastructure of the field, serving as brokers, dispute adjudicators, and rulemakers, as well as a clearinghouse for assessing the merits and reputation of potential partners.

Law and venture capital firms have served as bridging institutions, bringing scientists into contact with managerial talent, advising firms on intellectual property issues, and steering young companies through their early years. Even though in recent years venture capitalists have garnered greater returns on investments in information technology and Internet companies (where concerns with regulatory approval and protracted product development are much less salient), venture firms continue to be a critical part of the financing of biotech. Professors Josh Lerner and Robert Merges estimate that of the $40 billion in external financing of biotech firms over the period 1978–1995, approximately $9 billion came from venture capital and $10 billion from strategic alliances.[25] Thus, nearly half of the funds raised in the industry are associated with 'relationships'.

Venture capital support is vital because there are substantial challenges associated with financing start-up biotech firms. Because the primary asset of young companies is intellectual, and patent protection is both uncertain and complex, the main capability of a firm is not easily communicated to those

---

[24] See Mark Suchman, *On Advice of Counsel: Law Firms and Venture Capital Firms in the Structuration of Silicon Valley* (1994) (unpublished PhD. dissertation, Stanford University) (on file with Dept. of Sociology, Stanford University); Powell, n. 7 above (discussing the infrastructure for relational contracting).

[25] Lerner & Merges, n. 23 above. Other key sources of financing include initial public offerings ($7 billion) and follow-on offerings ($9 billion). In 1996, venture capital investments in biotech totaled $847 million. Ibid.

outside the field. Moreover, the long time-frame necessary for drug development means young firms will have a protracted need for external financing and complementary skills.

The mobilizing role of venture capital is highly influential at an early stage and leaves a huge footprint, but other parties fulfill important functions as well. Without research support from government institutes and universities, the science would not reach fruition. Pharmaceutical company money and expertise help drive product development, and more established biotech firms serve as talent scouts and risk-takers. Behind all this relational contracting is an emerging system of private governance in which a handful of law firms perform the essential tasks of relationship management, counseling, and dispute resolution, as well as serve as the source of relevant expertise in intellectual property law.[26]

To be sure, in its early years, biotechnology was rife with disputes over patent rights and inter-firm relationships that had gone sour. But the climate for managing interorganizational alliances changed markedly throughout the 1990s. A recent symposium on 'Stages of Biotech Growth' is illustrative.[27] The CEOs of two newer biotech companies offered insights into the complications and challenges of managing collaboration.[28] Robert Bishop of AutoImmune stressed the need to manage information flow and to maximize responsiveness when diverse organizations are involved on a project. Because it is more difficult to get information or services from people outside a company than from internal employees, it is critical to establish effective systems and open communication channels to enhance information flow. Bishop also noted that collaboration entails a constant process of negotiation, as things rarely go as first planned. Mark Shalensky of Geltex highlighted the need for constant communication and a communication infrastructure, as well as expert inhouse oversight. He too, stressed the importance of negotiation and mechanisms for rapid dispute resolution, noting that problems will always arise and a system for resolving disputes must be in place from the very beginning. Both executives emphasized the need at the outset of a relationship to set up mechanisms for settling disagreements. Waiting until issues arise delays product development while the respective managements attempt to solve the problem.

---

[26] To a considerable extent, patent filing and maintenance is 'outsourced' to a handful of law firms In our database of dedicated biotech firms, 266 companies have been assigned 3,126 patents over the period 1980–1996. Of this number, approximately 25 percent of the patents list corresponding addresses as that of the firm, while 65 percent are listed with law firms. (The remaining 10 percent are listed with such partners as a research university or large pharmaceuticals.) Eight law firms handle 30 percent of the patents in the field.

[27] Robert C. Bishop, Jose E. Gonzalez and Mark Skaletsky, *Is Virtual a Virtue?* 1 J BIOLAW & BUS. 17 (1997).

[28] See Robert Bishop, *Case Study: AutoImmune, Inc,* 1 J. BIOLAW & BUS. 28 (1997); Mark Shalensky, *Case Study: Geltex Pharmaceuticals, Inc.,* 1 J. BIOLAW & BUS. 31 (1997).

As small firms move from R&D into clinical trials and eventually manufacturing and marketing, they face a host of challenges. In the past, the lack of expertise and money led many biotechs to hook up with large pharmaceuticals, often in relationships in which the lion's share of the eventual profits were bargained away. But here, too, a transactional infrastructure is being built around third-party provision of services. In part, the availability of these services is a product of the huge layoffs that have accompanied restructurings and mergers among the big pharmaceuticals. Tens of thousands of employees have been let go by large pharmaceuticals as they have consolidated and tried to shed excess capacity. As a consequence, there are now numerous service firms that small companies can turn to on a pay-for-service basis.

A difficult task for a small firm is evaluating the potential market and the competition for its products in advanced stages of research. Market research companies, staffed by people trained in large companies, are now available to provide analysis and prioritization of product development portfolios. Historically, manufacturing was also a significant stumbling block. Firms faced the dilemma of building an expensive facility in advance only to have the product fail to obtain regulatory approval (as happened with Centocor's drug Centoxin), or receiving regulatory approval but lacking manufacturing capacity to provide the market with sufficient product (as happened with Chiron's Betaseron, which had to be rationed through a lottery). The development of contract manufacturing organizations with substantial capacity for manufacture of protein-based drugs now offers firms an alternative.

Running successful phase I and II clinical trials, where new medicines are tested for efficacy and safety, is also expensive and demanding for small firms. But research hospitals, university medical centers, and clinical research organizations (CROs) have stepped in and now provide this service. CROs, staffed by physicians and experts with years of pharmaceutical experience in clinical trials and working with regulatory authorities, now offer an expertise that young companies cannot match. The next stage, phase III clinical trials and product launch, was simply beyond the financial means of biotech firms that did not already have revenue-generating products on the market. Firms that had managed to get a product this far on their own often turned at this stage to a partner with deep pockets, most typically an established pharmaceutical with the financial clout and marketing muscle. But now there are alternatives here, too: contract sales organizations with specialized staff in particular therapeutic areas. On the financing side, relational creativity abounds as well. New solutions to financing stage III trials and product launch that involve the sharing of costs and profits among biotech firms and the various professional service firms that participated in the drug development pipeline are being forged.

In sum, the transactional infrastructure of drug research and development now affords access to a wide array of relevant skills and necessary resources that allow biotech firms to remain specialized and not take on expensive internal staff. But there is always a narrow line to walk here, as inhouse expertise is necessary to evaluate and oversee the quality of external services. As the field grows, the various participants develop reputations for the quality of their services and their skill at managing partnerships and resolving disputes, and these reputations in turn shape the structure of subsequent collaborations.

III. Will They Kill the Goose that Laid the Golden Egg?

To a student of organizations, law, or economics, the biotech industry is fascinating because of the density of the relationships and the speed and complexity of its organizing processes. Early commentators often averred that the industry would soon shake out and shed its complexity and uniqueness, and either be absorbed by the pharmaceutical industry or consolidated into a smaller number of dominant firms. Yet, prophecies of consolidation have missed a basic point about the structure of the field. Mergers do occur, and some young DBFs fail. But the rate of new foundings has outpaced exits, and most mergers involve the joining of small DBFs. The diversity of sponsorship that DBFs can avail themselves of, and the dense webs of collaboration that sustain these firms, appear to set the industry on a different trajectory. Rather than being absorbed by traditional sectors, the field operates more as a conduit for a wide range of surrounding organizations to access fundamental new technologies. The number and density of participants drawn to the field of biotechnology reflect not only opportunities for medical research and commercial benefit, but the strong motivation of a wide range of public, private, and nonprofit organizations to play a key role in the development of the field.

The critical challenge, then, as the science and technology continue to develop in a highly promising manner, is whether it will continue to enjoy a sense of common membership in a technological community, now that so many participants are attracted to the field. Already some of the participants are pursuing goals that depart from the roles they played in the industry's origins. For example, research universities are now much more concerned with the commercialization of their basic science discoveries and more involved in exclusive proprietary relationships than in the past.[29] This sea change in the focus of life science' basic research has its upside, as ivory

---

[29] See David Blumenthal, *Academic-Industry Relationships in the Life Sciences—Extent, Consequences, and Management*, 268 J AM. MED. ASS'N (1992); David Blumenthal, et. al., *Relationships between Academic Institutions and Industry in the Life Sciences· An Industry Survey*, 334 NEW ENG. J. MED. 368 (1996) (discussing academic-industry relations in the life sciences); Etzkowitz & Webster, n. 13 above (discussing changing academic norms); Powell & Owen-Smith, n. 2 above (discussing patenting and commercialization).

tower attitudes are shed and more concerted attention is given to technology transfer. But movement too far in this direction runs the risk of undermining public science, supplanting openness with secrecy and proprietary concerns, which, if in place at the outset, would have either prevented or delayed the founding of the field.

This tension can already be observed in the recent technological trajectory of biotechnology. The recombination of DNA and the production of monoclonal antibodies represent biotechnology's first and second technology platforms. Both are still robust and viable methods for product development. The advances in gene splicing leading to genomics and gene therapy represent a third technology platform. The explosion of interest in genomics has been accompanied by the founding of numerous new firms, considered to be technology companies as opposed to product-oriented companies.[30] But the stampede into genomics entails several key risks. One temptation is for companies to abandon well-conceived product development strategies based on first and second generation technologies in favor of the genomics bandwagon, without recognizing that converting promising new technology into products will take time and a great deal of effort. Such moves will also result in a long lapse in the introduction of new products.

A second concern highlighted by Professors Michael Heller and Rebecca Eisenberg, and dubbed the 'tragedy of the anticommons', is the growing fragmentation of intellectual property claims and the timing of their assertion.[31] The question of when to seek patent protection on a gene sequence is a complex matter. A wide array of parties—including, back in 1991, the NIH, which later reversed its position, as well as research universities and private firms— are filing hundreds of patent applications on newly identified DNA sequences, including gene fragments, before identifying any biological function, much less a medical product. Similar moves are afoot for various research tools, including the use of PCR technology and vectors that allow the targeting and analysis of gene function.

Some commentators stress that the past history of biotech points to ample precedent for the licensing of patents for fundamental inventions. But consider how differently the field would have evolved if the original Cohen-Boyer patent on recombinant DNA technology had not been licensed in a manner that kept the technology open.[32] The concern is that more parties today are likely to opt for either exclusive licenses or erect costly toll booths, imposing charges on those who need to make use of genomic information to create

---

[30] See Jürgen Drews, *Biotechnology's Metamorphosis into a Drug Discovery Industry*, 16 NATURE BIOTECHNOLOGY 22 (1998); Anne & Herbert Schoemaker, *The Three Pillars of Bioentrepreneurship*, 16 *Nature Biotechnology* 13 (1998).

[31] Michael Heller & Rebecca Eisenberg, *Can Patents Deter Innovation? The Anticommons in Biomedical Research*, 280 SCI 698 (1998).

[32] See Kenneth Sutherlin Dueker, *Biobusiness on Campus: Commercialization of University Developed Biomedical Technologies*, 52 FOOD DRUG L.J. 453 (1997).

viable new medicines. Whether such tolls will deter or delay innovation is unclear. But what is striking is how actively universities and firms are seeking to privatize new information. In their defense, neither universities nor technology-based firms will ever produce new medicines and reap the rewards from these innovations. They hope instead to profit from the supply of information or data analysis. Some observers worry that as the human genome project reaches fruition, the new information may not be widely available. The recent joint announcement by the two rival groups in the genome race reflects a truce and suggests that public availability of genome databases is considered a priority.

IV. Conclusion

In fields such as biotech, where knowledge is advancing rapidly and the sources of knowledge are widely dispersed, organizations enter into an array of relationships to gain access to different competencies and knowledge. Progress with the technology goes hand-in-hand with the evolution of the industry and its supporting institutions. In short, the science, the organizations, and the associated institutional practices are coevolving. Universities are now more attentive to the commercial development of research, DBFs are active participants in basic science inquiry, and pharmaceuticals are more keyed into developments at DBFs and universities.

Dedicated biotechnology firms have created organizational capabilities well out of proportion to their relatively small size by building relationships with external parties to gain access to resources, knowledge, and skills in support of an array of functions from R&D to distribution. Given the variety of activities for which collaborations are used, interorganizational ties not only enhance discovery efforts, they provide an opportunity for cross-fertilization both inside and across organizations. Firms with more experience at managing collaboration, especially in R&D, appear to be able to leverage that expertise and become more centrally connected. Consequently, central DBFs increase their collaborative capacity: they engage in more subsequent linkages and expand their portfolios of relationships and their competencies; they grow more rapidly; and they are among the industry leaders in bringing new medicines to the marketplace. More centrally connected firms have more extensive patent portfolios and show stronger performance, measured in terms of sales and nonoperating income.[33]

But the advantages that accrue from centrality and connectedness depend on the viability of the larger community. That community has been sustained by informal rules of the game that promote knowledge spillovers, or the

[33] See Powell et al, n. 4 above; Powell et al., n. 7 above.

investments in R&D by universities, government, and private corporations that are publicly available and thus spill over for third parties to exploit.[34] Generalized standards for dispute resolution and for the sharing of knowledge and research tools have made possible a set of organizational arrangements that has greatly facilitated the development of basic science discoveries. This achievement is recognized by even the largest participants in the field. For example, Daniel Vasella, CEO of Novartis, the giant Swiss firm formed from the merger of Sandoz and Ciba-Geigy, observes that 'external alliances accelerate the pace of drug discovery far more rapidly than a company establishing research capabilities solely in-house'.[35] Yet when the most talented participants in a field spend their time and energy trying, to use the vernacular, to get a piece of the action rather than creating new action, effort is wasted on disputes, duplication, and discord, and the larger community suffers and possibly unravels. Were this to occur, the nature of rivalry would shift from cooperative competition to turf wars, with rival networks of partners looking to delay, deter, and defend themselves against competitors and poachers rather than advancing both their efforts and those of the overall field.

[34] Clearly, some participants are better equipped to take advantage of third party research than others. Firm productivity is positively correlated with scientific publication rates once investment levels were controlled for. See Gambardella, n. 18 above. Firms that promote key researchers according to their standing in the larger scientific community are more productive than their rivals. See Rebecca Henderson & Iain Cockburn, *Scale, Scope, and Spillovers: The Determinants of Research Productivity in Drug Discovery*, 27 RAND J. ECON. 32 (1996). Thus there are substantial differences in the ability of some organizations to obtain value from the work of others, and those well placed in a research community with open norms of publishing are most able to utilize knowledge spillovers.

[35] Vasella, n. 8 above, at 485.

11

A POLITICAL ECONOMY OF THE PUBLIC DOMAIN: MARKETS IN INFORMATION GOODS VERSUS THE MARKETPLACE OF IDEAS

YOCHAI BENKLER*

I. The Free Republic Problem

Here's one for freedom of the press. The Washington Post and the Los Angeles Times are trying to get the government to prevent some readers from debating the political implications of their stories on a web-based forum. Well, not quite, but too close for comfort. The website is called Free Republic. It includes a forum where conservatives share news clippings and exchange opinions online. Users who read articles they think deserve comment cut and paste them onto the forum. They then post a comment, and

* I owe thanks to Diane Zimmerman for her comments on this chapter and to Rochelle Dreyfuss, who read an earlier version of the argument. The core arguments of the chapter were presented at the Engelberg Center for Innovation Law and Policy conference, Intellectual Products: Novel Claims to Protection and Their Boundaries (La Pietra, Italy, June 25–27, 1998), and I thank the participants in the conference for their comments and thoughts. Needless to say, I alone am responsible for whatever deserves criticism in the chapter. The research was supported by the Filomen D'Agostino and Max E. Greenberg Research Fund of the New York University School of Law.

other users participate in a discussion of the article.[1] In October 1998 the Washington Post and the Los Angeles Times decided that public discourse may well be a good thing, but not when someone else uses *their* stories to evoke it. So they brought a copyright action to prevent the users of Free Republic from posting the newspapers' stories to their political forum.[2]

The Free Republic suit crystallizes a pervasive tension between property in the information economy and the freedom to exchange ideas in the information society.[3] This tension has two core components.

First, enforcing property rights in information goods requires government to prevent its citizens from using information that they want to use in ways that they want to use it.[4] This is not a regrettable side effect of property rights. It is in the very nature of the institutional design of property rights in information.[5] In order to make possible a market in information goods, government must delineate the boundaries of what is the 'unit' of an 'information good', and must commit to prevent, at the behest of the owner, anyone other than the owner from using that 'unit' of information. This commitment to prevent

---

[1] See www.freerepublic.com, browse to Forum.

[2] See Pam Mendels, *Newspaper Suit Raises Fair Use Issues* (October 2, 1998) at <http://wwwnytimes.com/library/tech/98/10/cyber/articles/02papers.html>.

[3] In focusing on this tension, this chapter follows Rosemary J. Coombe, *Objects of Property and Subjects of Politics: Intellectual Property Laws and Democratic Dialogue*, 69 TEX. L. REV. 1853 (1991); Niva Elkin-Koren, *Cyberlaw and Social Change: A Democratic Approach to Copyright Law in Cyberspace*, 14 CARDOZO ARTS & ENT. L.J. 215 (1996); Neil Netanel, *Copyright and a Democratic Civil Society*, 106 YALE L.J. 283 (1996); James Boyle, *A Politics of Intellectual Property: Environmentalism for the Net?*, 47 DUKE L.J. 87 (1997). A more complete statement of my argument here is Yochai Benkler, *Free As the Air to Common Use, First Amendment Constraints on Enclosure of the Public Domain*, 74 N.Y.U. L. REV. 354 (1999).

[4] The speech-restricting character of copyright and its potential conflict with the First Amendment's speech clause is discussed in Diane Leenheer Zimmerman, *Information as Speech, Information as Goods· Some Thoughts on Marketplaces and the Bill of Rights*, 33 WM & MARY L. REV. 665 (1992); L. Ray Patterson & Stanley F. Birch, Jr., *Copyright and Free Speech Rights*, 4 J. INTELL. PROP. L. 1 (1996); Mark A. Lemley & Eugene Volokh, *Freedom of Speech and Injunctions in Intellectual Property Cases*, 48 DUKE L.J. 147 (1998).

[5] Defining the term 'information' is tricky, and formal definitions tend to change across disciplines and methodological uses. For purposes of the policy-oriented analysis we engage in as legal commentators, I use 'information' to refer to the potential content of communications among human beings—including the meaning attached to the communication by either its originator or its recipient. This definition is broad, and obviously includes the subject matter of copyright. It also includes the subject matter of patent, in that a new way of obtaining a result in the world is 'information' to the extent that it can be encoded in a manner capable of transmission from one person to another. The definition hence includes all potential objects of the law that propertizes the content of human communication, but not all that is 'information' in this sense is necessarily subject to protection—eg, raw data. This is what makes the definition useful for discussions about how much of the universe of information should and should not be the subject of exclusive rights. While deliberately broad, the definition is also more limited than other common definitions of the term. For example, genetic information enters into my definition of information when it refers to what scientists do to encode their understanding of genetics in humanly-meaningful terms—including their internal conversations about it—but not to the relationship between the genes and the body, which usually is also described by microbiologists as transmission of information.

some beneficial uses of the information is what makes possible a market in information goods, because permission to engage in the prohibited uses serves as the 'goods' sold in that market.

Secondly, the choice presented by the Free Republic case involves not merely a local choice between two speakers, but a systemic choice between two *types* of speakers. Holding for the newspapers will benefit speakers like the newspapers—professional, commercial producers who seek to appropriate the benefit of their production by selling permission to access and use their information products. Conversely, it will make more difficult amateur discussions like those on the Free Republic forum, which require access to some existing information as an input into their own conversation but do not seek to appropriate the social benefits that their conversation creates. Though neither side would necessarily cease operation if it lost the suit, the dispute nonetheless requires a choice between two very different types of information production, responding to very different incentives, and perhaps most importantly from a normative perspective, providing very different types of content.

I suggest that the choice represented by the Free Republic case is not only, or even primarily, between having more or less information in the long run, but also about *what kind of organizations or individuals* will produce information in the long run. This choice about what type of organizations or individuals will be producing information is present whenever we shift the respective boundaries of the enclosed and public domains. Furthermore, because people and organizations who produce information for different motivations and with different organizational constraints are likely to produce different types of information content, decisions about property rights in information must be held to a normative accounting in terms of their effects on the patterns of, strategies for, and ultimately the location and content of information production in our society.

Part II offers a positive analysis that modifies the standard understanding of the effects of property rights in information to provide a prediction of the effects of changes in property rules on the organization of information production. Part III then outlines the normative implications of this prediction.

II. Effects of Intellectual Property Rights on the Organization of Information Production

A. Background economics

We live in an intellectual environment that permits the propagation of silly statements such as 'the best prescription for connecting authors to their audiences is to extend rights into every corner where consumers derive value from literary and artistic works. If history is any measure, the results should be to promote political as well as cultural diversity, ensuring a plenitude of voices, all with the chance to be heard'.[6] The statement is silly because it states an economic prediction that has no basis in any competent economic theory of intellectual property. It is dangerous because it can be stated with a straight face, and accepted as plausible by enough people that it threatens to become the basis for our approach to regulating a core sector of economic activity in our society—the production, manipulation, and distribution of information. Indeed, this kind of thinking—that more property rights necessarily lead to the production of more, and more diverse, information—has been used in varying degrees to justify a phenomenal expansion of intellectual property rights in sundry directions over the past few years.[7] And that dramatic expansion marks a radical realignment of how our society produces knowledge.

There are, roughly speaking, two general economic approaches to understanding the production of information—welfare economics and neo-Schumpeterian economics. The *locus classicus* of the welfare economics approach to intellectual property is Arrow's discussion of patents.[8] Information is nonrival and partially nonexcludable,[9] and is both input and

---

[6] PAUL GOLDSTEIN, COPYRIGHT'S HIGHWAY: FROM GUTENBERG TO THE CELESTIAL JUKEBOX 236 (1994).

[7] Examples include the Sonny Bono Copyright Term Extension Act, Pub L. No. 105–298, 112 Stat. 2827 (1998), the Digital Millennium Copyright Act, Pub. L. No. 105–304, 112 Stat. 2860 (1998), and the drive to protect the information content of databases, to name a few prominent examples.

[8] Kenneth J Arrow, *Economic Welfare and the Allocation of Resources for Invention*, in THE RATE AND DIRECTION OF INVENTIVE ACTIVITY: ECONOMIC AND SOCIAL FACTORS 609, 623–25 (1962). In copyright, this tradeoff was applied in William M. Landes & Richard A. Posner, *An Economic Analysis of Copyright Law*, 18 J. LEGAL STUD. 325 (1989). Earlier discussions of the economics of copyright include ARNOLD PLANT, THE NEW COMMERCE IN IDEAS AND INTELLECTUAL PROPERTY (1953); Robert M. Hurt & Robert N. Schuchman, *The Economic Rationale of Copyright*, 56 AM. ECON. REV. 421 (1966); Stephen G. Breyer, *The Uneasy Case for Copyright: A Study of Copyright in Books, Photocopies, and Computer Programs*, 84 HARV. L. REV. 281 (1970). For important economic discussions of fair use, see Wendy J. Gordon, *Fair Use as Market Failure. A Structural and Economic Analysis of the Betamax Case and Its Predecessors*, 82 COLUM. L. REV. 1600 (1982); William W. Fisher III, *Reconstructing the Fair Use Doctrine*, 101 HARV. L. REV. 1659 (1988).

[9] See Paul M Romer, *Endogenous Technological Change*, 98 J. POL. ECON. S71, S73–S74 (1990). Every economic good can be defined by the degree to which it is excludable, and the degree to which it is rival. A good is excludable to the extent that its producer can appropriate its benefits by excluding those who benefit from it unless they pay a price. A good is rivalrous to the extent that its use by one person prevents (rivals) its use by another person. The former is a function of the available technology for exclusion, and the institutional (legal) framework that permits or facilitates such technically feasible exclusion. The latter is purely 'technological'. It is an attribute of the good itself: it either can, or cannot, as a practical matter, be used by many people without degradation or rivalry. A pure private good is one that is excludable and rivalrous. A pure public good is one that is nonexcludable and nonrivalrous. When a good is public in the sense of being nonexcludable, it is so because no firm can capture its social value. It must therefore be provided publicly, if at all. By definition, a nonrivalrous good is one that can be used by one person without preventing or degrading its use by any other person. Any additional person who uses the good imposes no social cost. Its optimal demand price is therefore zero. At that

output of its own production process.[10] Because of the nonrival nature of information, in a static analysis property rights that increase excludability reduce efficient consumption of information by permitting its price to be raised above its efficient demand price (a price equal to its marginal cost, which is zero). This short term loss is justified, if at all, by the need for dynamic efficiency—the need to permit producers to receive a benefit from producing information by charging a price for their information outputs. This dynamic effect, in turn, faces its own internal limits because information is input, as well as output of its production process. This creates a conflict between first and second generation producers, because the greater the rights (and hence incentives) of the first generation, the greater the costs (and hence the lower the incentives, or benefits net of costs) of the second generation.[11] Since every generation is both 'the first' to future producers, and 'the second' to prior producers, the conflict is pervasive and sets limits on the extent to which, even in a dynamic analysis, it is efficient to recognize and enforce rights in information products. As Arrow put it, 'precisely to the extent that [property rights in information are] successful, there is an underutilization of the information'.[12] Now, none of this means that traditional welfare economics argues against property rights in information products. But mainstream economics very clearly negates the superstition that if some property rights in information are good, then more rights in information are even better. That is decidedly contrary to prevailing economic wisdom.

The second strand of economics that focuses on information production, in particular on innovation, is the neo-Schumpeterian literature.[13] This is a somewhat loose category of work that focuses on market structure as the engine of innovation, in contrast to the neoclassical concern with efficient allocation of resources. It includes both theoretical and empirical work, the thrust of which is that market structure—through monopoly/oligopoly-based

price, however, it would not be produced by private interests, and must be provided publicly. At a higher price, which would induce private production, it will be underutilized.

[10] See Arrow, n. 8 above, at 618 ('Information is not only the product of inventive activity, it is also an input—in some sense, the major input apart from the talent of the inventor').

[11] This is also sometimes referred to as the 'on the shoulders of giants' problem See Suzanne Scotchmer, *Standing on the Shoulders of Giants: Cumulative Research and the Patent Law*, 5 J. ECON. PERSP. 29 (1991).

[12] See Arrow, n. 8 above, at 617.

[13] The name derives from its reliance on Schumpeter's basic insight that capitalist production is typified by dynamic, technology-driven growth over time, rather than by the static allocation efficiency emphasized by the neoclassical model See JOSEPH A. SCHUMPETER, CAPITALISM, SOCIALISM, AND DEMOCRACY (1942). Schumpeter introduced the idea that the incentive to gain a post-innovation legal monopoly was *not* the primary determinant of investment in technology, but rather that a concentrated market structure with large scale firms was the precondition to innovation-driven growth. The economic studies of innovation that followed Schumpeter's challenge have, in many ways, refuted, as well as elaborated, his insights. But this extensive literature has provided an alternative picture of information production as an economic phenomenon to that provided by welfare economics. For a compact review of the literature, see F.M. Scherer, *Schumpeter and Plausible Capitalism*, 30 J. ECON. LITERATURE 1416 (1992).

price discipline coupled with some competition or at least contestibility to drive and diversify effort—is what promotes innovation. Innovation, in turn, rather than efficient allocation, is the primary engine of productivity and growth. Again, within this second, alternative economic model, property rights are significantly less important than the superstition holds, because the market structure that *precedes* the information production and the market structure imposed by using the information are more important than property rights as incentives for innovation.

B. Overview of the effects of intellectual property approaches to organizing information production

If the current frenzy of propertization of information products is not prescribed by contemporary economic models, what do these models suggest will happen because of it? In this part, I present a relatively simple modification to the standard welfare economics model that explains some of the phenomena observed in the descriptive literature.[14] This, in turn, suggests an analytic framework for predicting how enclosure of our intellectual environment will effect the way our society produces information.

The core claim is this. Many people in society engage in information production. They produce and exchange information for a variety of reasons, and use a variety of strategies to appropriate the benefits of their production. This is the major variation from the traditional model, which assumes that all producers have the same strategy: they buy information inputs, sell outputs, and hope to maximize the difference between their cost and their revenue. A more detailed topology follows, but it is important to understand three major divides in the distribution of strategies used by information producers in our economy.

First, there is the division between commercial and noncommercial producers. Unlike the case with the production of wheat or automobiles, the noncommercial sector is of crucial importance in our information production system. Universities, government (both through direct investment in government labs or research institutes and through indirect investments such as National Science Foundation grants), political and civic organizations, and amateurs are all integral parts of the production of information on both large and small scales. Secondly, there is a division within the commercial sector between those who appropriate the benefits of their investment by relying on property rights, and those who appropriate the benefits of their production by relying on early access to the information (for example, wire services) or by

---

[14] The two most wide-ranging empirical studies are quite old by now. See Richard C. Levin et al., *Appropriating the Returns from Industrial Research and Development*, 3 BROOKINGS PAPERS ECON. ACTIVITY 783, 794–96 (1987); Edwin Mansfield et al., *Imitation Costs and Patents: An Empirical Study*, 91 ECON. J. 907 (1981).

giving the information for free and appropriating the benefits through relationships created around the information (such as lawyers who write for the
National Law Journal). Thirdly, and finally, there is a division within those
who sell 'information goods' in reliance on rights between those who produce
information on a small scale, like individual authors, and those who integrate
new production with ownership of large inventories of existing information,
like Disney or Time-Warner.

The core point to understand about property rights in information is that
they have different effects on these different strategies, and changes in the
institutional content of property rights can help some of these strategies *at the
expense* of others. In particular, increases in the scope and reach of property
rights benefit commercial producers who sell information goods, at the
expense both of noncommercial producers and of producers who appropriate
the benefits of their production by means other than the sale of rights. The
primary culprit forcing this tradeoff is the somewhat unique fact that
information is both input and output of its own production process. Increases
in appropriability cause a simultaneous increase both in expected ability to
appropriate the value of outputs and in input costs. By endogenizing the
strategies used by information producers, my approach underscores that,
while expansion of rights increases the input costs of all producers, and
thereby increases the production *costs* of all, such expansion benefits, and
hence increases production *incentives* of, only those producers who sell
information goods in reliance on rights. Expansion of rights increases the
returns to commercial producers who sell permission to use. But, by raising
input costs, it discourages production by producers who do not sell rights—
either because they are noncommercial, or because they appropriate the benefits of their information production by means other than sale of permission.

Moreover, increases in the scope and reach of property rights favor large
scale organizations that own information inventories over small scale organizations (including individuals) that do not own such inventories. The mechanism for this effect is as follows. Input costs increase because now more uses
of information that previously were not subject to anyone's right (in other
words, were available from the public domain at their marginal cost of zero)
must be purchased. An organization that owns a large inventory of existing
information can respond to the loss of public domain inputs by intensifying
reutilization of its owned inventory, and will do so to the extent that its inventory provides even rough substitutes for information inputs otherwise available only by purchase from others. Since the marginal cost of reutilization is
zero (information is nonrival), but the (supply) price at which information is
available from the market must be positive, a firm will face lower costs if it
uses its own inventory rather than information it does not own—even though
the social cost of using intrafirm resources is identical to the social cost of
utilizing market-purchased inputs. This is so because of the nonrivalry,

independent of and cumulative to any transaction costs effects. Organizations and individuals that do not have such an inventory do not have the reutilization option, and are forced to cover from the market information inputs no longer available from the public domain. This increases their input costs more rapidly than the rise in input costs of large scale vertically integrated organizations.

In other words, when Congress passes a statute like the Digital Millennium Copyright Act[15] or the Sonny Bono Copyright Term Extension Act,[16] or when the European Commission passes its database Directive,[17] it is favoring particular types of information producers. It is choosing to increase the costs of academic scholars, whose libraries must decide whether to buy more publications or more access rights to a smaller number of publications, to increase Reed Elsevier's returns. It is choosing to increase the costs of amateurs—like children who would put together web-based projects about their favorite cartoon characters—in order to increase the returns to Disney. It is choosing to raise the economic barriers facing participants in the Free Republic forum in order to increase the returns to the Washington Post.

C. The effects of intellectual property in more detail

In this analysis I assume that information producers are rational and well informed about their expected costs and benefits, and that when they engage in information production, they do so in order to maximize the difference between their costs and benefits.[18] I use the common assumption that the costs of information production are the sum of the costs of human capital[19] and of the cost of information inputs.[20] Intellectual property rights affect costs by affecting the cost of information inputs. I therefore focus solely on the cost of information inputs.[21]

---

[15] Pub L. No. 105–304, 112 Stat. 2860 (1998).

[16] Pub L. No. 105–298, 112 Stat. 2827 (1998).

[17] Council Directive 96/9/EC, 1996 O.J. L77 20 (on the legal protection of databases).

[18] In other words, I do not rely on claims about bounded rationality, or lack of information, or incommensurability between the motives of noncommercial producers and commercial producers.

[19] By human capital I mean creative effort. While this is difficult to measure, Romer defines human capital as acquired educational capabilities. See Romer, n. 9 above. This is useful when focusing on industrial or scientific innovation, and may make analysis more easily quantifiable, but the element that human capital 'gets at' is creativity, as distinguished from the application of work, money, or existing information to a productive enterprise.

[20] For a discussion of the plausibility of this focus in analyzing the economic effects of intellectual property, see Romer, n. 9 above, at S73-S74. See also Arrow, n. 8 above (two most important inputs are creative talent and existing information). This assumption ignores costs of labor and capital in the more traditional sense because these parameters are not affected by intellectual property rights in information production.

[21] To the extent that the ratio between information input costs and human capital costs is very low, changes in property rights will have a relatively low effect on the overall cost, and hence the effect I describe in the text would be muted. One might imagine activities that require more or

Existing information (available to be used as information input) can be owned or unowned, depending on the rules of intellectual property law in place. If owned, existing information can belong to the firm deciding whether, how, and what to produce, or it can be owned by another firm. If information is owned by another firm, that firm may sell it at a positive price (or withhold it), or give it away at its marginal cost of zero. Hence, the cost of information inputs is comprised of the cost of information inputs available at a positive, above-marginal-cost market price, those available at marginal cost from non-market (including intrafirm) sources, and those available from other firms that choose to barter or share their information. A firm will seek to minimize its costs by using, to the extent possible, inputs available from nonmarket sources, either internal or from the public domain.

To explain why any owned information inputs would be purchased at market price as long as unowned inputs exist in the public domain, I assume heterogeneity in the suitability of inputs to producing a given new product, given available human capital inputs. In order not to bias the analysis in favor of one type of input or another, I further assume that any given unit of existing information has a knowable probability of being the best input to be combined with human capital to produce a product, and that this probability is independent of whether the input is owned or unowned, owned by the firm making the decision or by another firm. I assume that the firm knows the probability that an input will be the right input, and that this probability assessment is what causes a firm to value a given input highly enough to pay a positive price for it, despite the availability of alternative inputs from non-market sources.

It should now be fairly intuitive to see how increases in the scope and content of intellectual property increase the cost of information production. A change in law that increases property rights—say, an extension of the term of copyright protection that keeps information out of the public domain for another 20 years—decreases the quantity of inputs available from the public domain, and makes those same inputs available only from owned sources. Unless the firm happens to own the inputs that, but for the change in law, would have been available at zero cost from the public domain, it will see these inputs as available only at a positive market price (or, at best, available through barter) and thus as increasing its information costs.

less creativity—say, the difference between writing a sonnet and writing a news report about a specific event. To the extent that a productive activity has a very high human capital cost component, the implications of the analysis that follows are attenuated. But even poets borrow from the works of other poets, and I will assume that for most activity that would fall within Kuhn's concept of 'normal science', the ratio between information inputs and human capital is high enough that the effects of intellectual property on the magnitude of information costs are large enough to affect overall cost. For purposes of this chapter I assume that the ratio between the quantity of information inputs and the quantity of human capital used in producing a given information product is exogenous (say, determined by the nature of the information product and the way in which the discipline of producing this type of information mixes information inputs with creative talent).

By specifying the components of cost, one gains the ability to see that an increase in property rights has different effects on the costs of firms in the market, based on the size of their existing information endowment at the time of the change in law. The larger a firm's endowment, the higher the likelihood that the input it needs is within its own endowment. In turn, this increases the likelihood that the firm will be able to continue to produce new products using inputs at their marginal cost, or that it will have something with which to barter for inputs. The smaller a firm's endowment, the higher the likelihood that the loss of inputs will increase the firm's costs of new production by forcing it to use inputs at market price. This effect is independent of the *distributive* windfall effect—increases in protection retroactively increase the value of any endowment existing at the time of the increase. It has to do with the probability that a firm will be able to use the most suitable information inputs in new products at their marginal cost rather than at some above-marginal-cost supply price.

Benefits of information production can be appropriated directly or indirectly. By 'direct' appropriation, I mean that the benefits of production are appropriated by selling or withholding permission to use the information output in reliance on the legal right to permit or refuse the use of information to those to whom it is useful.[22] 'Indirect' appropriation refers to any means by which the producer can obtain a benefit from producing and distributing the information other than selling permission to use it.

Indirect appropriation can be attained in a number of ways. It could result from correlative gains in the sale of another product or service as a result of the information production. It could be a side supply-effect in a correlated market, where the producer itself gains advantage through early access to the information. For example, first mover advantages in industrial research and development can permit a firm to convert early access to information into a production and sales advantage. It could also be a demand side-effect, when giving others access to the information increases demand for other products or services offered by the information producer. Indirect appropriation could also be attained through benefits to firm knowhow, or at the individual creator level as educational and reputational gains. We might also think of creative individuals as having a measure of taste for creation. Any professional scholar who could command higher personal income in practice than in an academic setting has made a personal choice to prefer some combination of

---

[22] This definition specifically uses the intended economic function of intellectual property law to define two classes of benefits: those that rely on legal protection (direct) and those that do not (indirect) To 'rely on legal protection' means to sell (or refuse to sell) permission under a system of formal property rights. A producer who relies purely on direct appropriation must sell the permission at least at a price sufficient to cover all development costs, including the cost of failed attempts. This is in fact the price usually assumed by the standard economic model to be the minimal price at which information goods will be sold.

educational, reputational, and hedonic gains in exchange for reduced direct payment for that person's ability to produce information.

Different combinations of the sources of cost reduction or benefit appropriation enable us to imagine multiple strategies for maintaining positive producer welfare from information production. First, there is the divide between organizations that appropriate the benefits of their production directly and those that do so indirectly. Within those that appropriate benefits directly, one could divide between those who own inventory (and hence can minimize costs by utilizing intrafirm inputs) from those who do not own inventory (and must rely either on public domain or on inputs purchased at an above-marginal-cost market price). Of those who appropriate benefits indirectly, some rely on supply-side benefits of early access to information, and hence on retaining control of the information (these could, if they chose, rely on barter to obtain information inputs) while others rely on demand-side benefits of wide access by the public, and thus disseminate the information widely instead of retaining it for barter or sale. And, finally, within those who rely on demand-side effects of access to the information, we could imagine a divide between those who derive a directly-correlated monetary benefit—let's call them 'commercial' providers—and those 'noncommercial' providers who derive correlated nonmonetary benefits.

Following these divisions among potential strategies of appropriation, we would come up with a distribution of strategies for obtaining information inputs and appropriating the benefits of information production that comports with the strategies generally described in the empirical and case study literature that studies information production markets.[23] Table 11.1 summarizes the topology, which is comprised of five ideal-type strategies for organizing information production.

The first two are variants of what the traditional economic model assumes to be the usual appropriation strategy. Appropriation is achieved by selling permission to use the information that these organizations produce, or by excluding competition through assertion of rights. These organizations depend on legal rights that define the information uses subject to their permission. The first type of organization owns an inventory of information, and vertically integrates sale and management of this inventory with the production of new information. Disney or Time-Warner are examples. Let us call this strategy 'Mickey'.

The second type of organization does not own inventory but does sell permission to use its information outputs. It sells either directly to consumers or to inventory managers, including Mickey organizations. This category includes organizations that sell a single piece of software, or a single patented gadget, or authors who sell publication or movie rights, or independent code

---

[23] See sources cited, n. 14 above.

Table 11.1: Five information production strategies

	Mickey	Romantic maximizer	Quasi-rent seeker	Studious lawyer	Joe Einstein
Production	vertically integrated new production and inventory management	new production separated from inventory management	new production separated from inventory management	new production separated from inventory management	new production separated from inventory management
Output	sells permission to use	sells rights to inventory management organizations; sells permission to use	maintains secrecy; sells time-sensitive access; shares information	makes information freely available	makes information freely available
Input	public domain materials purchases reuse of existing inventories	public domain materials purchases	public domain materials purchases information received in sharing	public domain materials purchases	public domain materials purchases
Revenue/Appropriation	sales and resales of new and old inventory	royalties from sale to inventory management firm; sales of new products	early access quasi-rents: exclusive access early access of pool participant sales of time-sensitive access	access *by others* to information produced positively correlated with sales of a different product	reputational gains; nonmarket grant funding; or no appropriation expectation
Examples	Disney, Time-Warner; Drug companies	authors of novels independent software developers inventors with small companies that sell their inventions	companies that rely on lead-time instead of patents Merck & Co's funding of public domain basic research newspapers, wire services nineteenth century US publishers of books from England	lawyers who publish in trade papers or produce newsletters Netscape's browser strategy	teaching and research institutions 'letters to the editor' Linux development of HTML participants who post comments to the Free Republic forum

writers who sell to a larger software company. Because they fit the traditional conception of an author laboring in expectation of royalties, I call users of this strategy 'the romantic maximizers'. Both strategies depend on acquisition of information inputs at marginal cost—zero—from the public domain, and, where necessary and possible, purchase of information inputs owned by other organizations. Mickey organizations have access to their own inventory as a source of information inputs. This characteristic distinguishes them from romantic maximizers and users of other strategies.

The third strategy seems to be the most common among companies that conduct industrial research and development, except for the pharmaceutical industry.[24] The distinguishing feature of this approach is that it relies on time-based advantages created by the producer's early access to the information to appropriate the benefits of production, rather than on the sale of permission or the assertion of legal rights to exclude competitors. These organizations may obtain their information inputs from the public domain by purchasing owned information, or by sharing information with similar organizations to capture economies of scale, or by sharing with organizations in different industries similarly invested in information production to capture economies of scope.[25]

Output management by these organizations is very different from that of Mickeys or romantic maximizers. These organizations do not sell information directly or assert rights to exclude competitors. They use early access to the information, gained by their investment in information production, to collect quasi-rents in a market that permits above-normal profits to those who have early access to the information. This can be done, as is the case with many process innovations, by increasing production efficiency relative to competitors while keeping the information secret.[26] It can also be done by participating in an oligopolistic pool, entry into which is reserved for those who have sufficient information production capacity to 'pay' for participation. Participants might barter their information for access, or simply be part of a small group of organizations with enough knowledge to exploit the information generated and informally shared by the group.[27] Rents are obtained from the concentrated market structure, not from assertion of property rights.[28] I

---

[24] See Levin et al., n. 14 above.

[25] See Richard R. Nelson, *The Simple Economics of Basic Scientific Research*, 67 J. POL. ECON. 297, 303 (1959); Powell, Chapter 10 above.

[26] See Levin et al., n. 14 above, at 794–96 (secrecy not as effective as lead time and learning curve advantages, but more effective than patent, as regards process innovations). The secrecy need not be kept forever, as long as new innovations can be made and kept secret for a while, creating recurring time windows in which above-normal profits are available. The search for these time windows is what drives innovation.

[27] See Wesley M Cohen & Daniel A. Leventhal, *Innovation and Learning: The Two Faces of R&D*, 99 ECON. J. 569 (1989).

[28] See, eg, F.M. Scherer, *Nordhaus' Theory of Optimal Patent Life: A Geometric Reinterpretation*, 62 AM. ECON. REV. 422 (1972).

call those who pursue this strategy 'quasi-rent seekers'. An equivalent strategy in the copyright industries is used by news organizations that rely on the timeliness and accuracy of their information, rather than on long term control over it. Similarly, nineteenth century publishers in the United States relied on first mover advantages to profit from the sale of works published in England, which were not then protected under domestic copyright law. They paid the English authors for advance copies of their galley proofs so as to be first to the American market with the new book; these payments often exceeded what the authors received from copyright royalties in England.[29]

The fourth type of organization relies on a positive correlation between the information it produces and demand for other sorts of products or services that it also sells. Doctors or lawyers who publish in trade journals are an instance of this strategy. In their honor, I call it 'the studious lawyer'. This model of appropriation was heralded a few years ago by Esther Dyson[30] and John Perry Barlow[31] as the way content would be produced in the digitally networked environment. When Netscape disseminates the source code for its browser, it does so in order to capture the standard of, and the market in, browsers, which, in turn, are given away for free. All this is done so as to capture other markets—the market in server-side software or the market in advertising to consumers who use whatever portal their browser's default home page is set to.[32] These organizations, like romantic maximizers, obtain information inputs from the public domain and by purchase. They do not, however, sell their outputs, but distribute them for free to maximize their utilization, and hence their effect on the positively-correlated market. Some release their products directly into the public domain; others distribute them free of charge, while maintaining intellectual property rights to prevent use harmful to their correlated product.

The fifth and last category lumps together what is in fact a diverse group of nonmarket actors. It includes universities and other research institutes, government research labs, individual academics, authors and artists playing to 'immortality', as well as a host of amateur endeavors, ranging from contributors to the op-ed page, to amateur choirs, to participants in mailing list. I call this strategy 'Joe Einstein', denoting the breadth of its coverage from the citizen/amateur ('Joe') to the highly professional noncommercial information producer or innovator. This is the strategy used to produce most basic science

---

[29] The story is told in Hurt & Schuchman, n. 8 above at 427; and Breyer, n. 8 above, at 282–83, as a cautionary tale against the assumption that in the absence of protection, production will suffer.

[30] Esther Dyson, *Intellectual Value*, WIRED, July 1995, at 307.

[31] John Perry Barlow, *The Economy of Ideas*, WIRED, March 1994, at 203.

[32] See Denise Caruso, *Netscape's Decision to Give Away Code Could Alter the Software Industry*, NY. TIMES, Feb. 2, 1998, at D3. See also John Markoff, *Sun Microsystems is Moving to an 'Open Source' Model*, N.Y. TIMES, Dec. 8, 1998, at C6 (describing similar strategy adopted by Sun).

and political argument (political parties and civic advocacy groups are Joe Einstein organizations), among other important information goods. Joe Einsteins obtain information inputs from the public domain and by purchasing owned information. They make information outputs freely available to the public. They appropriate the benefits of their investment, if at all, through reputational gains, research grants, charitable contributions, teaching positions rationed by publication-based reputation, or from desirable behavioral adaptations by audiences. Amateurs cross-subsidize their information production with revenues unrelated to the information production function they fulfill. Some production in this model may occur with no expectation of appropriation.

Both cost and revenue increases differ as among the five strategies identified in Table 11.1. These differential effects make Mickey better suited to thrive in an increasing-property rights environment than is any competing strategy. Table 11.2 summarizes the differential effects.

Mickey: Costs will increase because the organization must cover inputs lost from the public domain, and these lost inputs must be made up for by purchases of owned information. This effect is mitigated because Mickey organizations can cover a portion of the inputs lost from the public domain by intensifying reuse of their owned inventory. A side-effect of the expansion of property rights is, therefore, an increase in the value of owned inventory: it substitutes for information inputs previously in the public domain, as well as for potential inputs presently in the public domain discounted by the probability that they will in the future be enclosed. Inventories are likely to exhibit scope economies for organizations that vertically integrate new production with inventory management, because a larger inventory represents more varied inputs available at marginal cost for a given pool of human resources.[33] These attributes will tend to support consolidation of Mickey organizations and acquisition of romantic maximizers in order to internalize inputs, both information inventory and human capital.

Mickey organizations also experience the largest increase in revenue. They can now charge a positive price for uses they did not control prior to the change.[34] For example, a change in law might permit them to charge for personal photocopying of journal articles where such copying was previously permitted, or to enforce licenses to prevent or charge for reutilization of raw data contained in a compilation where, previously, reutilization of raw data could neither be licensed nor prevented, and hence could not be charged for. Mickey organizations will also be able to increase the price of uses that had

---

[33] This is an application of Romer's point that information production in an economy is an increasing returns activity. See Romer, n. 9 above, at S94–S95.

[34] For simplicity, I do not set out fully the parallel effect on ability to exclude competitors by asserting rights not previously available, but assume that this effect will be reflected in the producer's reservation price.

Table 11.2: Effects of increased intellectual property rights on organizations employing different strategies

	Mickey	Romantic maximizer	Quasi-rent seekers	Studious lawyers	Joe Einstein
Input costs	Increase, **mitigated by inventory reuse**	Increase	Increase, mitigated by sharing/barter	Increase	Increase
Revenue	Large increase: new sales higher prices because of absence of public domain substitutes **inventory windfall**	Increase: new sales higher prices because of absence of public domain substitutes	No effect	No effect, decrease, or increase, depending on strategic response and information and correlated markets	No effect

been under their control before the change in law, to the extent that the change decreases the supply of near-substitutes available from the public domain. Insofar as rents on the use of preexisting inventories can also be increased in these ways, Mickey organizations receive a windfall on existing inventory.[35]

Romantic maximizers: Costs increase for the same reasons as they do for Mickey organizations, but at greater magnitude, because lost public domain inputs cannot be covered by intensified reuse of owned-inventory resources. Like Mickeys, romantic maximizers see an increase in revenue, but without the windfall, because they do not own inventory. Overall costs rise more, and revenues increase less, than for Mickeys.

Quasi-rent seekers: Costs increase as they do for romantic maximizers, except that the subset of quasi-rent seekers who share their outputs as part of an R&D pool will have the effect mitigated through sharing. The magnitude of the effect on information input costs is therefore mitigated to the extent that shared information is the dominant information input. Because these organizations rely on time-based advantages, not on rights enforcement, they do not reap benefits from the increase in property rights. For some quasi-rent seekers, costs may increase less than for romantic maximizers or even Mickeys. But revenues will not increase at all. Thus, even if the expansion of property rights would be considered productive under traditional analysis— it increases the expected returns of producers more than it increases their costs—it would be a net loss to quasi-rent seekers.

Studious lawyers: Costs increase to the same extent as they do for romantic maximizers. There is no direct effect on revenue from information production, because studious lawyers do not sell information for revenue. In response to increased costs, these organizations can do one of three things. They can decrease information output in order to keep overall costs fixed. This would cause a decline in revenue in the correlated market. Were that not so, presumably they would have restricted their information output prior to the change to decrease their information production costs, since they would not have lost revenue in the correlated market by doing so. Alternatively, these organizations could maintain their level of information production, and attempt to pass the increased costs on to consumers in the correlated market. This would act as an upward shift in the marginal cost curve in that market. Finally, studious lawyers could try to adopt a mixed romantic maximizer/studious lawyer strategy, by charging a positive price for access to their information. This would decrease the quantity consumed, and result in a decline in the

---

[35] The increased inventory value is a 'windfall' because the information has already been produced or purchased by the organization prior to the change in rules. The organization's allocation decision—to produce or purchase the inventory—cannot be affected by the change in rules. The change, nonetheless, has distributive effects that permit an organization to appropriate greater benefits from the inventory than were necessary to give it the incentive to invest in acquiring the inventory in the first place.

correlative market similar to that which would be expected if the organizations had restricted output. An organization would adopt this approach if revenue from selling permission to access its information would exceed the decrease in revenue in the correlated market. But to the extent that it adopts the latter response, the organization shifts to a romantic maximizer strategy.

Joe Einsteins: Costs increase as they do for romantic maximizers. If amateur production has highly elastic demand for inputs, this increase will be expressed primarily as a decrease in the quantity of inputs utilized and hence, presumably, in lower output. There is no effect on revenue.

Given these effects on payoffs, studious lawyers and Joe Einsteins lose the most from an increase in property rights, and Mickeys and romantic maximizers stand to gain the most. Mickeys, however, do better than romantic maximizers. Their revenues increase more and their costs increase less. Thus, romantic maximizers will reach the point at which the standard economic model predicts that increased protection leads to declining productivity sooner than will Mickey organizations. Before aggregate productivity declines, romantic maximizers will shift to (be bought out by) Mickey organizations. This is an important and counter-intuitive consequence of the analysis: rights are often thought to benefit small scale and individual producers who do not have alternative means of appropriating benefits of their investments, such as control over distribution channels.

Given these payoffs, we should expect an increase in property rights in information to lead to the greatest increase in information production using Mickey strategies and the greatest decline in information production using studious lawyer and Joe Einstein strategies. Some quasi-rent seekers, studious lawyers, and Joe Einsteins may cease operations or shift to Mickey or romantic maximizer strategies. Some romantic maximizers may cease operations or be bought out by / hired by Mickey organizations. The overall number of Mickey organizations may decline, however, because consolidation of inventories will yield greater benefits to integration. This is so for two reasons. First, integration avoids transaction costs associated with purchase of information inputs owned by others. Secondly, information inventories have economies of scope as sources of inputs for new production. The larger and more diverse an inventory, the higher the probability that it will contain an input necessary to produce a new piece of information. Two organizations that combine their creative workforces and give each member of the combined workforce access to the joint inventory are likely to be more productive—have better suited information inputs available at marginal cost to complete a given project with a given pool of human capital—than the same two organizations when each workforce utilizes only its organization's independently-owned inventory.[36]

[36] It is important to underscore that the behavioral adaptations outlined arise from the decline in availability of information for use at marginal cost (zero). They are not primarily a response

The initial expected responses to an increase in intellectual property protection would likely have feedback effects that amplify the direction of the shift in strategies. A larger ratio of new information will be produced by organizations whose output is owned. This increases the probability that an input that has recently been minted will be owned by either a Mickey or a romantic maximizer, and will not be in the public domain. The increased probability that necessary inputs will be owned mimics and amplifies the effect of the initial extension of property rights. This feedback effect will be particularly pronounced in areas of production where *new* information is independently important as input, eg, where development is incremental (as with most of science and software development) or where fashion is important, as in entertainment. Furthermore, more investments will be made in producing consumer demand for information of the type produced by reuse of existing inventories. More investments will also be made in further institutional changes that make ownership of inventory and integration of new production with inventory management more profitable. Finally, organizations that expect these developments will more rapidly shift to the dominant strategies. The sum total of these effects will be to amplify, speed up, and lock in the effects of enclosure predicted by this analysis.

III. Normative Implications: The Free Republic and the Distribution of Capacity to Make Meaning

There are two types of normative implications to enclosure of the public domain. The first is a negative liberty concern—that a restriction on free speech is necessarily implied by a regime of property rights in information. The second directly flows from the prediction that enclosure systematically

to an increase in transaction costs that accompanies the expansion of rights. Even if information were licensed through an institutional mechanism that eliminated transaction costs altogether, it would still be licensed at a price above its marginal cost, because suppliers that license their information products must see a positive price in order to supply their products. Any organization choosing between an information input available from its owned inventory and an information input that must be licensed will see a demand price equal to marginal cost for inputs from its own inventory, and an above-marginal-cost demand price for external inputs. Similarly, any organization that previously obtained information inputs from the public domain at marginal cost will see an increase in cost if those inputs become subject to licensing. The presence or absence of sophisticated licensing mechanisms, whether technological or through collective rights organizations (CROs), will therefore affect the magnitude, but not direction, of the effects of increases in intellectual property on the payoffs to the strategies described here The negative incentive effects identified in this chapter persist even in an environment perfectly regulated by the most efficient CROs and contracts. The primary proponent of the position that effects on transaction cost-reducing mechanisms like CROs can justify stronger property rights in information than the traditional model would normally prescribe is Robert P Merges. See Robert P. Merges, *Contracting into Liability Rules: Intellectual Property Rights and Collective Rights Organizations*, 84 CAL. L. REV. 1293 (1996); Robert P. Merges, *Intellectual Property and the Costs of Commercial Exchange, A Review Essay*, 93 MICH. L. REV. 1570 (1995).

prefers commercial to noncommercial producers; prefers commercial producers who sell information goods to commercial producers who give information away for free in expectation of income-producing relationships; and prefers large scale organizations that integrate new production with management of existing information inventories to small scale independent producers. This latter prediction suggests a systematic loss of personal autonomy by individuals in society as they become increasingly dependent on a small number of commercial organizations to understand the world in which they live and the range of options open to them in the conduct of their lives. Large commercial organizations increasingly control the information environment and shape it either by reference to their owners' goals—partly displacing the individual's will with that of the owner—or by reference to a set of imperfect market incentives—impoverishing the information environment within which individuals must choose how to live their lives.

The negative liberty concern regarding freedom of speech is that property rights in information goods have practical effect only when they prohibit someone from using information in a way that that person wants to, and, as a practical matter, could use, but for the legal prohibition. This prohibition on making beneficial use of information undergirds the market in information goods, for that market is in fact a market in permissions to make such beneficial uses of information. What is important to understand is that, to the extent that a society bases its information environment on producers who rely on sale of permission—Mickeys and romantic maximizers—the society must commit to prevent everyone else from using the information those producers sell. In the United States, this commitment stands in stark tension with the constitutional commitment to refrain, insofar as possible, from regulating the use of information. Or, as Nimmer put it, the difference between Blackacre, whose ownership necessitates state prohibition on use of many pieces of land, and *Black Beauty*, whose ownership necessitates prohibition on use of many pieces of information, lies in the First Amendment.[37]

This negative liberty concern does not mean that copyright protection is automatically 'unconstitutional'. It does mean, however, that the same reasons that force legislatures and judges to be very careful when they enact or enforce rules that prevent individuals from accessing and communicating information apply with full force to any decision about whether to extend intellectual property rights. In the institutional structure of the United States, judges must pass on the reason and measure with which legislatures have enacted a set of intellectual property rules as they pass on other rules that restrict speech. Just as the government may tell a cable operator that it may not program certain of its channels, but must instead lease the channel to a

---

[37] Melville B Nimmer, *Does Copyright Abridge the First Amendment Guaranties of Free Speech and the Press?*, 17 UCLA L. REV. 1180, 1193 (1970).

broadcaster[38] or an unaffiliated program provider,[39] so, too, may the government tell a user that he or she may not copy or redistribute information that she would like to copy or distribute. But just as the government must explain its decision to a court with a great deal of care in the case of the constraint placed on the cable operator, so too must it explain its decision to constrain the user who wishes to access or communicate information.[40] Indeed, for those who believe that human beings have a greater claim to freedom of speech than corporations, the need for careful judicial scrutiny of intellectual property rights—which place significant constraints on individual users—is greater than the need to scrutinize media regulation measures that fall entirely on corporate actors.

The standard reaction to this First Amendment concern with property rights in information goods might be called the *Harper & Row* response. Faced with a First Amendment challenge to a copyright suit brought to prevent a journal from publishing politically relevant materials, the Supreme Court held that: '[T]he Framers intended copyright itself to be the engine of free expression. By establishing a marketable right to the use of one's expression, copyright supplies the economic incentive to create and disseminate ideas'.[41] In other words, the caution required when regulating speech through property rights has been built into the copyright law itself. Astonishingly tone-deaf to the censorial effects of its decision, and oblivious to the censorial role played by its own niggardly application of the copyright law's fair use defense in that case, the Court's majority minimised the First Amendment concern with copyright even as it recognized it. [42]

The vulgar quantitative version of the *Harper & Row* argument—copyright will lead to more information goods, and more is also better from the perspective of the First Amendment—has two important failings. First, it overstates the confidence with which one can assume that property rights increase production. As explained above, no standard economic model supports a general claim that increases in the amount of property rights will always increase, rather than decrease, aggregate production. At the very least, the vulgar quantitative version of the *Harper & Row* argument ought to require the government to show that the specific rule in question actually does increase, rather than impede, aggregate information production.

Second, and more fundamentally, the quantitative version of the *Harper & Row* argument conflates the production of 'information goods' with the production of information of the type that animates the free speech

---

[38] See *Turner Broad Sys., Inc. v. FCC*, 512 U.S. 622 (1994); *Turner Broad. Sys., Inc. v. FCC*, 520 U.S. 180 (1997).

[39] See *Denver Area Educ Television Consortium v FCC*, 518 U.S. 727 (1996).

[40] See Benkler, n. 3 above.

[41] *Harper & Row, Publishers, Inc v. Nation Enters.*, 471 U.S. 539, 558 (1985).

[42] Compare Justice Brennan's spirited dissent, in particular ibid at 589–90, 604 (Brennan, J., dissenting).

principle—information necessary for autonomous choice and self-governance. 'Information goods' are those instances of information that can be bought and sold as economic goods. What can or cannot be sold is contingent on the law and technology that make a given unit of information excludable.[43] The technological contingency upon which the excludability of information depends makes 'information goods' a technologically defined category. Information relevant for autonomous choice—whether personal or collective—is the product of a culturally contingent process of exchanging symbols that causes us to hold one or another set of beliefs about how we should organize our lives as individuals or as a polity. It is a culturally defined category. No necessary correlation exists between the cultural contingency that defines what information is relevant to autonomy or self-governance, and the technological-legal contingency that constrains what information can be demarcated and sold as goods. We, therefore, have no basis for assuming that rules put in place to take advantage of technologically-contingent tollbooth opportunities will encourage the production of information defined as important by its culturally-contingent 'political' valence.

There is a more sophisticated version of the *Harper & Row* argument.[44] This one suggests that information goods produced in reliance on market incentives are qualitatively better as sources of 'politically relevant information' than information produced by alternative sources. They are produced free of the bonds of patronage and government, the two alternative sources of funding for information producers. And they are produced in response to the market, that is, in response to what people define as relevant to themselves as consumers of information goods. In other words, commercial production is preferable to noncommercial, and market signals are preferable to other sources of incentive and direction to produce. My analysis of the effects of property in information on the organization of information production is most relevant to this sophisticated version of the *Harper & Row* defense of property in information. If, as my analysis suggests, intellectual property rights suffer from the Free Republic problem—they prefer some kinds of producers to others—then to sustain the sophisticated version of the *Harper & Row* response, one must prefer the Los Angeles Times to the users of the Free Republic forum.

I would argue that the systematic preference for commercial over noncommercial production is unwarranted. Noncommercial production is not primarily comprised of government or patronage-dependent propaganda. It includes in large measure the most independent and diverse sector of all, the amateur sector. If you hear of a news story or political scandal from a friend by the water cooler, you have received information from an amateur source

---

[43] See Romer, n. 9 above.

[44] A stark statement of this defense appears in GOLDSTEIN, n. 6 above, at 232. A more nuanced version can be found in Netanel, n. 3 above, at 342–62 (1996).

who relied on and interpreted other sources, which may have been more, or less, commercial. The selection of the materials for presentation, and the views expressed, were entirely unconstrained by either legal or market discipline. The participants in the Free Republic forum are beholden to no one when they select the stories on which they comment and when they write their opinions and exchange them. In this sense, amateur production is the source of the least constrained and most diverse information. In fact, some more organized and 'professional' portions of the noncommercial production system have created institutional frameworks to separate funding from content control. 'Tenure' and 'academic freedom' come to mind as obvious institutional devices to assure that scholars who rely on government or private funding are insulated from the preferences of the funding parties as to the information content they produce. To prefer commercial to noncommercial information production is to ignore, even in the political arena, the importance of production motives other than monetary appropriation based on sale of goods. It is also to ignore the ways our society has found to permit creators to live by their pens without depending on market success, and largely insulated from the power of the purse.

Second, unless the scale economies of information goods production (large first copy, small marginal per copy, costs) change radically, commercial producers will systematically 'aim for the middle', or for those products that will gain the most attention from the widest group of consumers. This is so for reasons explained in the body of literature critical of our polity's excessive reliance on commercial broadcasting.[45] Producing only for mass audiences should, it would seem, be mitigated by an environment that permits an infinite number of 'channels' that allow companies to focus on niche markets. Nonetheless, other scarcities, like human capital on the supply side and human attention on the demand side, suggest that a commercial product will be produced only if it has an audience large enough, given the intensity of its members' preferences and their wealth, to pay for the product's development and production costs. A noncommercial product, however, may be developed simply as an expression of its maker's thoughts, or to capture the attention of all those who value the expression highly enough to spend their time reading or listening, but who cannot or will not, alone or in concert, spend the money to buy it.

The cost of information inputs could, in an increasing-rights environment with low communications costs, supplant the high cost of mass communications equipment as the entry barrier to noncommercial producers and could lead to information-goods-sales-focused producers who cater to the mainstream only. This would homogenize discourse and eliminate the

---

[45] See, eg, C. Edwin Baker, *Giving the Audience What It Wants*, 58 Ohio St. L.J. 311 (1997); Jerome A. Barron, *Access to the Press—A New First Amendment Right*, 80 Harv. L. Rev. 1641 (1967); Owen M. Fiss, *Why the State?*, 100 Harv. L. Rev. 781 (1987).

opportunity created by the declining cost of communications both to decentralize information production and to give individuals the freedom to make their own information environment. Moreover, these effects cannot be cordoned off as pertaining only to 'new' uses of information, leaving unaffected the freedoms of users of older media. The new enclosure movement includes extensions of intellectual property rights into previously public domain areas, like raw data or time, and stronger rights that apply only to the digital environment. The former extensions constrain the freedom of users in any environment. Furthermore, once digital networks supplant mass mediated analog media as the core of our information environment, the rights-extensions into the 'exotic' area of digital information exchange may result in the loss not only of the liberating *opportunities* of the digitally networked environment, but also of *existing* freedoms that users enjoy because of the technological limitations that analog media place on the capacity of rights-holders to monitor use of, and prevent access to, their information goods.

Thirdly, if, in fact, enclosure benefits large scale organizations *at the expense* of small scale producers, then the *Harper & Row* argument can justify enclosure only if, *from a normative perspective*, information produced by such large scale organizations is preferable to information produced by small scale producers who do not own information inventories. There are two types of reasons to think the contrary.

First, what makes large scale organizations more robust in a dynamic increasing-rights environment is their ability to access and reutilize large pools of their own preexisting information. Increasing rights give these organizations reasons to search for ways to reuse information they own because they own it, not because it is the most suitable way to make the best new product given available human capital. Disney employees work with Mickey and Goofy. Warner Brothers employees work with Bugs and Daffy. What one would predict, in effect, is increased output of the Lethal Weapon IV, Mickey Mouse band aid, and 'best of' or blooper show variety. Organizations that do not own inventories see all available inputs of preexisting information at their (above marginal cost) market price, and will not likely have a similar bias. They are, in other words, more likely to produce using the most suitable information inputs given available human capital.

Furthermore, since producers will distort their production choices relative to consumer preferences based on the contents of their owned inventory, and since they will try to find the recombinations that will appeal to the largest possible segments, the probability that a given consumer will actually find his or her first-best preferred good is relatively low. Putative consumers faced with this behavior will therefore not invest in producing a first-best preference ordering of their interests. Instead, rational consumers will wait for producers to 'invent' a menu, and choose a second-best solution from the available menu.[46] Both the constraint created by reutilization of inventory and the rational absence of consumer first-best preferences weakens the *Harper & Row* argument that commercial producers effectively serve diversity by responding well to consumer preferences.

Secondly, a democratic deficit emerges when a small number of organizations or individuals gain too large a share of the power to control the content of the information available to the polity. This too has been a traditional criticism of commercial concentration in broadcasting,[47] and is exemplified by the reported suppression of a news report about security failures in Disney World prepared for 20/20, a news magazine aired on Disney's subsidiary, ABC.[48] An information production system composed of many small scale producers, commercial and noncommercial, will have less of a tendency to be dominated by narrow political or other agendas than one populated by a small number of large scale organizations.

IV. The Free Republic Problem Revisited: Conclusion

The Free Republic problem is one that all market-based democracies must face when they think of information policy. To make markets in information goods possible, governments must prevent many of their constituents from reading and speaking in ways that would be beneficial and feasible to them. This choice, to sacrifice individual interests in using information to further the social policy goal of making markets in information goods, raises serious normative concerns in liberal democracies.

These concerns are compounded when the effects of intellectual property rights on the organization of information production are considered. Introducing heterogeneity of production strategies into our understanding of the way that intellectual property affects the costs and benefits of information producers allows us to make a few observations previously obscure to the economic analysis of information production. Strong rights favor commercial producers who own large inventories of information goods, minimize their costs by reusing their owned inventory, and rely on sale of permission to use their information goods at above marginal cost prices to recoup the costs of production. Such rights hurt producers, both commercial and noncommercial, who do not own such large inventories, as well as producers who do not benefit from the strong rights because they do not rely on selling permission

---

[46] For a more detailed description of this problem as it arises in broadcasting, see Yochai Benkler, *Overcoming Agoraphobia: Building the Commons of the Digitally Networked Environment*, 11 HARV J.L. & TECH. 287, 365–68 (1998).

[47] See sources cited, n. 45 above. See also C. Edwin Baker, *Private Power, the Press, and the Constitution*, 10 CONST. COMMENT. 421 (1993).

[48] See Lawrie Mifflin, *An ABC News Reporter Tests the Boundaries of Investigating Disney and Finds Them*, NY. TIMES, Oct. 19, 1998, at C8.

to use the information to recoup their production costs. These effects suggest that increasing the scope and coverage of intellectual property rights will foster the development of large scale commercial information producers who benefit most from these rights.

My analysis suggests that broadening intellectual property rights may perpetuate, or even extend, the problematic aspects of the mass media model of producing our information environment, even as the communication costs of distributing information that underlay that model's emergence are disappearing. The new entry barriers, unlike the old, are not a result of economies of scale imposed by the cost of large scale presses or powerful transmitters, but rather (like poorly conceived spectrum policy) by a regulatory regime, the rapidly expanding enclosure of the public domain.

Responding to pressures from rent-seeking inventory owners, relying on questionable economic pronouncements with little basis in the standard economics of information production, and blind to the normative concerns involved in enforcing property rights in information, Congress, other legislatures, and many courts push forward to enclose increasing portions of the public domain. Recognizing the Free Republic problem, however, requires that we adopt a studied skepticism toward new rights in information goods and the imposition of new restraints on users' capacity to access information. New rules that enclose the public domain ought to be rigorously tested to show both the likelihood that a particular proposed rule will increase aggregate production, and to understand who will be producing more under this new rule and who will be producing less. Even if a rule seems likely to increase aggregate production—all negative effects considered—the aggregate welfare effects must be weighed against the probable costs to freedom of speech and diversity of discourse.

PART IV

IMPLEMENTING INNOVATION POLICY FOR THE INFORMATION AGE

The previous sections made a strong case for expanding intellectual property protection to respond to technological change in ways that are sensitive to the needs of users and subsequent innovators. The main issue for Part IV is how that balance should best be achieved. Thomas Dreier argues that as continental and Anglo-American intellectual property regimes have coalesced over time, they have developed ample tools for balancing public and private concerns. Adjusting rights within this framework creates law that is coherent and capable of tracking developments as they occur. In contrast, Bernt Hugenhotz, Susan DeSanti, and Hanns Ullrich argue that other areas of law are also important sources of innovation policy. Bernt Hugenholtz looks at values emanating from human rights laws; Susan DeSanti makes the case for competition policies embodied in national antitrust legislation; while Hanns Ullrich looks at the international competitive environment.

BALANCING PROPRIETARY AND PUBLIC DOMAIN INTERESTS: INSIDE OR OUTSIDE OF PROPRIETARY RIGHTS?

THOMAS DREIER*

As the previous chapters have demonstrated, there is little consensus—possibly less than ever before in the history of intellectual property protection—as to what constitutes an adequate balance between proprietary intellectual property rights and the public interest. Such debates are by no means new. Ever since the inception of modern intellectual property law, the monopoly character of exclusive rights has been subjected to examination. In repeated waves of criticism, both the rationale for granting intellectual property protection to intangibles and the details of this protection, have undergone scrutiny. So far, intellectual property rights have more than resisted these attacks: indeed, the last decades have seen a trend of ever increasing protection. The crucial question now is whether intellectual property can withstand the attacks of the future. The answer depends on the extent to which intellectual property law will be capable of accommodating nonproprietary interests and on the extent to which public values must be safeguarded by legal instruments outside of intellectual property protection.

What generally holds true for all intellectual property rights (patents, trademarks, and design rights, to name just the most important ones), is particularly true for copyright law. Here, the development of digital and networking communication technologies has made the current debates

* Professor of Law, University of Karlsruhe.

particularly heated. Thus, the present wave of criticism can be traced back to the case of computer programs, which seem to have been the first object of protection of a digital nature. Once the die was cast in favor of copyright at the international level, the fiercely debated question was how far this protection should go: where to draw the line between proprietary and user interests; between the interests of market leaders and second sources; and between program creators and providers of value-added products and services. More recently, databases have become the object of concern. The drafting of European-style sui generis protection provoked a storm of protest amongst scientists, libraries and other user communities in the United States. Although European user groups did not initially voice objections, they eventually joined their American counterparts in raising a general question about how to adapt copyright laws first developed for an analog world to a newly digitized and networked environment.

In some ways, however, it is curious that these debates are so intense. After all, copyright law has always proved able to adapt to new subject matter (photography, phonograms, film) and to new dissemination techniques (radio, television, magnetic tape recorders, VCRs, copy machines, cable and satellite). Perhaps the problem is that this time, the changes are more far-reaching in nature. Digitization and networking affect both the subject matter of protection and the means of its dissemination. They affect subject matter because all categories of protected works can be transformed into a digital format that permits the creation of new composite—often multmedia—works. They affect dissemination by opening up the possibility of easy copying at low (or virtually no) cost, and in almost no time. Finally, at least in theory, works need to be fixed only once; worldwide demand can then be satisfied through networking.

As a result of these developments, rightholders are caught in a bind. While they hope to benefit from the new markets that these technologies open, they also see the technologies as associated with a loss of control. Thus, they are left with a fear that the application of traditional copyright provisions to the digital and networking context will lead to severe underprotection. Given this point of view, it is logical for them to call for a strengthening of legal protection, and to argue that the application of traditional copyright principles to the digital context turns the mere use of a protected work, such as reading or viewing, into infringement—into a form of reproduction that is subject to the rightholder's consent. In contrast, users of copyrighted works reason that because these activities are copyright-free in the analog world, the application (or strengthening) of existing principles will lead to overprotection and will undermine the delicate balance copyright law strikes between proprietary and public or other interests.

To put this in economic terms, we appear to be faced with two competing scenarios, both negative. On the one hand, it is claimed that insufficient protection will mean that valuable subject matter will be withheld from distribution in digital form and via the Internet. This, in turn, might jeopardize investment in digital and networking technology. On the other hand, it is claimed that strengthening protection will annihilate the benefits created by new technologies: that it will exclude users from activities they were permitted in the analog environment, and that value-added activities beneficial to society as a whole will be blocked.

Undoubtedly, both views suffer from a certain degree of short-sightedness. Emphasis on the proprietary nature of intellectual property rights neglects the conditions under which copyrighted materials are used. Conversely, emphasis on public policy interests ignores the conditions necessary for their creation. Under both perspectives, the 'public' interest is increasingly seen as something outside of, and opposed to, copyright: either the proprietary aspect embodied in copyright seems to be opposed to public policy considerations from without, or the public policy aspect is seen as threatened by the copyright monopoly and thus perceived as something to be distinguished from copyright considerations.

To complicate matters, while the term 'public interest' is often cited, there is a certain vagueness inherent in it. Who is, or who represents, the 'public'? In some instances, the reference is to the 'general' public, ie to society as a whole. In other instances, the reference is to the interest of a certain subgroup of society: for example, end-users, who are viewed as in opposition to the interests of the rightholders. Furthermore, the label 'public' is sometimes used to mask private—often commercial—interests; by the same token, denial of a 'public interest' can be a mask for unfettered individualistic interests. In fact, post-modern discourse has made it clear that every one of us forms part of several 'publics', each of which has its own unique interests.

The only way out of this confusion is through a fair and open description of the criteria entailed in describing a position as 'in the "public" interest'; it being understood that 'public' may refer both to society as a whole and to various subgroups within it. Moreover, in discussing the accommodation of 'public' interests, it should be borne in mind that copyright law accommodates more than just proprietary and user interests; it also sets a framework for the relationship between competitors by serving as the basis for trading rights in protected works—for securing, dividing and exploiting markets. In sum, it does not do justice to the full reality of the legal copyright framework to view copyright as only a property right isolated from any public policy considerations, or to view it merely as a disguised criminal law that 'polices' the average citizen's use of protected material.

It is not, however, the purpose of this chapter to judge these different points of view, to balance the interests at stake, or even to enter into a discussion of details. Rather, the purpose is to describe how, inside and outside of the body of copyright law, conflicting interests are—and can be—accommodated, and to show that as a general rule, the 'public' interest is best safeguarded within intellectual property rather than through other positive laws. Part I compares the Anglo-American copyright system to the *droit d'auteur* system characteristic of continental Europe and demonstrates the remarkable convergence they have achieved, especially regarding the variety of interests (including those of proprietor, user, and competitor) that these rights are understood as furthering. Part II demonstrates that in both systems, balancing these interests internally (within the body of the law creating the right) is preferable for a variety of reasons: because copyright law already includes a series of carefully constructed accommodations; because there is value in preserving a coherent body of law on information policy; and because antitrust law is too blunt an instrument to draw fine lines at the boundaries of copyright protection that are required. Part III illustrates these points with the specific example of allocating rights in digital products.

I. Convergence of the Anglo-American and Continental European Traditions

Despite the fact that international law uses the term 'copyright' to refer to both the *droit d'auteur* approach to intellectual property protection familiar on the Continent and to the exclusive rights regimes found in the United Kingdom, the United States, and the Commonwealth states, it is important to recall that there are fundamental differences between the two systems. Somewhat simplified, it may be said that the Anglo-American system—the one I shall henceforth refer to as the 'copyright' system—has retained much of its initial character as a limited monopoly, expressly granted in order to serve the public interest. In contrast, the continental system—which I shall call the '*droit d'auteur*' system—has developed in the course of the nineteenth century under the influence of German idealistic philosophy and French legal doctrine, from a mere printer's and publisher's right into a right based on natural justice, a right that is now understood as emanating from the inalienable personality of the author.[1]

But notwithstanding these historical differences, both systems have from their inceptions been concerned with the same set of interests. In both cases, the great debates have centered on the merits of protection, its advantages and disadvantages; the quest for the right balance between the scope of the monopoly granted to the individual and its effects on the dissemination and availability of protected subject matter. In both, each new technology has

---

[1] A comprehensive comparative analysis of the history of the two systems from a European perspective is undertaken by ALAIN STROWEL, DROIT D'AUTEUR ET COPYRIGHT (1993). See also Jane Ginsburg, *A Tale of Two Copyrights: Literary Property in Revolutionary France and America*, 147 REVUE INTERNATIONALE DES DROITS DE L'ANTIQUITE 125 (1991).

spawned political fights between creators and those who advocate a broad public domain. Moreover, both have generated an abundant theoretical literature on the rationale for exclusive protection of goods that are, by their very nature, ubiquitous: appropriable by third parties without depriving the initial creator of his or her own use.[2]

In the copyright system, the importance attributed to public policy considerations is explicitly enshrined in the US Constitution, which directs Congress to grant exclusive monopoly rights in order to benefit the general public.[3] This understanding has been carried into case law, where it is used, sometimes in combination with constitutional guarantees, such as the right to freedom of speech, to determine the exact scope of exclusive copyright prerogatives conferred upon authors and rightholders by the Copyright Act.[4] However, it is important to note that this approach does not go so far as to justify a *general* 'right' of end-users to obtain free or even easy access to all creative material.

In contrast to copyright, *droit d'auteur*'s public policy rationale is harder to discern. This view anchors the rationale for granting exclusive protection in the personality of the author and has its roots in the natural law tradition that is now reflected in the Universal Declaration of Human Rights.[5] Under this *'droit moral'* (moral rights) approach, the author is seen as having full control over the work and as having no obligation to publish or exploit it. By deeming creative works *'la propriété la plus sacrée'* (the most sacred property), *droit d'auteur* regimes make proprietary interests appear to be paramount. But this view needs to be corrected in several respects.

First, it should be noted that the moral rights ramification of *'la propriété la plus sacrée'* was not originally the exclusive reason for granting *droit d'auteur* protection. Thus, seminal French intellectual property laws do not mention *droit moral* at all. Rather, they were exclusively concerned with exploitation rights, aiming to remedy the problems of music, literature and opera 'pirating'. Their goal was to give artists adequate benefits from the

---

[2] See, eg, Zechariah Chafee, *Reflections on the Law of Copyright*, 45 COLUM. L. REV. 503 (Part I) & 719 (Part II) (1945); Stephen Breyer, *The Uneasy Case for Copyright: A Study on Copyright in Books, Photocopies and Computer Programs*, 84 HARV. L. REV. 281 (1970); Seve Ljungman, *The Function of Copyright in the Present Day Society*, 88 REVUE INTERNATIONALE DES DROITS DE L'ANTIQUITE 51 (1976); William Landes & Richard Posner, *An Economic Analysis of Copyright Law*, 18 J. LEGAL STUD. 325 (1989); Wendy Gordon, *Fair Use as Market Failure. A Structural and Economic Analysis of the Betamax Case and its Predecessors*, 82 COLUM. L. REV. 1600 (1982); GILLIAN DAVIES, COPYRIGHT AND THE PUBLIC INTEREST 135 (1994).

[3] U.S. CONST. Art. I, § 8 empowers Congress '*to promote the progress of Science . . . by securing for limited times to authors . . . the exclusive right to their respective writings*' (emphasis added).

[4] 17 U.S.C §§ 100. See, eg, *Harper & Row Publishers, Inc. v. Nation Enterprises*, 471 U.S. 539, 554 (1985); *Mazer v. Stein*, 347 U.S. 201, 219 (1954).

[5] Under Art. 27 (2) of the Universal Declaration of Human Rights, 'everyone has the right to the protection of the moral and material interests resulting from any scientific, literary or artistic production of which he is the author': G.A. Res. 217A, UN Doc. A/810 (1948)

proceeds of the exploitation of their works, so that they could afford to create new works for the instruction and enlightenment of the public.[6] Similarly, other early laws were directed at giving publishers sufficient lead time to recapture their investments and earn adequate profits through the exploitation of published works.[7]

Secondly, while it is undoubtedly true that at a later stage the philosophical emphasis shifted to *droit moral*, the underlying reason for recognizing proprietary rights, at least in Germany, was probably economic.[8] At the time of the shift, Germany had one common language area and an elaborate network of commercial roads. However, politically it was splintered into a great number of territories, each having its own legislation and judicial authorities. As a result, there was an urgent need for transborder intellectual property protection. In the absence of international conventions, the politically most expedient way to compel states to adopt intellectual property rights was to emphasize their natural law quality. Rather than forcing states to 'create' intellectual property protection, this move allowed states simply to 'recognize' rights.[9] In sum, then, the aim in Europe was not so different from that of the United States: *droit d'auteur* secured a framework for orderly book dissemination, it excluded piracy, offered legal certainty to publishers, and thus benefitted the public, which could then obtain access to publishers' products.

In addition, there are several instances where the structure of *droit d'auteur* protection is explicitly based on public policy considerations. Consider, for example, the Berne Convention. It is certainly more influenced by continen-

---

[6] See Décret des 13–19 janvier 1791 relatif aux spectacles et Décret des 19–24 juillet 1793 concerning writers, composers and painters. For the historical development in France, see, eg ANDRÉ LUCAS & HENRI-JACQUES LUCAS, PROPRIÉTÉ LITTÉRAIRE ET ARTISTIQUE 11 (1994).

[7] In France and Germany, authors' rights legislation came to include moral rights as such only in 1957 and 1965, respectively, in both cases to reflect judicial developments. The protection of investment made by publishers had been the motive for the grant of the earlier privileges, such as the first privilege granted to Johann von Speyer by the Signoria of Venice in 1469. See *generally* LUDWIG GIESEKE, DIE GESCHICHTLICHE ENTWICKLUNG DES URHEBERRECHTS IN DEUTSCHLAND (1957); LUDWIG GIESEKE, VOM PRIVILEG ZUM URHEBERRECHT (1995); JOSEF KOHLER, URHEBERRECHT AN SCHRIFTWERKEN UND VERLAGSRECHT (1907); GERHARD SCHRICKER AND MARTIN VOGEL, URHEBERRECHT Einleitung, nn. 52 et seq. (2nd ed. 1999).

[8] For a detailed history of *droit moral*, see generally, STIG STROMHOLM, LE DROIT MORAL DE L'AUTEUR EN DROIT ALLEMAND, FRANÇAIS ET SCANDINAVE Vol. I and II/1 (1967), and Vol. II (1973). It should be noted that *droit moral* is part of almost all continental European states. In 1988, it was recognized in the United Kingdom. See Copyright, Designs and Patents Act 1988, s. 77 (Eng.). Since its 1928 revision, Art. 6bis of the Revised Berne Convention obliges Member States to grant authors 'the right to claim authorship of the work and to object to any distortion, mutilation or other modification of, or other derogatory action in relation to, the said work, which would be prejudicial to his honour or reputation'. See Berne Convention for the Protection of Literary and Artistic Works, September 9, 1886, Art. 6bis.

[9] Thus, the reproduction of books without the consent of the author (so-called '*unerlaubter Büchernachdruck*') appeared to be illegal even absent a grant of a particular privilege to the author and/or publisher. See, eg, GERHARD SCHRICKER & MARTIN VOGEL, URHEBERRECHT Einleitung, n. 59 (2nd ed. 1999).

tal European than by Anglo-American thinking.[10] Yet it protects works by non-Berne Convention nationals only when they are published for the first time (or within 30 days after their first publication abroad) within a Member State. The reason for this limitation is clearly related to the public interest and not to the rights of authors: by making the benefits of the Convention contingent on local publication, non-member nationals are encouraged to make their works known to Berne Convention nationals.[11] Likewise, the preferential treatment granted to developing countries in the Annex to the Berne Convention adopted at the Paris Conference in 1971, reflects the special educational needs of these countries.[12] Finally, the Convention permits Member States to create other public interest safeguards. These include compulsory licensing provisions, such as the traditional sound recording license[13] and the modern restraint favoring collective dealings.[14] Finally, even when countries rely on *droit d'auteur* to justify the existence of copyright, they nevertheless see constitutional freedoms as the basis for imposing legal limitations on the exclusive rights recognized.[15]

These commonalities in the rationale and theory for protection have led to an astonishing convergence of the two systems at the practical level as well. In some ways, the convergence has favored proprietary interests. Thus, for example, the copyright system has adopted moral rights protection to a certain, albeit limited, extent.[16] But the main areas of convergence have been public-regarding. For example, both systems now recognize, within the body of the legislation creating the exclusive rights regimes, a first sale doctrine that mediates between the interests of creators and end-users.[17] That is, both the

[10] See, eg, SAM RICKETSON, THE BERNE CONVENTION FOR THE PROTECTION OF LITERARY AND ARTISTIC WORKS: 1886–1986 39 et seq. (1987); Berne Convention for the Protection of Literary and Artistic Works, Sept. 9, 1886, *as last revised*, July 24, 1971 (*amended* 1979), 828 U.N.T.S. 221.

[11] See Berne Convention, n. 10 above, Art. 3(1)(b), (4). Regarding the reason for this provision see, eg Federal Supreme Court of Germany, IIC 1976, vol. 7, 134, at 137 ('a publication of the work which provides sufficient opportunity for attracting the attention of the public counts; the work must be accessible and attainable by the public'); similarly, Federal Supreme Court of Germany, IIC 1973, vol. 3, 245, at 249 ('the decisive criterion for the publication of a motion picture is not causing the film to become well-known by presentation, but rather the fact that the motion picture is released for regular distribution and thereby made accessible to the general public'). See also WILHELM NORDEMANN & VINCK HERTIN, INTERNATIONAL COPYRIGHT AND NEIGHBORING RIGHTS LAW art. 3/4 BC, n. 8 (1990).

[12] See, eg, ADOLF DIETZ, URHEBERRECHT UND ENTWICKLUNGSLANDER (1981).

[13] See, eg, Berne Convention, n. 10 above, Art. 13(1) (on compulsory licenses for sound recordings).

[14] See, eg, German Copyright Administration Law, September 9, 1965, §§ 11(1), 12 (requiring collecting societies to 'grant exploitation rights or authorizations to any person so requesting on equitable terms in respect of the rights they administer').

[15] See below.

[16] See 17 U.S.C. § 106A; 15 U.S.C. § 1125(a), which are cited by the USA as conforming to the moral rights requirements of the Berne Convention, n. 10 above, Art. 6bis.

[17] See, eg, 17 U S.C. § 109(a); German Copyright Act, September 9, 1965, § 17(2). In Europe, the community-wide exhaustion results from the fundamental freedoms of movements of goods and of services see, 25 March 1957, Treaty Establishing the European Economic Community,

copyright and the *droit d'auteur* systems strengthen the proprietary aspect of the law by distinguishing a property interest in the intangible content (the work) from a property interest in the material copy (the book). Since, as a rule, the transfer of the property in the material copy does not entail any transfer of rights to the intangible work, the rightholder continues to control the intangible work, even after he or she has parted with a copy. However, under the first sale doctrine, the rightholder cannot object to the resale of a material copy once it has been put on the market with his or her consent.[18] If, then, a user is willing to wait, he or she can gain access to the contents of copyrighted works without the author's express consent—by reading a used copy after it is sold or given away by the initial purchaser, or by patronizing a public library.[19]

Similarly, both systems now increasingly see intellectual property rights as part of the legislation that sets the framework for commercial activities. The scope of protection is thus made as broad as needed to create incentives to production, but not so broad as to hinder access and competition any more than is necessary to achieve the incentive goal.[20] To adjust the balance, several countries, including some with a *droit d'auteur* tradition, rely on doctrines like misuse: exclusivity gives rightholders flexibility in the marketplace to earn back returns on their investment, but the misuse doctrine permits courts to step in and limit these prerogatives when a rightholder has used his or her proprietary interest in an abusive way.[21]

261 U.N.T.S. 140, Arts 28, 30 and 49 (formerly Arts 30, 36 and 59); Case 78/70, *Deutsche Grammophon v. Metro*, [1971] E.C.R. 487; Cases 55, 57/80, *Musik-Vertrieb membran v. GEMA*, [1981] E.C.R. 147. Admittedly, former French authors' rights law contained a so-called '*droit de destination*', which gave the author the right to control any use act, including the act of further distribution. However, this right seems to have never been enforced in practice.

[18] Exceptions to this rule mainly concern works of the visual arts. See, eg, *Urheberrechtsgesetz* 9.9.1965 (BGB1.1 S. 1273) (hereinafter the German Copyright Act) § 44 (2), which allows the owner of the original of a work of the visual arts to publicly display it, provided the author has not excluded this right at the time of the sale of the work of art. The same is true in the USA, see 17 U.S.C. § 106(6) (giving the artist the right to control public displays of the work).

[19] The European Union Directive on Rental and Lending Right allows Member States to derogate from the exclusive rental rights of copies sold in respect of public lending, provided that authors obtain remuneration for such lending: Council Directive 92/100/EEC, arts. 1(1), 5(2), 1992 O.J. L346.

[20] See Ullrich, Chapter 15 below. The maximization of quality would also seem to be a desirable goal, but it is largely ignored, except in so far as market mechanisms promote quality; otherwise both systems rely entirely on the selective choices made by creators.

[21] See, eg, *Code de la propriete intellectuelle* (Law No. 92–597 of July 1, 1992, J.O., July 3, 1992, p. 8801); (hereinafter the French Law on the Intellectual Property Code) art. L. 121–3 regarding an abuse after the death of the author of the moral rights, and art. L. 122–9 of the same Law, of exploitation rights. Although the doctrine of misuse of rights is generally known in German civil law as well, it seems not to have been applied to moral rights cases in German copyright law, where, however, the aspect of misuse might influence the general weighing of conflicting interests and tip the balance to the disfavor of the rightholder. As to contractual relationships between the author and a user of the work, see the German Copyright Act, § 39 (2) which

The trend towards convergence of the two systems is especially apparent at the international level in the Agreement on Trade-Related Aspects of Intellectual Property Rights (the TRIPS Agreement) and its inclusion in the General Agreement on Tariffs and Trade.[22] The TRIPS Agreement is significant because it demonstrates a willingness to set aside the irreconcilable aspects of national intellectual property regimes, such as the wider scope given in Europe to moral rights and US public policy considerations which favor nonproprietary interests, in order to increase trade, employment, and economic benefits. Of course, the old differences are likely to resurface as new forms of use of protected material are considered. Indeed, this is exactly what seems to have happened in the debate on digital copyright, where American users, libraries and telecommunications companies are demanding more attention be paid to the public interest, whereas the Europeans have been strengthening exclusive rights.[23] But for the purposes of this chapter, there still seems to be enough common ground to consider the instruments for balancing interests as addressing a single problem, with solutions applicable to regimes throughout both copyright and *droit d'auteur* systems.

II. Balancing Proprietary and Other Interests: Legislative Techniques

Having established that *droit d'auteur* and copyright systems share similar sets of concerns, we now take up the primary issue, which is determining how national legislation should balance these interests. Until now, and irrespective of system differences, most of the balancing has been achieved within the framework of intellectual property law (the fair use and misuse limitations discussed above are examples); the question is whether this strategy should continue, or whether nonproprietary interests should be protected externally, through such devices as contract and/or competition law.

A. Balancing within intellectual property

Within the bodies of both copyright and *droit d'auteur*, there are a variety of mechanisms for accommodating interests. Balance can be achieved by carefully defining the subject matter of protection, the prerequisites of originality, the idea/expression dichotomy, and the rules governing derivative works; by limiting the duration of the monopoly; by restricting the scope of the

expressly stipulates that 'modifications in the work and its title which the author cannot in good faith refuse shall be permissible'. For an American comparison, see, eg, *Lasercomb v. Reynolds*, 911 F.2d 970 (4th Cir. 1990) (enunciating a doctrine of copyright misuse).

[22] Agreement on Trade-Related Aspects of Intellectual Property Rights, April 15, 1994, Marrakesh Agreement Establishing the World Trade Organization, Annex 1C, 33 I.L.M. 1197 (1994) (hereinafter TRIPS Agreement).

[23] See, eg, Council Directive 96/9/EC, arts. 7 et seq., 1996 O.J. L77.

exclusive rights granted; and, most important, by laying down exceptions and limitations to the exclusive rights. Each mechanism has its strengths and weaknesses.

1. Subject matter

One key limitation is contained in the definition of subject matter.[24] Not every intangible object resulting from a human creative activity is protected by law; admittedly, at times such an exclusion from protectable subject matter (examples are sports plays and circus acts)[25] is rather arbitrary. More important, however, is the criterion of originality. In some countries, originality means little more than 'not copied';[26] but in others, this requirement excludes trivial creations, usually on the theory that protection of minor productions would divert creators from the socially desirable goal of preparing works of greater originality and would at the same time hinder creations which draw from pre-existing material.[27] Likewise, the idea/expression dichotomy—or comparable instruments of national copyright doctrine—define the border between what can be appropriated and what cannot.[28] Creators must be able to use ideas and derive inspiration from protected works, for otherwise innovative activity would come to an end or be unduly stifled. At the same time, however, there are limits on the amount of taking that is permitted: receiving inspiration is not thought to require the right to freely appropriate, adapt, or mod-

---

[24] The classic definition of copyrightable subject matter as contained in the Title, Preamble and Art. 1 of the Revised Berne Convention, n. 10 above, refers to 'literary and artistic works', thus excluding inventions (covered by patent laws), trademarks (covered by trademark laws) and discoveries (not covered by intellectual property laws at all). National laws sometimes exclude subject matter which might be regarded as 'creative' in a broader sense, such as representations of performing artists (in authors' rights jurisdictions mostly covered by a neighboring right); see Art. 7 of the Rome Convention on the Protection of Performing Artists, Producers of Phonograms and Broadcasting Organizations, Oct. 26, 1961, 496 U.N.T.S. 43, as well as Chapter II of the WIPO Performances and Phonograms Treaty (WPPT), Dec. 20, 1996, 36 I.L.M. 76, Art. 16(2) (1997). The American tradition is the reverse: it includes objects which from a *droit d'auteur* perspective appear as objects of neighboring rights into the ambit of copyright protection. See 17 U.S.C. § 102(b).

[25] See, eg, *National Basketball Association v. Motorola, Inc*, 105 F.3d 841 (2d Cir. 1997). Cf French Copyright Act, art. L. 112–2(4) (now expressly *including* 'circus numbers').

[26] This has been especially true for UK copyright law. See, eg, *University of London Press v. University Tutorial Press* 2 Ch. 601, 608 (1916); *Macmillan v. Cooper* 93 L.J.P.C. 113, 117 (1923). For the standard in US law, see *Feist Publications, Inc. v. Rural Telephone Service Co., Inc.*, 499 U.S. 340, 345 (1991).

[27] See, eg, Thomas Dreier & Gunnar Karnell, *Originality of the Copyrighted Work: A European Perspective*, 39 J. Copyright Soc'y U.S. 289 (1992). See also *Gracen v. Bradford Exchange*, 698 F.2d 300, 304 (7th Cir. 1983) (Posner J.) ('the concept of originality in copyright law has as one would expect a legal rather than aesthetic function—to prevent overlapping claims').

[28] See, eg, *Harper & Row Publishers, Inc. v. Nation Enterprises*, 471 U.S. 539, 556 (1985); *Baker v. Selden*, 101 U.S. 99, 103 (1879). Comparable doctrines, such as in Germany and France, focus on the distinction between form and content. See, eg, Gerhard Schricker & Ulrich Loewenheim, Urheberrecht § 2 nn. 27 et seq. (2nd ed.1987): Pierre-Yves Gautier, Propriété Littéraire et Artistique 50 et seq. (3rd ed. 1999).

ify existing works. Rather, most intellectual property laws require the consent of the holder of the rights in the first work to prepare a derivative work, or at least to market one.[29]

2. Duration

Another important limitation contained within both *droit d'auteur* and copyright legislation is the term of the exclusive right. This limitation is a marked departure from the way in which property rights in tangible objects are handled: there, rights are not temporally circumscribed. The idea in intellectual property law is that once the author (and, where the term extends *post mortem auctoris*, his or her heirs) has had sufficient opportunity to exploit a particular work, that work should fall into the public domain. In this way, both competing publishers and the public benefit, for the end of the monopoly provides an opportunity to produce new editions at a cheaper price and hence with wider circulation.

Admittedly, duration has tended to rise over time, and is much longer for creative works than for industrial property.[30] It can also be argued that current terms of protection postpone the occasion for improving innovations for far too long;[31] that what may be appropriate for one kind of work (novels, which can have a highly entertaining character) may be inappropriate for another (computer programs, which in general have a highly functional character);[32] and that what is best for most works within a category need not necessarily be true for all of them (adaptations of books of information substantially add to public knowledge, whereas society has a comparatively small interest in the incremental improvement of novels). Moreover, the economics of innovation cannot explain terms measured by the length of the author's life, which is the most common measurement in both *droit d'auteur* and copyright systems.[33]

However, for administrative reasons, some broad generalizations must be made. Moreover, the economic implications of changing an existing term can be difficult to assess, as a particular change can have both positive and

[29] See, eg, 17 U.S.C. § 106(2); French Law on the Intellectual Property Code, art. L. 122–4. Section 23 of the German Copyright Act permits the preparation, but not the dissemination of a derivative work other than a work of cinematography, visual art, or architecture.

[30] See Council Directive 93/98/EEC, 1993 O.J. L290 (harmonizing the term of protection of copyright and certain related rights); 17 USC § 101 (the 1998 Sonny Bono Copyright Term Extension Act).

[31] See the discussion of the 1983 Draft Treaty on the Legal Protection of Computer Software, prepared by the International Bureau Group of Experts, Copyright 1993, at 276 (suggesting that the duration of protection for software should not exceed 10 to 15 years 'because, amongst other reasons, a longer period would create difficulties for the users of the software in view of the need to further develop the software').

[32] See WIPO Model Provisions on the Protection of Computer Programs, Copyright 1978, § 6 (1977) (protection for 20 years after commercialization and a maximum of 25 years after creation of the software); 35 U.S.C. § 154 (20 year term for patents in the USA).

[33] See, eg, 17 U.S.C. §§ 302(a) & (b).

negative implications for the overall economy. Thus, while shortening the term enables producers to come up with new, and most likely cheaper editions (which appeals to the public interest in access), it generates less income and thus may be a disincentive to invest in new creations. Conversely, a longer term generates extra income (which appeals to the public interest in encouraging economic activity and increasing knowledge), but it forces users—including future innovators—to spend more.

In the end, attaining an 'appropriate', 'just', or 'adequate' balance is not only a question of adapting the term to innovation needs: the decision is ultimately political. Here, it must be recalled that reality follows its own imperatives. For example, the prime reason given for prolonging the term of protection within the EU was the desire for harmonization. While economic considerations in each country played a role in determining duration, what won in Europe was the idea of the single market. The concept of using law to shape the creative environment had to step back in the political process.

3. Scope of exclusive rights granted

The scope of the exclusive rights (ie, the limits of what counts as infringement) is also an important tool for striking the balance between proprietary interests on the one hand, and competitors and public user interests on the other.[34] The set of exclusive rights granted to the author tends to be defined as rather complete where the property aspect is the starting point (or, using a metaphor, as solid land which possibly contains some lakes), whereas the author is granted only a number of distinct use rights where the aspect of public policy is emphasized (which resembles more the idea of an ocean with several islands, many of them connected and several of them as big as continents).

It might be thought that the general theory utilized will make a substantive difference in the level of protection accorded. Thus, it could be argued that where the property aspect is the starting point, the legislature will tend to define the scope of exclusive rights rather broadly; when there is doubt, the courts will grant authors protection by way of a broad statutory interpretation. But where the general theory emphasizes public policy, the legislature will be reluctant to extend new rights and courts will interpret existing ones narrowly. It is not, however, clear that the scope of protection turns on the theoretic approach that a country adopts. Outcomes largely tend to be the same in both cases. Differences appear to be largely a matter of national drafting technique: the same level of accommodation between public and private interests can be achieved under either regime.

---

[34] See, eg, 17 U.S.C. § 106; German Copyright Act, §§ 15 et seq.; French Law on the Intellectual Property Code, art. L. 122–1 et seq.

4. Exceptions and limitations

However, for both *droit d'auteur* and copyright, the key instruments for fine-tuning property rights and balancing interests are statutory 'exceptions' and 'limitations' (again, the choice of terminology appears to have little importance). User interests typically accommodated in this way include news reporting;[35] critical analysis and comment;[36] scientific research;[37] the needs of administrative and judicial proceedings;[38] communications by certain favored user groups;[39] and protection of privacy and facilitation of private use.[40] Competing proprietary interests, such as the interests of cable and satellite companies, restaurants, and jukebox operators are likewise safeguarded through limitations, although these are sometimes more circumscribed in nature, particularly in *droit d'auteur* systems.[41]

Of course, there is some overlap among these interests. Since many (in the analog world, most) end-uses are outside the scope of protection, the beneficiaries of these exceptions are the entities that reproduce, distribute, or communicate the copy of a work to the end-user. In such cases, however, the general public benefits, albeit indirectly. For example, a producer who need not ask permission to produce and offer a work, who may even be exempt from payment, benefits the public because he will not withhold the work from public enjoyment and may make it available at a lower price. Even limitations that directly benefit competitors, such as the decompilation privilege in the EU computer program directive, are public-regarding in that they facilitate access and achieve cost reductions.[42]

The exceptions and limitations provisions of both *droit d'auteur* and copyright are, on the whole, tailored to specific conflicts of interest. These can be roughly classified into three categories: exceptions that serve overriding public interests (such as constitutionally protected interests); those serving less crucial public interests; and those that respond to situations of perceived

---

[35] See, eg, German Copyright Act, §§ 48–50 (public speeches, newspaper articles and broadcast commentaries, news reporting).

[36] See, eg, German Copyright Act, § 51 (quotations).

[37] See, eg, German Copyright Act, §§ 53(1) & (2), 87(c) (copying for personal scientific use, or to be included in personal files). In the USA, all of the interests cited above are accommodated through fair use. See 17 U.S.C. § 107 (preamble).

[38] See, eg, German Copyright Act, § 45 (administration of justice and public safety).

[39] See, eg, German Copyright Act, §§ 46, 52 (collections for religious, school or instructional use; certain public communication); 17 U.S.C. §§ 108 (libraries), 110(1) (instructional use), 110(3) (religious services), 110(8) (transmissions to the blind).

[40] See, eg, German Copyright Act, §§ 53 et seq. (reproduction for private and other personal uses).

[41] Competitor limitations are particularly prevalent in the copyright system. See, eg, 17 U.S.C. §§ 111 (cable transmissions), 116 (jukeboxes), 119 (satellite transmissions). Compare German Copyright Act, §§ 55, 56, 58 (limited use ancillary to the operation of certain commercial enterprises).

[42] See Council Directive 91/250/EEC, arts. 5 (3), 6, 1991 O.J. L122 (on the legal protection of computer programs). For the purpose of these provisions, see, eg, BRIDGET CZARNOTA & ROBERT HART, LEGAL PROTECTION OF COMPUTER PROGRAMS IN EUROPE 74 et seq. (1991).

market failure.[43] Of course, all are in some way public-regarding, for they all more or less involve the communicative process. They ensure that once a work is created and protected, it enters public discourse, where it can be enjoyed, fully examined, discussed, and used as the basis for the creation of new works.

Note that there are several legislative techniques available to implement these exceptions. There is an all-or-nothing approach, which gives the public free use of the work and provides the rightholder with no remuneration.[44] But there are also other possibilities. The exclusive right can relieve the user of the need to obtain consent, but require that the rightholder be paid adequate and fair remuneration.[45] Alternatively, the exception or limitation can subject the parties to a duty to negotiate (which, in some instances, is backed up by a duty to arbitrate).[46] In some instances, remuneration is fixed by law.[47] In sum, the legislature has at its disposal a whole instrumentarium of non-voluntary licenses, from a legal license to a duty to contract, from a pure property rule to something resembling a liability rule. Which tool is deployed depends on the conflict being addressed. Thus, in the case of the first category (overriding public interests), the usual solution is to eliminate both the authorization requirement and the rightholder's entitlement to remuneration. In contrast, where the exclusive right is limited due to market failure (the third category), it would seem unjustified to deny the rightholder remuneration.[48] There is, however, no generally established rule regarding the second category.[49]

Finally, mention should be made of the so-called 'three-step test' adopted at the international level to secure a measure of international harmonization.[50] According to this test, the exceptions and limitations that can be made

---

[43] See INSTITUUT VOOR INFORMATIERECHT & LUCIE GUIBAULT, CONTRACTS AND COPYRIGHT EXEMPTIONS 14 et seq. (1997); Wendy Gordon, n. 2 above.

[44] See, eg, German Copyright Act, §§ 46, 48, 50, 51; 17 U.S.C. § 107.

[45] See, eg, German Gopyright Act, §§ 27(2), 46, 49(1), 53 et seq. (the blank tape levy, the levy on audio and video recorders, copy machines, remuneration for certain press clippings, reproduction in collections for religious, school or instructional use, claims for public lending).

[46] See, eg, Council Directive 93/83/EEC, art. 12, 1993 O.J. L248; 17 U.S.C. §§ 116 (juke boxes), 119 (satellite transmissions); German Copyright Act, § 46(4) (inclusion in collections for religious, school or instructional use), § 47(2) (remuneration for records of school broadcasts kept for more than one school year), § 52(1) (remuneration for certain public communications).

[47] See, eg, German Copyright Act, § 54d (1), Annex.

[48] For the rationale of the introduction of the German levy system see the explanatory memorandum of the draft Copyright Amendment Law of 1985, BT-Drucks. 10/837, A I (introduction of the levy for blank tapes and of the levy for reprography).

[49] Compare, eg the German privilege for the publisher of school books in § 46 of the German Copyright Act (no authorization, but prior information and possibility to object; payment of remuneration) with the decompilation provisions of art. 6 of the Council Directive 91/250/EC of 14 May 1991 on the legal protection of computer programs 1991 O.J. L122/42 (no authorization within rather narrowly defined limits, and likewise no remuneration).

[50] See Berne Convention for the Protection of Literary and Artistic Works, Sept. 9, 1886, *as last revised*, July 24, 1971 (amended 1979), 828 U.N.T.S. 221, Art. 9(2); TRIPS Agreement, n. 22 above, Art. 13; WIPO Copyright Treaty (WCT), Dec. 20, 1996, 36 I.L.M. 65, Art. 10(2) (1997); WIPO Performances and Phonograms Treaty (WPPT), Dec. 20, 1996, 36 I.L.M. 76, Art. 16(2) (1997).

available in local laws are confined to: (1) certain special cases that (2) do not conflict with a normal exploitation of the work and that (3) do not unreasonably prejudice the legitimate interests of the rightholder. This differentiated approach, which permits each nation to respond to its own particular traditions, economic conditions, and factual situations, implicitly shows that there is general recognition of the multiple meanings of 'public'. More important for our purposes, it demonstrates that there is substantial international consensus that public interests are an integral part of intellectual property law and should be accommodated from within. Finally, the flexibility of these international instruments, their responsiveness to a variety of local public needs, and especially the durability of the Berne Convention, strongly point in the direction of balancing interests within rather than outside the body of intellectual property legislation. As we have just seen, there are ample instruments in each nation's laws to do so, even though each may work somewhat imperfectly.

B. Balancing outside intellectual property

It is certainly true that the interests taken into consideration when it comes to balancing are in general in opposition to the idea of exclusive rights. However, they are all more or less linked to the logic of recognizing rights in that in most cases, the goals are to create new works and disseminate them to the public. Although other legal regimes have features that can also serve to further these same purposes, the logical linkage to copyright and *droit d'auteur* is not always as present as is the case of copyright legislation. This logical disjuncture, as well as other constraints, prevent even seemingly applicable public interest safeguards from performing as effectively as the instruments of accommodation discussed in the previous section.

1. Constitutional law

Constitutional law is one case in point.[51] Of course, due to its superior norm rank in many countries, constitutional rules and principles serve as binding 'outside' guidelines for the interpretation of copyright and droit d'auteur prerogatives. Nevertheless, in some countries, these can be 'read into' the intellectual property law to limit its applicability and protect public interests.[52]

In other countries, however, constitutional guarantees are primarily understood as protecting citizens against acts of the state. Since intellectual property cases typically involve only private parties, this understanding might

---

[51] But see Hugenholtz, Chapter 14 below.

[52] See, eg, *Harper & Row Publishers, Inc. v. Nation Enterprises*, 471 U.S. 539, 556 (1985) (assuming that constitutional principles apply to state enforcement of copyright law against individuals). See also Melville Nimmer, *Does Copyright Abridge the First Amendment Guarantees of Free Speech and Press?*, 17 UCLA L. REV. 1180 (1970).

prevent the use of constitutional principles to protect nonproprietary interests when resolving intellectual property disputes. Even in Germany, for example, where the courts are under a legal obligation to interpret statutory norms in the light of the fundamental constitutional guarantees and the objective order of values created by them, civil courts cannot apply constitutional guarantees directly to a case involving only private parties, against an explicit statutory regulation. Rather, it is up to the Constitutional Court to declare a particular statute unconstitutional and to void it. Moreover, there is a general presumption that an Act voted upon by Parliament is in conformity with the Constitution.[53] Thus, even when intellectual property protection is overprotective, it has only rarely been found to violate users' fundamental constitutional guarantees.

There is another barrier to the use of constitutional principles in limiting copyright and *droit d'auteur* prerogative: constitutional law is general whereas intellectual property laws are specific. Since the latter are presumably designed by the legislature in view of, and taking into consideration, the constitutional framework, relying on general law in order to override specific provisions amounts to a shift in institutional competency from the legislature to the judiciary. Some countries regard such a shift as itself unconstitutional, unless the legislature decided otherwise. But even in countries that accept the shift, there is often a reluctance to void particular applications of specific laws on the basis of vague constitutional language.[54]

2. Media, contract, and consumer laws

There is a certain—small—amount of balancing taken care of outside of intellectual property law in other legislation (and, in federal systems, state laws). Most are media regulations, such as 'must carry' provisions;[55] rules concerning the mandatory deposit of a certain number of copies in state libraries;[56] or provisions regarding the preservation of artworks in the public interest.[57]

---

[53] See Federal Constitution, Art. 100(1); German Act on the Constitutional Court, arts. 78, 82, 95(3).

[54] In the USA, eg, there are few cases that explicitly rely on the First Amendment to avoid the application of intellectual property law. But see *LL Bean, Inc. v. Drake Publishers Inc.*, 811 F.2d 26 (1st Cir. 1987) (finding the application of a trademark antidilution law unconstitutional).

[55] See, eg, Austrian Broadcasting Regulation, (formerly) § 21(3) (which grants a legal right to obtain a license to retransmit broadcasts, provided that the cable operator retransmits the programs of the Austrian national broadcaster); § 20 Abs. 1 BGBl 1977 (which provides that a licensed cable operator must retransmit the signals simultaneously, unaltered and unabridged).

[56] See, eg, the French Act No. 92–546 of 20 June 1992, J.O. of 23 June 1992. In Germany, there are both federal and state regulations to this effect; for the deposit requirement at the German Library (Deutsche Bibliothek, Berlin) see Law on the German Library, § 18 et seq., 31.3.1969 (BGBl. I S.265); German Unification Treaty, 23.9.1990 (BGBl. II S.885). In the USA, however, the deposit requirement is contained in copyright legislation. See 17 U.S.C. § 407.

[57] Such provisions mainly result from monument preservation legislation, although in practice the vast majority of objects generally concerned by such legislation will no longer be protected by copyright. See, eg, CAL. CIV. CODE §§ 987(c), (e)(1) (the 'California Art Preservation Act').

In some instances, even more general laws, such as contract and consumer laws, also affect intellectual property interests.[58]

One problem with relying on these provisions is that it is rare for a legislature to consider explicitly the interaction between these laws and copyright or *droit d'auteur* prerogatives.[59] When conflicts arise in the course of litigation, courts resolve them with traditional methods of analysis, such as the doctrines of *lex specialis*, *lex posterior*, or in the case of state law, preemption.[60] But these are formal approaches; they resolve conflicts of legislative competency rather than material law questions regarding the relationship among rightholders, their competitors, and end-users. Thus, these doctrines are not capable of responding directly to the substantive problem of accommodating proprietary and nonproprietary claims as effectively as copyright or *droit d'auteur* legislation. Dealing with the balancing of opposed interests in one single set of rules has other important advantages. By keeping together that which belongs together, the law is made user-friendly (relevant legislation can be found easily). It is also more transparent (it is possible to understand what the legislature has done), and—in all likelihood—more acceptable (the legislature is accountable for its actions).

In sum, addressing issues relevant to *droit d'auteur* and copyright in other legislation does not really add to the instrumentarium. Instead, it tends to fragmentize and obscure what should be a coherent body of law. Perhaps most important, it undermines the integrity of the legislative process. That is, when opposing interests are considered in copyright or *droit d'auteur* legislation, the political process will engage all of those concerned in meaningful bargaining. If, however, innovation interests are considered outside intellectual property, voices can be missed, leading to legislative compromises that fail to give due consideration to a balancing of all relevant positions. Furthermore, it risks achieving outcomes that depend on accidental compromises among parties who are only partially concerned with the question at hand.

3. Antitrust law

Finally, there is the question of the role that antitrust (competition) law should play. This law is designed to ensure that market conditions are maintained. Since its prime function is to prevent abuses of monopolies that already exist, be it by way of abusing a dominant market position or by

---

[58] See, eg, Uniform Computer Information Transaction Act (UCITA), <http://www.nccusl. org/uniformact_factsheets/uniformacts-fs-ucita.htm>.

[59] Again, the classic example are media law 'must carry' rules, which oblige the operator of a cable system to carry certain programs as prescribed by law. See, eg, the Austrian Supreme Court of 12 November 1979, IIC 1981, vol. 12, 105, at 107 (norms found in media law 'are mainly technical regulations rather than copyright rules', and therefore 'do not help' the defendant's position).

[60] See, eg, 17 U.S.C. § 301.

unduly restricting competition in contractually-exercised exclusive rights, antitrust law could be viewed as a direct complement to intellectual property law and, in fact, as the proper instrument for dealing with issues like misuse.[61]

But despite its role in setting a framework for market activities, antitrust law cannot be fully adapted to accommodating the interests involved in intellectual property. It does not generally prescribe where in copyright or *droit d'auteur* regimes to draw the boundaries of the legal monopolies granted. It does not specifically address issues of information policy or concern itself directly with the question of how far the intellectual property monopoly should extend. Most important, because it does not contain the instrumentarium of approaches available in *droit d'auteur* and copyright regimes, antitrust law is, on both the level of legislation and on the level of practical application, too 'heavy-handed' to achieve the fine-tuning of interests that can be accomplished in intellectual property law.[62] Antitrust remedies should therefore be reserved for exceptional situations where intellectual property law has failed.

III. The Example of Digital Products

These remarks can be illustrated by considering the issues raised by the fundamental changes brought about by digital communication technology. With this technology, the mere use of a protected work in digital form requires an act—downloading, storing—that almost always will be an act of reproduction, requiring the consent of the rightholder. Since this is not true for analog works, the transition to digitization can turn end-users into reusers and alter all of the relationships in the author/producer/end-user chain.

One question raised by these developments is how the balance between the entities in this chain should be struck. That issue is discussed generally by other contributors in this volume.[63] The current question is where the instruments of balance should be contained: inside the legislation that creates the right (ie intellectual property law), or outside it (eg, in general contract law or consumer protection law).

A. End-use subject to exclusive intellectual property rights

As regards the end-use of copyrighted material in digital format, three scenarios are worthy of consideration. The first one concerns the end-user who has legitimately acquired the work. He or she wishes to utilize it in a manner contemplated by law or authorized by way of a contractual agreement, but in

---

[61] Cf Shapiro, Chapter 4 above and Merges, Chapter 6 above.
[62] See also Ullrich, Chapter 15 below.   [63] See eg Elkin-Koren, Chapter 8 above.

order to do so, must commit one or even several acts of reproduction, acts that are arguably violations of the reproduction right. Here, it would seem appropriate to deal with the question whether separate consent is required within copyright or *droit d'auteur* legislation, to provide explicitly in this body of law that all technical reproduction acts made in the course of legitimate use are outside the scope of the exclusive right. Indeed, models for such an exception are contained in both the EU Computer Program Directive[64] and in the EU Database Directive.[65]

The second scenario involves a potential user who, before taking a use license, wants to 'browse', that is, obtain information about the material to be potentially licensed and used. On the one hand, intellectual property laws generally allow the rightholder to decide whether or not he or she wants to authorize specific types of uses. Since browsing will sometimes substitute for use of the work, it is easy to understand why a rightholder may want to restrict it, at least in certain instances, depending on the nature of the work. On the other hand, it is difficult to understand what sort of contract can be concluded between the rightholder and the potential user when the latter has not been able to obtain information about what he or she is contracting for.

Because there is tension in this scenario between the goals of the user and legitimate proprietary interests of the rightholder, it is difficult to decide exactly how to draw this line; it is a question that will require more attention than it has so far attracted. But it is much easier to choose the body of legislation where the line-drawing should be done. The browser is not so different from the legitimate user of the first scenario. In both cases, the line-drawing question is closely linked to the issue of the proper scope of the exclusive right. Thus, the only appropriate place to deal with this question is the same place that dealt with the first issue. It should be treated within, rather than outside of, copyright and *droit d'auteur*.

The third scenario concerns the user who wants to make what, in the analog world, would be considered a free use of a protected work, but who in the digital environment finds the same use restricted by contract. The issues raised by this scenario concern the circumstances in which such contracts should be enforceable. Should they always be enforced? Does enforcement turn on whether the restriction is in a standard-form contract? On whether

---

[64] Council Directive 91/250/EEC, art. 5(1), 1991 O.J. L122 (providing that in the absence of a specific contractual provision, the acts of reproduction and alteration of a computer program shall not require authorization by the rightholder 'where they are necessary for the use of the computer program by the lawful acquirer in accordance with its intended purpose, including for error correction').

[65] Council Directive 96/9/EC, arts. 6(1), 8(1), 1996 O.J. L77 (providing that the performance by the lawful user of a database of any of the acts restricted by an exclusive right shall not require the authorization of the author of the database, if it is 'necessary for the purposes of access to the contents of the database and normal use' of its contents; a similar exception is provided for the sui generis right).

the contractual provision restricts uses that the legislature specifically exempted from the scope of the exclusive right?

Although contractual agreements are generally regarded as valid so long as they are entered into by the free will of the parties, there is hot debate about how to handle contracts that undermine legislatively-determined information policy. For us, however, the issue once again is where restrictions on the freedom to contract should be imposed. The solution here seems less obvious than in previous two scenarios. Such restrictions only concern dealings in copyright and *droit d'auteur*, making their incorporation into these statutes seemingly appropriate. Thus, the resolution could be to recognize user 'rights' through well-defined provisions that specifically limit the general freedom to contract.[66] A model is the EU Computer Program Directive, which provides that a person having a right to use a computer program may not be prevented by contract from making necessary back-up copies and permits rightful users to observe, study or test the functioning of the program in the course of normal use, in order to determine the ideas and principles which underlie the program.[67] Similar exceptions in favor of legitimate users are found in the EU Database Directive.[68] At the same time, however, strong arguments can be made that these kinds of user restrictions should be unenforceable only when imposed through nonnegotiated standard form contracts. If the approach adopted is one that is tied to the method by which the contract is made, then the appropriate vehicle for regulation is, perhaps, contract law legislation on standard terms and agreements.

It may also be tempting to think that the problem with some of these restrictions is that the contract goes beyond the bounds of intellectual property rights. If so, it may seem that the appropriate locus of regulation would be antitrust law. However, antitrust law mainly comes into play when policies specific to antitrust law are transgressed, or when imposing the restriction is an abuse of a dominant market position. Thus, it is unlikely that antitrust law will ever be the source of substantial amounts of regulation in this area.

---

[66] It should, however, be noted that this is not a 'right' in the strict sense of the term as used in civil law. A 'right' in civil law is characterized as a legal relationship between a subject and an object, to the effect that the object is in respect of all or some of its possible uses exclusively reserved to the subject and owner of the exclusive right. By definition, then, such 'exclusivity' has an effect against certain or all third parties, which is not the case where a user may commit certain acts, but does not have the legal power to exclude others from committing similar acts. Here the 'right' is simply a freedom to act.

[67] Council Directive 91/250/EEC, arts. 5(2), 5(3), 1991 O.J. L122. See also art. 9(1), second sentence, which expressly declares any contractual restriction contrary to the decompilation provisions of art. 6 or to the exceptions provided for in art. 5(2) and (3) null and void. It may be presumed that such mandatory rules cannot be sidestepped by the parties' choice of another applicable law which does not contain similar restrictions.

[68] Council Directive 96/9/EC, art.15, 1996 O.J. L77.

B. The end-user as reuser

Another new problem stems from the perfect quality of digital copies. The ease of, for example, transmission over the Internet, increasingly turns end-users into reusers. Historically speaking, this fundamental change does not derive from the digital format as such, but emerged earlier: magnetic tape, VCRs, and copy machines all shifted the production function from publishers to end-users. Nonetheless, if one believes the likes of Negropente and Bill Gates, digital and networking technologies will make this phenomenon so ubiquitous and so much the prevailing mode of using protected materials in the future, that a major reassessment of the issue is needed.

The ultimate question is whether these rather private uses, which were formerly outside the scope of exclusive rights (or not easily prevented by rightholders), should now be considered infringement. Should the law give way to the control interests of so called content providers? Or, should access interests prevail? If so, to what extent? Since digitization and networking make unnecessary two of the fundamental activities of traditional producers (production and distribution), it can be argued that the provisions of law that work for the benefit of producers should now be restructured to benefit those end-users who assume the roles that were played by publishers in the analog world.

But no matter how this substantive question is decided, this is once again a problem that is clearly best left to resolution within copyright and *droit d'auteur*. It is too closely related to information policy to imagine other laws capable of generating an appropriate response. And significantly, intellectual property laws and treaties already contain the seeds of solution: the only problem is that the references may not currently go far enough. Thus, authors and rightholders can claim that excepting such use from the scope of their rights violates the three-step tests of the international agreements, which, as noted earlier, confine exceptions to special cases that do not interfere with the normal exploitation of the work or unreasonably prejudice the legitimate interests of the rightholder. Of course, applying the test is not easy in this circumstance. When does reuse by third parties infringe upon the normal exploitation of the work: in cases where a new use is just emerging, how can 'normal' be determined? By the same token, what are the criteria for recognizing the legitimate interests of the author where new markets are emerging?[69] It makes little sense to effectuate such a recognition and allocation of markets solely on the basis of a literal application of legal texts, especially texts originally formulated to balance conflicting interests under earlier technologies and other economic circumstances. However, it may be advisable to

[69] For interpretation of these criteria of the three-step test see now WTO Dispute Settlement Panel Report WT/DS160/R, avaliable at the WTO website (www.wto.org).

stick to the legal texts until new criteria emerge. Otherwise, restriking the balance will only mask a more or less arbitrary allocation of markets. Besides, the interests at stake are those of end-users, libraries, telecommunications providers, and other commercial players. So long as they understand that the political process for expounding on the solution will be targeted at intellectual property legislation, they can easily focus their attention on that arena. Influencing the legislative agenda involving more general measures would be much harder.

IV. Conclusion

The rationale for granting both copyright and *droit d'auteur* takes into consideration not only proprietary interests, but also the interest of the public in production, dissemination, and access to protected subject matter. Although this dynamic is more visible in legislation of the Anglo-American copyright type than in the laws of the continental European *droit d'auteur* tradition, there are nevertheless many indications pointing towards convergence. Balancing proprietary against public and other interests is a concern that should mainly be addressed by intellectual property legislation, by defining an adequate scope of protection including appropriate exceptions to the exclusive rights granted.

This is not to say that adjusting the balance will be easy, especially not in a digital and networked world. Indeed, the main difficulties are highly predictable. First, there is vagueness in the notion of the 'public'. Secondly, the effects of legislative changes in this area are hard to assess because both psychologic features (incentives to create) and economic models (on production and distribution) come into play. Neither is well understood and their effects will vary according to the marketing situation at hand. Thirdly, the statutes and treaties use concepts such as 'appropriate', 'adequate', 'equitable', and 'just', which are not easily defined in the case of conflict. Fourthly, because the law cannot foresee individual cases, and because the perception of fairness depends on agreeing to rules before conflicts arise, balancing must be carried out in a rather abstract and generalized way. Fifthly, as the fundamentals of information production change, the interests of those involved in the communication process must be rebalanced, yet the very activity of striking the balance creates, allocates, and limits the markets in which these new roles are being defined.

It is, in the end, difficult to know what compromises will ultimately be reached. What it is easier to say is that they should continue to be struck within rather than outside the framework of intellectual property legislation.

COMPETITION TO INNOVATE: STRATEGIES FOR PROPER ANTITRUST ASSESSMENTS

SUSAN DeSANTI AND WILLIAM COHEN*

Innovation is enormously important to the increased productivity and global competitiveness of US companies and to economic growth in general.[1] Consequently, competition policymakers and enforcers in recent decades have consistently emphasized the importance of not impairing the incentives of firms to innovate. At the same time, increasing claims of anticompetitive conduct designed to dampen innovation competition have required antitrust

* Susan DeSanti is Director and William Cohen is Deputy Director of Policy Planning at the US Federal Trade Commission (FTC). The views expressed in this chapter are their own and do not necessarily reflect those of the Commission or any Commissioner. We would like to thank Hillary Greene of Policy Planning, and Nancy Dickinson and Brian Grube, formerly of Policy Planning, for their substantial assistance in the preparation of this chapter.

[1] Many have found that innovation accounts for a large—perhaps even the primary share—of economic growth in the United States. See eg, Kenneth W. Dam, *The Economic Underpinnings of Patent Law*, 23 J. LEGAL STUD. 247 (1994); Janusz A. Ordover, *A Patent System for Both Diffusion and Exclusion*, 5 J. ECON. PERSP. 43 (1991); Suzanne Scotchmer, *Standing on the Shoulders of Giants: Cumulative Research and the Patent Law*, 5 J. ECON. PERSP. 29 (1991); Suzanne Scotchmer & Jerry Green, *Novelty and Disclosure in Patent Law*, 21 RAND J. ECON. 131 (1990); Richard J. Gilbert & Carl Shapiro, *Optimal Patent Length and Breadth*, 21 RAND J. ECON. 106 (1990).

enforcers to determine whether enforcement action might be necessary in order to protect the incentives and ability of firms to innovate. Debate has emerged about the proper parameters of any such enforcement action.

Some economists and lawyers have pointed out that antitrust has the benefit of an economic model of price competition around which there is a fairly large degree of consensus; that is not the case for innovation competition, for which there is no generally agreed-upon economic model to reflect how competition in innovation occurs. In the absence of a consensus on the relevant economic theory, some urge that the agencies refrain from action. Others respond that action is appropriate where specific facts indicate a likelihood of competitive harm and antitrust enforcers will not have another opportunity to prevent the elimination of R&D competition. US antitrust agencies have, in fact, become more active in pursuing claims that certain business conduct harms innovation competition. In this chapter, we both describe and endorse that role.

One of the critical tools for analyzing competition in innovation is 'innovation markets', a measure of the area in which innovation competition is occurring that is analogous to the 'product markets' that antitrust uses to measure the area of competition on price and other competitive variables. This concept emerged in the mid-1990s when antitrust agencies focused on mergers of competing R&D efforts to develop products not yet on the market. Since no products were yet in existence, the definition of a product market was difficult; rather, the agencies sometimes alleged 'innovation markets' in which the merger would substantially lessen competition.[2]

In roughly the same time period, the concept of 'innovation markets' was explicated in the *Antitrust Guidelines for the Licensing of Intellectual Property*[3] (hereinafter 'Intellectual Property Guidelines'), issued jointly by the US Department of Justice ('DOJ') and the Federal Trade Commission ('FTC' or 'Commission'). The underpinnings of the approach were thoroughly aired and debated during the FTC's 1995 Hearings on Global and Innovation-Based Competition, and were extensively analyzed in the ensuing FTC Staff Report, *Anticipating the 21st Century: Competition Policy in the New High-Tech, Global Marketplace*, issued in May 1996. Finally, innovation market analysis was extended to a broader variety of competitor collaborations by the FTC/DOJ (collectively, 'the Agencies') *Antitrust Guidelines for Collaborations Among Competitors*[4] (hereinafter 'CC Guidelines'), issued in April 2000.

Drawing on all of these sources, this chapter first provides an overview of the debate about whether competition fosters or deters innovation. It next

---

[2] See Thomas N. Dahdouh & James F. Mongoven, *The Shape of Things to Come: Innovation Market Analysis in Merger Cases*, 64 ANTITRUST L.J. 405, 441 (1996).

[3] *Reprinted in* 4 Trade Reg. Rep. (CCH) ¶ 13,132.

[4] *Reprinted in* 4 Trade Reg. Rep. (CCH) ¶ 13,160.

outlines some activity of the US antitrust agencies regarding innovation competition to improve existing products—cases which highlight innovation competition yet remain amenable to handling under more conventional antitrust analysis. The chapter then describes and assesses the use of 'innovation markets' for products not yet in existence. It concludes that antitrust law has a role in maintaining rivalries within the context of R&D generally, and innovation market analysis is an appropriate tool for use within that context.[5]

I. The Relationship Between Innovation and Competition

Economists, business persons, legislators, and jurists all provide valuable insights into the relationship between innovation and competition.

A. Theoretical and empirical economic work on the relation between market concentration and level of innovation

No consensus exists as to how economics should develop a theoretical model of the 'socially optimal' level of innovation, a point amply reflected in the testimony presented at the FTC hearings. One economist asserted that the amount of R&D that is 'best' is not known, so one can not be certain whether a cutback in R&D helps or harms welfare.[6] He pointed out that in patent races, each rival invests to maximize its chance of success, whereas society only cares that someone succeed; in his view, therefore, the competitive level of R&D may be socially 'excessive'.[7] In contrast, other economists noted empirical evidence which would suggest that promoting additional research and development is likely to be beneficial.[8]

---

[5] See generally, Robert Pitofsky, Chairman FTC, *Challenges in the New Economy: Issues at the Intersection of Antitrust and Intellectual Property*, Remarks Before the American Antitrust Institute (June 15, 2000) 3–4 (addressing and rejecting the argument that the difficulty in measuring incentives to innovate requires the government to pursue a 'hands-off policy' regarding the protection of innovation competition).

[6] Richard T. Rapp, Testimony before FTC Hearings on Global and Innovation-Based Competition (Oct. 25, 1995) at 918 (transcript available at FTC Headquarters and at FTC website, http://www.ftc.gov/opp/gic.htm) (hereinafter 'Tr'.).

[7] Richard T. Rapp, *The Misapplication of the Innovation Market Approach to Merger Analysis*, 64 ANTITRUST L.J. 19, 34–35 (1995) (submitted for the hearings record).

[8] Dennis Carlton, Statement submitted for the record before FTC Hearings on Global and Innovation-Based Competition (Oct. 25, 1995) at 6–7 (statements available at FTC Headquarters and at FTC website, http://www.ftc.gov/opp/gic.htm) (hereinafter 'Stmt'.); Richard J. Gilbert & Steven C. Sunshine, *Incorporating Dynamic Efficiency Concerns in Merger Analysis: The Use of Innovation Markets*, 63 ANTITRUST L.J. 569, 573–74, 593–94 n.60 (1995) (hereinafter 'Gilbert & Sunshine') (submitted for the hearings record); Thomas M. Jorde & David J. Teece, *Rule of Reason Analysis of Horizontal Arrangements: Agreements Designed to Advance Innovation and Commercial Technology*, 61 ANTITRUST L.J. 579, 583–88 (1993) (submitted for the hearings record).

The witnesses agreed that there is no unambiguous economic theory or empirical showing to support a general proposition that increased market concentration leads to reduced innovation activity.[9] Nevertheless, some stressed that a specific merger between R&D competitors might remove powerful incentives for R&D rivalry,[10] pointing to Kenneth Arrow's finding that a monopolist, which already extracts a monopoly profit, has less to gain from an innovation that would cannibalize its existing earnings than a firm in a competitive industry, which begins with zero economic profit.[11] Moreover, several participants noted that particularized industry studies do suggest causal linkages between market structure and innovation.[12]

Other participants pointed to Joseph Schumpeter's findings that large firm size and high market share may better support R&D efforts.[13] They noted that small changes in the underlying economic models reverse Arrow's results.[14] Several witnesses asserted that losses from decreased rivalry could be easily offset, for example, through synergies from combining R&D programs that would encourage even greater R&D efforts or by reduction of the extent to which the innovators' rivals share in the gains from innovation.[15] Some contended that the uncertainty inherent in R&D strategies and the high risk associated with being late to market typically prevent a firm's

[9] David J. Teece, Tr. 874 (Oct. 24, 1995); Rapp, Tr. at 918; Carlton, Tr. at 930 (Oct. 25, 1995); Carlton, Stmt. at 8–9; Michael Sohn, Tr. at 993 (Oct. 25, 1995); James F. Rill, Stmt. at 14–15 (Oct. 12, 1995); Janet L. McDavid, Stmt. Mergers 1995 at 9 (Dec. 5, 1995). Wesley M. Cohen and Richard C. Levin observe: 'The empirical results concerning how firm size and market structure relate to innovation are perhaps most accurately described as fragile. The failure to obtain robust results seem to arise, at least in part, from the literature's inadequate attention to the dependence of these relationships on more fundamental conditions'. *Empirical Studies of Innovation and Market Structure* in HANDBOOK OF INDUSTRIAL ORGANIZATION 1078 (Richard Schmalensee & Robert D. Willig eds., 1989).

[10] Robert J. Gilbert, Tr. 914–15 (Oct. 25, 1995); Gilbert & Sunshine, n. 8 above, at 593; Dennis Yao, Stmt. at 5 (Oct. 25, 1995).

[11] See Gilbert & Sunshine, n. 8 above, at 575–76. See below.

[12] Gilbert, Tr. at 914; Yao, Tr. at 955, 1067–68 (Oct. 25, 1995); Gilbert & Sunshine, n. 8 above, at 579–81. One study that has yielded interesting results is Josh Lerner's examination of the computer disk drive industry from 1971 to 1988 to test the hypothesis that market leaders innovate less than followers: Josh Lerner, *An Empirical Exploration of a Technology Race*, 28(2) RAND J. ECONOMICS 228 (Summer 1997). Lerner measured innovation in terms of a drive's ability to read more densely packed disks. Improvements in density, like other aspects of the drives, were typically not patented. Lerner found that firms 'in the middle of the followers' at the beginning of a year were more likely than the firms in the top quartile to introduce during that year a drive with greatest technological improvements. Lerner's study suggests that where a market has numerous participants and in which intellectual property enforcement is generally unavailable for intermediate or final discoveries, market followers are likely to overtake market leaders in relatively short order.

[13] Carlton, Tr. at 930 & Stmt. at 7 (citing Joseph Schumpeter).

[14] Carlton, Tr. at 930–31 (observing that a monopolist has greater incentives to innovate than a competitive firm if the monopolist fears loss of its monopoly profit), Stmt. at 7–8; Sohn, Stmt. at 4 (noting that Arrow's model 'depends on the assumption that the subject of the innovation relate to existing products or processes').

[15] Gilbert, Tr. at 913; Carlton, Tr. at 930 & Stmt. at 8; Sohn, Tr. at 995; Yao, Tr. at 1017–18, 1021; Rill, Stmt. at 15.

net incentive from favoring reduced R&D effort.[16] They conceded, however, that this was less certain in a transaction that would combine a firm with a current product and a firm innovating to create a next-generation product that would compete with the incumbent's current product.[17] Moreover, some have questioned the operation of Schumpeter's hypotheses in particular industries. For example, Johannes Bauer argues that 'infrastructure industries' such as energy and telecommunications do not fit the Schumpeterian model; he contends that the evidence in the United States of innovation in the telecommunications industry shows that a dynamic and flexible industry organization stimulates innovation.[18] His observations coincide with testimony from an AT&T Corporation representative who described the 1982 Department of Justice antitrust consent decree requiring AT&T to restructure and divest certain of its businesses as 'one of the most successful remedies in antitrust history', in part because 'innovation has burgeoned' as a result of the decree.[19]

In sum, agreement exists only for the general proposition that economic empiricism and analysis have not conclusively demonstrated—*one way or the other*—whether there is a causal link between increased concentration and decreased innovation.

B. Business testimony about competition as an incentive for innovation

Business participants who addressed this issue were emphatic that competition is a primary incentive for innovation, and that continuous innovation is critical for success in increasingly global markets.

1. Competition as a driver of continuous and diverse innovation

Competition forces unceasing attention to innovation. A 3M representative reported that 'innovation can give you a market position, but it's fleeting, and unless you continue to innovate, you cannot maintain your market position in any market'.[20] Competition rivalry has driven companies to invest greater

---

[16] Summanth Addanki, Tr. at 944–46 (Oct. 25, 1995); Sohn, Tr. at 995.

[17] Addanki, Tr. at 944–48; Sohn, Stmt. at 5–6; Pfizer, Stmt. at 9–10. Cf Judy Whalley, Tr. at 1057 (Oct. 25, 1995) ('in most circumstances, not all, but most circumstances' the incentive of a merged company will favor continuing separate research paths).

[18] Johannes M. Bauer, *Market Power, Innovation and Efficiency in Telecommunications. Schumpeter Reconsidered,* 31(2) J. Econ. Issues 557 (June 1997). Bauer discusses ways in which network industries and rate-regulated infrastructure industries may not meet certain assumptions, including ease of entry, contained in Schumpeter's model.

[19] Mark Rosenblum, Stmt. at 11, 14 (Nov. 30, 1995).

[20] William Coyne, Tr. at 205 (Oct. 17, 1995). Various representatives from the computer or computer-related industries concurred. In discussing competition in high-tech industries, a representative of IBM Corporation stated: '[I]nnovation is the preeminent factor . . . R&D generates incredible increases in performance': Marshall Phelps, Stmt. at 3 (Nov. 30, 1995); Emery Simon, Stmt. at 1 (Nov. 30, 1995)

amounts in more diverse research approaches. An Eastman Kodak Company representative reported that competition from digital imaging technology led Kodak to spend $3 billion over 15 years on R&D directed toward electronic imaging.[21] A leader of a pharmaceutical study conducted at the Massachusetts Institute of Technology explained how pharmaceutical biomedical research today requires more diverse approaches:

[T]o develop very targeted drugs in the most efficient competitive way, you need to invest a fair amount of money into understanding the molecular basis of disease . . . This requires some diversity in research . . . As a consequence multiple therapies have evolved . . . When the opportunity is big and it's an important target, that diversity, I think, is important to competitiveness.[22]

Competition's role in stimulating innovation is not confined to high-tech or research-intensive industries.[23] In the United States, manufacturing-intensive industries like steel and auto have reemerged largely due to innovations developed in response to the pressure from increased competition.[24] The idea that competition drives innovation was also articulated by participants in consumer goods industries.[25]

2. The need to be first to market
Competition to innovate also includes winning the race to bring a new product to market. Being successful often means being the first to market; therefore, businesses focus on rapid product development:

If you miss the market window, no matter how good that product is, you have lost in that marketplace. You have to be the first to market in most innovations, and so we do a lot in our company to make sure that we have the systems in place to bring products to the market as fast as possible.[26]

A director of a Sloan Foundation study of the computer industry observed that the computer marketplace is characterized by 'a competition process in the short run whereby firms race, [and] time to market is extremely important'.[27]

---

[21] Terence W. Faulkner, Tr. at 510 (Oct. 19, 1995).

[22] Charles Cooney, Tr. at 701–02 (Oct. 23, 1995).

[23] See Dahdouh & Mongoven, n. 2 above , at 409 ('In many industries innovation is so rapid and so important a focus of competition that firms compete more on the basis of product attributes like new models and expanded capabilities, both important results of innovation, than price'.).

[24] Daniel Roos, Tr. at 266–69, 275, 291 (Oct. 18, 1995); Richard Fruehan, Tr. at 457–70 (Oct. 19, 1995). A Sloan Foundation study of the US steel industry concluded that, in a manner similar to the auto industry, aggressive foreign and national competition ultimately led to product and process innovations by US steel manufacturers: Fruehan, Stmt.

[25] For example, a representative of the Grocery Manufacturers of America (GMA) stated, 'There can be little question that . . . the increasingly global scale of competition raises the importance of innovation to unprecedented levels': William C. MacLeod, Stmt. at 1, 2, 4–5 (Nov. 27, 1995).

[26] Coyne, Tr. at 209.

[27] Timothy Bresnahan, Tr. at 3514 (Nov. 30, 1995). See also David Mowery, Tr. at 754–55 (Oct. 24, 1995) (semiconductor industry); Richard Donaldson, Tr. at 786–87 (Oct. 24, 1995).

Moreover, first movers in network industries have significant advantages. They may gain control of the technical standards of the network as well as controlling follow-on innovation because of the need for innovations to be backward compatible with the existing technological infrastructure.[28]

3. Shortened product life cycles

Competition to be first on the market has resulted in shortening product life cycles, at least in high-tech industries. Hewlett-Packard Company's chief executive officer observed that the typical product life cycle is six-to-12 months, whereas in the past the average product life cycle was three-to-five years.[29] 3M measures its innovation through its annual sales of new products. Several years ago, the company targeted 25 percent of annual sales to come from 3M products on the market less than five years.[30] 3M has raised that goal, however, explaining 'we have found out that rate of innovation was not fast enough for today's markets, and we have raised it to 30 percent and [4] years, and . . . that isn't even enough'.[31]

4. Customer relationships

From high-tech industries to consumer goods industries, customer demands also affect competition to innovate. An IBM executive testified that 'today unrelenting consumer demands for additional computing capability and techniques . . . [a]re fueling the impetus for even further innovation by the [information technology] industry. Consequently, innovation and commercialization of new technologies are proceeding at a breakneck pace'.[32]

C. Legislative history and legal precedent regarding competition and innovation

Perhaps as a reflection of this practical business sense of how competition fosters innovation, Congress, the courts, and the antitrust agencies have

---

[28] See Bauer, n. 18 above, at 560. Of course, first mover advantages need not be insurmountable. See, eg, CARL SHAPIRO & HAL R. VARIAN, INFORMATION RULES 29–32, 180–82 (1999) (noting that WordStar's and VisiCalc's early advantages in word processing and spreadsheet software were overcome and that the *Encyclopedia Britannica*s of the world can be displaced by technology advances).

[29] Lewis E. Platt, Tr. at 35 (Oct. 12, 1995). IBM also noted that product development cycles have become significantly shorter: Phelps, Tr. at 3534. But see CHRISTOPH FRIEDRICH VON BRAUN, THE INNOVATION WAR (Prentice Hall, 1997). Von Braun argues that shorter product life cycles have a tendency to decrease incentives to innovate over time in what is known as the 'acceleration trap'. The 'acceleration trap' is a phenomenon under which a firm's incentive to increase revenues by developing innovative product lines decreases because, as product life cycles becomes shorter and shorter, eventually the market reaches a limit in how much product obsolescence it will tolerate.

[30] Coyne, Tr. at 206.   [31] Coyne, Tr. at 206.

[32] Phelps, Stmt. at 2. The Sloan Foundation steel study found that customer demands are driving much innovation in the US steel industry: Fruehan, Tr. at 465, 478. Attention to customer demands is also critical in consumer goods industries, where firms must 'innovate or die', according to a representative of GMA: MacLeod, Stmt. at 5.

consistently applied antitrust law to maintain a 'competitive level' of innovation. When Congress gave limited relief from the antitrust laws to registered research joint ventures by enacting the National Cooperative Research Act of 1984 ('NCRA') and subsequent amendments,[33] it directed that registered ventures be reviewed for their 'effects on competition in properly defined, relevant *research, development*, product, process, and service markets'.[34] The legislative history of the NCRA expressly recognized competition as a key stimulant of innovation:

Competition is as important in R&D as it is in any other commercial endeavor. Indeed, in many industries, particularly those that are based on rapidly evolving technology, remaining competitive in R&D may be crucial to success . . .

In general, reducing the number of separate R&D efforts may increase the costs to society of mistakes in R&D strategy because there will be fewer other businesses pursuing different and potentially successful R&D paths.[35]

So, too, when writing for the court in *Federal Trade Commission v. PPG Industries, Inc.*,[36] which involved a proposed merger between two participants in a high-technology market for aircraft window transparencies, Judge Bork recognized that direct competition between the merging parties existed 'at the stage of research and development as transparency [window] manufacturers try to influence airframe customers about types of transparencies for future generations of aircraft'.[37] The court relied in part on a likelihood of a substantial lessening of competition in this high-technology market[38] to grant the FTC's request for a preliminary injunction. Similarly, more than 30 years ago, the DOJ recognized the importance of competition at the product innovation stage in its suit against the Automobile Manufacturers Association[39] challenging an agreement among four auto manufacturers and their trade association that allegedly would delay the development, as well as the manufacture and installation, of pollution control devices in motor vehicles.

---

[33] National Cooperative Research and Production Act of 1993 (NCRPA), Pub. L. No. 103–42, 107 Stat. 117 (1993) (amending National Cooperative Research Act of 1984 (NCRA), Pub. L. No. 98–462, 98 Stat. 1815 (1984)) (current version at 15 U.S.C.A. §§ 4301–4306 (West 1997)).

[34] 15 U.S.C.A. § 4302 (West 1997) (emphasis added).

[35] National Cooperative Research Act of 1984, JOINT EXPLANATORY STATEMENT OF THE COMM. OF CONF., 98th Cong., 2d Sess. 9 (1984), *reprinted in* 1984 U.S.C.C.A.N. 3131, 3133–34.

[36] *FTC v. PPG Indus., Inc.*, 798 F.2d 1500 (D.C. Cir. 1986).

[37] *PPG*, 798 F.2d at 1505.

[38] The district court had employed similar reasoning. See *FTC v. PPG Indus., Inc.*, 628 F. Supp. 881, 885 (D.D.C.), *aff'd*, 798 F.2d 1500 (D.C. Cir. 1986).

[39] *United States v. Automobile Mfrs. Ass'n*, 307 F. Supp. 617 (C.D. Cal. 1969), *final judgment published* in 1969 Trade Cas. ¶ 72,907 (CCH) (C.D. Cal. 1969), *modified sub nom United States v. Motor Vehicle Mfrs. Ass'n*, 1982–83 Trade Cas. ¶ 65,088 (CCH) (C.D. Cal. 1982). Even earlier, Judge Learned Hand explained that, 'possession of unchallenged economic power deadens initiative, discourages thrift and depresses energy; that immunity from competition is a narcotic, and rivalry is a stimulant, to industrial progress': *United States v. Aluminum Co. of Am.*, 148 F.2d 416, 427 (2d Cir. 1945).

II. Innovation Competition to Improve Existing Products

To assess a transaction's likely competitive effects on innovation competition in markets in which goods or services[40] are currently bought and sold, a focus on the existing relevant product market usually suffices.[41] The Antitrust Division's complaint in the *Pilkington* case[42] articulates the basic theory that harm to competition in an existing product market may reduce innovation as well as raise price or reduce output. The Antitrust Division alleged that Pilkington, the world's largest float glass producer, had entered patent and knowhow license agreements with all of its principal competitors that provided a framework for a worldwide float glass cartel.[43] According to the complaint, the agreements enabled Pilkington to exercise control over float glass markets, including control over 'the extent to which float process innovations were permitted to be commercially exploited'.[44]

The complaint stated that '[c]ompetition to design and construct float glass plants, if not restrained, creates or increases demand for innovations in float glass-making technology. Such innovations tend to reduce the manufacturing cost and improve the quality of float glass'.[45] However:

Pilkington's territorial and use restrictions discouraged competitor licensees from developing and using their own innovations in float glass technology. The territorial restrictions discouraged the development of competing technology by geographically limiting the opportunities for economic exploitation of innovations. The use restrictions had a similar effect since, according to Pilkington, the use of its technology to develop a new or broader range of float glass technology was a violation of the licensing agreement. The consequent reduction in innovation in float glass technology deprived consumers of the benefits of more efficient production techniques and higher quality glass.[46]

Similarly:

the reporting and grant-back provisions in the Pilkington license agreements disadvantaged competitors in creating and competitively marketing float glass technology that could be used free of Pilkington's licensing restrictions *by eliminating or reducing economic incentives to innovate*.[47]

---

[40] Hereinafter, the term 'goods' also includes 'services'.
[41] See IP Guidelines § 3.2.3, 4 Trade Reg. Rep. (CCH) at 20,378 (an innovation market will be defined only when an arrangement has competitive effects on innovation that cannot be adequately addressed through the analysis of goods or technology markets); see also CC Guidelines § 3.32(c) (adopting a similar limitation on the use of innovation markets).
[42] *United States v. Pilkington plc*, CV 94–345, WDB (D. Ariz. May 24, 1994). Complaint available at the DOJ website, http:/www.usdoj.gov/atr/cases/f0000/0014.htm.
[43] *Pilkington*, Complt. ¶¶ 15, 19, 25.   [44] *Pilkington*, Complt. ¶ 25.
[45] *Pilkington*, Complt. ¶ 17.   [46] *Pilkington*, Complt. ¶ 20.
[47] *Pilkington*, Complt. ¶ 21 (emphasis added).

Importantly, the complaint emphasized that Pilkington's maintenance and continued enforcement of its license restraints was not justified by any intellectual property rights claims, since Pilkington's core float glass technology was in the public domain (some patents had long ago expired, and unpatented Pilkington float glass technology had been publicly disclosed in substantial part).[48]

Another example how anticompetitive conduct can jeopardize incentives to innovate is shown in the FTC's suit against Intel Corporation. In its complaint, the FTC alleged that Intel had used its monopoly power in the worldwide market for general purpose microprocessors, inter alia, to coerce three of its leading customers to cross-license certain of their intellectual property to Intel. More specifically, Intel allegedly withheld advanced technical information and product samples, both of which were ordinarily provided to similarly situated customers in the normal course of Intel's business, and, more importantly, were critical to each customer's ability to market effectively products using Intel microprocessors, until the customers acceded to Intel's demands for licenses.[49] The circumstances relating to one of the three instances of alleged misconduct illustrate the threat to innovation Intel's alleged conduct created.

Digital Equipment Corporation ('Digital') was an original equipment manufacturer of personal computers ('PCs') and purchased a substantial quantity of general purpose microprocessors from Intel. (General purpose microprocessors are the 'brains' of PCs and thus their most significant component.) Digital also designed and manufactured microprocessors, which it actively marketed under the brand-name 'Alpha'.[50] Digital filed a patent suit in 1997 against Intel, alleging that Intel's Pentium Pro® microprocessors infringed its patented Alpha technology.[51] In response, Intel, inter alia, demanded the return of technical information relating to its microprocessors and refused to provide further advanced technical information or product samples, notwithstanding that Intel allegedly held no reasonable belief that Digital had in any way misused such information or samples or disregarded the terms of any relevant nondisclosure agreements.[52] Intel's conduct 'had a significant adverse impact on Digital's ability to develop and bring to market in a timely manner new computer systems based on Intel microprocessors, and would have posed an even more significant long-term threat to Digital's

---

[48] See *Pilkington*, Complt. ¶¶ 23–24. The consent decree in the case eliminated all territorial and use restrictions imposed on licensees and prohibited Pilkington from enforcing related licensing provisions. See *United States v. Pilkington plc*, 1994 Trade Cas. (CCH) ¶ 70,842 (D. Ariz. 1994). The Ninth Circuit subsequently permitted a potential Pilkington competitor to proceed with certain claims that Pilkington and its licensees violated the Sherman Act by conspiring to thwart the potential competitor's attempts to enter the engineering and consulting end of the plate glass industry: *Int'l Technologies Consultants, Inc. v. Pilkington PLC*, 137 F.3d 1382 (9th Cir. 1998).

[49] Statement of Chairman Robert Pitofsky, et al., *In re Intel Corp.*, Dkt. No. 9288 (April 15, 1999).

[50] Ibid at ¶¶ 16–17.   [51] Ibid. at ¶ 18.   [52] Ibid. at ¶ 19.

business'.[53] According to the FTC's complaint, Intel withheld its advanced technical information and product samples from Digital for the purpose of forcing Digital to license its Alpha microprocessor technology.[54]

The alleged anticompetitive effects resulting from this conduct were two-fold. First, by securing access to Alpha and incorporating its advances into its own products, Intel had effectively removed any competitive advantage between the two companies' products and thus maintained its monopoly.[55] Secondly and more importantly here, Intel discouraged innovation competition. By its conduct, Intel allegedly diminished the incentives of (potential) rivals to invest in competing microprocessor technologies.[56] Why would a potential innovator invest in microprocessor technology where there exists a substantial risk that Intel will exercise whatever leverage it may have over the innovator to take its innovations notwithstanding the innovator's intellectual property rights and without adequate compensation?

The consent agreement between the FTC and Intel ensures that disputes over intellectual property rights will be adjudicated in the courts by law rather than through an exercise of market power. Intel fully retains the right to withhold its advanced technical information and product samples for 'considerations unre-lated to the existence of [an] IP Dispute'.[57] However, Intel is forbidden to with-hold or threaten to withhold 'access by any microprocessor customer to [advance technical] information . . . or [to base] any supply decisions . . . upon the existence of an IP dispute'.[58] Thus, the agreement provides substantial assur-ances to potential innovators that their technologies will be accorded their due intellectual property protections, and thereby guards innovators' incentives.[59]

III. The Assessment of Competitive Effects on Innovation Toward Products Not Yet in Existence

Where there is no product yet in existence, the likely impact of business con-duct on levels of innovation, as opposed to price or output, is not as readily

---

[53] *Intel*, Cmplt. at ¶ 21.   [54] *Intel*, Complaint ¶ 13.

[55] Statement of Chairman Robert Pitofsky, et al., *In re Intel Corp.*, n. 49 above.

[56] Ibid.

[57] Agreement Containing Consent Order, *In re Intel Corp.*, Dkt. No. 9288 (Final Order March 17, 1999) at IIB (available at FTC website, http://www.ftc.gov/os/1999/ 9903/d09288 intelagree-ment.

[58] Ibid at IIA.

[59] Alleged anticompetitive effects on innovation are also among the issues being litigated in the case brought by the DOJ against Microsoft. In *United States v. Microsoft, Corp.*, the federal dis-trict court found that the defendant had demonstrated it would use its 'prodigious market power' and 'immense profits to harm any firm that insists on pursuing initiatives [including R&D] that could intensify competition against one of Microsoft's core products'. 84 F.Supp. 2d 9, 111 (D.D.C. 1999) (findings of fact), 87 F.Supp. 2d 30 (D.D.C.2000) (conclusions of law), 97 F.Supp. 2d 59 (D.D.C. 2000) (final judgment), *appeal denied and cause remanded*, 121 S.Ct. 25 (2000), *appeal docketed*, Nos. 00–5212, 5213 (D.C.Cir. June 13, 2000). The ultimate assessment of these issues awaits the outcome of the appeals process.

susceptible to analysis through traditional antitrust paradigms. Antitrust guidance on how to assess possible anticompetitive reductions of innovation towards products not yet extant is still evolving. The FTC and the DOJ first provided guidelines for the assessment of innovation issues with regard to licensing agreements and their treatment under the FTC and Sherman Acts.[60] That methodology, which was shaped by the experience of both agencies in assessing merger-related innovation issues, was largely adopted in the CC Guidelines.[61]

A. The concept of an 'innovation market'[62]

1. Competitor collaboration guidelines
The CC Guidelines provide:

An innovation market consists of the research and development directed to particular new or improved goods or processes, and the close substitutes for that research and development. The Agencies define an innovation market only when the capabilities to engage in the relevant research and development can be associated with specialized assets or characteristics of specific firms.[63]

The CC Guidelines define 'close substitutes' as the 'research and development efforts, technologies, and goods[64] that significantly constrain the exercise of market power with respect to the relevant research and development, for example by limiting the ability and incentive of a hypothetical monopolist to retard the pace of research and development'.[65] This methodology establishes certain constraints on the agencies' analyses. The R&D at issue must be 'directed to particular new or improved goods or processes'.[66] The transaction's likely competitive effects on those goods or processes cannot be adequately assessed within markets for the existing goods.[67] Moreover, the agencies will not use an innovation market definition unless 'the capabilities

---

[60] See IP Guidelines, 4 Trade Reg. Rep. (CCH) ¶ 13,132.   [61] CC Guidelines § 3.32(c).

[62] *SCM Corp. v. Xerox Corp.*, 645 F.2d 1195 (2d Cir. 1981), *cert. denied*, 455 U.S. 1016 (1982), has been cited for the proposition that there can be no relevant market for antitrust purposes without a commercial transaction. See Robert J. Hoerner, *Innovation Markets: New Wine in Old Bottles*, 64 ANTITRUST L.J. 49, 53–55 (1995). The case in fact holds only that where a relevant current product market is alleged, there must be some current production. The court was not presented with an alleged market for research and development. See *SCM*, 645 F.2d at 1199 n.1, 1201, 1208, & 1211. See also Dahdouh & Mongoven, n. 2 above, at 412–15; Gilbert & Sunshine, n. 8 above, at 597–601; Richard J. Gilbert & Steven C. Sunshine, *The Use of Innovation Markets: A Reply to Hay, Rapp, and Hoerner*, 64 ANTITRUST L.J. 75, 78–80 (1995) ('Gilbert & Sunshine Reply').

[63] See also IP Guidelines § 3.2.3, 4 Trade Reg. Rep. (CCH) at 20,738.

[64] The IP Guidelines explain that: 'For example, the licensor of research and development may be constrained in its conduct not only by competing research and development efforts but also by other existing goods that would compete with the goods under development': § 3.2.3 n.25, 4 Trade Reg. Rep. (CCH) at 20,738.

[65] CC Guidelines § 3.32(c) (adopting IP Guidelines § 3.2.3).   [66] Ibid.   [67] Ibid.

to engage in the relevant [R&D] can be associated with specialized assets or characteristics of specific firms'.[68] These restrictions should also apply in the context of merger analysis. They are useful screens to keep the focus only on innovation efforts that require some degree of specialization and for which few substitutable R&D efforts may exist, and to avoid unnecessary antitrust investigations in the area of very basic R&D, where it is more likely that substitutable R&D is readily available or could be fairly easily assembled.

2. Agency consent orders

The FTC has found several circumstances in which it concluded that analysis of likely competitive effects required delineation of innovation markets. Each of those transactions would have combined one innovation effort with either a competing innovation effort or a competing, first generation good. Each innovation effort was directed toward development of a specific product or category of products.[69] As a result of such merger-induced changes in incentives or abilities, consumers could be harmed significantly through at least two anticompetitive effects. First, the next generation product might not reach consumers as quickly or with the same quality or diversity as would be the case absent the merger. Secondly, consumers might be deprived of the potential price competition in either the current or future goods market. Some of the transactions involved mergers of firms that had been competing to develop new products not yet in existence. In *The Upjohn Company and Pharmacia Aktiebolag*,[70] for example, the merging parties were two of only a very small number of companies in the advanced stages of developing a particular drug for colorectal cancer, and no competing product was currently on the market. Upjohn's product was allegedly the closest to FDA approval and was expected to be the first such drug marketed in the USA. Pharmacia's product was allegedly a few years behind Upjohn's in the FDA process.[71] The basic competitive concern was that, after the merger, Upjohn would have reduced incentives to develop and commercialize Pharmacia's product as quickly as possible;[72] one can imagine that, once it had put a new product on

---

[68] Ibid.

[69] All but one of the transactions involved biotechnology, pharmaceutical, or other products subject to a stringent approval process by the Food & Drug Administration (FDA). The requirement that a product under development pass through the FDA approval process turns out to be significant for antitrust purposes because it typically eliminates the probability of timely entry by substitutable R&D. In general, any new innovation effort would have to start at the beginning of the FDA process and thus would usually be required to conduct several years of testing before it could catch up with any current R&D efforts. Moreover, because the FDA is willing to cooperate with the antitrust agencies, FTC staff had a wealth of information on the status, approach, and likely effect of each innovation effort relevant to these investigations that may have been difficult to obtain otherwise.

[70] *The Upjohn Co. and Pharmacia Aktiebolag*, 123 FTC 47 (1995) (hereinafter *Upjohn*).

[71] *Upjohn*, Complaint ¶ 8, 121 FTC 44, 46 (1996).

[72] See Dahdouh & Mongoven, n. 2 above, at 425.

the market, the merged firm would have limited, if any, incentive to introduce a competing product that might cannibalize sales of the first product. The FTC's complaint defined the relevant market as 'the research, development, manufacture and sale of topoisomerase I inhibitors for the treatment of colorectal cancer'.[73] The complaint alleged that the merger might eliminate 'actual, direct and substantial competition in research and development', might 'potentially decreas[e] the number of [R&D] tracks for the [drug]', and, even if both Upjohn's and Pharmacia's drugs were eventually approved, might eliminate potential future price competition between the Upjohn and Pharmacia drugs.[74] The allegations were resolved by consent order, as has been the case in similar matters.[75]

Other investigations have involved proposed acquisitions where one party was already selling a drug with FDA approval, while the other was still conducting R&D on a drug that was projected to compete with the first party's product once approved by the FDA. In such situations, in addition to alleging harm to innovation competition, the FTC has alleged that the proposed acquisition would eliminate potential competition for the first party's drug by removing a potential competitor from the FDA pipeline.[76]

An FTC investigation of non-FDA regulated products involved electronic article surveillance (EAS) systems,[77] in which a tag on a product sets off an alarm if the product is removed from the store with the tag still attached. Historically, retailers had attached EAS tags to products as they were shelved. The research at that time, however, was directed toward developing labels that manufacturers instead could attach during the production process. The proposed acquisition involved firms with competing but incompatible systems that were developing future EAS labels that could be attached by manufacturers. For the next generation product, buyers would likely require

---

[73] *Upjohn*, Complaint ¶ 5, 121 FTC at 45.

[74] *Upjohn*, Complaint ¶ 10, 121 FTC at 46.

[75] *Upjohn*, 121 FTC 44 (1996). See, eg, Pfizer Inc. and Warner-Lambert Co., C–3957 (June 17, 2000) (merger of the two pharmaceutical companies would 'increase . . . the likelihood that the merged entity would unilaterally delay, deter or eliminate competing programs to research and develop EGFr-tk inhibitors for the treatment of cancer, potentially reducing the number of drugs reaching the market and thus resulting in higher prices for consumers'); Glaxo plc, 119 FTC 815 (1995) (R&D of non-injectable drugs for the treatment of migraine); American Home Prods. Corp., C–3557, 5 Trade Reg. Rep. (CCH) ¶ 23,712 (FTC Feb. 14, 1994) (Comm'r Azcuenaga *concurring*) (R&D of a rotavirus vaccine).

[76] See, eg, Hoechst AG, C–3629, 5 Trade Reg. Rep. (CCH) ¶ 23,895 (FTC Dec. 5, 1995) (allegation that merger would eliminate competition or reduce potential competition in the direct thrombin inhibitor market when the proposed merger involved the only firm successfully to commercially develop the drug in question and the only firm in the final stages of obtaining FDA approval); Boston Scientific Corp., 119 FTC 549 (1995) (Comm'r Azcuenaga *concurring in part & dissenting in part*) (allegation that acquisition of SCIMED would eliminate the only potential competitor).

[77] Sensormatic Elecs. Corp., 119 FTC 520 (1995) (Comm'r Azcuenaga *concurring in part & dissenting in part*). See also Dahdouh & Mongoven, n. 2 above, at 424–25.

greater compatibility with existing receivers or migrate to a de facto standard, because any one manufacturer's product containing an EAS label would be sold to multiple retailers. A competitive concern was that the merger would increase incentives to stop one of the innovation efforts in order to avoid competition to select the de facto standard. The consent order essentially prohibited Sensormatic from acquiring patents and other exclusive rights pertaining to the next generation technology.[78]

The Department of Justice has also acted to protect innovation competition.[79] For example, the Department of Justice initially withheld approval of Monsanto Company's acquisition of DeKalb Genetics Corporation until Monsanto spun off certain biotechnology rights to an independent entity and agreed to license certain genetic material to 150 of its customers.[80] Involved there was 'transformation technology', used to insert a desirable genetic trait into corn seed. DeKalb held intellectual property relating to the leading method of corn transformation, biolistics. According to the Department, the proposed combination of DeKalb's intellectual property in biolistics with Monsanto's claims to intellectual property in the newly emerging agrobacterium method raised concerns about competition for corn transformation. DOJ found that biotechnology developers, introducing new traits into corn seed, need access to transformation technology on competitive terms. Monsanto was required to spin off its agrobacterium claims to the University of California at Berkeley, an independent entity with experience in the exploitation of such intellectual property, thus ensuring that biotechnology developers would not be deprived of future competition in corn transformation technology. DOJ also found the combination of the corn germplasm held by each company raised competitive concerns. Corn germplasm is the type of corn genetic material that is used to breed the hybrid seed that farmers plant, and biotechnology developers wanting to introduce improvements in corn require access to elite germplasm such as that held by the two firms. DOJ found that Monsanto's agreement to license its corn germplasm to 150 of its current customers for use in creating corn hybrids with transgenic improvements would ensure that the merger did not reduce competition in biotechnology developments in corn.

B. The validity of innovation market analysis

There have been two basic categories of objections to the use of 'innovation market' analysis to assess the likelihood of a delay in, or elimination or

---

[78] Ibid.

[79] See, eg, *U.S. v. General Motors Corp.*, Civ. Action No. 93–530 (D. Del. filed Nov. 16, 1993).

[80] See *Justice Department Approves Monsanto's Acquisition of DeKalb Genetics Corporation* (DOJ press release issued Nov. 30, 1998) (available online at </www.usdoj.gov/atr/public/press_releases/1998/2103.htm/>).

reduction in quality or diversity of, innovation as a result of lessened innovation competition. The first challenges the existence of any systematic relationship between concentration and innovation, while the second questions the ability of any firm to monopolize innovation.

1. The link between concentration and innovation

The absence of an unambiguous theoretical or empirical link between increased concentration and decreased innovation has been cited as a reason not to attempt antitrust analysis in this area.[81] At the FTC's hearings there was agreement that, in theory, one could analyze potential increases in market power over innovation and potential anticompetitive effects from reduced innovation efforts.[82] Nevertheless, significant concern was expressed that, since any mistake could inhibit or deter innovation rather than further it, antitrust should refrain from acting in order to avoid costly mistakes.[83]

A closely related argument, put forth by several witnesses, carefully distinguished between R&D expenditures (an input to accomplish innovation) and innovation (the output), and pointed out that if R&D expenditures were used more efficiently, they could be reduced without slowing or reducing innovation.[84] Another witness articulated a similar idea concerning the loss of a different research path, questioning whether an enforcement agency could judge whether a company's decision to shut down one of two research tracks, to focus its resources on just one track, would likely be procompetitive or anticompetitive.[85]

On the other hand, witnesses argued that in the factual context of particular mergers, antitrust enforcers would be able to distinguish anticompetitive from efficient reductions of innovation.[86] Such testimony expressed concern that reductions of so-called 'duplicative' R&D may actually represent the elimination of diverse research paths that could lead to different results and further cautioned that even if research paths were identical, different R&D researchers in different companies might draw different inferences from them, and hence achieve different results from the same discovery.[87]

---

[81] Rapp, Tr. at 918; Carlton, Tr. at 930; Sohn, Tr. at 993; Rill, Stmt. at 14–15; McDavid (Stmt: Mergers 1995) 9.

[82] Carlton, Tr. at 926 ('As a matter of logic, antitrust policy could be used to prevent mergers that would harm consumers by concentrating an innovation market').

[83] Rapp, Tr. at 917–19, 922. See Carlton, Tr. at 926, 930; Sohn, Tr. at 995–96.

[84] Rapp, Tr. at 917–19; Carlton, Tr. at 929; US Chamber of Commerce, Stmt. of Non-Participant at 3–4 (statements of non-participants available at FTC Headquarters and at FTC website, http:/www.ftc.gov/opp/non_part.htm).

[85] Sohn, Tr. at 995–96.

[86] Gilbert, Tr. at 909, 915; Yao, Tr. at 955–56; Thomas Rosch, Tr. at 3838–39 (Dec. 1, 1995) (in biotechnology transactions it is 'pretty easy' to assess claims of complementarities and 'fairly easy to determine whether or not redundancies exist whose elimination can yield efficiencies').

[87] Roger Noll, Tr. at 1230–33 (Oct. 26, 1995); Yao, Stmt. at 5; Gilbert & Sunshine, n. 8 above, at 579.

The objections to conducting antitrust analysis in this area appear over-stated. Although it may be difficult to distinguish between procompetitive and anticompetitive combinations of innovation efforts, it is hardly impossible.[88] There are ways in which the analysis can be focused so as to increase significantly the likelihood of a correct result. As one witness pointed out, there are a number of theoretical models that suggest when a monopolist may have a disincentive to invest in research and development.[89] Antitrust enforcers can examine whether the facts of a specific matter are generally consistent with a particular theoretical description.[90] Indeed, the facts of some of the FTC's challenges appear consistent with the insights of Arrow's theoretical model of a monopolist that would have the incentive to eliminate, delay, or reduce an innovation effort if it would otherwise lead to a product that could cannibalize sales of the monopolist's current product.[91] The CC Guidelines expressly recognize and account for the dynamic Arrow posited.[92] Several witnesses acknowledged that the monopolist's incentives to eliminate, delay, or reduce innovation in such situations would be quite clear.[93]

Similarly, although a reduction in R&D expenditures may reduce duplica-tive, unnecessary costs, it also may eliminate promising alternative research. A careful, intense factual investigation is necessary to distinguish which applies to any given situation.[94] More fundamentally, antitrust enforcers should not equate R&D expenditures—or any other single measure—with a fail-safe measure of either the significance of current competition in innova-tion or likely postmerger effects on innovation. And in fact, FTC staff cast a wide net in assessing current innovation competition, also seeking evidence on 'buyers' and market participants' assessments of the competitive signifi-cance of innovation market participants'.[95]

Finally, it is important to note that a loss of innovation competition poses a somewhat unusual disjuncture between the timing and source of anticompeti-tive conduct and anticompetitive effects. Most typically, antitrust has been con-cerned with the anticompetitive conduct and anticompetitive effects that occur

---

[88] See Gilbert, Tr. at 914–15; Yao, Tr. at 955–56, 958–59, 1017; Whalley, Stmt. at 5; Carlton, Stmt. at 10 ('a study of an individual industry over time could well find a stable empirical rela-tionship between concentration and R&D activity, all else equal'); Gilbert & Sunshine Reply, n. 62 above, at 77–78.

[89] Gilbert, Tr. at 914.   [90] Ibid.   [91] See, eg, *Upjohn*, discussed above.

[92] CC Guidelines § 3.31(a) (finding a greater likelihood of competitive concern when R&D col-laborations or its participants 'already possess a secure source of market power over an existing product and the new R&D efforts might cannibalize their supracompetitive earnings').

[93] Addanki, Tr. at 946–47; Sohn, Tr. at 993 (but he emphasized that the incentives depend on innovation occurring 'with respect to and in close proximity to a good that's being monopo-lized'); Gilbert (Stmt: *Should Antitrust Enforcers Rely on Potential Competition Analysis or the Concept of Innovation Markets*) 2.

[94] Under the IP Guidelines, R&D expenditure data are used only if they 'accurately reflect the competitive significance of market participants': IP Guidelines § 3.2.3, 4 Trade Reg. Rep. (CCH) at 20,738.

[95] Ibid.

at essentially the same time and inhere in effectively the same conduct: anti-competitive price increases. By contrast, the anticompetitive conduct of slowing (or ending) an innovation effort would only manifest its anticompetitive effects in the future, and then only as 'non-events', that is, a product would not appear as soon as it otherwise would (or would not appear at all). Similarly, an anti-competitive limitation of the scope of innovation efforts would only manifest its anticompetitive effect as a later, 'non-event', that is, products would not come into existence offering the qualities that otherwise might have been achievable. These 'non-events' do constitute consumer harm, but it is quite difficult to assess their competitive significance.[96] This analysis counsels that antitrust should focus on the likelihood of anticompetitive conduct, not just the likelihood of anticompetitive effects, when assessing possible consumer harm from a reduction in innovation competition. Moreover, once the firms have merged and innovation efforts are in the control of the merged firm, antitrust enforcers could hardly recreate innovation competition even if they were certain that some had been lost. Thus, the best chance that antitrust has to evaluate and prevent significant consumer harm from a loss of innovation competition in the merger context comes when the merger is presented for agency review during the Hart-Scott-Rodino premerger notification process.[97]

2. The difficulty of monopolizing innovation

A second basic objection to innovation market analysis asserts that it is extremely difficult to monopolize innovation, and so competitive problems are rare and the use of innovation market analysis to assess a transaction's competitive effects is unnecessary. Some testimony at the FTC hearings emphasized that there are likely many other technologies from which alternatives to current innovation efforts could develop.[98] Even if a line of R&D were briefly monopolized, it was argued, its components likely could be reassembled elsewhere.[99] Other testimony stressed the view that little real-world evidence exists to suggest that research is being anticompetitively sup-

---

[96] In theory, the price that consumers would experience in these circumstances could be viewed as reflecting the anticompetitive effect of substantially lessened innovation competition. Since consumers generally make price/quality tradeoffs, see Whalley, Tr. at 851–53, one might argue that continued higher 'quality-adjusted prices' will reflect any losses from decreased innovation competition.

Although such an approach is theoretically possible, it would be difficult to implement practically—how could, and at what point should, one assess whether 'quality-adjusted prices' are higher than they would have been, absent elimination of an innovation effort? We prefer an analysis that focuses more directly on the conduct that could produce such an anticompetitive effect and that is likely to emerge first (that is, whether the merged firm likely will abandon an existing innovation effort or innovate more slowly or less diversely or at a lower quality than would the two firms if they remained independent).

[97] See Dahdouh & Mongoven, n. 2 above, at 411–12.

[98] Addanki, Tr. at 943–44. See also Rapp, Tr. at 921–22.

[99] Addanki, Stmt. at 5–6; US Chamber of Commerce, Stmt. at 4; Rapp, n. 7 above, at 36.

pressed, thus confirming the small likelihood that competitive harm will occur.[100]

To be sure, in many situations it is unlikely that innovation could be monopolized. Testimony at the hearings confirmed that even experienced innovators may not know about all the sources of alternative, equivalent R&D. For instance, the 3M witness testified that 3M invests in venture capital companies so that 3M can find out about competing innovation efforts.[101] In these types of situations, it may truly be unlikely that innovation could be monopolized.

There are other examples, however, where it is clear that innovation could be monopolized for significant periods of time. The most obvious situation, one expressly addressed by CC Guidelines § 3.31(a), potentially arises 'when a regulatory approval process limits the ability of late-comers to catch up with competitors already engaged in the R&D'. For example, suppose a proposed merger would combine two innovation efforts competing toward the development of drugs for the same indication, and each innovation effort was within two years of FDA approval, with a third effort about seven years away from FDA approval. In such circumstances, the merged firm could slow innovation efforts for as much as five years before any other firm could catch up (although, of course, the incentive of the merged firm to do so should be examined). Because the FDA approval process requires a series of clinical trial periods, data collection and analysis from those clinical trials, and expenditures of significant resources over a period of many years, in general no entrant could 'leap-frog' into the drug product market or significantly catch up with merging innovation efforts.[102]

Another example involves the situation where other firms with the specialized assets necessary to conduct competing research have no incentive to do so. This situation might occur where the specialized assets already were committed to an area of research believed by the other firms to be more promising than the R&D likely to be lost through the merger. In some investigations, FTC staff have conducted interviews to find out whether there are other firms with 'core competencies'[103] that would permit them to replace any R&D that likely would be lost through the merger. Even where firms had core competencies and specialized assets that would give them the ability to undertake comparable R&D, many were unlikely to do so, because they considered participation in the ultimate product market undesirable for their firm.

[100] Sohn, Tr. at 990–91. See Rill, Tr. at 4157–58 (Dec. 12, 1995).
[101] Coyne, Tr. at 218–19.   [102] eg, *Upjohn*, n. 70 above, at Complaint ¶ 9.
[103] Yao, Tr. at 956 ('[C]ore competence is a business strategy concept that is intended to force managers to understand what unique set of skills and technologies their company or organization possesses that will allow them to compete successfully in current and more importantly in future markets'.). Cf Coyne, Tr. at 209 (3M views its core competencies as 'technologies and technology platforms from which [it] can build new businesses'.).

A third example involves a situation where 'R&D competition is confined to firms with specialized characteristics or assets, such as intellectual property'.[104] Indeed, the FTC encountered such circumstances in the case of *In re Ciba-Geigy*.[105] There, two merging parties, Ciba-Geigy and Sandoz, controlled the critical proprietary rights necessary to commercialize gene therapy products and possessed the technological, manufacturing, clinical, and regulatory expertise and manufacturing capability to develop commercially gene therapy products.[106] Each company controlled a variety of critical gene therapy intellectual property portfolios, including patents, patent applications, and knowhow.[107]

No gene therapy products were available in the market at the time of the merger, and the FTC's complaint defined one relevant market as 'gene therapy technology and research and development of gene therapies, including ex vivo and in vivo gene therapy'.[108] The competitive concern in this market was that '[w]hereas before the merger third parties might have had the option of licensing one party's patents or challenging the validity of the other's, . . . the merger created a "killer patent portfolio", so broad as to eliminate that option'.[109] The merged firm had a disincentive to license third parties, while the separate firms premerger 'had the incentive and did act as rival centers from which others could obtain needed intellectual property rights. Ciba/Chiron and Sandoz would grant limited intellectual property rights to other developers and researchers in return for receiving marketing or other valuable rights back from them'.[110] As proposed, the merger allegedly would have heightened barriers to entry by resulting in one entity holding an even more extensive portfolio of patents and patent applications, together with a reduced incentive to license, which would impede the ability of other gene therapy researchers and developers to continue developing their products. Competitive concerns also arose from the fact that each company was one of only a few companies either in clinical development or near clinical development for the treatment of certain medical problems for which there were large unmet medical needs[111] and that the barriers to entry to the markets for gene therapy R&D were very high.[112]

---

[104] CC Guidelines § 3.31(a).

[105] *In re Ciba-Geigy Ltd.*, 123 FTC 853 (1997) (hereinafter *Ciba-Geigy*).

[106] *Ciba-Geigy*, Complt. ¶ 14, 123 FTC 842, 846 (1996).

[107] *Ciba-Geigy*, Complt. ¶ 15, 123 FTC at 846–47.

[108] *Ciba-Geigy*, Complt. ¶ 9, 123 FTC at 844–45.

[109] *Ciba-Geigy*, Sep. Stmnt. (Chmn. Robert Pitofsky et. al.) at 2 (FTC Mar. 24, 1997) (available at FTC Headquarters).

[110] *Ciba-Geigy*, Analysis to Aid Public Comment (Chmn. Robert Pitofsky et. al.) at 2 (FTC Dec. 17, 1996) (available at FTC Headquarters).

[111] *Ciba-Geigy*, Complt. ¶ 14–19, 123 FTC at 846–47.

[112] See *Ciba-Geigy*, Complt. ¶ 26, 123 FTC at 850. Rather than requiring divestiture, which could have had disruptive effects on the parties' ongoing research, the Commission ordered a remedy of patent licensing to a competing pharmaceutical company, Rhône-Poulenc Rorer

In sum, notwithstanding general propositions about the difficulty of monopolizing innovation, antitrust enforcers should not close their eyes when confronted with specific fact situations that suggest the likelihood of consumer harm. Although the cautions raised are important and appropriate, they should not deter a continuation of the agencies' careful approach to these issues.

C. The application of innovation market analysis

Keeping in mind the sensitivity and importance of innovation, a conservative approach to the use of innovation market analysis is appropriate.

1. Threshold considerations: market participants and the degree of current competition

The agencies recognize that competitor collaborations are often procompetitive and, as such, they have established 'safety zones' to encourage such activity. Safety zones are not meant to discourage collaborations that fall outside of the zones, but rather identify those situations in which the agencies presume the arrangements to be lawful.[113]

For R&D situations analyzed in terms of innovation markets, the agencies will not challenge competitor collaborations 'where three or more independently controlled research efforts in addition to those of the collaboration possess the required specialized assets or characteristics and the incentive to engage in R&D that is a close substitute for the R&D activity of the collaboration'.[114] Consequently, the safety zone will shelter an R&D collaboration with approximately a 25 percent market share. In contrast, the safety zone for other collaborations extends only to a 20 percent market share.[115] The Commission may wish to apply a similar 'safety zone' for mergers analyzed in terms of innovation markets, because four independent and closely substitutable innovation efforts, in general, should be sufficient competitive pressure and because competing innovation efforts may continue to emerge over time. Of course, the usual caveats should apply, that is, extraordinary circumstances might warrant a challenge even in 'safe harbor' circumstances.

In terms of how to define the scope of an 'innovation market', the CC Guidelines, like the IP Guidelines, focus on 'research and development directed to particular new or improved goods or processes'.[116] To determine whether independent R&D efforts are close substitutes, the CC Guidelines

Inc. The Commission also mandated that the merged firm license specific patents of Ciba and Sandoz to any interested person at a reasonable royalty: *Ciba-Geigy*, Dec. & Order at IX, 123 FTC at 876.

[113] CC Guidelines § 4.1.   [114] CC Guidelines § 4.3.
[115] CC Guidelines § 4.2. Neither safety zone applies to agreements that are per se illegal or that 'would be challenged without a detailed market analysis': CC Guidelines §§ 4.2–.3.
[116] CC Guidelines § 3.32(c); IP Guidelines § 3.2.3.

consider 'the nature, scope and magnitude of their R&D efforts; their access to financial support; their access to intellectual property, skilled personnel, or other specialized assets; their timing; and their ability, either acting alone or through others, to successfully commercialize innovations'.[117]

2. Threats to competition from unilateral and coordinated activities
Once an agency has determined that the current degree of competition does not place a transaction beyond concern, it must then decide whether, given that context, the proposed combination of innovation efforts may be pro-competitive or anticompetitive. The hearings testimony clearly stressed that unilateral anticompetitive effects, rather than coordinated interaction, are much more likely to be the problem in the context of innovation combinations.[118] Coordinated interaction among innovation efforts is likely to be difficult.[119] Monitoring an agreement may be impractical, given the secrecy of much R&D activity.[120] Cheating on an agreement may be attractive and difficult to deter, because of the magnitude and duration of potential gains and the likely absence of timely and effective punishment mechanisms.[121] The more expansive 25 percent safety zone applied to innovation market analysis by the CC Guidelines may be a reflection of the greater difficulty of achieving coordinated interaction.

Nevertheless, coordinated interaction regarding innovation is clearly not impossible. For example, effective punishment may be available if the parties are in repeat relationships or if there is an ability to punish in a goods market.[122] Therefore, although the agencies may find that anticompetitive effects are primarily unilateral, the possibility of coordinated interaction should not be rejected without factual analysis of the particular situation.

3. Ease of entry
In almost all of the settings where the Commission has applied an innovation market analysis, it has been clear that entry would not constrain anticompetitive conduct. As noted above, these cases typically involved circumstances where regulatory processes permitted identification of the potential entrants and relatively secure conclusions that they would be unable to constrain anticompetitive conduct. Other settings, however, may require additional atten-

---

[117] CC Guidelines § 4.3.
[118] See, eg, Addanki, Tr. at 940; Gilbert, Tr. at 985; Whalley, Tr. at 1004, 1007, 4123; Yao, Tr. at 1014–17, 1022.
[119] See CC Guidelines § 3.31(a) ('Although R&D collaborations also may facilitate tacit collusion on R&D efforts, achieving, monitoring, and punishing departures from collusion is sometimes difficult to achieve in the R&D context.').
[120] CC Guidelines § 3.31(b). See also, Rapp, Tr. at 919; Carlton, Tr. at 932; Addanki, Tr. at 940; Gilbert, Tr. at 984; Sohn, Tr. at 996; Whalley, Stmt. at 10.
[121] CC Guidelines § 3.31(b). See also, Carlton, Tr. at 932; Addanki, Tr. at 940; Sohn, Tr. at 996; Rapp, n. 6 above, at 30 n.37.
[122] Gilbert, Tr. at 984–85.

tion to entry issues raising topics addressed by the CC Guidelines.[123] The CC Guidelines adopt the principles of entry analysis employed in the 1992 Horizontal Merger Guidelines[124] and begin the job of applying those entry principles to collaborations, including R&D collaborations. A flexible application of the Horizontal Merger Guidelines—informed by the considerations identified in the hearings—should permit a reasonable entry analysis in the context of R&D collaborations.

The Horizontal Merger Guidelines state that '[a] merger is not likely to create or enhance market power or to facilitate its exercise, if entry into the market is so easy that market participants, after the merger, either collectively or unilaterally could not profitably maintain a price increase above premerger levels'.[125] To assess whether entry is 'so easy', the Horizontal Merger Guidelines require an inquiry into whether 'entry would be timely, likely, and sufficient in its magnitude, character and scope to deter or counteract the competitive effects of concern'.[126] For possible effects on innovation, the fundamental question therefore becomes whether entry into a substitutable innovation effort would occur to deter or counteract any anticompetitive conduct.

The Horizontal Merger Guidelines consider entry only when timely, that is, 'only those committed entry alternatives that can be achieved within two years from initial planning to significant market impact'.[127] The CC Guidelines maintain the two-year time-frame and specify that '[t]o be timely, entry must be sufficiently prompt to deter or counteract [anticompetitive R&D reductions]'.[128]

The likelihood of entry into innovation markets raises difficult issues, and the 1996 FTC staff report emphasized the need for additional research into the mechanisms that induce firms to enter into new innovation efforts.[129] Witnesses at the 1995 hearings generally approached the issue from two perspectives. Some essentially viewed entry as exogenous to the innovation decisions of the merging or collaborating firms.[130] Others analogized more closely

---

[123] CC Guidelines, § 3.35.

[124] US Department of Justice and Federal Trade Commission, *Horizontal Merger Guidelines* (1992), *reprinted in* 4 Trade Reg. Rep. (CCH) ¶ 13,104.

[125] Horizontal Merger Guidelines § 3.0, 4 Trade Reg. Rep. (CCH) at 20,573–9 to –11.

[126] Ibid.   [127] Horizontal Merger Guidelines § 3.2, 4 Trade Reg. Rep. (CCH) at 20,573–10.

[128] CC Guidelines § 3.35.

[129] *Competition Policy in the New High-Tech, Global Marketplace* (1996), at ch. 7 p. 38.

[130] See, eg, Addanki, Tr. at 944. Some testimony addressed the possibility of 'drastic' entry, which would effectively capture the market rather than merely provide incremental innovation, such as when a breakthrough technology supplants incumbents who fail to keep pace: Gilbert, Tr. at 1029. An incumbent might be constrained from reducing innovation efforts if doing so might induce 'drastic' entry: Sohn, Tr. at 998; Gilbert, Tr. at 1029. On the other hand, 'drastic' entry might occur without regard to the incumbent's conduct, so in some circumstances its possibility might not be any kind of constraint: Gilbert, Tr. at 1032–33. As a major producer of pharmaceutical drugs stated: '[I]ncumbent firms do not constrain their behavior to avoid the entry of new drug therapies, whose introduction they often view as unpredictable in timing (due to FDA review) but otherwise inevitable': Pfizer, Stmt. at 5.

to the treatment of entry in goods markets, where it has been viewed as a response to profit opportunities flowing from the anticompetitive effect of concern.[131]

The CC Guidelines leave room for both possibilities. They recognize that 'widespread availability of R&D capabilities and the large gains that may accrue to successful innovators often suggest a high likelihood that entry will deter or counteract anticompetitive reductions of R&D efforts'.[132] 'Nonetheless', they continue, 'such conditions do not always pertain'.[133] If the level and type of R&D efforts in the relevant market are typically known and observable,[134] then the likelihood of entry may be assessed in light of the extent to which there are firms that have '(1) core competencies (and the ability to acquire any necessary specialized assets) that give them the ability to enter into competing R&D and (2) incentives to enter into competing R&D'.[135] On the other hand, there may be cases where the R&D in the relevant market is typically secret and unobservable by other firms.[136] Where rival firms have no knowledge that the R&D is occurring or where they would make no presumption about the likelihood of post-agreement reductions in innovation efforts, there is little reason to assume either that entry would occur in response to reduced innovation efforts, or that such entry, even if it did occur, would be observed by the incumbent. In such a situation, a reduction of R&D would not trigger new entry that would deter or counteract any anticompetitive conduct.

The 'sufficiency' of likely and timely entry also should be evaluated in a pragmatic way. Whether the entering innovator's effort would be 'sufficient' to deter or counteract a loss of innovation competition might depend on fac-

---

[131] See, eg, Sohn, Tr. at 997–98; Yao, Tr. at 1021. The entry analysis of the Horizontal Merger Guidelines is premised on the notion that entry sufficient to counteract the adverse effects of the merger (ie, sufficient to return pricing to premerger levels or below) is likely to be induced if a firm outside the market sees a profitable sales opportunity. A reduction in output due to a merger, for example, may make entry profitable even after accounting for the costs of the entrant's sunk investments and the effect of its entry on prices: Horizontal Merger Guidelines § 3.3, 4 Trade Reg. Rep. (CCH) at 20,573–11.

[132] CC Guidelines § 3.35.   [133] Ibid.

[134] Some witnesses reported that R&D in certain industries is relatively well known through patent applications, scientific journals, and other sources: William G. Green, Tr. at 684, 697–98 (Oct. 23, 1995) (biotechnology); Allen Bloom, Tr. at 724–27 (Oct. 23, 1995) (biotechnology). One witness indicated that clinical testing resulted in reduced levels of secrecy for medical devices and pharmaceuticals but argued that secrecy may endure long enough to undermine collusion: Sohn, Stmt. at 9. Another witness noted that, in places like the Silicon Valley where employees from different companies interact regularly, employees may share information about the R&D paths or tracks that they are pursuing: Yao, Tr. at 1013–15.

[135] CC Guidelines § 3.35.

[136] The CC Guidelines explain: '[T]he extent to which an agreement creates *and enables identification* of opportunities that would induce entry and the conditions under which ease of entry may deter or counteract anticompetitive harms may be more complex and less direct than for mergers and will vary somewhat according to the nature of the relevant agreement': ibid (emphasis added).

tors such as whether the potential entry would involve the same or a different research track from that of the collaboration or merged firm, and whether the potential entry would involve resource commitments sufficient to make the innovation effort likely to succeed.

4. Efficiencies

The hearings did not specifically focus on the evaluation of efficiencies in the context of innovation markets. Nonetheless, the record suggests that many combinations of innovation efforts are likely to generate efficiencies. For example, there could be important synergies from combining complementary assets (tangible or intangible) or research skills.[137] At the same time, the testimony suggested a need for caution in distinguishing some claimed efficiencies from reductions in valuable research and development efforts. We advocate a focus on credible efficiencies in keeping with the principles recently articulated in § 4 of the Horizontal Merger Guidelines and §§ 3.36–.37 of the CC Guidelines.

IV. Conclusion

Given the critical and ever-increasing importance of innovation in the economy, it is not surprising that antitrust law would address innovation competition and, in particular, the concept of an innovation market within the contexts of mergers, intellectual property, and competitor collaborations. The agencies' reliance upon innovation market analysis has been incremental and case-based. The CC Guidelines, issued in 2000, draw upon this established analytical framework and extensive body of experience, and are solicitous of innovation efforts.[138] Undoubtedly, antitrust theory regarding innovation competition will continue to evolve and the course of that evolution will be one of the cardinal developments in competition law in the coming decade.

[137] See, eg, Yao, Stmt. at 5; US Chamber of Commerce, Stmt. at 4; Gilbert & Sunshine, n. 8 above, at 594.

[138] See Pitofsky, n. 5 above, at 4 (the CC Guidelines continue to avoid 'unnecessary interference' with innovation). See CC Guidelines § 3.31(a) (terming '[m]ost' joint R&D agreements 'pro-competitive').

COPYRIGHT AND FREEDOM OF EXPRESSION IN EUROPE

P. BERNT HUGENHOLTZ*

Concern over the steady proliferation of intellectual property rights, or, conversely, the declining public domain is no longer limited to the United States. In recent years, an increasing number of prominent European scholars and judges have expressed their anxiety over the seemingly unstoppable growth of copyrights, neighboring rights, sui generis rights, trademarks, and other rights of intellectual or industrial property.[1] Can the rising tide of copyright and related rights be stopped? Recent court decisions from Europe seem to suggest that freedom of expression and information, as guaranteed inter alia in the European Convention on Human Rights ('ECHR'),[2] may under specific circumstances limit overbroad protection. Article 10 ECHR,[3] long overlooked

---

* The author wishes to thank Professors Neil Netanel, Gerard Schuijt, Jan de Meij, and Diane Zimmerman for useful comments, references and inspiration.

[1] See, eg, J.H. Spoor, De gestage groei van merk, werk en uitvinding [The Steady Growth of Trademark, Work of Authorship and Invention] (1990); D.W.F. Verkade, Intellectuele eigendom, mededinging en informatievrijheid [Intellectual Property, Competition and Freedom of Expression and Information] 11–15 (1990); T. Koopmans, Intellectuele eigendom, economie en politiek [Intellectual Property, Economics and Policy], Informatierecht/AMI 110–111 (1994); H. Laddie, Copyright: Over-Strength, Over-Regulated, Over-Rated?, Eur. Intell. Prop. Rev. 253 (1996).

[2] Convention for the Protection of Human Rights and Fundamental Freedoms, November 4, 1950, Europ. T.S. No. 5 (hereinafter ECHR).

[3] '1. Everyone has the right to freedom of expression. This right shall include freedom to hold opinions and to receive and impart information and ideas without interference by public authority and regardless of frontiers . . . 2. The exercise of these freedoms, since it carries with it duties

by scholars and courts alike, may serve, perhaps, not as a dike, but as a lifebuoy for bona fide users drowning in a sea of intellectual property.[4]

Whereas copyright grants owners a limited monopoly with respect to the communication of their works, freedom of expression and information, guaranteed under Article 10 ECHR, warrants the 'freedom to hold opinions and to receive and impart information and ideas'.[5] Assuming that every copyrighted work consists, at least in part, of 'information and ideas',[6] a potential conflict between copyright and freedom of expression is apparent.[7] Nevertheless, as recently as 2000, the European Court of Human Rights (the 'European Court') has yet to decide its first case dealing with this issue.

There are a number of explanations for the late development of European interest in the potential copyright/free speech conflict. One important factor is the natural law mystique that traditionally has surrounded copyright (*droit d'auteur*) on the European continent.[8] Unlike the law of the United States, where utilitarian considerations of information policy are directly reflected in the Constitution ('to promote science and the useful arts'),[9] continental-European authors' rights are based primarily on notions of natural justice: 'authors' rights are not created by law but always existed in the legal consciousness of man'.[10] In the pure *droit d'auteur* philosophy, copyright is an essentially unrestricted natural right reflecting the 'sacred' bond between the author and his personal creation.[11]

and responsibilities, may be subject to such formalities, conditions, restrictions or penalties as are prescribed by law and are necessary in a democratic society, in the interests of national security, territorial integrity or public safety, for the prevention of disorder or crime, for the protection of health or morals, for the protection of the reputation or rights of others, for preventing the disclosure of information received in confidence, or for maintaining the authority and impartiality of the judiciary': Art. 10 ECHR.

   [4] Early European commentators include: E.W. PLOMAN & L. CLARK HAMILTON, COPYRIGHT: INTELLECTUAL PROPERTY IN THE INFORMATION AGE 39 (1980); M. Löffler, *Das Grundrecht auf Informationsfreiheit als Schranke des Urheberrechts*, NEUE JURISTISCHE WOCHENSCHRIFT [NJW] 201 (1980); H. Cohen Jehoram, *Freedom of Expression in Copyright and Media Law*, GEWERBLICHER RECHTSCHUTZ UND URHEBERRECHT, INTERNATIONALER TEIL[GRUR INT.] 385 (1983); H. Cohen Jehoram, *Freedom of Expression in Copyright Law*, EUR. INTELL. PROP. REV. 3 (1984).

   [5] Art. 10 ECHR.

   [6] See P.B. HUGENHOLTZ, AUTEURSRECHT OP INFORMATIE (1989) (discussing informational nature of work of authorship).

   [7] For the United States, see Melville B. Nimmer, *Copyright vs. the First Amendment*, 17 BULL. COPYRIGHT SOC'Y 255 (1970); Lionel S. Sobel, *Copyright and the First Amendment: A Gathering Storm?*, 19 COPYRIGHT L. SYMP. (ASCAP) 43 (1971). For more recent discussion, see Neil Weinstock Netanel, *Asserting Copyright's Democratic Principles in the Global Arena*, 51 VAND. L. REV. 217 (1998); Stephen Fraser, *The Conflict Between the First Amendment and Copyright Law and its Impact on the Internet*, 16 CARDOZO ARTS & ENT. L.J. 1 (1998).

   [8] See F. Willem Grosheide, *Paradigms in Copyright Law*, in OF AUTHORS AND ORIGINS: ESSAYS ON COPYRIGHT LAW 203, 207 (Brad Sherman & Alain Strowel eds., 1994).

   [9] U.S. CONST. art. I, § 8, cl. 8.

   [10] Ploman, n. 4 above, at 13; F.W. GROSHEIDE, AUTEURSRECHT OP MAAT 130 (1986).

   [11] See Grosheide, n. 8 above, at 207. Admittedly, other rationales underlying the copyright equation (economic efficiency, protection of culture, dissemination of ideas) are recognized as well in Europe. See Grosheide, n. 10 above, at 129–143.

Another factor explaining the paucity of copyright versus free speech case law and literature is a certain reluctance on the part of European national courts and scholars to apply fundamental rights and freedoms in so-called 'horizontal' relationships, ie in conflicts between citizens.[12] Also, unlike the situation in the United States, constitutional courts with the power to over-turn national legislation that violates provisions of the constitution are absent in many European countries. An important exception is the federal constitutional court in Germany, the Bundesverfassungsgericht, that, since 1948, has displayed a measure of constitutional activism comparable to that of the US Supreme Court. Furthermore, because constitutional protection for free speech in Europe nearly always expressly leaves room for restrictions imposed by national legislatures, courts in Europe will be faced with issues of constitutionality only in exceptional cases.

This chapter will describe the state of European law concerning the conflict between copyright and freedom of expression. To set the stage, I will first set out the constitutional basis of copyright (or the absence thereof) in various countries in Europe. Next, I shall describe the law governing free speech, and in particular the workings of Article 10 ECHR. The analysis will thereafter focus on the copyright versus free speech case law that has recently emerged from a number of continental European countries (especially Germany, France and the Netherlands), and from the former 'gate-keeper' to the European Court, the European Commission of Human Rights (the 'European Commission').[13] In closing, I will speculate, on the basis of the case law

---

[12] In view of freedom of expression's primary function as a safeguard against undue state intervention, horizontal application appears unlikely. Indeed, most commentators accept that constitutional freedoms only rarely affect or create rights and obligations between citizens directly. However, both doctrine and case law have gradually recognized that private relationships may be affected *indirectly* under a variety of legal theories. Under German constitutional law, fundamental freedoms reflect essential social values, and thereby must be taken into account when interpreting existing legal norms. See text accompanying n. 24 below. The principle of interpretation in conformity with the constitution is widely applied by courts in Europe. Sometimes, constitutional freedoms serve as benchmarks for interpreting general notions of private law, such as unlawfulness (tort) or good faith. Also, constitutional freedoms may play a role in assessing cases of abuse of law or abuse of a dominant position (competition law). In sum, even though horizontal application stricto sensu is probably ruled out, in practice freedom of expression will play an important role in relationships ruled by private law. See F. FECHNER, GEISTIGES EIGENTUM UND VERFASSUNG 188 (1999); J.M. DE MEIJ, UITINGSVRIJHEID 82 (2nd ed. 1995); E.A. Alkema, *De reikwijdte van fundamentele rechten. De nationale en internationale dimensies*, 125 HANDELINGEN NEDERLANDSE JURISTEN-VERENIGING 22, 22–32 (1995) (referring to Article 25(1) of the Swiss Constitution, 'Legislature and judiciary see to it that fundamental freedoms become effective between private persons'). Before the European Court, the question of horizontal application is rarely an issue. The Court does not deal with proceedings between private parties; complaints must be directed against states that allegedly have not complied with the European Convention. Thus, 'horizontal' conflicts become 'vertical' ones automatically.

[13] Until November 1, 1998 the European Commission of Human Rights decided the admissibility of complaints of human rights infringement; only cases deemed admissible by the Commission were brought before the European Court. The European Commission has since then become part of the European Court.

discussed in this chapter and of general ECHR jurisprudence, how the European Court might eventually decide a case in which copyright and free speech interests come into conflict.

I. Free Speech and the Copyright Paradigm

A. Constitutional basis of copyright in Europe

Even within the European Union, copyright law in Europe is still very much regulated on a country-by-country basis. Each independent state has its own law that protects copyrights, or 'authors' rights' as the European mainland prefers it, much in the same way as the Copyright Act of the United States. The Member States of the European Union have, until today, preserved their autonomy in this field, but must comply with a handful of harmonization directives that the European Council and Parliament have adopted since 1991.[14]

To fully appreciate the weight given to copyright interests in a case involving fundamental freedoms, it is first important to consider the constitutional basis underlying copyright in Europe. The specific constitutional foundation on which copyright rests in the United States (the Copyright Clause in the US Constitution)[15] does not have a parallel in most European countries. As a 'natural' right based on a mix of personality and property interests, copyright in continental Europe has its constitutional basis, if at all, either in provisions protecting rights of personality or in those protecting property. The ECHR does not expressly recognize copyright or intellectual property as a human right. Although neither the European Court nor the European Commission has ever been called upon to consider copyright as such, arguably, a fundamental rights basis for copyright may be construed both from the 'property clause' of Article 1 of the First Protocol to the ECHR[16] and from the 'privacy clause' of Article 8 ECHR.[17]

---

[14] See Council Directive 91/250/EC, 1991 O.J. L122/42 (on the legal protection of computer programs); Council Directive 92/100/EC, 1992 O.J. L346/61 (on rental and lending rights and certain rights related to copyright in the field of intellectual property); Council Directive 93/83/EC, 1993 O.J. L248/15 (on the coordination of certain rules concerning copyright and rights related to copyright applicable to satellite broadcasting and cable retransmission); Council Directive 93/98/EC, 1993 O.J. L290/9 (harmonizing the term of protection of copyright and certain related rights); Council Directive 96/9/EC, 1996 O.J. L77/20 (on the legal protection of databases).

[15] U.S. CONST. art. I, § 8, cl. 8.

[16] The First Protocol to the ECHR, Paris, 2 March 1952, Article 1 reads: 'Every natural or legal person is entitled to the peaceful enjoyment of his possessions. No one shall be deprived of his possessions except in the public interest and subject to the conditions provided for by law and by the general principles of international law. The preceding provisions shall not, however, in any way impair the right of a State to enforce such laws as it deems necessary to control the use of property in accordance with the general interest or to secure the payment of taxes or other contributions or penalties'.

[17] ECHR, Article 8 reads: '1. Everyone has the right to respect for his private and family life, his home and his correspondence. 2. There shall be no interference by a public authority with the

Only the Swedish constitution (*Regeringsform*) expressly refers to copyright. Article 19 of Chapter 2 provides that '[a]uthors, artists and photographers shall own the rights to their works in accordance with provisions laid down in law'.[18] Because, according to the explanatory memorandum, the rationale for this constitutional provision is promotion of 'the free formation of opinion', the constitutional protection does not cover producers' rights, such as the neighboring rights of phonogram producers or broadcasters.[19]

Case law and doctrine recognizing an implied constitutional underpinning for copyright are particularly well developed in Germany.[20] The moral rights element, which according to German doctrine is an indivisible part of copyright, is deemed protected under articles 1(1)[21] and 2(1)[22] of the Federal Constitution (*Grundgesetz*). The copyright owner's economic rights are protected by Article 14(1)[23] which secures private property, subject to the limits set by the law. Article 14(2)[24] expressly recognizes that property rights serve a social function, thus providing a constitutional basis for limiting overbroad copyright protection. In a series of landmark cases initiated by rightholders, the German Federal Constitutional Court (*Bundesverfassungsgericht*) was invited to test the validity of a number of copyright limitations against Article 14 of the Constitution.[25] The Court has held that Article 14 justifies certain limitations on the rightholder's monopoly for the public good. Thus, even without directly addressing free speech considerations, the German constitution has been held to require that a balance be struck between protecting copyright and the public interest.[26]

In recent years, however, this concern for social welfare has gradually given way to a more protectionist approach. As Leinemann observes, this

exercise of this right except such as is in accordance with the law and is necessary in a democratic society in the interests of national security, public safety or the economic well-being of the country, for the prevention of disorder or crime, for the protection of health or morals, or for the protection of the rights and freedoms of others'.

[18] Chapter 2, article 19 of the Swedish Constitution (*Regeringsform*).

[19] See Jan M. de Meij, *Copyright and Freedom of Expression in the Swedish Constitution: An Example for The Netherlands?*, in INTELLECTUAL PROPERTY AND INFORMATION LAW—ESSAYS IN HONOUR OF HERMAN COHEN JEHORAM 315 (Jan J.C. Kabel & Gerard J.H.M. Mom eds., 1998).

[20] See F. LEINEMANN, DIE SOZIALBINDUNG DES 'GEISTIGEN EIGENTUMS' 52–58 (1998); FECHNER, n. 12 above.

[21] Article 1(1) of the German Constitution reads: 'The dignity of man is inviolable. To respect and protect it shall be the duty of all public authority'.

[22] Article 2(1) of the German Constitution reads: 'Everybody has the right to self-fulfillment in so far as they do not violate the rights of others or offend against the constitutional order or morality'.

[23] Article 14(1) of the German Constitution reads: 'Property and the right of inheritance shall be guaranteed. Their substance and limits shall be determined by law'.

[24] Article 14(2) of the German Constitution reads: 'Property entails obligations. Its use should also serve the public interest'.

[25] See, eg, *Kirchen-und Schulgebrauch*, German Federal Constitutional Court, 7 July 1971, 31 BVerfGE 229; *Kirchenmusik*, German Federal Constitutional Court, 25 October 1978, 49 BVerfGE 382.

[26] See Leinemann, n. 20 above, at 58.

development seems to run against the tide of history. Whereas the scope of other property rights increasingly is limited by the realities of the modern social welfare state, copyright just keeps expanding.[27]

Article 5 of the German Constitution[28] is another source from which a constitutional 'right' to copyright protection might be derived. This provision protects both the 'freedom of art' and the 'freedom of science'. Because Article 5 guarantees freedom of expression and information as well, it also constitutes an additional constitutional basis for *limiting* the scope of copyright.

Elsewhere in Europe, the protection of copyright as a human right also is thought to be implicit in constitutional provisions that guarantee private property, rights of privacy and personality, artistic freedoms, and so forth. In addition, protection for copyright follows directly from Article 27(2) of the Universal Declaration on Human Rights or Article 15(1)(c) of the United Nations Covenant on Economic, Social and Cultural Rights.[29]

B. Freedom of expression and information in europe

A right to enjoy freedom of expression and information has been embodied in various international treaties and instruments. From a European perspective, Article 10 of the ECHR is, by far, the most relevant. The freedom of expression and information protected under Article 10 ECHR includes the right to foster opinions, as well as to impart, distribute and receive information without government interference.[30] The provisions of the ECHR may be invoked directly before the courts of the states that are party to it, subject to review by the European Court.

---

[27] Ibid at 163–4.

[28] Article 5 of the German Constitution reads: '(1) Everybody has the right freely to express and disseminate their opinions orally, in writing or visually and to obtain information from generally accessible sources without hindrance. Freedom of the press and freedom of reporting through audiovisual media shall be guaranteed. There shall be no censorship. (2) These rights are subject to limitations embodied in the provisions of general legislation, statutory provisions for the protection of young persons and the citizen's right to personal respect. (3) Art and scholarship, research and teaching shall be free. Freedom of teaching shall not absolve anybody from loyalty to the constitution.'

[29] Article 27(2) of the Universal Declaration on Human Rights reads: 'Everyone has the right to protection of the moral and material interests resulting from any scientific, literary or artistic production of which he is the author'. Article 15(1)(c) of the United Nations Covenant on Economic, Social and Cultural Rights reads: 'The States Parties to the present Covenant recognize the right of everyone . . . c) To benefit from the protection of the moral and material interests resulting from any scientific, literary or artistic production of which he is the author'. See also F. Dessemontet, *Copyright and Human Rights* in INTELLECTUAL PROPERTY AND INFORMATION LAW—ESSAYS IN HONOUR OF HERMAN COHEN JEHORAM 113 (Jan J.C. Kabel & Gerard J.H.M. Mom eds., 1998); M. Vivant, *Le droit d'auteur, un droit de l'homme*, 174 REVUE INTERNATIONALE DU DROIT D'AUTEUR 60 (1997); A Kéréver, *Authors' Rights are Human Rights*, 32 COPYRIGHT BULL. 18 (1999).

[30] See Caroline Uyttendaele & Joseph Dumortier, *Free Speech on the Information Superhighway European Perspectives*, 16 JOHN MARSHALL J. COMPUTER & INFO. L. 905, 912 (1998).

Article 10 ECHR is intended to be interpreted broadly. It is phrased in media-neutral terms, applying to old and new media alike.[31] The term 'information' includes, at the very least, the communication of facts, news, knowledge, and scientific information. Whether or not, and to what extent, Article 10 ECHR protection extends to *commercial* speech has been a matter of some controversy.[32] However, the European Court of Human Rights has made it clear that information of a commercial nature is indeed protected, albeit to a lesser degree than political speech.[33]

According to Article 10(2) ECHR, the exercise of freedom of expression and information 'may be subject to such formalities, conditions, restrictions, or penalties as are prescribed by law and are necessary in a democratic society . . . for the protection of the . . . rights of others'. Boukema has argued that the term 'rights of others' necessarily refers only to the fundamental rights recognized by the Convention itself. It would undermine the meaning of the Convention, he wrote, if human rights and freedoms could be overridden by any random subjective interest.[34] However, doctrine and case law have never accepted Boukema's interpretation. Instead, the 'rights of others' have been held to include a wide range of subjective rights and interests, certainly including the rights protected under copyright.[35]

Judging from the European Court's recent case law, the 'rights of others' has become a broad and unspecific justification for limiting freedom of expression and information. For example, in the *Groppera* case the European Court considered a restriction of the retransmission of foreign radio broadcasts imposed by the Swiss Government. The Court upheld the restriction as protecting 'the rights of others', based on the Government's alleged interest in fostering pluralism on the airwaves.[36] As interpreted by the Court, the 'rights of others' has become almost synonymous with the public interest at large. Commentators have concluded it has lost much of its meaning as part of the test applied by Article 10(2) ECHR to speech restrictions.[37]

The more important test, however, remains. Regulations that restrict the freedom of expression and information must be 'necessary in a democratic

---

[31] See *Antelecom Els*, Dutch Supreme Court, 26 February 1999, NEDERLANDSE JURISPRUDENTIE 716 (holding that Article 10 ECHR is applicable to public telephone network in view of its increasing importance for the exchange of information and ideas).

[32] See J.J.C. KABEL, UITINGSVRIJHEID EN ABSOLUTE BEPERKINGEN OP HANDELSRECLAME 39 (1981).

[33] See, eg, *Barthold*, 90 Eur. Ct. H.R (ser. A) (1985); *Markt intern*, 165 Eur. Ct. H.R. (ser. A) (1989); *Casado Coca*, 285 Eur. Ct. H.R. (ser. A) (1994); *Hertel*, 1998-V Eur. Ct. H.R. (ser. A) (1998). See also J. Steven Rich, *Commercial Speech in the Law of the European Union: Lessons for the United States?*, 51 FED. COMM. L.J. 263 (1998).

[34] P.J. BOUKEMA, ENKELE ASPECTEN VAN DE VRIJHEID VAN MENINGSUITING IN DE DUITSE BONDSREPUBLIEK EN IN NEDERLAND 258 (1966).

[35] See *Chappell*, 152 Eur. Ct. H.R. (ser. A) (1989) (*Anton Piller* order not considered infringement of privacy right protected under Article 8 ECHR).

[36] *Groppera*, 173 Eur. Ct. H.R. (ser. A) (1990).

[37] See E.A. ALKEMA, NEDERLANDSE JURISPRUDENTIE 738 (1990).

society'. In determining whether a restriction is necessary, the European
Court has granted the parties to the Convention a measure of discretion, a
so-called 'margin of appreciation'. Restrictions are deemed 'necessary in a
democratic society' if they answer 'a pressing social need' and are proportional to the legitimate aim of the restriction. In this regard, the European
Court has to consider whether the reasons adduced by the national authorities to justify the restriction are 'relevant and sufficient'.[38] In practice, the latitude allowed to national governments varies from case to case, depending
largely on the interests at stake and the composition of the Court. States enjoy
considerable discretion to restrict freedom of speech in cases involving morality and commercial speech. In cases involving the core freedoms protected
under Article 10, such as political speech, however, the 'margin of appreciation' will be drawn more narrowly.[39]

The free speech provisions found in most national constitutions in Europe
are pale in comparison to the broad scope of Article 10. Many of these provisions date back to the nineteenth century and are phrased in antiquated,
media-specific terms. As a result, in some countries, instead of resorting to
outdated 'local' constitutional freedoms, citizens may prefer to invoke Article
10 ECHR freedoms directly before their national courts. The post-war constitution of the Federal Republic of Germany is a notable exception. It provides a sophisticated three-tiered freedom formulation covering freedom of
opinion, freedom of the media, and a right to be informed.[40] Another noteworthy exception is Sweden; besides a broadly-worded provision protecting
freedom of expression in the general constitution (*Regeringsform*), it provides
for two special constitutions that contain elaborate provisions protecting
freedom of the press and of the electronic media.[41]

II. Limits to Copyright Imposed by Free Speech Considerations

A. Late recognition of conflict in doctrine

As I noted at the beginning of this chapter, the potential conflict between
copyright and free speech has long been ignored in European law. Most
handbooks are either entirely silent on the issue or mention freedom of
expression only fleetingly in the context of certain statutory limitations. The
arguments against the existence of a conflict are well known. Copyright does
not limit the use of 'information'. Copyright does not monopolize ideas.

---

[38] *Handyside*, 24 Eur. Ct. H.R. (ser. A) (1976); *Sunday Times*, 30 Eur. Ct. H.R. (ser. A) (1979).
[39] See text accompanying n. 94 below.
[40] See German Constitution (*Grundgesetz*), art. 5.
[41] See Jan de Meij, *Uitingsvrijheid naar Zweeds model: een overladen menu van grondwettelijke delicatessen?*, Mediaforum 44 (1998).

Copyright and freedom of expression are consistent because they both promote speech.

Perhaps the most convincing of these arguments is that copyright, as codified, already reflects a balance between free speech and property rights. In other words, the conflict between copyright and freedom of expression has been 'internalized', and presumably solved, within the framework of the copyright laws. Proponents of this argument point to various aspects of the copyright system for evidence of this balancing: the concept of the work of authorship,[42] the idea/expression dichotomy,[43] the limits to the economic rights,[44] the limited term of protection,[45] and, particularly, the limitations or exceptions to copyright discussed below.

More recent European literature on copyright has, however, begun to recognize the independent relevance of freedom of expression.[46] Even the monumental German handbook on copyright, *Urheberrecht Kommentar*, contains an elaborate discussion of the limits freedom of expression imposes on the scope of copyright.[47]

The proposed expansion of the reproduction right, contained in the proposal for a European Copyright Directive,[48] has generated particular concern among legal commentators. In commenting upon the Green Paper that preceded the proposal, the Legal Advisory Board (the 'LAB'), the body that advises the European Commission on questions of information law, observed:

the LAB notes with concern that considerations of informational privacy and freedom of expression and information are practically absent from the Green Paper. The LAB wishes to underline that these are basic freedoms expressly protected by Articles 8 and

---

[42] Most European copyright laws protect only works that are creations in the sense that they are 'original' and have 'personal character'.

[43] The idea/expression (or in Europe, the form/content) dichotomy implies that ideas, theories and facts as such remain in the public domain; only 'original' expression/form with 'personal character' is copyright protected.

[44] The economic rights protected under copyright normally include the rights of reproduction, adaptation, distribution and communication to the public (in all media), but not the reception or private use of a work.

[45] In the European Union the term of protection has been harmonised; copyright normally expires 70 years after the death of the author. See Council Directive 93/98/EC, art. 1(1), 1993 O.J. L290/9 (harmonizing the term of protection of copyright and certain related rights).

[46] See, eg, HUGENHOLTZ, n. 6 above, at 150–70 (discussing potential conflict between copyright in information and freedom of expression and information); D.W.F. VERKADE, INTELLECTUELE EIGENDOM, MEDEDINGING EN INFORMATIEVRIJHEID 38–39 (1990) (closed system of limitations may call for direct application of Article 10 ECRM); D. Voorhoof, *La parodie et les droits moraux. Le droit au respect de l'auteur d'une bande dessinée· un obstacle insurmontable pour la parodie?*, in DROIT D'AUTEUR ET BANDE DESSINÉE 237, 243–47 (1997) (Article 10 ECHR may provide defense in parody cases).

[47] See URHEBERRECHT KOMMENTAR § 97, nos. 19–25 (G. Schricker ed., 2d ed. 1999).

[48] Commission of the European Communities, *Amended Proposal for a European Parliament and Council Directive on the harmonisation of certain aspects of copyright and related rights in the Information Society*, 21 May 1999, COM (1999) 250 final

10 of the European Convention on Human Rights, and therefore part of European community law. In the opinion of the LAB, the extent and scope of these rights are clearly at stake, if as the Commission suggests (Green Paper, p. 51–52), the economic rights of right holders is to be extended or interpreted to include acts of intermediate transmission and reproduction, as well as acts of private viewing and use of information . . . *The LAB therefore recommends that the Commission give sufficient attention and weight to issues of privacy protection and freedom of expression and information when undertaking any initiative in the area of intellectual property rights in the digital environment . . . . According to the LAB, the broad interpretation of the reproduction right, as advanced by the Commission, would mean carrying the copyright monopoly one step too far.* Freedom of reception considerations may, perhaps, not carry much weight in respect of computer programs. However, the information superhighway will eventually carry the very works for which Articles 8 and 10 of the European Convention of Human Rights were written.[49]

The proposed Copyright Directive has also caused free speech concerns by attempting to 'harmonize' copyright limitations ('exceptions') in the European Union through an exhaustive list of exceptions that national legislatures may apply. Commentators are worried that the directive, if adopted, will deny Member States the flexibility they need to accommodate the public interest, especially in the dynamic environment of the Internet. It is reasonable to predict that removing the 'safety valve' of discretion to create new exceptions in the laws of the Member States—where copyright limitations tend to be express, exhaustive and narrowly interpreted—will put the copyright versus free speech conflict firmly on the map in Europe.

B. Open rights, closed exemptions

The essential difference between the American notion of a 'utilitarian' copyright and Europe's conception of 'natural' authors' rights is immediately visible in the way US and continental European law is expressed. As Strowel has observed, in Europe economic rights are generally expressed in flexible and 'open' terms, allowing courts to recognize a wide spectrum of protected forms of exploitation.[50] On the other hand, limitations on copyright tend to be rigorously defined and 'closed'. The opposite is true for copyright in the United States: the copyright owner's economic rights, generally, are narrowly defined, whereas the exemption for *fair use* leaves a wide latitude for a variety of unauthorized uses. Courts and commentators in Europe—in contrast to the American tradition—also have a 'natural' tendency where possible to

---

[49] *Reply to the Green Paper on Copyright and Related Rights in the Information Society, Legal Advisory Board* (September 1995) <http://www.ipso.cec.be/legal/en/ipr/ipr.html>. See generally P. Bernt Hugenholtz, *Adapting Copyright to the Information Superhighway*, in THE FUTURE OF COPYRIGHT IN A DIGITAL ENVIRONMENT 81–102 (P. Bernt Hugenholtz ed., 1996).

[50] A. STROWEL, DROIT D'AUTEUR ET COPYRIGHT. DIVERGENCES ET CONVERGENCES 144–47 (1993). See also A. LUCAS, DROIT D'AUTEUR ET NUMÉRIQUE 173 (1998).

construe economic rights broadly while construing limitations, or 'exceptions', as narrowly as possible.[51]

Also, because the copyright limitations presently existing in various European laws are generally considered, both by courts and commentators, to be exhaustive,[52] and because they do not contain catch-all provisions like fair use, the laws do not provide 'safety valves' to deal with hard cases. Courts have been reluctant to imply exemptions or even to apply existing exemptions to new situations by analogy.[53] A recent decision by the Dutch Supreme Court, however, may signify a breakthrough in this regard. The case involved the reproduction of copyrighted perfume bottles in advertisements by a retailer offering parallel-imported goods for sale. The Court agreed that no express exemption applied to the facts of the case, but went on to hold that there was room to move *outside* the existing system of exemptions, by balancing interests on a rationale similar to that underlying the existing exemptions.[54]

According to some commentators, the *Dior v. Evora* judgment may have opened the door to an American-style fair use defense; others, more cautiously, interpret the Dutch Court's decision merely as a form of reasoning by analogy of a sort well known in private law.[55] The *Dior* decision has, however, inspired the Dutch Copyright Committee, an advisory body to the Ministry of Justice, to suggest the adoption of a fair-use provision in the law which would allow for a variety of unauthorized uses[56] under circumstances consistent with Article 9(2) of the Berne Convention.[57] The Minister of Justice has responded favorably to the proposal.[58]

---

[51] See, eg, LUCAS, n. 50 above, at 171; URHEBERRECHT KOMMENTAR § 45, no. 15; § 51, nos. 8–9 (G. Schricker ed., 2d ed. 1999), but see *Kirchenmusik*, German Federal Constitutional Court, 25 October 1978, 49 BVerfGE 382 (no reason to construe narrowly copyright limitations). See also P. Bernt Hugenholtz, *Fierce Creatures· Copyright Exemptions Towards Extinction?* (October 1997) <http://www.imprimatur.net/legal.htm> (whether use is permitted by limiting scope of economic right or by express limitation is largely matter of legislative technique; copyright exemptions are not, necessarily, *exceptions*).

[52] See Jaap H. Spoor, *General Aspects of Exceptions and Limitations to Copyright: General Report* in THE BOUNDARIES OF COPYRIGHT: ITS PROPER LIMITATIONS AND EXCEPTIONS (L. Baulch, M. Green, & M. Wyburn eds. 1998).

[53] Cf *Manifest,* Supreme Court of Sweden (Högsta Domstolen), 23 December 1985, GRUR Int. 1986, 739 (even if infringing use were justifiable, courts are not allowed to overrule legislature).

[54] See *Dior/Evora*, Dutch Supreme Court, 20 October 1995, NEDERLANDSE JURISPRUDENTIE 682.

[55] See F.W. Grosheide, *De commercialisering van het auteursrecht*, INFORMATIERECHT/AMI 43 (1996).

[56] Commissie Auteursrecht, *Advies over auteursrecht, naburige rechten en de nieuwe media* (The Hague, 18 August 1998).

[57] Article 9(2) of the Berne Convention reads: 'It shall be a matter for legislation in the countries of the Union to permit the reproduction of such works in certain special cases, provided that such reproduction does not conflict with a normal exploitation of the work and does not unreasonably prejudice the legitimate interests of the author'.

[58] *Letter from Minister of Justice to the Second Chamber of Parliament* (10 May 1999) <http://www.ivir.nl/Publicaties/engvert1.doc>.

As they currently exist, national laws in Europe reveal a bewildering variety of limitations on copyright, often very detailed.[59] In many cases, the limitations take the form of outright exceptions to the copyright owner's exclusive rights. Less often, they are in the form of statutory licenses, offering a right to equitable remuneration. These latter schemes are usually complemented by a regulatory framework for the collective administration of rights. Many of the limitations found in European acts are inspired, either explicitly or implicitly, by concern over freedom of expression and information.[60] Most countries allow, for example, copying for personal use, news reporting, quotation and criticism, scientific uses, archival purposes, library and museum uses, and for access to government information. Many of these would continue to be permitted by the proposed Copyright Directive (Article 5(2)(3)), in some cases in the form of statutory licenses requiring payment of compensation.

C. Copyright versus freedom of speech: selected decisions from national courts

Just as there has been a paucity of legal literature on the potential conflict between copyright and free speech, so, too, has there been a dearth of relevant case law. Even so, national courts are beginning to recognize that copyright must, under exceptional circumstances, give way to the freedom of expression guaranteed by national constitutions and the European Convention.[61] Cases, mostly from Germany, France and the Netherlands, indicate that courts may curtail copyright, especially when freedom of the press—traditionally the 'hard core' of freedom of expression and information in Europe—is at stake. Freedom of expression defenses have been especially successful in cases where literal copying was considered essential—for purposes of quotation, for example, or in cases of 'live' broadcasting of works of art. However, courts have shied away from direct application of constitutional law or even of Article 10 ECHR, preferring instead to treat freedom of expression as a normative principle to be used in interpreting existing statutory limitations.[62]

---

[59] See P. BERNT HUGENHOLTZ & DIRK J.G. VISSER, COPYRIGHT PROBLEMS OF ELECTRONIC DOCUMENT DELIVERY, REPORT TO THE COMMISSION OF THE EUROPEAN COMMUNITIES (1995).

[60] See Council of Europe Steering Committee on the Mass Media, *Discussion Paper on the Question of Exemptions and Limitations on Copyright and Neighbouring Rights in the Digital Era* (prepared by L. Guibault), September 1, 1998, MM-S-PR (98) 7 rev, 22–27. Arguably, limitations reflecting constitutional freedoms cannot be overridden by contract. See *L Guibault, Contracts and Copyright Exceptions in* COPYRIGHT AND ELECTRONIC COMMERCE (P.B. Hugenholtz ed. 2000).

[61] At least one British court now seems to have acknowledged the conflict between copyright and freedom of speech. See Clive D. Thorne, *The Alan Clark Case—What It Is Not*, EUR. INTELL. PROP. REV. 194 (1998).

[62] See Löffler, n. 4 above, at 204; URHEBERRECHT KOMMENTAR § 97, no. 23 (G. Schricker ed., 2nd ed. 1999).

1. Germany

German courts, beginning in the 1960s, have decided a number of copyright cases in which free speech limitations have been recognized.[63] In 1962, the Berlin District Court permitted an unauthorized rebroadcasting by West Berlin television of parts of a news item produced in the German Democratic Republic, on the ground that freedom of expression, as guaranteed by Article 5 of the Federal Constitution, provided an extra-statutory justification.[64] Similarly, the Berlin Court of Appeal in 1968[65] held that the republication by a Berlin periodical, without permission, of cartoons stereotyping students was justified. The copying occurred in the context of a critical analysis of the way left-wing Berlin students were being portrayed by the Springer press. The Court held that publication for this purpose did not infringe the cartoonist's rights, even though the requirements of the statutory quotation right[66] were not met. The Court said that copyright law should be interpreted in the light of the free speech norms reflected in Article 5 of the Constitution.

Referring to the 1968 decision, the District Court of Berlin in 1977 similarly allowed the broadcast by German public television of four copyrighted photographs of members of the Baader-Meinhof terrorist group (RAF), previously published in Der Spiegel, in a critical news report on Der Spiegel's purported role as a vehicle of RAF publicity. Again, although the facts of the case did not square neatly with the criteria set out in the statutory exemption, the fact that the broadcast involved political speech weighed heavily in the determination that a copyright violation had not occurred.[67] The District Court in Munich went a step further in 1983 by allowing a television station to show a photograph from a pharmaceutical brochure in a program critical of pharmaceutical advertising aimed at juveniles. Although this case did not involve political speech, the Court found that, here, too, the principles underlying Article 5 of the German Constitution also provided a defense.[68]

The German Supreme Court (Bundesgerichtshof) has been somewhat more cautious in recognizing free speech limitations on copyright. An example is the Court's *Lili Marleen* decision of 1985,[69] the unauthorized publication of the 'Lili Marleen' song lyrics in newspaper articles on a forthcoming film portraying the 'real' Lili Marleen (Lale Anderson). The Supreme Court said that Article 5 of the Constitution did not provide a separate defense because protection for freedom of the press was already incorporated into the

---

[63] See Urheberrecht Kommentar, n. 62 above, at § 97, no. 24.

[64] See *Maifeiern,* Landgericht Berlin, 12 December 1960 [1962] GRUR 207.

[65] See *Bild Zeitung,* Court of Appeal (Kammergericht) Berlin, 26 November 1968, [1969] 54 UFITA 296.

[66] See German Copyright Act, art. 51.

[67] *Terroristenbild,* Landgericht Berlin, 26 May 1977, [1978] GRUR 108.

[68] *Monitor,* Landgericht München, 21 October 1983, [1984] ARCHIV FÜR PRESSERECHT 118.

[69] *Lili Marleen,* German Federal Supreme Court, 7 March 1985, [1987] GRUR 34.

German Copyright Act. Even so, the Court did accept in principle that 'under exceptional circumstances, because of an unusually urgent information need, limits to copyright exceeding the express statutory limitations may be taken into consideration'.[70]

A similar outcome can be found in the two *CB-Infobank* cases decided by the German Supreme Court in 1997. The defendant operated a commercial research database containing abstracts of articles published in professional periodicals, and also offered a document delivery service providing full-text copies. The Court found that the public interest in accessing information did not justify departing from the rule that statutory limitations on copyright be narrowly construed. The Court underlined, however, that copyright does not protect information as such, and that information services, therefore, remain free to provide facts, data and bibliographical information.[71]

2. Austria

In 1996, the Austrian Supreme Court, in a decision that has received criticism,[72] declined to allow freedom of expression, as protected both under Article 13 of the Austrian Constitution and Article 10 ECHR, to be used as a defense in a case involving the unauthorized publication of a contract for the sale of stocks in a magazine article critical of the sale. In 1997, in a case involving the unauthorized use of copyrighted cartoons to illustrate a news feature, the Supreme Court again refused to accept a free speech defense. The Court asserted that the free speech values involved were sufficiently acknowledged in the relevant statutory limitation.[73]

3. The Netherlands

Under Dutch law, acts of Parliament (formal laws) are not subject to being tested against the Constitution. As a result, freedom of expression defenses rely solely upon Article 10 ECHR, which has direct application and supersedes statutory law. Courts in the Netherlands have long been hesitant, however, to apply Article 10 ECHR in copyright cases. A few recent court decisions may be signs of a change in attitude.

The first, decided in 1994, involved an interview, published in the daily newspaper De Volkskrant, with a well-known corporate raider.[74] The piece was illustrated by a photograph taken in the interviewee's office. Prominent

---

[70] Cf *Pelzversand*, German Federal Supreme Court, 10 January 1968, [1968] GRUR 645 (freedom of speech may impose limits on unfair competition).

[71] *CB-Infobank I*, German Federal Supreme Court, 16 January 1997, [1997] GRUR 459 at 463; and *CB-Infobank II*, German Federal Supreme Court, 16 January 1997, [1997] GRUR 464, at 466.

[72] *Head-Kaufvertrag*, Austrian Supreme Court, 17 December 1996, [1997] MEDIEN UND RECHT 93, at 95. See comment by M. Walter, ibid; and R. Schanda, *Pressefreiheit contra Urheberrecht*, [1997] MEDIEN UND RECHT 97.

[73] *Karikaturwiedergabe*, Austrian Supreme Court, 9 December 1997, [1998] GRUR Int. 896.

[74] *Boogschutter*, District Court of Amsterdam, 19 January 1994, [1994] INFORMATIE-RECHT/AMI 51. See comment by P.B. Hugenholtz, [1994] NJCM BULLETIN 673.

in the photograph was one of the many works of art on display in the office—a statuette of an archer, aiming, as it would seem, at the head of its collector. The Dutch licensing society for visual arts, Stichting Beeldrecht, claimed damages for copyright infringement. De Volkskrant admitted that no statutory copyright limitation was applicable—Dutch law does not recognize a fair use defense. Instead, the defendant invoked the protection of Article 10 ECHR. Although it ultimately found for the plaintiff, the Court agreed that under certain circumstances copyright may conflict with Article 10. In doing so, the Court expressly noted the shift that has occurred in legal doctrine since the 1980s. Nevertheless, the Court considered it unnecessary to invoke Article 10 in the case before it because it concluded that depicting the work of art in such a prominent manner was not really necessary for the purpose of De Volkskrant's news reporting. A year later, in the *Dior v. Evora* decision previously discussed,[75] the Dutch Supreme Court confirmed that, in principle, trademarks and copyrights may conflict with Article 10 ECHR.

Most recently, in a 1998 decision concerning the missing pages of Anne Frank's diary, reprinted without authorization by the Dutch newspaper Het Parool, the Amsterdam Court of Appeals decided that the freedom of expression and information guaranteed under Article 10 did not override the copyright claims of the Anne Frank Foundation, owner of the copyrights in the diary.[76] After carefully weighing the public interest in having the pages divulged against the interest of the Foundation in protecting, inter alia, the reputation of the Frank family members described in the diary fragments, the Court found for the Foundation, reversing the decision of the District Court.[77]

4. France

Not surprisingly, French courts, long among the strongest advocates of authors' rights, have been extremely hesitant in accepting free speech defenses in copyright cases. In the seemingly endless string of *SPADEM v. Antenne 2* cases concerning the scope of the freedom to display protected works of art briefly during television broadcasts, not a single French court saw fit to even mention a concern with freedom of expression.[78]

Only recently, in 1999, has a French court applied Article 10 ECHR directly. The Utrillo estate brought infringement claims against the national

---

[75] *Dior/Evora*, Dutch Supreme Court, 20 October 1995, NEDERLANDSE JURISPRUDENTIE 682. See text, accompanying nn. 55 and 56 above.

[76] *Anne Frank Fonds/Het Parool*, Court of Appeal, Amsterdam, 8 July 1999, [1999] INFORMATIERECHT/AMI 116.

[77] *Anne Frank Fonds/Het Parool*, President District Court of Amsterdam 12 November 1998, [1999] MEDIAFORUM 39.

[78] See *T.G.I. Paris*, May 15, 1991, 150 REVUE INTERNATIONALE DU DROIT D'AUTEUR 164; *rev'd*, C.A. Paris, July 7, 1992, 154 REVUE INTERNATIONALE DU DROIT D'AUTEUR 161; *aff'd*, Cass. ass. plén., July 4, 1995, 167 REVUE INTERNATIONALE DU DROIT D'AUTEUR 263. The case eventually came before the European Commission, whose decision is discussed below. See also Cass. ass. plén., July 4, 1995, 167 REVUE INTERNATIONALE DU DROIT D'AUTEUR 259.

television station, France 2, for showing twelve copyrighted paintings in a news item on a Utrillo exhibition. The Paris Court pointed out that Article 10 ECHR is superior to national law, including the law of copyright, and then went on to conclude that, in the light of Article 10, the right of the public to be informed of important cultural events should prevail over the interests of the copyright owner.[79]

D. Copyright versus free speech before the European Court

The European Court has never been called upon to consider the conflict between copyright and freedom of expression, or opine on the potential 'necessity' of copyright. The European Commission, formerly the gateway to the European Court, has, however, faced the problem twice.

1. De Geïllustreerde Pers N.V. v. The Netherlands

The case of *De Geïllustreerde Pers N.V. v. The Netherlands*[80] concerned the Dutch public broadcasters' monopoly in radio and television program listings. Before the Commission, publisher De Geïllustreerde Pers complained that the Dutch copyright in (non-original) program listings, and the broadcasters' refusal to license, were at odds with Article 10 ECHR. The Commission, however, concluded that the broadcasters' copyright did not restrict freedom of expression and information, and, thus, did not implicate Article 10(2). The Commission's rationale for this conclusion is difficult to fathom. Although it acknowledged that the program listings were 'information' within the meaning of Article 10, the Commission observed:

In the first place, such lists of programme data are not simple facts, or news in the proper sense of the word . . . The characteristic feature of such information is that it can only be produced and provided by the broadcasting organisations being charged with the production of the programmes themselves . . . The Commission considers that the freedom under Art. 10 to impart information of the kind described above is only granted to the person or body who produces, provides or organises it. In other words, the freedom to impart such information is limited to information produced, provided or organised by the person claiming that freedom being the author, the originator or otherwise the intellectual owner of the information concerned. It follows that any right which the applicant company itself may have under Art. 10 of the Convention has not been interfered with where it is prevented from publishing information not yet in its possession.[81]

---

[79] See *T G.I Paris*, 23 February 1999, 184 Revue internationale du droit d'auteur 374 (2000).
[80] *De Geïllustreerde Pers N.V. v. The Netherlands*, 8 Eur. Comm'n H.R. Dec. & Rep. 5 (1976); cf *KPN/Kapitol*, President District Court Dordrecht, 8 September 1998, [1999] INFORMATIERECHT/AMI 7 (copyright in telephone subscriber listings not considered infringement of Article 10 ECHR because (a) freedom of the public to receive information not impeded, and (b) listings could be licensed).
[81] *De Geïllustreerde Pers N V v. The Netherlands*, 8 Eur. Comm'n H.R. Dec. & Rep. 5 (1976)

The Commission added that 'the free flow of such information to the public in general' was not at stake, since Dutch audiences could obtain the information from a variety of mass media.

The *Geïllustreerde Pers* decision has been criticized by many commentators.[82] The Commission's conclusion that third parties may never invoke Article 10 freedoms with respect to 'single-source' data is obviously erroneous. Freedom of expression under Article 10 is not confined to speech that is original with the speaker. Moreover, the Commission was arguably wrong in suggesting that freedom of expression and information is not restricted as long as the free flow of information to the public in general is not impeded. The existence of alternative communications channels may be an element in measuring the 'necessity' of a restriction, but to declare that no restriction exists if alternative channels are available is clearly at odds with the meaning and purpose of Article 10.

2. France 2 v. France

The second, more recent, European Commission decision involving potentially overbroad copyright claims is equally disappointing in its reasoning.[83] During a television news broadcast by France 2 (Antenne 2), covering the reopening, after major restoration work, of the theatre on the Champs-Elysées, the camera focused several times, for a total duration of 49 seconds, on the theatre's famous frescos by Edouard Vuillard. The visual arts collecting society, SPADEM, representing the Vuillard estate, demanded, and eventually obtained compensation.[84] The Cour de Cassation held that France 2 could not defend itself by invoking the statutory right to quote briefly from copyrighted works for informational purposes.[85] The Court ruled that communicating an entire work to the public does not, by definition, amount to a 'brief quotation' within the meaning of the law.

Before the European Commission, France 2 complained that the Cour de Cassation's analysis was at odds with Article 10 ECHR. The Commission disagreed. Although it acknowledged that, in principle, copyright is a restriction on the freedom of expression and information protected under Article 10, the Commission rightly observed that copyright law is 'prescribed by law' for the purpose of protecting the 'rights of others'. The Commission then added, rather surprisingly:

---

[82] See H. Cohen Jehoram, [1979] 28 ARS AEQUI 153; P. VAN DIJK & G.J.H. VAN HOOF, DE EUROPESE CONVENTIE IN THEORIE EN PRAKTIJK 358 (2d ed. 1982).

[83] See *France 2 v. France*, App. No. 30262/96, Eur. Comm'n H.R. (1997); [1999] INFORMATIERECHT/AMI 115.

[84] See text, accompanying n. 77 above.

[85] See article 43–1 of the French Copyright Act of 11 March 1957 (currently article L 111–1 of the Code of Intellectual Property).

[I]t is normally not for the organs of the Convention to decide, in respect of Article 10 (2), possible conflicts between the right to communicate information freely, on the one hand, and the right of the authors of the works communicated, on the other hand.[86]

The Commission then found that the principles of copyright and free expression were both satisfied by awarding royalties to SPADEM. The Commission held 'that under the circumstances of the case the French courts had good reason to take into account the copyrights of the author and the right holders in the works that were otherwise freely broadcast by the applicant'.[87]

In its reasoning and outcome, the France 2 case is similar to the European Commission's decision in the case of *Nederlandse Omroepprogramma Stichting (NOS) v. The Netherlands.* Here, the Commission was invited to consider the scope of real property rights in the light of Article 10.[88] Plaintiff, the Dutch national public broadcasting organization, complained that the right of the Dutch Football Association (KNVB) to financial compensation for radio and television coverage of football matches held under its auspices, violated its right to receive and impart information. Previously, the Dutch Supreme Court had ruled that the KNVB was entitled to compensation because of its property rights in the stadiums where the matches take place.[89] The European Commission dismissed the complaint:

[I]t cannot be considered an interference with the right to freedom of expression as guaranteed by Article 10 of the Convention if the organiser of a match limits the right to direct reporting of the match to those with whom the organiser has concluded agreements on the conditions for such reporting.[90]

III. Conclusion

How will the European Court eventually decide a conflict between copyright and freedom of expression? Both the national cases and the decisions by the European Commission discussed in this article provide a number of clues. Also, we may learn from the vast body of Article 10 ECHR cases decided by the Commission and the Court in noncopyright matters.

The somewhat related field of unfair competition law has generated a number of interesting decisions by the European Court.[91] The recent case of

---

[86] Translation from French by the author.
[87] Ibid (translation by the author).
[88] *NOS v. The Netherlands*, App. No. 13920/88, Eur. Comm'n H.R. (1991).
[89] See *NOS/KNVB*, Dutch Supreme Court, 23 October 1987, NEDERLANDSE JURISPRUDENTIE 310.
[90] *NOS v. The Netherlands*, App. No. 13920/88, Eur. Comm'n H.R. (1991).
[91] See *Barthold*, 90 Eur. Ct. H.R. (ser. A) (1985); *Markt intern*, 165 Eur. Ct. H.R. (ser. A) (1989).

Hertel v. Switzerland is particularly noteworthy.[92] Swiss scientist Hertel had published an article in a popular journal on the potential health hazards of consuming food prepared in microwave ovens. The article suggested that microwave cooking has a carcinogenic effect. According to the national courts, Hertel's behavior amounted to an act of unfair competition, since the publication had a potential negative effect on microwave oven sales. Before the European Court, Mr Hertel invoked his right freely to express his scientific opinions.

The Court reiterated that Member States enjoy a wide 'margin of appreciation' in balancing freedom of expression and information against principles of unfair competition law, and agreed that unfair competition law could be applied to such noncompetitive behavior as scientific publishing. Nevertheless, the Court found that Mr Hertel's freedom of expression was unnecessarily restricted because there was no evidence that microwave oven sales had effectively declined as a result of Mr Hertel's publication.

The *Hertel* decision confirms that speech relating to commercial interests enjoys only limited protection in Europe.[93] The European Court allows Member States a wide latitude in restricting speech to serve the interests of commercial law and the law of unfair competition. This line of cases suggests that Article 10 will allow the unauthorized use of copyrighted works for predominantly commercial purposes only in exceptional cases.

Clearly, not all content-related speech restrictions are treated equally by the European Court. In a long line of cases not concerning copyright, the European Commission and the European Court have consistently granted a higher level of protection to political speech than to 'ordinary' expression. In doing so, they have either implicitly or expressly recognized the democracy-enabling function of the freedoms protected by Article 10.[94] The Commission and the Court also appear to have given artistic speech a preferred position, even though artistic freedoms are not expressly recognized by the Convention and an *exceptio artis* that would have made creative artists immune from restrictions has never been accepted.[95]

Not surprisingly, the traditional 'core' of freedom of expression and information, freedom of the press, has generally been well protected. In several cases the Court has emphasized the special role the press has to play in

---

[92] *Hertel*, 1998-VI Eur. Ct. H.R. (ser. A) (1998). See also A. Kamperman Sanders, *Unfair Competition Law and the European Court of Human Rights. The Case of Hertel v. Switzerland and Beyond* (paper presented at 7th Annual Conference on International Intellectual Property Law and Policy, Fordham University School of Law, New York, April 8–9, 1999) (paper on file with the author).

[93] See text accompanying n. 33 above.

[94] See C. McCrudden, *The Impact on Freedom of Speech,* in The Impact of the Human Rights Bill on English Law 90 (Basil Markesinis ed., 1998).

[95] See Dirk Voorhoof, *Critical Perspectives on the Scope and Interpretation of Article 10 of the European Convention on Human Rights* 35, Mass Media Files, No. 10 (1995).

society as public watchdog.[96] The Commission and the Court have been especially critical of acts of government censorship, even though Article 10, in contrast to many national constitutions, does not contain an express ban on censorship.

In deciding whether speech regulations meet the test of necessity 'in a democratic society' (proportionality), the following factors have been taken into account.[97] First and foremost, the degree of public interest in the speech appears to play a crucial role; restrictions on political speech will more easily be found unwarranted than impediments to communications on commercial subjects. A second factor is the substantiality of the restrictions: minor impediments will more easily meet the test than major ones. A third factor appears to be the purpose of the regulation; for instance, a restriction for reasons of national security will more readily be judged proportional than restrictions on other grounds. A fourth factor is the level of European consensus: if similar restrictions exist in most other Member States, the European Court will be hesitant to find infringement of Article 10.[98] This does not mean, however, that national deviations will never meet the test of necessity. Especially in areas of the law where norms tend to diverge, such as morality and unfair competition, the Court will allow a wide 'margin of appreciation'.

In sum, our analysis of European case law suggests that freedom of expression arguments are likely to succeed against copyright claims aimed at preventing political discourse, curtailing journalistic or artistic freedoms, suppressing publication of government-produced information or impeding other forms of 'public speech'. In practice, this might imply that the Court would be willing to find violations of Article 10 if national courts fail to interpret broadly or 'stretch' existing copyright limitations to permit quotation, news reporting, artistic use or reutilization of government information. The Court might also be willing to find national copyright laws in direct contravention of Article 10 if they fail to provide exceptions for uses such as parody.[99]

In contrast, the European Commission has been reluctant to accept freedom of expression and information arguments in cases where property rights in information are asserted merely to ensure remuneration, and the flow of information to the public is not unreasonably impeded.

---

[96] See *Handyside*, 24 Eur. Ct. H.R. (ser. B) (1976); *Sunday Times*, 30 Eur. Ct. H.R. (ser. A) (1979); McCrudden, n. 94 above, at 98-99.

[97] See J.G.C. SCHOKKENBROEK, TOETSING AAN DE VRIJHEIDSRECHTEN VAN HET EUROPEES VERDRAG TOT BESCHERMING VAN DE RECHTEN VAN DE MENS 220 et seq. (1996).

[98] See ibid at 226; Colin Warbrick, *'Federalism' and Free Speech: Accommodating Community Standards—the American Constitution and the European Convention on Human Rights*, in IMPORTING THE FIRST AMENDMENT 183 (Ian Loveland ed., 1998).

[99] Except for France and Belgium, copyright laws in Europe do not provide for express parody exemptions.

European case law also suggests that speech restrictions in line with European consensus will more readily be accepted than those reflecting national peculiarities. Considering the increasingly important role of the European Union as pan-European copyright legislator, this is a sobering conclusion. Even if, according to many commentators, recent European Directives have upset the 'delicate balance' between copyright and the public interest, it is improbable the European Court, in light of its deference to consensus, will be easily convinced to apply Article 10 in order to restore the equilibrium.

For European legislatures the message is clear: as long as licenses are made avaliable under reasonable conditions, or statutory licenses apply, the European Court is unlikely to find that copyright and Article 10 collide.

European case law also suggests that speech restrictions in line with European consensus will more readily be accepted than national peculiarities. Considering the increasingly important role of the European Union as pan-European copyright legislator, this is a sobering conclusion. Even if, according to many commentators, recent European Directives have upset the 'delicate balance' between copyright and the public interest, it is improbable the European Court, in light of its deference to consensus, will be easily convinced to apply Article 10 in order to restore the equilibrium.

15

INTELLECTUAL PROPERTY, ACCESS TO INFORMATION, AND ANTITRUST: HARMONY, DISHARMONY, AND INTERNATIONAL HARMONIZATION

HANNS ULLRICH*

The purpose of this chapter is to examine the question whether the 'expanding bounds of intellectual property' also require expanding control of the exercise of intellectual property rights by antitrust laws. Such an expanded control may be a matter not only of substantive law, but also of the international reach of antitrust law and, as a consequence, of harmonizing its rules on the international level. However, the need for expanded control can only be determined by reference to the existing level of control. In this respect, conventional wisdom is based on the assumption that there is a conflict between the exclusivity that intellectual property affords to the owner of protected subject matter and the kind of unrestricted competition that the antitrust laws are intended to safeguard. In particular, the conflict potential is thought to result from the risk that the exploitation of intellectual property by contract is used as an opportunity to restrain competition beyond the restrictive effects that are inherent in the exclusivity. In this perspective, the role of antitrust law is simply to contain the exercise of intellectual property rights within their bounds and limits. A whole body of intellectual property-related rules of antitrust law has been developed to deal with this conflict, and it has been developed along different lines in different countries.

In more recent analysis, however, the concept of a conflict-ridden antitrust/intellectual property interface tends to be replaced by the view that intellectual property forms an integrated element of and, indeed, an instrument driving the evolutionary process of dynamic competition. If this is true, then there may be no need any longer for antitrust law rules specifically for

* Professor at Universitat der Bundeswehr Munchen, Neubiberg Germany.

intellectual property. Therefore, rather than simply restating the existing rules, the investigation must also be expanded. The very basis of antitrust control over the exercise of intellectual property needs to be reexamined (see Part IIA below).

To the traditional conflict between antitrust and intellectual property has been added a new concern. There is now a tendency towards 'over protecting' traditional subject matter and expanding availability of intellectual property rights to 'works of low authorship',[1] such as 'subpatentable' inventions or copyrights for almost any computer program or database. Antitrust law, rather than being called upon only to contain the exercise of exclusive rights, might be a means to correct seemingly excessive intellectual property protection by, eg, requiring access to and free use of protected information. This would reopen the by now almost forgotten debate about the incompatibility of 'monopoly' rights with free competition since it implies that, as a matter of 'natural or genuine competition', information is freely accessible for everybody, but will be artificially foreclosed if subject to protection by intellectual property. Antitrust answers for these problems, if any, are likely to be slow in coming, very fact-specific, and probably even contradictory or varying from country to country. How then may antitrust law ever present a general cure for unsatisfactory intellectual property law developments? In fact, existing case law is not very promising, and there is little reason to assume that antitrust law may remedy problems that intellectual property legislation has left unsolved. The reason is that the relationship between intellectual property and antitrust law is not one of a balance between conflicting or one of complementary systems principles, but one of different levels of market regulation (see Part IIB below).

A third overarching issue is international harmonization. This issue is particularly speculative. First, harmonization in the field of intellectual property is taking place at a much faster pace and on a broader scale (and with no respect for concerns of adequate international competition) than in the area of antitrust law. Secondly, the rudimentary international antitrust rules that exist and that might form a starting point for further harmonization actually sound the wrong signal by implicitly giving a priority to intellectual property protection and by allowing antitrust law to apply only exceptionally to the exercise of the exclusive right. Although the first-mentioned aspect, as well as the circumstance that information is ubiquitous and competition global, should militate for an equally rapid harmonization of the antitrust law rules relating to intellectual property, the second-mentioned aspect, as well as the general uncertainties and controversies surrounding the intellectual property/antitrust relationship, suggest a more cautious approach (see Part II below).

---

[1] See Ginsburg, Chapter 3 above.

I. Information, Competition, Intellectual Property, and Antitrust Law

A. Intellectual property for competition

1. The issue: intellectual property paradigms, paradoxes, and antitrust

There is general concern about the effects that expanding intellectual property rights may have on the creation of precisely those 'intellectual' or intangible goods that are the subject matter of these new or extended forms of intellectual property.[2] Assuming that competition is at the root of such creative efforts, the real questions, then, might be these. First, given the presence of so much intellectual property, will competition really work so as to give birth again to sufficient new subject matter, or will so much protection rather obstruct new creation? Secondly, in which way should antitrust law be applied? A conventional approach to this problem may be simply to ask whether a given intellectual property right is exercised illegitimately, so as to restrict unduly the production of new and necessary intellectual property. This, of course, is the same kind of question that is asked in the seemingly dissimilar context of maintaining competition for tangible products when such products are covered by intellectual property, a question that has given rise to so much controversy.

The two questions appear to be dissimilar. The first concerns the general systemic relationship between intellectual property and competition. It addresses the risk of a self-defeating process whereby excessive protection of intangible subject matter impedes or impairs its use for the creation of other intangible subject matter. The second question approaches the interface between intellectual property and competition rather indirectly via the application of the antitrust laws. Generally, it has been asked only with respect to a rather narrowly defined situation, namely that of the anticompetitive use of intellectual property which, by definition, has been granted in order to allow some control of competition in the market for tangible goods, but which, as such, would not block the use of its intangible subject matter for the development of other intangible subject matter. Quite to the contrary, as a quid pro quo for the grant of exclusivity over the tangible goods, this intangible subject matter of protection must be publicly disclosed in order to allow competitors any experimental use for and discovery of substitutable (intangible and tangible) 'products'.

This is the patent paradigm, which has formed all our thinking on the relationship between intellectual property and antitrust.[3] It seems to contrast

---

[2] See Introduction above, and also Gustavo Ghidini, *'Protektionistische' Tendenzen im Gewerblichen Rechtsschutz*, 1997 GEWERBLICHER RECHTSSCHUTZ UND URHEBERRECHT—INTERNATIONALER TEIL 773, 780 et seq.

[3] Thus, both the inherency and the reasonable-reward doctrine have been transposed to copyright and trademark licenses with little respect for the differences of operation existing among the

with the copyright paradigm to the extent that copyright has become a preferred way of protecting much of the information technologies.[4] This contrast, however, results from oversimplification, on the one hand, and from contradictions existing in copyright protection, on the other. For one thing, the primary purpose of patents also is to protect an intangible 'good', the invention as a technological instruction; protection of the tangible embodiments of the invention is only a secondary form granted in view of the nature of the markets from which the inventor's reward is obtained traditionally. This is obvious for process patents, but is no less true for product patents. Conversely, copyright protection also extends to the embodiments of the work, and it is only recently that trade in the intangible form of works has become more important than trade in their embodiments. For another thing, copyright protection has been extended to subject matter that, in its very essence, is different from the traditional subject matter of copyright. But the operation of protection has not been changed in any fundamental way so as conform to the nature of the new subject matter (except for strengthening the exclusivity). As a result, the inherent communication function of copyright has been severely undermined; reproduction of computer programs or of data compilations is defined so as to foreclose third parties from actual access to the content of the protected work. Put differently, protection of the form of the work is used to protect its underlying ideas, whatever declarations to the contrary the legislators have made as a matter of legalistic window-dressing.[5]

Competition involving the use of intellectual property has always taken place on two levels, that of the market for tangible goods and that of the market for intangible subject matter which, indeed, also represents a 'good'. However, there has been antitrust experience in dealing with the restrictive

various forms of protection except insofar as even more immunity from antitrust scrutiny is advocated, see for references Hanns Ullrich, in IMMENGA & MESTMACKER, EG WETTBEWERBSRECHT, 1387 et seq.; 1396 et seq. (1997).

[4] It may be noted en passant that there is something of an irony in the historical development of the protection of computer programs since these have been refused patent protection out of fears of overprotection (see Art. 52(2)(c) of the European Patent Convention 1973; s. 1(2)(3) of the German Patent Act; as to the development in the USA, see Randall M. Whitmeyer, *A Plea for Due Processes: Defining the Proper Scope of Patent Protection for Computer Software*, 85 Nw. U. L. REV. 1103 (1991)); the result being that, by twisting both copyright and the exception to patent protection, computer programs now enjoy double protection under both copyright and patent law, see Art. 9 of Directive 91/250/EC on computer program protection and the increase of computer program patents not only under US and EPC law, but also under the formerly restrictive German Law: DEUTSCHES PATENTAMT, ANNUAL ACTIVITY REPORT 1997 at 9 (Munich 1998).

[5] See K.E. Wenzel, *Problematik des Schutzes von Computer-Programmen*, 1991 GEWERBLICHER RECHTSSCHUTZ UND URHEBERRECHT 105, 110 (calling the EC Directive's claim of granting genuine copyright protection (rather than a copyright-related right) to computer programs a 'printed lie'). For a recent analysis see Sean E. Gordon, *The Very Idea!: Why Copyright Law Is an Inappropriate Way to Protect Computer Programs*, 20 EUR. INT. PROP. REV. 10 (1998).

exercise of intellectual property mainly with respect to maintaining competition on product markets. The question, therefore, is whether, due to the interdependency of these markets,[6] one may apply the antitrust rules that have been developed with respect to the restrictive exploitation of intellectual property on the market for tangible goods to restrictive conduct on the market for intangible products as well. Unfortunately, notwithstanding the long history of antitrust control over anticompetitive practices of intellectual property exploitation, there is not even consensus as to what is a proper approach to intellectual property-related conduct on product markets.[7] It is, of course, generally accepted that collective arrangements between competitors on how they will exploit their intellectual property as regards prices, territories, quantities or product specification are subject to the same antitrust rules that generally apply to horizontal restraints of competition.[8] But such arrangements do not constitute the most representative form of restrictive intellectual property exploitation. Moreover, where intellectual property is central to collective arrangements or joint ventures on the product markets, eg, in cases of patent pools or of cooperative research and development, the general antitrust principles nowadays must frequently give way to considerations like transaction cost minimization[9] or precompetitive cooperation.[10] The common denominator is that enterprises are allowed to determine

---

[6] Enforcement practice tends to examine only the product markets, see Federal Trade Commission, *Antitrust Guidelines for Licensing of Intellectual Property, reprinted in* 4 Trade Reg. Rep. (CCH) ¶ 13,132, at 3.2 (1995).

[7] For an account of the doctrinal development see Hanns Ullrich, *Lizenzkartellrecht auf dem Weg zur Mitte,* 1996 GRUR INT 554; Willard K. Tom & Joshua A. Newberg, *Antitrust and Intellectual Property: From Separate Spheres to Unified Field,* 66 ANTITRUST L.J. 167 (1997).

[8] See s. 20(4) of the *Gesetz gegen Wettbewerbsbeschränkungen* (GWB) as published on 28 February 1990 (LEGAL GAZETTE Part I, p. 235) and referred to in this text as the German Act Against Restraints of Competition; Ullrich, n. 3 above, at 1218 et seq. (EC law).

[9] See Merges, Chapter 6 above. The problem in assessing patent pools is that they are generally not instituted as a generally accessible 'board of trade' but as clubs seeking to accumulate patents, and that it is not patents as property rights that are traded, but exclusivities covering and attributing markets. At any rate, patent pools or exchanges will rarely be more than second-best solutions to two problems, that of an ill-conceived, because overprotectionist, intellectual property system, and that of enterprises doing research that yields intellectual goods and property that does not fully correspond to their needs. Put differently, pools tend to reduce individual R&D competition to competition for participation in the pool, and are justified mainly on grounds of product competition. That, however, is a form of market organization by industry (possibly with the assistance of a state's industrial policy concepts) made on the basis of a tradeoff between technological and product competition that is almost impossible to assess correctly because how do we know what technological competition would have yielded would there be no opportunity for escape into pooling agreements?

[10] For a comparative law examination of this Trojan horse of industrial policy, see ANDREAS FUCHS, KARTELLRECHTLICHE GRENZEN DER FORSCHUNGSKOOPERATION (1989); HANNS ULLRICH, KOOPERATIVE FORSCHUNG UND KARTELLRECHT (1988); as regards EC law, see Ullrich & Konrad, in IMMENGA & MESTMACKER, n. 3 above, at 1415 et seq.; Hanns Ullrich *Patents and Know-how, Free Trade, Inter-Enterprise Cooperation and Competition within the Internal Market,* 23 INT'L REV. INDUS. PROP. & COPY. L. 587, 610 et seq. (1992).

collectively the conditions under which they enter into competition on the market rather than having to accept the conditions of competition the market would impose on their individual conduct.

Regardless of the outcome of applying general rules of antitrust law to such cases, the principle is that the existence of the exclusive right as such does not modify the antitrust rules or their application. It is the very essence of horizontal restraints of competition that they result in concerted action by competitors. Such concertation may be justified, but the justification may never be based on the existence of intellectual property, and even less so on the fact that the concertation relates to the exercise of the exclusivity. As any piece of property, intellectual property is supposed to be used in competition as a matter of autonomous determination and conduct.[11] However, this unmitigated application of antitrust law to the exercise of intellectual property is no longer maintained when it comes to 'vertical' agreements associating third parties with the exploitation of intellectual property, in particular licensing agreements. Such agreements are looked upon with favor as they 'unlock' the exclusivity or promote technology transfer.[12] Whatever restriction they provide for as regards the exploitation of the subject matter by the other party, they are assessed by reference to the scope and/or purpose of the intellectual property right. The precise criteria to be applied have varied as the controversies over the correct determination of the intellectual property/antitrust interface have developed over the years and as competition policy objectives differ from country to country[13] or change over time. The so-called inherency doctrine and the reasonable reward approach, which to varying degrees immunize any restrictive covenant that is reasonably within the scope of the exclusivity or justified by the purpose underlying the grant of the exclusivity, gave way[14] to more vigorous antitrust enforcement until economic analysis

---

[11] See ECJ decisions: February 18, 1971, Case 40/70, *Sirena/EDA*, [1971] Rep., 69; Case C-9/93, *IHT Internationale Heiztechnik GmbH v. Ideal-Standard GmbH*, [1994] E.C.R. I-2789 (holding any exercise of the intellectual property right to be illegal which is the object, means, or result of a cartel agreement).

[12] See Commission Regulation 240/96 of January 31, 1996 on the application of Article 85(3) of the Treaty to certain categories of technology transfer agreements, 1996 O.J. L31/26–27 IIC 675 (1996), in particular Recitals 3, 8, 10. The concept pursuant to which restrictive licensing agreements nevertheless 'unlock' the exclusivity has been propagated by LIEBERKNECHT, PATENTE, LIZENZVERTRAGE UND VERBOT VON WETTBEWERBSBESCHRANKUNGEN (1953), and has become very popular in Germany in the intellectual property community.

[13] The best known example is that of the treatment of territorial restrictions under EC competition rules, see Barry E. Hawk, *La révolution antitrust américaine: une leçon pour la Communauté Economique européenne?* 1989 REV. TRIM. DR. EUR. 5; M. Waelbroeck, in commentary J. MÉGRET, LE DROIT DE LA CE, Vol. 4 'concurrence', 7 et seq., 19 et seq. (Brussels 1997); Hanns Ullrich, *Lizenzverträge im europäischen Wettbewerbsrecht—Einordnung und Einzelfragen*, 1998 MITT. PAT. ANW. 50, 52 et seq.

[14] Richard M. Buxbaum, *Restrictions Inherent in the Patent Monopoly: A Comparative Critique*, 113 U. PA. L. REV. 633 (1965); 1966 WIRTSCHAFT UND WETTBEWERB 193 needs to be

introduced the market value or the intellectual property's bargaining power as a yardstick of legitimate contractual restraints in relations between non-competing parties.[15] In particular, Chicago School representatives[16] generally assume the relationship between the licensor and the licensee to be of a vertical nature, and they justify the latter's integration into the exploitation of the exclusivity by the licensor as a market-determined and, therefore, legitimate restrictive practice.

These approaches, of course, cannot explain why the same kind of limitations on the exploitation of exclusivity by the licensor or by the licensee are accepted in one country and not in another,[17] or why the same kind of limitation is assessed differently over time.[18] The standards actually applied are really normative and uncertain because they depend on the development of antitrust concepts rather than on the relatively stable nature of intellectual property law. In fact, none of the proposed tests has ever corresponded to either the reality of competition or, worse, to the function that intellectual property fulfils in a market economy (although all the approaches attempt to limit antitrust in the name of intellectual property). As a matter of realistic assessment, hardly any agreement associating third parties with the exploitation of intellectual property simply and unilaterally 'unlocks' the exclusivity; rather it represents 'a deal' over the joint or shared exploitation of the exclusivity, whereby both parties determine their market options and conduct. Moreover, agreements between enterprises acting on the product market hardly ever are made on a strictly vertical basis implying no competitive relationship. Rather they result from strategic decisions as to whether the licensor should enter the market alone or whether the licensee should develop the subject matter of protection (or a substitute to it) all by himself; ie, the relationship between licensor and licensee mostly is one of potential competitors.

2. Intellectual property protection for, not from, competition
The more important problems result from the way these doctrines introduce considerations of intellectual property into the application of antitrust rules. They all do it, indeed, on the assumption that there is some contradiction or conflict between, on the one hand, the exclusivity provided for by intellectual property and, on the other, free competition. There is, however, no such

mentioned here, but with respect to German Law also WALZ, DER SCHUTZINHALT DES PATENTRECHTS IM RECHT DER WETTBEWERBSBESCHRANKUNGEN (1973).

[15] See in particular William F. Baxter, *Legal Restrictions on Exploitation of the Patent Monopoly. An Economic Analysis*, 76 YALE L.J. 267 (1966).

[16] See, eg, WARD SIMON BOWMAN, PATENT AND ANTITRUST LAW: A LEGAL AND ECONOMIC APPRAISAL (1973).

[17] See also n. 13 above (territorial restrictions).

[18] For example, the different treatment of tie-ins, grantback clauses, or no challenge clauses under the various EC group exemption regulations for patent licenses, knowhow agreements and technology transfer agreements, see Ullrich, n. 3 above, at 1336 et seq., 1339 et seq., 1357 et seq.

contradiction or conflict.[19] For one thing, competition, whether static or dynamic, is not a natural phenomenon occurring all by itself with respect to all kinds of goods. Rather it is a complex evolutionary system that is deliberately established and maintained to make the market mechanism work for goods that, by virtue of their economic nature, lend themselves to being produced according to market rules. In this sense markets have undergone an evolution from manufacture of and trade in homogenous natural goods to markets for highly diversified and artificial tangible or intangible goods, and similarly competition has changed from rivalry by production and natural imitation to an evolutionary process of systematic creation and innovation. The ever-increasing forms and numbers of intellectual property titles, the banalization of the standards of protection and the territorial broadening of the scope of protection only mirror in law the diversity of the goods actually offered in competition, and they testify to the normality of such competition. They simply constitute the means by which enterprises may operate in competition, and, by the same token, they determine the objects and the organization of competition.

It is this latter aspect that is most frequently misunderstood. Due to a long history of justification of intellectual property on grounds of natural justice, morality, or simply polito-economic expediency,[20] these grounds have acquired the status of overarching, omnipresent principles that pervade legal thinking whenever rules—like antitrust law rules—are discussed that may limit the exploitation of such property. Unfortunately, this inferiority complex and need for justification also overshadows the practical reasons underlying the establishment of intellectual property that are much more directly relevant to its relationship with antitrust. Whereas such legitimization of intellectual property represents nothing but the legislative motifs of protection (but frequently fails to limit its application properly),[21] the practical

---

[19] The following text is based on Hanns Ullrich, *Wissenschaftlich-technische Kreativität zwischen privatem Eigentum, freiem Wettbewerb und staatlicher Steuerung, in* KREATIVITÄT— WIRTSCHAFT—RECHT 203 (Harabi, ed. Zürich 1996); Ullrich, *Lizenzkartellrecht,* n. 7 above, at 561 et seq.; HANNS ULLRICH, INTERNATIONAL EXHAUSTION OF INTELLECTUAL PROPERTY RIGHTS: LESSONS FROM EUROPEAN EXPERIENCE (Mélanges Waellbrooek, Brussels 1999), 205.

[20] For a good general discussion see PETER DRAHOS, A PHILOSOPHY OF INTELLECTUAL PROPERTY 13 (1996).

[21] The exhaustion principle, for example, and its extension to the international level in particular, though in pure logic deducible from the objectives of protection by way of teleological construction of the reach of the exclusivity, has never gained general recognition and will never do so unless it becomes imposed as a mandatory rule following from broader principles of market organization (or integration, respectively), see Ullrich, *International Exhaustion,* n. 19 above. Being elevated to the status of private 'property', intellectual property becomes a self-relying legal institution with rules the construction of which tends to be dissociated from the objectives that have motivated its institution. This holds true even in the United States where the constitutional basis of patents and copyright provides more directly influential guidelines of construction. But these are not precise enough to control the development of intellectual property (as is made obvious by this conference) or to protect the misuse doctrine, its most exposed concretization, against attempts of referral to the status and limits of an antitrust remedy, see below.

reasons for the establishment of intellectual property protection do explain its relationship to competition since they simply result from the economic nature of its subject matter.

The subject matter of intellectual property, however diverse, always is some form of information: a technical instruction in the case of inventions; an aesthetic or emotional appeal or a way of presenting a human, political, philosophical, or scientific idea in the case of literary or artistic works; a message on the origin and/or quality of goods and services in the case of trademarks or service marks, etc. Modern economic theory[22] has pointed out the specific economic features of information, namely the risk of its production, the (total or relative) absence of natural appropriability, and nonrivalry of and nonconsumption by use. As a result it needs to be 'artificially' transformed into an appropriable, scarce 'good' that may be valued according to market rules. Indeed, in the absence of such artificial transformation, if information is created at all, it will not be created according to demand and at competitive costs. It is the exclusivity conferred by intellectual property protection that brings about such transformation into an economic good. This means that by operation of the law intellectual property establishes the protected subject matter as an economic good. But that is all it does. Contrary to a very common but rather misleading form of expression, it is not the grant of an intellectual property right that represents an incentive for the creation of its subject matter or promises a reward, considerations which are generally used to justify restrictive intellectual property exploitation. Exclusivity is a hollow right that takes on value only in accordance with competition.[23] Indeed, it is competition alone that provides the incentives and determines the value of the subject matter and the reward for its creation in accordance with the demand that may be caught by the subject matter. The only, but very important, function exclusivity has in this respect is an intermediate one; that of attributing the opportunities for a reward (the incentives) and the actually available reward to the owner of the right, ie to the 'creator' (inventor, author) or his successor in title. Consequently, competition is a prerequisite to the well functioning of the intellectual property system which, in its absence, has no purpose. Intellectual property, indeed, represents nothing else than a means of competition, an opportunity to act in competition according to the market rules of profit maximization. It grants protection *for* competition, not *from* competition.

---

[22] See generally Kenneth Arrow, *Economic Welfare and the Allocation of Resources for Inventions*, in THE RATE AND DIRECTION OF INVENTIVE ACTIVITY 609, 614 et seq. (National Bureau of Economic Research ed., 1962). For a recent account, see Paul A. David, *Intellectual Property Institutions and the Panda's Thumb: Patents, Copyrights and Trade Secrets in Economic Theory and History*, in GLOBAL DIMENSIONS OF INTELLECTUAL PROPERTY RIGHTS IN SCIENCE AND TECHNOLOGY 19, 24 et seq. (Mitchel B. Wallerstein et al. eds., 1993).

[23] See Baxter, n. 15 above, at 269 et seq. (1966); HANNS ULLRICH, EUROPEAN STANDARDS OF PATENTABILITY 105 et seq. (1977).

This analysis in no way reduces the importance of intellectual property, but simply puts it into the appropriate perspective. As an institutional arrangement for the proper operation of markets for intangible subject matter, it is exempt from antitrust control. In this sense, intellectual property law represents a framework regulation for markets and competition. As a piece of individual property, however, it is fully subject to general antitrust principles,[24] because what is conferred upon its owner is precisely that autonomy of decision in competition and freedom of contracting according to individual preferences[25] that results from any private property, and that is the object of and connecting factor for restraints of competition. Indeed, even though due to their economic characteristics intellectual goods may offer more opportunities of exploitation, the freedom of decision and contracting granted is neither different from general freedom of contract nor is it based on any different rationale, namely the recognition by law of the legitimacy of pursuing individual profit-maximizing interests through contract transactions. Therefore, antitrust control must and does apply to intellectual property-related restraints in the same way as it applies to any other restraint. General rules and principles or objectives of antitrust law, not intellectual property, determine whether intellectual property-related restraints of competition are acceptable. If antitrust law recognizes intrabrand restraints for the sake of interbrand competition, then such restraints must be tolerated in licensing agreements as well. If, however, in the interest of consumer choice, free trade, or market access, vertical restraints are subject to limits set by antitrust law, then these must equally apply to license restrictions. The exclusivity, which anyway is only directed against infringing conduct by third parties but is not intended to serve as a mechanism for interest-sharing among legitimate users of the intellectual good, may not be used as an excuse for restrictive covenants.

Conversely, the approach advocated here explains why license restrictions that are not directly related to the legally recognized purpose of intellectual property, such as quality control, supply exclusivities, or improvement exchanges, are accepted as well and on the basis of the same criteria, namely, on the basis of those that follow from general antitrust principles of furthering innovative competition.

---

[24] The DOJ/FTC Antitrust Guidelines for Licensing, see n. 6 above, also are based on the assumption that intellectual property should be treated as any other property, but fail to explain the reasons and, therefore, to make the necessary distinctions. Ultimately, therefore, they again suffer from an unavowed, but obvious intellectual property reward/incentive bias.

[25] See Case 19/84, *Pharmon BV v. Hoechst AG*, [1985] E.C.R. 2281 (compulsory licenses may not be equated to consent under the principle of exhaustion because compulsory licenses deprive the patent owner of his right 'to freely determine the conditions upon which he wishes to put his products into circulation').

3. The implications of the foregoing analysis

First, the analysis is valid as regards both the market for intangible goods and the market for those tangible goods that embody protected intangible subject matter. On the one hand, the test proposed above directly mirrors the specific characteristics of intangible goods and their transformation into market goods by operation of the law. On the other hand, as the markets for embodied subject matter represent only one level of exploitation of intellectual property (the level of concretization of intellectual goods), they may not, as a matter of principle, be subject to any different yardsticks. It is, indeed, one doctrinal advantage of the antitrust test proposed here that the analysis does not start from the effects that the intellectual property exclusivity may or may not create on product markets, but from the function an intellectual property right is legally intended to perform, namely, that of establishing (competitive) markets for informational goods in the first place.

Secondly, the proper distinction between intellectual property as a framework regulation of markets, on the one hand, and, on the other, antitrust control over the use that is made of the intellectual property's guarantee of entrepreneurial and contractual autonomy means at least two things. One is that intellectual property, although it has been largely harmonized on the international level, does not yield any common standard for the international harmonization of the antitrust rules that may apply to the exploitation of intellectual property. There is, in fact, neither reason nor need for any specific harmonization of intellectual property-related antitrust. Rather, such harmonization will only result from a general harmonization of national antitrust laws.[26] The other implication is that the distinction between intellectual property as a framework regulation of markets and antitrust control over the restrictive exercise of intellectual property on such markets means that antitrust law applies independently from the specific configuration the law has given to a particular form or kind of intellectual property.

At first glance, this latter point seems to be a rather simple, albeit practically important one. It may best be illustrated by the way antitrust law applies to license limitations made on the basis of the divisibility of intellectual property rights. Under both US law[27] and harmonized national law of EU Member States,[28] as well as under Community intellectual property law,[29] license limitations along the lines of such divisibility of the exclusivity

---

[26] Therefore, the Munich Draft International Antitrust Code, in particular its Art. 6 (reprinted in 1994 Aubenwirtschaft 310, 313; see also Fikentscher & Immenga, The Draft International Antitrust Code (Baden-Baden 1996)) is misconceived, but undeniably may very well anticipate the results of misdirected international harmonization efforts.

[27] See 35 U.S.C. § 261 (2000).

[28] Art. 2(2) of the EC Trademark Directive 89/104 of December 21, 1988, 1989 O.J. L40/1).

[29] Art. 22(2) of the Community Trademark Regulation 40/94 of December 20, 1993, 1994 O.J. L11, 125 IIC 735 (1994); see also Art. 42(2) of the Community Patent Convention 1989 O.J. L401/1).

produce effects erga omnes. Their transgression by the licensee represents not only a violation of the contract as such, but also an infringement of the intellectual property right, the result being that excess products or excess sales are illegal as a matter of intellectual property law. Any third party that subsequently acquires such products and uses, resells or keeps them in possession commits an infringement, and it may be sued on that account.

Put differently, as the consent to sales is limited by the license limitation, the exhaustion rule does not apply, so that the distribution of the product may be controlled or pursued all along the distribution line. Consequently, determination of what is a lawful division of intellectual property, which, if cast into license terms, produces such an effect erga omnes, becomes an economically highly important question. However, it is generally not answered in terms of free trade[30] or of its compatibility with competition requirements, but according to well-established practices of the trade and/or in terms of transparency of the division and legal security.[31] It is a matter of intellectual property law, more specifically, of the rules relating to intellectual property as a piece of property that may be transferred or otherwise exploited by contract. Therefore, the lines of divisibility of this property follow national perceptions of intellectual property and contracts.[32] However, as a matter of contract law, divisibility of the right is only an enabling quality, which in no way excludes or predetermines the application of the antitrust rules.[33] These may very well result in confining the limitation on the ground of unjustified restrictive effects, whether as a matter of general competition policy, eg territorial limitations under competition rules,[34] or as a matter of market conditions, eg, in view of a high degree of concentration or of industry practice that results in market foreclosure to new entrants.

Conversely, antitrust law may recognize restrictive covenants in sales or license agreements which are intended by the parties to compensate for failing or insufficient intellectual property protection. A well-known example is the sale or licensing of computer programs that is accompanied by limitations

---

[30] For a critical examination see Ullrich, n. 3 above, at 1179 et seq.

[31] See GERHARD SCHRICKER, KOMMENTAR ZUM URHEBERRECHT [Comment on Copyright], before ss. 28 ff, annot. 47 et seq. (1987) (with respect to copyright where the divisibility lines have not been set by legislative act, but by case law and legal opinion).

[32] With respect to US law, see James B. Kobak, Jr., *Contracting Around Exhaustion: Some Thoughts About the CAFC's Mallinckrodt Decision*, 75 J. PAT. & TRADEMARK OFF. SOC. 550 (1993); Richard H. Stern, *The Unobserved Demise of the Exhaustion Doctrine in US Patent Law*, 15 EUR. INT. PROP. REV. 460 (1993), both critically commenting on *Mallinckrodt Inc. v. Medipart Inc.*, 976 F.2d 700 (Fed. Cir. 1992) which, however, was a case of post-exhaustion infringement. At least under European and German intellectual property law, exhaustion applies only to the right of distribution, not to the separate privilege of exclusive manufacture (eg repair cases) or use (eg trademark in advertising), but there are a large number of borderline situations (eg, repackaging of trademarked goods for parallel resale).

[33] For an early critique, see Baxter, n. 15 above, at 348 et seq.

[34] See Art. 1 of Commission Regulation 240/96 1996 O.J. L31/2, granting a group exemption to specified territorial limitations only.

on the use of the program. Most limitations are, of course, covered by the exclusive (copy) right even when a standard program is sold rather then leased. Indeed, although the sale, but not the lease, results in exhaustion of the exclusivity, the sale still exhausts only the distribution right, not the right to control the reproduction of the program, ie, its use. This distinction is legitimate in view of the intangible or intellectual nature of the good sold,[35] ie, in view of the risk that a resale will not necessarily result in the first vendee being fully substituted by the following vendee as the only user. The intriguing problem, however, is that the vendee or the licensee may be subject to all kinds of restrictions of use. These limitations will be a matter of contract law rather than copyright law because it is controversial and unclear under EC law (Article 4(2) of EC Directive 91/250 on protection of computer programs) which acts of use of the program constitute a reproduction. Most limitations of use, however, are legitimate in view of the fact that, economically, it is not the copyright aspect of the program that matters (its expression), but its concept, ie, its value as a method of solving technical, administrative, or other organizational problems on the basis of electronic data processing.[36] For the program vendor to appropriate fully the value of the program as a service rendered to the vendee, the vendor must be able to control the use the latter makes of the program, whatever the terms of his/her intellectual property right. Antitrust should recognize this by qualifying the relevant use restrictions as lawful per se: it is only by such restrictions that the intellectual achievement of the programmer is transformed into an economic good that may be fully valued by the market.[37]

Finally, the distinction between intellectual property as a regulatory system establishing the conditions of the markets for intellectual goods, and antitrust as a control over the exercise of contract autonomy also explains why essentially the same antitrust law rules apply to conduct relating to intellectual subject matter protected only by contractual confidentiality clauses or simply by tort law. The best known example is secret knowhow. Contrary to what is generally taught, it is not the 'factual monopoly' resulting from secrecy that justifies such equal treatment of, eg, patent licenses and knowhow licenses. In view of the broad definition of trade secrets,[38] and in accordance with general

---

[35] Similarly, if the computer program were patented, there would be no exhaustion as the sale of patented processes does not entail exhaustion, at least not as regards their subsequent use; the underlying reasons are the same as in the case of copyright protection.

[36] For details see Hanns Ullrich, in ULLRICH & KORNER, DER INTERNATIONALE SOFTWAREVERTRAG, Part I, No. 4, 421 et seq. 424 et seq. (Heidelberg 1995).

[37] For similar reasons, all 'restraints' that are solely intended to establish or maintain the integrity of an intellectual good as a protected economic good are per se lawful under the antitrust law, see, eg, Case 27/87, *SPRL Louis Erauw-Jacquery v. La Hesbignonne SC* [1988] E.C.R. 1919. Other examples are sublicensing prohibitions and prohibitions on use once the license (of patents or knowhow) has been terminated.

[38] See Art. 10 (1)–(3) of Regulation 240/96, n. 34 above.

monopoly definitions,[39] in most cases there simply is no monopoly position that could justify a restraint. Rather, just as in the case of intellectual property-related restraints, trade secret-related restraints must be justified under the antitrust rules on the basis of their own merits, eg, because they are indispensable for technology transfer or contribute to technological progress.[40]

However, antitrust law does not only apply independently of the precise configuration of intellectual property. The distinction also means that antitrust law cannot remedy whatever deficiencies, misconceptions or excesses a given intellectual property system may have. This is so as a matter of principle, because antitrust law is never supposed to function as a mechanism for revising the regulatory framework of markets; and it is also the case because of a fundamental difference of function and operation of both bodies of law. As already mentioned,[41] intellectual property law operates as a system attributing 'bare' legal exclusivities. It is intended to remain neutral with respect to the markets and interests it covers, in that the rights are equally available to everybody and valued exclusively according to the commercial merits of a given subject matter or 'intellectual good'.[42] Intellectual property protection operates, so to speak, in the abstract in order to maintain the non-interventionist character of the grant of the right. Competition is to determine the economic yield of the system, and this system has been conceived by the legislators specifically in view of how they think the market will or should operate. Construction and application of intellectual property law must follow and implement this legislative intent. Since the legislature has acted upon the assumption that the market will yield the expected results because it operates on the basis of competition, antitrust law must make sure that competition will, in fact, work properly. But that is the only function of antitrust law. Just as it may only maintain, but not arrange or interfere with competition, it may not be used to modify intellectual property as a regulatory system that

[39] As is well known, the 'legal monopoly' resulting from patents or copyrights also has to be distinguished from the position the goods—tangible or intangible—hold on the relevant market. See Cases C–241/91 P and C–242/91 P, *Radio Telefis Eireann v. Commission of the European Communities* (hereinafter *Magill*), [1995] E.C.R. I–0743, at ¶ 46; Case 78/70, *Deutsche Grammophon Gesellschaft mbH v. Metro-SB-Großmärkte GmbH & Co.* KG [1971] E.C.R. 487 (copyright); Case 24–67, *Parke, Davis & Co. v Probel* [1968] E.C.R. 81 (patents). This well-accepted distinction between the legal and the economic monopoly is just another reason to separate antitrust analysis from intellectual property law criteria.

[40] This is not to say that the same rules and principles always lead to the same results, since the conditions of protection may require distinctions, eg, secrecy of knowhow results in both specific needs of safeguards and specific dependencies. See for an ill-conceived solution as regards improvement grantbacks, Art. 2(4) of Regulation 240/96, n. 34 above, and my critique, see Ullrich, n. 3 above, at 1339 et seq.

[41] See n. 23 above.

[42] Put differently, intellectually property only allows capturing legally unsecured market opportunities that result from demand and from the inventor's or author's competitive performance on the supply side of the market. As a result, the patent and the copyright systems clearly have a bias for commercially attractive inventions and works, but hardly stimulate public interest inventions or works.

defines the means of competition (however imperfect this definition may be). In particular, antitrust law is limited to controlling contractual or concerted restraints of trade or restrictive unilateral conduct in view of the specific conditions of competition existing in a given market. It may not alter or 'improve' the general conditions of competition that the intellectual property system establishes.

This principle, as most principles, seems to be clear as a statement of doctrine, but it may be difficult if not disappointing in its practical application. An example is the US doctrine of 'misuse', in particular the misuse of the copyright exclusivity.[43] Misuse doctrine rests on two assumptions: first, that the general purpose of establishing a given form of intellectual property also controls the individual exercise of that property, and, secondly, that this purpose is sufficiently stable and well defined to direct such control. Whether these assumptions hold true or not,[44] such a rule of intellectual property-related contract law is clearly distinct from antitrust law under which, with respect to the same contractual arrangement, entirely different, and certainly more specific, questions, would be asked, namely, whether there is an identifiable and perceptible restraint amongst actual or potential competitors or some foreclosure of market opportunities based on some definite market power, and whether or not the anticompetitive effects are outweighed by pro-competitive effects. This is a stricter test, directly depending on the effect the agreement has on actual competition, and it is independent and distinct from a test of the general compatibility of the individual contract with the abstract legislative purpose of a given intellectual property. It is not surprising, therefore, that the misuse doctrine has become the object of lively controversy, as the understanding of intellectual property as private property tends to replace its understanding as public policy.[45] On the Continent, where there are hardly

[43] See *Alcatel USA, Inc. v. DGI Techs.*, 166 F.3d 772, 792–95 (5th Cir. 1999); *Data Gen. Corp. v Grumman Sys. Support Corp.*, 36 F 3d 1147, 1169–70 (1st Cir. 1994); *Lasercomb America, Inc. v. Reynolds*, 911 F.2d 970 (4th Cir. 1990). See also *Morton Salt Co. v. G.S. Suppiger Co*, 314 U.S. 488 (1952) (patent misuse); *Practice Mgmt. Information Corp. v. American Medical Ass'n*, 121 F.3d 516 (9th Cir. 1997).

[44] The attempts to subject copyright to a reward or incentive rationale that is analogous to the incentive/reward rationale of patent law appear to derive much more strength from US constitutional language (if not myth) than from economic reality. See Wendy J. Gordon, *An Inquiry into the Merits of Copyright: The Challenges of Consistency, Consent, and Encouragement Theory*, 41 STAN. L. REV. 1343 (1989); Robert A. Kreiss, *Accessibility and Commercialization in Copyright Theory*, 43 UCLA L. REV. 1 (1995); Richard A. Posner & William M. Landes, *An Economic Analysis of Copyright Law*, 18 J. EC. STUD. 325 (1989). But see Stewart E. Sterk, *Rhetoric and Reality in Copyright Law*, 94 MICH L. REV. 1197 (1996). See generally Lloyd L. Weinreb, *Copyright for Functional Expression*, 111 HARV. L. REV. 1149, 1211–17 (1998). For the moderate Continental view, see Gerhard Schricker, *Urheberrecht zwischen Industrie- und Kulturpolitik*, 1992 GRUR 242, who also points to quite a different framework of discussion, which is beyond this chapter's scope; in this respect, see also Benkler, Chapter 11 above; Neil Weinstock Netanel, *Copyright and a Democratic Civil Society*, 106 YALE L.J. 283 (1996).

[45] See, eg, Troy Paredes, *Copyright Misuse and Tying: Will Courts Stop Misusing Misuse?*, 9 HIGH TECH. L.J. 271 (1994); Toshiko Takenaka, *Extending the New Patent Misuse Limitation to*

any constitutional overtones to intellectual property protection—other than those of private property[46]—that would guide the construction and application of intellectual property, no comparable misuse doctrine has ever found acceptance.

Arguably, the misuse doctrine and antitrust law may coexist in a relationship of complementarity,[47] since the misuse doctrine provides only a defense vis-à-vis infringement claims, and since the application of antitrust law indirectly contributes to the attainment of intellectual property law objectives. However, antitrust law will not so assist intellectual property where intellectual property-related contracts are concluded which, rather than stretching intellectual property considerations, tend to fall short of achieving the full purpose of protection. Thus, under German copyright law, licensing contracts are subject to a principle of the law of copyright contracts according to which the scope of the license is to be construed in view of the purpose for which the license is granted, and the presumption is that rights that have not been licensed by express covenant are not included in the license.[48] This rule, as well as the prohibition of assignments of as yet unknown modes of copyright exploitation,[49] aims at ensuring full participation of the author in whatever profit potential his work has, and, ultimately, it is aimed at ensuring the best possible exploitation of the work in accordance with the communication (and arguably the reward) function of copyright.[50] The principle, however, is not of a mandatory nature and, thus, may be contracted around by simply listing all presently known and conceivable modes of exploitation in the 'assignment section' of the license. The result, of course, may be an underexploitation of copyright. Antitrust provides no remedy against such contracts except if a specific (and unreasonable) restraint of competition is shown (and even then the prevailing opinion is more than reluctant to admit a violation)[51] or if the agreement is the result of an undue exercise of market power (rather

---

Copyright: Lasercomb America, Inc. v. Reynolds, 5 SOFTWARE L.J. 739 (1992). But see, eg, Ramsey Hanna, *Misusing Antitrust: The Search for Functional Copyright Misuse Standards*, 46 STAN. L. REV. 401 (1994); Note, *Is the Patent Misuse Doctrine Obselete?*, 110 HARV. L. REV. 1922 (1997).

[46] There is, of course, a discussion of broader issues especially as regards copyright, see Badura, *Zur Lehre von der verfassungsrechtlichen Institutsgarantie des Eigentums, betrachtet am Beispiel des 'geistigen Eigentums'*, FESTSCHR. MAUNZ 1 (Munich 1981).

[47] See Robert H. Lande & Sturgis M. Sobin, *Reverse Engineering of Computer Law Software and U.S. Antitrust Law*, 9 HARV. J.L. & TECH. 237, 248–50 (1996) (pointing to the different procedural functions and substantive criteria of the misuse defense and antitrust claims).

[48] See s. 31(5) of the *Urheberrechtsgesetz* 9.9.1965 (BGBl.I S. 1273) as last amended by the Law of July 24, 1996; and referred to in this text as the German Copyright Act; Schricker, n. 31 above, ss. 31, 32, annot. 9 et seq., 31 et seq.

[49] See s. 31(4) of the German Copyright Act; this rule has mandatory character.

[50] See HANNS ULLRICH, PRIVATRECHTSFRAGEN DER FORSCHUNGSFORDERUNG IN DER BUNDESREPUBLIK DEUTSCHLAND, 127 et seq. (1992).

[51] For references and a critique see Ullrich, n. 3 above, at 1398 et seq.

than merely the result of the imbalance of bargaining positions, which is typical for many copyright contracts).

B. Information access and antitrust

1. From system friction to redress of system failure?

The question whether there should be exceptions to the principle that antitrust not be applied to correct misconceived intellectual property law may best be addressed as a problem of adequate access to information covered by an intellectual property right. It is, indeed, with respect to information access that intellectual property is most frequently characterized as overprotectionist and self-defeating.[52] Typical conflict areas are presented by situations of dependency between patents for too broadly protected principal inventions and for improvement inventions respectively, or between basic and follow-on patents when the field of application of the basic invention has not been sufficiently specified.[53] Other examples relate to copyright protection for computer programs where reverse engineering in view of developing complementary or substitute programs or technology is impeded by a broad definition of the concept of reproduction,[54] or where modular systems programming requires the 'use', ie, reproduction (and eventually distribution) of other programs.[55] Finally, database protection on the basis of copyright and, in particular, of a 'sui generis right' approach is another matter of

[52] See nn. 1–2 above. See also Hugh Laddie, *Copyright: Over-strength, Over-regulated, Over-rated?*, 18 Eur. Int. Prop. Rev. 253 (1996). A more optimistic position is defended by Anthony Mason, *Developments in the Law of Copyright and Public Access to Information*, 19 Eur. Int. Prop. Rev. 636 (1997).

[53] See John H. Barton, *Patents and Antitrust: A Rethinking in Light of Patent Breadth and Sequential Innovation*, 65 Antitrust L.J. 449 (1997); see also Howard F. Chang, *Patent Scope, Antitrust Policy, and Cumulative Innovation*, 26 Rand J. Econ. 34 (1995). The phenomenon of sequential or cumulative innovation, familiar to patent lawyers, has found much interest among economists, see, eg, Dominique Foray, *Production and Distribution of Knowledge in the New System of Innovation: The Role of Intellectual Property Rights*, 1994 STI-Rev. (1) 119, 127 et seq; *Knowledge Distribution and the Institutional Infrastructure: The Role of Intellectual Property Rights*, in Albach & Rosenkranz, Intellectual Property and Global Competition, 77, 87 et seq. (Berlin 1995); Suzanne Scotchmer, *Standing on the Shoulders of Giants. Cumulative Research and the Patent Law*, 5 J. Ec. Persp. 29 (1991). In biotechnology the problems are aggravated by a loose practice of granting patents for inventions without requiring a showing of specific utility, see Joseph Straus, *Abhängigkeit bei Patenten auf genetische Information—ein Sonderfall?*, 1998 GRUR 314; see generally Barbara Looney, *Should Genes Be Patented? The Gene Patenting Controversy: Legal, Ethical, and Policy Foundations of an International Agreement*, 26 L. & Pol'y Int'l. Bus. 231 (1994).

[54] See, eg, *Mai Systems Corp. v Peak Computer Inc.*, 991 F.2d 511 (9th Cir. 1993); *DSC Comm'n Corp. v. DGI Technologies, Inc.*, 81 F.3d 597 (5th Cir. 1996); the cryptic definition of infringement in Art. 4 (2) of the Computer Program Directive 91/250 of May 14, 1991, 1991 O.J. L122/42, arguably making 'running', ie, using the program, an infringement, see Ullrich, in Ullrich & Korner, n. 36 above, Part 1, annot. 22, with references.

[55] This is the starting point of analysis for Pamela Samuelson et al , *A Manifesto Concerning the Legal Protection of Computer Programs*, 94 Colum. L. Rev. 2308 (1994).

concern.[56] The claim is that conventional intellectual property avenues for information access, such as experimental use in patent law[57] or fair use in copyright, do not afford adequate relief and that, therefore, antitrust law remedies should be made available.[58] Sometimes the legislative bodies themselves seem uncertain and simply refer to the availability of unspecified antitrust remedies.[59]

A first problem with these claims is that it is difficult to tell, in particular in today's 'information age', when seemingly reasonable or adequate intellectual property protection actually turns 'overprotectionist'.[60] In particular, it is hard to tell whether it will do so due to the sheer number of available forms of intellectual property. In fact, broad protection of pioneer inventions[61] or dependency situations between patents do have a long tradition, and they have been dealt with differently in various countries without any of the national systems having proved to be definitely superior or inferior as a matter of general

---

[56] See Ginsburg, n. 1 above; J.H. Reichman & Pamela Samuelson, *Intellectual Property Rights in Data?*, 50 VAND. L. REV. 51 (1997).

[57] For an optimistic view see Straus, n. 53 above, at 318; see also David Gilat, *Experimental Use and Patents 1995*, 18 EUR. INT. PROP. REV. 579 (1996).

[58] See, eg, Barton, n. 53 above. The problem of such approaches is that they interfere with the patent system's neutrality vis-à-vis small or great, commercially successful or less successful inventions and, therefore, with competition for small or great and successful inventions; ie, they modify the game and withdraw the jackpot from the lottery. Put differently, they substitute their model of (rational) competition with that which the legislators assumed would underlie the intellectual property system (or else the legislators would have defined the property differently).

[59] See COPYRIGHT OFFICE, REPORT ON DATABASE PROTECTION, Executive Summary, sub VII F (*reprinted in* 54 BNA-PTCJ 374 (1997)).

[60] For one thing, the empirical data even on how the patent system really works (it is the best investigated of all intellectual property forms) are inconclusive, see generally Harabi, *Appropriability of Technical Inventions—An Empirical Analysis*, 24 RES. POL. 981 (1995). For another, the patent scope discussion (see n. 61 below) seems to indicate that scope decisions should differentiate according to type of inventions, nature of industry, structure of the markets and forms and tradition of competition, see FRANKE, DIE BEDEUTUNG DES PATENTWESENS IM INNOVATIONSPROZEß—PROBLEME UND VERBESSERUNGSMÖGLICHKEITEN 307, 319 et seq. (1993). That, however, would require substitution of the rule-of-law-oriented patent granting procedure by an interventionist technology and market-assessment mechanism (for which there may be arguments, see John R. Thomas, *The Question Concerning Patent Law and Pioneer Inventions*, 10 HIGH TECH. L.J. 35 (1995)). In law, however, diversity of interests may be better served by a diversity of forms of protection (which exists, in particular in Europe, contra: Lester Thurow, *Needed: A New System of Intellectual Property Rights*, 1997 HARV. BUS. REV. 95, 103).

[61] While lawyers tend to look with favor on pioneer patents, economists are split as to whether and how to limit broad patents, see Welte, DER SCHUTZ VON PIONIERERFINDUNGEN 168 et seq. (1991); Robert P. Merges & Richard R. Nelson, *Market Structure and Technical Advance: The Role of Patent Scope Decisions*, in ANTITRUST, INNOVATION AND COMPETITIVENESS 185 (Thomas M. Jorde & David J. Teece eds., 1992); Carmen Matutes et al., *Optimal Patent Design and the Diffusion of Knowledge*, 27 RAND J. EC. 60 (1996); Janusz Ordover, *A Patent System for Both Diffusion and Exclusion*, 5 J. EC. PERSP. 43 (1991); Paul Klemperer, *How Broad Should the Scope of Patent Protection Be?*, 21 RAND J. EC. 113 (1990); Yusing Ko, *An Economic Analysis of Biotechnology Patent Protection*, 102 YALE L.J. 777 (1992).

policy.[62] While the unrestricted tendency to grant ever more protection at ever lower thresholds seems to be new, it should also be noted that many countries provide protection for 'subpatentable' inventions and have fared well,[63] and that the transaction function of intellectual property, which allows dependency situations to be overcome, generally has worked out well. It may even have a potential for still more use.[64] All this, of course, is not to deny the risk of counter-productive intellectual property configurations and systems[65] or to deny the obvious failure of the legislature to define the exceptions of protection in terms proportionate to the broadening of protection. After all, protection ought to be directed only at risks of parasitic imitation, not at risks of creative rivalry.[66] It is, indeed, appropriate to recall that the safeguards for the functionality of intellectual property must be built into the system itself, in particular the safeguards necessary to exploit the multifunctionality of its subject matter. Too much or too easy reliance on antitrust relief will never solve deficiencies that the intellectual property system is likely to show. Antitrust remedies, by their very nature, tend to be specific to the facts of a given case rather than offer general solutions. They may help in some singular cases as emergency (or escape) solutions, but they will never really compensate on a broad scale for the inefficiencies of a system of intellectual property protection, let alone guarantee the efficiency of a faulty system.

---

[62] Thus, it would be interesting to see (but difficult to investigate) whether countries with a tradition of narrow interpretation of claims (UK) actually have done better or poorer than, eg, Germany with its reputation for broad interpretation, or whether countries providing for compulsory licensing of principal and depending patents show better or poorer results than countries which, like the US or Germany, are reluctant to grant compulsory licenses, see for Germany, Federal Supreme Court, December 5, 1995, 1996 Mitt. PatAnw. 82.

[63] eg, countries providing for utility model protection as an alternative to or alongside patent protection; see Häusser, *Utility Models: The Experience of the Federal Republic of Germany*, 1987 IND. PROP. 314; utility model protection has been extended over the years and is likely to be introduced Community-wide, see Commission, *Proposal for a Directive on the Harmonization of the Law Relating to the Protection of Inventions by Utility Models*, 1998 O.J. C36/13; EC Commission, *Greenbook: Utility Model Protection in the Internal Market*, COM (95) 370 final, but has not met with acclaim in all Member States or by all interested parties.

[64] For an empirical investigation of the willingness of industry to license patents and on licensing practices see Greipl & Täger, WETTBEWERBSWIRKUNGEN DER UNTERNEHMERISCHEN PATENT- UND LIZENZPOLITIK (1982); Arora, *Patents, Licensing, and Market Structure in the Chemical Industry*, 26 RES. POL. 391 (1997); for an optimistic outlook see Mark A. Lemley & David W. O'Brien, *Encouraging Software Reuse*, 49 STAN. L. REV. 255 (1997).

[65] The example of the excessive copyright term, in general, and for computer programs, in particular, immediately comes to mind: there is no attempt made to determine the tradeoff between exclusion and diffusion which a broad patent literature would suggest (see David, n. 22 above, at 36 et seq.), at least not in Convention law or EC law, and the arguments used to justify the length of 70 years have caused irony, see Patrick Parrinder, *The Dead Hand of European Copyright*, 15 EUR. INT. PROP. REV. 391 (1993). The fine ideas forwarded by Dreier, Chapter 12 above, represent ideals that have never been put into reality, either on the political or the legislative level.

[66] See the reiterated conditioning of the reverse engineering exception on the safeguard of the copyright owner's interest by Art. 6 of Directive 91/250/EC on computer program protection, and the equivalent limitation of the exceptions in Arts 13, 17, 30 of the TRIPS Agreement or Art. 10 of the WIPO Copyright Treaty and Art. 16 of the WIPO Performances and Phonogram Treaty.

The second problem with these antitrust claims for correction of intellectual property 'at the borderline' is that the 'overprotectionist' features of
patent law or, in particular, of copyright law that are so much criticized, are
not marginal or exceptional, but systemic. However, any conceivable
antitrust-based 'rectification' will be available only in those extreme situations where antitrust remedies may directly interfere with existing market
conditions, namely, when, due to a monopolistic structure of the market,
competition has in fact broken down and needs to be restored. Such restoration of competition normally does not take the form of a restructuring of the
markets, but of a strict, quasi-interventionist antitrust control of the conduct
of market-dominating enterprises, these being held to a particular responsibility for the preservation of that 'left-over competition' that is existing on the
market.[67] In guise of a prohibition of abusive exploitation of the dominant
position, such quasi-interventionist antitrust control subjects the enterprise to
a duty of sound and transparent, namely nondiscriminatory, business conduct. Such control may also outlaw unreasonable refusals to deal, including
refusals to license intellectual property,[68] but only in cases of market domination, ie, when the legal monopoly has grown into a factual monopoly on
the market. This, however, means that it is not the exclusive right or the operation of the intellectual property that is at stake, but the use that is made of it
in the absence of competition. The antitrust rules that apply are those that
apply to monopolistic conduct in general; they are not specific to intellectual
property.[69] Where the legal monopoly amounts to a factual monopoly, competition-based intellectual property protection can no longer meet its purpose
nor operate as intended. This then means that the control attaches to the way
an intellectual good, whether protected or not, is exploited. The true problem,
therefore, is how the control of the abusive exploitation of market power may
be exercised with respect to information as an economic good in general.

---

[67] See ECJ: February 13, 1979, Case 85/76, *Hoffmann-La Roche*, 1979 Rep. 461, No. 3891;
December 11, 1980, Case 31/80, *L'Oréal/De Nieuwe Amck*, 1980 Rep. 3775 12 IIC 693 (1981), No.
27; November 9, 1983, Case 322/81, *Michelin/Commission*, 1983 Rep. 3461, No. 29, 57, 70; for an
analysis and references see Möschel, in IMMENGA & MESTMÄCKER, n. 3 above, at 720 et seq.
    [68] See n. 110 below.
    [69] This follows *e contrario* from the principle that as such the exercise of the exclusive intel-
lectual property right does not amount to an abuse of the dominant position the holder of the
right may have on the relevant market, see Case 24–67, *Parke, Davis & Co. v. Probel* [1968]
E.C.R. 81; ECJ: June 15, 1976, Case 96/75, *EMI Records/CBS Schallplatten*, 1976 Rep. 811 No.
34; May 23, 1978, Case 102/77, *Hoffmann La Roche/Centrafarm*, 1978 Rep. 1139 No. 16; Case
238/87, *AB Volvo v. Erik Veng (UK) Ltd.* [1988] E.C.R. 6211, [1989] 4 C.M.L.R. 122; October 5,
1988, Case 53/87, *CICRA/Renault*, 1988 Rep. 6089 No. 15, 20 IIC 186 (1989); Cases C–241/91 P
and C–242/91 P, *Radio Telefis Eireann v. Commission of the European Communities* [1995] E.C.R.
I–0743, at ¶ 49.

2. Controlling abuse or abusing control?

Information access problems are not new to antitrust law enforcement. Early cases involved suppression of a competitor's offer of information,[70] collective refusal of admission to a system of communication,[71] or to a system of information gathering and exchange.[72] These cases have been dealt with on the basis of conventional antitrust control of individual boycotts by monopolists or of group boycotts. Except for the *Associated Press* case,[73] they have not raised concerns for the safeguard of proprietary interests in information that characterize the recent cases, where the concern is about the exercise of monopoly power over information to which access is claimed to be indispensable for the operation of the business of generally small competitors. These cases are of two kinds.

In the European Community considerable controversy[74] has arisen concerning the Commission's intervention against British Broadcasting Corporation (BBC) and Independent Television Publications (ITP), a subsidiary of a group of independent broadcasters acting under the authority of the Independent Broadcasting Authority (IBA).[75] BBC and IBA are the major public broadcasters in the United Kingdom, the broadcasts of which also have a large audience in Ireland. They both published weekly magazines covering their own, and only their own, programs. However, they also made so-called program listings available to newspapers and magazines, ie, simple information on the content of programs that are scheduled some weeks ahead of broadcasting. This they do on condition that the newspapers publish the program only one or two days ahead of actual broadcasting. Claiming their copyright over the program listings, BBC and ITP individually refused to supply Magill TV-Guide, an Irish company which wanted to publish weekly magazines covering the programs of all receivable broadcasters. The Commission enjoined BBC and ITP[76] to supply the program listings on nondiscriminatory terms. The Tribunal of First Instance[77] rejected BBC's and ITP's action against the Commission's decision. Upon appeal the European Court of Justice affirmed, reasoning that the broadcasters hold a monopoly position with respect to the program listings since they make the program and, therefore, are the only source of information on these

---

[70] See *Lorain Journal Co. v. United States*, 342 U.S. 143 (1951).

[71] See *Silver v. New York Stock Exchange*, 373 U.S. 341 (1963).

[72] See *Associated Press v. United States*, 326 U.S. 1 (1945).

[73] See *Associated Press*, 326 U.S. at 29 (Roberts, J., dissenting) (emphasizing the joint effort to acquire the news on the basis of members' efforts and expenses).

[74] See Herman Cohen Jehoram & Kamiel Mortelsman, *Zur'Magill'-Entscheidung des Europäischen Gerichtshofs* [The 'Magill' Decision of the European Court of Justice], 1997 GRUR Int. 11; Ullrich, n. 3 above, at 1251 et seq.; Waelbroeck, n. 13 above, at 830 et seq.

[75] See Decision of December 21, 1988, 1989 O.J. L78/43.

[76] The decision also related to the similar conduct of Radio Telefis Eireann Authority (RTE), the Irish public broadcaster.

[77] See Judgment of July 10, 1991, Cases T–70/89 et al., *BBC/Commission*, 1991 Rep. II 485.

programs. Withholding this 'basic information' constituted an abuse of the monopoly position, because it resulted in the non-availability of a new product—weekly magazines—for which there was a demand, which they themselves did not meet.[78] At least one similar case has arisen and has been decided the same way on similar, though simpler, grounds in Germany.[79] However, the scope of this approach remains unclear since the Tribunal subsequently refused to apply it to a refusal to license TV-coverage of horse races in France to a chain of horse race betting offices which wanted to present live information of the races to its clients.[80]

In another series of cases it is not so much the information as such, but its timely supply to competitors, that is critical for competition. Typically these cases turn on a market-dominating enterprise's practice not to announce in advance the introduction of new products, or the modification of existing ones, to the industry supplying complementary products or services. The antitrust claim for a duty of market-dominating enterprises to 'predisclose' their innovations to enterprises acting on related submarkets[81] is made on the assumption that by withholding the information the monopolist is enabled to transfer its market power to the adjacent market, thereby obtaining an unfair advantage in competition for innovation. However, this claim has been enforced much more successfully by settlement agreements with IBM in the EU[82] than within courtrooms in the United States where Kodak won over Berkey on this account,[83] and where similar actions against IBM have been unsuccessful or withdrawn.[84]

Both lines of cases present difficult problems of market definition, determination of market power and ascertainment of market power transfer to adjacent or dependent markets[85]—a matter that has attracted much attention due to

---

[78] See Cases C–241/91 P and C–242/91 P, *Radio Telefis Eireann v. Commission of the European Communities* [1995] E.C.R. I–0743.

[79] See Hamburg Court of Appeals of May 15, 1997, WuW E OLG 5861 (*Pro 7 v. TV Today*).

[80] See Trib. 1st Inst. of June 12, 1997, Case T–504/93, *Tiercé Ladbroke/Commission*, 1997 Rep. II 923.

[81] Conversely, premature innovation announcement may amount to predatory conduct, see Fleischer, *Mißbräuchliche Produktionsankündigungen im Monopolrecht*, 1997 WuW 203; Janusz Ordover & Robert D. Willig, *An Economic Definition of Predation: Pricing and Product Innovation*, 91 YALE L.J. 8 (1981).

[82] See EC COMMISSION, 15TH REPORT ON COMPETITION POLICY 1984, No. 94 et seq. (Luxembourg 1985), [1984] 3 C.M.L.R. 147 (the disclosure requirements were not very far-reaching and easily manageable).

[83] See *Berkey Photo, Inc. v. Eastman Kodak Co.*, 603 F.2d 263 (2d Cir. 1979).

[84] See Kenneth L. Glazer & Abbott B. Lipsky, Jr., *Unilateral Refusals to Deal Under Section 2 of the Sherman Act*, 63 ANTITRUST L.J. 749, 776 (1995); Eleanor M. Fox, *Monopolization and Dominance in the United States and the European Community: Efficiency, Opportunity, and Fairness*, 61 NOTRE DAME L. REV. 981, 1013 et seq. (1986).

[85] For this market power leverage-approach see Roger D. Blair & Amanda K. Esquibel, *Some Remarks on Monopoly Leveraging*, 40 ANTITRUST BULL. 371 (1995); FLEISCHER, BEHINDERUNGSMIßBRAUCH DURCH PRODUKTINNOVATION, 53 et seq., 127 et seq., 138 et seq., 151 et seq. (1997).

Eastman Kodak v. Image Technical Services,[86] and that, fortunately, is outside the scope of this chapter. However, in the predisclosure cases, the analysis relates to markets for tangible goods or for services; whereas in the *Magill* type of cases, it is the market for information that has to be analyzed. Such analysis apparently induces short-circuit thinking. Both the European Court of Justice and the German Court of Appeals in Hamburg have been victims of such thinking in that they qualified the TV program listings as 'basic information' and then concluded that, because the broadcaster makes the program and, therefore, is the sole (or only original?) source of the listings, it also holds a monopolistic position with respect to the information.[87] However, every author of information and every person of interest to the media are the sole source of information on his/her internal matters and intentions. Therefore, the court's conclusion, which produces innumerable monopolies,[88] cannot be the end of the analysis. It is, of course, true, that listings of programs of one TV-broadcaster may not be substituted by listings of other broadcasters, and that, according to the subjective relevant market test that is applied under Community and German antitrust law,[89] it is the consumer's need or demand that determines the substitutability of goods and, therefore, the relevant market. However, such an analysis must fail to the extent that each piece of information is individual and specific, thus excluding substitutability in almost all cases. Yet reality teaches that just as inventions, whether patented or not, do have competitive substitutes, so do information items. The real problem is that information hardly lends itself to an objective test of substitutability. But this difficulty is no sufficient reason to accept the consequences of the test used by the European Court of Justice, which is that the essential element of competition in the information market, namely, competition for access to information, simply is totally neglected. In fact, the relevant market for the supply of goods, services or, for that matter, information is not only determined by what the consumers ask for and accept as substitutes, but by the form and vigor of competition on the demand side as well, since consumers competing for supply may be more ready to accept substitutes.[90] There will be no such competition on the demand side if,

[86] See *Eastman Kodak Co. v. Image Technical Servs. Inc.*, 504 U.S. 451 (1992); *Image Technical Servs., Inc. v. Eastman Kodak Co*, 125 F.3d 1195 (9th Cir. 1997). See also Joseph Kattan, *Market Power in the Presence of an Installed Base*, 62 ANTITRUST L.J. 1 (1993)

[87] See Cases C–241/91 P and C–242/91 P, *Radio Telefis Eireann v. Commission of the European Communities* [1995] E.C.R. I–0743, at ¶ 47; Hamburg, Court of Appeals, n. 79 above, WuW E OLG at 5863 (using an even simpler approach in stating that since the publisher of the TV-program magazine was interested in precisely the program listings of Pro 7, which only Pro 7 can supply, there is no other source of supply and, therefore, market domination exists).

[88] At least all the royal and aristocratic families, movie and sports stars, artists, etc that interest the gossip media would be in such a monopoly position, certainly so if they address that press by 'news from the royal court'.

[89] See Möschel, in IMMENGA & MESTMACKER, n. 3 above, at 696 et seq.; Hamburg, Court of Appeals, n. 79 above, 87 expressly relied on this '*Bedarfsmarktkonzept*'.

[90] The consideration necessarily follows from the dependency test of market domination which, with respect to refusals to deal, inquires into whether an enterprise is the natural and necessary

due to a formalistic determination of information interchangeability, market power is held to exist and, consequently, a claim to equal access to any piece of information is admitted as a matter of principle.[91] Put differently, such a one-sided approach sacrifices demand side competition in the interest of the competitiveness of demand side enterprises on their downstream sales markets. This, however, implies a difficult tradeoff that risks neglecting that competition is a system that forces enterprises to optimize their efficiency only when they are exposed to it on all sides of their activities, upstream and downstream.

This is not the place to develop a relevant market/monoply test for information markets. Sometimes the downstream markets for products or services embodying the information will yield sufficient indicia of interchangeability,[92] sometimes the event to which information relates will also determine the value of the latter.[93] In other cases the practice of the industry concerned will provide criteria. Generally speaking, the relevant market test is itself a normative concept and not a merely phenomenological one. Therefore, it must be applied with a view to the kind of competition the antitrust laws are intended to protect in a given case.[94] The test must be such as to overcome the paradoxes that result from the nature of information as an economic good. Its value (at least, private value) may increase if access is difficult. At any rate, the criteria establishing information as an economic good cannot automatically be the criteria for the relevant market. Value and inaccessibility of information increase the more specific, in particular competitor-specific, it is: at the margin each enterprise is a monopolist with respect to information on its own activity. This, however, cannot automatically make it a monopolist in an antitrust law sense. As with the subject matter of intellectual property in general, the individual character of information and the monopolistic nature of its position on the market are quite different things.

partner (supplier) of another (see *Waelbroeck*, n. 13 above, at 245 et seq., who, however is critical of this concept). The prevailing opinion, however, undertakes the analysis from the perspective of the market of the alleged monopolist, see Möschel, in IMMENGA & MESTMACKER, GWB, Kommentar zum Gesetz gegen Wettbewerbsbeschränkungen, s. 22 annot. 22 et seq. (2d ed. Munich 1992); but see ECJ of November 9, 1983, Case 322/81, *Michelin/Commission*, 1983 Report 3461 at No. 37 et seq.

[91] Quite apart from the fact that such an approach results in there being no basis for determining the price for the information, with all that this means in terms of interventionist control.

[92] This will normally be the case for inventions, see [DoJ] FTC-Guidelines n. 6 above, but also for software or other works as a product or a service, see Case 78/70, *Deutsche Grammophon Gesellschaft mbH v. Metro-SB-Großmärkte GmbH & Co. KG* [1971] E.C.R. 487.

[93] This may be the case for TV-transmission rights covering sports or entertainment events, see Commission decision of June 11, 1993 (EBU-Eurovisionsystem, 1993 O.J. L179/23; Trib. First Inst. of July 11, 1996, Cases T–528/93 et al., *Métropole Télévision/Commission*, 1996 Rep II 649.

[94] This is uncontroversial, see Möschel, in IMMENGA & MESTMACKER, n. 90 above; German Act Against Restraints of Competition, s. 22, annot. 19 et seq. (and obvious when market power is determined according to the dependency doctrine, see n. 90 above): markets are determined so as to allow control, eg, ECJ of November 13, 1975, Case 26/75, *General Motors Continental*, 1975 Rep. 1367.

Moreover, the multifunctionality of information means that its value depends on the use that is made of it. But enterprises may not be turned into monopolists simply because they hold information that their competitors find to be useful for their own purposes. The qualification of information as 'basic' is not helpful in this context either, but rather contributes to confusion by an obviously simplistic analogy to 'raw material' which monopolists may be obliged to supply to their competitors on downstream markets.[95]

A possible way out of all these dilemmas may be simply to reverse the relevant market test, and to take the consequences of market power as indicia of its existence. This is the rationale underlying the dependency test.[96] Consequently, one test could be to ask whether there are reasonably acceptable opportunities to obtain the information (or functionally comparable information) from other sources and/or whether nonsupply of the information substantially affects the competitiveness of the enterprise requesting it. In the *Magill TV-Guide* case where BBC and ITV programs had large market shares in Ireland, and where Magill's offer of a weekly TV-Guide, reasonable in itself, would not have been competitive if it did not cover these programs, several of the tests proposed were met. Their application would have been more convincing than the test used by the Court[97] or the Tribunal.[98]

It is, however, not only the relevant market that has to be defined normatively with a view to the kind of competition that the law seeks to protect. Rather, due to its being protected by law, competition itself is a normative concept. This is clearly illustrated by the predisclosure cases, since a predisclosure requirement plainly is at odds with what has been the generally accepted concept of competition under the antitrust laws, namely, that enterprises should not inform competitors of their competitive moves. But, then, this is just another change in the legal concept of competition underlying antitrust law. Agreements on the exchange of market data or business data have first been tolerated or authorized. They have even been made indirectly mandatory as a matter of maintaining transparency in the market for the sake of perfect competition.[99] Subsequently, they have come under antitrust scrutiny to the extent that transparency on oligopolistic markets for homogenous products disfavors an enterprise's willingness to make individually

---

[95] The Court (n. 78 above, at 56) expressly referred to ECJ of March 6, 1974, Cases 6/73 and 7/73, *Commercial Solvents/Commission*, 1974 Rep. 223, which is the leading case on the duty of a market-dominating manufacturer of raw material to supply its downstream competitors.

[96] See ECJ of November 11, 1986, Case 226/84, *British Leyland/Commission*, 1986 Rep 3263, at No. 9; s. 20(2)(2) of the German Act Against Restraints of Competition.

[97] Trib. First Inst. of July 10, 1991, n. 77 above at No. 48 et seq., 51 correctly distinguishes between the determination of the relevant market and that of market domination, but simply equates the latter with the 'monopoly' of the copyright in the program listings, ie, it does not even examine the importance of the copyrighted subject matter on the relevant market.

[98] See n. 78 above, at ¶ 47.

[99] See Arts 4, 60, 63 European Community for Steel and Coal (ECSC) Treaty (price information obligations); *Maple Flooring Mfrs. Ass'n v. United States*, 268 U.S. 563 (1925) (USA).

competitive moves, eg, price reductions. 'Arcane competition' became the catchword.[100] The principle behind the change of antitrust approach was that industry might not itself arrange the ways and forms according to which competition should operate by concertedly or collectively internalizing market information. Predisclosure claims relate to market information, namely, to data on the position and the competitive moves of other enterprises.[101] Whether they may be justified by the fact that, due to one enterprise's domination of the market, it internalizes the information needed by the entire market, so that its proprietary knowledge turns into knowledge affected by a public interest, depends not so much on an objective analysis of the market mechanism for innovation,[102] but on the idea which enforcement agencies and courts make themselves of competition for innovation. 'Undisclosed' criteria, such as litigation evidence, historical experience, personal attitude and general information relating to markets and economic systems they are familiar with,[103] will tend to influence their judgment. Diverging opinions are the result, and necessarily so. There is no definite answer to the relevant issues of competition for innovation like the necessary lead-time or the incentive/reward needed in terms of the number and/or scope of 'appropriable' markets.[104] The courts, though frequently deciding ex post, must take an ex ante view of these issues and of how competition could have developed, and they may with good reason prefer to substitute such uncertain or, worse, preten-

---

[100] German Federal Supreme Court: January 29, 1975, WuW E BGH 1337, 1341 et seq. (*Aluminiumhalbzeug*); November 18, 1986, WuW E BGH 2313 (*Baumarktstatistik*). For the USA see *US v. Container Corp. of America*, 393 U.S. 333 (1968); for the EC recently, Trib. First Inst. of May 14, 1998, Case T–338/94, *Finnish Board Mills Ass.-Finboard/Commission*, Rep. 1998 II 1617; ECJ of May 28, 1998, Case C–7/95 P, *John Deere Ltd./Commission*, Rep. 1998 I 3111; for a general discussion LAMPE, WETTBEWERB, WETTBEWERBSBEZIEHUNGEN, WETTBEWERBSINTENSITAT, 191 et seq. (1979); Johan Carle & Mats Johnsson, *Benchmarking and E.C. Competition Law*, 19 EUR. COMP. L. REV. 74 (1998).

[101] These 'market data' may and frequently will represent business secrets, both as regards the time and the object of individual innovation. Again, this shows the multifunctionality of information.

[102] This is a vast subject in itself with many antitrust issues relating to information that cannot be dealt with here, eg, information-sharing agreements as a (doubtful) justification for research and development joint ventures. See, eg, THOMAS M. JORDE & DAVID J. TEECE, INNOVATION, COOPERATION AND ANTITRUST, IN ANTITRUST, INNOVATION AND COMPETITIVENESS 47 (1992); David J. Teece, *Information Sharing, Innovation, and Antitrust*, 62 ANTITRUST L.J. 465 (1994); Monopolkommission, Hauptgutachten 1988/1989, No. 974 et seq. (Baden-Baden 1990).

[103] Compare *Berkey Photo, Inc. v. Eastman Kodak Co.*, 603 F.2d 263 (2d Cir. 1979) with the Commission's position in the IBM case, n. 82 above.

[104] Thus, there is so little political consensus as to whether spare-part markets (whether separate markets or submarkets in antitrust law terms or not) should be attributed to the owner of a car design that legislation on harmonization of design protection in the EC actually has been blocked for years, see G. Riehle, *Kapituliert Europa vor der Ersatzteilfrage?*, 1997 EuWiStR 361; Helmut Eichmann, *Kein Geschmacksmusterschutz für must-match Teile?*, 1997 GRUR INT. 595. Note that Case 238/87, *AB Volvo v. Erik Veng* (UK) Ltd. [1988] E.C.R. 6211, [1989] 4 C.M.L.R. 122 allowed Volvo to monopolize the spare-parts market on the basis of its design protection.

tious knowledge[105] by assuming that, due to its self-healing effects, dynamic competition will over a period of time reinstall competitive structures.[106]

However, such logic is far from being generally accepted. Not only industrial economics and publicly funded R&D policy, but commonsense insight into human mentality teach that it is difficult simply to accept the operation of innovation competition and to withstand the temptation to both influence its progress and to prevent or to cure its 'injustices'. Divergent national competition policies simply mirror the nations' different attitudes towards the social problems raised by competition.[107] Therefore, they will continue to exist, and so will fundamental competition policy controversies within countries. As recent history of antitrust law in the USA, EU and Germany shows, application of the antitrust laws follows these controversies with some time-lag. In fact, for the sake of what is expected from the operation of the market, antitrust law even accepts clear manipulation of the concept of competition.[108] Antitrust treatment of information access seems to be just another example of how antitrust does (but should not?) follow a volatile 'normative' concept of which competition ought to be protected.

Market domination may entail a duty to respect specifically the existence and survival of any remaining competition.[109] In particular, the monopolist is expected to behave competitively, ie, on the merits of its efficiency and innovative achievements. Therefore, the monopolistic enterprise is and must be entitled to adhere to precisely the conduct it would follow under conditions of workable competition, including the autonomous exercise of the exclusive right vis-à-vis infringements and the autonomous decision about whether and with whom to make contracts, eg, to refuse to grant contractual licenses.[110] However, as a monopolist may be tempted to take special advantage of its position on the market, antitrust law will control its conduct as to its possibly abusive, anticompetitive nature. Since under conditions of competition the

---

[105] See HAYEK, DER WETTBEWERB ALS ENTDECKUNGSVERFAHREN (1968).

[106] Independently of systems analysis, such optimism may simply be based on actual experience of the transitory effect of innovation-related restraints of competition, see Fleischer, Behinderangsmißbrauch durch Produkt innovation (Baden-Baden, 1997), at 143 et seq., 156 et seq.

[107] See John Haley, Culture, Competition, and (De-) Regulation: Japan's Challenge to International Harmonization of Competition Law, in COMPARATIVE COMPETITION LAW: APPROACHING AN INTERNATIONAL ANTITRUST LAW SYSTEM 93 (Hanns Ullrich ed., 1998).

[108] As regards the concept of 'precompetitive R&D' and the definition in the GATT/WTO subsidies code, see Art. 8(2) n. 7 (transformation of the results of industrial R&D into plans for innovative products, process and services, including prototype building); Ullrich, n. 3 above, at 1419 et seq.

[109] See n. 67 above and accompanying text.

[110] See Case 238/87, AB Volvo v. Erik Veng (UK) Ltd. [1988] E.C.R. 6211, [1989] 4 C.M.L.R. 122 (refusal to contract not abusive exercise of exclusivity right); Data Gen. Corp. v. Grumman Sys. Support Corp., 36 F.3d 1147 (1st Cir. 1994); Image Technical Servs., Inc v. Eastman Kodak Co., 125 F.3d 1195 (9th Cir. 1997). For a discussion see Shiraishi, Unfair Competition Law and Competition Policy, in COMPARATIVE COMPETITION LAW, n. 107 above, at 141, 145 et seq. See also n. 111 below.

enterprise would deal fairly with all its business partners, arbitrary discrimination of and refusal to sell or license enterprises in the course of a trade it generally maintains with other enterprises will be considered abusive.[111] This is a well-accepted principle, though determining arbitrariness (or simply 'discrimination') may not always be easy. Market-dominating broadcasters, for example, which do offer their program listings to all newspapers and TV-magazines, must have special reasons when they stop selling to one of them.[112] Certainly, the existence of copyright protection (assuming program lists do qualify for copyright)[113] by itself is no such business justification. Copyright affords an opportunity to do business by contract, but that is all it does. Invoking copyright as a ground justifying a refusal to license, which, due to the monopoly position of its owner needs justification, plainly is a circular argument, albeit one that is frequently used.[114]

A rule of antitrust law directed against discrimination in trade by monopolists appears to be sound as a principle ensuring a level playing field for enterprises competing with the market-dominating firm and for enterprises dependent on it as regards their own business. Difficulties arise only where nondiscrimination is determined indistinctly or by reference to 'orderly' competition rather then by reference to free and dynamic competition.[115] But these are difficulties of application, not of principle. By contrast, the antitrust rule against predatory conduct, which is another form of abusive behavior by monopolists, gives rise to fundamental divergences of judgment. As such, many acts of predation represent basically innocent competitive moves that are considered to be abusive only because they emanate from market-dominating enterprises, ie, market power tends to make all the difference. But still, particular circumstances must be present that make the conduct unlawful. Predisclosure cases are a good illustration of the difficulties in determining such qualifying circumstances.[116] But refusals to sell or license by market-dominating enterprises that do not (and never did) trade in the goods or intel-

---

[111] See Arts. 86(c) of the EC Treaty; ss. 19(4)(3); s. 20(2) of the German Act Against Restraints on Competition.

[112] See n. 79 above.

[113] Some commentators have explained the ECJ's *Magill* decision as a judicial critic of excessive copyright protection, see, eg, Götting, note commenting to ECJ of April 6, 1995, n. 78 above, 1996 JZ 307; Doutrelepont, *Mißbräuchliche Ausübung von Urheberrechten?*, 1994 GRUR INT. 302, 307.

[114] But see *Image Technical*, n. 110 above, 125 F.3d at 1195.

[115] See generally MESTMACKER, DER VERWALTETE WETTBEWERB, 5 et seq., 31 et seq. (1984).

[116] Fleischer, n. 106 above, at 110 et seq. lists a number of criteria relating to the structure of the market, the technical or aesthetic necessity or character of the innovation, the incentive/appropriability requirements for making the innovation (inclusion of the reward from related markets?), the necessary lead-time (which is hard to specify, see *Berkey Photo, Inc. v. Eastman Kodak Co.*, 603 F.2d 263, 282 (2nd Cir. 1979) pointing to the difficulties of specifying necessary predisclosure terms), the intent of the monopolist (as evidenced, eg, by arbitrary technical changes), etc.

lectual property asked to be sold or licensed are no less difficult,[117] in particular, when information goods are at stake. In its *Magill* judgment,[118] the
Court based its verdict on the refusal to supply the program listings on two
circumstances, first, that the refusal blocked the offer of a new product (ie,
weekly magazines with full coverage of all broadcasters) developed from the
'basic information' (ie, creation of a 'plus value') for which there is a demand,
and secondly, that the market dominating enterprise did not meet this
demand for fear that it would lose profits on a market which, for it, was secondary (broadcaster-specific TV-magazines).[119] These, of course, are circumstances of importance. They are even recognized by intellectual property law
as circumstances legitimizing withdrawal of protection or curtailment of the
exclusivity. At least patent law frequently makes exclusivity of protection
dependent on adequate use of the invention,[120] and it may also provide for
compulsory licenses in cases of dependency.[121] As far as copyright is concerned, its communication function was at stake in the *Magill* case, and copyright protection for technological subject matter arguably should be subject
to principles analogous to those of patent law such as use requirement,[122] at
least if it actually results in protection of the idea. The flaw of the decision as
a leading case, however, may precisely be that rather than applying tests of
antitrust law it relied on intellectual property philosophy. There was no
weighing at all of the interests of Magill vis-à-vis those of the broadcasters
as competitors on the markets for TV-magazines,[123] let alone any factual

---

[117] Thus, the circumstances listed by Case 238/87, *AB Volvo v. Erik Veng (UK) Ltd.* [1988]
E.C.R. 6211, [1989] 4 C.M.L.R. 122 with respect to the goods markets (arbitrary refusals to supply spare parts to independent repair stations, excessive prices for such parts or termination of
spare-parts production when the main product is still in general use) are ambivalent, see Ullrich,
n. 3 above, at 1258 et seq.

[118] See n. 78 above, at ¶ 52 et seq.

[119] This second argument is really related to a third argument, which the Court also used,
namely the market power leverage argument that the broadcasters tried to protect the 'derivative
market' for weekly TV-magazines; however, whether 'appropriation' of derivative markets is ille-
gitimate is a problem in itself, see n. 104 above and Ebenroth & Bohne, *Gewerbliche Schutzrechte
und Art 86 EG-Vertrag nach der Magill-Entscheidung* 1995 EuWiStR 397, 403.

[120] See Arts 45, 46 of the Community Patent Convention (CPC); ECJ of February 18, 1992,
Case C–30/90, *United Kingdom/Commission*, 1992 Rep. I 829 (id. at 858 *Italy/Commission*); Art
L 613–11 of the *Code de la propriété-intellectuelle*.

[121] See Art 47 CPC; Art L 613–15, of the *Code de la propriété intellectuelle* (Law No. 92–597
of July 1, 1992, J.O., July 3, 1992, p. 8801); as amended by Law (No. 92–1336) of December 16,
1992; as amended by Law (No. 94–102) of February 5, 1994; s. 48(3)(d) (ii) of the UK Patents
Act 1997; Art. 31(l) of the TRIPS Agreement; see also n. 62 above.

[122] See for a general approach John Shepard Wiley, Jr., *Copyright at the School of Patent*, 58
U. CHI. L. REV. 119 (1991).

[123] Quite to the contrary, by a 'normative' approach of determining the relevant market, the
Trib. First Inst., n. 80 above, managed to subdivide the markets for TV-program information
into two: the market for successful weekly magazines, and the market for less successful magazines specifically for broadcasters (and daily newspaper information, which is incidental to news
reporting anyway).

assessment of these interests. Rather, the Court only made a peremptory statement of the novel character of a weekly magazine (which, after all, was nothing more than the transfer of a commercial idea that was in practice in other EC countries), and it totally neglected the profits the broadcasters would lose on the TV-magazine market.[124]

In fact, in the case of refusal to supply information, specific consideration must be given to the circumstance that information markets may not easily be separated into upstream and downstream markets or into information markets and unrelated goods markets. Due to the multifunctionality of information, these markets generally are linked together by interdependency. For instance, the way the program information is used and presented by enterprises on the TV-magazine market may directly affect the broadcasting market. In the *Pro 7* case, Pro 7 complained of misleading reports being made on Pro 7's production activities. This may be a matter of media law,[125] but qualitatively correct reporting is a matter of high interest to the broadcaster, which, in the analogous case of the distribution of goods by unqualified trade, would justify a refusal to deal.[126] Put differently, to the plus-value the TV-magazine creates in publishing the program schedule might correspond a loss of money for the broadcaster's broadcasting activities, particularly so in the case of commercial broadcasters living exclusively on income based on the value of their programs for advertisers.[127]

An even more problematic issue is raised when there is direct interdependency due to information being exploited through the same modes of use by competitors. In these cases compulsory access modifies the scarcity relations that the law seeks to protect by transforming information into an appropriable economic good. As a result, the value the information has on the market and as a means of competition may be more or less heavily affected by giving extra rights to access.[128] As already mentioned, in the *Magill* case the European Court of Justice did not even mention the fact that obliging broadcasters to supply their program listings to TV-magazine publishers meant a

---

[124] See also the critique by Waelbroeck, in MEGRET, n. 13 above, at 832 et seq.; Ebenroth & Bohne, n. 119 above, at 402 et seq.

[125] Hamburg, Court of Appeals n. 79 above, used this as a ground to disregard arguments based on the misleading or disparaging character of TV-Today's report.

[126] For the right of the market dominating enterprise to opt for a selective distribution system, see Markertj, in IMMENGA & MESTMACKER, n. 90 above, s. 26(2) annot. 223.

[127] This circumstance should, in fact, have cautioned Hamburg, Court of Appeals n. 79 above, because a commercial broadcaster living on advertising income will not block information of its program to the potential audience without having substantial reasons.

[128] It was with good reason, therefore, that German Supreme Court decision of November 6, 1984, WuW E BGH 2134 (Schufa) accepted a kind of collective refusal by the credit information agency of commercial banks to admit independent credit brokers to the information it collected on the financial reliability of debtors. Of course, the argument that as clients for the information the brokers were not in the same line of business as are banks (see German Act Against Restraints of Competition, s. 26(2)), was all too easy and merely obscured the true reasons.

modification of these scarcity relations and, in fact, a devaluation if not an expropriation of the program listings in the hands of the broadcasters: the buying public lost any interest in the public broadcaster's own TV-magazine, and the duty of TV-magazine publishers to pay a royalty to the broadcaster, by definition, will never result in a full compensation for the expropriation.[129] Information is simply a good that is not consumed by use, but only rendered useless by lapse of time, ie by obsolescence. If it is not really transferred, but made accessible to joint use, then the value of use may be maintained, but its market value will drastically decrease, and so will the incentive to create the information—a circumstance that did not make itself felt in the *Magill* case for the simple reason that the program listings merely are a necessary by-product of the broadcasting activity.

The qualification of information by the term 'basic', and the popular comparison of the difficulties in the supply of advanced software with a 'bottle-neck' situation and of information with natural resources are all factors that have contributed to the antitrust law analysis of information markets recently having been enriched by the introduction of the essential facilities doctrine.[130] This doctrine is much in vogue as a key that opens a door to networks for the transportation of tangible or intangible goods.[131] Whatever the merits of the doctrine are as regards access to such networks,[132] its application for the purpose of breaking up information monopolies, whether legally protected by an intellectual property right or not, should be looked at rather critically. The

---

[129] A license royalty may never exceed the value of the use the licensed information has for the licensee; if it were to cover the losses a competing licensor suffers as a result of the compulsory license, it would be prohibitive. Typically, therefore, licenses are granted with respect to markets the licensor does not or cannot supply himself. As to the effect of compulsory licensing of program listings see Doutrelepont, n. 113 above, at 306.

[130] See Montag, *Gewerbliche Schutzrechte, wesentliche Einrichtungen und Normung im Spannungsfeld zu Art 86 EGV*, 1997 EuZW 71; Mennicke, '*Magill'—Von der Unterscheidung zwischen Bestand und Ausübung von Immaterialgüterrechten zur 'essential facilities'-Doktrin in der Rechtsprechung des Europäischen Gerichtshofs?*, 160 ZHR 626 (1996); Deselaers, *Die'Essential Facilities'-Doktrin im Lichte des Magill-Urteils des EuGH*, 1995 EuZW 563; Temple Lang, *Defining Legitimate Competition: Companies' Duties to Supply Competitors and Access to Essential Facilities*, 1994 FORD. CORP. L. INST. 244, 303 et seq. (B. Hawk, ed., 1995).

[131] See German Act Against Restraints of Competition, s. 19(4); Bundesregierung, Entwurf eines 6. Gesetzes zur Änderung des Gesetzes gegen Wettbewerbsbeschränkungen, Bundesratsdrucksache 852/97, at 37 et seq.

[132] See Case C–7/97, *Oscar Bronner GMBH & Co KG v. Mediaprint Zeitungs- und Zeitschriftenverlag GmbH & Co. KG* [1998] E.C.R. 1–7791, and the analysis of the doctrine by Advocate-General Jacobs; Klimisch & Lange, *Zugang zu Netzen und anderen wesentlichen Einrichtungen als Bestandteil der kartellrechtlichen Mißbrauchsaufsicht*, 1998 WuW 15; Möschel, in IMMENGA & MESTMACKER, n 3 above, at 765 et seq.; v Weizsäcker, *Wettbewerb in Netzen*, 1997 WuW 572. But see Bunte, *6. GWB-Novelle und Mißbrauch wegen Verweigerung des Zugangs zu einer wesentlichen Einrichtung*, 1997 WuW 302. It should be noted that the German legislature has limited the scope of application of the doctrine to *infra*structure facilities by substituting this term with the term 'essential facilities' in the original Bill. This is remarkable, because the Government Bill expressly mentioned intellectual property as an example of an essential facility (see Bundesratsdrucksache 852/97 at 38).

essential facilities doctrine has been reactivated after decades of oblivion[133] as an instrument for reorganizing markets that, for various reasons, are structured monopolistically. It is particularly well suited for this purpose, as it is a doctrine that, by its very definition,[134] is aimed at market power as such rather than merely at the abuse of such power. If applied to information as an economic good, it will again, and merely because of the coincidence of the legal and the factual monopoly, tear down the scarcity relation, which the law has established. While this may be an arguable proposition with respect to some preexisting information for which there is no substitute at all,[135] it is hardly defensible with respect to new or creative information, let alone with respect to individual or specific information in general. In addition, due to the multifunctionality of information and the interdependency links it creates between markets, it will be difficult to control all the effects resulting from granting compulsory access. Finally, compared to what happens when the essential facilities doctrine is applied to infrastructure networks for the transportation of tangible goods, giving access to information means that the

---

[133] See *United States v. Terminal R.R. Ass'n of St. Louis*, 224 U.S. 383 (1912); Glazer & Lipsky, n. 84 above, at 756 et seq. (1995) (doctrinal development); Venit & Kallaugher, *Essential Facilities· A Comparative Law Approach*, 1994 FORD. CORP. L. INST. 314 (B. Hawk, ed., 1995) (recent application of essential facilities doctrine); Teague I. Donahey, *Terminal Railroad Revisited: Using the Essential Facilities Doctrine to Ensure Accessability to Software Standards*, 25 AIPLA Q.J. 277 (1997); David Reiffen & Andrew N. Kleit, *Terminal Railroad Revisited: Foreclosure of an Essential Facility or Simple Horizontal Monopoly?*, 33 J.L. & ECON. 419 (1990) (generally critiquing essential facilities); Richard Gilbert, *An Economic Analysis of Unilateral Refusals to License Intellectual Property and International Competition Policy*, speech delivered at the conference on Competition Policy for an Integrated World Economy Oslo, June 13–14, 1996 (Norwegian Competition Authority) (applying essential facilities doctrine to intellectual property).

[134] Although definitions vary somewhat, they may be summarized as follows: (i) the facility to which access is refused must be essential and controlled by a monopolist, criteria which tend to merge, (ii) the essential character is determined by reference to the interest of the enterprise seeking access, because it must be practically or reasonably impossible for this enterprise to duplicate the facility although it is vital to its competitiveness (again the criteria tend to merge), and (iii) provision of the facility must be feasible for the monopolist, ie, not disruptive of its own use of the facility, this last criterion being of course the most critical and controversial, see Venit & Kallaugher, n. 133 above, at 322 et seq.; STEPHEN F. ROSS, PRINCIPLES OF ANTITRUST LAW, 96 et seq. (1993) and the somewhat more flexible definition in s. 19.(4) of the German Act Against Restraints of Competition. Two questions are not asked: (i) what are the reasons the monopolist has for refusing access, ie, its pro- or anticompetitive intent, and (ii) what are the merits the monopolist has had in establishing the essential facility in the first place, ie, the issue of incentive and dynamic competition. Both 'refusals of inquiry' cause the doctrine to result in a definition of an 'abuse per se' or, as said in the text, that it is aimed at market power as such.

[135] *Terminal Railroad*, n. 133 above, 224 U.S. at 383, is typically cited as a natural (physical) monopoly case (which it was not), and that is also what makes the case appealing as a matter of equity. Exclusive rights over mere discoveries of laws of nature would then be analogous information cases; see the exception to patentability in Art. 52(2)(a) EPC. However, delimitation becomes rapidly difficult, eg, the development of commercial and business methods which Art. 52(2)(c) EPC excludes from patentability could very well be made appropriable, at least if well defined as to their scope of protection, see *State Street Bank & Trust Co. v. Signature Financial Group, Inc.*, 149 F.3d 1368 (Fed. Cir. 1998).

information as such actually is adopted by a third party. Rather than serving merely as a means of transportation, the essential facility in this case de facto falls into coownership by third parties. These third parties most likely are competitors who may simultaneously use it as a good, albeit possibly as an intermediate good only, on the same or on related markets.[136] The doctrine, therefore, is faced with the same problems that generally surround the determination of the abusive character of a refusal to grant information access.

In fact, the essential facilities doctrine seems to contribute little to the antitrust law analysis of information-related unilateral restraints of competition. For one thing, both in Germany[137] and in the United States,[138] cases of non-access to essential information have been convincingly handled without taking resort to the doctrine, at least where access related to information that constituted only an auxiliary, albeit indispensable, means of competition. For another thing, the essential facilities doctrine, probably in part due to its suggestive name, tends to substitute thorough analysis of the alleged anticompetitive effects by vague and indeterminate criteria of reasonableness. Although reasonableness should be defined by reference to competition, it tends to be determined by reference to what may be expected from, on the one hand, the monopolist and, on the other, from the party requesting access. Court decisions may become unpredictable as the emphasis shifts from competition to fairness between the parties.

This unpredictability is particularly striking in cases after *Magill*.[139] For example, the Tribunal of First Instance[140] refused to apply the *Magill* doctrine in the *Tiercé Ladbroke* case on the ground that live TV-reporting of the French horse races is not essential for competition among betting offices, because bets are made before the races, and not after. In our age of audio-visual communication, and in view of the added value that such reporting would have brought to the entrepreneurial competition between betting offices (TV-reporting of

---

[136] Which means that the feasibility of access-criterion, see n. 134 above, is not met with, at least not if applied strictly (which precisely is the problem), see *Hecht v. Pro-Football, Inc.* 570 F.2d 982, 992 et seq. (D.C. Cir. 1977) (refusal is justified if shared use would be 'impractical or would inhibit the defendant's ability to serve its customers adequately').

[137] See Düsseldorf Court of Appeals, March 13, 1994, WuW E OLG 685 *Funk-tax-ibesitzerverein* (access to call centers for taxis); Federal Supreme Court, June 28, 1977, WuW E BGH 1485 *Autoruf-Genossenschaft*; Court of Appeals Munich, January 22, 1980, WuW E OLG 2287. In the EU, access to commercial fairs has been a related issue that has been dealt with on the basis of Art. 85 EC, see Emmerich, in IMMENGA & MESTMACKER, n. 3 above, at 204 (Art. 85(1)-Fallgruppen, annot. 25).

[138] See *Associated Press v. United States*, 326 U.S. 1 (1945); *Silver v. New York Stock Exchange*, 373 U.S. 341 (1963), and generally the very circumstantiated analysis by Glazer & Lipsky, n. 84 above, at 765 et seq., from which the unworkability of the vague essential facilities approach becomes apparent. Under German, European and probably also US antitrust law, rules on (group) boycotts, discrimination or deliberate monopolization provide adequate remedies, see, eg, *Aspen Skiing Co. v. Aspen Highlands Skiing Corp.*, 472 U.S. 585 (1985) (preferring deliberate monopolization to the essential facilities doctrine).

[139] See n. 78 above.   [140] See n. 80 above.

British horse races was possible), such a distinction really is one of a sliding scale rather than one of a quality jump. Therefore, the essential facilities doctrine contributes little to solving the main problem, which is to develop precise tools for a competition-specific analysis of information access cases rather than continue to rely on equity judgments.[141] What is worse, due to the instrumental character of the essential facilities doctrine and its static perspective, its application does, indeed, bear the risk that the advantages of dynamic, market-modifying competition are foregone for the sake of restructuring presently noncompetitive markets. This is true for network competition since networks develop and may be exposed to substitute competition, and it is even more true for competition in intellectual goods, which so heavily depends on the existence of adequate market prospects or 'incentives'.[142]

II. So Much and So Little Harmony

Turning, in conclusion, to international harmonization, the most striking discrepancy is that between the state of harmonization in the field of intellectual property protection, on the one hand, and that in the antitrust law area, on the other. This is not the place to describe in any detail the harmonization of intellectual property that has been achieved through the traditional international Paris and Berne Conventions and the recent GATT/WTO Agreement on the Trade-Related Aspects of Intellectual Property.[143] Some points, however, merit particular attention.

First, harmonization of intellectual property protection progresses at a surprisingly rapid pace closely following technological development, to wit the WIPO Copyright Treaty and the WIPO Performances and Phonograms Treaty.[144] These harmonization efforts are accompanied by regional block-

---

[141] Compare Cases C–241/91 P and 242/91 P, *Radio Telefis Eirann and Independent Television Publications, Ltd. v Commission of the European Communities* [1995] E.C.R. I–0743 with Case 238/87, *AB Volvo v. Erik Veng (UK) Ltd.* [1988] E.C.R. 6211, [1989] 4 C.M.L.R. 122.

[142] See Temple Lang in COMPARATIVE COMPETITION LAW, n. 107 above , at 175, 193 et seq.; with respect to access to R&D joint ventures FUCHS, n. 10 above, at 449 et seq., and n. that the German Federal Government Bill to revise the Act Against Restraints of Competition not only took account of the problem but ultimately narrowed the scope of application of the essential facilities doctrine so as not to encompass intellectual property, see n. 132 above.

[143] For an overview of the background, purpose, and structure of the TRIPS Agreement see J.H. Reichman, *Universal Minimum Standards of Intellectual Property Protection under the TRIPS Component of the WTO Agreement*, 29 INT'L LAW. 345 (1995); MICHAEL J. TREBILCOCK & ROBERT HOWSE, THE REGULATION OF INTERNATIONAL TRADE 248 (1995). For a detailed analysis see FROM GATT TO TRIPS: THE AGREEMENT ON TRADE-RELATED ASPECTS OF INTELLECTUAL PROPERTY RIGHTS (Friedrich-Karl Beier & Gerhard Schricker eds., 1996); UNITED NATIONS CONFERENCE ON TRADE AND DEVELOPMENT (hereinafter UNCTAD), THE TRIPS AGREEMENT AND DEVELOPING COUNTRIES (1996); J.H. Reichman, *Compliance with the TRIPS Agreement: Introduction to a Scholarly Debate*, 29 VAND. J. TRANSNAT'L L. 363 (1996).

[144] Texts in 36 Int'l. Leg. Mat. 65, 76 (1996) and 1998 O.J. C165/8, 13; see also Jorg Reinbothe, *The New WIPO Treaties: A First Résumé*, 19 EUR. INT. PROP. REV. 171 (1997).

building and intensification of harmonization, notably in the European Union and its neighboring Eastern European countries.[145]

Secondly, harmonization is directed at enhancing and extending protection, not at defining the exceptions, let alone at making the exceptions coextensive with enhanced protection and with the needs of access to information as a basis for creating new intellectual goods.[146] While the vague definition of the exceptions may be welcome by nation states as a matter of leaving them some discretion for the development of national intellectual property policies, such vagueness may also result in divergencies and hesitations of members to develop the exceptions further. This is all the more true as every exception is accompanied by a caveat in favor of protection. Thus, the TRIPS Agreement has been concluded with the purpose 'to promote effective and adequate protection of intellectual property rights',[147] which the TRIPS Council will not lose sight of when reviewing the operation of the Agreement (Article 68). In fact, the Council is invited to promote international harmonization by opening the TRIPS Agreement to harmonization that has been achieved in other international fora (Article 71(2)).

Thirdly, an even more intriguing feature of international harmonization of intellectual property is that it aims at securing undistorted competition on a global level, but actually operates on a national basis, namely on that of an unmitigated application of the principle of territoriality.[148] This means that, while the availability of international protection is increased and will even be further improved for patents,[149] actual protection may be used according to the territorial interests of the owner of an exclusive right. This is true not only

---

[145] Under the so-called Europe Agreements associating Eastern European countries to the EU, the former have to adopt EU standards of intellectual property protection, see eg, for Poland the Agreement of 1991/1994, Art 66 and Annex XIII, 1993 O.J. L348/1; for a general analysis see Govaere, *Convergence, Divergence and Interaction of Regional Trade Agreements and the Agreement on Trade-Related Aspects of Intellectual Property Rights (TRIPs)*; in REGIONALISM AND MULTILATERALISM AFTER THE URUGUAY ROUND 465 (Paul Demaret, Jean-Francois Bellis & Gonzalo Garcia Jiminéz, eds., 1997).

[146] See n. 66 above, significantly authors examining the TRIPS Agreement mostly do give only little attention to the exceptions from protection (eg, given Katzenberger, in Beier & Schricker, n. 143 above, at 59, 90; more extensive, but concentrating primarily on compulsory licenses, Straus, ibid, at 160, 202 et seq.), a notable exception being the UNCTAD analysis, see n. 143 above.

[147] See Preamble to the TRIPS Agreement, first introductory sentence.

[148] See Hanns Ullrich, *TRIPS: Adequate Protection, Inadequate Trade, Adequate Competition Policy*, 4 PAC. RIM L. & POL'Y J. 153, 186 (1995); Hanns Ullrich, *Technology Protection According to TRIPS Principles and Problems*, in Beier & Schricker, n 143 above, at 357, 360 et seq.

[149] WIPO actually examines ways for the granting of international patents on the basis of the Patent Cooperation Treaty, which means that patent granting procedures would become as international as those existing for trademarks under the Madrid Agreement for the International Registration of Trademarks and its Protocol, see Curchord, *Future Development of the PCT System: The View of the International Bureau of WIPO—A Proposed Protocol on 'PCT Patents'*, speech delivered at the WIPO International Symposium on the PCT System in the 21st Century, Beijing 1998 (WIPO-Doc. PCT/SEM/368/2 (IV)).

as regards exhaustion,[150] but also as regards enforcement against infringement and defense against invalidation, with all that this means in terms of opportunities for segregating world trade according to nationally differing profit potentials.[151]

International antitrust law is not at all prepared to cope with these developments. Not only is cooperation in international antitrust law enforcement still at the beginning stages,[152] but as a matter of substantive law, in antitrust enforcement the effects of internationally harmonized and enhanced intellectually property protection seem to be uncritically accepted. Obvious examples are presented by territorially limited licensing (with erga omnes protection in case of violation of the limitation of the license) or by international strategic R&D alliances (with their potential for market divisions).[153] Attempts to harmonize antitrust law internationally do not hold much promise for improving the situation since they modestly are geared only to minimum rules of general character, primarily rules directed at per se unlawful horizontal restraints of competition, and to an indeterminate obligation of Member States to provide for a national system of antitrust law.[154] This approach is, indeed, not very far-reaching as most countries do have some antitrust law and, as such an obligation does not at all rule out conflicts of antitrust law policies. The risk of such conflicts is just as obvious as is the

[150] See TRIPS Agreement, Art. 6; for the resulting controversy over the international exhaustion of intellectual property see Ullrich, Chélanges Waelbroek n. 19 above.

[151] Leaving aside the challenge of cyberspace and which largely is a problem of copyright and trademark law; for a fine analysis see David R. Johnson & David Post, *Law and Borders—The Rise of Law in Cyberspace*, 48 STAN. L. REV. 1367 (1996) (proposing to separate cyberspace law from territorial law); the tendency, however, is to find adequate rules of jurisdiction and choice of law that are developed on the basis of the principle of territoriality, see the reports by Ginsburg and Lucas to the WIPO Group of Consultants on the private international law aspects of the protection of works and objects of related rights transmitted through global digital networks, Geneva 1998.

[152] As regards the number, scope, and effectiveness of agreements between states regulating cooperation in extraterritorial antitrust enforcement, see Nina Hachigian, *Essential Mutual Assistance in International Antitrust Enforcement*, 29 INT'L LAW. 117 (1995); Romano, *First Assessment of the Agreement Between the European Union and the U.S.A Concerning the Application of their Competition Rules*, 1997 Rev. dr. aff. int. 491; Zäch, *International Cooperation Between Antitrust Enforcement Agencies: A View From a Small Country*, in COMPARATIVE COMPETITION LAW, n. 107 above, at 257. A nucleus of an international agreement on antitrust enforcement cooperation is contained in TRIPS Agreement. Art. 40(3). This is very welcome in view of the international character of most licensing policies of enterprises.

[153] In addition, strategic R&D alliances raise serious concerns to the extent that they are integrated in or associated to a national technology policy or are based on the ground that national markets are too small or international competition too strong to be faced by one enterprise alone: global intellectual property protection affords the legal security necessary for large R&D investments, see Ullrich, n. 148 above, at 197 et seq.

[154] See for the view of the European Union, which is the main protagonist of international harmonization within the framework of WTO, Karel Van Miert, *The WTO and Competition Policy: the Need to Consider Negotiations, Address before Ambassadors to WTO*, Geneva, April 21, 1998 (press release European Commission); Communication from the Commission to the Council, *Towards an International Framework of Competition Rules*, COM/96/284/fin.1996/06/18/31p.

general need to harmonize intellectual property-related antitrust law internationally so as to meet the de facto global reach of protection. Predisclosure requirements by one nation will nullify the nondisclosure policy of another;[155] compulsory access to standardized information or to telecommunication systems will be of no use if other countries allow intellectual property protection of such standards.

It is true that the TRIPS Agreement itself does recognize 'that some licensing practices or conditions pertaining to intellectual property rights which restrain competition may have adverse effects on trade and may impede the transfer and dissemination of technology' (Article 40(1)). But the Agreement, rather than harmonizing these rules, simply refers Member States to their national law, and it does so without really preventing conflicts of enforcement and policy, except, arguably, for an unwelcome limitation to the effect that national antitrust law may only control 'abuses' in the exercise or licensing of intellectual property.[156] This then points to the risks of international harmonization of intellectual property-related antitrust law rules, in particular if they would be developed within the framework of TRIPS or on its basis:[157] as even academic proposals for such rules foreshadow,[158] it is most likely that harmonization will be attempted along the lines of the inherency and/or reasonable reward doctrines that are ill-conceived and outdated, that have not helped to settle the former technology transfer debate,[159] and that, at any rate, cover only a part of the issues—and probably not the most important ones—namely, only restrictive licensing contracts. The risk is all the more serious as international harmonization would be made on the basis of a convention which, even if of a plurilateral nature rather then merely of a multilateral one, ie, even if linked to the trade-sanction mechanism of the WTO, will have the kind of standstill effect for antitrust law development that is common to all such international harmonization measures. The entire purpose of this chapter, however, is to show that intellectual property-related

[155] See Eleanor M. Fox, *Competition Law and the Agenda for WTO: Forging the Links of Competition and Trade*, 4 PAC. RIM L. & POL'Y J. 1, 26 et seq. (1995).

[156] See Eleanor M. Fox, *Trade, Competition, and Intellectual Property—TRIPS and Its Antitrust Counterparts*, 29 VAND. J. TRANSNAT'L L. 481, 497 (1996). But see UNCTAD, n. 143 above, at 54 et seq. (No. 267 et seq.). However, Art. 31(k) of the TRIPS Agreement accepts compulsory licensing as an antitrust remedy.

[157] For contrary views, see Richard H. Marschall, *Patents, Antitrust, and the WTO/GATT· Using TRIPs as a Vehicle for Antitrust Harmonization*, 28 LAW & POL'Y INT'L. BUS. 1165, 1191 et seq. (1997); see also Fox, n. 156 above, at 494 et seq. (1996) (advocating a trade-related approach to harmonization specific to intellectual property).

[158] See n. 26 above.

[159] Paul Kuruk, *Controls on Technology Transfer: An Analysis of the Southern Response to Northern Technology Protectionism*, 13 MD. J. INT'L L. & TRADE 301 (1989); UNCTAD, *Negotiations on an International Code of Conduct on the Transfer of Technology*, TD/Code TOT/60 of September 6, 1995 (recommending suspension of Code negotiations in view of the change of circumstances and of the legal environment); UNCTAD, n. 143 above, at 53 et seq.; S.K. Verma, *TRIPS—Development and Transfer of Technology*, 27 IIC 331, 364 (1996) (showing that the long-existing conflicts still exist).

antitrust law is general antitrust law, and that this general antitrust law is not harmonious and is not well settled, but follows the evolutionary lines of competition and divergent national competition policies. Furthermore, from analyzing both the intrinsic limits of antitrust and its external bounds, a message should have come forward, namely, that antitrust laws cannot help to maintain the efficiency of the intellectual property system when the legislature fails to care sufficiently for its legitimacy.

PART V

VIEWS FROM THE BENCH

WHO DECIDES THE EXTENT OF RIGHTS IN INTELLECTUAL PROPERTY?

FRANK H. EASTERBROOK*

Who decides whether intellectual property claims are sound? Making claims is easy, but how should we resolve them? Frightened by the idea of a patent on the human genome and drugs developed from it? Should we just declare that all such knowledge and products are in the public domain,[1] or require scientists and drug developers to license their discoveries and products at 'reasonable' (ie, low) prices? Unsettled by the prospect that books and articles distributed over the Internet will be tagged or encrypted so that the authors or publishers can collect payment each time they are read or redistributed? Should we just forbid the newfangled devices (or contracts that consent to them), declaring that authors can't be allowed to violate the rules for 'fair use' or to profit from information that 'ought' to be available to everyone for free?[2] Frustrated by a software license that forbids the disassembly of object code in search of the source code, which could help other programmers write competing or complementary products? Should we just tell the author that in the public interest the law won't enforce onerous terms which conflict with the public's presumptive right to engage in reverse engineering—and leave it to the judiciary to determine which terms are too onerous?[3]

I am a skeptic about the proposition that new developments in technology imply the need for new laws or rules.[4] I am skeptical for two fundamental reasons. First, we know so little about the effects of our current intellectual property regime on the production and use of traditional intellectual property

---

* Judge, United States Court of Appeals for the Seventh Circuit; Senior Lecturer, The Law School, The University of Chicago.

[1] See *Moore v. Regents of the University of California*, 51 Cal. 3d 120, 793 P.2d 479 (1990).

[2] See, eg, Yochai Benkler, *Free as the Air to Common Use: First Amendment Constraints on Enclosure of the Public Domain*, 74 N.Y.U. L. REV. 354 (1999); Wendy J. Gordon, *Intellectual Property as Price Discrimination: Implications for Contract*, 73 CHI.–KENT L. REV. 1367 (1999); Niva Elkin-Koren, *Copyright Policy and the Limits of Freedom of Contract*, 12 BERKELEY TECH. L.J. 93 (1997).

[3] See *Sony Computer Entertainment, Inc. v. Connectix Corp.*, 203 F.3d 596 (9th Cir. 2000).

[4] See Frank H. Easterbrook, *Cyberspace and the Law of the Horse*, 1996 U. CHI. LEGAL F. 207; Frank H. Easterbrook, *Intellectual Property is Still Property*, 13 HARV. J.L. & PUB. POL'Y 108 (1990). See also *ProCD, Inc. v. Zeidenberg*, 86 F.3d 1447 (7th Cir. 1996); *Hill v. Gateway 2000, Inc.*, 105 F.3d 1147 (7th Cir. 1997).

that it is silly to suppose that we have the information essential to prescribe new regimes for new kinds of intellectual property. Secondly, when flailing around in the dark, it is much easier to come up with 'solutions' that harm the development of intellectual property than it is to devise rules that help. Ignorance thus should lead us to leave well enough alone. (As Edmund Burke remarked: 'Don't talk to me of reform; things are bad enough as they are').

Consider for a moment the world of perfect competition in classical economics. Price everywhere equals marginal cost, so all decisions about producing, purchasing, and using goods are both privately and socially optimal. Now consider the problem for intellectual property: an idea, a book, a poem, or a piece of software can be used without being used up. The marginal cost of producing a new example, after the work has been created, is not zero, but it is low—substantially below average total cost. To recover its investment, a producer of intellectual property must be able to sell at average total cost or more; but if marginal cost is under average total cost, the price is 'too high' to be socially optimal, for the high price discourages at least some purchases even though the consumer values the work at more than the cost of producing an extra copy. That is the problem with which the law of intellectual property grapples,[5] and no solution can be praised unconditionally.

Patent law, copyright law, trademark law, and the law of contracts (of which trade secrets are a branch) create or employ property rights in information so that the producer of intellectual property can charge more than marginal cost, and thus cover the total cost of producing and disseminating the works. Would-be consumers who value the work at more than marginal cost but less than average total cost lose out; but if the law were otherwise different consumers would lose (and lose even more) because producers would not develop and distribute as many innovations, plays, drugs, and programs. Just *how much* above marginal cost should the price be? No one knows. A patent gives the inventor the right to exclude competition for 20 years, and thus to collect an enhanced price for that period. Is 20 years too long, too short, or just right? No one knows. A copyright lasts the life of the author plus an additional period that Congress keeps increasing in response to producers' lobbying. What is the right length of a copyright? No one knows. A trademark lasts forever (or at least for as long as the product is made, and the name does not become generic in the public's mind). A trade secret (such as the formula for Coca-Cola, or the source code of a computer program) lasts as long as the developer can keep the secret. Are these durations optimal? No one knows. How much use, and by whom, should be permitted without compensation under the fair use doctrine? No one knows.

By 'no one' I mean more than just legislators and judges. The best academic students of the subject disclaim knowledge. If we do not know the

[5] See William M. Landes & Richard A. Posner, *An Economic Analysis of Copyright Law*, 17 J. LEGAL STUD. 325 (1989).

answers to these traditional questions, how can we hope that a new set of rules for a new century to cover a new generation of intellectual property will be an improvement?

Who can be trusted to come up with better rules is a separate question. Should we rely on the academy? You cannot pick up a law review these days without encountering a proposal for revamping the law of intellectual property. But there is very little overlap between the authors of these proposals and serious students of markets in intellectual property. Most good scholars recognize that we don't know the answers to the current generation of questions and therefore are poorly situated to prescribe alterations. Bad scholars are less aware of their limitations and make bold proposals—but these are the people of whom we should be most wary.

Should we rely on inventors (or industry in general) to tell us what protections are 'needed'? Most authors and inventors think, like John L. Lewis, that the answer is 'more' (just as many consumers think that the answer is 'less'); self interest taints the response. Anyway, it turns out that inventors and authors are lousy prophets. Most inventions receive no royalties; about 10 percent earn significant returns, and a very few have huge payoffs.[6] Most books have few sales. Most songs are never sung in public. Similarly, most academic proposals for change in the law (like most genetic mutations) have negative value. A very few patents, novels, plays, songs, symphonies, and law-reform proposals have high value, but ex ante it is hard to tell the good innovations from the retrogressions.

What we do know about the market calls into serious question many proposals for regulation. If only 10 percent of patents earn substantial royalties, and if the bulk of returns come from a few great successes, this means that most inventors are slaving away in the hope of hitting a jackpot. It is the prospect of a big payoff that spurs development. Proposals for compulsory licenses, at 'reasonable' rates, expanded 'fair use' doctrines, or antitrust remedies would cut down the return from the big winners in the innovation game, without compensating the other inventors. (Nor would we *want* to compensate the inventors of products that flop in the market! Why subsidize losers?) Curtail the top returns, and the whole structure of rewards changes for the worse.

All too many proposals commit the Nirvana Fallacy. They take the form: 'The existing legal regimen has the following costs and flaws; therefore my proposal is better. Patents raise price and discourage use; this is a flaw because some consumers who value the product at more than marginal cost can't afford it; therefore *my* proposal to [fill in the blank] should be adopted.' That's a non sequitur. Every way of handling intellectual property is costly and imperfect. All of these costs must be toted up and compared; and, as I have stressed, no one knows how to do that.

---

[6] See Scherer, Chapter 1 above.

Even careful study of a question about innovations does not ensure success. Before Xerox Corporation made a fortune selling photocopiers employing Chester Carlson's great innovation, his (patented) corona-charging mechanism, Carlson's original licensee, the Battelle Institute, tried to raise development funds by selling a 50 percent interest in the invention to leading makers of office equipment. One potential buyer was International Business Machines Corporation. IBM commissioned a study by the best consulting firm money could buy; the consultants determined that there was no market for plain-paper photocopying, and after receiving this assessment IBM declined to invest. This was a spectacular blunder, but only in retrospect. Other, less noticed, errors occur when firms invest heavily in technologies that turn out to be busts. Anyone remember Federal Express's 'ZapMail', a two-hour delivery service brought to market at great expense just as businesses were installing fax machines, or Polaroid's 'Polavision', a technologically splendid instant-development motion-picture system that came out about the same time as the first handheld videotape cameras? If firms that put millions of dollars on the line cannot make reliable decisions about technology, what would make us think that scholars with *no* money on the line do well at devising legal rules to govern technology?

Perhaps, then, development of rules should be left to the legislature. Elected representatives have political legitimacy, but do they have the knowledge? Legislatures have no private information that is unavailable to scholars. And recent legislative efforts in the law of intellectual property have been adversely affected by the tugging and hauling of interest groups.

For a long time, the statutory law of intellectual property has been general. There was one term for all patents, one term for all copyrights—all against the background of a common law of contracts that is indifferent to the industry involved. When the law of intellectual property is general, most people are apt to support the best possible set of legal rules. Universities don't lobby to eliminate copyright protection—even though that would make it much cheaper to buy journals for their libraries—because they are also producers of intellectual property. General Motors pays substantial royalties to inventors, but it also receives royalties as a patent holder. When people are, or are likely to be, on both sides of a class of transactions, they tend to support legislators who favor efficient rules.

Not so when the rules can be made industry-specific. Recent amendments to the copyright statutes provide special rules (and benefits) for semiconductor chip producers, management systems, and digital audio devices. Special patent regimes have been created for drugs and plant varieties. Drug producers and drug buyers reflect very different interests. Industry-specific rules are the playgrounds of interest groups, and once factions get to work it is predictable that at least some of the laws will favor concentrated groups at the expense of a broader public.

Narrow laws also tend to detract from the force of competition among producers of intellectual property and thus magnify their own shortcomings. More general statutes have been contract-enabling: they create property rights that set the stage for competition and contract. General laws about intellectual property tend to promote competition. Most patents, books, songs, and so on receive low rewards because of competition—not because they are bad ideas on an absolute scale, but because other people have come up with many equally good ideas, and competition among them has the beneficial effects of all economic competition. Newer laws tend to be contract-defeating (substituting, say, a Copyright Royalty Tribunal for bilateral agreements), which means that if the statutes don't get things exactly right (and they don't), people can't transact around the errors.

How about courts as the source of newer and better rules? Information about rules' effects is as much a problem for judges as for other actors—worse, actually, and for four reasons: first, courts are run by judges; second, judges are lawyers; third, lawyers are ignorant; fourth, courts are incoherent.[7]

1. Courts are run by judges

Judges are smart people, who unsurprisingly tend to think well of their ideas. This is, alas, a drawback, because, as I have emphasized, most new ideas are bad. An academic who has a new idea subjects it to the test of scholarly interchange, and it often takes decades to confirm or refute new theses. A lawmaker who has a new idea submits it to the political marketplace, where those injured by the proposal can set up a defense (and an information campaign). A capitalist who has a new idea submits it to the test of the market—and as I have mentioned the market rejects (or at least does not reward) most new ideas and products. But a judge who has a brainstorm can write it directly into law.

Entrepreneurs and politicians who churn out more bad ideas than good ones can be evicted from office. A business manager who does not get tossed out may suffer a great decline in income as bonuses or the value of stock options fall. People recognize that because it is so hard to separate good from poor ideas ex ante, substantial rewards for success and penalties for failure are vital in business. Firms are at pains to devise methods to align the interests of managers with those of investors.[8] But what is vitally important in business (and political life) is forbidden in the judiciary. Judges do not reap rewards for devising better rules, and they do not pay a penalty for failure. Even the simplest reward structure—a bonus when your decision is affirmed,

---

[7] See Frank H. Easterbrook, *What's So Special About Judges?*, 61 U. Colo. L. Rev. 773 (1990).

[8] See Candice Prendergast, *The Provision of Incentives in Firms*, 37 J. Econ. Literature 7 (1999).

a penalty when the Supreme Court reverses—is missing. Viewed as legal entrepreneurs, therefore, judges are unlikely to excel.

2. Judges are lawyers

Lawyers are generalists. They are intermediaries and professional agents, dealing with a sweep of problems, from drug control to antitrust regulation, that no other profession covers. This means that even the most intelligent and dedicated members of the bar are not experts—and I began, recall, by contending that even experts in intellectual property don't know what rules would be optimal. Trained to cope with so many different kinds of problems, lawyers (and thus judges) are not steeped in the methods of science. My point is not that judges lack degrees in biochemistry or economics. It is that they are not comfortable with the scientific approach of testing hypotheses by collecting data and subjecting it to statistical analysis. Lawyers tend to think that disputes can be solved by evaluating the credibility of witnesses, an approach no scientist would adopt. Law schools teach future lawyers to make and evaluate arguments verbally, not empirically. But talk is cheap, hypotheses many, and confirmation hard. Simply put, if IBM and leading scientists can't reach answers about major problems in the domain of intellectual property, then neither can lawyers.

3. Lawyers are ignorant

This is just a different slant on the second point, but at retail rather than wholesale. Because lawyers are generalists (at least, judicial lawyers are generalists) who spend most of their time on cocaine prosecutions and social security disability cases, they lack the time necessary to fine-tune complex bodies of rules. The broader the portfolio of subjects, the more shallow the practitioner is doomed to be with respect to each.

4. Courts are incoherent

Today there are more than 650 federal district judges and more than 150 federal appellate judges. They were appointed by different Presidents and have exceptionally diverse backgrounds. It is unrealistic to suppose that the federal judiciary will coalesce around any one approach to a topic that has been highly contentious among specialists. Although the Supreme Court, with nine Justices, is much smaller, it still makes decisions by majority vote, and for reasons that I lack time to develop here any institution that decides by voting is bound to sacrifice either consistency or some other important aspect of the judicial process.[9]

Do not despair! Ignorance is normal. What's the right price of wheat? How many computers should be installed in a high school classroom? What is the

---

[9] See Frank H. Easterbrook, *Ways of Criticizing the Court*, 95 HARV. L. REV. 802 (1982).

right substitution between automobiles and housing for a family with an income of $50,000 per year? These enormously complex questions lack right answers. When there is no one right answer—and when people bear the costs of their actions—we rely on those affected to make their own decisions. Markets make it possible for different people, at different times, with different information and different objectives, to make different decisions. Legal rules often deny them that luxury. Markets and the price system are at their best when knowledge is diffuse and hard to organize.[10] Let me give you a theorem: the more complex the problem, the more the 'right' answer varies over time and the affected population; and the easier it is to address the problem by private contract, the less we should attempt to resolve it by law.

That theorem isn't mine, and it has a famous name: the Coase Theorem.[11] If bargaining is costless, then the outcome of private bargaining will be a Pareto-optimal solution and the rule of law will be irrelevant. Now bargaining is never costless, but whether to bear the costs of transactions is itself an economic decision. Unless costs are imposed on third parties who do not (and cannot) engage in transactions, then the contractual solution is most efficient at taking all costs (including those of bargaining) into account.

In the world of intellectual property transactions costs are falling, which improves the comparative advantage of contract over regulation. Today people communicate cheaply and easily, and they can strike deals electronically at low cost. Publishers could offer a menu of terms for rights you acquire to use and copy, say, music encoded in MP3 format, and you could set a preference in your web-browser or MP3 player about what kind of deal to accept. Patent pools, global standards, blanket licenses after the fashion of ASCAP, and other contractual devices have reduced the cost of bargaining about intellectual property.

It is ironic that just as a global network and automation are reducing the costs of contracting, and moving us closer to the world in which the Coase Theorem prevails, people promote more and more contract-defeating schemes. One is tempted to think that they are concerned not about market failures but about market successes—about the prospect that the sort of world people prefer when they vote their own pocketbooks will depart from the proposers' ideas of what people *ought* to prefer. Next thing you know, why, economic transactions between consenting adults will break out *right in public view*!

My principal suggestions follow from this understanding about the relative competence of public and private actors. Three propositions sum up what I know, or think I know, about wise public policy.

a. Make rules clearer, to promote bargains: 'We' don't know what is best, but in a Coasean world the affected parties will by their actions establish what is best

---

[10] See generally Thomas Sowell, Knowledge and Decisions (1980).
[11] See R.H. Coase, *The Problem of Social Cost*, 3 J.L. & Econ. 1 (1960).

It is awfully hard to know what the optimal compensation package for authors is. When there is ignorance, it is best to give more rights to authors. Why? Because if the best arrangement turns out to be free distribution, then private transactions may produce this result when the statute assigns the rights to authors; but if the best arrangement turns out to be some fee for distribution and a lower price for copying, it is extremely hard to get to this state of affairs if the statute cancels the distribution right. Private transactions could move the right back to authors only if the parties have contractual relations (for example, patrons of the opera may agree not to tape the performances). We must bear in mind the high possibility of error in the original specification of entitlements—a risk especially high in a legislative world dominated by interest-group politics. The risk of error should lead to initial assignments that are easy to reverse, so that people may find their own way with the least interference.

b. Create property rights, where now there are none—again to make bargains possible   One common response to a proposition of this sort is that holders of rights in intellectual property are bound to use them to cut out low valuing users, or to squeeze profits from information already in the public domain. I find it odd that this response appears so often in the law reviews, where it is self-refuting. Every law review article is copyrighted. This means that the author *could* insist that the law review pay, say, $5,000 for publication rights, and that Lexis pay another $5,000 (plus $100 per 'hit') for the right to make the text available electronically. But of course authors don't do this. They submit articles without payment, from either law reviews or the electronic services. Perhaps one could infer that the authors know something about the value of their intellectual property. But another possible inference is that when free distribution is socially optimal, people will not enforce their property right to withhold publication or demand fees. If you start from property rights you can negotiate for free distribution; if you start from an absence of property rights, it is very hard to get to the best solution when a charge is optimal.

c. Create bargaining institutions   Computers offer many opportunities to do, at next to no cost, the sort of thing the Copyright Clearance Center has tried and failed to do for photocopies. Consider, for example, the question whether a publisher of content on the Internet wants to authorize the making of copies—and, if so, the making of copies that can be recopied, or a single copy for use on a local computer, or only wants to authorize viewing on screen. All are logical possibilities, each rational for some authors, or for any given author at different times. How is it possible to specify which is which and to collect payment?

The answer lies in a convention, a protocol under which each file contains its own instructions on this question, and programs know how to interpret them. You are familiar with such conventions. When your modem calls a remote modem, the two devices engage in elaborate interrogation to discover what speed to use and what compression and error-correction algorithms are in place. An international standards-setting organization agreed on the language; private firms all over the world have decided whether, and to what extent, to use this agreed language for communications. Some firms have come up with their own extensions, outside the organization's framework. Just so with the Internet's core communications protocol (TCP/IP) and page-description language (HTML). Encryption technology is similar. You may notice that when your browser enters a particular corner of the Web a symbol appears on the screen to show that the client and the server have agreed on an encryption protocol, securing the session. There are several available protocols.

So can it be with copying. A standards-setting organization could prescribe, say, 20 different copying rules—sets of permission and payment terms. There may be competing organizations, with their own standards. Each server and client would understand these terms and carry out the negotiation automatically, remitting any payment to an agreed depository by secure methods. Your future electronic copy of *Moore's Federal Practice* may come tagged with instructions that tell your computer how many times it can be copied, and to whom it may be redistributed. Or you may receive a copy that is locked to your hard disk (using an approach such as Adobe's WebBuy). And you will be better off for it, because the alternative is more costly, less convenient, or both.

These, then, are my propositions. We live in a world of ignorance. We can expect ignorance about the full consequences and optimality of legal rules to be as prevalent in the twenty-first century as it has been in the past. We can expect academics, legislators, and judges to have in the future the same comparative disadvantages, vis-à-vis the market, that they have had in the past. In a world of imperfect knowledge—that is, in our world—you can benefit from clear rules, property rights, and institutions that promote negotiation.

THE ONWARD MARCH OF INTELLECTUAL
PROPERTY RIGHTS AND REMEDIES

HON. SIR ROBIN JACOB*

Persons in the position of the Defendants, that is, of agents for an American publisher, must be taken to know that Americans are in the habit of printing and exporting piratical works, and they must therefore know that they import books from America at the risk of their containing what is piratical, and of thus committing an unlawful act, and of being liable to be sued without notice.

So said Sir George Jessel, the Master of the Rolls in 1880.[1] An English copyright owner was seeking an injunction against a dealer in pirate copies of his work. To establish liability it was necessary under the then law to prove that the dealer had knowledge that the copies in which he dealt were piratical. That was the court's robust answer.

How far the United States has come since those days; and most of the distance has been covered in the last 40 years—at an accelerating pace. It was only in 1988 that the USA finally acceded to the Berne Convention[2] and we, in Europe, stopped having little legends in our paperbacks 'For copyright reasons this edition is not for sale in the United States or Canada'. It was only in 1982 that the US Court of Appeals for the Federal Circuit was created[3] with the result that US patents started being probably valid[4] rather than very likely invalid.[5]

We, in Europe, have seen a similar explosion in recent years, though it is fair to say that we were probably never quite as anti-patentee as the United States once was, and have also been fairer to foreign copyright holders for much longer. I readily confess that when I started as a barrister, my early days (and those of other young aggressive lawyers—a new breed so far as IP was concerned) were very much spent in pushing forward IP rights. Then they seemed a good thing and the more they were and the stronger they were the better. We had a new Patents Judge (Mr. Justice Graham) who seldom held patents

---

* Judge of the Patents Court of England and Wales.

[1] *Cooper v. Whittingham*, (1880) 15 Ch. D. 501.

[2] Berne Convention Implementation Act of 1988, Pub. L. No. 100–568, 102 Stat. 2853 (1988).

[3] See Federal Courts Improvement Act of 1982, Pub. L. No. 164, 96 Stat. 25 (1982).

[4] See Donald R. Dunner et al., *A Statistical Look at the Federal Circuit's Patent Decisions: 1982–1994*, 5 FED. CIRCUIT B.J. 151 (1995).

[5] The only patent that is valid is one which this Court has not been able to get its hands on': *Jungerson v. Ostby & Barton Co.*, 335 U.S. 560, 570–71 (1949) (Jackson J., dissenting).

invalid. We discovered an unintended consequence of our copyright legislation, which had a profound effect. It was an infringement of the copyright in a design drawing to copy an article made from that drawing.[6] The result was that copying almost anything, however trivial, of a mechanical nature was unlawful. We had that law for nearly 20 years and have indeed retained it in diminished scope and period.[7] At the same time new remedies were devised: first a new readiness in the court to grant interlocutory injunctions, the remedy of *information* (particularly the name) about wrongdoers,[8] the civil search warrant in all but name of the *Anton Piller* remedy.[9] Other developments in remedies also came about from the Commercial Court, particularly the *Mareva* injunction (asset freezing),[10] and remedies in tracing property.

Apart from the general rise of IP rights, Europe has been involved in another major development: the harmonisation—some would call it 'federalisation'—of our IP laws. We started with substantive patent law, harmonised by the European Patent Convention of 1972 and brought alive by the founding of the European Patent Office in 1978.[11] After a pause during the 1980s we have had a flood of European IP measures (Directives requiring States to bring their laws into line) and Regulations. We now have a European Trademark Office.[12] Before long there will be a European registered design (a sort of design patent). There is much (to my mind alarming) talk of a European 'utility model', an unexamined 'petty patent' which lasts for 10 years and has hardly any requirement of nonobviousness. Copyright got extended in all European countries for the self-evidently unnecessary period of 70 years from the year of death of the author in the name of harmonisation, and the fear that requiring Germany to lower its period to that of the other countries (50 years from death) would involve destruction of property.[13]

---

[6] See *L. B. (Plastics) Ltd. v. Swish Prods. Ltd.* [1979] R.P.C. 551; *British Leyland Motor Corp. v. Armstrong Patent Co. Ltd.* [1984] 1 All ER 850, as to how the courts interpreted the Copyright Act 1956 so as to reach this result.

[7] Whether it did or does any good remains completely open to question and are certainly worthy of study.

[8] See *Norwich Pharmacal v. Commissioners of Customs and Excise* [1973] 2 All E.R. 943.

[9] *Anton Piller KG v. Manufacturing Processes Ltd.* [1976] 1 All E.R. 779. Now it is called a 'search order'.

[10] *Mareva Compania Naviera SA v. International Bulkcarriers SA (The Mareva),* [1975] 1 All E.R. 213. See also *Bankers Trust v. Shapira* [1980] 3 All E.R. 353. The US Supreme Court recently struck down the use of *Mareva* injunctions in US federal courts. See *Grupo Mexicano de Desarrollo, S. A. v. Alliance Bond Fund, Inc.,* 527 U.S. 308 (1999).

[11] Convention on the Grant of European Patents (European Patent Convention), October 5, 1973, 13 I.L.M. 270, 1978 Gr. Brit. T.S. No. 20 (Cmnd 7090). The European Patent Office was founded as a result of the European Patent Convention entering into force on October 7, 1977, after Luxembourg ratified the Convention.

[12] The European Trademark Office (alternatively referred to as the Community Trade Mark Office and the Office for Harmonization in the Internal Market) is located in Alicante, Spain and was founded pursuant to Council Regulation 40/94 of 20 December 1993 on the Community Trade Mark, art. 2, 1994 O.J. L11/1; I.E.L. V–0015.

[13] Unfortunately it is much easier to ratchet IP rights up than down.

For some time I have been worried by the onward march of IP rights and remedies. I am near sure that its push into countries that get no or little benefit from IP laws by the TRIPS Agreement is likely to prove unfortunate. It may be all right for the 'flimflam' products of the designer world, such as those products sold under famous trademarks, which have achieved the status of snob marks. But in the large scheme of things, particularly third world poverty, I cannot see it doing any good. When our countries were young and backward the last thing we needed was our fledgling industries under a yoke of foreign rights. On the contrary, in the United Kingdom we gave patents to people who went abroad to 'steal' ideas from foreigners, and the USA only gave copyright rights for works first published in the United States—if first published elsewhere Americans were free to pirate. One must have a lot of sympathy for the point of view of a lady who spoke at the WIPO Arab Section meeting on TRIPS in March 1998, which I attended. She said, 'Our children cannot afford to pay full Western prices for computer programs—so if they cannot copy how will they ever learn?'

Returning to developed countries, particularly Europe and the United States, the onward march of IP is undoubtedly worthy of study. That is why the subject of this book and of the preceding conference in Florence is so important. I found some of the ideas wholly new, for instance Professor Scherer's suggestion that the IP rights resulting from research should be regarded as bets.[14] He points out, rightly, that most IP rights (even nonautomatic ones such as patents which have to be applied for and paid for) turn out to be of little or no value. His argument, that in order to encourage expenditure on R&D (ie, betting) courts should give IP rights wide scope (ie, bigger prizes), is fascinating. I do not go along with it myself, for two reasons. First it must never be forgotten that each IP right given to one enterprise is a potential stumbling block for its rivals. As an old sage in my chambers used to say, 'We are the grit in the wheels of industry'. Most IP departments of large companies spend more time on IP right evasion than on prosecuting the company's own rights. Secondly I question the assumption that the prospects of an even bigger prize (when existing prizes for winners are already very large) will result in proportionately more money being bet. I just do not know whether it is right. Nor do I know whether it is possible to test the assumption. I do not intend to give patent claims overwide construction on the basis of that assumption.

Another idea that I had not seen before is the possible use of the European Convention on Human Rights to rein in overpowerful copyright rights, as suggested by Bernt Hugenholtz.[15] We in the United Kingdom are now making this Convention part of our domestic (and hence daily) law. Positive rights are new to us—we have no history of a written constitution, which makes these things second nature to lawyers in many, if not most, countries. If IP

[14] See Scherer, Chapter 1 above.   [15] See Hugenholtz, Chapter 14 above.

rights continue to grow as they have in the past then I foresee much more of this sort of thing. There is a point when the law must find a way to say, 'enough is enough'.

I could go on about other articles in this really interesting collection. But I am not supposed to be writing a review, I am supposed to be giving a judge's perspective. Interestingly I fasten on much of what Judge Diane Wood has said.[16]

Take the role of experts. Those who support 'reform' take for granted that any dispute resolution system would be adequately provided with expert opinion. But there is a cost and there are real problems. In the common law world each side finds an expert who supports their case. Anyone in practice is familiar with the search for the expert who can plausibly support the cause for which he or she is hired. At its best the system works well: but it depends on having judges who are unmoved by experts bald conclusions and who are able to assess their reasons. It is very expensive because it also depends upon effective cross-examination. I am by no means convinced that it works well in a substantial number of cases. The use of a single expert[17] as used on the Continent also has major problems, mainly I suspect because there is inadequate opportunity for testing the opinion, and sometimes because the expert really is not an expert or sets about answering the wrong question. We in England may soon start experimenting with single experts (not, yet, in IP matters). It will be interesting to see how we get on.

More generally, IP rights are normally complex juristic things. Inherently they have very fuzzy edges: compare for instance the precision of land law with the almost subjective test of nonobviousness for patents or sufficient artistic input for copyright. And very often the factual matrix (both technical and economic) in which IP laws operate is also very complex. Judge Wood's contribution invites consideration of the judicial machinery by which disputes are to be determined. The same question is increasingly being asked in Europe. We in England have specialist patent judges. So do Germany, Sweden, and to some extent a few other countries. But many other countries do not. Inexperienced judges lead to litigation: it is always worth running or defending a lousy case if there is a serious chance that the judge will not spot it. Moreover a plaintiff has much less to lose if he loses than the defendant; and the gain if the plaintiff wins (injunction, damages, etc.) makes it worth a bet against the odds. Thus inexperienced and uncertain courts increase the power of the IP haves against the IP have-nots.[18] This fundamental fact of the

---

[16] See Wood, Chapter 19 below.

[17] Advocated by Learned Hand as long ago as 1900, before he was a judge. See Learned Hand, *Historical and Practical Considerations Regarding Expert Testimony*, 15 HARV. L. REV. 40, 55–58 (1901).

[18] I believe it to be, for instance, one of the reasons for the increase in jury trial of patent actions in the USA. And I suspect a major unarticulated premise of the decision in *Markman v. Westview Instruments, Inc.*, 52 F.3d 967 (Fed. Cir. 1995), was that it is dangerous to leave to a jury something as important as a decision on the width of a patent.

real world is at best wildly underestimated but normally wholly ignored by legislators. Anyone who proposes changes in an IP regime—and especially a change by way of an increase in IP rights—ought to consider as an integral part of the proposal, what dispute resolution mechanisms exist.

I believe that economists call the sort of factors involved in obtaining or enforcement of IP rights 'transaction costs'. What is needed at an international level is a major effort aimed towards reducing these. It is not enough for patent offices to reduce costs of obtaining patents—indeed there is something to be said in favor of quite significant fees for keeping patents in force; otherwise they amount to an overgrown jungle through which industry can find its way only with the aid of an army of patent attorneys. What, as a judge, I concentrate on is enforcement machinery. The present European (and indeed) world systems are not good enough. Frankly, patent enforcement by jury is, if it were not real, laughable.[19] Nor is it much better to entrust it to judges inexperienced in patents. That is why, so far as Europe is concerned, the current proposals[20] (national courts with appeal to a central European Patent Court as part of the Court of First Instance) are not good enough. We will one day have to have a European Patent Court of First Instance—if you like to call it a 'Federal' court you can. The name does not matter, but what it will do and *how* it will do it does. Much the same applies to other IP rights. The more and bigger they are, the greater is the imperative for a court system which is relatively cheap, really quite speedy, and above all predictable. Without the last, intellectual property litigation will develop into an international lottery, if it is not that already. One day we may have to be looking for a truly international litigation system.

---

[19] It is a tribute to the strength of the US economy that it can withstand its litigation (and particularly its patent litigation) system.

[20] Currently supported by the Commission and a Committee of the European Parliament. See Opinion of the Economic and Social Committee on *Promoting Innovation Through Patents: Green Paper on the Community Patent and the Patent System in Europe*, O.J. C129/8 (April 27, 1998); *Resolution on the Commission Green Paper on the Community Patent and the Patent System in Europe. Promoting Innovation Through Patents*, O.J. (C379/268 (November 19, 1998).

ACADEMIA AND THE BENCH: TOWARD A MORE PRODUCTIVE DIALOGUE

HON. JON O. NEWMAN*

In thinking about intellectual property issues for 20 years as a federal appellate judge, particularly copyright issues that place in tension the claims of authors and of those who advocate a broad public domain, I have been struck by the gulf that often exists between scholars writing and thinking hard about these questions and judges obliged to decide discrete controversies. Judges are a considerable distance from the factual information that most scholars have at their fingertips, such as the arcana of computer technology, and most of us are somewhat removed from the doctrinal familiarity of intellectual property scholars.

Perhaps, in a minor way, I can illustrate our remoteness by mentioning a case that I worked on many years ago. It was the *Tarzan* case,[1] a copyright and contract dispute in which a major issue was whether the Bo Derek/John Derek remake of the original 'Tarzan' film was 'substantially similar' to the original; the contract rights at issue entitled the Dereks to produce a remake of the old 'Tarzan' picture, provided the remake was 'substantially similar' to the original. So the three judges on the appellate panel dutifully watched both movies and read both scripts, and we considered such grave questions as whether this elephant scene was just like that elephant scene. In the end, after giving the matter due consideration, we decided that the remake was substantially similar to the original in its essential details and plot outline, and so the Dereks won. When we were about to file the opinion, I sent a memo to the panel, which read: 'Well, I think we have it right, but it does occur to me that

---

* Judge on the US Court of Appeals for the Second Circuit

[1] *Burroughs v Metro-Goldwyn-Mayer, Inc.*, 683 F.2d 610 (2d Cir. 1982).

only three appellate judges in the quiet confines of the Second Circuit could conclude that there is no substantial difference between Maureen O'Sullivan fully clothed and Bo Derek in the nude'.

The important details of that particular dispute were not so difficult for us to comprehend, but often we judges are rather removed from much of the facts and theories, especially those in emerging technologies, that are readily familiar to scholars in the field.

I. The Roles of the Academic Critic and the Judge

I am often struck by the extent to which the scholarly debate in intellectual property today is essentially legislative and policy-oriented, and has so little to do with the business of courts. As judges, we usually have a choice between only two outcomes: somebody comes to court and either wins or loses. Maybe at the remedies stage we can be a bit more inventive—at least I could when I served in the trial court; I could craft an injunction, or I could gently prod the lawyers toward a somewhat creative settlement. But by the time a case reaches the appellate court, usually the choice is either to affirm or to reverse.

Judges do not get to take positions on such issues as whether they wish to protect broadly the original author, the compiler, or the inventor, each of whom is creating something new, or, instead, the second comer, who also might sometimes be contributing something new to human understanding, even though some degree of infringement occurs.

When judges decide a particular copyright case, or any intellectual property case, the outcome, at most, is going to be one little blip on the screen that might indicate a tiny, and likely transitory, shift towards either protection of authors or enlargement of the public domain.

But, in my view, it is not the role of a judge to approach these issues and decide specific cases in an effort either to side with those who want more protection for authors, or to side with those who are raising serious cautions about the narrowing of the public domain. Even if privately I share some of these concerns, whether about authors or the public domain, I do not think I am entitled, as a judge, to say: 'Yes, one of those sides is right, and the next time I get a case I am going to do everything I can to decide the case in favor of that position because in the long run that will promote the greater good'.

Federal judges ruling on intellectual property disputes usually have statutes to apply. We are not common law judges in the seventeenth century. We are statutory judges in almost every case—occasionally constitutional judges—but generally statutory judges. If a statute governs the case, judges must interpret it and apply it. Academics, on the other hand, have the luxury of thinking about what the statutes ought to provide.

A. Critical comment from the Academy

Let me turn briefly to another aspect of the relation between a judge's work and that of an academician. For the most part, scholars' informed criticism of what we do as judges is very useful to us. Indeed, a special source of strength in the judicial process is the reaction of knowledgeable critics to judicial opinions, criticism that calls our attention to weaknesses in our reasoning and points the way to better opinions in the future. Sometimes, however, there is something of a disconnect between what judges do and what scholars say. Let me offer two examples from a recent conference of copyright scholars I was privileged to attend. A participant took on one of my favorite cases, one involving an alleged copying of a group of published baseball statistics.[2] The plaintiff, George Kregos, claimed a copyright in his selection of baseball statistics; the Associated Press had come along and 'borrowed' his selection of information rather literally. Writing the opinion for the Court of Appeals for the Second Circuit, I ruled there was a copyrightable interest in Kregos's selection of statistics.

The critic at the conference argued, first, that my opinion had 'gotten around' the opinion of the US Supreme Court in the *Feist* case.[3] That argument distressed me, because heaven forbid I should try to 'get around' a Supreme Court decision! In fact, I thought I had followed *Feist* assiduously. Nevertheless, my critic said that the way I had gotten around *Feist* was to protect Kregos's 'method' of compilation,[4] and 'methods' are generally not copyrightable.

That criticism was intriguing to me, first, because it certainly is not what I thought I had done. (That does not necessarily mean I did not do it. I think judges sometimes do things they have no awareness that they are doing). But then, when I started to reflect on the criticism, I wondered: 'What does this critic mean? What "method" of Kregos's did I protect?' All our Court said was that out of the large universe of available baseball statistics, Kregos's selection of a few of them had exhibited that minimal originality that the copyright law requires as a condition for protection. So I am not sure the criticism was valid or helpful in that instance.

In another instance, a commentator said that Judge Pierre Leval's decision in a case dealing with lists of car values[5] had overemphasized the need to preserve incentives to create new works and undervalued the competing interest

---

[2] *Kregos v Associated Press*, 937 F.2d 700 (2d Cir. 1991).

[3] *Feist Publications, Inc v. Rural Telephone Service Co., Inc.* 499 U.S. 340 (1991). In *Feist*, the Court held that a telephone directory lacked originality in its selection and arrangement of information and, hence, was not a copyrightable compilation.

[4] Compilations are protected under §103 of the Copyright Act 17 U.S.C. §103. A compilation, to be covered by the statute, must be 'selected, coordinated, or arranged in such a way that the resulting work as a whole constitutes an original work of authorship': 17 U.S.C. §101.

[5] *CCC Information Services, Inc v. MacLean Market Reports, Inc.*, 44 F.3d 61 (2d Cir. 1994).

in encouraging subsequent authors to improve on the old. I wondered: 'Well, that certainly might be a fault, but then, how much emphasis is too much, and how are we too know when we have gone too far?' Perhaps the critic simply disagreed with the Court's conclusion. Only criticism spelling out a flaw, if there is one in an opinion, and offering some detailed analysis will be helpful to judges.

I mention these examples not to quarrel with the critics, but to indicate that sometimes what scholars say in their comments about our last case may not help us reach a better outcome in our next case.

B. Continued relevance of the old terminology

One important contribution the academy could make to the crafting of opinions would be a reexamination of the continued usefulness of old doctrines and terminology in resolving issues arising in contexts of new technology, and, where needed, pointing us to new doctrines and new terminology. In copyright law, for example, I despair of the fact that we are still trying to apply doctrines fashioned 300 years ago to technologies that did not then exist and that do not now readily benefit from analysis under those doctrines.

I realize that some commentators disagree and argue that the old doctrines continue to work well when applied to new subject matters.[6] But I find it a bit unsettling to try to use something like the 'idea and expression dichotomy', developed in the context of written text, to identify what is copyrightable in a computer software program. I wonder what is the unprotectable 'idea' and what is the protectable 'expression' in computer source code. The 'idea'/ 'expression' terminology was reasonably helpful when we were trying to decide whether one author's short story borrowed too much from an earlier author's short story, but computer programs are not so easily divided into 'ideas' and 'expression'.

Now, judges can read the old cases—and we do—and we can benefit from the helpful commentary of scholars, but when I am told that I am supposed to work with what Judge Learned Hand said about 'abstractions' in deciding an infringement case involving a play and a screenplay,[7] to distill levels of

---

[6] See, eg, 4 MELVILLE B. NIMMER & DAVID NIMMER, NIMMER ON COPYRIGHT §13.03[F][1], 13–121 (1998) ('Although the abstractions test was created for literary works, it is readily adaptable to analyzing computer software').

[7] In *Nichols v Universal Pictures Corp.*, 45 F.2d 119, 121 (2d Cir. 1930), Judge Hand, in attempting to explain the distinction between an idea and the expression in a literary work, observed: 'Upon any work, and especially upon a play, a great number of patterns of increasing generality will fit equally well, as more and more of the incident is left out. The last may be no more than the most general statement of what the play is about, and at times consist only of its title; but there is a point in this series of abstractions where they are no longer protected, since otherwise the playwright could prevent the use of his "ideas", to which, apart from their expression, his property never extended. Nobody has ever been able to fix that boundary, and nobody can'.

'abstractions' from a piece of software,[8] I say to myself: 'That just isn't what Hand was talking about at all. He probably would have been dismayed if he could have foreseen that we would be forcing into such extended service his generalized comments in a case involving whether one dramatist's work infringed another's work'.

In the first place, the thought that it was an abstractions 'test' at all, I think, would have distressed him. He did not enunciate it as a 'test'. Rather, he simply made the observation that there is a continuum from an 'idea' down to details of its 'expression', and that we ought to be aware of that continuum. That was a useful insight, somewhat startling in its day.

But now when software infringement cases arise, some experts have begun drafting what they call 'abstraction exhibits'. They say to the trial judge and later to the appellate judges, 'This is the key "abstraction exhibit", and here is another "abstraction exhibit" '. As a judge, I want to say: 'Wait a minute. I thought Hand's concept was that there is a continuum running from a generalized idea to its particularized expression. How does something called an "abstraction exhibit" fit on that continuum? Are we even using the right words?'

Courts need more refined analytical tools than the idea/expression dichotomy to deal with cases involving modern technology. Along with all the attention to broad issues concerning the public domain, proprietary rights, and how best to provide incentives to create, it would be helpful if the academic community would spend some time thinking about new doctrinal tools that will help us deal with the issues that arise in computer and technology cases.

I have even been uncomfortable using the old terminology in copyright cases involving a claimed infringement of music, although I have gotten used to it in that context. Since nobody has given me any better analytical tools for such cases, I use the old ones. But I would welcome new techniques for deciding music and also audio-visual cases. I am fairly comfortable with the old doctrines and terminology in cases involving written texts because the familiar doctrines arose in that context and their vocabulary can still be applied reasonably well. But I am not so sure the terminology works well elsewhere.

C. Developing precise statutes

One of the major problems faced by courts—one on which academic expertise can be very helpful—is that the pertinent statutes in the copyright field, like many statutes that deal with hard problems, are so imprecise. For example, as Professor Jane Ginsberg properly points out,[9] one of the problems with the proposed statute to protect databases is that the various drafts

---

[8] See n. 5 above.   [9] See Ginsburg, Chapter 3 above.

'fudge' on the key questions. One of the proposed Bills, H.R. 2652,[10] provided protection for certain databases, using as one criterion whether the compilers had made a 'substantial investment'.

But the Bill does not tell us how we are to determine when an investment is 'substantial'. In retrospect, I begin to think we are fortunate that Congress told us specifically what the duration of a copyright is.[11] After all, they might have just said, 'A copyright lasts for a substantial period of time'. Then judges would have struggled to define 'substantial period of time' in a series of cases, perhaps upholding 40- or 50-year durations as substantial and rejecting 90- or 100-year durations as excessively long. We might have ended up with an interpretation of 'substantial period of time' that was about 75 years. Similarly, if the legislators tell judges that a database merits protection only where the plaintiff has made a 'substantial investment' of money or other resources, judges will have to interpret that phrase for several years until they reach an eventual consensus about which investments are substantial and which are not.

For my part, I would welcome intellectual property legislation that is more specific on matters amenable to specificity, such as the substantiality of an investment. Unfortunately, such laws are rarely enacted. The contending forces are in such serious disagreement on the hot-button issues that the legislature generally cannot enact a precise law. Indeed, I recall spending some interesting years in a legislative staff capacity being paid a modest wage to figure out what vague language I could come up with that would resolve whatever dispute was on the floor of the US Senate that day; that was part of my job. Often, the goal was not to bring clarity to a proposed Bill, but to make it sufficiently ambiguous so that it could be enacted.

As scholars raise large policy-oriented questions, they also need to confront the problem of particularity. It will not do simply to say: 'Be careful about too much protection; be careful about restricting the public domain'. That might be a useful caution and might be somewhat helpful to legislators. But they also need to know specifically how a statute should be drafted to reach the recommended balance between protecting authors and subsequent users of their work. Legislators will have to decide, ultimately, most of the policy issues, and they need help in doing so with as much precision as possible.

Some scholars have helpfully pointed out that no one solution is going to resolve all problems.[12] That is a very useful insight. But then we need com-

---

[10] 105th Cong, 2d Sess. (1998).

[11] In general, the term of a copyright in a work created after January 1, 1978, is the life of the author plus 70 years. See 17 U.S.C. §302(a).

[12] See, eg, Pamela Samuelson et al., *A Manifesto Concerning the Legal Protection of Computer Programs*, 94 COLUM. L. REV. 2308, 2310–11 (1994) ('Most of the considerable controversy about software protection, within the software industry and the legal community, has arisen when software developers have tried to use existing legal regimes to protect . . . program innovations. The authors have been among those who have opposed efforts to stretch the bounds of existing legal regimes to protect these aspects of programs') (footnotes omitted).

mentators to provide examples of specific statutes that would make sense in various differing contexts. Unless commentators offer such examples and legislators enact some of them, judges will be left to interpret old statutes of such vagueness that they will often reach a series of random results unlikely to provide a satisfactory resolution of difficult issues.

D. A clear rule versus a multi-factor rule

Another issue often faced by judges, especially in the absence of a clear statute, is whether they should formulate a precise rule to decide the pending and future cases or should adopt a more open-ended rule that tries to balance a number of relevant factors. This choice can be illustrated, for example, by the proposed legislation that would protect databases created by a 'substantial investment'. If a Bill is enacted with that language, courts asked to apply the statute and interpret that phrase will face an important threshold choice. On the one hand, judges could reason that, in this context, certainty is important, and therefore rule that a precise number, $5 million, for example, is a 'substantial investment'. I imagine some commentators would criticize that approach. They will say that courts have taken an arbitrary approach and will ask, 'How did you know it was $5 million? Why wasn't it $4 million, or $6 million?' But many people potentially affected by the new law might well have a different reaction, saying: 'Thank goodness. Now we know that the line has been drawn at $5 million, and we can predict our liability or our level of protection'.

On the other hand, courts could conclude that selecting a precise amount is an ill-advised way to interpret the statutory term 'substantial investment'. Instead, they could reach results in each case only after identifying and analyzing several relevant factors and then claiming to 'weigh' these factors to determine, on balance, whether the investment is 'substantial'. (Of course, judges do not really 'weigh' factors because they do not have scales to put the factors on, or even useful criteria to assess the relative importance of factors they consider. I have long thought that 'weighing' the relevant factors is one of the law's more unfortunate metaphors).

Judges often say they are 'weighing' factors, for example, in deciding a claim of fair use.[13] When courts purport to 'weigh' the four statutory fair use factors,[14] it is often difficult to predict the outcome, especially if two of the factors tip the 'scale' in one direction and two tip it in the other direction.

---

[13] See, eg, *Campbell v Acuff-Rose Music, Inc.*, 510 U.S. 569, 578 (1994) ('All [the relevant factors] are to be explored, and the results weighed together.').

[14] These factors are: (1) 'the purpose and character of the use [of the copyrighted material]', (2) 'the nature of the copyrighted work', (3) 'the amount and substantiality of the portion used in relation to the copyrighted work as a whole', and (4) 'the effect of the use upon the potential market value for or value of the copyrighted work': 17 U.S.C. §107.

Judges could do something similar by identifying and analyzing many factors that bear on the substantiality of an investment in the creation of a database and then announcing a conclusion that, on balance, the investment in a particular case was either substantial or insubstantial. After such a decision, it would be difficult to predict how the next case will be decided. However, once several cases have been decided, the line between 'substantial' and 'insubstantial' would begin to become clear, if not precise. One virtue of using a multifactor approach in this and other contexts is that, despite its lack of predictability, courts do not freeze the law, but instead allow it to evolve.

In any event, whenever courts are confronted with the need to apply some imprecise standard, they always have to decide whether to make that standard more precise or leave it amorphous. Courts would benefit from scholarly input on which is the better approach in particular contexts. Is predictability better in some contexts, and is the avoidance of rigid rules better in others?

My own view is that in some contexts, fair use for example, a lack of predictability is preferable to a rule framed in nearly absolute terms. A standard somewhat lacking in predictability permits courts to reach a nuanced decision in resolving each dispute. Of course, the risk of this approach is that, in the absence of precise guidance, some future writers thinking about copying portions of a prior author's work will be deterred in circumstances where copying would have been allowed. Others will unfairly copy without paying a price because some authors, uncertain as to whether they could win an infringement suit, will not sue even though their suit would have succeeded. But if courts tried to develop a more specific fair use 'rule', they would likely lurch too far in one direction or the other, either broadly permitting copying as fair use or broadly prohibiting it. In this context, I think some unpredictability of outcomes is preferable to the risk of either of those consequences.

The problem is summed up very well by Judge Frank Easterbrook in an opinion for the Court of Appeals for the Seventh Circuit. In *Nash v. CBS, Inc.*,[15] he wrote:

[E]very author is simultaneously a creator in part and a borrower in part. In these roles the same person has different objectives. Yet, only one rule[16] can be in force. This single rule must achieve as much as possible of these inconsistent demands. Neither Congress nor the courts has the information that would allow it to determine which is best. Both institutions must muddle through using, not a fixed rule, but a sense of the consequences of moving dramatically in either direction.[17]

I believe that point of view is sound and ought to guide judges as they approach most hard questions of intellectual property.

---

[15] 899 F2d 1537 (7th Cir. 1990).
[16] I am not sure I like the word 'rule' in this otherwise useful paragraph
[17] *Nash*, n. 15 above.

E. Legislating and reading court decisions with caution

I think legislators, too, ought to act somewhat tentatively when resolving issues that bear on the relative protection to be accorded creators and subsequent users. Often, one of the most useful provisions in any statute is a sunset provision, stating that the statute will expire after five years, or perhaps some longer period. That would avoid a contentious battle over whether or not to repeal the statute, and might lead to a useful legislative reconsideration on a regular basis of the costs and benefits of legislation first enacted on the basis of untested predictions.

A few years ago, when the Second Circuit Court of Appeals was considering aspects of our in banc rehearing practice,[18] I even suggested, somewhat (but not entirely) facetiously, to the Court that we should have a *judicial* sunset rule whereby every decision of our Court would cease to have precedential effect after a long period, perhaps 40 years, and an issue arising again, which had been decided in a very old case, would be considered a new issue. My colleagues did not think this was a very good idea.[19]

A more serious suggestion for judges, and for those who read our opinions, is to remain very clear about the difference between holding and dictum. That is an old truth, but an important one. If all the specific language in a judicial opinion is taken literally when subsequent cases are decided, courts risk freezing the law and inhibiting its evolution. Often, we judges do not have a sufficiently full understanding of each of the areas of law in which a case arises to appreciate the full implication of every sentence we write. Of course, we take great care in determining the holding of the case, but sometimes the dictum represents the opinion writer's intellectual rumination rather than a definitive statement fully endorsed by all three members of the appellate panel. Consider the decision of the US Court of Appeals for the Second Circuit in a computer software copyright infringement case known as *Altai*.[20] Ever since the case was decided, I have heard various thoughtful commentators discuss what they understand are different points made in the Court's opinion: '*Altai* says this', '*Altai* says that', '*Altai* says something else'.

---

[18] After a decision of a court of appeals has been rendered by a three-judge panel, the appeal may be reheard by the full court if a majority of the active judges of the court vote for such a rehearing. See 28 U.S.C. §46(c).

[19] In fact, however, our Court has used a technique, somewhat similar to my sunset approach, that enables the Court, without the burden of a full-dress in banc rehearing, to discard an old decision that has outlived its usefulness. A panel's draft opinion, proposing to disregard an old precedent, is circulated to all the active judges of the Court, and is permitted to be filed in the absence of objection, thereby announcing a new point of law for the Circuit. See, eg, *Trapnell v. United States*, 725 F.2d 149, 151–55 (2d Cir. 1983) (panel opinion, circulated to active judges prior to filing, rejected 'farce and mockery' standard of prior precedent in favor of 'reasonable competence' standard for assessing whether defendant in criminal case received constitutionally required effective assistance of counsel).

[20] *Computer Associates International, Inc v. Altai, Inc.*, 982 F.2d 693 (2d Cir. 1992).

I would caution that *Altai* definitively says only one, albeit very important, thing: that the District Judge who ruled that no wrongful copying occurred in that case was correct. That is the holding of that case. In the course of reaching that conclusion, the appellate court explained that it was applying what it called a 'three-step procedure' that involved 'abstraction', 'filtration', and 'comparison'.[21] Whether that procedure is a wonderful idea, or not so wonderful, or needs some refinement, are matters distinct from the holding. The Court's reasoning was surely important to its outcome, but should not be read as a mandatory direction to trial judges to use the suggested procedure in all its detail to decide all similar cases. Indeed, the *Altai* opinion wisely cautioned that 'our opinion should not be read to foreclose the district courts of our circuit from utilizing a modified version' of the abstraction-filtration-comparison procedure.[22] Of course, I am bound to follow the *Altai* holding in subsequent similar cases, but I will feel free to fiddle with (perhaps I should say 'refine') the procedure it described. As new cases arise, I want to think more about the appropriate way to consider whether one software program infringes the copyright in another, and then explain the reasoning process I will use to decide whether a software owner claiming copyright infringement wins or loses. And I hope that the judges who write opinions after mine will feel similarly free to disregard my language or, if they are so inclined, to borrow any parts they find useful. In that way, in the common law tradition (even though we are ultimately construing a statute), we may inch along and bring some increased measure of clarity and coherence to the law.

II. Conclusion

As with all areas of law, scholars in the field of intellectual property share with legislators and judges the task of helping to evolve new solutions to emerging problems. Legislators, obliged to consider a bewildering array of issues, cannot possibly be fully informed on all of them. And judges, though focusing on discrete controversies, cannot possibly have a comprehensive understanding of all the issues they confront. We need a great deal of help from the knowledgeable commentators who reside in domains to which we are only occasional visitors. The challenge of any legal system is to assure the evolution of doctrines that will be applicable to new disputes arising in new contexts we have barely begun to imagine.

[21] See *Computer Associates International, Inc v. Altai, Inc.*, 982 F.2d 693 (2d Cir. 1992) at 706–12.
[22] See ibid at 706.

19

INTELLECTUAL PROPERTY IN THE COURTS: THE ROLE OF THE JUDGE

DIANE P. WOOD*

Judges are not the principal architects of intellectual property, nor are they even the principal creators of intellectual property law. What, then, do judges have to add to discussions like those we have enjoyed throughout this symposium? Skeptics, including some on the bench, might suggest that generalist judges are at best philosopher kings, who bring little value added to the table. And yet, there is no denying the importance of the role the judiciary plays in bringing to life the type of property known as 'intellectual'. Self-help measures may suffice to keep trespassers away from Blackacre, but there are few substitutes for the courts if someone needs to prevent poaching of patent rights, trade secrets, copyrights, or other forms of intangible property rights. It is therefore helpful to understand how intellectual property rights are handled in the courts, and how advances in understanding can be carried over from the academic world and the business world to the judiciary.

Even though I have been on the federal bench only since 1995, I have already often been asked how judges cope with the bewildering array of subject matters that reach our desks. No one knows everything, and no one comes to the bench with expertise in every area of the law, yet every federal judge is expected to handle competently cases raising questions about complex regulatory regimes, such as tax law, antitrust, securities regulation, pension law, environmental law, or labor law; or cases about fundamental constitutional issues of due process, equal protection, abortion rights, freedom of speech and the press; or those touching on the operation of our criminal justice system at both the federal and (less directly, but still importantly) state levels. It is a daunting task, no doubt: the perfect job for the Type A workaholic whose idea of a good time on Saturday afternoon is to read slip opinions or to draft her own opinions. But cope we do, and I have expressed the opinion elsewhere that there are real advantages to having generalists deal with issues like intellectual property, that cut across so much of our economy.[1]

---

* Circuit Judge, US Court of Appeals for the Seventh Circuit; Senior Lecturer in Law, The University of Chicago Law School. The comments in this chapter are personal.

[1] See Diane P. Wood, *Generalist Judges in a Specialized World*, 50 SMU L. REV. 1755 (1997).

Initially, I should note that intellectual property is not being treated as a unitary subject matter in the courts, and this may have a deleterious effect on the coherence of the law that is being developed. Intellectual property rights, or IPRs, come in all shapes and sizes. Patents, copyrights, trademarks, trade secrets, and a host of privately created rights embodied in countless contracts, all fall within the scope of our subject. In spite of this fact, when a case reaches the appellate courts, we do not have a unitary system for handling it. Instead, in the United States, there is now a split in competence in the federal judiciary. Since 1982, the Court of Appeals for the Federal Circuit has had exclusive appellate jurisdiction over cases arising under the patent laws, while the regional courts of appeals have jurisdiction over cases involving any other kind of IPRs. Inevitably, this means that neither the Federal Circuit nor the other courts of appeals see the full picture. Whether it is nevertheless wise to have a singular court for all patent cases may be another matter, which is well beyond the scope of these remarks. I proceed here from the assumption that the patent cases are securely within the power of the Federal Circuit, and no one should assume this is my call to bring them back to the Seventh Circuit or any other general court. My only point is that the institutional allocation of responsibility for IPR cases probably has some effect on the way each court understands these issues.

Apart from institutional influences, what else affects a judge's understanding of a complex intellectual property problem? How, specifically, in real cases before real judges would one go about implementing the kinds of suggestions being made in this area? How are we to implement a sound cost-based system for compensation of IPRs, or define relevant markets for intangibles, or distinguish procompetitive cooperation and complementary arrangements from anticompetitive cartels? Is it realistic at all to entrust such complex matters to judges, who are on average not likely to know much about them, as Judge Frank Easterbrook wonders?

The principal guides through the maze of information that often exists in these cases are the expert witnesses. Although it is typically done otherwise in most countries, in the United States experts are part of the adversary process. One set of experts comes in and tells the court (and sometimes the jury) one version of the story, and another set of experts comes in and recounts the opposite version—or at the very least, a different one. Occasionally the court will appoint its own expert, but that is rare, and after the decision of the D.C. Circuit in *United States v. Microsoft,*[2] it may become rarer still. This raises a question that is a cousin to the old saw 'who will guard the guardians': how is a nonexpert judge to decide which of two or more sets of experts has the sounder view, assuming she does not appoint an objective court expert or master?

---

[2] 147 F.3d 935, 955–56 (D.C. Cir. 1998) (overturning the district court's decision to appoint Professor Lawrence Lessig as a special master).

Part of the answer has come in the increasingly rigorous standards the federal courts are applying to the qualification of experts and the admission of expert testimony. In *Daubert v. Merrell Dow Pharmaceuticals*,[3] the Supreme Court stressed the gatekeeping role of the judge and emphasized the judge's duty to exclude so-called junk science. Effective lawyers will make sure that the experts they are presenting have analyzed the facts using valid methodologies, that the person's background is suitable for the question at hand, and that the person is actually applying her expertise to the issue. No one needs to hear even a Nobel Prize-winning economist talk about the amount of stress a bridge can take. In the Seventh Circuit, we have put the point this way: if the person claiming to be an expert simply comes into the courtroom and says 'trust me, I'm an expert, and I'm going to tell you what the relevant market is', we will reject that testimony. If instead the person applies the same analytical techniques, and demands the same rigor, that he or she would do in noncourtroom work, then the testimony is not only admissible, but genuinely helpful.[4]

The remainder of the answer harks back to our faith in the adversary system. This places a tremendous burden on the attorneys in a complex case to explain accurately, but in lay language, whatever needs to be understood. If both sides can live up to that standard, there is a good chance the court will discern where the truth lies. (It would be wrong to call this a game, because the stakes are too high, but there are aspects of gamesmanship at work. Side A persuasively tells the court one thing; Side B says the opposite; and the judge tries to make sense of it, often concluding that neither side is wholly right or wholly wrong).

Given the institutional reasons why most US judges will not develop independent expertise in the field of IPRs (or anything else, for that matter, unless it is the Sentencing Guidelines), and given the imperfect ways we have of transmitting expert information to judges, how are decisions really made? Once the judge has done her best to understand the case, she may be left with some uncertainty. How can one tell if a certain strategy is procompetitive or anticompetitive? Is it possible to say for sure whether a first-generation patent should be understood to have very broad scope, or to be narrower? At that point, both formal and informal strategies for dealing with uncertainties move to the fore, and they are the final tiebreakers.

The most well known of these strategies are the various legal presumptions and conventions about burdens of proof, both production and persuasion. These devices reflect the important policy choices in any area. To take an antitrust example (it is the area I know best), if we decide that our primary

---

[3] 509 U.S. 579 (1993).
[4] See, eg, *People Who Care v. Rockford Bd. of Educ., Sch. Dist. No. 205*, 111 F.3d 528, 537 (7th Cir. 1997); *Braun v. Lorillard Inc.*, 84 F.3d 230, 235 (7th Cir. 1996). See also *City of Tuscaloosa v. Harcros Chemicals, Inc.*, 158 F.3d 548, 566 (11th Cir. 1998).

concern is with market power in firms and the harm it may cause in our competitive economy, then we should adopt presumptions and burdens of proof that will resolve uncertainties in favor of regulating that market power. Such a decision will also affect the kinds of remedies that are thought to be proper. Perhaps, with such a policy baseline, courts should tell monopolists what prices they can charge, or on what terms they can deal, or whom they should license, or what the boundaries of their IPR are. There are clear risks in this approach, of course: risks of error in the initial characterization of the practice as anticompetitive, as well as risks of adopting cures that are worse than the disease. But if in the end society makes the judgment that it is more important to preserve competitive opportunities in the market, then this is the kind of presumption that might be adopted. If, on the other hand, the greater concern is that courts are likely to misunderstand business behavior, that a judicial error condemning something is harder to correct than an error permitting something (because the market will frequently correct the latter sort of error on its own), and that competition is more vigorous, perhaps because of globalization, than it may seem, then the relevant lawgiver should adopt a presumption in favor of permitting ambiguous acts to go unpunished.

These rules are critical to the role of a judge. Judge Easterbrook has pointed out that there are more than 700 federal district judges, and in excess of 175 appellate judges. These people come from every imaginable background, and they represent every possible philosophical bent. The same is true, only to a lesser degree, in systems that use specialized courts. It will always be the case, no matter what, that no judge will be as expert and competent in the subject matter as the scientists and businesspeople who are actually creating the new IPRs. No matter what the system of courts, therefore, the set of presumptions that govern this area of law is pivotal to its implementation.

The political level at which laws, with their accompanying rules for dealing with uncertainty, are made is another important variable for the judge. Within the United States, we are familiar with both horizontal choice of law questions (ie does Illinois law or California law apply) and vertical choice of law questions (ie does federal law or some state's law apply). Today, however, we are increasingly facing a further vertical dimension, the international level.

International regulations have existed for many years in the field of intellectual property. Examples include the Paris Convention[5] and the Berne Convention,[6] and more recently the WTO's Agreement on Trade Related Intellectual Property Rights.[7] Nevertheless, it is still true that the basic rights

    [5] Berne Convention for the Protection of Literary and Artistic Works, September 9, 1886, *as last revised*, July 24, 1971 (*amended* 1979), 828 U.N.T.S. 221.

    [6] Paris Convention for the Protection of Industrial Property, March 20, 1883, *as last revised*, July 14, 1967, 21 U.S.T. 1583, 828 U.N.T.S. 305; *revised*, July 24, 1971, 828 U.N.T.S. 221.

    [7] Agreement on Trade-Related Aspects of Intellectual Property Rights, April 15, 1994, Marrakesh Agreement Establishing the World Trade Organization, Annex 1C, 33 I.L.M 1197 (1994).

themselves are nationally granted and territorial in scope. Important competitive consequences flow from that fact. Markets can be divided in the name of protecting nominally separate rights, gray market pricing can arise, and transaction costs of operating internationally under the same trademarks and business formulae can be high. Offenses are possible precisely because the IPRs have been segregated along national lines.

Consider, for example, patent pools. Some patent pools are certainly pro-competitive: they bring together all sorts of inputs, some of which are competitive, some of which are complementary, and the creative effort may be enhanced through the mixture. Some patent pools, however, may look quite different: Company A has the US patent for widgets, and Company B has the French patent for widgets, and they agree on a cross-license whereby A agrees to stay out of France, and B agrees to stay out of the United States. That looks a lot like the old international market divisions condemned in cases like *Timken Roller Bearing Co. v. United States*,[8] and *United States v. National Lead Co.*:[9] garden variety, illegal, international cartels. In short, the procompetitive story is much harder to believe if the parties are just manipulating the fact of jurisdictional differences in patent coverage.

That is certainly not to say that international efforts have been harmful to competition. Ordinarily, quite the opposite is true. Globalization is leading to harmonization of products and services, and harmonization is opening up more markets to more competition every day. As Carl Shapiro points out, international standard-setting organizations have become practically ubiquitous.[10] The WTO has a hand in this too, with an interest in guarding against product standards that in reality operate as impediments to international trade. Recall the famous story in trade law about the Japanese standard for making baseball bats, under which only baseball bats made in Japan could be certified as suitable for use there and baseball bats made in the United States did not comply.[11] The economic analyses we have heard about network efficiencies and complementarily have literally nothing to do with this kind of trade barrier: it was protectionism, pure and simple, and it worked because the government helped to enforce it.

Put a little differently, the effort to exclude US baseball bats worked because of national boundaries. The standard-setting organization was entitled to define a baseball bat for all of Japan, even though it had no such power over bats made in and for other markets, such as the United States or Cuba. In the area of private orderings and product standards, this kind of national segmentation is slowly breaking down (although not completely, as the debates over genetically altered foods and hormone-fed beef illustrate).

---

[8] 341 U.S. 593 (1951).   [9] 332 U.S. 319 (1947).

[10] See Shapiro, Chapter 4 above.

[11] See Bart S. Fisher & Ralph G. Steinhardt, III, *§ 301 of the Trade Act of 1974: Protection for U.S. Exporters of Goods, Services and Capital*, 14 LAW & POL'Y INT'L BUS. 569, 611 (1982).

Although private efforts to coordinate national patents, or national copyrights, are also having the practical effect of reducing the importance of boundaries, it is my impression that there is still much more to be done before we will have truly international intellectual property rights.[12] The most we have done thus far is to create systems that permit filings to apply internationally and that have begun to harmonize the level of protection national laws give to the IPR in question. That is a good start, but it may not be enough over the long run, given the inherently state-less quality of ideas.

The last influence on the judge's task I want to mention relates to the clarity of the law, once it has been identified properly and the right experts have been assembled to explain the *facts* of the situation. We need clarity in several different ways. First, clarity in the boundaries of IPRs is crucial, even if elusive. This is the difference between 'Blackacre' and 'Thoughtacre'. A great deal of litigation that arises in this area reaches the courts because a company is not sure whether the new gizmo it wants to manufacture will or will not infringe a patent or copyright, compromise a trade secret, or conflict with a trademark. Secondly, we need to know exactly what bundle of rights each type of IPR entails. Does the holder have, to take the real property analogy, a fee simple absolute, or just an easement or a license? Does the right of exclusivity extend from the depths of the earth to the heavens, or is it a surface right, or a mineral right, or an air right? These would not be the terms used in discussing most IPRs, naturally, but analogous subdivisions exist and are often efficient ways of exploiting the property. There is no right or wrong way to configure the rights, and, to take Becky Eisenberg's example for a moment, I would find it practically impossible to say ex ante whether IPRs should be able to pass through a wide mesh screen, or if they should be restricted somehow so that they will only pass through the fine mesh. I assure you that, as a judge, I would find it difficult to identify a principle that let me choose the proper size of the mesh.[13]

I would conclude by observing that the 'big think' this volume of essays represents is of the highest importance. Such efforts filter into real cases, real business decisions, and real litigation, even if the process is often slow and indirect. Look at what happened to antitrust from 1970 to the present time. Better understanding of business practices began in the economics departments and the law schools, and it moved into the courts and the legislatures. Statutes like the National Cooperative Research and Production Act[14] came

---

[12] Note that the idea of international property rights of any kind remains a radical notion. This was one of the sticking points for years in the Law of the Sea negotiations over rights to the deep-sea bed; it has come up in the Antarctica Treaty; and it is an issue in the various treaties governing use of near earth space and the Moon. Cf Diane P. Wood, *Who Should Regulate the Space Environment: The Laissez Faire, National, and Multinational Options*, in PRESERVATION OF NEAR-EARTH SPACE FOR FUTURE GENERATIONS (John A. Simpson, ed. 1994).

[13] See Eisenberg, Chapter 9 above.   [14] 15 U.S.C. §§ 4301 et seq.

about because of this work; decisions like *United States v. General Dynamics Corp.*,[15] *Continental T.V., Inc. v. GTE Sylvania Inc.*,[16] *Broadcast Music, Inc. v. Columbia Broadcasting System, Inc.*,[17] and *Business Electronics Corp. v. Sharp Electronics Corp.*,[18] all prominently bear the mark of this work. In the area of intellectual property too, the vocabulary of the advocates will change; the content of the expert testimony will shift to reflect new learning; and the judges—with any luck—will incorporate the new thinking into their decisions as they play their part in creating innovation policy for the coming years.

[15] 415 U.S. 486 (1974).   [16] 433 U.S. 36 (1977).
[17] 441 U.S. 1 (1979).   [18] 485 U.S. 717 (1988).

INDEX

Lightning Source UK Ltd.
Milton Keynes UK

177376UK00001B/14/A